THE PURPOSE OF RELATIONSHIPS

BY JOSHUA EZE

THE PURPOSE OF RELATIONSHIPS

Learn More On Page 374

TABLE OF CONTENTS

INTRODUCTION

In the intricate tapestry of human existence, relationships stand as the threads weaving together the narrative of our lives. Intricately designed by the Creator, relationships were birthed with divine intent, mirroring God's own relational nature.

In its broadest sense, a relationship refers to the way in which two or more concepts, objects, or people are connected, or the state of being connected. This definition extends beyond interpersonal connections and includes any form of association, whether it be between ideas, entities, or individuals.

In the sacred Garden of Eden, where the fabric of human connection was once woven in perfection, we embark on a journey to unpack the profound narrative of brokenness. Genesis 3 unfolds a pivotal moment in the human story, revealing the intricate details of Adam and Eve's encounter with the serpent—an adversary seeking to exploit the vulnerabilities within the very essence of their beings.

Unseen holes—those vulnerabilities and weaknesses lurking beneath the surface— persist, quietly influencing the dynamics of relationships. As we delve into the exploration of self-awareness, we begin the process of unveiling and addressing these relationship holes,

Authenticity, the first pillar of relatability, is a profound commitment to living in alignment with one's true self. To be authentic is to shed the layers of pretense and societal expectations, revealing the raw and genuine essence within.

RELATIONSHIP WITH GOD

In the vast expanse of the heavens, amidst the cosmic dance of stars and galaxies, there exists a divine desire pulsating from the very heart of God – a desire for an intimate and personal relationship with each individual.

RELATIONSHIP WITH SPOUSE

NAVIGATING TOWARDS SHARED HORIZONS IN YOUR RELATIONSHIP 319

Shared Mission and Desired Outcome
Just as a ship needs a destination, marriages thrive when couples have a shared mission – a collective purpose that unites them in the pursuit of common goals. This shared mission becomes the wind in their sails, propelling them forward through the challenges and triumphs of their journey.

RELATIONSHIP WITH CHILDREN

A FATHERS PERSPECTIVE 333

NURTURING A GROWTH ENVIRONMENT FOR CHILDREN 334

Parenting, from a biblical perspective, is not merely a biological or societal role but a sacred and divine calling. It transcends the physical act of bringing a child into the world; it is a stewardship of a precious life entrusted by God.

GOD'S ORIGINAL DESIGN FOR PARENTING: EMBRACING BIBLICAL PRINCIPLES 336

Delving into the pages of the Bible reveals profound insights into God's original design for parenting. From the creation narrative to various teachings and examples throughout scripture, the Bible offers timeless wisdom on the role of parents and the principles that guide the upbringing of children.

SCAN THE QR CODE BELOW FOR COACHING OR SUPPORT IN THIS AREA.

START HERE

Introduction: Relationship Sacrifices: Assessing the Costs of Neglect

In the intricate connections of life, our relationships with God, self, spouse, and our children are interwoven with the various facets of our endeavors in business, ministry, and creativity. These relationships form the foundation upon which we build our lives, influencing our perspectives, priorities, and pursuits. However, in the modern world driven by material success and external validation, there's a tendency to prioritize achievements in business, ministry, or creative pursuits over the nurturing of our spiritual, familial, and personal well-being.

God's version of success transcends the narrow confines of worldly achievements, encompassing holistic growth and fulfillment in every aspect of our lives. While professional success and accomplishments in business or ministry are important, they should not overshadow the significance of our relationships with God, self, spouse, and children. True success, according to God's standards, is measured by the depth of our spiritual maturity, the health of our familial bonds, and our commitment to living out His love and truth in all areas of life.

Unfortunately, the prevailing systems and structures in society often emphasize external markers of success, such as wealth, status, and recognition, while neglecting the importance of spiritual and relational well-being. As a result, many individuals excel in their careers or creative pursuits but struggle in their relationships with God, themselves, and their families. They may possess impressive skills and achievements in their professional endeavors but lack the emotional intelligence, empathy, and spiritual depth needed to nurture healthy, thriving relationships.

In God's economy, success is not defined by material wealth or accolades but by the quality of our relationships and our obedience to His will. Jesus Christ exemplified this holistic understanding of success, prioritizing His relationship with the Father above all else and demonstrating unconditional love, humility, and sacrificial service in His interactions with others. His life serves as a model for us to emulate, reminding us that true fulfillment and significance are found in aligning our lives with God's purposes and priorities.

To cultivate success in our relationships with God, self, spouse, and our children, we must prioritize spiritual growth, emotional well-being, and relational harmony alongside our professional pursuits. This requires intentional effort to invest time, energy, and resources into nurturing these foundational relationships, seeking guidance from God's Word and His Spirit to lead us in wisdom and discernment. It entails cultivating virtues such as love, patience, forgiveness, and humility, which are essential for building healthy, thriving relationships that honor God and bless others.

Ultimately, the success of our lives is not determined solely by our achievements in business, ministry, or creativity, but by the depth of our relationship with God and our commitment to loving and serving others. As we align our priorities with God's heart and seek His guidance in all areas of life, we can experience a profound sense of fulfillment, purpose, and joy that transcends the fleeting pleasures of worldly success. Let us strive to live out God's version of success, embracing His holistic vision for our lives and relationships, and allowing His love to transform us from the inside out.

Prioritizing Divine Order: The Key to Harmonious Relationships

Prioritization is not merely a matter of arranging tasks in order of importance; it's a fundamental principle that governs the balance and well-being of our lives. In God's divine order, our relationships are structured in a specific hierarchy, each serving as a conduit for His love and grace to flow into our lives and those around us.

At the top of this hierarchy stands our relationship with God—the cornerstone upon which all other connections are built. By nurturing this sacred bond, we open ourselves to receive His guidance, provision, and wisdom, laying a foundation of spiritual strength and stability that permeates every aspect of our existence.

Following closely behind is our relationship with ourselves—an often overlooked yet indispensable component of our well-being. Self-care is not selfish; it's an act of stewardship over the precious vessel that houses our spirit, mind, and emotions. By prioritizing self-love and self-care, we cultivate the resilience and vitality needed to navigate life's challenges with grace and authenticity.

Next in line are our relationships with our spouses and children, if applicable. These sacred unions are designed to mirror the divine love and unity found within the Godhead, serving as crucibles for growth, intimacy, and mutual support. When nurtured with intentionality and devotion, these relationships become sources of profound joy, fulfillment, and purpose.

At the bottom of God's divine order lies our business, ministries, or creative pursuits—extensions of our purpose and passion in the world. However, these endeavors must always remain subordinate to our primary relationships, lest they become idols that usurp God's rightful place in our lives.

When this divine order is upheld, each relationship becomes a conduit for God's love and grace to flow freely, creating a synergistic fabric of connection and purpose. The nutrients of God's love, grace, and guidance cascade down from our relationship with Him, nourishing our souls and igniting a fervent self-love that fuels our capacity to love and serve others.

This symbiotic relationship between God, self, and family radiates outward, infusing every facet of our lives with divine favor and purpose. In the marketplace, our unwavering commitment to God's divine order becomes a beacon of light, attracting opportunities and blessings that exceed our wildest dreams.

In essence, prioritizing God's divine order is not just a matter of personal preference—it's a blueprint for abundant living and lasting fulfillment. As we wholeheartedly invest in our relationship with God, ourselves, and our families, we unlock the fullness of God's promises and purpose for our lives, ensuring that every area of our existence flourishes in His grace and love.

The Cost of Neglect: The Price of Prioritizing Success Over Relationships
In the pursuit of success, it's easy to lose sight of what truly matters—the relationships that form the bedrock of our lives. When individuals neglect their connections with God, self, spouse, and children in favor of chasing worldly achievements, they often find themselves paying a steep price in the long run.

One of the most significant regrets people face is realizing they sacrificed their spiritual well-being for material success. Neglecting their relationship with God leaves them feeling spiritually bankrupt, disconnected, and unfulfilled. Despite their outward success, there is a nagging sense of emptiness—a void that cannot be filled by worldly accolades or possessions.

Furthermore, neglecting one's relationship with oneself can lead to a profound sense of discontent and inner turmoil. Individuals who prioritize external success over self-care often find themselves burnt out, overwhelmed, and struggling with issues like anxiety, depression, and low self-esteem. They may come to regret not investing more time and energy in self-reflection, personal growth, and nurturing their mental, emotional, and physical well-being.

In the realm of marriage and family, neglect can have devastating consequences. Spouses who prioritize their careers or personal ambitions over their relationship often find themselves facing marital discord, communication breakdowns, and ultimately, divorce. The pain of fractured relationships, broken homes, and the loss of intimacy and connection can leave lasting scars on both partners and children, impacting their emotional health and well-being for years to come.

Similarly, neglecting the needs of children can result in profound regret and sorrow. Parents who prioritize work or other pursuits over spending quality time with their children may miss out on crucial moments of bonding, growth, and development. As children grow older, they may harbor resentment or feelings of abandonment, straining the parent-child relationship and leading to a sense of loss and missed opportunities.

Ultimately, the true cost of neglecting relationships is immeasurable. While worldly success may bring temporary satisfaction or external validation, it pales in comparison to the richness and depth of meaningful connections with God, self, spouse, and children. As the old adage goes, "No one on their deathbed ever wishes they spent more time at the office." Instead, they long for reconciliation, restoration, and the opportunity to mend broken relationships—a priceless commodity that no amount of worldly success can buy.

In conclusion, the pursuit of success should never come at the expense of neglecting the relationships that matter most. True fulfillment and contentment are found not in the accumulation of wealth or achievements but in the love, connection, and intimacy shared with those we hold dear. By prioritizing our relationships with God, self, spouse, and children, we can avoid the pain of regret and experience the abundant life that comes from living in alignment with our true values and priorities.

Navigating the Pitfalls of Straying from Divine Order

When we stray from God's divine order of holistic success, pursuing worldly achievements such as business success, fame, or material wealth, we inevitably encounter a host of struggles that threaten our well-being and relationships. These challenges, born out of a misalignment of priorities, can wreak havoc on our lives if left unchecked. Here are some of the most common pain points we may encounter:

1. **Poor Time Management**: Without God's guidance and direction, we may find ourselves overwhelmed by competing demands and unable to effectively manage our time, leading to stress and frustration.
2. **Lack of Work-Life Harmony**: Pursuing success at the expense of our personal lives can result in a lack of balance and harmony, causing strain in our relationships and overall dissatisfaction.
3. **Unrealistic Expectations**: Straying from God's divine order may lead us to set unrealistic expectations for ourselves and others, setting us up for disappointment and resentment.
4. **Difficulty Disconnecting**: In our relentless pursuit of success, we may struggle to disconnect from work or other commitments, leading to burnout and exhaustion.
5. **Communication Breakdowns**: When our priorities are not aligned with God's divine order, communication breakdowns can occur, leading to misunderstandings and conflict in our relationships.
6. **Role Conflicts**: Neglecting our primary roles and responsibilities, such as those within our families, can result in conflicts and tensions that strain our relationships.
7. **Lack of Quality Time**: Without prioritizing our relationships with God, self, and family, we may find ourselves lacking quality time with our loved ones, leading to feelings of neglect and disconnection.
8. **Burnout**: The relentless pursuit of worldly success can lead to burnout, leaving us physically, emotionally, and spiritually depleted.
9. **Emotional Unavailability**: When we prioritize external achievements over our inner well-being, we may become emotionally unavailable to ourselves and others, hindering the depth and intimacy of our relationships.
10. **Isolation and Loneliness**: Straying from God's divine order can lead to feelings of isolation and loneliness, as we prioritize external validation over the nourishing connections found in our relationships.

Strategies for Overcoming These 10 Common Relationship Pitfalls

- **Poor Time Management:**
  - Relationship with God: Begin each day with prayer and meditation, seeking God's guidance on prioritizing tasks and managing time effectively.
  - Relationship with Self: Practice self-discipline and time-blocking techniques to allocate sufficient time for personal growth, self-care, and rejuvenation.
  - Relationship with Spouse: Collaborate with your spouse to create a shared schedule, ensuring that both partners have dedicated time for individual pursuits and quality time together.
  - Relationship with Children: Set aside designated periods for family activities and bonding moments, fostering a sense of structure and balance in your children's lives.
- **Lack of Work-Life Harmony:**
  - Relationship with God: Seek God's wisdom on finding a balance between work and personal life, trusting in His provision and guidance for both areas.
  - Relationship with Self: Prioritize self-care practices, such as setting boundaries, maintaining hobbies, and pursuing activities that bring joy and fulfillment outside of work.
  - Relationship with Spouse: Schedule regular date nights and prioritize open communication with your spouse to address any imbalances and ensure mutual support.
  - Relationship with Children: Involve your children in family decisions regarding time management and work-life balance, fostering a sense of inclusion and understanding.
- **Unrealistic Expectations:**
  - Relationship with God: Ground your expectations in God's promises and truths, seeking His perspective on your goals and aspirations.
  - Relationship with Self: Practice self-awareness and self-compassion, setting realistic and achievable goals that align with your values and capabilities.
  - Relationship with Spouse: Have honest discussions with your spouse about expectations, acknowledging each other's strengths, limitations, and mutual aspirations.
  - Relationship with Children: Encourage a growth mindset in your children, celebrating progress and effort rather than focusing solely on outcomes or achievements.

- **Difficulty Disconnecting:**
  - Relationship with God: Dedicate specific times for spiritual nourishment and rest, setting boundaries to ensure uninterrupted time with God.
  - Relationship with Self: Incorporate regular breaks and downtime into your schedule, engaging in activities that promote relaxation and rejuvenation.
  - Relationship with Spouse: Establish technology-free zones or designated "quality time" periods with your spouse to disconnect from external distractions and focus on each other.
  - Relationship with Children: Create technology-free family activities and bonding rituals, fostering meaningful connections and presence with your children.
- **Communication Breakdowns:**
  - Relationship with God: Seek God's wisdom and guidance in improving communication skills and resolving conflicts, prioritizing humility and empathy in your interactions.
  - Relationship with Self: Practice active listening and effective communication techniques, reflecting on your own communication style and areas for improvement.
  - Relationship with Spouse: Invest in couples' communication workshops or counseling sessions to enhance communication skills and address underlying issues.
  - Relationship with Children: Foster an open and supportive environment for communication, encouraging honesty, trust, and empathy in your interactions with your children.
- **Role Conflicts:**
  - Relationship with God: Seek God's wisdom on balancing your roles and responsibilities, prioritizing alignment with His purposes and values in all areas of your life.
  - Relationship with Self: Set clear boundaries and priorities, ensuring that your roles align with your values and personal well-being.
  - Relationship with Spouse: Have regular check-ins with your spouse to assess and realign roles and responsibilities, ensuring mutual understanding and support.
  - Relationship with Children: Establish clear expectations and boundaries with your children regarding roles and responsibilities within the family, fostering a sense of teamwork and cooperation.
- **Lack of Quality Time:**
  - Relationship with God: Prioritize dedicated time for prayer, worship, and spiritual reflection, nurturing your relationship with God and seeking His presence in your daily life.
  - Relationship with Self: Schedule regular "me time" for self-care activities and personal hobbies, replenishing your energy and nurturing your well-being.
  - Relationship with Spouse: Plan regular date nights and meaningful activities together, prioritizing quality time to strengthen your emotional bond and connection.
  - Relationship with Children: Create family traditions and rituals that promote quality time and bonding, such as game nights, outings, or shared meals.
- **Burnout:**
  - Relationship with God: Lean on God for strength and renewal, seeking His guidance on managing stress and finding rest in His presence.
  - Relationship with Self: Practice self-care habits and stress management techniques, prioritizing rest, exercise, and activities that promote mental and emotional well-being.
  - Relationship with Spouse: Support each other in recognizing signs of burnout and prioritizing self-care, offering encouragement, and assistance as needed.
  - Relationship with Children: Model healthy stress management and self-care behaviors for your children, prioritizing open communication and support within the family.
- **Emotional Unavailability:**
  - Relationship with God: Cultivate emotional intimacy with God through prayer, worship, and vulnerability, allowing Him to heal and strengthen your emotional well-being.
  - Relationship with Self: Practice self-awareness and emotional regulation, acknowledging and processing your feelings in healthy ways.
  - Relationship with Spouse: Prioritize emotional connection and vulnerability in your relationship, engaging in open and honest communication to deepen intimacy and understanding.
  - Relationship with Children: Create a safe and supportive environment for emotional expression and communication, modeling empathy and validation in your interactions with your children.

- **Isolation and Loneliness:**
  - Relationship with God: Draw comfort and companionship from your relationship with God, seeking solace and community in faith-based groups and communities.
  - Relationship with Self: Nurture meaningful connections with yourself through self-reflection, journaling, and engaging in activities that bring you joy and fulfillment.
  - Relationship with Spouse: Foster emotional intimacy and connection with your spouse, prioritizing quality time and shared experiences to combat feelings of isolation.
  - Relationship with Children: Create a supportive family environment where open communication and emotional support are encouraged, fostering a sense of belonging and connection within the family unit.

Relationship Assessment Worksheet

Please take some time to reflect on the following statements and rate yourself on a scale of 1 to 10, where:

1 = Strongly Disagree

10 = Strongly Agree

1. Poor Time Management: I effectively manage my time and prioritize tasks according to God's guidance and direction.
2. My Rating: _____
3. Lack of Work-Life Harmony: I maintain a healthy balance between work and personal life, ensuring that neither aspect dominates the other.
4. My Rating: _____
5. Unrealistic Expectations: I set realistic expectations for myself and others, avoiding unnecessary pressure and disappointment.
6. My Rating: _____
7. Difficulty Disconnecting: I can easily disconnect from work or other commitments to prioritize rest and self-care when necessary.
8. My Rating: _____
9. Communication Breakdowns: My relationships are characterized by open and effective communication, minimizing misunderstandings and conflicts.
10. My Rating: _____
11. Role Conflicts: I fulfill my primary roles and responsibilities, maintaining harmony within my family and other spheres of life.
12. My Rating: _____
13. Lack of Quality Time: I prioritize spending quality time with God, myself, and my family, fostering strong and meaningful connections.
14. My Rating: _____
15. Burnout: I take proactive steps to prevent burnout and maintain overall well-being, recognizing the importance of rest and self-care.
16. My Rating: _____
17. Emotional Unavailability: I am emotionally available and present in my relationships, fostering intimacy and connection with others.
18. My Rating: _____
19. Isolation and Loneliness: I actively seek nourishing connections with others, avoiding feelings of isolation and loneliness.
20. My Rating: _____

Scoring Area:

Add up all your ratings and divide by 10 to get your average score.

Average Score: _____
- 1-3: Your relationships may be struggling, and it's essential to seek support and make significant changes.
- 4-6: There are areas for improvement in your relationships. Consider focusing on these to strengthen your connections.
- 7-8: You're doing well in your relationships, but there's still room for growth and enhancement.
- 9-10: Congratulations! You have strong relationships and are effectively stewarding them according to God's divine order. Keep up the excellent work!

The Reward of Prioritizing Relationships in Success

As we reflect on the sobering consequences of neglecting our foundational relationships, it becomes evident that investing in these connections is not just a matter of personal fulfillment but also a strategic move towards achieving success in our business, ministries, and other endeavors. When these relationships are nurtured and prioritized, they serve as a powerful catalyst for growth, resilience, and achievement in every area of our lives.

- Relationship with God: Investing in our relationship with God is the ultimate source of strength, wisdom, and guidance in our journey towards success. By cultivating a deep, intimate connection with the Divine, we tap into a reservoir of supernatural resources that empower us to overcome obstacles, navigate challenges, and seize opportunities with confidence and clarity. Through prayer, meditation, and spiritual practices, we align ourselves with God's purpose and plan for our lives, unlocking doors of divine favor and provision that lead to unprecedented success and fulfillment.
- Relationship with Self: Self-awareness, self-care, and self-love are foundational principles that underpin our ability to achieve success in every aspect of our lives. When we prioritize our relationship with ourselves, we gain a deeper understanding of our strengths, weaknesses, and unique abilities, allowing us to leverage our potential for maximum impact and effectiveness. Investing in personal development, wellness practices, and self-reflection equips us with the resilience, confidence, and emotional intelligence needed to navigate the complexities of business, ministry, and leadership roles with grace and authenticity.
- Relationship with Spouse: A thriving marital relationship is a potent source of strength, support, and synergy that enhances our capacity for success in every area of life. When spouses prioritize their partnership, they create a harmonious and conducive environment for personal growth, mutual encouragement, and shared achievement. By fostering open communication, mutual respect, and collaborative decision-making, couples strengthen their bond and amplify their impact, laying the foundation for lasting success and fulfillment in their endeavors.
- Relationship with Children: The impact of positive parent-child relationships on our success cannot be overstated. When parents prioritize quality time, emotional connection, and meaningful interaction with their children, they sow the seeds of resilience, confidence, and purpose in their lives. Investing in the emotional well-being and holistic development of our children equips them with the tools and values they need to thrive in their own lives, creating a legacy of success that extends far beyond our individual achievements.

In summary, the rewards of prioritizing relationships in success are immeasurable. By investing in our relationship with God, self, spouse, and children, we unlock a wealth of spiritual, emotional, and relational resources that empower us to achieve our goals, fulfill our purpose, and leave a lasting legacy of impact and influence in the world. As you continue on your journey towards success, may you remember that true fulfillment and abundance are found not in the pursuit of external achievements but in the richness of meaningful connections with those we love and cherish.

The Purpose Behind the Pages

As you embark on this journey through the pages of "The Purpose of Relationships," it's important to understand the driving force behind this book. The purpose of writing this book is deeply rooted in the recognition of a profound truth: that sacrificing our relationships for the sake of worldly success ultimately leads to a hollow victory.

What good is it to gain the whole world, yet forfeit the soulful connections with God, family, and legacy? Our relationships, be it with God, ourselves, our spouses, children, or others, are not mere accessories to our success—they are the very fabric of it.

In crafting this book, my aim is to illuminate the invaluable treasures hidden within these relationships. God has packaged within them intangible riches like emotional support, love, accountability, and guidance, treasures that cannot be found anywhere else. These relationships are the compass guiding us towards true success—a success that transcends the fleeting allure of material gain and resonates with the eternal purpose of glorifying God.

So as you delve into the wisdom shared within these pages, may you be reminded of the sacred importance of nurturing and prioritizing your relationships. May this book serve as a beacon of light, illuminating the path towards a legacy built on enduring love, meaningful connections, and transformative impact. And may it equip you with the insights and tools needed to craft a legacy that is unforgettable, resonant, and eternally impactful.

How to Navigate the Book: You have the freedom to explore this book in a way that suits your needs. Whether you prefer to read it cover to cover or dive into specific areas of concern or interest, "The Purpose of Relationships" serves as both a toolkit and a comprehensive guide. Each section addresses a crucial aspect of relational dynamics, providing insights, activities, and reflection areas to aid your growth.

As you journey through these words, may your relationships be enriched, your soul nourished, and your legacy secured. And may the blessings of God's grace accompany you every step of the way.
With prayers for your relational journey, - **Coach**

If after reading this book or parts of it, you feel you need my assistance, don't hesitate to reach out to me at **mycoachjosh.com** to see how I can help you!

Before You Read This Book Assessment:
Take a moment to assess the current state of your relationships with God, yourself, your spouse or significant other, and your children (If Applicable). Rate each relationship on a scale from 1 to 10, with 1 being the lowest and 10 being the highest. After rating each relationship, reflect on where you would like these relationships to be and what improvements or growth you desire.

1. **Relationship with God:**
   - Current Rating: _____
   - Desired Rating: _____
   - Reflection: Consider how connected you feel to your spiritual life and the level of intimacy in your relationship with God. What changes or improvements would you like to see?

2. **Relationship with Self:**
   - Current Rating: _____
   - Desired Rating: _____
   - Reflection: Reflect on your self-awareness, self-compassion, and overall satisfaction with who you are. What aspects of your relationship with yourself would you like to enhance?

3. **Relationship with Spouse/Significant Other: (If Applicable)**
   - Current Rating: _____
   - Desired Rating: _____
   - Reflection: Evaluate the dynamics of your romantic relationship. What strengths or challenges do you currently face, and how would you like to see your relationship evolve?

4. **Relationship with Children: (If Applicable)**
   - Current Rating: _____
   - Desired Rating: _____
   - Reflection: Consider your interactions, communication, and connection with your children. What aspects of your parenting or the parent-child relationship would you like to improve?

Feel free to jot down additional thoughts, emotions, or specific areas you'd like to focus on throughout your journey with this book. This assessment serves as a starting point for self-reflection and personal growth in your relational journey.

THE PURPOSE OF RELATIONSHIPS

THE PURPOSE OF RELATIONSHIPS AND THE ESSENCE OF RELATABILITY

"The purpose of relationships is to nurture relatability within our connections with the shared aim of glorifying God through them."

In the intricate tapestry of human existence, relationships stand as the threads weaving together the narrative of our lives. Intricately designed by the Creator, relationships were birthed with divine intent, mirroring God's own relational nature. However, the contemporary struggle within relationships often echoes the age-old sentiment: Why do many relationships seem to sink, and why do people find it challenging to relate effectively?

The genesis of this challenge lies in our inability to embody relatability—an essential quality that permeates all spheres of our connections, be it with God, oneself, or others. It is the missing link that, when rediscovered, transforms mere interactions into profound bonds.

The Six Pillars of Relatability:
1. **Authenticity**: Genuine and transparent, authenticity forms the bedrock of relatability. It invites others to see and know us as we truly are.
2. **Respect**: Upholding respect for God, oneself, and others is the cornerstone that sustains vibrant and resilient relationships, fostering an atmosphere of honor and value.
3. **Empathy**: The ability to understand and share the feelings of others creates bridges of connection, fostering a deeper understanding in relationships.
4. **Humility**: Recognizing our imperfections and extending grace to others cultivates an environment of mutual respect and understanding.
5. **Communication**: Open, respectful communication is the lifeblood of relationships, ensuring that thoughts, feelings, and intentions are effectively expressed.
6. **Adaptability**: The willingness to adapt and grow, both individually and collectively, ensures that relationships remain vibrant and resilient.

13

A Return to the Garden:
To understand the profound importance of relatability, we journey back to the origins of human connection—the Garden of Eden. Adam and Eve, created in perfection, enjoyed unblemished relationship with God in His divine presence. However, a subtle shift occurred when the serpent introduced doubt and distorted truth, convincing them that God was withholding something vital. As they succumbed to temptation, the harmony of their relationship with God shattered.

Yet, in the midst of the brokenness, God unveiled a redemptive plan. Through Jesus, the cost of sin was paid, and the Holy Spirit became the catalyst for recreating an Eden within our hearts. Now, as we welcome God's Spirit into our lives, relatability is restored. We are made righteous through Christ's sacrifice, and the Holy Spirit endeavors to mold us into vessels of relatability in every facet of life.

Cultivating Stronger Relationships:
This journey is an invitation to rediscover relatability, to embody the divine essence within ourselves, and to extend it outwardly. It is my earnest desire to guide you through this exploration, helping you cultivate stronger relationships with God, yourself, and others—building bonds that stand unbroken against the trials of time. May this journey awaken a profound understanding of the purpose behind every relationship, propelling us toward deeper, more meaningful connections.

14

RELATIONSHIPS DEFINED.

Before delving into the core concepts of this book, let's establish a foundational understanding of relationships. The term "relationship" encompasses various dimensions, each contributing to the intricate nature of human connection.

In its broadest sense, a relationship refers to the way in which two or more concepts, objects, or people are connected, or the state of being connected. This definition extends beyond interpersonal connections and includes any form of association, whether it be between ideas, entities, or individuals. Understanding relationships in this context prompts us to explore the interconnectedness that underlies our existence.

Zooming into the realm of human interaction, another facet of the definition emerges: the way in which two or more people or groups regard and behave toward each other. This definition encapsulates the dynamic nature of interpersonal relationships, emphasizing not only the connection but also the attitudes, behaviors, and mutual perceptions that shape the quality of those connections.

In delving into the first definition of relationships, we uncover a vast landscape that extends beyond the realm of human connections. Our associations with concepts, objects, and entities play a significant role in shaping our perspectives, values, and daily choices. It's crucial to recognize that the impact of these non-human relationships can be profound, influencing not only our individual well-being but also the dynamics of our interactions with others.

People often form relationships with various entities such as companies, sports teams, products, places, and ideologies. These connections can be multifaceted, ranging from a sense of loyalty to a particular brand to identifying with a cultural or social movement. While these relationships may seem indirect, their influence on our lives can be substantial.

For instance, a person's allegiance to a sports team may contribute to a sense of camaraderie and shared identity with fellow fans. Conversely, a strong attachment to a brand or product can shape consumer behavior, impacting purchasing decisions and, in some cases, contributing to a sense of self-worth.

The places we associate with positive experiences hold sentimental value, influencing our emotions and memories. It is essential to assess the health of these non-human relationships, as they can significantly impact our overall well-being and, by extension, our interactions with others. Unhealthy attachments to brands or products, for instance, can lead to consumerism-driven behaviors, affecting personal finances and potentially straining relationships. Identifying and understanding these connections allows for intentional and mindful engagement, ensuring that our associations contribute positively to our lives and the relationships we cultivate with both people and the world around us.

In the intricate fabric of life, every thread of connection, whether with people or non-human entities, contributes to the broader narrative of our experiences. Being mindful of the quality and impact of these relationships empowers us to navigate the complexities of our interconnected existence more consciously and authentically.

Exploring the second definition of relationships delves into the intricacies of how individuals and groups regard and behave toward each other. This facet of relationships is profoundly significant, not just in our interpersonal dynamics but also in the broader spiritual and moral context.

The Bible emphasizes the importance of how we treat others. Our behavior and regard for others matter to God. In various scriptures, we find guidance on cultivating virtues such as love, kindness, and humility in our interactions with fellow human beings. For instance, Jesus emphasizes the command to love one another (John 13:34-35), and the Apostle Paul encourages believers to "be kind and compassionate to one another, forgiving each other, just as in Christ God forgave you" (Ephesians 4:32, ESV).

interactions with fellow human beings. For instance, Jesus emphasizes the command to love one another (John 13:34-35), and the Apostle Paul encourages believers to "be kind and compassionate to one another, forgiving each other, just as in Christ God forgave you" (Ephesians 4:32, ESV).

However, many individuals find themselves stuck in behavioral patterns that hinder the progress of their relationships. These patterns can include negative ways of communication, unresolved conflicts, or a lack of empathy. Being stuck in destructive ways can lead to strained relationships, causing emotional distance and, in some cases, irreparable damage. It is crucial to take a step back and evaluate our ways of interacting with others. Often, our behaviors are rooted in learned patterns, past experiences, or unaddressed wounds. Understanding the origins of our ways allows us to address the underlying issues, fostering personal growth and healthier relationship dynamics.

Excusing negative behaviors with explanations or placing blame on external factors can hinder personal development and strain relationships further. Instead, it's essential to take responsibility for our actions, seeking to align our ways with the values and virtues that God calls us to embody. This involves self-reflection, humility, and a willingness to change for the better.

Our ways impact how others feel, and planting excuses on top of negative behaviors only perpetuates a cycle of dysfunction. By acknowledging our shortcomings, seeking forgiveness where necessary, and actively working towards positive change, we can contribute to the restoration and flourishing of our relationships.

In essence, the way we regard and behave toward others is a reflection of our character and spiritual maturity. Aligning our ways with God's principles allows us to build relationships that honor Him and contribute to the well-being of those around us. As we navigate the complexities of human interactions, let us strive to cultivate ways that reflect the love, grace, and kindness modeled by our Creator.

Understanding the concept of relationship by breaking down the word "relationship" into "**relate-on-ship**" unveils a profound analogy likening relationships to ships. In this metaphorical voyage of life, relationships, friendships, and partnerships are akin to ships that traverse the seas of existence. Each ship, whether it be a friendship, familial tie, or romantic partnership, requires a collective understanding of its purpose and a shared vision of the promised land it aims to reach.

Boarding a "relation-ship" without a clear sense of purpose or a shared destination can lead to confusion, discord, and a journey adrift. The essence lies in understanding the purpose of the ship and the desired destination before embarking on the voyage. It is unwise to connect with individuals or entities that lack a sense of purpose, direction, or understanding of their intended journey.

Many people find themselves on relation-ships with no consideration for fundamental questions: What is the purpose of our voyage together? Where are we headed? Is this in alignment with God's will for our lives? Just as one would carefully consider boarding a physical ship, it is equally crucial to assess the relational ships we embark upon.
Before allowing someone to board our ship or joining another on their voyage, it's imperative to examine the vessel for any potential holes or weaknesses. These holes could signify unresolved issues, communication breakdowns, or areas of disagreement that may compromise the integrity of the relationship.

Furthermore, self-awareness is essential in this relational navigation. Understanding our own purpose and direction is key before extending an invitation for others to join us on our journey. Knowing where God is leading us is paramount, as it serves as a guiding force, steering our relational ship in alignment with His divine will.

Reflection becomes crucial in this process – have we considered the purpose of the relationships we are in or contemplating? Are we aware of any potential holes in these connections?

Who are we allowing to board our ship, and are they aligned with the direction God is sailing us towards?

In conclusion, the metaphor of the relation-ship underscores the importance of purpose, shared vision, and alignment with God's guidance in our relationships. By evaluating the ships we board or consider boarding, assessing their integrity, and ensuring a shared sense of purpose, we navigate the relational seas wisely, fostering connections that contribute to our individual and collective destinies.

Relational energy, in its essence, refers to the dynamic force produced by the thoughts, emotions, ideas, and actions exchanged in relationships. It is the invisible currency that flows between individuals, shaping the atmosphere and influencing the quality of connections. Understanding the impact of relational energy is paramount, as it can either generate synergy – a harmonious collaboration of positive energies – or sin-ergy – a discordant amalgamation of conflicting and negative forces.

Our thoughts, emotions, and ideas are not mere abstract concepts but potent energy-producing entities. When interconnected with others, these energies form a collective force that significantly affects the relational space. Synergy, the positive counterpart, emerges when individuals bring uplifting, loving, and God-centered energies into their interactions. It is a fusion of energies that amplifies the goodness within relationships.

On the contrary, sin-ergy manifests when negative energies, such as resentment, unforgiveness, envy, or any sinful disposition, intermingle with seemingly positive forces like love. This toxic combination produces an energy that can only yield negative outcomes, reinforcing destructive relational patterns and societal norms.

Relational energy is often rooted in past relationships, whether with ex-partners, family, or friends. Negative energies from previous connections can persist for years, influencing current relationships and affecting spouses, children, and others. Recognizing and addressing these lingering energies is essential for fostering healthy connections.

Synergistic relational energy is fueled by the Holy Spirit and the transformative power of God's Word. When individuals invest time in prayer, study the Scriptures, and allow the Holy Spirit to guide their thoughts and emotions, they contribute positive energy to their relationships. This synergistic energy becomes a beacon of hope and inspiration, radiating positivity not only within the relationship but also into the broader world.

Operating in high relational energy is a divine directive, as it creates atmospheres where relationships can breathe, thrive, and reflect the love and grace of God. By intentionally investing positive, God-inspired energy into our interactions, we contribute to the creation of environments that uplift, inspire, and foster growth. It is a conscious choice to align our relational energies with the principles of love, forgiveness, and the transformative power of God's grace.

God's Original Designs

It is crucial, much like constructing a building, to recognize the significance of having a blueprint before embarking on the journey of building relationships. God, the divine architect, holds the original designs for relationships in the palm of His omniscient hand.

Consider the analogy of a master architect meticulously crafting blueprints before the construction begins. In the realm of relationships, God is the ultimate Designer, and His blueprints serve as the foundational guide for building connections that reflect His relational nature. These blueprints embody transparency, trust, authenticity, and love—a divine framework meant to foster meaningful and lasting bonds.

Before God **assigns** relationships, He **aligns** individuals with His **designs**. It is a process of divine alignment, ensuring that the threads of connection are woven according to the patterns laid out by the Creator. God's design transcends the ephemeral and mundane, reaching into the spiritual and eternal realms of human connection.

God's Original Designs:
In exploring the concept of the divine design of relationships, we delve into the essence of God's original blueprints. These blueprints encapsulate the beauty of open communication, the strength of genuine authenticity, and the depth of empathy that surpasses human understanding.

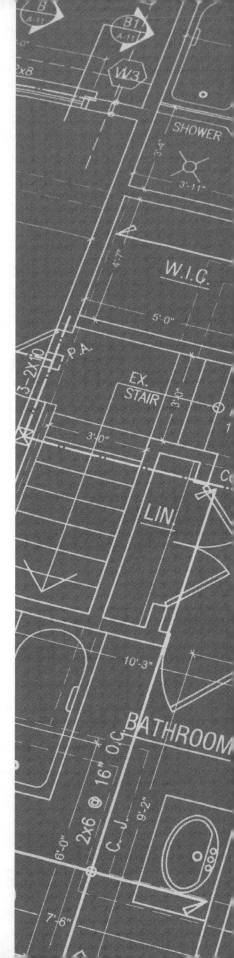

God's designs are not arbitrary; they are intentional, reflecting His desire for relationships to mirror the divine love and harmony found within the Trinity.

The Challenge of Alignment:
While God holds the perfect designs, the challenge lies in individuals aligning themselves with these divine patterns. The turbulence in many relationships often stems from a misalignment with God's designs. Understanding and embracing the blueprints require a willingness to submit to the divine wisdom that surpasses human comprehension.

Divine Alignment Process:
Before assigning relationships, God engages in a process of aligning individuals with His designs. This involves shaping hearts, renewing minds, and molding spirits to resonate with the divine frequencies of love, grace, and humility. It is a transformative journey that prepares individuals to enter into relationships not merely based on personal desires but rooted in the eternal purpose of reflecting God's glory.

The Transformative Power of Divine Alignment:
As individuals align themselves with God's designs, they experience a transformative power that goes beyond surface-level interactions. Relationships become vessels through which God's love and grace flow, creating bonds that withstand the tests of time and tribulations. In essence, the introduction of the divine design of relationships serves as an invitation to explore the beauty and purpose embedded in God's blueprints. It encourages individuals to align themselves with these designs, recognizing that true fulfillment in relationships comes from weaving connections according to the divine plan—a plan that stands as an eternal testament to the Creator's wisdom and love.

God's original designs for relational positions
In understanding God's original designs for various relationship positions, we unravel the intricate puzzle of divine intention woven into the roles of individuals. Each role contributes uniquely to the overarching purpose, creating a harmonious connection that reflects God's wisdom and design.

Son of God:
At the foundational level, every man must understand what it means to be a Son of God. This identity forms the bedrock of his existence, highlighting his worth, purpose, and connection to the Creator. As a Son of God, a man finds his true identity, significance, and belonging in Him. This foundational relationship lays the groundwork for understanding the divine attributes bestowed upon men. The Bible emphasizes this foundational relationship in passages like John 1:12 and Romans 8:16-17.

Manhood:
God's design for manhood encompasses qualities of leadership, strength, and responsibility. Men are called to reflect God's image through their character and actions. Scriptures like Genesis 1:27, Ephesians 5:25, and 1 Corinthians 16:13 outline the characteristics of godly manhood, emphasizing love, leadership, and steadfastness.

Husband:
In the context of marriage, a husband is designed to be a loving and sacrificial leader, mirroring Christ's relationship with the Church. Ephesians 5:25-33 provides a blueprint for husbands, emphasizing love, honor, and mutual respect within the marital relationship.

Father:
Fatherhood is a sacred responsibility bestowed by God, reflecting His role as our Heavenly Father. Fathers are called to provide, protect, and guide their children in the ways of the Lord. Scriptures like Proverbs 22:6, Ephesians 6:4, and Colossians 3:21 underscore the importance of nurturing children in the ways of God.

Purpose in the World:
Beyond familial roles, every man, as a Son of God, has a unique purpose in the world. God's design for each man extends to his broader impact on the world. Whether in careers, communities, or relationships, his purpose is intricately connected to God's overarching plan. Verses like Jeremiah 29:11, Ephesians 2:10, and Matthew 5:13-16 underscore his calling to be salt and light in the world, impacting it positively through his God-given purpose.

Understanding these relationships in light of God's original designs creates a holistic perspective that emphasizes the interconnectedness of these roles. By aligning with God's intentions, men contribute to a broader narrative that reflects His love, wisdom, and purpose in the world.

Daughter of God:
At the core of a woman's identity is her role as a Daughter of God. This foundational position emphasizes her inherent value, worth, and unique qualities designed by the Creator. Understanding herself as a beloved Daughter of God shapes her identity and provides a secure foundation. Scriptures like Psalm 139:13-16 and Galatians 3:26 underscore the significance of this foundational relationship.

Womanhood:
God's design for womanhood celebrates qualities of strength, grace, and nurturing. Women are called to reflect God's image through their character and contributions. Scriptures like Proverbs 31:10-31, Titus 2:3-5, and 1 Peter 3:3-4 highlight the virtues of godly womanhood, emphasizing wisdom, kindness, and reverence.

Wife:
In the context of marriage, a wife is designed to be a supportive and respectful partner, reflecting the unity and companionship found in the marriage covenant. Ephesians 5:22-33 provides guidance for wives, emphasizing mutual love, submission, and partnership within the marital relationship.

Mother:
Motherhood is a sacred and significant role given by God, reflecting His nurturing and caring attributes. Mothers are called to love, guide, and nurture their children in the ways of the Lord. Scriptures like Proverbs 31:25-30, 2 Timothy 1:5, and Isaiah 66:13 highlight the importance of a mother's influence in shaping the next generation.

Purpose in the World:
Beyond familial roles, every woman, as a Daughter of God, has a unique purpose in the world. God's design for each woman extends to her broader impact on the world. Whether in careers, communities, or relationships, her purpose is intricately connected to God's overarching plan. Verses like Jeremiah 29:11, Proverbs 31:20, and Matthew 5:14-16 emphasize her calling to be a light and influencer in the world, contributing positively through her God-given purpose.

Understanding these relationships in light of God's original designs empowers women to embrace their unique roles with confidence, purpose, and a deep sense of fulfillment. By aligning with God's intentions, women play a vital part in reflecting His love, wisdom, and purpose in the world.

Other Relational Positions
Friendship:
Friendship is a valuable and chosen connection between individuals, built on trust, loyalty, and shared experiences. Proverbs 17:17 highlights the essence of true friendship, stating, "A friend loves at all times, and a brother is born for a time of adversity." Godly friendships contribute to mutual growth, encouragement, and support.

Children (6-18):
As children grow and develop, their roles are marked by a season of learning, exploration, and shaping character. Proverbs 22:6 advises, "Start children off on the way they should go, and even when they are old, they will not turn from it." Parents, guardians, and mentors play a crucial role in guiding children through this formative stage, nurturing them with love, wisdom, and biblical values.

Reflection Questions:
1. Which of the relational positions mentioned above do you currently hold in your life? + On a scale of 1 to 10, how aligned do you feel with each of these roles?
   - _____ #_____
   - _____ #_____
   - _____ #_____
   - _____ #_____
   - _____ #_____
2. How do you believe your alignment with these roles impacts your overall well-being and fulfillment in life?
   _____
   _____
   _____
   _____
   _____

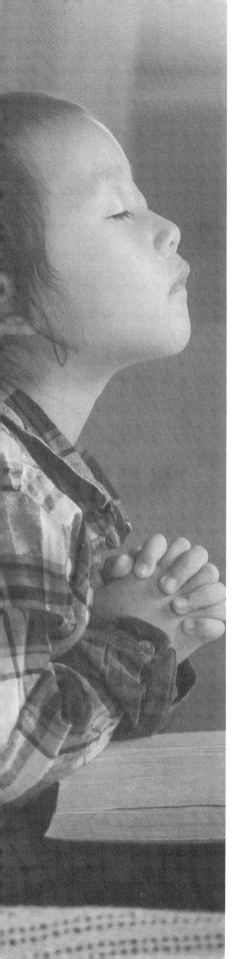

Foundational Relational Position: Sons and Daughters of God

At the core of all relational positions lies the foundational identity of being sons and daughters of God. This understanding shapes the lens through which we perceive ourselves and others, influencing the dynamics of every relationship. Sonship and daughterhood speak to our divine heritage, marking us as heirs to the Kingdom of God.

Defining Sonship:
Sonship is not merely a title; it is a profound relationship with the Creator. In Romans 8:15-17, the Bible says, "For you did not receive a spirit that makes you a slave again to fear, but you received the Spirit of sonship. And by him, we cry, 'Abba, Father.'" Sonship signifies a close, intimate connection with God as our loving Father. It is an invitation to approach Him with childlike trust, vulnerability, and dependence.

The Price and Process of Sonship:
The price of sonship was paid on the cross through the sacrifice of Jesus Christ. Galatians 4:4-7 underscores this, stating, "But when the set time had fully come, God sent his Son, born of a woman, born under the law, to redeem those under the law, that we might receive adoption to sonship." Through Christ's redemptive work, we are adopted into God's family, becoming His beloved sons and daughters. The process of sonship involves surrendering our lives to Christ, acknowledging our need for a Savior, and accepting the transformative work of the Holy Spirit. It requires shedding the old self and embracing the new identity found in Christ (2 Corinthians 5:17).

Enemy's Distortion of Fatherhood:
Recognizing the pivotal role of fatherhood in our understanding of God, the enemy seeks to distort this image. Negative experiences with earthly fathers, cultural influences, and societal trends contribute to misconceptions about God's fatherhood. Satan aims to erode trust, love, and dependency on God by clouding our perception of Him as a good Father.

Embracing Divine Fatherhood:
To safeguard all other relational positions, it is imperative to embrace God as a good Father. Jesus emphasized the importance of childlike faith in Matthew 18:3, "Truly I tell you, unless you change and become like little children, you will never enter the kingdom of heaven." When we grasp the depth of God's love as our Father, it becomes the bedrock for healthy relationships. Divine fatherly love infuses grace, forgiveness, and unwavering support into every connection, enabling us to navigate other relational positions with godly wisdom and compassion.

Understanding ourselves as sons and daughters of God is the linchpin that secures the fabric of all other relationships. As we anchor ourselves in this foundational identity, we become vessels of His love, extending grace and redemption to those around us.

God's Relational Nature:
As we delve deeper into the divine design of relationships, it becomes imperative to recognize the profound influence of God's relational nature on our connections. God, in His triune essence, embodies perfect harmony within the Father, Son, and Holy Spirit—a synergy that serves as the epitome of relational unity. Aligning ourselves with this divine harmony requires a holistic connection of spirit, soul, and body, mirroring the harmonious nature of the Trinity.

Harmony Within:
God's relational nature sets the standard for harmony within ourselves. The spirit, the eternal essence within us, seeks alignment with divine truth. The soul, encompassing the mind, will, and emotions, yearns for unity with God's wisdom and love. The body, the tangible vessel of expression, finds purpose in reflecting the grace and compassion inherent in God's triune nature. It is this holistic harmony that positions us to mirror God not only in our relationships but in every facet of our existence.

Impact on Various Relationships:
Understanding God's relational nature becomes the cornerstone for navigating relationships with profound purpose and meaning. In our connection with ourselves, aligning with the divine blueprint brings about self-awareness, self-acceptance, and a sense of purpose that transcends temporal desires. In spousal relationships, mirroring the love and unity within the Trinity fosters a foundation built on mutual respect, understanding, and shared purpose. Parental relationships, too, are transformed as parents seek to reflect God's nurturing and guiding nature.

The Importance of Relatability:
At the heart of God's relational nature lies relatability—a concept that transcends mere interactions and dives into the depth of connection. Relatability is the bridge that links the divine design to our daily interactions, making relationships not just a human endeavor but a sacred reflection of God's love. It is the key factor that transforms relationships from superficial engagements to profound, soul-enriching connections.

The Essence of Relatability:
Relatability is the ability to connect on a level that resonates with the core of our being. It involves genuine understanding, empathy, and authenticity—an embodiment of the very qualities found in God's relational nature. When we prioritize relatability, we open the door to meaningful connections that stand the test of time. It is a conscious choice to mirror God in our interactions, creating a ripple effect that extends beyond individual relationships to impact the broader essence of human connection.

Setting the Tone for Relatability:
As we journey through the exploration of God's design, let us set the tone for relatability in our relationships. Embracing the divine blueprint and mirroring God's relational nature allows us to navigate the intricate threads of connection with grace and purpose. Relatability becomes the compass guiding us through the intricacies of relationships, ensuring that every interaction echoes the divine harmony found within the Trinity.

In the next section, we will delve into the pillars that support relatability, exploring authenticity, respect, empathy, humility, communication, and adaptability. Following the brief explanations of the six pillars, we will journey through what broke relatability between God and man, as found in Genesis 3.

The Five Pillars of Relatability
In the journey of cultivating meaningful relationships, we encounter the foundational pillars that uphold the structure of relatability. These pillars, each essential in its own right, form the framework through which we tap into the full potential of our connections. Delving into the depths of authenticity, empathy, humility, effective communication, and adaptability, we explore how these qualities intertwine to create bonds that mirror the divine essence of relationships.

1. Authenticity:
Authenticity serves as the bedrock of relatability, the cornerstone upon which genuine connections are built. It involves presenting oneself without pretense, allowing others to witness the unfiltered truth of who we are. Authenticity invites vulnerability, fostering an environment where trust can flourish. When individuals embrace authenticity, relationships cease to be mere interactions; they become avenues for mutual understanding and acceptance.

2. Respect,

The second pillar of relatability shapes the landscape of our connections with others. It's the art of recognizing and honoring the intrinsic value of each person, fostering an environment where dignity and worth are paramount. In the fabric of relationships, respect is the thread that weaves understanding, courtesy, and empathy, creating a space where every individual is acknowledged and esteemed. Just as authenticity invites openness, respect invites a culture of honor and appreciation, allowing relationships to thrive in an atmosphere of mutual regard and valuing the uniqueness each person brings.

3. Empathy:

The third pillar, empathy, is the bridge that spans the gap between hearts. It goes beyond mere sympathy, diving deep into the ability to understand and share the feelings of others. Empathy cultivates a profound connection by acknowledging the emotions of those we interact with. In relationships, empathy creates a space where individuals feel heard, seen, and truly understood, nurturing a sense of belonging that transcends surface-level engagements.

4. Humility:

Humility, the fourth pillar, plays a transformative role in building resilient relationships. It involves recognizing our imperfections and extending grace to others. In the dance of humility, egos take a backseat, making room for mutual respect and understanding. When individuals embrace humility, conflicts become opportunities for growth, and relationships become arenas for the flourishing of grace.

5. Effective Communication:

The fifth pillar, effective communication, is the lifeblood of relationships. Open and respectful communication ensures that thoughts, feelings, and intentions are conveyed with clarity. It involves active listening, articulating emotions, and fostering a dialogue that deepens understanding. When communication flows seamlessly, relationships thrive, creating spaces for shared dreams, aspirations, and challenges.

5. Adaptability:

The sixth and final pillar, adaptability, is the key to navigating the ever-changing landscapes of relationships. It involves a willingness to grow, both individually and collectively, ensuring that connections remain vibrant and resilient.

Adaptability allows relationships to weather storms, embracing flexibility and fostering an environment where change becomes an opportunity for growth rather than a threat.

Tapping into the Potential:

As we delve into each pillar, it becomes evident that these qualities are not isolated but intricately interconnected. Authenticity lays the foundation for empathy, humility nurtures effective communication, and adaptability ensures the continued evolution of the relationship. Together, these pillars form a symphony that allows individuals to tap into the full potential of their connections.

_____
_____
_____
_____
_____
_____
_____
_____
_____
_____
_____
_____
_____
_____
_____
_____
_____
_____
_____
_____
_____
_____
_____
_____
_____
_____
_____
_____
_____
_____
_____
_____
_____
_____
_____
_____
_____

A RETURN TO THE GARDEN - UNDERSTANDING BROKENNESS

In the sacred Garden of Eden, where the fabric of human connection was once woven in perfection, we embark on a journey to unpack the profound narrative of brokenness. Genesis 3 unfolds a pivotal moment in the human story, revealing the intricate details of Adam and Eve's encounter with the serpent—an adversary seeking to exploit the vulnerabilities within the very essence of their beings.

The Serpent's Premise (Genesis 3:1):
In the subtle opening verse, the serpent enters the scene, sly and cunning. It addresses the woman, targeting the vulnerable aspects of her identity. This serpent, symbolizing the enemy, aims to engage with the weaker parts of ourselves, subtly undermining the strong areas of our lives. The serpent's premise is to create doubt and question God's intentions.

Knowing God's Original Design (Genesis 3:2):
The woman, representing humanity, is not oblivious to God's original design. She understands the divine blueprint of relationships, yet the serpent attempts to sever her connection by questioning God's word. The enemy insinuates that by partaking in the forbidden fruit, she wouldn't surely die, but that she can be like God, ruling her own life. Here, the serpent introduces the allure of autonomy, enticing the woman to step outside the boundaries of God's design.

The Temptation Angled for Every Key Area (Genesis 3:6):
As the woman succumbs to temptation, the narrative unveils how the enemy strategically tackles every key area of human existence. The forbidden fruit is declared "good for food, pleasant to the eyes, and desirable for gaining wisdom." This multifaceted temptation aims to contaminate not just one aspect but every dimension of our lives. In her choice, the woman unwittingly initiates the unraveling of the fabric of perfection. This unraveling, symbolized by the passing of the forbidden fruit to Adam, signifies the transfer of brokenness from the weaker side to the stronger areas, weakening their once harmonious connection with God.

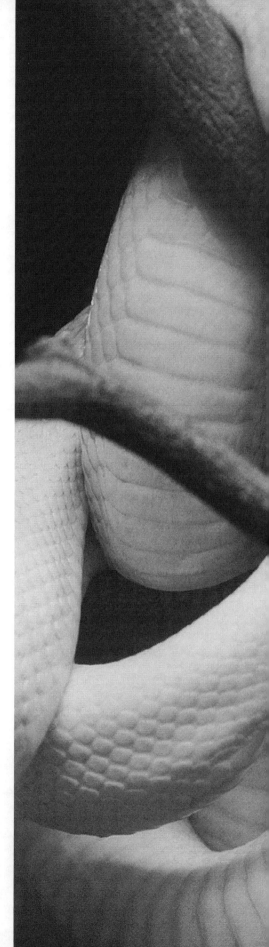

Entering Brokenness (Genesis 3:7):
Verse 7 marks the turning point. Their eyes are opened, and they become acutely aware of their vulnerability. Brokenness enters the scene, leading to shame and a desire to hide from God's presence. The enemy succeeds in convincing humanity to distance itself from the very source that sustains and provides insight for bettering relationships—the welcoming and acknowledging presence of God.

Blaming and Hiding (Genesis 3:9-12):
When God calls out to Adam, "Where are you?" it's not a question of geographical location but an invitation for Adam to assess his spiritual and emotional state. Adam's response, blaming the woman and indirectly blaming God ("the woman you gave me"), exemplifies a tendency inherent in broken relationships. We often deflect blame onto external factors, refusing to take responsibility for our decisions and actions.

Insights into Brokenness:
- Brokenness emerges when we entertain doubts about God's intentions and question His guidance.
- The enemy's strategy involves tempting us with the illusion of autonomy, leading to disobedience and broken connections.
- The multifaceted nature of temptation seeks to contaminate every key area of our lives.
- Hiding from God's presence perpetuates brokenness, hindering the transformative power of divine connection.
- Blaming others is a common response in broken relationships, deflecting responsibility and inhibiting growth.

This exploration of Genesis 3 unveils the root causes of brokenness—doubt, disobedience, and the allure of autonomy. As we navigate relationships, understanding these dynamics provides insight into the patterns that perpetuate broken connections and offers a path toward healing and restoration.

The Redemptive Plan through Jesus and the Transformative Role of the Holy Spirit:
In the midst of the brokenness that ensued in the Garden, hope emerges as we delve into the redemptive plan meticulously woven by God before the foundation of the world. The fall, rather than being a flaw in creation, becomes the canvas upon which God paints His masterpiece of grace and redemption.

The imperfection of the fallen world unveils God's redemptive and gracious qualities, as it is through brokenness that the transformative power of His plan is manifested.

God's Redemptive Plan Unveiled:
Before the foundations of the world, God already had a redemptive plan in place. The fall, rather than thwarting His purpose, becomes the perfect narrative to reveal God's character. The imperfection of a fallen world necessitates redemption, introducing God's gracious and loving intervention.

Jesus: Our Example and Representative (Hebrews 4:15):
Jesus stands at the center of God's redemptive plan, both our example and representative. As fully God and fully man, Jesus lived the life we couldn't and died the death we should. His humanity provides a relatable figure, a High Priest who understands every point of the human experience. Tempted at every point, yet without sin, Jesus becomes the bridge between broken humanity and a perfect God.

Key Points about Jesus:
- Jesus' life is a demonstration of the divine intent for relationships, showing us how to love, forgive, and embody the qualities essential for meaningful connections.
- As our representative, Jesus took upon Himself the consequences of sin, offering a path of reconciliation and restoration.

The Role of the Holy Spirit (John 16:7):
The Holy Spirit, an integral part of God's redemptive plan, plays a transformative role in the post-resurrection era. If Jesus hadn't paid the price for our sins, the Holy Spirit wouldn't have been released to enter us. Now, when the Father sees the blood on our lives and His Spirit in us, there is a connection. God, unable to relate to sin, has His Spirit within us to bridge the gap.

The Perfect Doorway for Jesus:
God, in His wisdom, designed the woman's womb with precision. The barrier preventing the mother's blood from crossing into the child's blood serves as a perfect doorway for Jesus to enter the world. This intentional design ensures the completion of God's redemptive plan through the incarnation of Jesus.

Transformation through the Holy Spirit:
With the Holy Spirit residing in us, the transformative journey begins. Each area of our lives is open to transformation, harmonizing with the divine blueprint of the Trinity. The Holy Spirit works within us, renewing our minds, reshaping our hearts, and aligning us with God's original designs for relationships.

In this section, we witness the unfolding of God's redemptive plan through Jesus and the transformative role of the Holy Spirit. The imperfection of the fallen world becomes the stage for God's gracious intervention, paving the way for the restoration of broken relationships and the harmonization of every aspect of our lives in the divine harmony of the Trinity.

RELATIONSHIP HOLES, REDEMPTION AND RETORATION.

Rediscovering Self-Awareness

In the intricate dance of relationships, self-awareness emerges as the choreographer, guiding each step with intention and clarity. To rediscover self-awareness is to embark on a transformative journey, peeling back the layers to reveal the subtle hindrances that impede the growth of connections. As we unravel the significance of self-awareness, we find that many traverse the intricate pathways of life blissfully unaware of the profound holes that punctuate their existence —open areas of vulnerability and weakness that silently impact relationships.

The Essence of Self-Awareness:

Self-awareness is the art of recognizing and understanding one's own thoughts, emotions, and behaviors. It involves peering into the mirror of the self with objectivity, embracing strengths, and acknowledging weaknesses without judgment. In the context of relationships, self-awareness becomes the foundation upon which meaningful connections are built—a lens through which individuals can navigate the intricate landscape of human interaction.

Unveiling the Unseen Holes:

Yet, for many, the journey into self-awareness remains uncharted territory. Unseen holes—those vulnerabilities and weaknesses lurking beneath the surface—persist, quietly influencing the dynamics of relationships. As we delve into the exploration of self-awareness, we begin the process of unveiling and addressing these relationship holes, starting with an understanding of the profound impact of generational patterns— the generational holes that intricately shape the narrative of our connections.

Generational Holes: Breaking Destructive Cycles. Generational holes are the silent echoes of the past that reverberate through the present, creating subtle yet profound impacts on relationships. These holes, often rooted in familial habits and traits, have the potential to shape the course of one's life, influencing the dynamics of connections across generations.

27

1. Repetition of Patterns:
Generational holes often manifest as a repetition of detrimental patterns. For instance, if a family has a history of unhealthy relationship dynamics—perhaps involving infidelity or unresolved conflict—there's a likelihood that these patterns will reemerge in subsequent generations. The repetition is not merely coincidental but a reflection of ingrained behaviors passed down through familial lines.

2. Inverse Reactions to Curses:
Interestingly, generational holes can also lead to inverse reactions. If a parent's behavior was excessively strict, it might create a hole in the next generation, tempting them towards a more lenient approach. This inversion can be a subconscious response to the perceived negative aspects of the past. Unaware of these generational patterns, individuals may unknowingly perpetuate or counteract the very behaviors they seek to avoid.

3. The Power of Recognition:
Addressing generational holes begins with recognition—a conscious awareness of the patterns and traits that have been passed down. Recognizing these familial influences provides the opportunity to break free from destructive cycles. It involves a courageous examination of one's own behaviors and a commitment to fostering positive change within the family lineage.

4. Intentional Transformation:
Breaking generational holes requires intentional transformation. Individuals must actively seek to replace negative patterns with positive, life-affirming behaviors. This may involve seeking therapy, engaging in self-reflection, and making intentional choices to break free from the chains of generational influence. The power of transformation lies in the awareness that change is not only possible but essential for building healthier relationships.

5. Breaking the Silence:
Generational holes often thrive in silence, with family narratives left unspoken. Breaking the silence is a key step in addressing these holes. Open and honest communication within families can unveil hidden patterns, fostering a collective commitment to positive change. By acknowledging the impact of generational holes, families can work together to rewrite their narrative and create a legacy of healthier, more fulfilling relationships.

In exploring generational holes, it becomes evident that self-awareness is the torch that illuminates the path toward transformation. Recognizing and addressing these patterns empower individuals to break free from destructive cycles, fostering healing within themselves and laying the foundation for healthier relationships across generations.

Workbook - Generational Holes Worksheet: Page 9

Emotional holes

As we journey deeper into the realms of self-awareness, we encounter emotional holes—those concealed openings in the fabric of our emotions that profoundly influence the course of relationships. Emotional holes, stemming from a lack of emotional intelligence or empathy, often go unnoticed, silently hindering the growth of connections with God, oneself, and others.

Understanding Emotional Holes:
Emotional holes are voids in our emotional intelligence, manifesting as difficulties in understanding and managing our own emotions or empathizing with the emotions of others. They emerge from various sources, such as unrealistic expectations leading to profound disappointments, experiences of abandonment, rejection, or abuse, and a myriad of other factors that contribute to emotional disconnection.

The Impact of Unrealistic Expectations:
Unrealistic expectations act as architects of emotional holes, creating chasms between desired outcomes and reality. When expectations are unmet, a void forms, and the emotional fabric is punctured. This rupture often leads to disappointment, frustration, and a diminished ability to navigate relationships with authenticity and understanding.

Contributing Factors to Emotional Holes:
Beyond expectations, emotional holes are often shaped by life experiences. The sting of abandonment, the scars of rejection, and the echoes of past abuse can leave lasting imprints on one's emotional landscape. These experiences, if unaddressed, create emotional blind spots that hinder the ability to forge deep and meaningful connections.

Hindering the Growth of Relationships:
Emotional holes act as barriers to the growth of relationships in various ways. A lack of emotional intelligence may result in an inability to communicate feelings effectively, leading to misunderstandings and conflict. The absence of empathy can create a disconnect in understanding the emotional experiences of others, impeding the development of compassion and genuine connection.

Addressing Emotional Holes:
To rediscover self-awareness is to embark on a journey of addressing and healing emotional holes. This involves recognizing the sources of emotional disconnection, whether rooted in unmet expectations or past traumas,

and intentionally working towards emotional intelligence and empathy. Through self-reflection, therapy, and a commitment to growth, individuals can mend these emotional holes, fostering healthier and more resilient relationships.

In the exploration of emotional holes, the significance of self-awareness becomes evident—a lantern guiding individuals through the labyrinth of emotions toward a deeper understanding of oneself and others. As we continue this journey, we uncover the intricacies of personal, generational, and emotional aspects, each playing a unique role in relational growth.

Workbook - Emotional Holes Worksheet: Page 10

Mental holes

Venturing further into the realm of self-awareness, we encounter mental holes—voids in our cognitive landscape that can profoundly influence relationships. These mental holes, born from ignorance, negative thoughts, haunting memories, and various other factors, operate silently, shaping the narrative of connections with God, oneself, and others.

Understanding Mental Holes:

Mental holes are gaps in our cognitive understanding and processing, manifesting as ignorance, negative thought patterns, or haunting memories. These voids, if left unaddressed, can hinder the growth of relationships and impact our ability to engage authentically with the world.

Ignorance as a Mental Hole:

Ignorance creates mental holes by limiting our understanding of the world and the perspectives of others. When we lack knowledge or awareness, assumptions and biases may fill the void, distorting our perceptions and leading to miscommunication and misunderstanding within relationships.

Negative Thought Patterns:

Negative thought patterns form mental holes through a continuous cycle of pessimistic thinking. These patterns, rooted in self-doubt, fear, or anxiety, create barriers to positive and constructive interactions. Persistent negative thoughts can erode self-esteem and hinder the development of healthy connections with others.

Haunting Memories:

Haunted by memories of past traumas or failures, individuals may experience mental holes that affect their present relationships. Unresolved issues from the past can influence behavior, communication, and overall emotional well-being, creating challenges in forming and maintaining meaningful connections.

Other Factors Contributing to Mental Holes:

- Limiting Beliefs: Fixed and limiting beliefs about oneself or others can create mental holes, constraining personal and relational growth.
- Lack of Mindfulness: A lack of mindfulness and presence in the moment can result in mental holes, as individuals may struggle to fully engage in and appreciate their relationships.
- Unhealthy Coping Mechanisms: Using unhealthy coping mechanisms, such as avoidance or substance abuse, can create mental voids that impede emotional and relational development.

Impact on Relationships:

Mental holes impact relationships by fostering misunderstandings, diminishing communication, and hindering personal and collective growth. Ignorance may lead to judgment, negative thought patterns can poison interactions, and haunting memories can cast shadows on the potential for genuine connection.

Dealing with Mental Holes:

Addressing mental holes involves intentional efforts toward self-awareness and cognitive growth. Strategies include:

- Education and Learning: Combat ignorance by seeking knowledge and understanding diverse perspectives.
- Trauma-Informed Approaches: Seek professional help for processing and healing from haunting memories.
- Mindfulness Practices: Cultivate mindfulness to stay present and engaged in the moment, reducing mental clutter.
- Healthy Coping Mechanisms: Replace unhealthy coping mechanisms with constructive strategies such as exercise, therapy, or creative outlets.

In the exploration of mental holes, the path to self-awareness becomes a transformative journey, guiding individuals through the complexities of their cognitive landscape toward healthier, more resilient relationships.

Workbook - Mental Holes Worksheet: Page 11

_____
_____
_____
_____
_____
_____
_____
_____
_____
_____
_____
_____
_____
_____
_____
_____
_____
_____
_____
_____

Physical holes

As we continue our exploration of self-awareness, we encounter physical holes—voids in our well-being that significantly impact relationships. These physical holes, often created by unhealthy habits, can pose challenges in keeping up with the unpredictability and rapidness of relationships. Understanding how physical fitness is intertwined with relational dynamics is crucial for cultivating meaningful connections with God, oneself, and others.

Unhealthy Habits as Physical Holes: Physical holes manifest through unhealthy habits that compromise our well-being. Sedentary lifestyles, poor nutrition, and inadequate sleep contribute to these voids, affecting our physical fitness and, subsequently, our ability to navigate the dynamic landscape of relationships.

Challenges of Unhealthy Habits:
1. Energy Depletion: Unhealthy habits can lead to fatigue and low energy levels, impacting our capacity to actively engage in relationships.
2. Mood Fluctuations: Poor physical health is often linked to mood swings and irritability, influencing the emotional tone of interactions.
3. Reduced Resilience: Physical unfitness diminishes resilience, making it challenging to cope with the rapid changes and uncertainties inherent in relationships.

Keeping Up with Relationship Dynamics:
Relationships are dynamic, requiring adaptability and resilience. Physical fitness enhances our capacity to keep pace with the unpredictability of connections. Regular exercise, a balanced diet, and sufficient rest contribute to increased stamina, improved mental clarity, and emotional stability—essential elements for navigating the twists and turns of relationships.

Why Physical Fitness Matters:
1. Vitality and Engagement: Physical fitness sustains vitality, allowing individuals to actively engage in relationships with enthusiasm and presence.
2. Stress Management: Exercise is a powerful stress reliever, aiding in the effective management of challenges within relationships.
3. Enhanced Mood: Physical activity triggers the release of endorphins, fostering a positive mood that contributes to healthier interactions.

4. Increased Resilience: A physically fit body enhances resilience, empowering individuals to bounce back from relationship setbacks with greater ease.

Addressing Physical Holes:
1. Regular Exercise: Incorporate physical activity into your routine to boost energy levels and improve overall well-being.
2. Nutrient-Rich Diet: Prioritize a balanced and nutritious diet to support physical health and mental clarity.
3. Adequate Rest: Ensure sufficient and quality sleep to rejuvenate the body and mind.
4. Mind-Body Practices: Explore mind-body practices such as yoga or meditation to integrate physical and mental well-being.

In the journey of self-awareness, recognizing and addressing physical holes is paramount. A physically fit body lays the foundation for resilient, vibrant relationships, enabling individuals to actively participate in the dance of connection with strength, adaptability, and enduring vitality.

Workbook - Physical Holes Worksheet: Page 12

_____
_____
_____
_____
_____
_____
_____
_____
_____
_____
_____
_____
_____
_____
_____
_____
_____
_____
_____
_____
_____
_____
_____
_____
_____
_____
_____
_____
_____
_____

Spiritual holes

As we delve deeper into the exploration of self-awareness, we encounter spiritual holes—voids that emerge from spiritual darkness, distance, and disobedience. These holes significantly influence relationships, highlighting the importance of drawing near to God, prayer, studying the Word, and fostering fellowship with the Holy Spirit for meaningful connections with God, oneself, and others.

Spiritual Holes:
Spiritual holes manifest through spiritual darkness, distance from God, and disobedience to divine guidance. These voids create a sense of spiritual disconnection, impacting the depth and authenticity of relationships.

Spiritual Darkness and Its Impact:
Spiritual darkness results from a lack of spiritual insight, wisdom, and understanding. It can lead to confusion, misguided priorities, and a diminished ability to navigate relationships with divine wisdom.

Distance from God:
Distance from God creates spiritual voids, hindering the awareness of His presence and guidance. A sense of spiritual distance can result from neglecting prayer, avoiding spiritual disciplines, or being entangled in worldly distractions.

Disobedience to Divine Guidance:
Disobedience to divine guidance creates holes in the spiritual fabric, disrupting the alignment with God's will. Ignoring God's directives may lead to relational challenges, as disobedience often stems from a self-centered rather than a God-centered perspective.

Importance of Drawing Near to God:
1. Biblical Foundation: Drawing near to God aligns with biblical principles, emphasizing the significance of a close relationship with the Creator for personal and relational well-being.
2. Divine Guidance: Proximity to God fosters a receptivity to divine guidance, providing clarity and wisdom in navigating relationships.
3. Transformation of Heart: Drawing near to God initiates a transformative process, aligning the heart with God's love, grace, and compassion.

Prayer and Word Study:
1. Communication with God: Prayer is the channel of communication with the Divine, fostering intimacy and a sense of connection.
2. Scriptural Wisdom: Studying the Word provides a foundation of biblical wisdom, guiding individuals in their interactions and decision-making within relationships.

Fellowship with the Holy Spirit:
1. Comfort and Counsel: Fellowship with the Holy Spirit brings comfort and counsel, aiding individuals in navigating challenges within relationships.
2. Fruit of the Spirit: The Holy Spirit produces fruits such as love, joy, peace, patience, kindness, goodness, faithfulness, gentleness, and self-control—qualities essential for healthy relationships.

Addressing Spiritual Holes:
1. Reconnecting through Prayer: Regular and earnest prayer serves as a pathway to draw near to God, fostering spiritual closeness.
2. Studying the Word: Delve into the Scriptures to gain spiritual insights and align personal values with biblical principles.
3. Seeking the Holy Spirit: Foster an ongoing relationship with the Holy Spirit through prayer, meditation, and a receptive heart.

In the realm of self-awareness, acknowledging and addressing spiritual holes is pivotal. A vibrant spiritual life not only deepens the connection with God but also enriches relationships with a divine perspective, love, and grace.

Workbook - Spiritual Holes Worksheet: Page 13

The chapters of our existence intricately weave together the threads of physical, mental, emotional, spiritual, and relational dimensions. Within this tapestry, these dimensions are not isolated; they are interdependent, forming a delicate balance that profoundly influences the quality of relationships. Neglecting, ignoring, or remaining unaware of a hole in one area sends reverberations through the others, creating a ripple effect. For instance, unhealthy physical habits can cast shadows on emotional well-being, impacting how individuals engage in relationships. Negative thought patterns, if left unaddressed, may permeate interactions, causing conflict and emotional strain.

Emotional scars, remnants of past wounds, can cloud mental clarity and decision-making, affecting relational dynamics. Neglecting spiritual practices may lead to fatigue, diminishing physical vitality and resilience. Relationships, acting as a nexus where all dimensions converge, hold the power to influence and shape the overall well-being of an individual. A strained relationship can exacerbate challenges in physical, mental, emotional, and spiritual realms, underscoring the profound interdependence of these facets. Recognizing this interconnectedness is key to a holistic approach to well-being, fostering integrated healing and resilient connections across all dimensions of life. In the journey of rediscovering self-awareness, understanding and addressing these interconnections become the guiding principles for cultivating a harmonious and balanced existence.

As we bring this chapter on self-awareness and relationship holes to a close, it's clear that our journey is one of interconnectedness and balance. The threads of physical, mental, emotional, spiritual, and relational aspects intricately weave the fabric of our lives. Neglected holes in any dimension cast a shadow over our relationships, affecting the delicate equilibrium of our existence. Yet, as we navigate the landscape of self-awareness, we uncover the transformative power of addressing these interconnected aspects. Healing and growth in one dimension reverberate through others, offering the promise of more resilient and fulfilling connections

THE SIX PILLARS EXPOUNDED

Authenticity, the first pillar of relatability, is a profound commitment to living in alignment with one's true self. To be authentic is to shed the layers of pretense and societal expectations, revealing the raw and genuine essence within. It involves embracing vulnerabilities, acknowledging imperfections, and daring to be transparent in a world that often encourages masks. Authenticity goes beyond mere honesty; it's a courageous unveiling of one's true identity, offering a genuine reflection for others to connect with. Being authentic means embracing both strengths and weaknesses, celebrating successes and acknowledging failures. It is the cornerstone of deep and meaningful connections, fostering an environment where individuals can truly see, understand, and resonate with each other's authentic humanity.

Embracing God's Design
In the divine fabric of creation, each individual is uniquely fashioned by the Creator. God's desire for authenticity stems from the recognition that He doesn't make copies; He crafts originals. Each person is a masterpiece, intricately designed with distinct qualities, purpose, and potential. Just as an artist cherishes the uniqueness of their creations, God celebrates the authenticity embedded within each individual.
Being authentic is not only a gift to ourselves but aligns with God's intention for genuine, unfiltered connection. The analogy extends to the notion that the things God has prepared for us are searching for our authentic selves. The blessings, opportunities, and meaningful connections ordained for our lives are intricately intertwined with our true identity.

When we present our authentic selves to the world, we become a magnet for the blessings that are tailored to our unique essence. It's a declaration that we are ready to receive what's authentically meant for us. God, the ultimate orchestrator of destinies, seeks to bless and guide us according to our true selves, for He knows the genuine desires of our hearts.

34

When individuals choose to be copies, mirroring societal expectations or conforming to a predefined blueprint, they inadvertently sabotage the potential for deep, authentic relationships. This reluctance to be authentic stems from the fear of standing alone as an original. In truth, the allure of being a copy might seem easier, providing a perceived safety within the familiar. However, this section unveils the detrimental impact of this conformity, particularly in the realm of relationships. Authenticity becomes the compass that guides individuals toward connections that resonate with their true selves. Many people, driven by the fear of rejection or societal judgment, compromise their authenticity, hindering the probability of finding a significant other or causing strain in existing relationships. The fear of embracing one's uniqueness often stems from a lack of guidance on how to stand alone as an original creation in God's grand design.

This section explores the challenges individuals face in breaking free from the mold, shedding light on the transformative power of authenticity in fostering genuine connections and attracting what has grace for the real, unfiltered self.

Romans 12:2 serves as a profound anchor in understanding the imperative of authenticity and the transformative power of renewing one's mind. The verse urges believers not to conform to the pattern of this world but to be transformed by the renewing of their minds. This counsel resonates with the idea that conformity to worldly norms can breed inauthenticity and hinder genuine connections. It emphasizes the call to resist societal pressures and expectations that may compromise one's true self. The transformative aspect, marked by the renewal of the mind, signifies a deliberate process of inner change and growth, aligning one's thoughts and perspectives with a higher, more divine standard. This resonates with the scripture in 1 John, cautioning against loving the world or its enticements. The conjunction of these scriptures underscores the importance of resisting conformity to worldly values and embracing a transformation that aligns with a higher spiritual truth. It signifies a profound shift in perspective, choosing authenticity over conformity, and aligning one's love and allegiance with higher, timeless principles rather than fleeting worldly desires.

Conforming to the world's norms can subtly erode the fabric of relationships, fostering inauthentic connections that lack depth and resonance. When individuals succumb to societal pressures and conform to external expectations, the genuine essence of who they are often gets overshadowed by a facade crafted to meet perceived standards.

This conformity weakens the bonds within relationships, creating a chasm between individuals and hindering authentic connection. On the contrary, the transformative journey of enhancing authenticity, inspired by the renewing of the mind as advocated in Romans 12:2, becomes a catalyst for profound positive change in relationships. Embracing one's true self, unburdened by societal expectations, fosters genuine connections built on transparency, trust, and mutual understanding. The commitment to authenticity becomes a cornerstone for flourishing relationships, where individuals feel seen, heard, and valued for who they truly are. This transformative shift not only benefits individual well-being but also contributes to the resilience and depth of connections, forming the bedrock for meaningful and enduring relationships.

Embracing our true selves proves to be an inherently simpler and more sustainable approach as we navigate the intricasies of relationships. Our authentic selves are a consistent thread that effortlessly weaves through different relationship domains, maintaining a coherence that resonates across various connections. The truth, after all, remains steadfast and doesn't require alteration to fit different contexts. In contrast, the complexity arises when individuals choose inauthenticity, attempting to be copies rather than embracing their unique selves.

The facade of conformity demands a constant juggling act, with the need to keep up appearances and maintain consistency in the ever-changing details of the charade. This exhausting endeavor not only strains personal well-being but also complicates interactions within different relationship spheres. God's design encourages simplicity and authenticity, making it abundantly clear that being true to oneself is not only easier but also aligns with the harmonious flow that He intended for our lives. In embracing our true selves, we find a natural ease in navigating the complexities of relationships, allowing for genuine connections to flourish without the burdensome weight of pretense.

Loving ourselves becomes an integral aspect of embracing authenticity, and it all starts with acknowledging and accepting the unwavering love that God has for each of us. Once we grasp the depth of God's love, understanding that we are fearfully and wonderfully made in His image, we unlock the pathway to genuine self-love.

God's love serves as the foundation upon which we can build a healthy and authentic appreciation for who we are. In this self-love, we discover a reservoir of compassion and kindness that allows us to extend love authentically to others. When we authentically love ourselves as God loves us, we gain clarity on how to navigate relationships with a genuine and compassionate heart. This authentic self-love becomes the wellspring from which we draw, enabling us to discern how and to whom we should distribute our love.

It becomes a harmonious flow—God's love leading to self-love, and self-love guiding the sincere distribution of love to those around us. This interconnected journey of love, starting with God's divine love, empowers us to authentically express love in all our relationships, fostering connections rooted in truth, compassion, and grace.

Understanding the authenticity of oneself carries the realization that not everyone is destined to be a part of our intimate relational spheres. Relationships, whether they be friendships, partnerships, or familial bonds, were never designed to be forced or desperately pursued. Instead, they were intended to unfold organically, in alignment with God's divine plan. Recognizing that not everyone is meant to be intricately woven into the fabric of our lives, and vice versa, is a powerful revelation. God, in His infinite wisdom, designed our relational connections before we were even created.

This understanding dismantles the urgency to race into relationships, as it unveils the divine orchestration behind every meaningful connection. Just as we are not meant for everyone, not everyone is meant for us. Embracing this truth liberates us from the pressure to force connections that may not align with God's intended plan. It allows relationships to blossom organically, fostering a space for genuine, authentic connections that stand the test of time and align with the divine blueprint that God laid out for our lives.

Standing alone as an original creation in God's grand design is a transformative endeavor that begins with cultivating a deep, personal connection with God. It involves understanding and embracing one's unique identity, acknowledging the gifts and talents instilled by the Creator. This journey entails seeking God's guidance in prayer and meditation, aligning one's purpose with His divine plan.

Before walking alongside someone else, it is crucial to stand alone with God, solidifying a foundation of strength and clarity. This solitary alignment with the Creator allows for an authentic understanding of self, fostering independence rooted in divine purpose. It is within this sacred solitude that individuals can find the courage to resist societal pressures and expectations, confidently embracing their originality. Standing alone with God is not a state of isolation but a deliberate choice to cultivate a profound connection that becomes the wellspring of authenticity. This intentional alignment allows individuals to enter relationships from a position of strength, bringing a whole and genuine self to the intricate dance of connections, grounded in the certainty of being an original creation in God's intricate design.

My Testimony:
More than ten years ago, I was deeply invested in discovering my true purpose. I was leading a Bible study program called Unplugged, which aimed to help individuals connect with their authentic selves. One Thursday evening, as I fully embraced the purpose designed for that phase of my life, something remarkable happened. Little did I realize that this evening would mark the beginning of an extraordinary journey - it was the night I met the woman who would later become my wife. If I had been merely imitating someone else's purpose or lifestyle, I might have missed this divine alignment. By embracing my true self, I not only attracted the purpose meant for me but, unexpectedly and beautifully, I also attracted the person who would share in this journey with me. This profound connection serves as a powerful reminder of the magnetic force of authenticity. When we have the courage to be genuine, we effortlessly align with what is truly meant for us.

To those wrestling with self-doubt or the pressure to conform, I empathize, for I, too, once struggled with dissatisfaction in the mirror. There was a time when I longed to mirror the athleticism, charisma, and charm of others, feeling that my innate gifts of advice-giving and empathy were somehow inferior. I allowed the applause of peers to dictate the worth of my unique abilities. However, the transformative journey toward authenticity led me to embrace and celebrate who I truly am. Now, echoing the sentiments of the Psalmist in Psalm 139, I declare, "I praise you, for I am fearfully and wonderfully made; wonderful are your works; my soul knows it very well."

This newfound perspective urges each of us to look in the mirror through the eyes of our Creator, acknowledging the intricate design and purpose woven into our being. It is a reminder that authenticity is not a weakness but a divine strength, an affirmation to embrace the unique gifts that make us fearfully and wonderfully made.

As we conclude this exploration of authenticity, let us recognize that the journey towards being our authentic selves is a continuous process intricately woven into the fabric of personal growth. It requires patience, self-reflection, and a willingness to embrace the transformative power of God's design. Surrounding ourselves with a supportive community that values authenticity becomes a pivotal aspect of this journey, providing shared experiences and encouragement.

Workbook - Authenticity Worksheet: Page 14

Self-Reflection on Authenticity:
- Reflect on moments in your life when you felt the pressure to conform or imitate others. How did this impact your sense of self? In what ways have you embraced your authentic self, and how has it positively influenced your relationships?
1. Embracing Divine Design:
   - Consider the idea that God crafts each individual as a unique masterpiece. How does this perspective resonate with you? In what ways can embracing your true identity align with God's design enhance your relationships and connections?
2. The Transformative Power of Authenticity:
   - Explore instances where authenticity played a transformative role in your relationships. How did being true to yourself contribute to the depth and resilience of those connections? How might embracing authenticity continue to shape your interactions with others?
3. The Journey of Standing Alone with God:
   - Reflect on the concept of standing alone as an original creation in God's design. How does cultivating a deep, personal connection with God contribute to your authenticity? In what ways can this intentional alignment with the Creator empower you in relationships?

Respect stands as the cornerstone of healthy and meaningful relationships, serving as the second pillar of relatability, following closely behind authenticity. At its core, respect begins with our reverence for God. Our level of respect or reverence for the Divine directly influences our self-respect and the manner in which we interact with others.

Scripture teaches us that the fear of the Lord is the beginning of wisdom. This principle underscores the importance of fearing or revering God in every aspect of our lives. When we hold God in the highest regard, it cultivates a deep sense of respect for His creation, including ourselves and those around us. However, in today's society, this concept of reverence has been distorted. The enemy seeks to invert our understanding of fear, encouraging us to fear everything except what God has made. We are bombarded with lies, perversion, and false ideologies, instilling fear in areas where God intends us to exercise trust and respect.

Yet, when we genuinely fear God, it aligns our perspective with His divine order. It teaches us to respect His creation at the level He intends for us. This includes respecting ourselves, our fellow human beings, and the world around us. In essence, our reverence for God lays the foundation for cultivating a culture of respect in all our interactions. It reminds us of the inherent value and dignity of every individual, guiding us to honor and esteem others as we would ourselves.

The fear of God serves as the catalyst for self-respect, instilling within us a deep understanding of our inherent worth and dignity. When we truly reverence God, we recognize ourselves as His beloved creation, fearfully and wonderfully made in His image. This realization fosters a profound sense of self-worth, rooted not in our accomplishments or external validation but in our identity as cherished children of God.

Moreover, our reverence for God shapes our perception of ourselves. Instead of comparing ourselves to societal standards or seeking approval from others, we find our validation in God's unconditional love and acceptance. This empowers us to embrace our strengths, acknowledge our weaknesses, and journey towards personal growth with confidence and humility.

Additionally, the fear of God compels us to uphold moral integrity and righteousness in our lives. As we reverence His holiness and righteousness, we are motivated to align our thoughts, words, and actions with His divine standards. This commitment to living in accordance with God's will cultivates a deep sense of self-respect, knowing that we are honoring our Creator and fulfilling our purpose. Furthermore, the fear of God guards us against the destructive influences of pride, arrogance, and self-centeredness. When we humbly acknowledge God's sovereignty and authority over our lives, we surrender our egocentric desires and ambitions. This humility fosters an authentic sense of self-respect, characterized by humility, grace, and a servant's heart.

In essence, the fear of God serves as the bedrock of self-respect, guiding us to value ourselves as God does and empowering us to live with integrity, humility, and purpose. As we cultivate a reverent awe of God, we discover the true depth of our worth and embrace the journey towards becoming the individuals He created us to be.

The fear of God extends beyond our relationship with ourselves and permeates every aspect of our lives, including our craft and relationships. When we approach our work with reverence for the One who has bestowed us with talents and abilities, we honor the divine source of creativity and excellence. This perspective instills a deep respect for our craft, compelling us to pursue excellence and steward our talents with diligence and integrity.

In marriage, the fear of God cultivates a deep respect for the sacred covenant between spouses. As we honor God's design for marriage, we prioritize mutual love, understanding, and support, valuing our partner's unique strengths and contributions. This respect creates a harmonious partnership where both spouses feel valued, affirmed, and empowered to flourish in their respective roles.

Similarly, the fear of God influences our parenting approach, instilling a profound respect for the gift of children entrusted to our care. When we reverence God as the ultimate authority and source of wisdom, we recognize the divine purpose and potential inherent in each child. This respect leads us to parent with love, patience, and discipline, nurturing our children's growth and development in a manner that honors their individuality and dignity.

Furthermore, in positions of leadership or influence, the fear of God compels us to lead with integrity, humility, and respect for those under our care. Whether in the workplace, community, or church, we steward our authority and influence responsibly, seeking the well-being and growth of those we lead. This respect creates an environment of trust, collaboration, and empowerment, where individuals are valued and supported in their journey towards personal and collective fulfillment.

Moreover, as we honor God through our relationships and interactions, His glory becomes evident in every story. Respect for God's divine order and authority ensures that His presence can flow seamlessly through every aspect of our lives, infusing our marriages, families, and spheres of influence with His love, grace, and wisdom. Ultimately, the fear of God leads us to prioritize His glory above all else, recognizing that true fulfillment and purpose are found in honoring Him in every area of our lives.

Reflection Questions
1. How does your understanding of the fear of God influence your level of respect for yourself and others in your daily interactions?
2. Reflect on a time when you felt challenged to demonstrate respect in a relationship. How did your reverence for God guide your response and actions?
3. Consider the impact of respect on your relationships with your spouse, children, or those under your influence. How can you cultivate a deeper sense of respect in these relationships to honor God's design and purpose?
4. Have you noticed any areas in your life where a lack of respect for God's creation or His design has led to discord or dissatisfaction in your relationships? Reflect on how you can realign your perspective to honor His creation and promote harmony.
5. How do you balance asserting your own needs and boundaries with showing respect towards others, particularly in moments of conflict or disagreement? Reflect on ways to maintain respect while advocating for yourself and fostering understanding and empathy towards others.

Empathy, far from a mere social courtesy, unfolds as a dynamic force that brings depth and authenticity to our relationships. It is the art of stepping into another's shoes, comprehending their emotions, and embracing their perspective with an open heart. This chapter invites us to unravel the transformative nature of empathy, acknowledging its role as a key pillar in the construction of meaningful connections. As we navigate the nuances of empathetic engagement, we discover that its essence lies not only in the acknowledgment of shared emotions but in the profound capacity to create a space where understanding and compassion flourish, paving the way for relationships to thrive in authenticity and depth.

In unraveling the essence of empathy, it is paramount to define this intricate and transformative concept that serves as a cornerstone in the realm of interpersonal dynamics. Empathy transcends the boundaries of mere sympathy, as it involves a profound and emotional connection with others that goes beyond surface-level understanding. At its core, empathy is the ability to step into another's shoes, not merely acknowledging their struggles but deeply understanding the emotions and experiences that accompany them.

Unlike sympathy, which may offer a compassionate glance at the surface of a person and their situation, empathy plunges into the depths of their feelings and perspectives. It is a dynamic engagement that requires a genuine curiosity about the intricacies of another's emotional world. Through this profound connection, empathy becomes a bridge, forging bonds that extend beyond the superficial, fostering a level of understanding that resonates at the very core of our shared humanity. It is in this understanding that relationships find fertile ground for growth, trust, and the shared experience of navigating the complexities of life.

Transitioning from the essence to the practical application of empathy, let's delve into the intricate realm of fostering empathetic communication. Empathy, as a dynamic force in relationships, finds its expression through deliberate and conscious communication. Breaking down the components of empathetic communication, it becomes evident that active listening stands as a cornerstone.

This involves not only hearing words but fully comprehending the emotions embedded within them. Additionally, emphasizing the validation of emotions becomes pivotal, as it acknowledges the legitimacy of the other person's feelings. It involves communicating not just an understanding of the words spoken but an affirmation of the emotions experienced. This intentional validation creates a safe and empathetic space where individuals feel heard, understood, and valued. As we delve into these components, we discover that empathetic communication is not merely a skill but a transformative art that deepens connections and lays the foundation for authentic relationships.

Let's journey from the theoretical framework of empathetic communication to tangible scenarios where its positive outcomes shine brightly. In the context of a marital relationship, imagine a scenario where one partner expresses feelings of overwhelm due to work-related stress. Through empathetic communication, the other partner actively listens, comprehends the emotional weight, and validates these feelings. This fosters a supportive environment, reinforcing the emotional bond between spouses.

In the realm of parenting, empathetic communication takes center stage when a child expresses fears or concerns. A parent who practices active listening, fully grasping the child's emotions and validating their feelings, creates a space for open dialogue. This not only strengthens the parent-child relationship but also nurtures the child's emotional intelligence.

In the realm of friendships, empathetic communication transforms conflicts into opportunities for understanding. Picture a situation where a friend shares a personal struggle.

Through active listening and validating their emotions, the friend fosters a deep connection, turning a moment of vulnerability into a strengthening bond. These real-life examples illuminate the transformative power of empathetic communication across diverse relationship scenarios, illustrating its ability to foster understanding, nurture emotional bonds, and contribute to the overall well-being of individuals within these connections.

As we embark on the journey of cultivating empathy, it is essential to bridge theory with practice through practical exercises that will empower you to enhance your empathetic skills. These exercises are not merely theoretical concepts but actionable steps that you can integrate into your daily life. One such exercise involves the intentional practice of active listening in everyday conversations. Focus on truly hearing the words spoken by others, attuning yourself to the emotional nuances behind the language.

Another practical exercise is to engage in perspective-taking, a transformative tool for deepening empathy. This exercise encourages you to step into the shoes of others, considering their unique experiences, challenges, and emotions. By doing so, you'll broaden your understanding and foster compassion.

Self-reflection and awareness emerge as vital components in the cultivation of empathy. Readers are encouraged to engage in introspective practices that illuminate their own emotional responses and biases. This self-awareness serves as a catalyst for empathetic growth, enabling you to navigate interpersonal dynamics with a heightened sensitivity to the diverse emotions at play.

In essence, these practical exercises extend an invitation for you to actively participate in the transformative journey of cultivating empathy. By integrating these exercises into your daily interactions and fostering self-reflection, you not only enhance your empathetic skills but also contribute to the creation of a more compassionate and understanding world.

Transitioning from the individual cultivation of empathy to its impact on relationships, let's delve into the vital role of compassion in nurturing stronger connections. Compassion, the natural offspring of empathy, acts as the glue that binds individuals within relationships. Its essence lies in the ability to recognize and respond to the suffering or joys of others, fostering a deep sense of understanding and shared humanity.

Within the relational context, empathetic gestures become the tangible expressions of compassion. Imagine a scenario where one partner, attuned to the emotional needs of the other, offers a comforting gesture during a challenging moment. This act of empathy transforms into a compassionate gesture, creating a more harmonious and supportive environment within the relationship.

Exploring further, we recognize that compassionate actions extend beyond grand gestures to everyday nuances. Small acts of kindness, empathetic listening, and genuine understanding collectively contribute to a relational ecosystem where individuals feel seen, valued, and supported. In essence, nurturing compassion in relationships becomes a reciprocal dance where empathetic gestures lay the groundwork for a more harmonious and interconnected relational environment, strengthening the bonds that hold individuals together in shared empathy and understanding.

Delving into the profound principles of empathy and compassion, we find a timeless guidance in the scriptural wisdom that encourages us to "weep with those who weep and rejoice with those who rejoice." This powerful verse encapsulates the essence of empathy by urging us to attune ourselves to the emotions of others, sharing in both their joys and sorrows. When someone is in pain, the call is not just to observe but to genuinely weep alongside them, acknowledging and validating their emotions. Conversely, in moments of celebration, the directive is not mere observation but active participation in the joy of others. This scripture goes beyond a mere acknowledgment of emotions; it calls for a transformative engagement that mirrors the compassionate heart of God.

Conversely, failing to adhere to this principle can be perceived as selfishness. When we withhold the empathy required, whether in sharing grief or joy, it weakens the bonds of relationships. When individuals sense that others are not connecting with them emotionally, it creates a rift, suggesting a lack of genuine empathy. The capacity to weep and rejoice with others becomes a barometer of our commitment to understanding and supporting those we are in relationship with. Thus, embodying the essence of this scripture becomes not only a spiritual practice but a foundational principle for building and sustaining meaningful connections.

In concluding this exploration of empathy, we unearthed its transformative power within the intricate fabric of relationships. The key takeaways resound with the understanding that empathy is not merely a sentiment but a dynamic force capable of fostering profound connections.

Through empathetic communication, intentional practices, and compassionate gestures, individuals can cultivate a relational environment where understanding and shared humanity thrive.

As you embark on your own journey of integrating empathy into your daily interactions, may you carry with you the realization that this transformative quality is not just a virtue but a catalyst for deeper connections. Let empathy be the guiding force that transcends differences, builds bridges, and nurtures the bonds that unite us in the shared experience of the human condition. In the symphony of relationships, empathy becomes the note that harmonizes understanding, compassion, and support, creating a melody of connections that withstand the tests of time and circumstance. May this chapter inspire you to embrace empathy as a cornerstone in the construction of meaningful and authentic relationships.

Workbook- Empathy Reflection Questions Page 15
1. Empathy in Everyday Scenarios:
   - Reflect on a personal experience where someone demonstrated empathy towards you in a challenging moment. How did their empathetic gestures impact your feelings, and what aspects of their behavior made you feel truly understood and supported?
2. Practical Exercises for Cultivating Empathy:
   - Consider engaging in the suggested practical exercises for cultivating empathy. How did intentional active listening, perspective-taking, and self-reflection influence your understanding of others and your own emotional responses? Share specific instances where these exercises made a difference in your interactions.
3. The Role of Compassion in Relationships:
   - Think about a relationship where compassion played a significant role. How did empathetic gestures contribute to the nurturing of compassion within that relationship? In what ways did small acts of kindness and understanding strengthen the bonds between you and the other person?
4. Embodying Scriptural Wisdom on Empathy:
   - Explore your experiences in adhering to the scriptural wisdom that encourages us to "weep with those who weep and rejoice with those who rejoice." How has embodying this principle impacted your relationships? Share instances where you actively engaged in both shared grief and joy, and the effects it had on the dynamics of those relationships.

These reflection questions are designed to deepen your understanding of empathy and its transformative impact on relationships. Take time to reflect on your experiences, insights, and personal growth as you integrate empathy into your daily interactions and strive to create more meaningful and authentic connections with others.

_____
_____
_____
_____
_____
_____
_____
_____
_____
_____
_____
_____
_____
_____
_____
_____
_____
_____
_____
_____
_____
_____
_____
_____
_____
_____
_____
_____
_____
_____
_____
_____
_____
_____
_____
_____
_____
_____
_____
_____
_____

Humility

In the exploration of humility within the realm of relationships, we embark on a comprehensive journey in this section: Unpacking Humility. Humility, in its essence, goes beyond a mere dictionary definition; it is a dynamic and multifaceted quality that plays a crucial role in the delicate dance of human connections. At its core, humility involves a profound self-awareness, a willingness to recognize one's imperfections, and an authentic openness to understanding and prioritizing others. The multifaceted aspects of humility within relationships extend beyond a surface-level understanding, delving into genuine respect, empathetic understanding, and an acknowledgment of shared humanity.

However, as we delve into this exploration, we confront the prevailing misconceptions that often obscure the true nature of humility. Misinterpreted as weakness by some, humility faces resistance in a world that may misjudge it as submissiveness. By unraveling these misconceptions, we aim to reshape perspectives and emphasize humility as a source of strength, fostering genuine connections. Additionally, we address the challenges associated with practicing humility, acknowledging the inherent difficulties in embracing vulnerability and surrendering the ego. This comprehensive exploration sets the stage for a deeper understanding of humility's transformative role, laying the foundation for resilient connections that withstand the complexities of human relationships.

In the complex web of relationships, the profound impact of humility unfolds prominently as individuals embrace and acknowledge their imperfections. Humility, as an authentic self-awareness, encourages a willingness to confront and recognize personal flaws. This acknowledgment becomes a pivotal step in fostering authenticity within relationships. When individuals openly admit to their imperfections, it creates an environment of vulnerability and honesty. This, in turn, lays the groundwork for genuine connections where both parties can relate to each other on a human level, free from the pretense of perfection.

Real-life examples abound, illustrating how acknowledging imperfections contributes to relational strength. Consider the scenario where a partner openly admits to struggling with communication. Instead of hiding this flaw, acknowledging it becomes an invitation for collaborative growth. The act of recognizing and embracing this imperfection opens the door for honest conversations and shared efforts to improve communication skills. In friendships or family dynamics, similar authenticity about imperfections can create spaces for mutual support, understanding, and ultimately, resilience in the face of challenges.

This transformative power of acknowledging imperfections aligns seamlessly with the essence of humility discussed in Section 1. Humility, with its multifaceted aspects, stands as the catalyst for individuals to recognize and embrace their imperfections, fostering deeper connections built on authenticity and mutual understanding. As individuals navigate the complexities of humility, they pave the way for a relational landscape that values honesty, vulnerability, and shared humanity.

Within the intricate dance of relationships, the role of grace emerges as a transformative force, contributing to the creation of an atmosphere steeped in mutual respect. Grace, in the context of relationships, involves extending kindness, forgiveness, and understanding even when faced with imperfections and shortcomings.

The essence of grace is deeply intertwined with humility, as it requires a recognition of one's own fallibility and a willingness to extend compassion to others in their moments of vulnerability. When individuals embrace grace, they move beyond a judgmental mindset and instead approach relationships with a spirit of understanding.

This approach fundamentally alters the dynamics, creating a space where mistakes are not met with condemnation but are opportunities for growth and learning.

Practical insights into extending grace further emphasize its significance in relationships. The act of forgiving and extending understanding becomes a tool for resolving conflicts and strengthening bonds. In moments of tension or disagreement, choosing grace allows individuals to step back, view situations through a lens of empathy, and respond with a generous spirit. This, in turn, paves the way for open communication, creating a foundation for mutual respect and sustained connection.

The interconnected nature of grace, humility, and acknowledging imperfections contributes to the holistic understanding of humility within relationships. As individuals navigate the complexities of extending grace, they contribute to the creation of a relational atmosphere where mutual respect thrives, and connections endure the test of time and challenges.

Conflict is an inevitable part of any relationship, but how individuals approach and navigate these conflicts can make all the difference. Humility becomes the guiding force that enables individuals to set aside ego, listen with an open heart, and seek resolution through understanding rather than dominance. Humility's role in conflict resolution is multifaceted. It involves acknowledging one's own contributions to the conflict, recognizing the validity of the other person's perspective, and approaching the resolution process with a genuine willingness to find common ground. Instead of seeking victory or vindication, humble individuals prioritize the health of the relationship and value the perspective of the other party.

In the arena of conflict, humility becomes a potent weapon against not only the tangible disputes between individuals but also the unseen forces that seek to sow discord and division. The enemy, often unseen, strives to turn the battleground of relationships into a chaotic field where individuals engage in a relentless struggle against each other. The insidious tactics of pride and the powers of darkness work hand in hand, aiming to escalate conflicts and divert attention from the true adversary.

Humility, as a formidable defense mechanism, acts as a shield against the arrows of pride and the schemes of darkness. It operates on a higher plane, recognizing that the true victory lies not in the defeat of the other person but in the preservation and enhancement of the relationship. By embracing humility, individuals disarm the enemy's tactics, refusing to be drawn into the quagmire of ego-driven conflicts.

When conflicts begin to escalate, it is crucial to discern the underlying forces at play—whether it be the unchecked pride within individuals or the subtle influence of dark powers seeking to destabilize relationships. Humility becomes the strategic countermeasure, defusing pride and preventing the escalation of conflict. It shifts the focus from winning at all costs to sustaining the relationship, recognizing that true victory is found in the mutual growth and understanding that emerges when ego takes a back seat.

In the battlefield of relationships, humility becomes the key to defeating the true enemy. It redirects the narrative from a self-centered pursuit of victory to a collaborative effort to nurture and strengthen connections. As individuals choose humility over pride, they not only overcome the immediate conflicts but also fortify themselves against the insidious forces that seek to undermine the bonds of relationships. The goal becomes clear – it is not the triumph of one over the other, but the victory of the relationship over the divisive forces that threaten its harmony.

The "Spicy Chicken Sandwich" technique offers a practical and intentional approach to defusing conflicts through humility and grace. Much like the layers of a sandwich, this method involves carefully constructing the conversation to ensure that the individual feels celebrated, heard, and understood.

The first layer, the "Bottom Bun," represents celebrating the person. Before delving into the spicy components of the conversation, take a moment to reflect on the positive aspects of your relationship with them. Acknowledge and appreciate their strengths and qualities. This initial step sets a positive tone and helps soften potential defenses.

The "Spicy Chicken" layer introduces the concern or conflict in a respectful and honest manner. Start by expressing gratitude and admiration, then delicately introduce the issue that needs addressing. By framing it as a concern rather than an accusation, you create an atmosphere of openness and receptivity.

The final layer, the "Top Bun", is crucial for concluding the conversation on a positive note. After addressing the spicy components, reaffirm your appreciation for the individual. Share empathy and understanding, emphasizing that the goal is not to diminish them but to strengthen the relationship. This closing celebration helps neutralize any lingering tension and fosters an environment of mutual respect.

Remember the wisdom found in Proverbs 15:1 – "A soft answer turns away wrath." Approach the conversation with a calm and gentle demeanor, allowing humility and grace to guide your words. The "Spicy Chicken Sandwich" technique provides a practical framework for navigating conflicts, promoting understanding, and building resilient relationships.

While humility is a powerful virtue in relationships, it's essential to strike a balance and avoid extremes, such as being overly humble or operating in false humility. Let's delve into the significance of finding this balance.

Avoiding Overly Humble Behavior:
Being too humble might involve constantly downplaying your strengths, achievements, or opinions. While humility encourages acknowledging imperfections and recognizing the value of others, it doesn't require diminishing your own worth. Overly humble behavior can lead to self-deprecation, eroding self-esteem, and preventing healthy self-expression. It's crucial to embrace humility without neglecting the importance of acknowledging your strengths and contributions.

A healthy balance ensures that you offer genuine humility while maintaining a confident and authentic self-awareness.
In the past, I found myself trapped in this pattern. I would downplay my accomplishments, books, and the evident favor of God in my life, thinking it was a way to avoid coming off as arrogant.

However, I learned a valuable lesson: it's not wise to dim a light that could inspire others. While genuine humility is essential, it doesn't require hiding the glory of God working through your life. Embracing humility without diminishing the impact of your journey can be both inspiring and authentic. It's crucial to acknowledge and celebrate the accomplishments and blessings, recognizing them as instruments through which God's grace shines.

Guarding Against False Humility:
False humility involves pretending to be humble while harboring pride or manipulative motives beneath the surface. It's a deceptive posture that can undermine genuine connections. False humility may manifest as insincere compliments, feigned vulnerability, or excessive self-sacrifice for external validation. This behavior can erode trust and authenticity in relationships. True humility stems from a genuine recognition of one's strengths and weaknesses, while false humility is a facade that conceals true intentions. Guarding against false humility involves cultivating authenticity and being transparent about your intentions in relationships.

The Importance of Balanced Humility:
Balanced humility allows you to acknowledge your strengths without arrogance and recognize your weaknesses without self-deprecation. It involves a genuine appreciation for others while maintaining a healthy self-respect. Striking this balance fosters authentic connections, as people can relate to your sincerity and vulnerability. It also ensures that you don't compromise your values or allow others to take advantage of your humility. Balanced humility promotes mutual respect, understanding, and the creation of resilient relationships.

In summary, finding the right balance in humility involves avoiding extremes of being overly humble or succumbing to false humility. Embracing a genuine and balanced humility contributes to the authenticity and strength of your relationships.

As we conclude our exploration of humility's role in building robust relationships, I invite you to embrace this powerful quality. Recognizing imperfections, extending grace, and navigating conflicts with humility paves the way for authentic connections that withstand the tests of time. Embracing humility isn't a display of weakness; instead, it serves as a wellspring of strength, unlocking the door to cultivate understanding, compassion, and forgiveness within the fabric of your relationships. May your journey be adorned with the richness of humility, creating bonds that reflect the transformative grace at the heart of genuine connections.

Workbook - Mental Holes Worksheet: Page 16

Reflection Questions:
1. **Self-Awareness and Imperfections:**
   - Reflect on a time when acknowledging your imperfections contributed to the strength of a relationship. How did embracing humility and vulnerability in that moment foster authenticity and mutual understanding?
2. **Grace and Conflict Resolution:**
   - Consider a conflict you've experienced. How did the application of humility and grace contribute to the resolution of the conflict? In what ways did humility serve as a shield against the unseen forces that seek to undermine relationships?
3. **The "Spicy Chicken Sandwich" Technique:**
   - Think about a challenging conversation you've had. How might applying the "Spicy Chicken Sandwich" technique enhance the communication process? How can humility and grace guide your words in navigating conflicts?
4. **Finding the Balance in Humility:**
   - Reflect on your own behavior in relationships. Have you ever observed instances of being overly humble or practicing false humility? How can you strike a balance to ensure genuine humility without compromising your self-worth or authenticity?

These reflection questions are designed to deepen your understanding of humility within the context of relationships. Take time to ponder each question, considering personal experiences and insights that contribute to your growth in cultivating authentic connections.

Effective communication stands as the lifeblood of healthy relationships, breathing vitality into the very essence of human connections. Within the complex interweaving of our interactions, it functions as the bridge that unites hearts, minds, and souls. The vital role it plays cannot be overstated, as it becomes the conduit through which understanding, trust, and intimacy flow. Healthy relationships thrive on the foundation of open and effective communication, creating a space where individuals can express their thoughts, share their feelings, and truly be heard. It is the compass guiding us through the labyrinth of human connection, illuminating the path towards deeper understanding and fostering an environment where relationships can flourish and withstand the tests of time.

Communication, in its essence, is the heartbeat of human connection—a dynamic process through which individuals exchange thoughts, feelings, and information. Signifying much more than the mere transmission of words, communication forms the cornerstone of relationship dynamics, shaping the nature and quality of interactions. Its significance lies not just in the exchange of information but in the creation of shared understanding, fostering connections that transcend the superficial.

Verbal communication, the most overt form of expression, involves the use of language, spoken or written, to convey messages. It encompasses the words we choose, the tone of our voice, and the clarity with which we articulate our thoughts. However, communication extends beyond the verbal realm, delving into the subtleties of non-verbal cues. Body language, facial expressions, gestures, and even silence are integral elements in the diverse mosaic of communication, frequently expressing subtleties and emotions that words alone may struggle to convey.

Exploring the various forms of communication reveals the intricate dance between spoken and unspoken elements. It is the interplay of words, tones, gestures, and expressions that breathes life into conversations, making them more than transactions of information but profound exchanges that shape the fabric of relationships. Understanding the essence of communication opens the door to unlocking the full potential of human connection, paving the way for relationships marked by depth, authenticity, and mutual comprehension.

Openness in communication stands as a cornerstone for fostering healthy and meaningful connections. This vital aspect emphasizes transparency, inviting individuals to express their thoughts, feelings, and ideas with authenticity. Transparency ensures that the intentions behind communication are clear, reducing the likelihood of misunderstandings and misinterpretations. When individuals engage in open communication, they create a space where honesty and trust can thrive. It involves willingly sharing one's perspective and being receptive to others' viewpoints, building a foundation for mutual understanding.

Vulnerability, an integral part of openness, adds depth to the communication dynamic. It involves the courage to share one's true self, including insecurities, fears, and aspirations. In the dance of effective communication, vulnerability fosters a sense of connection as individuals resonate with shared human experiences. This openness to being vulnerable builds bridges between people, creating a more profound and authentic connection. By embracing vulnerability, individuals contribute to an environment where communication is not just a surface-level exchange but an opportunity for genuine connection and growth.

Moving to the partner of openness in the dance of communication, respect plays a pivotal role in creating a conducive environment for effective dialogue. Respect involves recognizing and valuing the perspectives, opinions, and experiences of others. It is the foundational element that ensures every participant in the communication dance feels heard and acknowledged.

Respectful communication requires active listening, empathy, and a genuine appreciation for the diversity of thoughts and ideas. In a respectful dialogue, individuals feel safe to express themselves, knowing that their input is valued, and differences are treated with consideration. The combination of openness and respect sets the stage for a harmonious and enriching communication dance, where each participant contributes to the collective rhythm of understanding and connection.

Enhancing communication involves mastering both verbal and non-verbal aspects, creating a symphony of connection. In the realm of verbal communication, clarity is paramount. It's essential to express thoughts and ideas in a concise and articulate manner to ensure the intended message is effectively conveyed.

Choosing words carefully, avoiding ambiguity, and being mindful of tone contribute to the effectiveness of verbal communication. Moreover, active listening is a crucial component. It involves fully engaging with the speaker, demonstrating interest, and providing feedback to confirm understanding.

Non-verbal communication, often as impactful as spoken words, encompasses body language, facial expressions, and gestures. Maintaining eye contact, using appropriate facial expressions, and employing open body language enhance the non-verbal dimension of communication. These cues provide additional layers of meaning, adding depth and nuance to the spoken message.

The art of asking open-ended questions is a valuable tool in effective communication. Open-ended questions invite more than a simple "yes" or "no" response, encouraging the speaker to elaborate and share deeper insights. They foster a more expansive and meaningful conversation, opening avenues for exploration and understanding. Additionally, active listening complements the art of questioning, ensuring that responses are genuinely heard and acknowledged.

In the dance of effective communication, these practical tips act as choreography, guiding participants to move seamlessly through the intricate steps of verbal and non-verbal exchange. By incorporating these techniques, individuals can elevate their communication skills, creating a more engaging and enriching experience for all involved.

Active Listening:
Example: During a conversation, instead of interrupting or formulating your response while the other person is speaking, actively listen. Provide non-verbal cues such as nodding or maintaining eye contact to convey your engagement. Once they finish speaking, paraphrase or summarize what they said to ensure understanding.

Choosing Words Carefully:
Example: When expressing a sensitive opinion or providing feedback, select words that are constructive and non-confrontational. For instance, instead of saying, "You're wrong," you could express, "I see it differently, and I'd like to understand your perspective better."

Non-Verbal Cues:
Example: In a professional setting, maintain an open posture during meetings. Avoid crossing your arms, as it may convey defensiveness. Use facial expressions to show interest and understanding. For instance, smiling when appropriate or expressing empathy through facial cues.

Open-Ended Questions:
Example: Instead of asking, "Did you enjoy the event?" which could result in a simple "yes" or "no," pose an open-ended question like, "What aspects of the event did you find most interesting?" This encourages the person to share more detailed and personal insights.

Clarity in Verbal Communication:
Example: When giving instructions, be specific and clear. Instead of saying, "Complete the report soon," provide details like, "Please submit the report by 3 p.m. on Friday, and feel free to reach out if you have any questions."

Feedback Acknowledgment:
Example: When receiving feedback, whether positive or constructive, acknowledge it with appreciation. Respond with statements like, "Thank you for sharing your thoughts; I value your input," fostering a culture of open communication.

Implementing these examples in daily interactions contributes to a more effective and meaningful communication exchange. Effective communication is the lifeblood of healthy relationships, forming the cornerstone of connection, understanding, and mutual growth. To cultivate and refine these crucial skills, interactive exercises become invaluable tools, creating an environment where participants can actively engage, practice, and internalize the principles of effective communication.

One powerful exercise is the "Mirror Communication" activity. This exercise focuses on non-verbal communication, an often underestimated aspect of interpersonal dynamics. By mimicking each other's gestures and expressions, participants develop a heightened awareness of the unspoken messages they convey. This not only enhances non-verbal communication skills but also fosters a deeper understanding of the impact these cues have on relationships.

Another impactful exercise is the "Active Listening Role Play." Here, participants engage in scenarios where one person shares while the other practices active listening. The restriction on giving advice or sharing personal stories allows individuals to focus solely on understanding the speaker's perspective. This exercise is instrumental in developing empathetic listening skills, an essential component of effective communication.

"Expressing Feelings Through Art" provides a creative avenue for individuals to articulate emotions that may be challenging to express verbally. By translating feelings into visual representations, participants gain insight into their emotional landscape and learn alternative ways to communicate complex sentiments. This exercise encourages vulnerability and self-expression within a supportive context.

The "Perspective Swap" exercise challenges participants to defend perspectives that may differ from their own. By actively embodying varied viewpoints, individuals develop a profound sense of empathy and broaden their understanding of diverse opinions. This exercise promotes open-mindedness and helps participants navigate conversations with a more inclusive mindset.

The "Question Building Game" focuses on improving the art of asking open-ended questions. Effective communication is not just about expressing oneself but also about eliciting meaningful responses from others. This exercise hones the skill of formulating questions that encourage thoughtful and detailed answers, enriching the quality of conversations.

An example of an open-ended question is: Instead of asking, "Did you enjoy the movie?" (which can be answered with a simple "yes" or "no"),
You can ask, "What aspects of the movie did you find most interesting or captivating?"

This encourages the person to share their thoughts and opinions in a more detailed and open manner, fostering a richer and more meaningful conversation. Open-ended questions typically start with words like "what," "how," or "why" and invite the respondent to provide thoughtful and elaborate responses.

Lastly, the "Conflict Resolution Simulation" provides a safe space for participants to practice resolving conflicts through effective communication. By immersing themselves in simulated scenarios, individuals learn to navigate disagreements, express their feelings constructively, and work collaboratively toward resolutions. This exercise equips participants with practical conflict resolution skills applicable in various relationship contexts.

These communication exercises serve as dynamic platforms for enhancing skills, fostering empathy, deepening understanding, and refining the art of expression. Through active participation in these activities, individuals not only absorb theoretical principles but also internalize them through experiential learning, paving the way for more meaningful and resilient connections.

Communication within relationships is a dynamic and intricate dance that, at times, encounters challenges that can disrupt its harmonious flow. One common challenge is the lack of clarity or misinterpretation of messages. In the dance of communication, individuals may find themselves stepping on each other's toes, leading to misunderstandings and confusion. This can result from differences in communication styles, cultural nuances, or simply the choice of words. When these challenges arise, the dance partners must be equipped with strategies to navigate the complexities.

A key strategy in overcoming communication challenges is cultivating active listening skills. Just as a skilled dancer pays close attention to their partner's movements, active listening involves fully concentrating, understanding, responding, and remembering what is being communicated. This not only helps in grasping the intended message but also conveys respect and validation. Moreover, it opens up the opportunity for individuals to express themselves more clearly, reducing the likelihood of misinterpretation.

Another challenge often encountered in the dance of communication is the emotional aspect. Emotions can add layers of complexity to the exchange, leading to heightened sensitivities and potential conflicts. In such instances, it becomes crucial to introduce emotional intelligence into the dance.

Emotional intelligence involves recognizing, understanding, and managing one's emotions, as well as empathizing with the emotions of others. This skill allows individuals to navigate emotional hurdles with grace and sensitivity, fostering an environment where communication can continue to flourish.

Moreover, addressing challenges in communication requires a willingness to be vulnerable and transparent. Just as a dance involves trust between partners, effective communication thrives on a foundation of openness. Sharing thoughts, feelings, and concerns authentically creates a space for mutual understanding and connection. Vulnerability in communication does not imply weakness but rather a strength that allows for genuine and meaningful connections.

In summary, the dance of effective communication encounters challenges, but with the right strategies, individuals can overcome barriers, navigate emotional complexities, and foster an environment where understanding and connection can prevail. Communication, like a well-choreographed dance, requires practice, patience, and a commitment to continuous improvement.

Challenges in Communication:
Mismatched Communication Styles:
- Challenge: Individuals may have different communication styles, leading to misunderstandings.
- Strategy: Foster awareness of each other's communication preferences and adapt your style accordingly. Practice active listening to better understand each other's perspectives.

Assumptions and Mind Reading:
- Challenge: Making assumptions about what the other person is thinking or feeling can lead to misinterpretations.
- Strategy: Encourage open and honest communication. Clarify assumptions by asking questions rather than making conclusions. Be explicit about your thoughts and feelings.

Non-Verbal Communication Barriers:
- Challenge: Non-verbal cues, such as body language and facial expressions, can be misread or overlooked.
- Strategy: Pay attention to non-verbal signals and seek clarification if there's uncertainty. Use positive body language to convey openness and receptiveness.

Emotional Hotspots:
- Challenge: Certain topics may trigger emotional responses, making communication challenging.
- Strategy: Identify potential emotional triggers and approach these topics with sensitivity. Use "I" statements to express feelings without blaming the other person.

Timing and Environment:
- Challenge: Communication can suffer if it happens at inappropriate times or in unfavorable settings.
- Strategy: Choose the right time and place for important conversations. Ensure that both parties are in a receptive and focused state of mind.

Assumption of Shared Understanding:
- Challenge: Assuming that both parties share the same understanding of a situation can lead to miscommunication.
- Strategy: Clarify and confirm understanding by paraphrasing or summarizing key points. Ensure that both individuals are on the same page before moving forward.

Withholding Information:
- Challenge: Deliberately holding back information can hinder effective communication.
- Strategy: Encourage an environment of openness where both parties feel comfortable sharing information. Foster trust to reduce the tendency to withhold crucial details.

Reacting Defensively:
- Challenge: Defensive reactions can escalate conflicts and hinder productive communication.
- Strategy: Practice active listening and respond calmly without immediately getting defensive. Focus on understanding the other person's perspective before expressing your own.

By recognizing and addressing these challenges, individuals can nurture effective communication, creating a space for understanding, connection, and growth within relationships.

As we navigate the various nuances of communication, from openness and respect to practical strategies and exercises, the key takeaway is the profound impact it holds on the fabric of healthy connections. By defining communication, exploring its different forms, and delving into exercises that enhance empathetic expression, individuals gain the tools to fortify their relational dance. Challenges in communication are acknowledged and addressed with strategies that foster understanding amidst differences. As we conclude this exploration, the resounding message is clear: communication is the heartbeat of thriving relationships. Let the lessons learned guide you in embracing openness, respect, and practical approaches, transforming the way you engage with others. Enriched dialogue and profound understanding await those who heed the call to communicate with intention and authenticity.

Workbook - Navigating the Dance of Effective Communication Worksheet: Page 17
1. **Personal Communication Challenges:**
    o Reflect on a situation in your life where miscommunication or a lack of clarity impacted a relationship. What were the challenges faced, and how did they manifest? Consider the strategies discussed for overcoming communication challenges and identify how they could have been applied in that specific scenario.
2. **Emotional Intelligence in Communication:**
    o Think about a time when emotions played a significant role in a communication exchange. How did emotional intelligence, or the lack thereof, influence the outcome? Share specific instances where recognizing and managing emotions could have improved the dynamics of the conversation.
3. **Application of Communication Strategies:**
    o Choose one of the suggested communication strategies, such as active listening, clarity in verbal communication, or addressing emotional hotspots. Reflect on a recent interaction where you applied or could have applied this strategy. What changes did you observe in the communication dynamic, and how did it contribute to understanding and connection?

These reflection questions are designed to encourage self-awareness and deeper contemplation on the intricacies of effective communication. By considering personal experiences and applying the principles discussed, individuals can enhance their communication skills, fostering healthier and more meaningful connections with others.

51

In the intricate dynamics of relationships, **adaptability** emerges as a crucial factor in fostering strength and resilience. This chapter explores the vital role of adaptability, recognizing it as a dynamic and necessary aspect of relationship growth. Unlike a rigid structure, relationships demand flexibility to navigate the evolving challenges and changes that life brings. Adaptation is not merely a response; it is an intentional and ongoing process that contributes to the vibrancy and sustainability of connections. As we delve into this chapter, let us unravel the layers of adaptability, understanding it as an active and transformative element essential for the growth and flourishing of relationships.

Adaptability, in its essence, refers to the ability to adjust, evolve, and respond to the ever-changing dynamics of life. It holds significant importance in relationship dynamics, acting as a compass that guides individuals and partnerships through the various seasons of change and challenge.

Being adaptable is not merely about surviving change; it's about thriving amidst it. Relationships are not static entities but living, breathing organisms that require constant nourishment and adjustment. Adaptability allows individuals to embrace the ebb and flow of life, providing a framework for navigating the inevitable shifts in circumstances, priorities, and perspectives.

Consider a relationship faced with unexpected challenges, whether external pressures or internal shifts. The essence of adaptability lies in the capacity to reassess, recalibrate, and find new ways to connect and understand each other. It is the willingness to let go of rigid expectations and embrace the fluidity of growth. In this context, adaptability becomes the bridge that spans the gap between where a relationship is and where it can be, fostering an environment where both individuals can evolve together.

The significance of adaptability extends beyond mere survival; it is the catalyst for transformation and flourishing. Relationships that lack adaptability risk becoming stagnant or brittle when faced with the winds of change. On the contrary, those rooted in adaptability become resilient bonds that weather the storms and, in the process, discover new facets of connection and strength. As we embark on this exploration of adaptability, let us unravel its layers and understand its profound impact on the ever-evolving dance of relationships.

In my own journey, a significant chapter unfolded during a season of challenges in my marriage. My wife faced the complexities and uncertainties of pregnancy and childbirth, demanding a considerable shift in our dynamics. For nearly two years, I found myself shouldering a substantial portion of the responsibilities, adapting to new roles and sacrifices to support my wife and ensure the well-being of our growing family.

This period required a profound level of adaptability, where I had to navigate uncharted territories and embrace a role that demanded flexibility and selflessness. The weight of the marriage shifted, and rather than resisting, I chose to adapt, trusting that the outcomes were for the greater good. This season of adaptability not only strengthened our connection as a couple but also fostered personal growth. It revealed the depth of our commitment, our ability to weather storms together, and the transformative power of adaptability.

Real-life stories like these underscore the positive outcomes that emerge when individuals and relationships embrace adaptability. They showcase how navigating change with an open heart and a willingness to adjust can lead to strengthened connections, deeper understanding, and personal flourishing. As we explore these stories, let them serve as beacons of inspiration, illustrating the beauty that unfolds when adaptability becomes an integral part of the dance of relationships.

At the heart of every resilient relationship lies the indispensable quality of adaptability. Resilience and adaptability share an intimate connection, intertwining to form the sturdy foundation on which enduring connections are built. The ability to adapt is not merely a response to change; it is a proactive stance that fortifies relationships against the inevitable challenges and unexpected twists that life presents.

In the intricate dance of relationships, being adaptable empowers individuals and couples to navigate obstacles with grace and poise. Resilience, the capacity to bounce back from adversity, finds a formidable ally in adaptability. When faced with difficulties or unexpected shifts, adaptable individuals don't merely weather the storm—they adjust their sails.

This proactive approach ensures that challenges become opportunities for growth, and setbacks become stepping stones toward a more robust and resilient connection.

Consider a relationship as a living organism that requires constant adjustment to its environment. Just as a tree sways with the wind to avoid breaking, adaptable relationships flex and bend to absorb the shocks of life. The intertwined dance of resilience and adaptability creates a harmonious rhythm that allows connections to withstand the tests of time. By exploring and understanding this intricate relationship, individuals can cultivate a mindset of adaptability, contributing to the resilience that sustains and enriches their connections.

For both singles navigating the dynamic landscape of dating and couples seeking to fortify their bond, cultivating adaptability is a transformative journey that opens doors to enriched connections. One practical strategy involves fostering a mindset of openness to change. Embracing the reality that relationships, like life, are in a constant state of flux allows individuals to approach challenges with curiosity rather than resistance. Another actionable tip is to prioritize effective communication. Adaptability thrives in an environment where partners can openly express their needs, concerns, and aspirations. Regular and honest communication fosters a shared understanding of each other's evolving desires and dreams, creating space for adaptation without judgment.

Furthermore, couples can benefit from intentionally introducing novelty into their relationship. Whether it's trying new activities together, exploring different hobbies, or embarking on shared adventures, embracing new experiences enhances adaptability. Novelty injects energy into relationships and encourages individuals to grow together, fostering a resilient bond.

In the realm of dating, singles can practice adaptability by approaching relationships with a flexible mindset. Recognizing that expectations and circumstances may evolve over time allows individuals to adjust their perspectives and responses accordingly. Adaptability in dating involves being attuned to the ebb and flow of emotions and circumstances, creating space for organic growth and connection.

Ultimately, the benefits of embracing change and being open to new experiences in relationships are manifold. Adaptability not only strengthens the resilience of connections but also contributes to personal growth and a more profound understanding of oneself and one's partner. By integrating these practical strategies, individuals and couples can initiate a voyage of adaptability that enhances the fabric of their relationships.

For Parents
For parents navigating the intricate journey of raising children, adaptability is a crucial attribute that extends beyond accommodating the changing dynamics of a child's growth. It involves a profound commitment to allowing children the space to become the individuals God intended them to be. Rather than imposing preconceived notions or societal expectations, parents can adapt their parenting approach by recognizing and celebrating the unique qualities and purpose of each child.

A fundamental tip for parents is to refrain from stifling their children's natural inclinations and talents. Cultivating adaptability involves observing and appreciating the individual strengths and interests of each child, adjusting parenting strategies to support rather than restrict their innate gifts. This not only empowers children to flourish in their authenticity but also builds a foundation of trust and acceptance within the parent-child relationship.

Additionally, parents can foster adaptability by acknowledging that children, like adults, undergo phases of change and development. Being attuned to these shifts allows parents to adapt their guidance, providing the necessary support during different stages. Adaptability in parenting involves a willingness to learn alongside one's children, embracing the challenges and joys of each developmental milestone.

Furthermore, parents can encourage adaptability by creating an environment of open communication. Establishing a space where children feel free to express their thoughts, emotions, and aspirations fosters a trusting relationship. This adaptability in communication allows parents to understand the evolving needs of their children, adapting their guidance in response to the unique journey of each child.

In summary, the journey of parenting involves a continual process of adaptation. By celebrating the individuality of each child, refraining from imposing rigid expectations, and fostering open communication, parents can navigate the challenges of parenting with adaptability. This approach not only contributes to the resilience of the parent-child relationship but also allows children to blossom into the individuals God designed them to be.

In conclusion, the dance of adaptability within relationships, whether in dating, marriage, or parenting, is a harmonious journey of growth and resilience. Embracing adaptability requires a flexible mindset, open communication, and a willingness to navigate the evolving dynamics of life together. The essence of adaptability lies in acknowledging change not as a threat but as an opportunity for enrichment.

As individuals and couples nurture adaptability, they craft a rich collage of experiences that strengthens the fabric of their connections. From the thrill of new adventures to the challenges of parenting, adaptability allows relationships to weather storms and celebrate victories. It involves a commitment to learning, growing, and evolving alongside one another.

The stories of flexibility and growth serve as beacons, illuminating the positive outcomes that arise when individuals and couples embrace adaptability. Whether adapting to the nuances of dating, the complexities of marriage, or the joys and trials of parenting, the ability to navigate change becomes a transformative force that strengthens the bonds of connection.

As we conclude the exploration of adaptability, it is an invitation to dance with life's changes, recognizing that the steps may be unpredictable but that each adaptation adds depth and richness to the relational journey. With a mindset of openness, a commitment to effective communication, and a celebration of the uniqueness in ourselves and our loved ones, the dance of adaptability becomes a beautiful and resilient expression of love and growth.

Workbook - Adaptability Worksheet: Page 18
Reflection Questions: Embracing the Dance of Adaptability

1. Personal Adaptability Challenges:
   o Reflect on a specific instance in your life where you faced unexpected changes or challenges in a relationship. How did you respond to these changes, and what role did adaptability play in navigating through them? Consider the outcomes of your adaptability and the impact on the relationship.
2. Adaptability in Transformative Moments:
   o Think about a significant period in your life where adaptability was crucial, similar to the personal story shared in the text about challenges in a marriage. How did you or those involved adapt to the evolving circumstances? Reflect on the transformative power of adaptability during such moments.
3. Relationship Resilience Through Adaptability:
   o Consider a relationship you have been a part of that has endured various challenges or changes. How did the adaptability of individuals involved contribute to the resilience of the relationship? Reflect on specific actions, mindset shifts, or communication strategies that supported adaptability and resilience.
4. Parenting and Adaptability:
   o For parents, reflect on your approach to adapting to the changing dynamics of raising children. How do you celebrate the unique qualities of each child and adjust your parenting style accordingly? Consider specific instances where adaptability in parenting has positively influenced your relationship with your children.

RELATIONSHIP WITH GOD

RELATIONSHIP WITH GOD

In the vast expanse of the heavens, amidst the cosmic dance of stars and galaxies, there exists a divine desire pulsating from the very heart of God – a desire for an intimate and personal relationship with each individual. This chapter unfolds the sacred narrative of God's unwavering yearning for a connection with His beloved creation. It begins with the foundational truth that God desires a relationship with you, positioning this divine connection as the most crucial and significant bond in your life.

God's Yearning for a Personal Connection: God's longing transcends the cosmic expanse and zeroes in on the individual. In the intricate details of your existence, God desires a relationship that goes beyond the mere acknowledgment of His existence. It's an intimate communion, a dance of souls, where the Creator yearns to know and be known by His creation. This is not a distant, indifferent deity; rather, it's a God who actively pursues a connection with you.

God Wants a Relationship with You as Your Most Important Connection:
At the core of God's desire is the profound truth that He wants to be your most important connection. In the bustling complexity of life's relationships – family, friends, colleagues – God stands as the central figure, beckoning you to draw near. It's not a relationship of obligation but an invitation to the depths of divine love, where you find your truest identity and purpose.

This introduction lays the groundwork for a journey into the depths of cultivating a relationship with God. It sets the stage for exploring the attributes of God, understanding the role of these attributes in our spiritual connection, and embarking on practical steps to strengthen this sacred bond. The desire of God for relationship is not mere sentimentality; it is a eternal truth that echoes through the ages, inviting you to partake in the sacred dance of connection with the Divine.

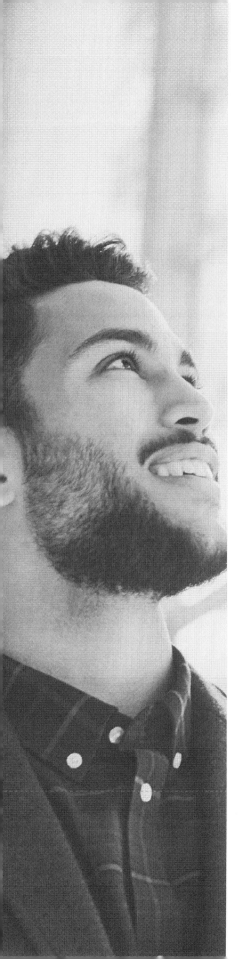

Interconnected Importance:
As we delve into the interconnected importance of our relationship with God, we unravel the profound truth that the state of our connection with the divine has a ripple effect on all other relationships. It's not a compartmentalized existence where our spiritual life is isolated from our interactions with family, friends, and colleagues. Rather, the vitality of our relationship with God serves as the nucleus, influencing the entirety of our relational landscape.

The Importance of Knowing God: The Pivotal Role of a Relationship with God: At the heart of this intricate dance of relationships is the pivotal role of knowing God. It's not merely an intellectual understanding of theological concepts but an experiential, intimate knowledge of the Divine. This relationship with God becomes the North Star, guiding our moral compass, shaping our character, and infusing our existence with purpose and meaning. As the central figure in the grand narrative of our lives, God's influence seeps into the very fabric of who we are.

The Impact on Other Relationships when God is Central: When God takes His rightful place at the center of our lives, the impact reverberates through our other relationships. Family dynamics, friendships, professional collaborations – all find a harmonious rhythm when anchored in the divine. The love, grace, and wisdom gleaned from our relationship with God become the wellspring from which we draw to navigate the complexities of human connections. In placing God at the center, we find the wisdom to love sacrificially, forgive generously, and extend grace abundantly.

This interconnectedness underscores the profound reality that our relationship with God is not an isolated journey; it's the nucleus that radiates transformative energy, shaping and enhancing every facet of our relational existence. As we embark on the journey of cultivating a thriving relationship with God, we discover the wellspring from which the waters of divine love flow into every nook and cranny of our interconnected relationships.

The Vine Parable: Exploring the Metaphor of the Vine and Its Significance in Our Connection with God:
The vine parable, a profound metaphor used by Jesus, paints a vivid picture of our relationship with God. In this allegorical tale, Jesus likens Himself to the vine, God the Father as the vinedresser, and believers as the branches. This metaphor holds profound lessons on dependence, growth, and the intricate dance of serving.

57

Understanding the Metaphor of the Vine

The metaphor of the vine encapsulates the essence of our connection with God. The vine serves as the source of life, nourishment, and vitality for the branches. In this symbiotic relationship, the branches draw their sustenance directly from the vine. It's a powerful image conveying the intimate connection we have with God. The vine is not merely a distant force; it's the lifeblood flowing through our spiritual veins.

Lessons on Dependence and Growth

Embedded in the vine parable are lessons on dependence and growth. The branches, representing believers, are entirely reliant on the vine for their sustenance. Similarly, our spiritual growth and vitality are contingent on our deep dependence on God. It's a call to relinquish the illusion of self-sufficiency and embrace the reality of our need for God's nourishment and guidance. The vinedresser, God the Father, plays a crucial role in tending to the vine and its branches. He prunes, cares, and nurtures to ensure optimal growth and fruitfulness. This illustrates the divine care and attention God invests in our lives when we are in a relationship with Him. The branches, in turn, bear fruit—a testament to the transformative power of being connected to the vine.

In this relational ecosystem, the vine, the branches, the vinedresser, and the fruit are all intertwined in a partnership of serving. The vinedresser tends to the vine and the branches, ensuring their health and productivity. The branches, in their connection to the vine, bear fruit – the natural outflow of a thriving relationship. This interconnected dance underscores the truth that serving is not an isolated act but an overflow of being in a vibrant relationship with God.

As we delve into the lessons of the vine parable, we glean insights into the beauty of dependence, the transformative nature of growth, and the profound reality that our service to others is an outflow of our intimate relationship with the divine vine. It's a call to be firmly rooted in the source of life, drawing sustenance and purpose from the vine, and in turn, bearing fruit that enriches the relational landscape around us.

Rating Reflection Question: On a scale of 1 to 10, how would you rate your current level of dependence on God for spiritual nourishment and growth, considering the insights gained from understanding the metaphor of the vine? #_____ After reading book #_____

Navigating the Perils: Building and Sailing Ships Without God

In the vast ocean of relationships, attempting to build and sail ships without God at the helm exposes individuals to profound consequences. The analogy of ships without divine guidance vividly illustrates the perilous journey that unfolds when relationships lack the foundation of spiritual connection and divine wisdom.

Consequences of a Ship Without God:

Embarking on the journey of relationships without grounding them in God's wisdom exposes them to a range of consequences. Picture a ship setting sail without a skilled navigator; it risks drifting into unknown and treacherous waters. Similarly, relationships without the divine compass may find themselves adrift in a sea of miscommunication, misunderstandings, and a lack of purpose. The absence of God's guidance leaves these relationships vulnerable to the storms of life, lacking the anchor of faith to weather challenges.

The Sinking Ships Analogy: A Descent into Chaos:

The imagery of sinking ships vividly captures the chaotic descent relationships face without divine guidance. In the absence of God's steady hand, these connections can become like ships navigating turbulent seas without a reliable captain. Unforeseen storms, treacherous waters, and the lurking threat of hidden reefs become insurmountable challenges. Attempting to sail the seas of life without God's guidance risks shipwreck, leading to the fragmentation and dissolution of connections that were meant to thrive.

The Danger of Drifting:

The true danger lies not only in facing external challenges but also in the internal drift that occurs without God as the anchor. Relationships without a spiritual foundation risk drifting away from shared values, purpose, and commitment – the essential elements for longevity. Much like a ship without an anchor, relationships may lose their direction, succumbing to the currents of worldly influences. This chapter emphasizes the profound impact of having God as the Captain of our relational voyages, urging individuals to recognize the perils of attempting relationships without divine guidance.

_____
_____
_____
_____
_____
_____

Cultivating a Relationship with God

In the pursuit of cultivating a deep and meaningful relationship with God, it becomes paramount to acquaint oneself with the attributes that define the very nature of the Divine. This chapter delves into the significance of getting to know God, unraveling ten key attributes that shape our understanding of the Almighty.

Defining Divine Attributes:

Before embarking on the exploration of God's attributes, it is crucial to grasp the concept of divine attributes. These are the inherent qualities and characteristics that define the nature and essence of God. Each attribute serves as a facet, revealing different dimensions of God's character. Understanding these attributes not only deepens our knowledge of God but also lays the foundation for a more profound and intimate connection.

Exploring Ten Key Attributes of God:

- Love: At the core of God's being is an unending and unconditional love. This attribute is the wellspring from which all other aspects of God's character flow. Understanding God's love allows us to approach Him with confidence, knowing that His love is a constant presence in our lives.
- Holiness: God's holiness speaks to His absolute purity and perfection. It sets Him apart from any form of impurity or sin. Recognizing this attribute inspires reverence and awe, shaping our approach to God with humility and respect.
- Omnipotence: God's omnipotence reveals His unlimited power and authority. Acknowledging this attribute instills confidence in His ability to bring about His divine purposes and assures us that nothing is beyond His control.
- Omniscience: God's omniscience highlights His infinite knowledge and wisdom. Understanding that God knows all things, including our deepest thoughts and desires, fosters a sense of intimacy and trust in our relationship with Him.
- Eternality: God exists beyond the constraints of time. His eternality underscores the unchanging nature of His character and His enduring commitment to His creation. This attribute provides a sense of stability and security in our connection with Him.
- Immutability: God's immutability signifies His unchanging nature. Amidst the shifting sands of life, recognizing this attribute assures us that God's promises and character remain steadfast, providing a firm foundation for our faith.

- Justice: God's justice ensures that righteousness prevails. This attribute underscores His commitment to fairness and equity, instilling confidence that God's judgments are guided by a perfect sense of right and wrong.
- Mercy: God's mercy extends unmerited compassion and forgiveness to humanity. Embracing this attribute offers solace and hope, knowing that God's compassion is readily available, even in our moments of weakness.
- Grace: God's grace goes beyond mercy, offering unearned favor and blessing. Recognizing this attribute fosters gratitude and humility, as we acknowledge the undeserved goodness that God pours into our lives.
- Faithfulness: God's faithfulness reflects His unwavering commitment to His promises. Trusting in this attribute provides a rock-solid foundation for our relationship with God, assuring us that He remains true to His word.
- In the subsequent sections, each attribute will be explored in depth, unraveling the profound implications and applications of these divine qualities in our journey of cultivating a flourishing relationship with God.

Love: The Unending and Unconditional Well of God's Being

At the very heart of God's essence lies a love that transcends human comprehension. It is a love that knows no bounds, extends infinitely, and operates without conditions. This attribute, often considered the cornerstone of God's character, serves as the wellspring from which every other facet of His nature flows. Understanding God's love transforms the way we perceive Him and, consequently, influences the dynamics of our relationships. It is a love that defies our finite understanding, surpassing the limitations of human love. God's love is not contingent upon our actions, merits, or shortcomings; it is an enduring force that remains steadfast, regardless of our circumstances.

Approaching God with the awareness of His unending and unconditional love is transformative. It shatters the misconception that we must earn His love through perfection or good deeds. Instead, it allows us to come before Him with confidence, knowing that His love is a constant, unchanging presence in our lives.

In our relationships with others, understanding God's love becomes a guiding principle. It becomes a model for the way we ought to love – selflessly, sacrificially, and without expecting reciprocation. It prompts us to extend grace and compassion, mirroring the divine love that first embraced us.

Moreover, God's love provides a source of comfort and assurance in the midst of life's challenges. Knowing that we are enveloped in a love that surpasses all circumstances offers solace and strengthens our resilience. It becomes a steady anchor, grounding us when the storms of life threaten to overwhelm.

In essence, God's love is a transformative force that permeates every aspect of our existence. It shapes our identity, influences our interactions, and serves as the foundation for cultivating healthy and meaningful relationships. As we grasp the depth of God's love, we are not only recipients but carriers of this divine love, radiating it to those around us, creating a ripple effect of grace and compassion in our relational spheres.

Jeremiah 31:3: "The Lord appeared to him from far away. I have loved you with an everlasting love; therefore, I have continued my faithfulness to you."

Romans 8:38-39: "For I am sure that neither death nor life, nor angels nor rulers, nor things present nor things to come, nor powers, nor height nor depth, nor anything else in all creation, will be able to separate us from the love of God in Christ Jesus our Lord."

1 John 4:16: "So we have come to know and to believe the love that God has for us. God is love, and anyone who abides in love abides in God, and God abides in him."

Ephesians 3:17-19: "So that Christ may dwell in your hearts through faith—that you, being rooted and grounded in love, may have strength to comprehend with all the saints what is the breadth and length and height and depth, and to know the love of Christ that surpasses knowledge, that you may be filled with all the fullness of God."

Zephaniah 3:17: "The Lord your God is in your midst, a mighty one who will save; he will rejoice over you with gladness; he will quiet you by his love; he will exult over you with loud singing."

1 Corinthians 13:4-7: "Love is patient and kind; love does not envy or boast; it is not arrogant or rude. It does not insist on its own way; it is not irritable or resentful; it does not rejoice at wrongdoing, but rejoices with the truth. Love bears all things, believes all things, hopes all things, endures all things."

John 3:16: "For God so loved the world, that he gave his only Son, that whoever believes in him should not perish but have eternal life."
Psalm 36:7: "How precious is your steadfast love, O God! The children of mankind take refuge in the shadow of your wings."

Lamentations 3:22-23: "The steadfast love of the Lord never ceases; his mercies never come to an end; they are new every morning; great is your faithfulness."

Psalm 103:8: "The Lord is merciful and gracious, slow to anger and abounding in steadfast love."
Feel free to explore these passages for a more in-depth understanding of God's love and how it impacts our relationship with Him and others.

God's Unconditional Love Scripture Study and Reflection Worksheet Page: 20

_____
_____
_____
_____
_____
_____
_____
_____
_____
_____
_____
_____
_____
_____
_____
_____
_____
_____
_____
_____
_____
_____
_____
_____
_____
_____

The Holiness Of God

God's holiness, characterized by His absolute purity and perfection, is a foundational aspect of His character. This attribute sets Him apart from anything tainted by impurity or sin, highlighting the divine standard of moral excellence. Understanding God's holiness profoundly influences how we relate to Him and engage in our relationships with others.

Reverence and Awe: Recognizing God's holiness evokes a sense of awe and reverence. It calls us to approach Him with humility, acknowledging the vast gap between our fallen nature and His perfect holiness. This awareness fosters a deep respect for the sacredness of our connection with the Almighty.

Transformative Impact: The acknowledgment of God's holiness has a transformative impact on our lives. It calls us to strive for moral excellence and purity in our actions, thoughts, and relationships. As we align ourselves with His holiness, we are inspired to pursue righteousness and live in accordance with His divine standards.

Repentance and Redemption: God's holiness illuminates our imperfections and sinfulness. In response, it leads us to repentance—a sincere turning away from sin and a desire for redemption. Through the redemptive work of Christ, we can approach the holy God with confidence, knowing that His grace covers our shortcomings.

Guidance for Relationships: The understanding of God's holiness provides a moral compass for our relationships. It encourages us to seek purity and righteousness in our interactions with others. As we recognize the holiness of God, we are inspired to treat others with dignity, respect, and love, reflecting the divine character in our human connections.

Humility and Gratitude: God's holiness humbles us, reminding us of our dependence on His grace. We approach Him not with entitlement but with gratitude for His mercy. This humility extends to our relationships, fostering an attitude of gratitude, empathy, and a willingness to extend grace to others.

Separation from Sin: God's holiness necessitates a separation from sin. This separation is not driven by a desire for distance but by the divine intention to protect and guide us toward abundant and righteous living. Embracing God's holiness empowers us to resist the destructive forces of sin in our relationships.

In summary, understanding and embracing God's holiness profoundly impact our relationships by shaping our character, guiding our moral choices, and fostering a deep reverence for the divine. It invites us into a transformative journey where the pursuit of holiness becomes the foundation for cultivating healthy, God-honoring connections with others.

- Isaiah 6:3: "And one called to another and said: 'Holy, holy, holy is the Lord of hosts; the whole earth is full of his glory!'"
- 1 Peter 1:15-16: "But as he who called you is holy, you also be holy in all your conduct, since it is written, 'You shall be holy, for I am holy.'"
- Revelation 4:8: "And the four living creatures, each of them with six wings, are full of eyes all around and within, and day and night they never cease to say, 'Holy, holy, holy, is the Lord God Almighty, who was and is and is to come!'"
- Exodus 15:11: "Who is like you, O Lord, among the gods? Who is like you, majestic in holiness, awesome in glorious deeds, doing wonders?"
- Psalm 99:5: "Exalt the Lord our God; worship at his footstool! Holy is he!"
- Leviticus 11:44-45: "For I am the Lord your God. Consecrate yourselves therefore, and be holy, for I am holy."
- Psalm 22:3: "Yet you are holy, enthroned on the praises of Israel."
- Revelation 15:4: "Who will not fear, O Lord, and glorify your name? For you alone are holy. All nations will come and worship you, for your righteous acts have been revealed."
- 1 Samuel 2:2: "There is none holy like the Lord: for there is none besides you; there is no rock like our God."
- Psalm 99:9: "Exalt the Lord our God, and worship at his holy mountain; for the Lord our God is holy!"

These verses provide a glimpse into the scriptural depiction of God's holiness and can serve as a starting point for meditation and reflection.

Embracing God's Holiness: A Personal Reflection Worksheet Page 22

_____
_____
_____
_____
_____
_____
_____
_____
_____
_____

Omnipotence, one of God's fundamental attributes, signifies His unlimited power and authority. This attribute reveals the magnitude of God's sovereignty and underscores the fact that there is no limit to His ability to accomplish His divine purposes. Understanding God's omnipotence has profound implications for our lives and relationships.

Confidence in God's Capability: Recognizing God's omnipotence allows us to approach Him with confidence. In times of uncertainty or difficulty, we can trust that God has the power to navigate us through any circumstance. This confidence becomes a source of strength in facing life's challenges.

Submission and Surrender: Embracing God's omnipotence encourages a spirit of submission and surrender. Knowing that God is all-powerful invites us to yield our own plans and desires to His higher and perfect will. This attitude fosters humility and a deeper connection with God.

Trusting Divine Timing: God's omnipotence assures us that His timing is perfect. In our relationships, we may encounter situations where we desire certain outcomes or changes. Understanding God's unlimited power encourages us to trust His timing, believing that He is orchestrating events according to His greater plan.

Overcoming Fear: The recognition of God's omnipotence helps us overcome fear. Instead of being paralyzed by anxiety about the future, we can rest in the assurance that God, who is all-powerful, is in control. This freedom from fear positively impacts our mental and emotional well-being.

Assurance in Prayer: When we pray, understanding God's omnipotence transforms our perspective. We pray not to a limited or distant deity, but to the One who holds all power. This assurance in prayer strengthens our communication with God and deepens our relationship with Him.

In relationships, the impact of God's omnipotence is profound. It shapes our attitudes, actions, and responses, fostering a sense of security, trust, and reliance on the Almighty in the intricate dance of human connections.

- Jeremiah 32:17 (ESV): "Ah, Lord God! It is you who have made the heavens and the earth by your great power and by your outstretched arm! Nothing is too hard for you."
- Matthew 19:26 (ESV): "But Jesus looked at them and said, 'With man this is impossible, but with God all things are possible.'"
- Isaiah 40:28 (ESV): "Have you not known? Have you not heard? The Lord is the everlasting God, the Creator of the ends of the earth. He does not faint or grow weary; his understanding is unsearchable."
- Ephesians 3:20 (ESV): "Now to him who is able to do far more abundantly than all that we ask or think, according to the power at work within us."
- Job 42:2 (ESV): "I know that you can do all things, and that no purpose of yours can be thwarted."
- Psalm 115:3 (ESV): "Our God is in the heavens; he does all that he pleases."
- Luke 1:37 (ESV): "For nothing will be impossible with God."
- Genesis 18:14 (ESV): "Is anything too hard for the Lord? At the appointed time I will return to you, about this time next year, and Sarah shall have a son."
- Revelation 19:6 (ESV): "Then I heard what seemed to be the voice of a great multitude, like the roar of many waters and like the sound of mighty peals of thunder, crying out, 'Hallelujah! For the Lord our God the Almighty reigns.'"
- Psalm 147:5 (ESV): "Great is our Lord, and abundant in power; his understanding is beyond measure."
- These verses collectively emphasize God's omnipotence, showcasing His unlimited power, authority, and ability to accomplish all things.

Embracing God's Omnipotence: A Personal Reflection Worksheet 24

God's **omniscience**, or all-knowing nature, is a profound aspect of His character that profoundly influences our relationship with Him and, by extension, our interactions with others.

Intimacy and Trust:
Recognizing that God knows every detail of our lives, including our thoughts, fears, and desires, fosters a unique intimacy in our relationship with Him. This knowledge assures us that we can approach Him with authenticity, without fear of judgment or misunderstanding. In human relationships, trust is often built on understanding, and God's omniscience provides a foundational trust that surpasses human comprehension.

Comfort in Prayer:
God's omniscience enhances the power and comfort of prayer. When we pray, we're not informing God of something He doesn't know; rather, we're engaging in a dialogue with a God who intimately understands our needs. This understanding prompts us to approach prayer with confidence, knowing that God comprehends even the unspoken nuances of our hearts.

Guidance and Wisdom:
Since God possesses infinite wisdom, His omniscience ensures that His guidance in our lives is perfect. As we navigate relationships, decisions, and challenges, we can rely on God's omniscient knowledge to lead us on the right path. This attribute becomes a source of wisdom, offering insights into situations that may seem complex or confusing to us.

Accountability and Transformation:
God's knowledge of our innermost selves holds us accountable in a loving way. It encourages self-reflection and a desire for positive transformation. Understanding that God knows us completely motivates us to align our lives with His principles, fostering growth and maturity in our character.

Gratitude and Surrender:
The awareness of God's omniscience invites gratitude. We can be thankful that God knows us intimately, loves us unconditionally, and desires the best for us. Surrendering to God's omniscience involves letting go of the need to control every aspect of our lives, trusting that His knowledge surpasses our finite understanding.

In essence, God's omniscience deepens our connection with Him by providing a profound sense of intimacy, trust, guidance, accountability, and gratitude. As we cultivate an awareness of this attribute, it transforms how we approach our relationship with God and, consequently, influences how we engage with others in the various relationships of our lives.

Psalm 139:1-4 (ESV):
O Lord, you have searched me and known me!
You know when I sit down and when I rise up;
you discern my thoughts from afar.
You search out my path and my lying down
and are acquainted with all my ways.
Even before a word is on my tongue,
behold, O Lord, you know it altogether.

Proverbs 15:3 (ESV):
The eyes of the Lord are in every place,
keeping watch on the evil and the good.

Hebrews 4:13 (ESV):
And no creature is hidden from his sight,
but all are naked and exposed to the eyes of
him to whom we must give account.

Matthew 10:29-30 (ESV):
Are not two sparrows sold for a penny?
And not one of them will fall to the ground
apart from your Father. But even the hairs of
your head are all numbered.

Isaiah 46:9-10 (ESV):
...for I am God, and there is no other;
I am God, and there is none like me,
declaring the end from the beginning
and from ancient times things not yet done,
saying, 'My counsel shall stand,
and I will accomplish all my purpose.'
These verses emphasize God's knowledge, understanding, and awareness of all things, showcasing the depth of His omniscience.

Embracing God's Omniscience: A Personal Reflection Worksheet 26

_____
_____
_____
_____
_____
_____
_____
_____
_____
_____

The attribute of God's **eternality** emphasizes that He exists beyond the limitations of time. It means that God is not bound by the past, present, or future; rather, He transcends time itself. This profound aspect of His nature holds significant implications for our relationship with Him.

Stability and Security:
God's eternality provides a foundation of stability and security for believers. In a world where circumstances change, relationships shift, and uncertainties abound, the eternal nature of God becomes an anchor. It assures us that His character remains constant, unaffected by the passing of time. This stability becomes a source of comfort and trust in our relationship with Him.

Enduring Commitment:
God's commitment to His creation is unwavering throughout all ages. His eternality reveals a timeless dedication to His people. This commitment is not contingent on temporal conditions; rather, it is rooted in His unchanging nature. Understanding God's eternality assures us that His love, promises, and purposes endure forever, fostering a deep sense of assurance and faith in our relationship with Him.

Perspective on Time:
As finite beings bound by time, we often struggle with temporal perspectives. God's eternality allows us to see our lives and circumstances from a broader, timeless vantage point. This broader view can bring clarity to challenges, offering the understanding that God's plans extend beyond the immediate and into the eternal. It encourages patience and trust as we navigate the complexities of life.

Connection Beyond Time:
Our relationship with God is not confined to specific moments or seasons. The eternal nature of God means that our connection with Him transcends time. Whether in moments of joy or seasons of trial, He remains present and accessible. Recognizing this eternal connection invites us into a continual and intimate communion with the timeless Creator.
In essence, the eternality of God enriches our relationship with Him by providing a stable foundation, assuring us of His enduring commitment, offering a timeless perspective, and inviting us into a connection that surpasses the confines of time.

Psalm 90:2 (ESV):
"Before the mountains were brought forth, or ever you had formed the earth and the world, from everlasting to everlasting you are God."

Isaiah 57:15 (ESV):
"For thus says the One who is high and lifted up, who inhabits eternity, whose name is Holy: 'I dwell in the high and holy place, and also with him who is of a contrite and lowly spirit, to revive the spirit of the lowly, and to revive the heart of the contrite.'"

Revelation 1:8 (ESV):
"'I am the Alpha and the Omega,' says the Lord God, 'who is and who was and who is to come, the Almighty.'"

Isaiah 40:28 (ESV):
"Have you not known? Have you not heard? The Lord is the everlasting God, the Creator of the ends of the earth. He does not faint or grow weary; his understanding is unsearchable."

Psalm 102:12 (ESV):
"But you, O Lord, are enthroned forever; you are remembered throughout all generations."

1 Timothy 1:17 (ESV):
"To the King of the ages, immortal, invisible, the only God, be honor and glory forever and ever. Amen."

Revelation 22:13 (ESV):
"I am the Alpha and the Omega, the first and the last, the beginning and the end."

Psalm 93:2 (ESV):
"Your throne is established from of old; you are from everlasting."

Hebrews 13:8 (ESV):
"Jesus Christ is the same yesterday and today and forever."

Micah 5:2 (ESV):
"But you, O Bethlehem Ephrathah, who are too little to be among the clans of Judah, from you shall come forth for me one who is to be ruler in Israel, whose coming forth is from of old, from ancient days."

These verses affirm the eternal nature of God and provide a biblical foundation for understanding His enduring existence beyond the constraints of time.

Immutability

The attribute of God's immutability, meaning His unchanging nature, has profound implications for our lives and relationships. In a world characterized by constant change and unpredictability, the unchanging nature of God stands as a source of comfort and assurance. It means that God's character, promises, and love remain steadfast, unaffected by the shifting circumstances of life. This immutability provides a firm foundation for our faith and trust in God.

Stability in an Unstable World:
God's immutability is like an anchor in the stormy seas of life. When everything around us is changing, God remains constant. This stability is a source of comfort and peace, especially in times of uncertainty and upheaval.

Trustworthiness of His Promises:
Because God does not change, His promises are unwavering. Every word spoken by God stands firm, offering us a reliable foundation on which we can build our lives and relationships. This fosters trust in His faithfulness.

Consistency in His Love:
God's love is not subject to fluctuations. It doesn't increase or decrease based on our actions or circumstances. His unchanging love provides a sense of security and acceptance, influencing the way we approach Him and others.

Encourages Dependence on God:
Understanding God's immutability encourages us to depend on Him wholly. We can confidently rely on His character, knowing that He won't change His mind, withdraw His love, or alter His plans for us.

A Model for Consistent Relationships:
This attribute of God serves as a model for how we can strive for consistency and reliability in our relationships. While human relationships may experience fluctuations, we can aim to emulate God's steadfastness in our commitments and love for others.

Foundation for Our Faith:
Our faith in God rests on the unchanging nature of His character. This attribute assures us that we serve a God who is the same yesterday, today, and forever, providing a solid foundation for our spiritual journey.

In essence, God's immutability brings a sense of constancy and reliability into our lives. It influences the way we approach Him in prayer, the confidence with which we claim His promises, and the manner in which we navigate our relationships, striving to reflect His unchanging nature in our interactions with others.

Malachi 3:6 (ESV): "For I the Lord do not change; therefore you, O children of Jacob, are not consumed."

James 1:17 (ESV): "Every good gift and every perfect gift is from above, coming down from the Father of lights, with whom there is no variation or shadow due to change."

Numbers 23:19 (ESV): "God is not man, that he should lie, or a son of man, that he should change his mind. Has he said, and will he not do it? Or has he spoken, and will he not fulfill it?"

Psalm 33:11 (ESV): "The counsel of the Lord stands forever, the plans of his heart to all generations."

Psalm 119:89-91 (ESV): "Forever, O Lord, your word is firmly fixed in the heavens. Your faithfulness endures to all generations; you have established the earth, and it stands fast. By your appointment, they stand this day, for all things are your servants."

Hebrews 6:17-18 (ESV): "So when God desired to show more convincingly to the heirs of the promise the unchangeable character of his purpose, he guaranteed it with an oath, so that by two unchangeable things, in which it is impossible for God to lie, we who have fled for refuge might have strong encouragement to hold fast to the hope set before us."

Psalm 102:25-27 (ESV): "Of old you laid the foundation of the earth, and the heavens are the work of your hands. They will perish, but you will remain; they will all wear out like a garment. You will change them like a robe, and they will pass away, but you are the same, and your years have no end."

Exploring God's Immutability: A Reflection and Scripture Study Page 30

God's **justice** is a reflection of His righteous and fair nature. This attribute assures us that God's judgments are perfect, unbiased, and guided by an unwavering sense of right and wrong. Understanding God's justice has profound implications for our relationships:

1. Assurance of Fairness: In our human interactions, justice is often a sought-after quality. The assurance that God is just provides comfort and confidence that, ultimately, righteousness will prevail. This assurance impacts our relationships by inspiring a commitment to fairness and integrity.
2. Guidance for Conflict Resolution: When conflicts arise, knowing God's justice becomes a guiding principle for resolving disputes. It encourages seeking resolutions that align with God's sense of justice, promoting reconciliation and healing in relationships.
3. Moral Compass: God's justice serves as a moral compass for our actions. It influences how we treat others, fostering a sense of responsibility to act justly in our interactions. This moral framework contributes to building trust and integrity in relationships.
4. Addressing Injustice: Understanding God's commitment to justice motivates us to address and correct injustices in our relationships and the world. It calls us to be advocates for those who are oppressed or treated unfairly, aligning our actions with God's justice.
5. Accountability and Repentance: The concept of divine justice reminds us that God holds us accountable for our actions. This accountability encourages self-reflection and repentance when we fall short, promoting personal growth and reconciliation in relationships.

Scriptures that highlight God's justice:

- Isaiah 30:18 (ESV): "Therefore the Lord waits to be gracious to you, and therefore he exalts himself to show mercy to you. For the Lord is a God of justice; blessed are all those who wait for him."
- Deuteronomy 32:4 (ESV): "The Rock, his work is perfect, for all his ways are justice. A God of faithfulness and without iniquity, just and upright is he."
- Romans 2:5-6 (ESV): "But because of your hard and impenitent heart you are storing up wrath for yourself on the day of wrath when God's righteous judgment will be revealed. He will render to each one according to his works."

Embracing God's justice in our relationships contributes to an environment of righteousness, fairness, and accountability, fostering healthier connections with others.

Understanding God's Justice: Reflection and Scripture Study Page: 32

66

God's **mercy** is a profound expression of His unmerited compassion and forgiveness. Embracing this attribute has transformative effects on us and our relationships:

1. Source of Solace and Hope: Knowing that God's mercy is readily available provides solace and hope, especially in moments of weakness, guilt, or despair. This understanding shapes our perception of God as a compassionate and forgiving source of comfort.
2. Foundation for Forgiveness: God's mercy sets a powerful example for how forgiveness operates. In our relationships, extending mercy becomes a foundation for forgiveness, fostering an atmosphere of grace and reconciliation. This attribute challenges us to mirror God's mercy in our interactions with others.
3. Encouragement for Personal Growth: God's mercy offers encouragement for personal growth and transformation. When we experience God's merciful love, it motivates us to reflect that mercy in our relationships. This leads to a continuous cycle of grace, forgiveness, and personal development.
4. Healing Brokenness: Mercy plays a vital role in healing brokenness within relationships. It encourages a spirit of understanding, compassion, and empathy, allowing us to extend grace to those who may have hurt us. Embracing God's mercy facilitates the restoration of broken bonds.
5. Transformation of Heart: The recognition of God's merciful nature prompts a transformation of the heart. It encourages us to let go of judgment, embrace humility, and approach others with compassion. This transformation contributes to the development of healthier and more loving relationships.

Scriptures highlighting God's mercy:

- Ephesians 2:4-5 (ESV): "But God, being rich in mercy, because of the great love with which he loved us, even when we were dead in our trespasses, made us alive together with Christ—by grace you have been saved."
- Psalm 103:8 (ESV): "The Lord is merciful and gracious, slow to anger and abounding in steadfast love."
- Lamentations 3:22-23 (ESV): "The steadfast love of the Lord never ceases; his mercies never come to an end; they are new every morning; great is your faithfulness."

Embracing God's mercy in our relationships allows us to cultivate a compassionate and forgiving spirit, fostering an environment of grace, healing, and transformation.

Embracing God's Mercy: Reflection and Scripture Study Page 34

God's **grace**, an attribute that extends beyond mercy, is a transformative force that significantly impacts us and our relationships:

1. Unearned Favor and Blessing: At the heart of grace is the concept of unearned favor and blessing. Embracing God's grace means recognizing that His goodness is freely given, not based on our merit. This understanding leads to a deep sense of gratitude for the undeserved blessings God bestows upon us.
2. Fostering Gratitude: The acknowledgment of God's grace cultivates gratitude in our hearts. Gratitude becomes a powerful force that shapes our attitudes and interactions in relationships. It encourages us to appreciate the goodness in others and express thankfulness for the blessings we share.
3. Humility in Relationships: Understanding God's grace fosters humility. As recipients of unearned favor, we learn to approach relationships with a humble attitude, recognizing that everyone is in need of grace. This humility dismantles pride and judgment, creating an environment where grace can flow freely among individuals.
4. Model for Relationship Dynamics: God's grace serves as a model for healthy relationship dynamics. In our interactions with others, extending grace becomes a key component of resolving conflicts, offering second chances, and fostering forgiveness. Grace allows relationships to thrive in an atmosphere of understanding and compassion.
5. Transformation of Character: Embracing God's grace contributes to the transformation of character. As we experience the depth of His unmerited favor, it inspires us to reflect that grace in our dealings with others. This transformative process shapes us into individuals who are quick to show kindness, empathy, and generosity in relationships.

Scriptures highlighting God's grace:

- Ephesians 2:8-9 (ESV): "For by grace you have been saved through faith. And this is not your own doing; it is the gift of God, not a result of works, so that no one may boast."
- 2 Corinthians 12:9 (ESV): "But he said to me, 'My grace is sufficient for you, for my power is made perfect in weakness.' Therefore I will boast all the more gladly of my weaknesses, so that the power of Christ may rest upon me."
- Romans 5:8 (ESV): "But God shows his love for us in that while we were still sinners, Christ died for us."

Embracing God's grace in our relationships enables us to create spaces of love, forgiveness, and humility, fostering connections that are rooted in the boundless goodness of God.

Embracing God's Grace: Reflection and Scripture Study Page: 36

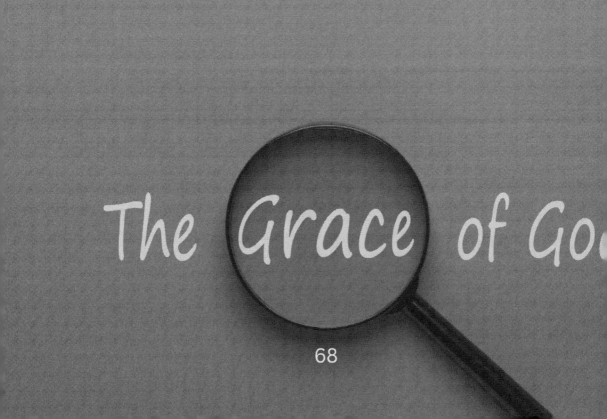

The Grace of Go

God's **faithfulness**, a steadfast attribute that reflects His unwavering commitment to His promises, profoundly impacts us and our relationships:

1. Rock-Solid Foundation: God's faithfulness provides a rock-solid foundation for our relationship with Him. Knowing that God remains true to His word gives us confidence and security in our journey of faith. This foundation becomes a source of stability, especially in the face of life's uncertainties.
2. Building Trust: The unwavering faithfulness of God serves as a model for building trust in our relationships. As we experience the constancy of His promises, we are inspired to cultivate trustworthiness in our interactions with others. Trust becomes a cornerstone in healthy relationships, fostering openness and vulnerability.
3. Consistency in Commitments: God's faithfulness is synonymous with His consistency in commitments. In our relationships, consistency is a key element for creating a sense of reliability and dependability. Being faithful to our promises and commitments contributes to the establishment of trust and reliability among friends, family, and acquaintances.
4. Navigating Challenges: Understanding God's faithfulness equips us to navigate challenges in relationships. Just as God remains faithful in all circumstances, we are encouraged to persevere through difficulties in our connections with others. This attribute inspires resilience and endurance in facing relational hurdles.
5. Promoting Reliability: God's faithfulness encourages us to be reliable individuals in our relationships. Reliability is essential for building strong connections, as it assures others that we can be counted on. Being faithful to our words and actions fosters an atmosphere of security and dependability.

Scriptures highlighting God's faithfulness:

- Lamentations 3:22-23 (ESV): "The steadfast love of the Lord never ceases; his mercies never come to an end; they are new every morning; great is your faithfulness."
- 1 Corinthians 1:9 (ESV): "God is faithful, by whom you were called into the fellowship of his Son, Jesus Christ our Lord."
- Psalm 33:4 (ESV): "For the word of the Lord is upright, and all his work is done in faithfulness."

God's faithfulness serves as a beacon of assurance, encouraging us to emulate this attribute in our relationships. By establishing trust, consistency, and reliability, we contribute to the creation of strong and enduring connections with those around us.

Building Trust Through God's Faithfulness: Relationship Development Worksheet Page: 38

69

LEARNING TO BUILD & SAIL RELATIONSHIPS: THE ANALOGY OF SHIPS

In our journey of building and sailing relationships, God desires to teach us the intricate art of constructing and navigating the vessels of connection. This analogy beautifully illustrates the progressive nature of our relationship with God and how it shapes the various "ships" we encounter in life.

Boats of Personal Growth: At the beginning of our relationship with God, we learn to construct smaller boats representing our individual lives. These boats symbolize our personal growth, resilience, and navigation through the challenges of life. As we allow God to guide us, we develop the skills needed to navigate the waters of self-discovery and character formation.

In the foundational stage of constructing our boats of personal growth, God invites us into a transformative journey. These boats, emblematic of our individual lives, serve as the vessels through which we navigate the vast and often unpredictable waters of our personal journeys. God's desire for a relationship with us is unveiled in this process of constructing these initial vessels. It is here that we first learn to trust His guidance and align our paths with His divine plan.

As we embark on the construction phase, we find that each plank and nail represents a facet of our character and self-discovery. God, the Master Shipbuilder, meticulously shapes and refines these elements, teaching us resilience and endurance in the face of life's challenges. Just as a boat must withstand the currents and storms, our lives, under God's guidance, develop the strength to weather the trials and tribulations of our personal odyssey.

Navigating these early boats calls for a partnership with God. Through prayer, introspection, and the study of His Word, we acquire the necessary skills to steer our vessels through the waters of self-discovery. The lessons learned during this phase become the building blocks for the larger ships and fleets God envisions for us. The intimate connection forged in constructing these personal growth boats sets the tone for the more expansive relationships that lie ahead, emphasizing the foundational importance of a consistent and evolving relationship with our Master Shipbuilder.

Workbook - Reflection Questions: Building Your Boats Page 40

Ships of Marriage: With a solid foundation in personal growth, God then teaches us how to build more substantial ships, symbolizing marriages. Marital relationships are intricate vessels requiring careful construction, teamwork, and the ability to weather storms together. God, as the Master Shipbuilder, imparts wisdom on communication, sacrifice, and mutual support, ensuring our marriage ships sail smoothly.

Moving beyond the construction of personal growth boats, God extends His guidance into the complex realm of building substantial ships, each symbolizing the sacred institution of marriage. Marital relationships, likened to these sturdy vessels, demand meticulous construction, emphasizing the importance of teamwork, resilience, and the capacity to navigate life's storms together. In this crucial phase of relationship-building, God assumes the role of the Master Shipbuilder, imparting invaluable wisdom that serves as the blueprint for harmonious and enduring marriages.

God's teachings in this endeavor delve into the intricacies of communication, an essential skillset for navigating the shared waters of matrimony. As the Master Shipbuilder imparts insights on effective communication, He equips couples with the tools needed to foster understanding and unity. Additionally, God imparts the art of sacrifice, emphasizing that true marital ships are built on foundations of mutual support and selflessness. These ships of marriage, constructed under God's watchful eye, serve as symbols of enduring commitment and unity.

As couples embark on the journey of constructing these marital vessels, the lessons learned become integral to the sustainability of the relationship. The Master Shipbuilder's guidance ensures that the marriage ships sail smoothly, fortified against the turbulent waters that may arise. The principles instilled during this phase set the course for the development of more expansive fleets, underscoring the interconnectedness of our relationships and the pivotal role of God as the guiding force in our journey.

- **Workbook - Preparing Your Personal Growth Boat: Page: 41**
- **Workbook-Construction of Marital Vessels Page: 42**

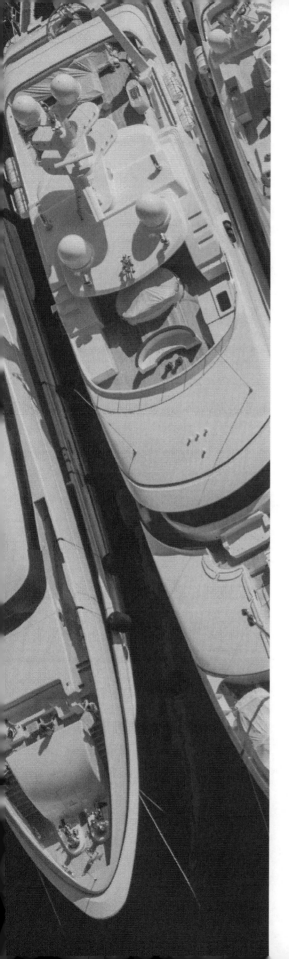

Leadership Fleets: For those whose journeys extend further, God desires to teach us how to lead and own fleets of ships. This represents the expansion of our influence and responsibilities, such as leading a family. God, as the Admiral, equips us with the qualities of leadership, mentorship, and responsibility, allowing us to guide multiple vessels toward a collective purpose.

Transitioning from the construction of marital ships, God's teachings then propel us into the expansive territory of leadership fleets. In this phase, God becomes our Admiral, instructing and empowering us to lead and own fleets of ships, each vessel representing an extension of our influence and responsibilities. This journey signifies a broader spectrum of relationships and roles, with a primary focus on leading a family.

As the Admiral of our leadership fleet, God imparts the qualities essential for effective leadership, mentorship, and responsibility. Just as a skilled Admiral navigates multiple vessels toward a collective purpose, God equips us with the wisdom and discernment needed to guide our family and those within our sphere of influence. The construction of leadership fleets is not merely about individual accomplishment; rather, it's about stewarding the interconnected relationships under our care.

This phase underscores the importance of God's role as the Admiral, providing guidance on leadership principles that transcend personal ambitions. The leadership fleet, constructed under God's tutelage, becomes a testament to the impact of purposeful and godly leadership on the lives entrusted to us. God's teachings in this context set the foundation for a lasting legacy, emphasizing the interconnectedness of relationships and the significance of leadership within the broader fleet of human connections.

Workbook -Reflection Questions on Leadership Fleets: Page 43

Navigating Warships Against Darkness: As the relationship with God matures, some are called to construct warships, representing our roles in spiritual warfare against the forces of darkness. These relationships involve a heightened level of spiritual preparedness, strategic thinking, and collaborative efforts with other believers. God, as the Commander, imparts insights into wielding spiritual weapons and defending against the enemy's attacks.

Advancing beyond the construction of leadership fleets, God's teachings propel us into the formidable realm of constructing warships, symbolizing our roles in spiritual warfare against the forces of darkness. In this phase of our relationship with God, He assumes the role of the Commander, guiding us in the intricate process of developing and navigating warships designed for strategic spiritual warfare. The construction of warships signifies a heightened level of spiritual preparedness and strategic thinking.

God, as the Commander overseeing this phase, imparts crucial insights into wielding spiritual weapons, discerning spiritual battles, and defending against the relentless attacks of the enemy. Just as a seasoned Commander equips soldiers with the skills and knowledge needed for warfare, God prepares us for the spiritual battles we face in a fallen world. Navigating warships against darkness involves collaborative efforts with fellow believers. God, in His wisdom, encourages unity and shared purpose within the spiritual army. This phase underscores the interconnected nature of our relationships within the Body of Christ, emphasizing the importance of standing together against the forces that seek to undermine the Kingdom of God.

As we engage in spiritual warfare under God's guidance, the construction and navigation of warships become a testament to His authority, power, and triumph over darkness. This phase of our relationship with God extends beyond personal growth and leadership influence, signaling a divine call to actively participate in the ongoing battle for spiritual victory.

Consistent relationship with God is the common thread woven through each stage of this analogy. It is the Master Shipbuilder's guidance and wisdom that empowers us to construct and navigate relationships of varying complexities. Whether steering a small boat or commanding a fleet, the relationship with God serves as the compass, ensuring our vessels stay true to their intended course.

Workbook: Reflection Questions on Navigating Warships Against Darkness Pages: 45

REPENTANCE

Embarking on the journey of developing a thriving relationship with God is akin to cultivating any meaningful connection—with disciplines, determination, and intentional investment yielding the richest harvest. Relationships, especially with the divine, thrive on the sincerity and depth of our engagement. In this section, we delve into the transformative steps that lay the foundation for a flourishing connection with God. It begins with the essential practice of repentance and turning away from sin, a pivotal step in the path toward divine intimacy. Just as the richness of a harvest is directly proportional to the care invested in the seeds sown, the growth of our relationship with God is a reflection of the sincerity and commitment we bring to its development. So, let us journey together, cultivating the fertile soil of repentance and turning from sin, as we seek to nurture a thriving relationship with the Creator.

Repentance, biblically speaking, is a transformative change of mind and heart that leads to a turning away from sin and a turning toward God. The Greek word for repentance in the New Testament is "metanoia," which implies a profound change in one's way of thinking, feeling, and living. It's not merely feeling sorry for one's actions but involves a sincere and deep-seated transformation.

The role of repentance in spiritual growth is fundamental and holds significant biblical weight. In various passages throughout the Bible, repentance is intricately linked with forgiveness, redemption, and a restored relationship with God.

Forgiveness and Cleansing: In Acts 3:19, the apostle Peter calls for repentance, promising that times of refreshing will come from the Lord. Repentance is the gateway to receiving forgiveness and experiencing the cleansing power of God.

Acts 3:19 (ESV): "Repent therefore, and turn back, that your sins may be blotted out."

Restoration and Renewal: The prophet Isaiah highlights the restorative nature of repentance, describing how sins can be transformed into purity through genuine repentance.

Isaiah 1:18 (ESV): "Come now, let us reason together, says the Lord: though your sins are like scarlet, they shall be as white as snow; though they are red like crimson, they shall become like wool."

Salvation and Turning to God: The call to repentance is often coupled with an invitation to turn to God for salvation. In Acts 26:20, Paul emphasizes the connection between repentance and deeds in keeping with repentance.

Acts 26:20 (ESV): "But declared first to those in Damascus, then in Jerusalem and throughout all the region of Judea, and also to the Gentiles, that they should repent and turn to God, performing deeds in keeping with their repentance."

A Change of Heart: The Bible emphasizes that true repentance involves a change of heart and a turning away from the old self.

Ezekiel 18:30-31 (ESV): "Repent and turn from all your transgressions, lest iniquity be your ruin. Cast away from you all the transgressions that you have committed, and make yourselves a new heart and a new spirit!"

Repentance, then, is not a one-time event but an ongoing posture of humility and surrender. It's an essential step in the process of spiritual growth, allowing believers to continually draw near to God, experience His mercy, and walk in the light of His transformative grace.

Let's delve deeper into the idea that repentance is not a one-time event but an ongoing posture of humility and surrender. This perspective aligns with the biblical concept of sanctification – the process of becoming more like Christ.

Ongoing Transformation: Repentance is not a checkbox but a continuous journey of transformation. As believers, we're called to examine our hearts regularly, allowing the Holy Spirit to reveal areas that need repentance. This ongoing process enables us to grow in Christlikeness.

2 Corinthians 3:18 (ESV): "And we all, with unveiled face, beholding the glory of the Lord, are being transformed into the same image from one degree of glory to another. For this comes from the Lord who is the Spirit."

Humility and Surrender: Repentance is an expression of humility, acknowledging our dependence on God's grace. It involves surrendering our will to His, recognizing that our understanding of righteousness falls short of His perfect standard.

James 4:6 (ESV): "But he gives more grace. Therefore it says, 'God opposes the proud but gives grace to the humble.'"

Drawing Near to God: The continual practice of repentance draws us into a closer relationship with God. It's an intimate acknowledgment of our need for Him and an openness to His transforming work in our lives.

James 4:8 (ESV): "Draw near to God, and he will draw near to you. Cleanse your hands, you sinners, and purify your hearts, you double-minded."

Fruit of Repentance: True repentance bears fruit in our lives. As we consistently turn away from sin and turn toward God, the evidence is seen in changed attitudes, behaviors, and a growing conformity to the image of Christ.

Matthew 3:8 (ESV): "Bear fruit in keeping with repentance."

In essence, repentance is a dynamic process of becoming more aligned with God's purposes. It's an invitation to a lifelong journey of spiritual growth, where we continually yield to God's transformative work, allowing Him to shape our character, attitudes, and actions. Through the ongoing practice of repentance, believers not only experience the joy of forgiveness but also participate in the beautiful process of becoming more like the One they follow.

let's explore what repentance is not and clarify its profound nature in the context of our relationship with God.

Repentance is not a Perpetual Indulgence: The apostle Paul addresses the misconception that grace gives us license to continue in sin. He emphatically states in Romans 6:1-2 (ESV): "What shall we say then? Are we to continue in sin that grace may abound? By no means! How can we who died to sin still live in it?"

Repentance is not a perpetual cycle of indulging in sin with the expectation that God's grace will cover it. Instead, it involves a genuine turning away from sin, recognizing its destructive nature, and embracing a new way of life in Christ.

Sincere vs. Insincere Repentance:
Insincere repentance may involve mere regret over consequences or a desire to avoid punishment. True repentance, on the other hand, is marked by godly sorrow and a genuine turning toward God. 2 Corinthians 7:10 (ESV) illustrates this distinction: "For godly grief produces a repentance that leads to salvation without regret, whereas worldly grief produces death."

Entrance into Relationship with God:
Repentance is the gateway into a relationship with God. It's not a matter of choosing God as if we hold the initiative. Rather, it's a response to God's goodness and pursuit of us. Romans 2:4 (ESV) emphasizes this: "Or do you presume on the riches of his kindness and forbearance and patience, not knowing that God's kindness is meant to lead you to repentance?"

Awareness of Need for God's Work:
Repentance involves an awakening to our need for God's transformative work in our lives. It's not about achieving righteousness on our own; rather, it's a surrender to God's gracious work within us. Ephesians 2:8-9 (ESV) affirms this: "For by grace you have been saved through faith. And this is not your own doing; it is the gift of God, not a result of works, so that no one may boast." In essence, repentance is a dynamic and transformative act that signifies a profound turning toward God. It's not a legalistic transaction but a relational response to the relentless pursuit of God's love and goodness. As we turn away from sin and embrace God's grace, we step into a journey of ongoing transformation and intimacy with our Creator.

Maintaining a Spirit of Repentance: A Dance of Forgiveness and Transformation

In the intricate dance of our relationship with God, maintaining a spirit of repentance becomes the rhythm that guides us through the steps of fumbling and making mistakes, receiving forgiveness that's already there, and growing to a place where frequent sin is no longer our practice.

Marriage of Mistakes and Forgiveness:
Just as a marital relationship undergoes growth and maturity, our connection with God involves a continual journey.

At the heart of this journey is the understanding that God's forgiveness is not a reaction to our repentance; it's a constant, unwavering presence. The marriage between our fumbling and God's forgiveness allows us to stumble, knowing that restoration is readily available.

Eternal Forgiveness through Christ's Sacrifice:
The forgiveness available to us through Christ's death on the cross has dealt with the eternal penalty of sin. Legally, we are saved from the eternal separation in hell for our sins when we repent and put our trust in Christ. However, the forgiveness we seek in our moments of weakness is more about reestablishing our relational posture with God. It's acknowledging that, though eternally secure, our sin can disrupt the flow of our partnership with Him on a day-to-day basis.

Maintaining Awareness of Sin's Impact:
Maintaining a repentant posture keeps us acutely aware of how sin, though not severing us from God's love, can impact our partnership endeavors. It serves as a gentle reminder that sin, while forgiven, disrupts the harmonious dance of flowing with God and being used by Him at a higher level.

God's Relentless Pursuit:
In this dance of forgiveness and transformation, God's relentless pursuit of us becomes evident. He doesn't need a relationship with us; we need a relationship with Him. In Him, we live, move, and have our being (Acts 17:28, ESV). Maintaining a spirit of repentance is not a burdensome requirement; it's an invitation to engage in the beautiful dance of transformation, where our mistakes are met with grace, and our journey unfolds in the light of God's unwavering love.

Steps of Repentance and Turning from Sin to Righteousness: A Transformative Journey Embarking on the transformative journey of repentance and turning from sin to righteousness involves deliberate steps that resonate with the rhythm of God's grace. Here's a guide to navigate this dance of spiritual renewal:

Audit Your Heart:
Begin by audaciously peering into the depths of your heart. Identify the root reasons that lead to sin. This introspection allows you to unearth the underlying motivations and desires that may contribute to your shortcomings.

Awareness of God's Goodness:
Cultivate a keen awareness of the goodness of God. Recognize His boundless grace and mercy that stand ready to embrace you, not as a reaction to your repentance but as an unchanging attribute of His character.

Impact of Sin:
Contemplate the impact of sin, both on your life and the lives of those around you. Understand the relational, emotional, and spiritual repercussions, fostering a genuine desire for transformation.

Collaboration with the Holy Spirit:
Engage in collaborative efforts with the Holy Spirit. Seek His guidance and wisdom in developing practical systems of action and accountability. Through this partnership, you empower yourself to resist temptation and build resilience against the allure of sin.

Developing Systems of Action and Accountability:
Construct intentional systems of action and accountability to fortify your defense against the vulnerability of falling into sin. This may involve setting boundaries, establishing regular spiritual disciplines, and surrounding yourself with a supportive community that encourages growth.

Embracing the Erasing Process:
Embrace the process of erasing poor habits and negative patterns. Understand that transformation is not a one-time event but a continual journey of growth. Develop resilience by learning from mistakes, adjusting your course, and allowing God's transformative grace to redefine your trajectory.

Continuous Repentance:
Finally, recognize that repentance is not a one-off action but a continuous posture of humility and surrender. It's a dynamic dance of turning away from sin and turning toward righteousness, guided by the ever-present grace of God.
In these intentional steps, the dance of repentance becomes a transformative journey where you not only turn from sin but step into the fullness of God's righteousness, ever-growing in His grace and becoming more aligned with His transformative purposes for your life.

Living Repentant: Nurturing Healthy Relationships
Living in a state of repentance, where one is consistently aware of the need for divine guidance and forgiveness, has a profound impact on relationships across the spectrum of human connections. Repentance, as a continual process, becomes a transformative force that nurtures healthy relationships in various dimensions.

In marriage, the practice of living repentant allows spouses to navigate conflicts with humility and a willingness to seek forgiveness and extend it. The acknowledgment of personal shortcomings fosters an environment where openness and vulnerability are valued. Couples who live repentant recognize that they are on a shared journey of growth, and the act of repentance becomes a bridge that brings them closer rather than a wall that separates them. Parenting is another realm where living repentant influences the dynamics of the relationship. Children observe and absorb the behavior of their parents, and when parents model a repentant lifestyle, it teaches children the importance of accountability, forgiveness, and the continual pursuit of personal growth.

The family becomes a laboratory where grace is not only spoken but tangibly experienced. Beyond the family unit, friendships and professional relationships also benefit from living repentant. A repentant heart is quick to acknowledge mistakes, seek reconciliation, and foster an atmosphere of understanding. It prevents the buildup of resentment and creates a culture where individuals are willing to learn from one another, strengthening the fabric of the relationship.

Living repentant is not a one-time event but a lifestyle that shapes the way individuals approach relationships. It emphasizes the importance of ongoing self-reflection, a willingness to admit faults, and a commitment to continual improvement. In this way, relationships become sanctuaries where grace flows freely, and individuals grow together in the shared journey of repentance and transformation.

Conclusion

In the fabric of spiritual growth and relational depth, genuine repentance emerges as the vibrant thread, knitting a flourishing connection with God. It is not merely a response to mistakes but a continual dance of humility and surrender, a melody that resonates with the grace and goodness of a loving Creator. Sincere repentance is the compass that keeps our hearts attuned to the divine, acknowledging our need for God's transformative work in our lives. As we audaciously audit our hearts, cultivate awareness of God's goodness, and collaborate with the Holy Spirit in the erasing process of poor habits, we pave the way for a thriving relationship. The dance of repentance is not a monotonous routine but a dynamic partnership, where the echoes of God's forgiveness and the transformative power of grace resonate. In the sincere turning away from sin, we step into the embrace of divine love, forging a resilient and thriving connection that withstands the tests of time and circumstance.

Reflection Question on Personal Repentance Page: 47

RIGHTEOUSNESS

In the intricate dance of cultivating a meaningful relationship with God, two profound challenges often emerge—condemnation and perfectionism. These formidable adversaries can cast a shadow on the vivid landscape of our spiritual journey, impeding our ability to wholeheartedly embrace the righteousness and grace that God offers.

In setting the stage for exploring these themes, it is crucial to recognize that condemnation often stems from a misunderstanding of God's nature and the purpose of conviction in our lives. Meanwhile, perfectionism, with its relentless pursuit of flawlessness, can leave us perpetually unsatisfied and distant from the understanding of God's grace.

The journey of embracing God's righteousness and grace is an invitation to cast aside the heavy burdens of condemnation and perfectionism, to step into the liberating light of God's love. It is an acknowledgment that, in our imperfection, God's righteousness covers us, and His grace empowers us to grow and thrive. As we embark on this exploration, let us navigate the delicate balance of understanding the weight of righteousness without succumbing to condemnation and the pursuit of excellence without falling into the trap of perfectionism. In doing so, we open the door to a harmonious and transformative relationship with God, where His righteousness and grace converge to illuminate our path.

Defining God's Righteousness and its Significance:
To comprehend God's righteousness is to grasp the very essence of His character. God's righteousness signifies His moral perfection and adherence to divine principles. It is not a rigid adherence to legalistic rules but an unwavering commitment to what is right and just. Embracing this aspect of God's nature provides a firm foundation for understanding His actions, judgments, and interactions with humanity. It is a righteousness that flows from His love and seeks the highest good for all. Recognizing God's righteousness dispels misconceptions, allowing us to approach Him with confidence, knowing that His nature is just and true.

Embracing God's Righteousness as a Foundation for a Thriving Relationship:
In the intricate dance of cultivating a thriving relationship with God, His righteousness becomes a foundational cornerstone. Embracing God's righteousness involves acknowledging our need for His moral guidance and aligning our lives with His principles. Rather than viewing God's righteousness as a harsh judge, we come to understand it as a beacon of light that illuminates our path.

This awareness fosters humility and dependence, creating a dynamic where we seek His righteousness in our lives. It becomes a transformative force that shapes our character, actions, and relationships, leading to a more harmonious and thriving connection with the Divine.

Imputed Righteousness Through Jesus: A Divine Exchange

In our relationship with God, the idea of imputed righteousness is like a crucial thread woven by Jesus Christ's sacrificial love.

This profound theological truth transforms the dynamics of our connection with God, bridging the gap between our fallen state and the holiness of the Almighty.

The journey begins with an understanding of humanity's inherent brokenness and separation from God due to sin. The apostle Paul, in his epistles, unfolds the narrative of how all have fallen short of God's glory. Yet, in this narrative, a divine intervention emerges—a redemptive plan initiated by God's unfathomable love for His creation.

Enter Jesus Christ, the sinless Savior, whose life, death, and resurrection set in motion the divine exchange. Jesus, the Lamb of God, takes upon Himself the sins of the world, bearing the weight of our transgressions on the cross. The transaction is not merely symbolic; it is a profound spiritual reality—our sin for His righteousness.

Through this divine exchange, Jesus imputes His righteousness onto us. The term "imputation" conveys a legal reckoning—a crediting of Jesus' righteousness to our account. As a result, we stand before God not in our own merit, stained by sin, but clothed in the righteousness of Christ. This positional righteousness is the foundation upon which our thriving relationship with God rests.

In the heavenly courtroom, God, the Righteous Judge, declares believers justified—made righteous—in Christ. This transformative act not only secures our forgiveness but grants us access to the Father's presence without shame or condemnation. It is an imputed righteousness that empowers us to boldly approach the throne of grace, knowing that our standing is not based on our performance but on Christ's finished work.

However, the divine exchange doesn't end with mere justification; it sets in motion a process of sanctification. Inspired by the imputed righteousness of Christ, believers embark on a transformative journey to grow into the likeness of their Savior. This ongoing work of the Holy Spirit within us shapes our character, molds our desires, and empowers us to live out the righteousness imputed to us.

Workbook - Reflection Questions on Righteousness 48

_____
_____
_____
_____
_____
_____
_____
_____
_____
_____
_____
_____
_____
_____
_____
_____
_____
_____
_____
_____
_____
_____
_____
_____
_____
_____
_____
_____
_____
_____

GRACE

Embracing God's Grace: A Transformative Journey
Defining God's Grace and Its Transformative Power
In the grand narrative of our relationship with God,
grace emerges as the divine elixir that transforms
our brokenness into a masterpiece of redemption.
Understanding grace requires us to delve into its
profound definition—a concept far richer than mere
favor or unmerited kindness.

At its essence, God's grace embodies His
unconditional love manifested in undeserved favor
and forgiveness. Grace is not earned through
human efforts; rather, it flows from the heart of a
benevolent Creator who extends His hand to fallen
humanity. This divine favor is not contingent upon
our performance; it is rooted in God's character and
His desire to reconcile us to Himself.

Grace is, in essence, a transformative force. It
reaches into the depths of our brokenness, offering
healing, restoration, and a new beginning. The
Apostle Paul, who experienced the radical
transformation wrought by God's grace, declares,
"For by grace, you have been saved through faith.
And this is not your own doing; it is the gift of
God" (Ephesians 2:8, ESV). Salvation, the ultimate
expression of God's grace, marks the inception of
our transformative journey.

Recognizing the Role of Grace in Our Spiritual Journey

Grace is not a one-time event but a continuous
stream that accompanies us throughout our
spiritual pilgrimage. As we navigate the terrain of
sanctification—the process of becoming more
Christ-like—grace is our constant companion,
nurturing growth, and empowering change.
The transformative power of grace is evident in its
ability to break the chains of guilt and shame. In a
world burdened by the weight of sin, grace
liberates believers from the oppressive yoke of
condemnation. The Apostle John encapsulates this
truth: "For the law was given through Moses; grace
and truth came through Jesus Christ" (John 1:17,
ESV).

Moreover, grace operates as a catalyst for spiritual
disciplines. It inspires gratitude, leading to a life
characterized by worship, prayer, and a hunger for
God's Word. The understanding that we stand
justified by grace prompts a response of love and
devotion.

As we embrace God's grace, our perspective on relationships undergoes a radical shift. Grace empowers us to extend mercy and forgiveness to others, creating an environment of love and acceptance. The transformative journey facilitated by grace extends beyond individual lives, permeating the fabric of our relationships, communities, and beyond.

In essence, embracing God's grace is not a passive acceptance but an active engagement with the transformative power of divine favor. It propels us forward on the path of spiritual growth, reshaping our hearts, minds, and actions. This transformative journey under grace is an ongoing process—a dance of redemption and renewal that continues to unfold throughout our earthly sojourn.

Perspectives on Amazing Grace and the Pitfalls of Abusing Grace: The Marvel of Amazing Grace

"Amazing Grace, how sweet the sound, that saved a wretch like me!" This iconic hymn captures the essence of the believer's awe and wonder at the boundless nature of God's grace. Amazing Grace is not just a theological concept; it is a profoundly personal experience that transforms lives.

Understanding the marvel of Amazing Grace begins with acknowledging our unworthiness. It's a recognition that we were lost, but now we're found; we were blind, but now we see. This divine favor, unearned and undeserved, is a beacon of hope that pierces through the darkest corners of our existence.

Amazing Grace is an invitation to a new way of life—a life liberated from the shackles of sin and guilt. It's an anthem of redemption, resonating through the corridors of human history, declaring that no one is beyond the reach of God's transformative love. This perspective on grace fosters gratitude, humility, and a deep sense of dependence on the Giver of this wondrous gift.

The Pitfalls of Abusing Grace

In juxtaposition to the marvel of Amazing Grace, there exists the perilous path of abusing grace. The Apostle Paul addresses this potential pitfall in Romans 6:1-2 (ESV), "What shall we say then? Are we to continue in sin that grace may abound? By no means! How can we who died to sin still live in it?" Abusing grace involves a misunderstanding or intentional manipulation of the concept. Some may fall into the trap of thinking that because grace abounds,

they can continue in a lifestyle contrary to God's will without consequence. This perspective tarnishes the sanctity of grace, reducing it to a license for unbridled indulgence in sin.

However, true grace, as Paul emphatically declares, does not endorse a lifestyle of sin. It is not a loophole to evade the call to holiness and obedience. Rather, it is the catalyst for a life transformed by the power of God. The danger of abusing grace lies in severing the connection between God's love and our response to that love. Instead of responding with gratitude and obedience, the abuser of grace divorces grace from righteous living. In contrast, embracing Amazing Grace aligns our hearts with God's redemptive purpose. It compels us to live in a manner worthy of the calling we have received (Ephesians 4:1, ESV). Instead of exploiting grace for self-indulgence, we respond to the gift of grace with a life marked by love, holiness, and a fervent pursuit of God's will.

Navigating the delicate balance between embracing grace and avoiding its abuse requires a steadfast commitment to living out the transformative power of grace. It is an ongoing journey of gratitude, obedience, and a deepening relationship with the One who extends this amazing grace to undeserving hearts.

God's Grace: Guiding in Sufficiency: The Sufficiency of Grace for Sanctification

Grace, in its essence, is not merely a divine favor extended to us in times of struggle; it is the transformative force that guides us through the journey of sanctification. The Apostle Paul experienced and testified to the sufficiency of God's grace in the midst of his own challenges. In 2 Corinthians 12:9 (ESV), the Lord's response to Paul's plea for the removal of a thorn in the flesh is profound: "My grace is sufficient for you, for my power is made perfect in weakness."

God's grace is not a limited resource; it's an abundant wellspring that flows ceaselessly. It is the very means by which we are sanctified, molded into the image of Christ. In moments of weakness, when we confront our inadequacies, God's grace doesn't merely cover our flaws; it empowers us to overcome them. This sufficiency of grace is the anchor of our sanctification, a continual process of becoming more like Christ.

God's Grace and the Pursuit of His Will

While God's grace is abundant for our sanctification, it does not operate as a blank check endorsing any endeavor we choose to pursue. God's grace is intricately linked to His will. When we align our lives with His purpose, grace becomes the guiding force, making the pursuit of His will seem effortless, smooth, and seamless.

However, when we attempt to pursue our own will and expect God's grace to empower our self-driven endeavors, we may encounter resistance. God's grace is not meant to fuel our personal ambitions divorced from His divine plan. It is not a resource to facilitate our success in ventures that are contrary to His purpose.

The confusion often arises when individuals grind themselves out trying to achieve what they believe God wants for them without seeking clarity. God is indeed the author of clarity, not confusion. His grace is most pronounced and effective when it aligns with His will.

In personal experiences, such as navigating the challenges in marriage, one can witness the profound impact of God's grace when it guides a union that is in accordance with His purpose. The journey may have its share of difficulties, but when God's grace is on the race, the path becomes smoother, and the challenges are navigated with a sense of divine guidance.

Therefore, the crucial question in every pursuit is, "Is God's grace on this race I am running?" Seeking God's will and aligning our endeavors with His purpose ensures that His grace is not only sufficient for our sanctification but also actively guiding us in the paths of righteousness.

The Importance of God's Grace in Relationships

The principle of God's grace guiding in sufficiency holds profound significance in the context of relationships, whether in marriage, parenting, or any other familial bonds. In the intricate dance of human connections, where flaws and imperfections are inevitably present, the sufficiency of God's grace becomes the glue that holds relationships together.

In marriage, for instance, understanding that God's grace is not just a safety net for when challenges arise but an active force guiding the union transforms the dynamics. When both partners recognize the sufficiency of God's grace for sanctification, it fosters an environment where forgiveness, understanding, and growth become the pillars of the relationship. Rather than expecting perfection from one another, spouses learn to extend the same grace that God showers upon them daily.

Parenting, with its inherent challenges and joys, also benefits immensely from this principle. Raising children is a complex journey filled with unexpected twists and turns. Embracing God's grace as the guiding force acknowledges that parents are not expected to be perfect but are equipped to navigate the journey with divine assistance. When parents operate in the sufficiency of God's grace, they model humility, forgiveness, and love, creating a home environment where children learn the transformative power of grace.

This principle ripples into every aspect of relational dynamics, reminding individuals that relationships are not about perfection but about growth, resilience, and navigating the journey together. It encourages a posture of humility, recognizing that, like the branches connected to the vine, we all need the continuous flow of God's grace to bear the fruit of love, patience, and understanding in our relationships. As relationships are sanctified through the sufficiency of God's grace, they become not only stronger but also reflective of the divine love that binds them together.

Breaking Free from Condemnation: Understanding the Difference Between Conviction and Condemnation

In the spiritual journey, understanding the nuanced difference between conviction and condemnation is pivotal for breaking free from the shackles of self-condemnation. Conviction and condemnation are distinct forces at play in the realm of the human conscience, and comprehending their characteristics empowers individuals to navigate their spiritual landscape with clarity and freedom.

Conviction: A Compassionate Call to Change
Conviction, often orchestrated by the Holy Spirit, is a gentle, compassionate nudge toward recognizing and rectifying behaviors misaligned with God's standards. It is a divine whisper that draws attention to areas of life where growth, transformation, or reconciliation is needed. Unlike condemnation, conviction does not berate or shame; instead, it lovingly guides individuals toward a path of righteousness.

When experiencing conviction, individuals are invited to participate in the redemptive work of God. It is an acknowledgment of divine care, a realization that God's standards are higher but accompanied by the assurance that His grace is sufficient to aid in the journey toward improvement. Conviction is an ally in the pursuit of spiritual growth, fostering a sense of hope and a desire for positive change.

Condemnation: The Destructive Voice of Accusation
Condemnation, on the other hand, emanates from a different source. It is a destructive force that accuses, berates, and fosters a sense of hopelessness. Unlike conviction, condemnation is not rooted in love but in the tactics of the enemy seeking to sow seeds of doubt, shame, and despair. It is a relentless voice that magnifies shortcomings without offering a pathway to redemption.

Condemnation thrives in darkness and isolation, driving individuals away from God's grace instead of toward it. It paralyzes, discourages, and creates a barrier between the individual and the loving embrace of a merciful God. Recognizing condemnation requires discernment, as it often masquerades as a divine response when, in reality, it is a counterfeit that seeks to undermine the transformative power of God's love.

Understanding the source of condemnation is crucial for discernment. In Revelation 12:10, it is revealed that Satan is the accuser of the brethren, constantly seeking to bring accusations against God's people. Why does he do this? Satan aims to create a sense of separation and distance between individuals and God, undermining their confidence in God's love and forgiveness. By recognizing the accusing voice as originating from the enemy, individuals can more effectively reject condemnation and embrace the liberating truth of God's grace.

In conclusion, breaking free from condemnation involves discerning the voice that speaks within. Embracing the compassionate call of conviction leads to growth, while rejecting the destructive accusations of condemnation paves the way for a liberated and grace-filled journey with God. By understanding these dynamics, individuals can foster a relationship with God that thrives on love, hope, and the transformative power of His grace.

Strategies for Overcoming a Condemning Mindset
Breaking free from a condemning mindset is a transformative process that involves intentional strategies to shift one's perspective and embrace the liberating truth of God's grace. Here are practical strategies for individuals seeking to overcome a condemning mindset:

1. Embrace the Truth of God's Word:
Immerse yourself in the Scriptures to understand and internalize God's perspective on forgiveness, redemption, and His unconditional love.
Memorize verses that emphasize God's grace and forgiveness, such as Romans 8:1, which declares, "There is therefore now no condemnation for those who are in Christ Jesus."

2. Practice Discernment:
Develop discernment to distinguish between the voice of conviction, which guides towards positive change, and the voice of condemnation, which brings shame and despair. Pray for wisdom and discernment, relying on the Holy Spirit to help identify and reject condemning thoughts.

3. Cultivate a Repentant Heart:
Maintain a repentant heart that acknowledges shortcomings and sins, but also trusts in God's forgiveness and grace.
Understand that genuine repentance leads to transformation and growth, while condemnation hinders progress.

4. Seek Accountability and Support:
Share your struggles with a trusted friend, mentor, or spiritual leader who can provide accountability and offer guidance from a biblical perspective.
Surround yourself with a community that understands the transformative power of God's grace and encourages each other in the journey.

5. Practice Self-Compassion:
Extend the same grace to yourself that God offers. Remember that everyone is on a journey of growth, and setbacks do not define your identity in Christ.
Challenge negative self-talk and replace condemning thoughts with affirmations grounded in God's love.

6. Meditate on God's Love:
Regularly meditate on the depth of God's love for you. Reflect on passages that highlight His unconditional love, such as John 3:16.
Allow the reality of God's love to permeate your thoughts and emotions, dispelling condemning narratives.

7. Challenge Distorted Beliefs:
Identify distorted beliefs about God's character and your worthiness of His love.
Replace distorted beliefs with biblical truths. For example, if you struggle with feelings of unworthiness, meditate on Ephesians 2:8-9.

8. Practice Gratitude:
Cultivate a heart of gratitude for God's mercy, forgiveness, and the opportunity for a renewed relationship with Him.
Regularly express thankfulness for the transformative work of God's grace in your life.

9. Engage in Worship:
Participate in worship activities, whether through music, prayer, or other forms of worship, to reinforce the truth of God's goodness and love.
Worship helps shift focus from self-condemnation to the magnificence of God's redemptive power.

10. Renew Your Mind:
Commit to renewing your mind daily through intentional prayer, meditation, and reflection on God's Word (Romans 12:2).
Allow God's truth to reshape your thought patterns and align them with His grace.
By implementing these strategies consistently, individuals can actively break free from a condemning mindset, experiencing the freedom and joy that come from embracing God's righteousness and grace.

Letting Go of Perfectionism: The Impact on Our Relationship with God
Perfectionism, the relentless pursuit of flawlessness, can significantly impact our relationship with God, hindering our ability to accept His righteousness and grace. Here's a thorough breakdown of the impact of perfectionism:

1. Impaired Understanding of God's Grace:
Perfectionism fosters an unrealistic expectation of flawlessness, making it challenging to comprehend and accept the depth of God's grace. Individuals trapped in perfectionism may struggle to acknowledge that God's grace extends to imperfections and shortcomings.

2. Fear of Rejection:
Perfectionists often fear rejection and condemnation, projecting these fears onto their relationship with God. This fear can lead to avoidance of God, thinking that imperfections will result in God's disapproval, thus straining the connection.

3. Conditional Self-Worth:
Perfectionism links self-worth to flawless performance, creating a conditional sense of value. When individuals fail to meet self-imposed perfectionist standards, they may perceive themselves as unworthy of God's love, hindering a genuine connection.

4. Legalistic Approach to Faith:
Perfectionism can foster a legalistic view of faith, where individuals attempt to earn God's love through flawless adherence to rules and rituals. This legalistic approach undermines the foundational truth that God's love is freely given and not based on human achievements.

5. Lack of Vulnerability:
Perfectionists often struggle with vulnerability, hesitant to expose their imperfections even to God. This lack of vulnerability impedes the depth of intimacy in the relationship, as vulnerability is crucial for authentic connection.

6. Striving for Self-Righteousness:
Perfectionism may lead to an unhealthy pursuit of self-righteousness, attempting to establish one's righteousness apart from God's grace. This striving undermines the core tenet of Christianity, which emphasizes reliance on God's righteousness through faith in Christ.

7. Inability to Extend Grace to Others:
Perfectionists, preoccupied with their own performance, may struggle to extend grace to others, fostering judgment and criticism. This lack of grace toward others reflects a distorted understanding of God's grace, inhibiting a harmonious relationship with fellow believers.

8. Anxiety and Burnout:

The constant pursuit of perfection can result in anxiety, burnout, and exhaustion. Individuals overwhelmed by these feelings may struggle to approach God with authenticity, as perfectionism hinders genuine connection in moments of vulnerability.

9. Idolizing Achievements:

Perfectionism often leads to the idolization of achievements and success, making it challenging to find fulfillment in God's love alone. This idolatry can divert attention from God's grace, hindering the experience of profound joy and contentment in the relationship.

10. Resistance to God's Transformative Work:

Perfectionists may resist God's transformative work in their lives, fearing that change implies acknowledging current imperfections. This resistance obstructs the growth and renewal that God's grace seeks to instigate.

Understanding the impact of perfectionism on our relationship with God is a crucial step toward embracing His righteousness and grace. By recognizing these hindrances, individuals can embark on a journey of letting go of perfectionism, opening the door to a deeper, more authentic connection with God. Letting go of perfectionism is not an admission of defeat but an invitation to experience the richness of God's grace in our ongoing development as individuals and as followers of Christ.

Authenticity as a Catalyst for Growth:

Authenticity is the cornerstone of genuine spiritual growth. It involves peeling away the layers of pretense and revealing our true selves before God. When we embrace authenticity, we create a space for God to work within the reality of our lives, addressing our struggles and guiding us toward growth. This raw honesty fosters a deeper connection with God, allowing Him to meet us where we are and lead us to where He desires us to be.

Imperfection as a Canvas for Grace:

Imperfection is not a hindrance to growth; rather, it is the very canvas upon which the brushstrokes of God's grace are painted. By acknowledging our imperfections, we open ourselves to the transformative power of grace that works within the messiness of our lives. God's redemptive work is most evident in our willingness to lay bare our imperfections, allowing Him to bring beauty from brokenness and growth from areas of weakness.

Letting Go of Perfectionism:

Perfectionism is a burdensome weight that stifles growth. When we release the unrealistic expectations of flawlessness, we free ourselves to experience God's transformative power. Letting go of perfectionism is not a lowering of standards but a shifting of focus from our own abilities to God's sufficiency. It is an acknowledgment that our journey of growth is marked by progress, not unattainable perfection.

Fostering Growth Through Vulnerability: Vulnerability is a key element in embracing authenticity and imperfection. It involves a courageous openness to share our struggles, doubts, and shortcomings with God and others. In this vulnerability, we find a fertile ground for growth, as it opens avenues for God's grace and the support of a community to uplift and nurture us. The act of sharing our authentic selves becomes a catalyst for mutual encouragement and collective growth.

The Beauty of Imperfect Progress:

True growth is not about reaching a state of flawlessness but about making progress in becoming more like Christ. Embracing authenticity and imperfection allows us to appreciate the beauty of imperfect progress. Each step, no matter how small, becomes a testament to God's work in our lives. It is a continuous journey of transformation, where God's grace meets us at every turn, shaping us into individuals who reflect His character.

In the realm of embracing authenticity and imperfection, growth is not a destination but a dynamic process. It's about allowing God to work within the authenticity of our lives, trusting in His transformative power, and recognizing that imperfection is not a stumbling block but a stepping stone toward spiritual maturity. As we let go of perfectionism and embrace the beauty of our authentic, imperfect selves, we unlock the door to a flourishing journey of growth in God's grace.

Workbook-Reflection Questions on God's Grace 49

THE BIBLE

In the vast library of literature that spans human history, one book stands unrivaled in its profound impact on relationships—the Bible. As the sacred and divinely inspired text, the Bible serves as the foundational guide for navigating the intricate web of connections that define our existence. Its principles, woven into the fabric of its verses, transcend time and culture, permeating every facet of human relationships. The Bible is not merely a book of eloquent sayings or poignant narratives; it is a transformative force that shapes the very essence of our interactions. Embracing its principles not only deepens our connection with the Divine but also molds us into individuals who mirror the character of God, fostering relationships that echo the grace, love, and compassion embedded in the scriptures. As we explore the transformative influence of the Bible on relationships, we embark on a journey of aligning our lives with timeless truths, a journey that leads us toward a more profound understanding of God and a more harmonious existence with one another.

Knowing God Through Scripture: A Journey of Revelation and Deepening Knowledge
God desires to be known by His creation. The first rays of divine revelation break through the clouds of mystery within the pages of Scripture. It is in this sacred text that God takes on the role of Author, revealing the depths of His character, the richness of His love, and the boundless nature of His grace. Scripture becomes the initial handshake in the divine introduction, inviting us to embark on a journey of profound discovery.

To know God is to trust Him, and trust stems from familiarity. The Bible serves as the stage where God introduces Himself, showcasing the splendor of His attributes and the consistency of His promises. In the verses, we encounter a God who is both sovereign and intimate, just and merciful, righteous and loving. It is through the lens of Scripture that we begin to understand the beautiful mosaic of His character, laying the foundation for a relationship grounded in knowledge and trust.

The journey of knowing God deepens as we dive into the scriptures with an open heart and a seeking spirit. The Bible is not a stagnant pool but a dynamic river, inviting us to wade into its depths. Each passage, story, and verse offers a revelation of God's nature, providing glimpses into His heart. The more we explore this divine library, the richer our understanding becomes. God's self-disclosure through Scripture is an ongoing narrative, and the turning of each page unveils new facets of His being.

In the sacred text, we find a treasure trove of wisdom, guidance, and love. It is not a mere manual of rules but a love letter penned by the Creator to His beloved creation. As we immerse ourselves in the words, we are drawn into a dance of discovery and revelation. The Bible becomes a mirror reflecting the image of God, and in the process of seeking Him, we find ourselves.

In the pursuit of a deeper relationship with God, the scriptures stand as the foundational wellspring. The more we know of Him through His Word, the more intimately we can walk with Him. It is a transformative journey where knowledge births trust, trust deepens into intimacy, and intimacy blossoms into a flourishing relationship with the Divine. The pages of the Bible, alive with the breath of God, beckon us to know Him more and walk hand in hand with the One who authored our story.

Applying Scriptural Principles: Empowering Lives Through Divine Authorization
In the symphony of life, the authorship of Scripture extends beyond the written word, transcending into the realm of divine authorization. The principles embedded within the verses are not just ink on paper; they carry the weight of authority, guiding and shaping lives. As we apply the wisdom imparted by the Author of the Scriptures, we step into a realm of divine authorization—a spiritual empowerment that enables us to function in alignment with biblical principles.

The application of scriptural principles is not a mere adherence to rules but a dynamic interaction between the written word and the human spirit. When we engage with the truths woven into the fabric of Scripture, something profound happens within our souls. The principles become more than guidelines; they transform into keys unlocking the dormant potential within us. Through divine authorization, we receive not only the authority to live according to God's Word but also the empowerment to do so.

As we apply the principles of Scripture to our lives, a beautiful exchange occurs. The timeless truths of the Bible resonate with the depths of our spirits, resonating with the divine frequency that echoes through creation. Our souls, once marred by the brokenness of the world, find renewal in the transformative power of God's Word. It is a renewal that goes beyond surface-level change;

it permeates the very essence of who we are, shaping us into vessels capable of holding our relational positions with grace and wisdom.

Cultivating a relationship with God through Scripture is the catalyst for this transformative process. The Bible serves as a blueprint, providing the architectural design for building our lives on the solid foundation of divine principles. It offers guidance on how to construct relationships, navigate challenges, and fulfill our purpose. Without this foundational relationship, attempting to live according to scriptural principles is like constructing a building without a blueprint—an endeavor destined for instability and uncertainty.

In essence, the application of scriptural principles, fueled by divine authorization, aligns our lives with the grand design authored by God. It empowers us not only to understand the principles but to embody them in our daily interactions. Through this divine partnership, we become co-authors of a narrative shaped by the wisdom of the Creator, living out a story that reflects the beauty of relationships and the transformative power of God's Word.
The Living Word: Active, Sharp, and Transformative

Within the intricate framework of divine revelation, the Bible stands out as an exceptional instrument, a dynamic and sharp tool of unmatched efficacy. Hebrews 4:12 beautifully articulates this concept, likening the Word of God to a living and active, sharper than any two-edged sword, whose sharpness and effectiveness far exceed any humanly devised implement.
Imagine instructing a child to clean a bathtub and specifying the cleaning agent. Instead of suggesting a regular bar soap, you would recommend a powerful cleanser like Comet, laden with active ingredients capable of tackling stubborn stains. Similarly, the Word of God stands out among the words of humanity, being active, alive, and endowed with a potency that transcends conventional communication.

The notion of the Word being 'active' implies a dynamic force, not merely static text on a page. It possesses the vitality to engage, transform, and penetrate the depths of our being. Unlike mundane words that may fall flat, God's Word resonates with a vibrancy that stirs the dormant aspects of our souls. Its active nature is not constrained by the limitations of language but is propelled by the Spirit of God, creating a connection between its purity and our impurities, making us clean and renewed. Moreover, the sharpness of God's Word is unparalleled. In the analogy of cleaning, it is as if God's Word is not just a cleanser but a precision instrument, capable of discerning and addressing the most intricate aspects of our lives. This sharpness serves a dual purpose – it separates and reveals. Like a surgeon's scalpel, it delicately separates what needs to be distinguished, creating a distinction between right and wrong, truth and falsehood. The Word, with its acute precision, exposes the hidden recesses of our hearts, laying bare the motives and intentions within.

The Word of God is not a passive collection of ancient wisdom but an active, living force that speaks directly into our existence. It is sharper than any humanly devised instrument, piercing through the layers of pretense and revealing the truth. As we engage with this living Word, we find ourselves transformed, cleansed, and sharpened by the divine revelation that transcends the limitations of mere human communication.

Renewing Minds through the Living Word
The transformative power of the Word of God extends beyond the realm of information to the profound renewal of our minds. The Bible emphasizes the renewal of the mind as a vital component of spiritual growth and flourishing relationships. In Romans 12:2, believers are urged not to conform to the pattern of this world but to be transformed by the renewing of their minds. This renewal is not a mere intellectual exercise but a holistic transformation that influences our perspectives, attitudes, and behaviors.
The renewal process begins with a deep dive into the Scriptures, where the living Word interacts with the recesses of our minds. As we immerse ourselves in the truth revealed in God's Word, it becomes a catalyst for a mental makeover. The Word acts as a mirror, reflecting our thoughts, intentions, and beliefs, and inviting us into a journey of self-discovery and alignment with divine perspectives.

One profound aspect of the Word's renewing work is its ability to challenge and reshape our thought patterns. Often, our minds are entangled with worldly philosophies, cultural norms, and personal biases that hinder our spiritual and relational growth. The Word serves as a corrective lens, offering a divine perspective that transcends human wisdom.

It challenges distorted thinking, dispels falsehoods, and guides our minds into alignment with God's truth.
The renewal of the mind through the Word also plays a crucial role in our relationship with God. As our minds are transformed, our understanding of God's character deepens, and our intimacy with Him grows. The Word reveals the heart of God, His desires for us, and the principles that underpin a flourishing relationship with Him. The more we grasp the truths of Scripture, the more our minds align with God's thoughts, fostering a profound connection with the Divine.

Furthermore, the impact of a renewed mind extends to our interactions with others. The principles of love, forgiveness, and humility found in the Word become the foundation for healthy relationships. The renewed mind learns to see others through the lens of grace, extending the same compassion and understanding that God has shown us. This transformation has a ripple effect, creating an atmosphere of grace and love in our interactions with family, friends, and even strangers.

In essence, the living Word acts as a renewing agent, breaking the chains of old thought patterns and ushering in a fresh perspective. As our minds are renewed, our relationship with God flourishes, and we become conduits of His transformative grace in the relationships that shape our lives.

The Infallible Word: Reliability of the Bible
As followers of Christ embark on the journey of understanding and applying God's Word, a critical foundation rests on the unwavering confidence that the Bible is not merely a collection of human writings but the divinely inspired and infallible Word of God. Let us take a thoughtful pause to explore key facts that substantiate the claim of the Bible as God's authoritative revelation. These foundational aspects will fortify your confidence, enabling you to engage with the Scriptures with assurance and trust in their reliability.

Firstly, the Bible declares its divine origin, asserting that it is "God-breathed" (2 Timothy 3:16). This profound claim sets the stage for understanding that the Scriptures are not products of human wisdom alone but are imbued with the breath of God, ensuring their accuracy, truthfulness, and reliability in communicating His message.

Beyond the claim of inspiration, the unity and coherence of the Bible across diverse genres and authors testify to its divine authorship. Though written by multiple human hands over centuries, the Bible presents a seamless narrative, revealing a consistent and harmonious message of God's redemptive plan. This remarkable unity points to the divine oversight that guided the writing of the Scriptures.

Furthermore, the Bible contains numerous prophecies that have been fulfilled with striking precision. Prophecies concerning the life, death, and resurrection of Jesus Christ, as well as other historical events, validate the supernatural foresight embedded in the Scriptures. Witnessing the fulfillment of these prophecies strengthens the believer's confidence in the reliability of God's Word. Among these prophetic declarations, one notable example is the prophecy concerning the birthplace of the Messiah. In the Old Testament book of Micah (Micah 5:2), a prophecy foretells that the Messiah would be born in Bethlehem, a prediction precisely fulfilled in the birth of Jesus Christ. Another powerful prophecy is found in Isaiah 53, describing the suffering and sacrificial death of the Messiah with astonishing detail—a prophecy that aligns remarkably with the crucifixion of Jesus. Additionally, the prediction of the destruction of Jerusalem and the scattering of the Jewish people, as foretold in Deuteronomy 28 and Leviticus 26, came to pass with the historical events surrounding the Babylonian and Roman conquests. These prophetic fulfillments not only affirm the reliability of the Bible but also point to the supernatural guidance behind its pages, strengthening our confidence in its divine origin.

Archaeological discoveries continually affirm the historical accuracy of the Bible. As spades unearth ancient artifacts and validate the Bible's accounts of people, places, and events, believers find external confirmation that aligns with the meticulous historical record presented in the Scriptures.
Among the Gospel accounts in the New Testament, the Book of Luke stands not only as a testament to the life and teachings of Jesus Christ but also as a recognized historical document of immense significance. Scholars and historians, both within and outside the Christian faith, regard the Gospel of Luke as a valuable historical record due to

its meticulous attention to detail, careful investigation, and dedication to presenting an orderly account of the events surrounding Jesus' life. Luke, known as a physician and companion of the apostle Paul, approached his Gospel with a commitment to accuracy and thorough research. His efforts in compiling a reliable historical narrative contribute to the enduring recognition of the Book of Luke as a pivotal and trustworthy document, providing invaluable insights into the life of Jesus and the cultural context of the time. This acknowledgment adds another layer of credibility to the overall reliability of the Bible as a historical and spiritual guide.

Additionally, the transformative power of the Bible in the lives of those who engage with its teachings stands as experiential evidence of its divine authenticity. Countless testimonies attest to the profound impact of the Word, influencing personal growth, guiding decisions, and providing comfort in times of trial.
In exploring these key facts, we delve into the foundations that instill confidence in the Bible as God's Word. As we navigate the Scriptures with this assurance, we embark on a journey of deeper understanding, transformative growth, and the cultivation of a thriving relationship with the Creator.

The Word of God is not merely a text for us to read; it is a living, breathing entity that desires to read us, to scan the depths of our hearts, minds, motives, and intentions. Hebrews 4:12 beautifully articulates this truth, stating that the Word of God is living and active, sharper than any two-edged sword, piercing to the division of soul and of spirit, discerning the thoughts and intentions of the heart. It's not a passive document but a dynamic force that seeks to engage with the very essence of who we are.

Unfortunately, many believers treat the Bible as a one-way street, merely reading its pages without allowing it to read them. The Bible functions like a scanner, revealing our vulnerabilities, strengths, weaknesses, and providing transformative principles that, when embraced, become part of our character. The challenge lies in opening up enough time and space for the Word to actively work within us. The Bible desires to write in us a living epistle —a tangible expression of its teachings. When people observe our lives, they should see the principles of Scripture at work. Our actions, body language, posture, character, integrity, and words become a living testimony of God's Word. The ultimate goal is to be God-breathed, embodying the principles of the Bible in such a way that, when others encounter us, they are drawn to read the Word for themselves.

Consider the idea of being a living epistle in your own life. As a role model, people should read your life and see if you've embraced the teachings of the Bible on topics like manhood, fatherhood, marriage, and more. When people read you, what are they reading? The Bible invites us into a transformative cycle where we read it, allow it to read us, and then live out its principles, creating a powerful ripple effect of positive change in the lives of those around us.

In conclusion, the Bible is not merely a collection of words on pages; it is a dynamic force that, when embraced, creates a profound ripple effect in our lives and relationships. It serves as the bedrock upon which we can build the structure of our existence. Beyond being God's love letter to humanity, the Bible provides timeless principles that, when followed, ensure that our relationships sail smoothly in the waters of God's wisdom. As we allow the Word to read us, shape us, and become a living epistle within us, the transformative power extends beyond our personal connection with God and permeates every interaction, fostering a harmonious symphony of love, grace, and righteousness in all our relationships. The Bible, then, is not just a book; it is the blueprint for a thriving life anchored in God's eternal truths.

- **Reflection Questions on Personal Bible Reading Habits 51**
- **Reflection Questions on What the Bible Has Read About You 52**
- **30-Day Bible Reading and Reflection Plan 53**

PRAYER

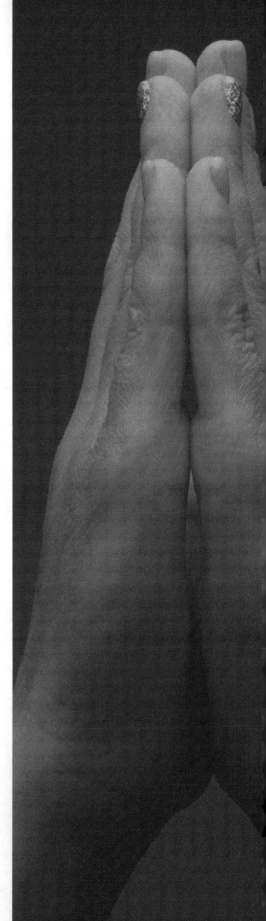

In the fabric of the human journey, a dimension beyond the tangible unfolds, where the soul yearns for a connection with a force greater than its own existence. This sacred space, often elusive yet profoundly transformative, is found in the art of open communication with God.

Imagine a realm where words echo in eternity, where the whispers of the heart are heard by the Divine. This is the sacred ground we tread upon as we seek to understand the profound importance of open communication with God. Beyond the rituals and routines, this is an invitation to enter into a genuine conversation with the One who intricately knows the depths of our being. It is an acknowledgment that within the weave of our existence, a strand of divine conversation patiently awaits integration into the fabric of our lives.

At the heart of this exploration lies prayer—an ageless practice that transcends religious boundaries and cultural differences. Prayer is more than a mere recitation of words; it is the cornerstone upon which a meaningful relationship with the Divine is built. It is the channel through which the human spirit connects with the transcendent, seeking solace, guidance, and an intimate understanding of the purpose that animates our existence. As we navigate the contours of this sacred journey, let us unveil the transformative power of prayer and recognize it not only as a spiritual discipline but as the vibrant heartbeat of a thriving relationship with God.

Prayer as a Cornerstone
Defining Prayer and Its Various Forms
At its essence, prayer is a profound and intimate conversation with the Divine—a dialogue that transcends the limitations of earthly communication. It is a spiritual language spoken from the depths of the heart, a language understood by the very soul it seeks to commune with. Prayer takes on various forms, extending beyond the traditional spoken words. It encompasses silent contemplation, the language of gratitude, the poetry of worship, and the unspoken longings of the heart. Grasping these varied manifestations unveils a portal to a vibrant network of connections, where the soul communicates through countless expressions, and the Divine attentively comprehends with limitless understanding.

The Transformative Power of Prayer in Deepening the Relationship with God
The transformative power of prayer is akin to the gentle yet persistent shaping of a sculptor's hands on clay. As we engage in this sacred dialogue, our relationship with God undergoes a metamorphosis, moving from transactional encounters to a profound

communion. Prayer becomes a transformative force, not only altering the external circumstances of our lives but reshaping the very core of our being. It has the capacity to soften hardened hearts, provide clarity in moments of confusion, and instill a sense of peace that transcends understanding. The depth of our connection with God is measured not in the eloquence of our words but in the authenticity of our hearts laid bare in prayer. It is in this vulnerability that the transformative dance between the finite and the infinite takes place, deepening the roots of a relationship that goes beyond the surface of mere requests and petitions.

The Multifaceted Nature of Prayer

Prayer, as a dynamic and multifaceted form of communication with the Divine, offers a spectrum of expressions that cater to the diverse needs, emotions, and spiritual depths of individuals. There is no one-size-fits-all approach, and the richness of prayer lies in its diversity. Each type of prayer serves a unique purpose, providing a powerful means of connecting with God and navigating the complexities of life.

Thanksgiving and Gratitude:

Thanksgiving is a form of prayer that celebrates the goodness and faithfulness of God. It involves expressing gratitude for blessings, both big and small, and recognizing the abundant provision in our lives. Regularly engaging in prayers of thanksgiving cultivates a spirit of appreciation and contentment, fostering a positive outlook on life.

Supplication:

Supplication is a heartfelt and earnest form of prayer where individuals bring their specific needs, desires, and challenges before God. It reflects a posture of humility, acknowledging human dependence on the Divine. Supplication invites individuals to cast their anxieties on God, trusting in His wisdom and provision.

Intercession:

Intercessory prayer extends beyond personal concerns to encompass the needs of others. It involves standing in the gap on behalf of friends, family, communities, or even nations. Intercession reflects a selfless and compassionate approach to prayer, embodying the principle of loving our neighbors as ourselves.

Silent Contemplative Prayer - Unspoken Longings of the Heart:

Silent contemplative prayer transcends words and invites individuals to dwell in the quiet presence of God. It's a form of prayer that acknowledges the limitations of language and embraces the mystery of the divine encounter. In the stillness, unspoken longings find expression, creating a sacred space for communion with the Divine.

Poetry of Worship:

Worship through poetry is a creative and expressive form of prayer that combines words, rhythm, and emotion to glorify God. Whether written or spoken, poetic prayers elevate the act of worship, offering a unique avenue for individuals to pour out their hearts in adoration and awe.

Warfare Prayers:

Warfare prayers acknowledge the spiritual battles that individuals may face. These prayers are assertive and intentional, seeking God's protection, deliverance, and victory over spiritual challenges. Warfare prayers recognize the authority believers have in Christ to confront and overcome spiritual opposition. In essence, the power and importance of these different types of prayers lie in their ability to cater to the diverse dimensions of the human experience. Whether in moments of celebration, supplication, intercession, silence, creative expression, or spiritual warfare, prayer becomes a versatile and transformative tool that deepens the connection between individuals and the Divine.

Prayer as Dialogue: Understanding God's Response

Prayer is not a one-way communication but a dynamic dialogue with the Divine. It involves not only pouring out our hearts but also listening attentively for God's response. Here are some ways in which God responds to our prayers:

1. Assurance through Scripture:
As we delve into the pages of the Bible, we often find verses that directly address our concerns or provide guidance. God uses His Word to offer comfort, correction, and affirmation.

2. Inner Peace and Stillness:
In moments of silent contemplation after prayer, God may bring a sense of peace that surpasses understanding. The stillness of the heart becomes a subtle yet profound response to our petitions.

3. Wisdom and Discernment:
Through prayer, God may grant us wisdom and discernment, helping us see situations from His perspective. The clarity that follows can be a direct response to seeking His guidance.

4. Promptings and Impressions:
God communicates through gentle nudges, prompting us to take specific actions or make decisions aligned with His will. Paying attention to these impressions is vital in understanding His response.

5. Circumstantial Shifts:
Sometimes, God responds by orchestrating changes in our circumstances. Doors may open, obstacles may be removed, or unexpected opportunities may arise, aligning with our prayers.

6. Insights and Revelations:
During prayer, God may grant insights or revelations that offer deeper understanding or fresh perspectives on situations we've been grappling with. These "aha" moments can be powerful responses.

7. Confirmations from Others:
God often uses people around us to affirm His response. Insights or advice from friends, mentors, or even strangers may align with what we've been praying about, serving as a confirmation.

Understanding that prayer is a two-way conversation transforms our approach, fostering an environment where we actively listen for God's responses, recognizing that He interacts with us in diverse and meaningful ways.

Overcoming Challenges in Prayer: Nurturing Consistency and Persistence
Prayer is a powerful weapon against the spiritual battles that surround us, but it's precisely this potency that the adversary seeks to undermine. Recognizing the importance of consistent and persistent prayer, we must address common challenges that hinder a vibrant prayer life:

1. Distractions and Busyness:
In our fast-paced lives, distractions and busyness can easily drown out the still, small voice of God. The enemy subtly lures us into a perpetual cycle of activity, making it crucial to intentionally set aside time for focused prayer.

2. Doubt and Disbelief:
Skepticism about the effectiveness of prayer can weaken our resolve. The enemy seeks to plant seeds of doubt, convincing us that our prayers are futile. Overcoming this challenge involves nurturing a confident faith in the power of prayer.

3. Lack of Discipline:
Maintaining a consistent prayer life requires discipline. The enemy exploits our struggle with self-discipline, tempting us to procrastinate or neglect regular prayer. Building a routine helps establish a foundation for consistent communication with God.

4. Unanswered Prayers:
When prayers seem unanswered, discouragement may set in. The enemy seizes this opportunity to sow seeds of disappointment and disillusionment. Understanding that God's timing and ways are beyond our comprehension helps navigate through this challenge.

5. Spiritual Warfare:
Engaging in prayer is an act of spiritual warfare, and the enemy will try to thwart our efforts. Persistent attacks, distractions, and discouragement can intensify during times of prayer. Standing firm in faith and using spiritual weapons counteracts these assaults.

6. Lack of Passion:
Passion in prayer often wanes due to various reasons, including routine, weariness, or complacency. The enemy seeks to extinguish the fire of enthusiasm for prayer. Cultivating a fervent spirit involves stirring up passion through worship, gratitude, and intentionally seeking God's presence.

7. Unconfessed Sin:
The enemy capitalizes on unconfessed sin to erect barriers between us and God. Addressing sin through repentance opens the channel for effective communication with the Divine.

8. Unrealistic Expectations:
Expecting instant, dramatic results from prayer can lead to disappointment. The enemy fuels unrealistic expectations, fostering impatience. Recognizing that God works in His timing helps overcome this challenge.

9. Lack of Understanding of God's Nature:
A distorted view of God's character can hinder effective communication. The enemy exploits misconceptions about God, fostering fear or distance. Studying and understanding God's nature deepens our connection with Him.

The Prey and the Prayer Analogy:
Imagine a dense forest where predators roam freely. Without the protection of a secure dwelling, individuals in the open become vulnerable prey. Similarly, when we neglect the fortress of prayer, we expose ourselves, and everything around us becomes susceptible to the prowling spiritual adversaries. Prayer serves as our refuge, a stronghold that safeguards not only our personal well-being but also the spheres of influence we inhabit. In the absence of prayer, we risk becoming prey to the attacks of the enemy, and the strength of our spiritual defenses weakens, leaving us and those around us vulnerable to the onslaughts of the adversary. It underscores the urgent need for consistent, intentional prayer to fortify our spiritual positions and secure the safety of our spiritual territories.

The Whisper of God: Nurturing Closeness in Prayer
In the symphony of life's clamor, God often chooses to whisper. His gentle whispers, like the soft rustle of leaves in a quiet breeze, beckon us to draw near, fostering an intimate closeness that transcends the noise of the world. The art of God's whispering holds profound significance for those attuned to His voice:
1. Sustaining Closeness:
A whisper necessitates proximity. In the same way, God's whispers are designed to sustain closeness. He speaks intimately to those who lean in, creating a sacred space where the soul can commune with the Divine. No one can hear a whisper from across a noisy room, just as no one can discern God's voice in the tumult of a distant, noisy life. Maintaining proximity to God through prayer positions us to catch His whispers and experience the profound connection that proximity brings.

2. The Desire to Listen:
God's whispers are not reserved for the indifferent or the distracted. They are reserved for those who possess a deep desire to listen. In the stillness of a receptive heart, God's whispers find a home. Prayer becomes the conduit through which our desire to listen transforms into a receptive posture, attuned to the nuances of His voice.

3. Staying Close vs. Drifting Away:
Just as one must stay close to hear a whisper, our spiritual closeness to God is vital. Drifting away, akin to moving to a distant corner of a room, diminishes the clarity of God's whispers. A consistent prayer life acts as the tether that keeps us close. The rhythm of prayer, like a steady heartbeat, maintains our spiritual proximity and enhances our ability to hear the divine whispers that guide, comfort, and counsel.

In the art of God's whispering, prayer becomes the sanctuary where proximity, desire, and attentiveness converge. As we lean in, the divine whispers become a source of sustenance, guiding our steps and enveloping us in the comforting presence of the Almighty. Prayer, then, is not just a monologue but a dialogue—a sacred exchange where God's whispers meet the listening heart in the quiet intimacy of sustained closeness.

The beauty of prayer lies in its innate flexibility, effortlessly blending into the individual threads that make up the fabric of our unique personalities. God, the Master Artisan, desires to engage with you in a conversation that mirrors the authentic essence of who you are. Here's how you can embark on the journey of developing a personal and authentic prayer life:

A. Encouraging Authenticity:
God wants you to pray like you. There's no need for pretense or elaborate words; authenticity is the currency of prayer. Whether you express yourself in simplicity or pour out your heart in intricacy, God cherishes the genuine outpourings of your soul. Encouraging individuals to embrace their authentic voice in prayer is an invitation to be real, vulnerable, and transparent before the Creator.

B. Developing the Prayer Muscle:
Much like a muscle that requires intentional exercise, prayer must be developed. It's an evolving discipline that unfolds and deepens over time. Start by exploring various forms of prayer—whether it's conversational, meditative, or written expressions. Just as every athlete has a unique training regimen, your prayer style can be tailored to resonate with your temperament. The key is consistency and a willingness to explore different facets of the prayer journey.

C. Establishing a Routine:
Routines provide a framework for consistency and growth. Establishing a regular time and space for prayer creates a rhythm in your spiritual life. Whether it's in the quiet hours of the morning or amidst the serenity of evening, find a time that aligns with your natural inclinations. This routine becomes the sacred ground where you meet with God, fostering a consistent and flourishing prayer life.

D. Finding Your Prayer Style:
Just as individuals resonate with different genres of music, people connect with varied prayer styles. Some may find solace in contemplative silence, while others express themselves through spoken words. Discovering your prayer style involves experimenting with different approaches, allowing you to identify what resonates most deeply with your spirit. It could be journaling, intercession, thanksgiving, or a combination that forms a unique symphony of communication between you and your Creator.

E. The Art of Exploration:
Consider prayer as an expedition—an exploration of the divine landscape. Delve into the richness of prayer practices, from ancient traditions to contemporary expressions. Each exploration contributes to the development of your prayer muscle, unraveling new facets of intimacy with God. Be open to the surprises, the revelations, and the transformative encounters that unfold as you navigate the expansive terrain of prayer. Cultivating a personal and authentic prayer life is an ongoing journey—a dynamic exchange that deepens as you engage with God in the raw authenticity of your being. Remember, God delights in the uniqueness of your voice, and the unfolding chapters of your prayer life weave a beautiful narrative of connection, growth, and intimate communion.

Prayer and Relationship Dynamics: Unveiling the Transformative Power in Connections

Exploring how prayer impacts other relationships in one's life:

Prayer, a divine dialogue between the soul and its Creator, transcends the individual sphere and permeates the intricate web of human relationships. As you engage in prayer, its transformative ripples extend far beyond your personal space, influencing the dynamics of every relationship you hold dear. Here's a profound exploration of how prayer intricately weaves into the fabric of your connections:

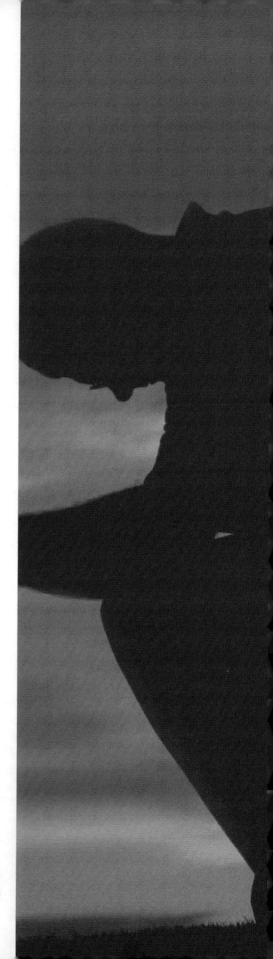

Fostering Empathy and Compassion:
Prayer has the remarkable ability to cultivate empathy and compassion within you. As you commune with the Divine, your heart becomes attuned to the needs, struggles, and joys of others. This newfound sensitivity becomes the driving force behind your interactions, allowing you to engage with genuine care and understanding in your relationships.

Creating a Culture of Forgiveness:
In the sacred space of prayer, forgiveness becomes a recurring theme. As you lay bare your own shortcomings before God, the grace you receive fosters a spirit of forgiveness in your heart. This cultivated forgiveness becomes a powerful force in your relationships, breaking down walls of resentment and paving the way for reconciliation.

Building Trust and Intimacy:
Trust is the cornerstone of any healthy relationship. Through prayer, you build trust not only in God but also in your interactions with others. As you seek guidance, share concerns, and express gratitude in prayer, a foundation of trust is laid, fostering a deeper sense of intimacy and connection in your relationships.

Aligning Values and Priorities:
Prayer serves as a compass, aligning your values and priorities with divine principles. This alignment has a ripple effect on your relationships, ensuring that your interactions are rooted in shared values, mutual respect, and a common purpose. It becomes a unifying force that transcends differences and strengthens the bonds you share with others.

- **Workbook-Reflection Questions on Assessing Prayer Life and Identifying Obstacles Page 56**
- **Workbook - Daily Gratitude Journal Page 58**
- **Workbook - Prayer List Worksheet Page 61**

97

Prayer Strategy: The 7 R's Approach

Reflect: Begin your prayer time by reflecting on the goodness of God. Take a moment to ponder His faithfulness, mercy, and love. Recall instances where He has shown kindness and provision in your life. Let your heart be filled with gratitude as you recognize the blessings that come from God's goodness.
- *Example: "Lord, I reflect on Your goodness. You've been my provider, my comforter, and my guide. I thank You for your faithfulness and unwavering love."

Rejoice: Move from reflection to rejoicing. Express your gratitude to God for all the good things He has done. Let your prayers be filled with joy as you acknowledge His blessings. Rejoicing in His goodness sets the tone for a positive and thankful conversation with God.
- *Example: "I rejoice in Your faithfulness, Lord. Thank You for the countless blessings, both big and small. My heart is filled with joy because of Your goodness."

Repent: After expressing gratitude, take a moment for repentance. Reflect on your actions, habits, and motives. Humbly confess any wrongdoings and ask for God's forgiveness. Repentance opens the door for a renewed and cleansed spirit.
- *Example: "Lord, I repent of any actions or thoughts that have not aligned with Your will. Forgive me, cleanse my heart, and guide me in the paths of righteousness."

Resourcefulness: Shift your focus to others. Pray for friends, family, and even those you may not know personally. Lift up their needs, challenges, and joys to God. Be resourceful in intercession, asking for God's provision, guidance, and blessings upon their lives.
- *Example: "I pray for those around me, Lord. May Your resources be poured out upon them. Guide, heal, and bless them according to Your perfect plan."

Request: Now, present your personal needs and desires before God. Having reflected, rejoiced, repented, and interceded, your requests are aligned with God's will. Ask for what you need with confidence, knowing that God hears the prayers of a heart aligned with His purposes.
- *Example: "Father, I bring my needs before You. I ask for [specific requests] in accordance with Your will. Grant me the wisdom to discern Your plans for my life."

Retaliation: Engage in spiritual warfare by retaliating against the enemy. Declare your authority in Christ, reclaiming what rightfully belongs to you. Pray against any negative influences or attacks, standing firm in the victory of Jesus.
- *Example: "In the name of Jesus, I retaliate against the enemy. I reclaim my peace, joy, and all that the enemy has sought to steal. I stand firm in Your victory, Lord."

Rejoice and Reflect Throughout the Day: As you go about your day, maintain an attitude of prayer. Continuously rejoice in the Lord's goodness and reflect on His presence in every situation. Keep a grateful heart, maintaining a constant connection with God.
- *Example: "Lord, I carry Your joy and reflect on Your goodness throughout my day. Thank You for Your constant presence and guidance."

This 7 R's approach creates a holistic and intentional prayer strategy that covers reflection, gratitude, repentance, intercession, personal requests, spiritual warfare, and maintaining a continuous connection with God throughout the day.

CREATING

At the heart of our identity as humans lies a profound truth—we are inherently creative beings. From the very opening lines of the Bible, God is introduced as the ultimate Creator, shaping the earth with divine artistry. This creative essence is woven into the fabric of our existence, reflecting our Maker. Engaging in creativity becomes a sacred act of connection with God, a pathway to strengthen our relationship with the Divine.

The invitation to co-create with God echoes through the narrative of Scripture. It extends beyond the mere act of creation to encompass every aspect of our lives. Whether we are cultivating relationships, solving problems, or pursuing our passions, we are called to collaborate with the Creator. Recognizing that God is the source of creativity encourages us to tap into this divine wellspring, infusing our endeavors with purpose and inspiration.

Co-creative collaboration with God transcends the conventional understanding of creativity. It's not confined to artistic pursuits but encompasses the whole spectrum of human existence. In our daily interactions, decision-making processes, and problem-solving moments, we have the opportunity to engage in co-creative endeavors with the One who breathed life into existence. This collaboration in creativity is a transformative journey. It aligns our hearts with the rhythms of divine inspiration and elevates our mundane activities into sacred acts. As we embrace our role as co-creators, we deepen our relationship with God, recognizing that our creativity mirrors the image of the Creator. Whether we express our creativity through art, innovation, or relational dynamics, each endeavor becomes a brushstroke on the canvas of our spiritual connection, illustrating the beauty of collaboration with the Divine.

Creativity is not merely a skill; it's a mindset, a way of perceiving the world as a canvas of endless possibilities waiting to be transformed. At its core, creativity is an openness to the act of creation itself—a receptivity to the divine spark that can turn ordinary moments into extraordinary masterpieces. When our minds are tuned to the frequency of creativity, we become co-creators with God, actively participating in the ongoing work of the Divine Artist.

This expansive mindset of creativity extends far beyond traditional artistic expressions. It involves creating conversations that foster connection, generating innovative solutions to challenges, and initiating moments of grace and kindness. The beauty of creativity lies in its ability to turn the intangible into tangible, to birth something new out of the raw materials of imagination and inspiration. However, this co-creative potential is not without opposition. The adversary seeks to divert our creative energy away from collaboration with God, steering it toward self-serving pursuits or destructive paths.

The enemy's agenda involves stealing our natural resources—gifts, talents, and energy—meant for divine collaboration. Staying in a creative rhythm with God becomes a spiritual safeguard, preventing the theft of our creative essence for purposes contrary to God's design. Being co-creators with God means constantly cultivating a creative mindset, a mentality that sees opportunities for creation in every moment. It involves consciously creating divine portals through our minds—gateways through which God's continuous creative flow can manifest in our lives. By staying connected to the Source of all creativity, we become vessels through which the Master Creator can continually shape and reshape the world around us.

Understanding God's creative nature is an awe-inspiring journey into the heart of the Divine Artist. From the very opening verses of the Bible, we encounter God as the ultimate Creator, fashioning the cosmos with the brushstrokes of His divine imagination. In Genesis, the narrative unfolds as God speaks, and creation responds to the call of its Creator. This biblical perspective emphasizes not only God's power to create but the intimate relationship between the Creator and His creation.

The book of Genesis paints a vivid picture of God's creative process—speaking light into existence, shaping the earth, and bringing forth life in its diverse forms. The beauty of this portrayal lies in the recognition that creativity is not merely an action but an intrinsic part of God's nature. God is not just a Creator; He is Creativity itself. His creativity is not limited to the act of creation but extends to the ongoing sustenance and renewal of all that exists.

Drawing inspiration from God's creative nature is an invitation to align our creative processes with the Divine. It's about recognizing that our ability to imagine, innovate, and bring forth something new finds its source in the Creator Himself. As we delve into the biblical narrative, we discover not only the "what" of creation but also the "how" and "why" behind God's creative acts. It's an exploration of the depth and intentionality with which God crafts each aspect of existence.

When we draw inspiration from God's creativity, we tap into a wellspring of divine ideas and concepts. It's not merely about replicating what God has done but allowing His creative spirit to infuse our individual and collaborative processes. This inspiration becomes a magnetic force, drawing individuals closer to God as they recognize the boundless possibilities within the Creator's mind. Just as a piece of art reflects the essence of its creator, our creative endeavors can reflect the divine touch when we draw from the well of God's creativity. The more we align our creative processes with God's, the more we find ourselves drawn into the intimate dance of co-creation with the One who spoke the universe into existence.

In the grand war between good and evil, Satan's strategic use of the idea of evolution as a tool to undermine the reality of creation is a profound and subtle tactic. The notion that life and humanity emerged from a random, purposeless process attempts to strip away the intentional design inherent in the biblical narrative of creation. From a Christian perspective, this strategic move by the adversary is not merely an assault on scientific theories but a calculated attempt to erode the very foundations of human identity, purpose, and intrinsic value.

At the core of Satan's ploy is the insidious suggestion that we are nothing more than accidental products of chance – soulless beings devoid of purpose or divine intent. If he can successfully implant the idea that our existence lacks meaning, then the natural progression is for individuals to question their inherent worth. The enemy knows that when we lose sight of our value, we become vulnerable to adopting a perspective that diminishes the sanctity of human life.

The biblical truth that we are fearfully and wonderfully made, crafted in the image of God, stands in direct opposition to the evolutionary narrative. Recognizing our status as intentional creations of a loving Creator grants us a profound sense of value and purpose. Our souls find security in the knowledge that we are not accidents but deliberate masterpieces shaped by the hands of the Almighty.

When we understand our inherent worth, it becomes the cornerstone upon which we build our moral framework and governing values. This awareness prompts us to see others as fellow image-bearers, each possessing a unique, God-given dignity. A society that embraces the truth of creation is more likely to foster an environment where individuals recognize and appreciate the inherent value in one another.

Satan's agenda, therefore, is not merely to propagate a scientific theory but to subtly chip away at the foundational understanding of human identity. By sowing seeds of doubt regarding our creation, he aims to break the cycle of recognizing and valuing each other as image-bearers and creative vessels of God. As believers, it is crucial to remain steadfast in the truth that our worth is not derived from the opinions or theories of men but from the eternal truth that we are fearfully and wonderfully made by the Creator Himself.

Incorporating creativity into our relationship with God is not a distant or abstract concept; it's a vibrant reality that can transform our daily lives. Here are some practical applications and examples of how individuals can actively collaborate with God in their everyday experiences:

A. Cultivating Creative Times with God:
One powerful way to engage in creative collaboration is by setting aside intentional times to connect with God in creativity. This could involve creating a sacred space for prayer and brainstorming, seeking divine inspiration for creative projects, or simply allowing God's creativity to flow through activities like journaling, drawing, or playing an instrument.

B. Developing a Creative Mindset:
Creativity is not confined to artistic pursuits; it permeates every aspect of our lives. Cultivating a creative mindset involves approaching challenges with an open heart, seeking innovative solutions, and embracing the idea that each moment is an opportunity to co-create with God. This mindset shift enables us to see the world through a lens of endless possibilities.

C. Collaborating in Problem-Solving:
God's creativity extends to problem-solving. When faced with challenges or dilemmas, seek divine insight and inspiration. Engage in prayerful reflection and invite God to guide your thoughts, offering fresh perspectives and creative solutions. The collaborative effort in problem-solving can result in outcomes that reflect divine wisdom.

D. Creative Synergy in Relationships:
As individuals tap into their God-given creative abilities, they contribute unique aspects of God's character to the collective synergy. In relationships, this creative synergy can lead to deeper understanding, innovative collaboration, and harmonious coexistence. Recognizing and appreciating the diverse creative expressions within a community fosters unity and enriches the overall experience.

E. Transformative Impact on Others:
Incorporating creativity into our relationship with God has a transformative ripple effect on those around us. Whether through acts of kindness, expressions of love, or sharing creative talents, the impact can be profound. A simple creative gesture can carry the imprint of God's love and spark inspiration in others. When individuals actively collaborate with God in their creative endeavors, they step into a realm where they are co-creators with the Creator.

This transformative journey not only enhances personal growth but also contributes to a larger narrative of divine creativity unfolding in the world. It's an invitation to align our creative energies with God's, tapping into the infinite wellspring of creativity that flows from the Author of all creation.
God has not only designed us but has poured a unique facet of His creativity into each individual. Each person carries a specific blend of talents, skills, and creative abilities that reflect a distinct portion of the divine Creator's genius.

It's as if God has filled our brim with a part of His creativity, shaping us with intentional purpose and unique attributes.

Whether you find joy in artistic expressions like drawing, have a knack for weaving words into compelling stories, possess a mind for business and administration, excel in mathematical intricacies, or showcase creativity in myriad other forms, these abilities are not random occurrences. They are intentional deposits of God's creativity into the very core of who you are.

This personalized infusion of creativity serves a dual purpose. First, it's an invitation to co-create with God. As stewards of the creativity He has poured into us, we have the opportunity to collaborate with the Creator in expressing His beauty, wisdom, and innovation in the world. This collaboration is not only a privilege but a responsibility — a divine partnership in which we contribute to the ongoing narrative of creation.

Second, the uniqueness of our creative endowment dispels the need for comparison or envy. God, in His infinite wisdom, has crafted each person with a specific contribution to make. Your way of creating, your distinct blend of talents, is an essential part of God's grand design. Embracing your creativity is an act of gratitude and stewardship, acknowledging the divine fingerprint on your abilities.

So, whether you're pondering over a canvas, crafting a business strategy, solving mathematical equations, or engaging in any creative endeavor, recognize it as a manifestation of God's creativity flowing through you. Own your creativity, not as a mere talent but as a divine deposit entrusted to you for a purpose. Ask God to guide and infuse His creative power into your unique abilities, transforming your creative expressions into a reflection of His character. In doing so, you become a conduit of God's creativity, allowing His uniqueness to shine through your individuality. The symphony of diverse creative expressions, each person contributing their part, creates a beautiful harmony that echoes the multifaceted nature of the Creator Himself. Embrace what God has poured into you, and let your creativity be a testament to the richness of His creative genius.

In the intricate web of our relationship with God, service naturally springs forth as a tangible expression of the dynamic and transformative connection we share with our Creator. God, who fashioned us with unique abilities and poured His creativity into our beings, has a purposeful intent behind this endowment. Part of that divine plan is the overflow of our creative essence into the lives of others.

As we cultivate a strong relationship with God, acknowledging His role as the ultimate Creator and our co-creator, the desire to serve others becomes woven into the fabric of our existence. This service is not a burdensome obligation but a joyful response to the love and creativity poured into us by God. Recognizing service as a natural extension of our relationship allows us to move beyond mere acts of kindness to a deeper, purposeful engagement with the needs of those around us. Exploring the Connection Between Serving Others and Deepening One's Connection with God:

Service becomes a dynamic link in deepening our connection with God. It transforms the abstract concept of a relationship with the divine into practical expressions of love, compassion, and impact. As we engage in acts of service, we become vessels through which God's creative love flows into the lives of others.

The connection between serving others and deepening our relationship with God is profound. Serving becomes a form of worship, an expression of gratitude for the abundance of creativity and love bestowed upon us. In reaching out to meet the needs of others, we reflect God's character, mirroring the selfless love that defines our Creator.

Moreover, engaging in acts of service opens channels for divine grace to flow. It is through our willingness to serve that we position ourselves to receive more of God's transformative power. The act of pouring out creatively into the world aligns us with the heart of God, who continually pours out His love and goodness.

In this reciprocal relationship, serving others not only becomes a way to impact the world but also a means to draw closer to God. The more we extend ourselves in service, the more intimately we connect with the source of our creativity and love. It's a beautiful dance of giving and receiving, a divine exchange that amplifies our relationship with God and magnifies the impact of our creative expressions on the lives of others.

In essence, service becomes a sacred rhythm in the symphony of our relationship with God. It's a melody of love and creativity that echoes the heartbeat of our Creator, resonating through the world as we pour out what has been creatively poured into us.

Addressing Common Challenges in Service:
In the pursuit of a creative partnership with God through acts of service, individuals may encounter a range of challenges that can hinder the free flow of creativity and love. Recognizing and addressing these obstacles is essential for overcoming barriers and fostering a more vibrant and impactful service-oriented relationship with God.

One common challenge is the fear of inadequacy. Many individuals hesitate to engage in acts of service because they doubt their abilities or feel ill-equipped to make a meaningful impact. This fear can be paralyzing, preventing them from fully embracing the creative potential God has poured into them. Overcoming this challenge involves acknowledging that God's grace is sufficient, and He equips us for the tasks He calls us to. By stepping out in faith, relying on His strength, individuals can navigate this fear and discover the richness of their creative partnership with God.

Another obstacle is the busyness of life. In the hustle and bustle of daily responsibilities, finding time for acts of service can seem challenging. Prioritizing and creating intentional space for service can be transformative. By recognizing that service is not an additional burden but an integral part of our relationship with God, individuals can overcome the challenge of busyness and infuse their lives with purposeful creativity.

Addressing Burnout:
Burnout is a prevalent challenge, particularly when individuals pour themselves into service without adequate self-care. The desire to help others may lead to neglecting personal well-being, resulting in exhaustion and disillusionment. Overcoming burnout involves setting healthy boundaries, recognizing personal limitations, and periodically taking moments of rest and reflection. God invites us into a sustainable rhythm of service, where our creativity flows from a place of spiritual and emotional wholeness.

Encouragement and Perseverance:
In the face of challenges, encouragement plays a crucial role. Sometimes, individuals may feel discouraged when they perceive minimal impact or encounter resistance. Realigning expectations and understanding that even small acts of service can have profound effects over time is essential. God values every effort, and perseverance in the face of challenges is a testament to the strength of one's commitment to the creative partnership with Him.

In overcoming challenges, individuals not only enhance their ability to serve but also deepen their creative partnership with God. These obstacles, when addressed with faith and resilience, become stepping stones toward a more profound and impactful expression of God's love and creativity in the world.
Conclusion:

In closing, the essence of a thriving relationship with God is beautifully encapsulated in the principles of creative collaboration and meaningful service. Recognizing our unique creative potential and expressing it through service becomes a profound way to engage with the Creator. This dynamic interplay forms a vibrant c, showcasing the beauty of divine partnership. As we embrace the invitation to co-create and serve, we discover that our lives become a masterpiece reflecting God's love and impacting the world with grace and compassion. May this journey of collaboration and service be a continual source of joy and purpose in our relationship with the Creator.

Workbook-Reflection Questions: Collaborating Creatively with God Page 64

UNDERSTANDING GRATITUDE

Gratitude, at its core, is a profound acknowledgment and appreciation for the positive aspects of life, recognizing the goodness that surrounds us. It goes beyond mere politeness or saying "thank you"; it involves a deep, heartfelt recognition of the blessings we receive. This transformative power of gratitude extends beyond a simple exchange of pleasantries and has the ability to reshape our perspectives, attitudes, and even our relationships.

From a biblical standpoint, gratitude is intricately woven into the fabric of faith. The Scriptures emphasize the importance of giving thanks in all circumstances, not as a mere ritual but as a reflection of a heart attuned to the goodness of God. The act of gratitude is portrayed as a fundamental aspect of faith, acknowledging God's sovereignty, provision, and grace in every situation.

In essence, gratitude is a spiritual posture that aligns our hearts with the divine. It fosters an atmosphere of humility, recognizing that every good and perfect gift comes from above. As we delve into the depths of defining gratitude, we uncover its transformative power to shape our character, enhance our relationships, and ultimately draw us closer to the divine source of all blessings.

The scripture "This is the day that the Lord has made; let us rejoice and be glad in it" (Psalm 118:24) serves as a powerful reminder of the gift of each new day bestowed upon us by God. It encapsulates the essence of gratitude as a deliberate choice and a response to God's continuous act of creation.

Gratitude is indeed a choice, a disposition of the heart that acknowledges the blessings and opportunities embedded within each day. When we internalize the truth that God has fashioned a new day specifically for us, it shifts our perspective. Every sunrise marks a fresh beginning, a canvas upon which we can paint our experiences, dreams, and aspirations.

The phrase "this is the day" underscores the immediacy and uniqueness of the present moment. It invites us to embrace the unfolding day with open hearts and minds, free from the burdens of past regrets or anxieties about the future. By acknowledging that God has made the day, we recognize His sovereignty and providence over our lives.

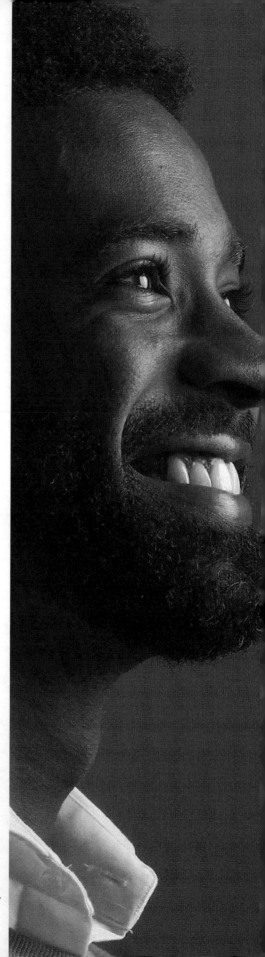

Moreover, the exhortation to "rejoice and be glad in it" emphasizes an active participation in the day's unfolding narrative. It is a call to intentionally seek out moments of joy, wonder, and gratitude amidst the ebb and flow of daily life. Rather than allowing circumstances to dictate our mood, we are invited to cultivate an attitude of gladness rooted in the recognition of God's goodness.

Consider the reality that somebody ran out of days, yet we are granted another opportunity to create, to live, and to experience the manifold blessings of existence. Each day is a precious gift, a testament to God's faithfulness and unfailing love. Gratitude, therefore, becomes our response to this divine generosity. It is a recognition of God's provision, protection, and presence in our lives. As we rehearse the truth of Psalm 118:24, we train our hearts to embrace the blessings hidden within the fabric of each day.

In essence, gratitude is not just a passive acknowledgment of blessings received; it is an active engagement with the present moment. By rejoicing and being glad in the day that the Lord has made, we honor God's creation, embrace His grace, and live fully in the abundance of His love. So, let us not be sad, mad, or bad, but glad in each day that God has graciously given us.

Incorporating gratitude into our everyday routines is a transformative practice that enriches our lives and strengthens our relationship with God. Here are practical strategies to cultivate gratitude on a daily basis:

Morning Gratitude Ritual:
- Begin your day with a gratitude ritual. Take a few moments each morning to reflect on the blessings in your life. Whether through prayer, journaling, or silent contemplation, express thanks for the new day, the breath in your lungs, and the opportunities ahead.

Gratitude Journal:
- Keep a gratitude journal where you document things you are thankful for daily. This intentional act of writing down blessings, both big and small, fosters a heightened awareness of the positive aspects of your life.

Gratitude Moments:
- Throughout the day, pause and intentionally acknowledge moments of gratitude. It could be the warmth of sunlight, the kindness of a colleague, or the taste of a delicious meal. Taking a moment to appreciate these small blessings can shift your focus and mindset.

Express Thankfulness:
- Verbalize your gratitude by expressing thanks to others. Acknowledge acts of kindness, appreciate the efforts of those around you, and share your gratitude openly. This not only blesses others but also reinforces a positive and thankful atmosphere.

Mindful Awareness:
- Practice mindfulness by being fully present in the moment. Engage your senses and appreciate the beauty around you. This awareness cultivates gratitude by helping you recognize the richness of your experiences.

Evening Reflection:
- Before bedtime, reflect on the events of the day and identify moments of gratitude. This reflection can serve as a peaceful conclusion to your day, fostering a sense of contentment and gratitude.

Gratitude Challenge:
- Challenge yourself to find something new to be thankful for each day. This can be a fun and creative way to explore the depth of blessings in your life and keep your gratitude practice dynamic.

Acts of Kindness:
- Engage in acts of kindness as a way of expressing gratitude. Whether through volunteering, helping a friend, or supporting a cause, acts of kindness create a positive cycle of gratitude in your life.

Gratitude Affirmations:
- Integrate gratitude affirmations into your daily routine. Affirm positive statements about your life, relationships, and circumstances. Speaking these affirmations aloud reinforces a mindset of gratitude.

Family or Group Gratitude Time:
- Foster a culture of gratitude in your family or social circles. Set aside time each day or week to share things you are thankful for. This collective practice strengthens the bonds of gratitude within the group.

By incorporating these practical strategies into your daily routines, you create a habit of gratitude that permeates your life. The consistent practice of acknowledging and appreciating the blessings around you will deepen your relationship with God and contribute to a more joyful and contented life.

Gratitude serves as a profound bridge that deepens our connection with God, creating a harmonious and transformative relationship. Here's an exploration of how gratitude enhances our spiritual connection:

Heart of Worship:

- Gratitude is a fundamental aspect of worship. When we express thanks to God for His goodness, provisions, and love, our hearts align with the essence of worship. Gratitude becomes a form of prayer, acknowledging God's role as the ultimate provider and sustainer.

Acknowledging God's Faithfulness:

- Gratitude is a powerful tool for recognizing and appreciating God's faithfulness throughout our lives. Reflecting on past blessings and answered prayers instills a sense of trust in God's continuous provision, fostering a deeper understanding of His unwavering commitment to His children.

Cultivating Trust:

- Gratitude strengthens our trust in God's plans and purposes. As we express thanks for both the blessings and challenges, we acknowledge God's sovereignty. This acknowledgment fosters a sense of trust that God is orchestrating every aspect of our lives for our ultimate good.

Transformative Perspective:

- Gratitude transforms our perspective, allowing us to see beyond immediate circumstances. In times of difficulty, expressing thanks redirects our focus from challenges to the opportunities for growth and God's grace in the midst of trials.

Spiritual Awareness:

- A grateful heart enhances our spiritual awareness. As we intentionally recognize and appreciate the blessings around us, we become more attuned to God's presence and the ways He actively works in our lives. Gratitude opens our eyes to the divine fingerprints in every aspect of our existence.

Fostering Humility:

- Gratitude fosters humility by acknowledging that every good gift comes from God. It humbles us to recognize our dependence on Him and shifts our hearts from entitlement to a posture of humility, where we receive His blessings with gratitude and awe.

Joyful Surrender:

- Gratitude paves the way for joyful surrender to God's will. When we express thanks in all circumstances, we surrender our desires and plans, trusting that God's purposes are higher and more significant. This surrender deepens our relationship by aligning our hearts with His divine will.

Creating a Culture of Appreciation:

- Infusing gratitude into our relationship with God creates a culture of appreciation. This culture extends beyond individual expressions of thanks to a collective acknowledgment of God's goodness within communities of believers, fostering a rich and vibrant spiritual atmosphere.

In essence, gratitude becomes a language of the soul, a continuous conversation with God that strengthens the bond between the Creator and His creation. As we embrace a heart of gratitude, our relationship with God flourishes, and we enter into a deeper communion marked by trust, joy, and an enduring awareness of His presence in every facet of our lives.

Overcoming challenges In cultivating gratitude is essential for maintaining a vibrant and thankful heart. Here's an exploration of common obstacles and practical solutions to nurture gratitude:

A. Addressing Common Obstacles:

Comparison Trap:

- Comparing our lives to others can hinder gratitude, leading to feelings of discontentment and envy. The constant comparison fosters a mindset of scarcity rather than abundance.

Adversity and Hardship:

- Difficult circumstances and adversity can overshadow gratitude, making it challenging to find blessings amidst trials. Pain, loss, and suffering may obscure our ability to see God's goodness.

Busyness and Distractions:

- Busy lifestyles and constant distractions often pull us away from mindfulness and reflection. The hustle and bustle of daily life can drown out moments of gratitude and appreciation.

Entitlement Mentality:

- An entitlement mentality breeds ingratitude, as it fosters expectations of privilege and entitlement rather than appreciation for blessings received. This mindset diminishes the capacity for genuine thankfulness.

Providing Practical Solutions:
Cultivate Mindfulness:
1. Practicing mindfulness enables us to live in the present moment, fully aware of God's blessings surrounding us. Engaging in mindfulness exercises such as deep breathing, meditation, and reflection helps center our hearts on gratitude.
Practice Daily Gratitude:
1. Intentionally setting aside time each day to practice gratitude cultivates a thankful heart. Keeping a gratitude journal, where we write down blessings and moments of thankfulness, serves as a tangible reminder of God's faithfulness.
Count Your Blessings:
1. Instead of focusing on what we lack, intentionally count and celebrate the blessings we already have. Reflecting on the abundance of God's provision shifts our perspective from scarcity to abundance.
Embrace Adversity as Growth Opportunities:
1. Viewing challenges and adversity through the lens of growth and resilience fosters gratitude. Every trial presents an opportunity for spiritual growth and refinement, deepening our trust in God's providence.
Practice Contentment:
1. Cultivating contentment involves accepting and appreciating our present circumstances, trusting that God's plans are perfect. Contentment acknowledges that true joy and fulfillment come from a relationship with God, not external possessions or achievements.
Engage in Acts of Service:
1. Serving others cultivates gratitude by shifting our focus from ourselves to the needs of others. Volunteering, acts of kindness, and generosity open our hearts to the blessings of giving and receiving.
Seek Community Support:
1. Surrounding ourselves with a community of believers who encourage gratitude and accountability fosters a supportive environment. Sharing testimonies of God's faithfulness and journeying together in gratitude strengthens our resolve to overcome challenges.

By addressing common obstacles and implementing practical solutions, we can overcome challenges in cultivating gratitude, nurturing a heart that overflows with thankfulness and appreciation for God's abundant blessings.

In conclusion, gratitude is a transformative force that deepens our relationship with God. By cultivating a grateful heart,

we acknowledge God's goodness in our lives and open ourselves to His blessings. Despite challenges, maintaining gratitude strengthens our faith and resilience. Let us continue to embrace gratitude as a spiritual discipline, fostering a vibrant connection with God built on thankfulness and trust.

- **Workbook-Reflection Questions: Understanding Gratitude Page 66**
- **Workbook-Daily Gratitude Journal Page 58**

THE HOLY SPIRIT

In the journey of relationship navigation, the Holy Spirit serves as our divine guide, offering unparalleled wisdom and insight. His role is foundational, shaping the course of our connections with others. The Holy Spirit is not merely an influence; He is God dwelling within us, providing a constant source of divine counsel.

II. God in Us: The Power of the Holy Spirit
Understanding the Holy Spirit as God in us transforms our perspective. His presence in our lives signifies a dynamic connection with the very essence of God. This recognition brings forth a profound awareness that we carry the divine within us, influencing our thoughts, actions, and interactions with others.

III. Importance of Fellowship with the Holy Spirit
Intentional fellowship with the Holy Spirit is crucial for relationship success. As we engage in this spiritual communion, we tap into the wellspring of God's wisdom and discernment. It's through this fellowship that we gain clarity, direction, and the ability to navigate the complexities of our relationships.

IV. Nurturing a Relationship with the Divine Guide
To nurture a relationship with the Holy Spirit, it's essential to cultivate an environment of receptivity and openness. Regular prayer, meditation, and reflection provide avenues for communion. Acknowledging the Holy Spirit's presence in our daily lives allows us to draw upon His divine guidance in both mundane and critical moments.

V. Guiding Principles for Relationship Navigation
The Holy Spirit's guidance is not a one-size-fits-all solution; it's personalized for our unique journeys. By seeking His counsel, we receive tailor-made insights for our relationships—whether in friendships, family dynamics, or romantic connections. This personalized guidance empowers us to navigate challenges with divine wisdom.

VI. The Transformative Impact on Relationships
Fellowship with the Holy Spirit transforms our relationships from mere human interactions to divine collaborations. His influence brings forth qualities such as love, joy, peace, patience, kindness, goodness, faithfulness, gentleness, and self-control—attributes that enrich and elevate our connections with others.

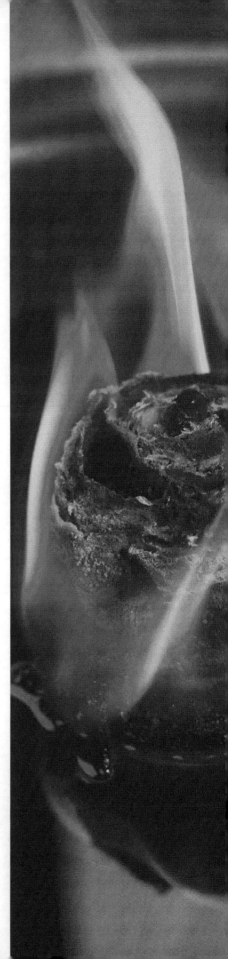

Fellowship with the Holy Spirit is not merely a religious concept but a vibrant reality that shapes the essence of our relationship with God. It transcends mere acknowledgment and delves into the depths of communion with the divine. Like a deep well within us, the fellowship with the Holy Spirit quenches the thirst of our souls, providing a constant connection to the divine network of God's presence. It's more than just having occasional encounters; it's about being continually immersed in the flow of God's spirit.

When we engage in fellowship with the Holy Spirit, we tap into a reservoir of wisdom, guidance, and revelation. The Holy Spirit, as the searcher of the deep things of God, unlocks mysteries and truths that transcend human understanding. It's through this fellowship that we gain insights into the heart and mind of God, enabling us to align our lives with His divine purposes. As we allow the Holy Spirit to search the depths of our being, He brings to light areas that need transformation and renewal, leading us into deeper intimacy with God.

Fellowship with the Holy Spirit is not a passive endeavor but an active engagement of our spirit with the divine presence. It's about being attuned to the still, small voice that speaks to our hearts, guiding us in the paths of righteousness. Through this fellowship, we experience the power of conviction, comfort, and empowerment that comes from the Holy Spirit. It's a relationship marked by sensitivity to His leading and obedience to His promptings.

In the journey of fellowship with the Holy Spirit, we discover the richness of God's love and the depth of His grace. It's in this fellowship that we experience the transformative work of God in our lives, as He molds us into vessels of His glory. As we yield to the Holy Spirit's leading, we are empowered to walk in the fullness of God's purposes, bearing fruit that reflects His character and nature.

Ultimately, fellowship with the Holy Spirit is the heartbeat of our relationship with God. It's the source of our strength, the wellspring of our joy, and the compass for our journey.

As we cultivate this intimate communion with the Holy Spirit, we find ourselves drawn deeper into the embrace of God's love, experiencing the fullness of life in His presence.

The Holy Spirit, often referred to as the Comforter or Counselor, holds a significant role in the life of a believer. This understanding is deeply rooted in the teachings of Jesus and the scriptures.

- Scriptural Foundation:
  - John 14:16-17 (ESV): "And I will ask the Father, and he will give you another Helper, to be with you forever, even the Spirit of truth, whom the world cannot receive, because it neither sees him nor knows him. You know him, for he dwells with you and will be in you."
  - John 16:7 (ESV): "Nevertheless, I tell you the truth: it is to your advantage that I go away, for if I do not go away, the Helper will not come to you. But if I go, I will send him to you."

Expediency of Jesus' Departure:

- Jesus expressed that it was advantageous for Him to leave so that the Holy Spirit could come. His departure paved the way for the permanent indwelling of the Holy Spirit in believers. While Jesus, in His earthly form, was limited by time and space, the Holy Spirit's presence is universally accessible and abiding.

Price Paid for the Holy Spirit:

- The coming of the Holy Spirit was made possible through Jesus' sacrificial death, resurrection, and ascension. The redemptive work on the cross opened the way for the Holy Spirit to dwell within believers, marking a new era of God's relationship with humanity.

Roles of the Holy Spirit:

  - Comforter and Counselor: The Holy Spirit is our Comforter in times of trouble, providing solace, guidance, and wisdom. (John 14:16, John 15:26)
  - Convicter of Sin: The Holy Spirit convicts the world of sin, righteousness, and judgment, leading people to repentance. (John 16:8)
  - Teacher of Truth: He guides believers into all truth, illuminating the understanding of God's Word. (John 16:13)
  - Indweller and Empowerer: The Holy Spirit takes residence in believers, empowering them for righteous living and equipping them with spiritual gifts. (Romans 8:9, Acts 1:8)
  - Witness to Jesus: The Holy Spirit testifies about Jesus, glorifying Him and magnifying His redemptive work. (John 15:26)

Understanding the Holy Spirit's multifaceted roles helps believers appreciate His profound impact on their lives. His presence brings transformation, assurance, and continual communion with the Triune God. The Holy Spirit is not merely a force or influence but a divine Person actively involved in the lives of believers.

Being filled with the Holy Spirit is a transformative and ongoing process for believers. When we accepted the gift of salvation, we received the fullness of the Godhead in us (Colossians 2:9-10). However, allowing the Holy Spirit to fill every area of our lives is a dynamic journey.

Locked rooms in our lives symbolize areas that we, consciously or unconsciously, withhold from the transforming work of the Holy Spirit. These closed-off spaces can represent aspects of our hearts and minds where we struggle to fully surrender to God's guidance and grace. They are spaces marked by reluctance, fear, and a desire to maintain control rather than yielding to the transformative power of the Holy Spirit. Identifying these locked rooms is crucial for recognizing the areas in which we may hinder the Spirit's work in our lives.

- Locked Rooms in Our Lives:
  - Unforgiveness: We may lock the door to past hurts, harboring unforgiveness and bitterness.
  - Fear and Anxiety: Locked doors of fear and anxiety keep us from fully trusting God with our future.
  - Pride and Self-Reliance: Some lock the door of pride, relying on their abilities rather than surrendering to God.
  - Hidden Sin: Doors locked to secret sins hinder the Holy Spirit's transformative work.
  - Broken Relationships: Unresolved conflicts may lock the door to reconciliation and unity.
- Reasons for Keeping Doors Locked:
  - Comfort Zone: Fear of change or stepping out of our comfort zones.
  - Shame and Guilt: A sense of shame or guilt that prevents us from inviting the Holy Spirit into areas of brokenness.
  - Lack of Awareness: Unawareness of the need for the Holy Spirit's intervention in specific aspects of our lives.
  - Control: Desire for control, resisting yielding complete control to the Holy Spirit.

- Importance of Unlocking Every Room:
  - Renewing Perspectives: Allowing the Holy Spirit into every area renews our perspectives, aligning them with God's truth.
  - Healing Wounds: His presence heals wounds, bringing emotional and spiritual restoration.
  - Shaping Character: Filling every room shapes our character, instilling virtues like love, joy, peace, patience, and kindness (Galatians 5:22-23).
  - Empowering Roles: The Holy Spirit empowers us to fulfill our roles in relationships, work, and service.
- The Sanctification Process:
  - Sanctification: It is the ongoing process of becoming more like Christ, allowing the Holy Spirit to transform us.
  - Cooperation with God: We cooperate by surrendering, confessing sins, and yielding to the Holy Spirit's leading.
  - Freedom and Empowerment: Unlocked rooms lead to spiritual freedom and empowerment for impactful living.

Embracing the Holy Spirit's filling is not a one-time event but a continual surrender, allowing Him access to every aspect of our lives. As we unlock each room, we experience the beauty of God's transformative work, enabling us to live out our divine roles with grace and purpose.

Cultivating Daily Fellowship with the Holy Spirit

Fellowship with the Holy Spirit is not a sporadic encounter but a continual, intentional engagement that transforms the mundane into the divine. To practically strengthen our relationship with the Holy Spirit on a daily basis, consider incorporating the following practices:

1. Communion Through Prayer:
Begin your day with a heart-to-heart conversation with the Holy Spirit. Share your thoughts, concerns, and dreams. In prayer, invite the Holy Spirit to guide your steps and align your will with God's purpose. This open line of communication establishes an ongoing dialogue throughout the day.

Scripture Inspiration: Ephesians 6:18 - "Praying at all times in the Spirit, with all prayer and supplication. To that end, keep alert with all perseverance, making supplication for all the saints."

2. Meditative Reflection:

Create moments of quiet reflection to meditate on God's Word. Invite the Holy Spirit to illuminate the scriptures, providing insights and revelations that apply directly to your life. This practice allows the Holy Spirit to guide your understanding and foster spiritual growth.

Scripture Inspiration: Psalm 119:105 - "Your word is a lamp to my feet and a light to my path."

3. Surrender in Worship:

Engage in worship as a form of surrender. Offer praises and thanksgiving, allowing the Holy Spirit to fill the atmosphere. In these moments of adoration, you create space for the Holy Spirit to minister to your heart, bringing comfort, joy, and a deep sense of God's presence.

Scripture Inspiration: John 4:24 - "God is spirit, and those who worship him must worship in spirit and truth."

4. Mindful Awareness:

Practice mindfulness throughout your day. Be attuned to the promptings of the Holy Spirit in various situations. Whether making decisions, interacting with others, or facing challenges, seek the Holy Spirit's guidance. Cultivate an awareness of His presence in the ordinary moments of life.

Scripture Inspiration: Galatians 5:25 - "If we live by the Spirit, let us also keep in step with the Spirit."

5. Gratitude and Acknowledgment:

Express gratitude to the Holy Spirit for His continuous presence and guidance. Acknowledge His work in your life and the lives of those around you. A heart filled with gratitude opens the door for deeper fellowship and an ongoing partnership with the Holy Spirit.

Scripture Inspiration: 1 Thessalonians 5:16-18 - "Rejoice always, pray without ceasing, give thanks in all circumstances; for this is the will of God in Christ Jesus for you."

By integrating these practices into your daily routine, you not only strengthen your relationship with the Holy Spirit but also foster a transformative connection that ripples into your relationships with others. The Holy Spirit becomes a constant companion, shaping your thoughts, actions, and interactions with the love and wisdom of God.

Workbook-Reflection Questions: The Holy Spirit Page 67

_____
_____
_____
_____
_____
_____
_____
_____
_____
_____
_____
_____
_____
_____
_____
_____
_____
_____
_____
_____
_____
_____
_____
_____
_____
_____
_____
_____
_____
_____
_____
_____
_____
_____
_____
_____
_____
_____
_____
_____
_____
_____

111

SIX PILLARS OF RELATABILITY WITH GOD.

Authenticity in Relationship with God: Embracing True Connection

In the realm of spirituality, authenticity becomes a profound catalyst for forging a genuine and intimate relationship with God. The essence of an authentic connection with the Divine lies in presenting our true selves without pretense or masks. Here's a contemplation on how authenticity enhances our relationship with God:

1. True Worship: Authenticity invites genuine worship. God desires our hearts, not a polished façade. When we bring our authentic selves into worship, our prayers, praises, and expressions become raw and real, fostering a deeper connection with the Almighty.

2. Vulnerability and Surrender: God desires our vulnerability. Authenticity allows us to approach Him with our doubts, fears, and insecurities. Surrendering our true selves brings forth a humility that acknowledges our dependence on God, creating space for His transformative power.

3. Honest Dialogue: Authenticity promotes honest dialogue with God. When we are authentic, we feel free to express our true feelings, share our struggles, and ask genuine questions. God welcomes such openness, fostering a relationship built on trust and transparency.

4. True Identity: God knows us intimately, and He desires for us to know ourselves authentically. When we embrace our true identity in Christ, understanding who we are and whose we are, our relationship with God flourishes. Authenticity aligns us with the truth of our created purpose.

5. Freedom from Performance: Authenticity liberates us from the need to perform for God's approval. God's love is unconditional, and when we stop striving to meet external expectations, we can rest in His love, fostering a secure and authentic relationship.

6. Healing and Restoration: God is in the business of healing brokenness. Authenticity opens the door for God to work in the deepest recesses of our hearts, bringing healing and restoration. When we allow God access to our authentic selves, His transformative grace brings about renewal.

Conclusion: In the journey of faith, embracing authenticity in our relationship with God is transformative.

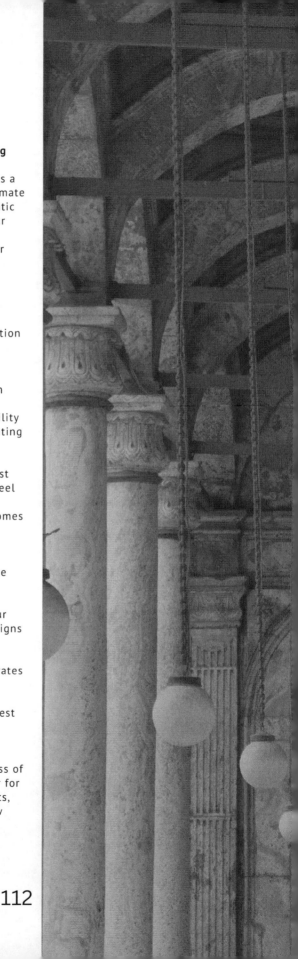

As we open our hearts honestly, share our joys and struggles, and surrender our authentic selves, we step into a realm where God's love, grace, and transformative power abound. Authenticity in our spiritual journey is not just an invitation; it's a pathway to a richer, more profound connection with the Divine.

Reflection Questions: Authenticity in Relationship with God Page 69

Reflecting on True Worship:
- Consider your worship practices and expressions towards God. How does the concept of authenticity influence the way you approach worship?
- In what ways have you experienced a deeper connection with God when your prayers and praises were raw and authentic, free from any external expectations?

1. **Exploring Vulnerability and Surrender:**
   - Reflect on moments in your spiritual journey when you embraced vulnerability before God. How did this openness impact your connection with Him?
   - Surrendering our true selves to God requires humility. In what areas of your life can you cultivate a greater sense of humility, acknowledging dependence on God's transformative power?

2. **Engaging in Honest Dialogue:**
   - Evaluate the nature of your dialogue with God. Do you feel free to express your true feelings, struggles, and questions authentically?
   - How can you enhance your ability to engage in honest and transparent conversations with God, fostering a relationship built on trust and openness?

3. **Discovering True Identity:**
   - Reflect on your understanding of your identity in Christ. In what ways does authenticity contribute to a clearer understanding of who you are and whose you are in God's eyes?
   - Consider any challenges or barriers you face in fully embracing your true identity in Christ. How can authenticity help align your self-perception with the truth of your created purpose?

These reflection questions are designed to encourage introspection and exploration of your authentic connection with God. They aim to guide you in evaluating your worship, vulnerability, dialogue, and understanding of identity in the context of your relationship with the Divine.

113

Respecting God: The Foundation of Wisdom in Relationship

Respecting God serves as the cornerstone of a meaningful and transformative relationship with the Divine. It goes beyond a mere acknowledgment of His existence; it involves a deep reverence that acknowledges His sovereignty and wisdom. Here's an exploration of how respect enhances our connection with God:

1. Definition of Respecting God: Respecting God is more than a passive acknowledgment. It involves an active reverence, awe, and deep honor for His character, attributes, and authority. It's a posture of humility that acknowledges His preeminence in our lives.

2. Reverence as the Beginning of Wisdom: The Scriptures teach that "The fear of the Lord is the beginning of wisdom" (Proverbs 9:10). Reverencing God is not rooted in fearfulness but in a profound respect that recognizes His infinite wisdom. When we approach God with deep respect, we position ourselves to receive His wisdom for navigating life's complexities.

3. Cultivating a Reverent Heart: Respecting God entails cultivating a heart of reverence in our daily lives. This involves acknowledging His holiness, seeking His guidance, and aligning our actions with His principles. A reverent heart continually seeks to honor God in thought, word, and deed.

4. Impact on Relationships: When we respect God, it naturally extends to how we treat others. The respect we show towards God influences our interactions with family, friends, and the broader community. It creates a ripple effect, fostering an atmosphere of honor and dignity in our relationships.

5. Deepening Connection with God: Respect builds a bridge for a deeper connection with God. As we acknowledge His majesty and trust in His plans, our relationship with Him deepens. Respect becomes the currency that fuels intimate conversations, heartfelt prayers, and a growing understanding of His character.

6. Alignment with God's Will: Respecting God involves aligning our will with His. It means surrendering our desires, plans, and ambitions to His higher purpose. This alignment with God's will positions us to receive His blessings and walk in the paths He has ordained for us.

7. Expressions of Respect: Respect for God is expressed through obedience, worship, and a surrendered heart. When we live in harmony with His teachings and honor His presence in our lives, we demonstrate the respect that enhances our connection with Him.

It's not a rigid formality but a dynamic posture that invites us into a relationship marked by wisdom, intimacy, and alignment with God's transformative grace. As we grow in our respect for God, the landscape of our spiritual journey becomes adorned with the colors of reverence, enhancing our connection with the One who deserves our highest regard.

Workbook-Reflection Questions: Respecting God - The Foundation of Wisdom in Relationship Page 70

Defining Respecting God:
- Reflect on your understanding of respecting God. How does it go beyond a passive acknowledgment and manifest as an active reverence, awe, and honor for His character, attributes, and authority?
- In what ways does viewing respect for God as a posture of humility enhance your relationship with Him?

1. **Embracing Reverence for Wisdom:**
   - Consider the wisdom found in the biblical statement, "The fear of the Lord is the beginning of wisdom" (Proverbs 9:10). How does reverence, rather than fearfulness, contribute to the acquisition of wisdom in your life?
   - Share instances where approaching God with deep respect has positioned you to receive wisdom for navigating complex situations in your life.

2. **Cultivating a Reverent Heart:**
   - Evaluate your daily practices in cultivating a heart of reverence. How do you acknowledge God's holiness, seek His guidance, and align your actions with His principles?
   - Identify specific areas in your life where cultivating a reverent heart can have a transformative impact on your thoughts, words, and deeds.

3. **Respect's Impact on Relationships:**
   - Explore the connection between respecting God and how you treat others in your relationships. In what ways does the respect you show towards God influence your interactions with family, friends, and the broader community?

Empathy: A Gateway to Divine Connection and Purposeful Impact

Empathy serves as a profound bridge that connects the human heart with the divine. It goes beyond understanding; it involves feeling the heartbeat of God and, in turn, extending that compassion to others. Here's an exploration of how empathy enhances our relationship with God:

1. The Essence of Empathy: Empathy transcends mere understanding; it's an emotional resonance with the experiences and emotions of others. In the context of our relationship with God, empathy involves attuning our hearts to His, feeling His joys, sorrows, and desires for humanity.

2. Feeling the Heartbeat of God: As we deepen our empathy, we become more attuned to the heartbeat of God. It's about aligning our emotions with His divine compassion for the world. This connection allows us to share in His love for humanity and empowers us to respond with empathy to the needs of those around us.

3. Transferring God's Compassion to Others: Empathy becomes a channel through which we transfer God's compassion to the world. When we feel what moves the heart of God, we are compelled to act in ways that mirror His love. This can manifest in acts of kindness, understanding, and selfless service to those in need.

4. Impact on Fulfilling Purpose: Understanding the heart of God through empathy plays a pivotal role in fulfilling our purpose. God's purposes are intricately tied to His deep love for humanity. By empathizing with His desires, we gain clarity on our unique role in advancing His kingdom and bringing healing to a broken world.

5. Empathy in Prayer and Worship: In our moments of prayer and worship, empathy allows us to connect with God on a deeper emotional level. It transforms routine religious practices into intimate conversations where we share in the joys and burdens of His heart. This empathetic connection enriches our spiritual journey.

6. Cultivating a Compassionate Spirit: Empathy cultivates a compassionate spirit within us. It prompts us to view others through God's eyes, fostering a genuine concern for their well-being. This compassionate spirit becomes a testimony of God's love working through us, drawing others closer to Him.

7. Strengthening Divine Connection: As we cultivate empathy, our connection with God strengthens. It's a reciprocal relationship where we not only seek to understand God but also to feel His heart. This mutual understanding deepens our trust in His plans and enhances the intimacy of our communion with Him.

8. Responding to Human Brokenness: Empathy equips us to respond to the brokenness in the world with God's healing touch. It empowers us to be agents of reconciliation, restoration, and love, mirroring the transformative power of God's empathy for humanity.

Conclusion: Empathy, as a spiritual practice, transforms our relationship with God into a dynamic and emotionally resonant journey. It propels us to align our hearts with His, empowering us to impact the world with divine compassion. Through empathy, our spiritual landscape becomes a canvas painted with the colors of understanding, love, and purposeful impact, bringing us closer to the heart of the Divine.

Workbook-Reflection Questions: Empathy And God 71

Understanding the Essence of Empathy:
- Reflect on your understanding of empathy in the context of a relationship with God. How does it go beyond mere understanding and involve an emotional resonance with God's experiences, joys, sorrows, and desires for humanity?
- Consider moments in your life where you've felt a deep connection with God's emotions. How did these moments shape your perspective on empathy in spiritual life?

1. **Aligning with the Heartbeat of God:**
   - Explore the concept of aligning your emotions with the heartbeat of God. How does deepening your empathy allow you to share in God's love for humanity?
   - Share specific instances where you've felt connected to God's compassion and how it influenced your response to the needs of those around you.

2. **Empathy as a Channel for God's Compassion:**
   - In what ways does empathy serve as a channel through which you transfer God's compassion to the world? Reflect on instances where your empathetic understanding led to acts of kindness, understanding, or selfless service.
   - How can you intentionally cultivate empathy to become a more effective conduit for expressing God's love to others?

Humility: The Gateway to Divine Connection

Here's a reflection on how humility enhances our connection with God:

1. Submission to the All-Knowing and All-Powerful: At the core of humility is the acknowledgment of God's omniscience and omnipotence. We recognize that God knows all things and is all-powerful, leaving us with no choice but to submit to His wisdom and authority. Humility opens the door to a relationship characterized by reverence and surrender.

2. Embracing Our Finite Understanding: Humility leads us to accept the limitations of our finite understanding in the face of God's infinite wisdom. We approach Him with a recognition that His ways are higher, His thoughts are beyond our comprehension, and our humility becomes a vessel for His divine revelation.

3. Trusting God's Sovereignty: A humble heart trusts in the sovereignty of God. It surrenders the illusion of control and embraces the truth that God is the ultimate orchestrator of all things. Humility allows us to release our grip on the steering wheel of life, placing our trust in the hands of the One who holds the universe.

4. Learning from Christ's Example: The embodiment of humility is found in the life of Jesus Christ. He, being God, humbled Himself to the point of taking on human form and submitting to the cross. By adopting Christ's humility, we align ourselves with His sacrificial love and servanthood, mirroring the very nature of God.

5. Acknowledging Dependency on God: Humility recognizes our dependency on God for every breath, every heartbeat, and every step we take. It brings us to a place of utter reliance on Him, acknowledging that apart from God, we can do nothing. In our dependence, we find strength, grace, and sustenance.

6. Receiving Grace with Gratitude: A humble heart is a receptive heart. It acknowledges its need for God's grace and mercy and receives these gifts with profound gratitude. Humility allows us to approach the throne of grace boldly, knowing that we are welcomed not because of our merit but because of God's abundant love.

7. Repentance and Transformation: Humility is the soil in which repentance and transformation flourish. It enables us to recognize our shortcomings, repent of our sins, and allow God's transformative power to work in our lives. Humility positions us to be vessels of God's grace, continually molded into His likeness.

8. Cultivating a Servant's Heart: Humility births a servant's heart. Just as Jesus washed the feet of His disciples, humility compels us to serve others selflessly. Through acts of humility and service, we reflect the character of God and embody the essence of His love for humanity. Conclusion: In the symphony of our relationship with God, humility plays the melody that resonates with divine harmony. It opens our hearts to the awe-inspiring majesty of God, fosters a deep trust in His sovereign plan, and positions us to receive the fullness of His grace. Humility is not a mark of weakness but a manifestation of strength, drawing us nearer to the heart of the Almighty.

Workbook-Reflection Questions: Humility and god Page 72

_____
_____
_____
_____
_____
_____
_____
_____
_____
_____
_____
_____
_____
_____
_____
_____
_____
_____
_____
_____
_____
_____
_____

Effective Communication: Building a Dialogue with the Divine

Communication is the lifeblood of any meaningful relationship, and when it comes to our connection with God, it forms the essence of a dynamic and transformative dialogue. Here's an exploration of how effective communication enhances our relationship with the Divine, along with practical ways to foster this vital connection:

1. Cultivating an Open Heart: Effective communication with God begins with an open heart—a heart willing to share its joys, concerns, hopes, and fears. Cultivate an environment within yourself that welcomes God's presence and invites Him into every aspect of your life.

2. Honest and Transparent Expression: God desires authenticity in our communication. Be honest and transparent in expressing your thoughts, emotions, and struggles. Authenticity fosters a genuine connection, allowing God to meet you exactly where you are.

3. The Power of Prayer: Prayer is the foundational language of our conversation with God. Regular, heartfelt prayers create a continuous line of communication, providing a space to express gratitude, seek guidance, and lay our burdens before the Lord.

4. Meditating on Scripture: God speaks to us through His Word, and effective communication involves not only speaking but also listening. Spend time meditating on Scripture, allowing God's truth to resonate within you. This practice nurtures a two-way conversation, where you absorb divine wisdom and respond with a receptive heart.

5. Active Listening: Communication is a two-way street. Develop the discipline of active listening in your relationship with God. Set aside moments of stillness to listen for His voice—through the Scriptures, in prayer, or through the prompting of the Holy Spirit.

6. Journaling as a Reflection Tool: Keep a spiritual journal as a tool for reflection. Write down your prayers, thoughts, and the insights you receive during your time with God. Journaling helps you track your spiritual journey and reinforces the communication loop.

7. Reflective Silence: Sometimes, effective communication with God is found in the quiet moments of reflective silence. Allow time for stillness, letting your heart commune with God without words. In the silence, you may find a depth of connection beyond verbal expression.

8. Worship as a Language: Engage in worship as a language of communication. Whether through song, praise, or gratitude, worship deepens the connection with God. It transcends verbal expression and reaches into the core of your spirit.

9. Seeking and Trusting God's Guidance: Effective communication involves seeking God's guidance and trusting His responses. Be attentive to His leading, trusting that His wisdom surpasses your own understanding. This trust strengthens the foundation of your relationship.

10. Embracing Patience: Communication with God unfolds over time. Embrace patience as a virtue in your dialogue with the Divine. Allow your relationship to develop, deepen, and mature as you persistently seek His presence.

In the symphony of communication with God, every word, every silence, and every prayer contribute to the melody of a relationship that grows stronger with each exchange. Cultivate the art of effective communication, and watch as your connection with God transforms into a rich and enduring dialogue.

Workbook-Reflection Questions: Effective Communication With God 73

Navigating Divine Seasons: The Art of Adaptation in Our Relationship with God

In the symphony of our spiritual journey, the ability to adapt becomes a crucial note that harmonizes through the various seasons, trials, and tribulations orchestrated by God. Embracing adaptability enhances our relationship with the Divine, allowing us to tap into the full potential of His guidance and purpose. Here's an exploration of how being adaptable enriches our connection with God and practical ways to cultivate this quality:

1. Surrendering to God's Timing: Adaptability in our relationship with God starts with surrendering to His timing. God's plans unfold according to His divine schedule, and being adaptable means releasing our own timelines and trusting in His perfect orchestration.

2. Embracing Change with Faith: God often leads us through changes, both internal and external. Embrace these shifts with faith, knowing that His plans are for our welfare. Trusting God's guidance in the midst of change enhances our adaptability and draws us closer to His purpose.

3. Flexibility in Prayer and Worship: Adaptability involves being flexible in our prayer and worship practices. While having routines is beneficial, being open to spontaneous moments of connection allows for a more dynamic and responsive relationship with God.

4. Learning from Different Biblical Characters: The Bible is rich with stories of individuals who navigated diverse challenges and changes. Study the lives of biblical characters like Joseph, Esther, and Paul to glean insights into their adaptability amid God's unfolding plan.

5. Remaining Open to Divine Lessons: Adaptability means remaining open to the lessons God seeks to teach us. Be receptive to His correction, guidance, and redirection. A teachable spirit fosters growth and a deeper connection with the Father.

6. Trusting God's Promises: Trust is at the core of adaptability. Trusting God's promises and believing in His unwavering love allows us to adapt to circumstances, knowing that He is faithful to fulfill His word.

7. Seeking the Holy Spirit's Guidance: The Holy Spirit is our divine guide, providing wisdom and discernment. Cultivate a relationship with the Holy Spirit through prayer and meditation, allowing His guidance to shape your responses to various situations.

8. Finding Strength in Vulnerability: Adaptability requires vulnerability—acknowledging our limitations and relying on God's strength. Finding strength in vulnerability deepens our dependence on Him and fosters resilience in navigating challenges.

9. Responding to God's Corrections: God corrects those He loves. An adaptable heart responds humbly to God's corrections, recognizing them as invitations to growth and refinement. Embracing correction enhances our spiritual journey.

10. Remaining Rooted in God's Word: The Bible is a steady anchor in our ever-changing lives. Remain rooted in God's Word, drawing strength and guidance from its timeless truths. The more grounded we are in His Word, the more adaptable we become.

As we navigate the ebb and flow of our relationship with God, adaptability emerges as a key ingredient for a thriving connection. In the symphony of divine seasons, our willingness to adapt allows us to move in harmony with God's purpose and experience the fullness of His transformative grace.

Workbook-Reflection Questions: Adapting To God 74

Reflecting on Surrender:
- How willing are you to surrender your own timelines and plans to God's perfect orchestration in your life? Consider specific areas where surrendering to God's timing might enhance your relationship with Him.

1. **Faith in the Midst of Change:**
- Reflect on your response to changes, both internal and external, in your life. How can you embrace these shifts with faith, trusting in God's guidance? Consider instances where faith can be the cornerstone of your adaptability.

2. **Dynamic Prayer and Worship:**
- In what ways can you introduce flexibility into your prayer and worship practices to make them more dynamic and responsive? Reflect on the role of spontaneity in your spiritual life and how it might deepen your connection with God.

3. **Learning from Biblical Characters:**
- Choose a biblical character who faced significant changes and challenges. How did their adaptability contribute to their journey with God? Reflect on the lessons you can learn from their experiences and apply to your own life.

As you ponder these questions, may your reflections guide you in cultivating adaptability in your relationship with God, enhancing your ability to navigate the diverse seasons orchestrated by the Divine.

The Foundation of All Connections:
The depth and vitality of our relationships with family, friends, and colleagues are intrinsically tied to the health of our relationship with God. As the foundational relationship, our connection with the Divine sets the tone for how we navigate and nurture all other bonds. Just as a building's foundation determines its stability, the strength of our connection with God determines the resilience of our relational edifice.

Navigating Life's Seas:
Consider life's journey as a vast sea, and relationships as the ships that navigate its waters. Without a sturdy and well-maintained vessel, the challenges of the sea become daunting. Likewise, without a thriving relationship with God, the voyage through life's uncertainties can be tumultuous. Cultivating this connection becomes the compass that guides our ships, offering direction, stability, and assurance in the face of turbulent waves.

The Anchor in Life's Storms:
Our relationship with God is the anchor that holds us steadfast when storms of life threaten to toss us adrift. In moments of uncertainty, grief, or joy, this connection provides a secure harbor. It is in the embrace of God's love and wisdom that we find solace, strength, and unwavering support, allowing us to weather the storms and emerge resilient.

The Source of Life-Giving Waters:
Just as a river nourishes the land through which it flows, our relationship with God is the source of life-giving waters that nourish every facet of our existence. From this spiritual wellspring, we draw the sustenance needed for growth, wisdom, and resilience. Without regular communion with this source, the landscape of our lives may become barren and arid.

The Ripple Effect:
As we cultivate a thriving relationship with God, the impact ripples into every other relationship we hold. It shapes the lens through which we view others, influencing our capacity for love, compassion, and understanding. A flourishing connection with the Divine fosters a spirit of grace and humility that enriches our interactions, creating a ripple effect of positivity and transformation.

Time to Cultivate:
In the busyness of life, it's easy to overlook the most foundational relationship – the one that fuels and sustains all others. Yet, the importance of dedicating time to cultivate this connection cannot be overstated. Just as neglecting a garden leads to withered plants, neglecting our relationship with God hinders the vibrancy of our entire relational landscape.

As we conclude this journey into the heart of relationships, let it be a clarion call to prioritize and invest in the most pivotal connection – your relationship with God. In the embrace of divine love, you find the strength to navigate life's waters, the anchor in its storms, and the wellspring that nourishes every aspect of your being. May this foundation empower you to build resilient ships that sail confidently through the seas of relationships, leaving a wake of grace, love, and transformative connection.

RELATIONSHIP WITH SELF

NURTURING THE RELATIONSHIP WITH ONESELF

Now is the opportune moment to turn our attention inward, where the intricate dance of self-discovery awaits. Before we embark on the journey of becoming exceptional partners, parents, or influential figures in our spheres of impact, a foundational truth beckons us. To foster greatness in our external relationships, we must first unravel the depths of knowing and loving ourselves. The purpose of this chapter is to guide you through the transformative process of cultivating a robust self-relationship. Recognize that the ability to stand confidently alone is the prerequisite for standing alongside others. Join this exploration, delving into the nuances of self-awareness and self-love, laying the groundwork for a resilient, authentic, and harmonious connection with the person you encounter in every reflection—yourself.

Exploring the Harmony of Body, Mind, and Spirit At the very core of our existence lies a profound revelation – we are fashioned in the image of God, a triune being. Just as the divine nature is revealed in the trinity of God as the Father, the Son, and the Holy Spirit, humanity mirrors this triadic essence through the components of body, mind, and spirit.. This divine blueprint serves as a guide for our harmonious coexistence. The intricate dance of our triune nature unfolds with the spirit housing our personality, gifts, and talents, resonating with the divine spark that reflects God's image within us. The soul, a repository of thoughts, memories, emotions, knowledge, ideas, perspectives, and skills, is the bridge between our spiritual essence and our physical reality.

Our bodies, with their myriad systems, serve as the vessel through which we experience the world. When aligned, these three dimensions operate in unity, akin to the seamless collaboration within the triune Godhead. However, for humanity, achieving such harmony is a perpetual journey. The spirit, the seat of God-consciousness, imparts purpose, while the soul offers self-consciousness, and the body, world-consciousness. Yet, the ongoing war among these elements can obstruct the purposeful flow intended by the Creator.

The call is to align our spirit, soul, and body in unified accord, just as the triune God works together for a common purpose. When our spirits are charged, the soul vibrates with peace, leading to a vitality that echoes through the body.

121

The interconnectedness of these facets is a delicate dance — a symphony of spiritual, mental, and physical well-being. As we delve into the understanding of this three-part being, we embark on a transformative journey towards self-discovery and divine alignment, fostering a state of holistic flourishing in every dimension of our existence.

Within the complex web of our existence, the spirit arises as the intangible abode, a sacred sanctuary where the core of our unique personality, abilities, and gifts establish their dwelling. This spiritual sanctuary serves as the abode of the Holy Spirit, permeating our innermost core. Yet, in the course of life's complexities, many individuals find these invaluable aspects of their spirit—personality, gifts, and talents—suppressed or obscured.

The adversary, in his relentless pursuit, seeks to assail our spiritual raw resources. His tactics involve suffocation or, more insidiously, theft for his malevolent purposes. The ultimate aim is to sever the profound connection between our spirits and the divine, plunging us into spiritual unconsciousness. One might ponder why activities that feed and nourish our spirits, such as prayer and diligent reading, are often overshadowed by the relentless demands on our souls and bodies.

The enemy's strategy is clear—he desires dominance of our souls and bodies, diverting attention from our spiritual well-being. The less we engage in activities that uplift our spirits, the more susceptible we become to spiritual dormancy or, worse, spiritual darkness due to separation from God. Now, let's embark on an exploration of the profound components housed in our spirit, commencing with the distinct and irreplaceable facets of our personality.

Personality

In the intricately designed essence of our being, our personalities emerge as unique and irreplaceable facets, intricately woven into the fabric of our spirits by the divine Creator. God, in His infinite wisdom, crafted each individual with a distinct set of traits, creativity, and expressions that are intrinsically wired within. The richness of your personality, the way you think, feel, and express, is a deliberate masterpiece designed by God.

You are not a duplicate; you are an original creation. God doesn't engage in replication; it is Satan who seeks to manufacture mere copies. The adversary desires to inundate individuals with soul-dominance, fostering an environment of comparison, fear, and embarrassment, leading them to forsake their true selves. Authenticity becomes a beacon in this context—an affirmation of the uniqueness bestowed upon you. It is cheaper to be yourself, embracing the authenticity of the original design.

The key question emerges: How are you wired? What intrinsic qualities, passions, and expressions make you uniquely you? These attributes are not random but purposefully installed within your spirit, becoming the very conduit through which divine purpose flows. Your spirit, housing your unique personality, is the epicenter where purpose resides. As you embrace your authentic self, you tap into the divine pipeline leading to your purpose. God intends for the light of your original design to shine through, attracting and resonating with a specific group. You were meticulously designed to attract what is destined for you, and by staying true to the original blueprint of your personality, you align with the divine purpose woven into the core of your being. The beauty of your personality, a distinct masterpiece, reflects the creativity of the divine Artist who crafted you in His image.

Personality Defined.

A personality, in its essence, is the unique blend of characteristics, traits, and expressions that form the distinctive individuality of a person. It encompasses how one thinks, feels, and interacts with the world, creating a nuanced and specific pattern that distinguishes one from another. The Creator, in His divine craftsmanship, intricately designed each person with a personality that reflects His creativity and purpose. God's intention is not only for individuals to recognize and embrace their personalities but also to utilize them as powerful tools for impact.

In the grand naof creation, every personality is a deliberate stroke of divine artistry, contributing to the broader masterpiece of human existence. Each personality trait, whether introverted or extroverted, analytical or creative, carries a unique purpose within the greater narrative of God's plan. It is through these distinct qualities that individuals can connect with others in profound and meaningful ways, fostering community, understanding, and love.

God's desire is for individuals to recognize that their personalities are not arbitrary but intentional components designed to fulfill a specific role within the larger framework of His purposes. Just as no two fingerprints are alike, no two personalities are identical, underscoring the uniqueness of each individual's contribution to the world. Embracing and understanding one's personality becomes a crucial step in aligning with God's plan for impact, as it opens doors for authentic connections and enables individuals to be vessels through which God's love and grace can flow into the lives of others.

When individuals fully understand and appreciate their God-given personalities, they become instruments through which the beauty and diversity of God's creation are displayed. Whether through a quiet and thoughtful demeanor or an outgoing and expressive nature, every personality trait has the potential to shine brightly for God's glory, leaving a lasting impact on those who encounter it. It is in the genuine expression of one's unique personality that the transformative power of God's love is vividly displayed, creating ripples of positive influence in the lives of others.

Workbook-Activity: Discovering Your God-Given Personality Page 76

Gifts and Talents

Gifts and talents, bestowed upon each individual by the divine Creator, are like precious gems embedded within the very fabric of our being. God, in His infinite wisdom and creativity, crafted these unique qualities and abilities as part of our inherent design. Unlike transient possessions, gifts and talents are immovable elements intricately installed within us, shaping our identity and contributing to the richness of the human experience. A gift, in its essence, is a special endowment or ability that surpasses ordinary aptitude. It is a distinctive quality or attribute, generously given by God, that carries the potential to bless, uplift, and contribute positively to the world. Talents, similarly, refer to inherent aptitudes or skills that individuals possess, often marked by a natural proficiency in a particular area. Both gifts and talents are intentional bestowals from our Creator, designed to serve a purpose beyond personal gratification.

God's act of fashioning us in our mothers' wombs involves the deliberate implantation of these divine endowments. Every individual is uniquely equipped with a set of gifts and talents, forming an integral part of their identity and purpose. These gifts are not arbitrary; rather, they are a manifestation of God's grace and provision for each person. Recognizing and acknowledging these innate abilities becomes a journey of self-discovery and an essential aspect of nurturing a strong relationship with oneself.

The purpose behind God's lavish gifting is profound. He endows individuals with specific gifts and talents not only for their personal fulfillment but also as a means to contribute to the well-being of others. Each person becomes a channel through which God's goodness flows into the world. The world, in turn, responds with reciprocal blessings, creating a beautiful cycle of divine exchange.

God desires for His children to steward their gifts and talents responsibly, utilizing them to bring glory to Him and blessings to those around them. The investment of these divine endowments in the service of others becomes a testament to God's generosity and an expression of His love through human vessels. In embracing and utilizing our gifts and talents, we align ourselves with God's purpose, becoming conduits for His transformative work in the world.s and talents

The Parable Of The talents

The Parable of the Talents, found in Matthew 25:14-30, unveils a profound message through its double entendre. In the cultural context of biblical times, a talent was a unit of currency, a significant sum of money. To understand the weight of this currency in today's terms, one talent is estimated to be equivalent to about 20 years' worth of wages for a common laborer. The master in the parable entrusts talents to his servants, indicating a substantial and valuable investment. The first two servants immediately engage with the master's resources in the marketplace, doubling their talents through wise investments. Their diligence and responsibility are evident, and they are rewarded accordingly. The master commends them, stating, "Well done, good and faithful servant! You have been faithful with a few things; I will put you in charge of many things. Come and share your master's happiness!" (Matthew 25:21).

However, the third servant adopts a different perspective. Fearing the master's character, he buries the single talent rather than putting it to work. This servant's perspective reflects a distorted image of the master—one characterized by fear rather than understanding. He makes excuses, claiming that he knew the master to be a hard man reaping where he did not sow. In this erroneous view, the servant justifies his inaction. The consequences for the third servant are severe. The master, upon his return, rebukes the servant for his fear and unproductive stewardship. The talent is taken from him and given to the servant with ten talents, emphasizing the principle that to those who use what they have, more will be given. In stark contrast, the one who buries his talent loses even what he has.

This parable carries a poignant message for us today. God has uniquely gifted each individual with talents and abilities. Rather than burying them due to fear, indifference, or a distorted perspective of God, we are called to invest our talents in the marketplace of life. Just as Jesus, at the age of twelve, was about His Father's business, we are to be actively engaged in God's work, using our gifts to further His kingdom.

The parable underscores the responsibility and reward associated with maximizing our talents for God's purposes. When we invest our unique abilities in the marketplace of life—whether in our careers, relationships, or communities—we not only contribute to the flourishing of others but also align ourselves with God's intended purpose. The warning is clear: to bury our talents is to squander the valuable resources God has given us, hindering the collective benefit for the Master, the marketplace, and ourselves. As faithful stewards, we are called to multiply and invest what we've been given for the glory of God.

Discovering and understanding your gifts and talents is a crucial aspect of recognizing the unique way God has designed you. Here are some steps to help you discern and harness your God-given abilities:

1. Self-reflection:
Begin by reflecting on your interests, passions, and activities that bring you joy. Consider the things you love to do, and take note of the areas where you naturally excel. Your talents often align with your genuine interests.

2. Seek feedback:
Ask friends, family, and those who know you well about the qualities or skills they observe in you. Sometimes, others can provide valuable insights into our strengths that we might not see in ourselves.

3. Identify patterns:
Look for recurring themes or patterns in your life. Notice the activities or tasks that consistently draw you in, and examine the skills you consistently develop or demonstrate. These patterns can offer clues about your inherent gifts.

4. Explore various activities:
Don't be afraid to try new things. Engage in a variety of activities, both within and outside your comfort zone. Experimenting with different pursuits can help you uncover latent talents or refine existing ones.

5. Assess your impact:
Consider the impact you have on others through your actions, words, or skills. Reflect on situations where you've made a positive difference or received acknowledgment. Your unique contributions often leave a positive imprint on those around you.

6. Spiritual guidance:
Seek God's guidance through prayer and meditation. Ask Him to reveal your gifts and talents and provide clarity on how He intends for you to use them. Trust in His wisdom to guide you on the path He has designed for you.

7. Personal assessments:
Utilize tools and assessments designed to identify strengths and talents. There are various resources available, such as personality tests, spiritual gifts assessments, or skills inventories, which can provide valuable insights into your unique attributes.

8. Embrace diversity:
Recognize that God has created a diverse range of talents and gifts. Embrace the uniqueness of your gifts, even if they differ from others. Comparing yourself to others can be counterproductive; instead, focus on cultivating the strengths inherent to your individual design.

9. Observe your energy levels:
Pay attention to the activities that energize you rather than drain you. Talents often align with areas that bring you fulfillment and vitality. Identifying where you find joy and a sense of purpose can help pinpoint your unique gifts.

10. Align with your values:
Consider your values and beliefs. Aligning your talents with your core values can lead to a more fulfilling and purpose-driven life. Your gifts are not just about what you can do but also about who you are becoming.

Remember that the process of discovering your gifts and talents is ongoing. It's a journey of self-discovery and growth, and God may continually reveal new aspects of your design as you navigate through different seasons of life. Be patient, open-minded, and receptive to the guidance of the Holy Spirit as you uncover and develop the unique gifts God has placed within you.

Workbook-Discover Your Divine Gifts and Talents Worksheet Page 78

Your Soul

Exploring the Depths of the Soul: The Essence of Awareness

Within the complex framework of our existence, the soul emerges as the second layer, a profound repository of thoughts, memories, emotions, ideas, knowledge, perspectives, and skills. Each component woven into the fabric of our soul plays a distinctive role, collectively shaping our awareness and influencing how we perceive and engage with the world.

1. Thoughts:

Our thoughts are the silent narrators of our internal dialogue. They reflect our beliefs, attitudes, and interpretations of the world around us. The mind, a powerful instrument within the soul, processes thoughts that mold our perception, guiding our actions and responses to external stimuli.

2. Memories:

Memories form the foundation of our past. They encapsulate experiences, lessons, and moments that have shaped us. The ability to recall memories not only anchors us in our personal history but also serves as a compass for navigating the present and future.

3. Emotions:

Emotions are the vibrant hues that paint the canvas of our soul. They express the depth and richness of our human experience—joy, sorrow, love, anger, and everything in between. Acknowledging and understanding our emotions allows us to navigate life's complexities with authenticity and resilience.

4. Ideas:

Ideas are the sparks of creativity that ignite within the soul. They represent our capacity to innovate, dream, and conceptualize. The soul, as the incubator of ideas, fosters imagination and fuels our aspirations, guiding us toward self-discovery and the pursuit of our passions.

5. Knowledge Bank:

The soul functions as a repository of knowledge, storing insights gained through learning and experiences. This knowledge bank serves as a resource for decision-making, problem-solving, and personal growth, enriching our perspectives and informing our understanding of the world.

6. Perspectives:

Perspectives are the lenses through which we view the world. Shaped by our unique combination of experiences, beliefs, and values, perspectives influence our judgments, interpretations, and interactions with others. Understanding diverse perspectives enhances empathy and fosters meaningful connections.

7. Skills:

Skills are the tools honed within the soul, empowering us to navigate life's challenges and contribute to the world. Whether intellectual, emotional, or practical, skills are manifestations of our potential and capabilities, allowing us to shape our personal and professional journey.

As we delve into the intricate layers of the soul, we uncover the profound significance of these components in shaping our awareness. The soul, with its multifaceted dimensions, serves as the lens through which we perceive and engage with the world—a canvas rich with the colors of our thoughts, memories, emotions, ideas, knowledge, perspectives, and skills.

Unveiling the Soul's Magnificence: A Closer Look at Psalms 139:14

In the sacred verses of Psalms 139:14, a profound truth is articulated: "I praise you because I am fearfully and wonderfully made; your works are wonderful, I know that full well." The soul, an intricate and delicate part of our being, plays a pivotal role in comprehending this divine truth. The psalmist declares, "I know that full well," underscoring the significance of the soul's awareness. Our souls, the custodians of thoughts, memories, emotions, ideas, knowledge, perspectives, and skills, hold the key to recognizing the marvelous craftsmanship of our Creator. However, the soul's awareness can be clouded, and its true value obscured.

At times, the soul becomes a repository of external influences, societal expectations, and personal insecurities that overshadow its inherent worth. The enemy cunningly seeks to manipulate the soul, steering it away from the profound truth that we are fearfully and wonderfully made. The soul, unaware of its magnificence, can inadvertently become a barrier to the free expression of the spirit's values.

The Battle for Soul Awareness:
The enemy's strategy involves creating soul holes—voids in the soul's understanding of its intrinsic value. These holes can manifest as doubts, insecurities, and distorted self-perceptions. When the soul is not rooted in the truth of its divine origin, it becomes susceptible to the enemy's schemes.

The Subtle Ploys:
The adversary endeavors to control the narrative within the soul, offering counterfeit affirmations that undermine the psalmist's proclamation. Fame, fortune, and worldly success are proffered as substitutes for the genuine acknowledgment of being fearfully and wonderfully made. The soul, if unaware of its authentic worth, may unwittingly trade the treasures of the spirit for transient and hollow achievements.

Navigating Soul Holes and Ties:
In the forthcoming section, we will delve into the intricate dynamics of soul holes and soul ties. Understanding these aspects is paramount for reclaiming the soul's awareness, reinforcing the truth that resonates within Psalms 139:14. As we explore the depths of the soul's vulnerabilities, we embark on a journey to mend the holes and break the detrimental ties that hinder the soul from fully embracing its fearfully and wonderfully made nature.

Unraveling Soul Holes and Ties: A Profound Exploration
Within the intricate design of our being lies the enigmatic realm of the soul—a repository of thoughts, memories, emotions, ideas, knowledge, perspectives, and skills. Yet, this profound sanctuary is not impervious to vulnerabilities. Soul holes and ties, intricately woven into the fabric of our innermost selves, demand a closer inspection.

Defining Soul Holes:
Soul holes are voids or gaps within the components of the soul. These openings can manifest as doubts, insecurities, and distorted perceptions that obscure the soul's true magnificence. For instance, a soul hole in the realm of emotions might be a deep-seated fear that inhibits the full expression of joy, hindering the embrace of one's true nature as fearfully and wonderfully made.

The Pervasive Impact:
Each component of the soul—thoughts, memories, emotions, ideas, knowledge, perspectives, and skills—can harbor these voids. A thought tainted by self-doubt, a memory haunted by past traumas, or an emotion restrained by unresolved pain—all contribute to the presence of soul holes.

Understanding Soul Ties:
Soul ties, on the other hand, are connections that bind the components of the soul to external influences. These ties can be positive or negative, shaping the trajectory of our lives. For instance, an unhealthy tie in the area of perspectives might be an attachment to societal norms that stifles individuality and distorts one's sense of purpose.

Examples of Soul Ties:
- *Thoughts:* A soul tied to societal expectations may grapple with intrusive thoughts that hinder the pursuit of personal aspirations, fostering self-doubt.
- *Memories:* Traumatic memories tied to past experiences can create emotional entanglements, impacting present relationships and hindering emotional well-being.
- *Emotions:* A soul tied to the pursuit of external validation may experience emotional turmoil when faced with perceived rejection or criticism.
- *Ideas:* Ties to cultural norms can limit creative ideas, stifling individual expression and innovation.
- *Knowledge Bank:* A soul tied to a rigid belief system may resist the acquisition of new knowledge, impeding personal growth and enlightenment.
- *Perspectives:* An individual tied to toxic relationships may adopt skewed perspectives on love and connection, perpetuating a cycle of unhealthy ties.
- *Skills:* A soul tied to societal standards of success may misuse skills for personal gain, neglecting the greater purpose of contributing positively to the world.

Navigating the Complex Landscape:
Understanding soul holes and ties is paramount for reclaiming the soul's true awareness and potential. In the upcoming sections, we will embark on a journey to explore strategies and insights that facilitate healing, empowering us to mend soul holes and break detrimental ties that hinder the soul from aligning with its fearfully and wonderfully made essence.

Navigating Soul Holes and Ties: The Impact on Relationships

In the intricate fabric of our souls, composed of thoughts, memories, emotions, ideas, knowledge banks, perspectives, and skills, the presence of soul holes and ties can profoundly influence the course of our relationships. These components, when compromised, act as invisible weights that can disrupt the smooth sailing of our connections with others.

1. Thoughts:
Soul Holes: Negative thought patterns, self-doubt, and destructive self-talk can bore soul holes, allowing insecurities and fears to leak into our interactions.
Soul Ties: Unhealthy thought ties might connect us to past hurts, limiting our ability to trust and fostering a lens of skepticism in our relationships.

2. Memories:
Soul Holes: Traumatic or unresolved memories can create holes, allowing past pain to resurface unexpectedly and taint our present interactions.
Soul Ties: Ties to negative memories might cause us to project past grievances onto current relationships, hindering forgiveness and reconciliation.

3. Emotions:
Soul Holes: Suppressed or unaddressed emotions can create holes, leading to emotional outbursts, mood swings, or an inability to express and manage emotions healthily.
Soul Ties: Emotional ties to past experiences may result in unhealed emotional wounds that impact our ability to connect authentically in new relationships.

4. Ideas:
Soul Holes: Limiting beliefs and rigid ideologies can puncture soul holes, restricting openness to diverse perspectives and hindering the growth of mutual understanding.
Soul Ties: Ties to narrow-minded ideologies may strain relationships by fostering an environment resistant to change and compromise.

5. Knowledge Bank:
Soul Holes: Lack of self-awareness or ignorance can create knowledge gaps, preventing us from understanding and empathizing with others.
Soul Ties: Ties to misinformation or prejudiced views can lead to judgment and misunderstanding, straining relationships.

6. Perspectives:
Soul Holes: Closed-minded perspectives and an unwillingness to see others' points of view can create holes, hindering effective communication and mutual respect.
Soul Ties: Ties to narrow perspectives may limit our ability to appreciate the diversity of thoughts and ideas, impacting the richness of our relationships.

7. Skills:
Soul Holes: Deficiencies in communication or conflict resolution skills can create holes, leading to misunderstandings and unresolved issues.
Soul Ties: Ties to ineffective or destructive relational skills may result in patterns of unhealthy behavior that impact the sustainability of relationships.

Navigating the Waters:
- Self-Reflection: Regularly assess the health of your thoughts, memories, emotions, ideas, knowledge bank, perspectives, and skills.
- Healing: Address unresolved issues, traumas, or negative patterns through therapy, counseling, or personal development.
- Communication: Openly discuss potential soul holes and ties with trusted individuals, fostering understanding and support.
- Continuous Growth: Commit to ongoing self-awareness and improvement, ensuring that soul holes and ties are identified and addressed promptly.

By acknowledging and addressing these soul vulnerabilities, we can fortify our relationships, fostering an environment where understanding, empathy, and connection can flourish.

Healing the Soul: A Journey to Wholeness

Embarking on a journey to heal each facet of the soul is a profound and transformative endeavor. Here's a guide to nurture and restore vitality to different areas of your soul:

- **Thoughts: Nurture Positive Self-Talk**
  - Embrace Affirmations: Speak life-giving affirmations over yourself daily, reinforcing positive beliefs about your identity and purpose.
  - Gratitude Practices: Cultivate a habit of gratitude by regularly acknowledging and appreciating the blessings in your life.
  - Challenge Negative Thoughts: Actively challenge and replace negative thoughts with constructive and empowering alternatives.
  - Scripture for Meditation: "Finally, brothers, whatever is true, whatever is honorable, whatever is just, whatever is pure, whatever is lovely, whatever is commendable, if there is any excellence, if there is anything worthy of praise, think about these things." - Philippians 4:8 (ESV)

- **Memories: Shifting Perspective on the Past**
  - Positive Light: Aim to see your past in a positive light, viewing challenges as opportunities for growth and resilience.
  - Pain into Gain: Investigate ways God can turn past pain into gain, recognizing the redemptive power of His grace.
  - Memory Bank as a Reference Library: Transform your memory bank into a reference library for learning and growth rather than a dwelling place for past hurts.
  - Scripture for Meditation: "I will ponder all your work, and meditate on your mighty deeds." - Psalm 77:12 (ESV)

- **Emotions: Developing Emotional Intelligence**
  - Emotion Assessment: Write down your top emotions, assessing the root causes and identifying patterns in emotional responses.
  - Counteract with Gratitude: Counteract negative emotions with gratitude, redirecting your focus toward the positive aspects of your life.
  - Scripture for Meditation: "Rejoice always, pray without ceasing, give thanks in all circumstances; for this is the will of God in Christ Jesus for you." - 1 Thessalonians 5:16-18 (ESV)

- **Ideas: Fostering Open-Mindedness**
  - Growth Mindset: Cultivate a growth mindset, actively seeking diverse perspectives and embracing continuous learning.
  - Challenge Preconceived Notions: Challenge and evolve your ideas by being open to new information and perspectives.
  - Scripture for Meditation: "Get wisdom; get insight; do not forget, and do not turn away from the words of my mouth." - Proverbs 4:5 (ESV)

- **Knowledge Bank: Strategic Learning**
  - Strategic Knowledge: Be intentional about acquiring knowledge that aligns with God, your purpose, and personal growth.
  - Remove Unnecessary Knowledge: Discern and eliminate knowledge that adds no value or aligns with your purpose.
  - Scripture for Meditation: "The fear of the Lord is the beginning of knowledge; fools despise wisdom and instruction." - Proverbs 1:7 (ESV)

- **Perspectives: Cultivate Empathy**
  - Cultivate Empathy: Practice putting yourself in others' shoes, seeking to understand their perspectives. Engage in dialogues with people from diverse backgrounds to broaden your worldview. Also, allow the Word of God to shift your perspectives in areas where you may have a poor perspective. By aligning your viewpoint with biblical principles, you gain a foundation for empathetic understanding and compassion toward others.
  - *Scripture for Meditation: "Have this mind among yourselves, which is yours in Christ Jesus, who, though he was in the form of God, did not count equality with God a thing to be grasped, but emptied himself, by taking the form of a servant, being born in the likeness of men." - Philippians 2:5-7 (ESV)*

- **Skills: Invest in Personal Development**
  - Invest in Personal Development: Enhance your relational skills through courses, workshops, or self-help resources. Develop effective communication, conflict resolution, and interpersonal skills to navigate relationships skillfully. Recognize that personal growth is an ongoing process, and investing in your skills contributes not only to your well-being but also to the enrichment of your relationships.

129

○ *Scripture for Meditation: "Do your best to present yourself to God as one approved, a worker who has no need to be ashamed, rightly handling the word of truth." - 2 Timothy 2:15 (ESV)*

If you are seeking a deeper understanding of soul ties, explore the insights provided in my book, "The Purpose of Freedom." It delves into the intricacies of soul connections and offers valuable perspectives on nurturing healthy relationships with yourself and others.

Healing the Soul: Patching Up Soul Holes And Undoing Soul Ties Worksheet 81

Caring for the Vehicle of Purpose: Nurturing Our Physical Well-being

In the intricate mechanics of our existence, our physical bodies function as the vehicles propelling us through the journey of purpose. Much like a well-maintained car, our bodies require careful attention and intentional care to fulfill their purpose effectively. Let's explore the significance of tending to our physical well-being, drawing parallels between our bodies and vehicles and understanding the divine call to stewardship:

1. The Vehicle of Purpose: Consider your body as the vehicle that transports you through the roads of life's purpose. Just as a driver cares for their vehicle to ensure a smooth journey, we are entrusted with the responsibility to care for our bodies to fulfill the purpose God has set before us.

2. Stewardship and Worship: Caring for our bodies is an act of worship and stewardship. Recognizing that our bodies are fearfully and wonderfully made by God, we honor Him by maintaining and nurturing the physical temple He has given us. Stewarding our bodies is an expression of gratitude for the gift of life.

3. The Driver's Role: As the drivers of these intricate vehicles, we play a pivotal role in determining how well our bodies function. Our choices in nutrition, exercise, rest, and overall lifestyle directly impact the mileage we can achieve in our earthly journey. God entrusts us with the agency to make choices that honor our bodies.

4. Holistic Wellness: Physical well-being encompasses more than just the absence of illness. It involves holistic wellness—addressing the interconnected aspects of our health, including mental, emotional, and spiritual dimensions. A healthy body supports a vibrant and purpose-driven life.

5. Purposeful Nutrition: Just as fuel powers a vehicle, nutrition fuels our bodies. Purposeful nutrition involves making choices that nourish and sustain our physical health. Consider the quality of the "fuel" you provide your body to ensure it operates at its best.

6. Regular Maintenance: Routine maintenance is essential for any vehicle's longevity. Similarly, regular exercise, adequate sleep, and self-care routines contribute to the overall maintenance of our bodies. Prioritize habits that foster physical well-being.

7. The Journey of Fulfillment: Our bodies are not just vessels; they are active participants in the journey toward fulfillment. Maintaining physical health enhances our ability to actively engage in purpose, pursue passions, and contribute meaningfully to the world around us.

8. Temple of the Holy Spirit: The Bible refers to our bodies as temples of the Holy Spirit. Recognizing this sacred connection underscores the importance of treating our bodies with reverence. A well-cared-for temple is a conducive space for the Spirit to dwell and work through us.

9. Preventive Care and Wisdom: Proactive and preventive care is an expression of wisdom. Regular health check-ups, screenings, and preventive measures contribute to longevity and enable us to fulfill God's purpose without unnecessary hindrances.

10. An Offering of Self: Ultimately, our bodies are offerings of self to God. By actively caring for our physical well-being, we demonstrate a commitment to stewarding the gift of life responsibly. A healthy body becomes a vessel through which God's purpose can be expressed more fully.

In embracing the analogy of our bodies as vehicles of purpose, we discover the importance of maintaining and nurturing these intricate vessels. As stewards of the divine gift of life, let us honor God by prioritizing our physical well-being, recognizing that a cared-for body enhances our capacity to journey toward fulfillment and purpose.

The Temple of the Holy Spirit: Cultivating a Sacred Dwelling

Our bodies, intricately woven and fearfully made, stand as the sacred temple of the Holy Spirit. It is within these mortal frames that the divine resides, and from here, He seeks to manifest His power, love, and purpose. In contemplating the condition of our bodily temple, we are invited to reflect on the quality of the environment we provide for the Spirit's habitation.

Imagine your body as a home. Is it cluttered with unhealthy habits, diseased by neglect, or struggling with a sickly disposition? Alternatively, is it clean, optimized, and well-cared-for, ready to be a vessel for divine purposes? These questions prompt us to consider whether our bodies are places of healing or constant battlegrounds in need of restoration.

The Holy Spirit's desire is to heal through us, not perpetually fight against us. He seeks a harmonious dwelling, free from the disarray of poor health or self-destructive habits. As we acknowledge our bodies as both the dwelling and the tool of the Spirit, it becomes clear that He longs for an effective instrument—healthy, energized, skilled, and strong enough to bear the weight of our divine purpose.

Honoring our bodies as temples involves adopting practices that cultivate vitality and well-being. Whether through nourishing food choices, regular exercise, sufficient rest, or mindful habits, we actively participate in creating a hospitable environment for the Holy Spirit. Let us embark on a journey to optimize our physical homes, recognizing that in doing so, we align ourselves with the divine purpose and power that flows through us.

Satan's Assault on the Body: A Strategic Weakening

In the grand design of creation, God designed our bodies as vessels for His purpose, temples for the Holy Spirit to dwell. Understanding the significance of this divine dwelling, Satan, in his cunning strategy, seeks to weaken these vessels to the point of dysfunction. His malevolent tactics are aimed at hindering the flourishing of God's purpose within us.

One of Satan's primary weapons is the cultivation of unhealthy habits that gradually erode the vitality of our bodies. Whether through addictions to substances, overconsumption of harmful foods, or the neglect of essential self-care practices, he strategically weakens our physical frames. These vices act as corrosive agents, gradually deteriorating the well-being of the temple God intended to be resilient and robust.

Furthermore, Satan employs the chaos of the world to bury individuals under the weight of stress, anxiety, and relentless busyness. These external pressures can lead to a weakened immune system, chronic illnesses, and an overall breakdown of physical health. The adversary's insidious aim is to use the cares of the world as a burial ground, suffocating the potential for growth and purpose within us.

Additionally, Satan understands the profound connection between the body and purpose. He is aware that premature death not only robs individuals of the fullness of life but also extinguishes the potential for generational impact. By attacking the physical vessel, he seeks to cut short the fruitful tree God intended, preventing it from bearing the fruit that could nourish generations to come.

To counteract Satan's strategy, it is essential to fortify our bodies through intentional care and attention. Recognizing the subtle traps laid before us allows us to resist the erosion of our physical well-being. By embracing practices that promote health, we not only thwart the enemy's plans but also position ourselves to fulfill the purpose God has embedded within our mortal frames.

How to Optimize your HEALTH.

1. **Hydration:**
   - Drinking ample water daily is vital for bodily functions, as water is involved in various physiological processes.
   - Proper hydration supports digestion, nutrient absorption, and the elimination of toxins from the body.
   - It helps maintain skin health, joint lubrication, and overall cellular function.

2. **Exercise:**
   - Regular physical activity strengthens muscles, enhances cardiovascular health, and boosts overall well-being.
   - Exercise improves circulation, contributing to better oxygenation of cells and removal of waste products.
   - It plays a crucial role in maintaining a healthy weight, reducing the risk of chronic diseases, and promoting mental well-being.

3. **Abundant Nutrition:**
   - Consuming a balanced and nutrient-rich diet provides the body with essential vitamins, minerals, and antioxidants.
   - Whole foods, including fruits, vegetables, lean proteins, and whole grains, support optimal functioning of organs and systems.
   - Proper nutrition is fundamental for energy production, immune function, and the prevention of nutritional deficiencies.

4. **Lifestyle Balance:**
   - Prioritizing sufficient sleep allows the body to rest, recover, and rejuvenate, contributing to overall health.
   - Managing stress through mindfulness practices, meditation, and enjoyable activities helps maintain hormonal balance.
   - Balancing work, relationships, and personal time fosters mental and emotional well-being.

5. **Trusting God's Timing:**
   - Trusting in God's timing reduces stress and anxiety, positively impacting mental and emotional health.
   - Recognizing that God is in control can alleviate the pressure to meet unrealistic deadlines, leading to a more balanced and peaceful life.

6. **Holistic Approach:**
   - Incorporating mental and emotional well-being into the health routine through practices like counseling or self-reflection.
   - Positive relationships and social connections contribute to overall life satisfaction, impacting mental health positively.
   - Recognizing the interconnectedness of physical, mental, and spiritual aspects fosters a comprehensive approach to well-being.

By integrating these principles, individuals can create a holistic and sustainable approach to health that aligns with God's design for their well-being. Each element plays a crucial role in achieving optimal health and fulfilling the purpose embedded within our physical bodies.

Workbook-Body Care Worksheet Page 86

Harmony among the three parts of our being—body, mind, and spirit—is not only a concept aligned with the divine design but a crucial aspect of our overall well-being. Each part plays a distinct role, contributing to the synergy required for a balanced and purposeful life.

1. Highlighting the Role of Each Part:
Spirit: The spirit serves as the anchor, the connection to the divine. Its role is to stay attuned to heaven, receiving guidance, renewal, and purpose. As the conduit to the spiritual realm, the spirit provides the necessary strength and direction for navigating life's journey.

Soul: The soul embodies the heart and mind. It's the seat of our emotions, thoughts, and intellect. In essence, the soul serves as the bridge between the spiritual and the earthly, allowing us to connect with ourselves, others, and, most importantly, with God. The soul ensures that our actions align with divine principles and purposes.

Body: The body acts as the vessel, the tangible instrument through which the will and purpose of God are manifested. It is the delivery vehicle for our spiritual essence and the means by which we interact with the physical world. A healthy and robust body is essential for enduring the challenges of life and effectively carrying out the tasks assigned by God.

When each part functions in harmony, a powerful synergy emerges. The spirit receives divine guidance, the soul embodies God's wisdom and love, and the body executes God's purposes in the world. This cohesive functioning creates an unstoppable force, aligning our entire being with the divine plan.

2. Exploring Imbalance and its Consequences:
Spiritual Imbalance: Being excessively focused on spirituality while neglecting practical earthly matters can lead to an imbalance. The Bible warns against being "so heavenly-minded that we are of no earthly value." It emphasizes the importance of translating spiritual insights into practical, impactful actions that benefit both ourselves and others.

Emotional Imbalance: Overindulgence in emotions, whether through unchecked passions or negative thought patterns, can disturb the harmony. Emotions are essential, but an imbalance, whether through excessive worry, anger, or unfettered desires, can hinder spiritual connection and impair decision-making.

Physical Imbalance: Neglecting the body's well-being, whether through unhealthy habits or excessive focus on physical pursuits, can also disrupt harmony. A neglected body may struggle to endure the challenges of life, hindering the effective execution of God's purposes.

In summary, maintaining harmony among the three parts involves recognizing and honoring the unique roles of each component. Striking a balance ensures that our spiritual, emotional, and physical aspects work in tandem, fostering holistic well-being and enabling us to fulfill our divine calling in a purposeful and impactful manner.

Biblical Insight on Achieving Harmony in Body, Mind, and Spirit:
The Bible provides profound guidance on achieving harmony within our tripartite nature—body, mind, and spirit. The sacred text emphasizes the interconnectedness of these facets and offers timeless principles for fostering balance and well-being.

1. Spiritual Practices:
Daily Prayer and Meditation (Philippians 4:6-7): "Do not be anxious about anything, but in every situation, by prayer and petition, with thanksgiving, present your requests to God. And the peace of God, which transcends all understanding, will guard your hearts and your minds in Christ Jesus."
Scripture Reading (Psalm 119:105): "Your word is a lamp for my feet, a light on my path." Regularly immersing ourselves in God's Word illuminates our spiritual path and aligns our thoughts with divine wisdom.

2. Emotional Well-being:
Mindfulness and Self-Awareness (Proverbs 4:23): "Above all else, guard your heart, for everything you do flows from it." Cultivating mindfulness aligns our thoughts with God's truth, promoting emotional well-being.

Journaling (Psalm 139:23-24): "Search me, God, and know my heart; test me and know my anxious thoughts. See if there is any offensive way in me and lead me in the way everlasting." Journaling allows introspection and invites God into our emotional spaces.

3. Physical Well-being:
Balanced Nutrition (1 Corinthians 6:19-20): "Do you not know that your bodies are temples of the Holy Spirit, who is in you, whom you have received from God? You are not your own; you were bought at a price. Therefore, honor God with your bodies." Nourishing our bodies honors the temple God entrusted to us.

Regular Exercise (1 Timothy 4:8): "For physical training is of some value, but godliness has value for all things, holding promise for both the present life and the life to come." Recognizing the value of physical well-being aligns with biblical principles.

4. Holistic Practices:
Nature Connection (Psalm 19:1): "The heavens declare the glory of God; the skies proclaim the work of his hands." Spending time in nature allows us to witness God's creation, fostering a sense of connection and peace.

5. Rest and Recovery:
Adequate Sleep (Psalm 4:8): "In peace, I will lie down and sleep, for you alone, Lord, make me dwell in safety." Prioritizing rest acknowledges God's role in providing security and peace.
Mindful Rest (Matthew 11:28): "Come to me, all you who are weary and burdened, and I will give you rest." Mindful rest aligns with Christ's invitation to find solace in Him.

6. Community and Relationships:
Positive Connections (Proverbs 27:17): "As iron sharpens iron, so one person sharpens another." Healthy relationships contribute to mutual growth and sharpening.
Serve Others (Galatians 5:13): "Serve one another humbly in love." Serving others aligns with the biblical call to love and selflessly contribute to the well-being of those around us.

7. Continuous Learning:
Personal Development (Proverbs 18:15): "An intelligent heart acquires knowledge, and the ear of the wise seeks knowledge." The pursuit of knowledge is encouraged in the pursuit of wisdom and understanding.

Harmony among body, mind, and spirit is deeply rooted in biblical principles. As we heed the wisdom found in Scripture, we embark on a journey towards holistic well-being, aligning ourselves with God's design for a purposeful and harmonious life.

At the heart of our being lies the profound essence of purpose—an intricate composition woven with our identity, gifts, talents, and unique calling. Purpose is not a mere abstraction; it is the inherent reason for our creation, the compass guiding our journey through life. Understanding and embracing our purpose is central to personal development, a journey that commences with unraveling the layers of our existence.

Defining Purpose:

Purpose, in its essence, is the profound realization that our lives are imbued with significance and intentionality. It is the divine blueprint that orchestrates our existence, shaping our character, influencing our choices, and propelling us toward a destiny crafted by the Creator. In the intricate design of our being, purpose is the thread that weaves together the fabric of our identity, granting us a sense of direction and fulfillment.

The Spiritual Archive of Purpose:
Within the recesses of our spirit lies the full divine file of our purpose and potential. Every nuance of our calling, every fragment of our unique giftings and talents, is housed in this sacred archive. The challenge often lies not in the absence of purpose but in our awareness and acknowledgment of it. Our spirit, illuminated by the indwelling presence of the Holy Spirit, serves as the repository of divine revelation regarding our purpose.

Obvious Purpose Pieces:
Our purpose is not an enigmatic puzzle; rather, it is a mosaic of obvious pieces waiting to be assembled. These pieces manifest in the form of our unique giftings, talents, and passions. Yet, the journey toward embracing our purpose is not always straightforward. Many have had their purpose suppressed by the opinions of others, their calling dismissed or discouraged, leading to a stifling of their innate gifts. Rediscovering and embracing these purpose pieces often involves breaking free from the chains of external expectations and allowing the authenticity of our divine design to emerge.

Revelation Over Time:
While some purpose pieces may be obvious, the full scope of our purpose often unfolds gradually. God, in His wisdom, reveals the intricacies of our purpose over time, unveiling purpose places, purpose people, and purpose positions. This gradual unfolding invites us to trust in the divine timing of revelation and to cultivate a deep relationship with God, who, as the author of our purpose, holds the key to its unfolding.

In my personal journey, I have come to realize the profound interconnectedness of the various roles I embody. As a husband and a father, I recognize that the effectiveness and anointing upon my calling as a speaker and writer are intricately tied to my faithful stewardship in these foundational roles. It is not merely about compartmentalizing these aspects of my life but understanding that the authenticity and depth with which I fulfill my responsibilities as a husband and father directly influence the impact of my broader purpose.

The integrity and anointing of my words and teachings find their source in the genuine love, care, and guidance I provide within the sacred walls of my family. It is within the context of being a devoted husband and a present father that I discover the nuances of leadership, compassion, and sacrifice, which, in turn, enrich and empower my capacity to speak and write with authenticity and depth.

This revelation underscores the importance of holistic living and alignment with God's purposes in every sphere of life. My journey as a husband and a father is not a separate entity from my journey as a speaker and a writer; rather, they are intertwined threads in the fabric of my purpose. It serves as a constant reminder that the effectiveness of my public calling is intimately linked to the genuine expression of love, wisdom, and grace within the private sanctuary of my family life.

In conclusion, uncovering the significance of purpose in personal development is an ongoing journey of self-discovery and alignment with God's divine design. As we delve into the depths of our being, acknowledge the obvious purpose pieces, and trust God's unfolding revelation, we step into the fullness of our purpose—a purpose intricately connected to the very heartbeat of our Creator.

Understanding and embracing our individual purposes is a transformative journey that extends far beyond personal fulfillment; it profoundly impacts the quality and dynamics of our relationships. The interconnectedness of personal purpose and relational well-being becomes evident as we navigate our roles in various spheres of life.

Pursuing our God-given purpose aligns us with divine timing and intentionality, fostering a sense of harmony in our lives. This harmony extends to our relationships, as the clarity and fulfillment derived from living out our purpose positively affect how we engage with others. When we are aligned with our purpose, we bring authenticity, passion, and a sense of direction to our interactions, creating a positive ripple effect on those around us.

Conversely, neglecting or misaligning with our purpose can strain relationships. Pursuing endeavors outside of God's will or timing may lead to overworking relationships, causing unnecessary stress and tension. When individuals are disconnected from their purpose, they might feel unfulfilled, leading to dissatisfaction that can spill over into their interactions with others. This misalignment can result in a lack of clarity, direction, and authenticity in relationships, hindering their potential for growth and connection.

The impact of purpose on relationships extends beyond the personal realm to the roles we fulfill in various capacities. Those who actively pursue their purpose within the roles of a spouse, parent, friend, or colleague bring a sense of dedication and intentionality to their interactions. They understand the divine significance of each role and seek to fulfill them with excellence. In contrast, individuals who neglect their purpose within these roles may inadvertently undermine the potential for positive, impactful relationships.

In essence, understanding and living out our purpose is not just an individual journey but a communal one. The transformative influence of purpose on the quality of relationships highlights the intricate dance between personal fulfillment and relational dynamics, emphasizing the significance of purpose-driven living in fostering healthy, meaningful connections with those around us.

Here is a list of biblical purposes for various roles that individuals commonly hold in relationships and the marketplace:

- Husband/Father: Purpose: To love and lead their families sacrificially, providing spiritual guidance and support. Biblical Reference: Ephesians 5:25, Joshua 24:15
- Wife/Mother: Purpose: To support and complement their husbands, nurturing and guiding their children in the ways of the Lord. Biblical Reference: Proverbs 31:10-31, Titus 2:4-5
- Parent: Purpose: To train and discipline children in the ways of the Lord, shaping their character and instilling godly values. Biblical Reference: Proverbs 22:6, Deuteronomy 6:6-7
- Friend: Purpose: To provide support, encouragement, and accountability, reflecting the love of Christ in relationships. Biblical Reference: Proverbs 17:17, Ecclesiastes 4:9-12
- Employee/Colleague: Purpose: To work diligently and ethically, serving others with excellence and reflecting Christ's character in the workplace. Biblical Reference: Colossians 3:23-24, Ephesians 6:5-8
- Employer/Leader: Purpose: To lead with integrity, providing a positive and fair work environment, and fostering the personal and professional growth of employees. Biblical Reference: Colossians 4:1, Proverbs 29:2
- Teacher/Mentor: Purpose: To impart knowledge, wisdom, and character, guiding others toward personal and spiritual growth. Biblical Reference: Proverbs 9:9, Matthew 28:19-20
- Neighbor: Purpose: To show love and kindness to those around, actively seeking their welfare and sharing the hope of Christ. Biblical Reference: Luke 10:27-37, Matthew 5:16
- Citizen: Purpose: To contribute positively to society, obeying governing authorities, and being a source of justice and righteousness. Biblical Reference: Romans 13:1-7, Jeremiah 29:7
- Church Member: Purpose: To actively participate in a local body of believers, using spiritual gifts for the edification of the church and reaching out to the community. Biblical Reference: 1 Corinthians 12:12-27, Hebrews 10:24-25

Understanding and aligning with these biblical purposes for various roles can provide a foundation for individuals to live out God's original intent in their relationships and the marketplace.

Understanding and embracing our individual purposes is a transformative journey that extends far beyond personal fulfillment; it profoundly impacts the quality and dynamics of our relationships. The interconnectedness of personal purpose and relational well-being becomes evident as we navigate our roles in various spheres of life.

Pursuing our God-given purpose aligns us with divine timing and intentionality, fostering a sense of harmony in our lives. This harmony extends to our relationships, as the clarity and fulfillment derived from living out our purpose positively affect how we engage with others. When we are aligned with our purpose, we bring authenticity, passion, and a sense of direction to our interactions, creating a positive ripple effect on those around us.

Conversely, neglecting or misaligning with our purpose can strain relationships. Pursuing endeavors outside of God's will or timing may lead to overworking relationships, causing unnecessary stress and tension. When individuals are disconnected from their purpose, they might feel unfulfilled, leading to dissatisfaction that can spill over into their interactions with others. This misalignment can result in a lack of clarity, direction, and authenticity in relationships, hindering their potential for growth and connection.

The impact of purpose on relationships extends beyond the personal realm to the roles we fulfill in various capacities. Those who actively pursue their purpose within the roles of a spouse, parent, friend, or colleague bring a sense of dedication and intentionality to their interactions. They understand the divine significance of each role and seek to fulfill them with excellence. In contrast, individuals who neglect their purpose within these roles may inadvertently undermine the potential for positive, impactful relationships.

In essence, understanding and living out our purpose is not just an individual journey but a communal one. The transformative influence of purpose on the quality of relationships highlights the intricate dance between personal fulfillment and relational dynamics, emphasizing the significance of purpose-driven living in fostering healthy, meaningful connections with those around us.

Here is a list of biblical purposes for various roles that individuals commonly hold in relationships and the marketplace:

- Husband/Father: Purpose: To love and lead their families sacrificially, providing spiritual guidance and support. Biblical Reference: Ephesians 5:25, Joshua 24:15
- Wife/Mother: Purpose: To support and complement their husbands, nurturing and guiding their children in the ways of the Lord. Biblical Reference: Proverbs 31:10-31, Titus 2:4-5
- Parent: Purpose: To train and discipline children in the ways of the Lord, shaping their character and instilling godly values. Biblical Reference: Proverbs 22:6, Deuteronomy 6:6-7
- Friend: Purpose: To provide support, encouragement, and accountability, reflecting the love of Christ in relationships. Biblical Reference: Proverbs 17:17, Ecclesiastes 4:9-12
- Employee/Colleague: Purpose: To work diligently and ethically, serving others with excellence and reflecting Christ's character in the workplace. Biblical Reference: Colossians 3:23-24, Ephesians 6:5-8
- Employer/Leader: Purpose: To lead with integrity, providing a positive and fair work environment, and fostering the personal and professional growth of employees. Biblical Reference: Colossians 4:1, Proverbs 29:2
- Teacher/Mentor: Purpose: To impart knowledge, wisdom, and character, guiding others toward personal and spiritual growth. Biblical Reference: Proverbs 9:9, Matthew 28:19-20
- Neighbor: Purpose: To show love and kindness to those around, actively seeking their welfare and sharing the hope of Christ. Biblical Reference: Luke 10:27-37, Matthew 5:16
- Citizen: Purpose: To contribute positively to society, obeying governing authorities, and being a source of justice and righteousness. Biblical Reference: Romans 13:1-7, Jeremiah 29:7
- Church Member: Purpose: To actively participate in a local body of believers, using spiritual gifts for the edification of the church and reaching out to the community. Biblical Reference: 1 Corinthians 12:12-27, Hebrews 10:24-25

- Entrepreneur/Business Owner: Purpose: To steward resources wisely, create value for society, and operate the business with integrity and fairness. Entrepreneur is called to impact the marketplace positively, using their skills and innovation to contribute to the well-being of employees, customers, and the community. Biblical Reference: Proverbs 16:11, Colossians 3:23-24, Proverbs 22:29, Luke 16:10

Understanding and aligning with these biblical purposes for various roles can provide a foundation for individuals to live out God's original intent in their relationships and the marketplace.

Discovering our general purpose involves a journey of self-discovery and a deep connection with God. Here are practical steps to guide you in finding your purpose:

1. Cultivate a Relationship with God: Begin by strengthening your relationship with God through prayer, meditation, and studying His Word. Seek His guidance and wisdom in understanding your unique purpose.

2. Reflect on Your Passions: Take time to reflect on what truly excites and energizes you. Your passions often provide clues to your purpose. Consider the activities that make you lose track of time or those that bring you deep fulfillment.

3. Identify Your Natural Abilities: Assess your innate talents and abilities. God often aligns our purpose with the skills and gifts He has already bestowed upon us. What comes naturally to you? What are you naturally good at?

4. Explore Life Experiences: Examine your life experiences, both positive and challenging. These experiences can shape your purpose and contribute to how you can impact others positively. Your unique journey holds valuable insights.

5. Seek Wise Counsel: Engage with mentors, counselors, or spiritual leaders who can provide guidance and offer insights into your strengths and potential purpose. Their external perspective can bring valuable clarity.

6. Pursue Personal Development: Invest in your personal development by acquiring new skills and knowledge. Sometimes, God reveals our purpose progressively as we grow and develop in various aspects of our lives.

7. Test and Explore: Be open to testing different paths. Sometimes, purpose becomes clearer through practical exploration. Volunteer, engage in different activities, or take on new challenges to see where your passion aligns with impacting others.

8. Listen to Inner Promptings: Pay attention to your inner promptings and convictions. God often communicates with us through our intuition and conscience. Trusting these inner nudges can lead you closer to your purpose.

Remember that discovering your purpose is often a journey, not a destination. Be patient with yourself and trust that God is guiding you every step of the way. As you align your life with Him, clarity about your general purpose will unfold.

Workbook Pages
- **Purpose Discovery Worksheet Page 91**
- **Purpose Journal Page 93**
- **Intuition Journal Page 97**

Personal Development

Personal development is not just a trendy concept; it is a profound aspect of our journey towards becoming the best versions of ourselves. The process of personal development is pivotal because it shapes who we are and influences the impact we have on the world around us. When we neglect personal development, we do a disservice not only to ourselves but also to those in our sphere of influence.

One of the critical areas where personal development plays a crucial role is in relationships. Individuals who resist personal growth and remain stuck in their ways can inadvertently sabotage relationships. The unwillingness to reflect, learn, and make necessary changes hinders the depth and growth of connections. A stagnant person in a relationship creates an environment where learning, understanding, and adaptability become challenging.

Embracing personal development is, in essence, embracing the power of becoming. Life is not about pursuing what's already developed but about growing in such a way that opportunities and experiences pursue us. The concept of "becoming" holds within it the words "be" and "come." The more we focus on being—developing our character, skills, and mindset—the more life-transforming experiences and opportunities will come our way. It's a principle that echoes the truth that we attract not what we desire but what we are.

As human beings, not human havings or human desirings, the essence of our being defines the outcomes we attract. The question becomes: Who are you being? Because what you be will determine what comes to you. Investigating your desired next level is essential to understand what that level requires. It's about aligning yourself with the weight and responsibility of the next level. Just as God won't put more on us than we can bear, personal development ensures that we are equipped to manage and balance the weight of our responsibilities.

In essence, personal development is a journey of self-discovery, growth, and refinement. It enables us to navigate the complexities of life with resilience, adaptability, and wisdom. By investing in our personal development, we not only enhance our own lives but also contribute positively to the relationships and communities we are a part of. It's an ongoing process that propels us toward our purpose and allows us to make a meaningful impact in the world.

Embracing Belovedness: From God to Self-Love

At the core of our identity lies the profound truth that we are beloved by God. This recognition, deeply rooted in biblical principles, forms the bedrock of our understanding of self-love and self-care. The Scriptures abound with verses that affirm God's love for us, inviting us to embrace our status as His beloved children.

One such scripture is found in Zephaniah 3:17, where we are reminded that the Lord rejoices over us with singing and delights in us. This imagery paints a vivid picture of a loving Father expressing joy and affection towards His cherished children. The Gospel of John, in 1 John 4:16, declares that God is love, and whoever abides in love abides in God, and God abides in them. This profound truth underscores the inseparable connection between God's nature and the essence of love itself.

Romans 8:38-39 encapsulates the powerful assurance of God's unwavering love for us: "For I am convinced that neither death nor life, neither angels nor demons, neither the present nor the future, nor any powers, neither height nor depth, nor anything else in all creation, will be able to separate us from the love of God that is in Christ Jesus our Lord." This scripture stands as an unshakable foundation, emphasizing the enduring and all-encompassing nature of God's love, reinforcing the truth that nothing can separate us from His boundless and eternal love.

As we delve into the recognition of ourselves as God's beloved, we must also turn to the words of Jesus in Matthew 22:39, where He commands us to love our neighbors as ourselves. This command assumes a foundational self-love that flows from our understanding of being loved by God. Recognizing our belovedness is not a self-centered endeavor but a transformative realization that propels us to love ourselves in a way that aligns with God's perspective.

The Apostle Paul, in Ephesians 5:29, provides a compelling analogy, stating that no one hates their own body but feeds and cares for it. This draws a parallel between our relationship with ourselves and the care God desires for us. Accepting ourselves as beloved by God lays the groundwork for fostering a healthy self-love that acknowledges the inherent value and worth placed upon us by our Creator.

In the upcoming sections, we will explore the profound impact of God's love on our ability to love ourselves and engage in self-care. This journey towards embracing belovedness extends beyond sentimentality; it is a foundational principle that shapes our attitudes, actions, and relationships. As we recognize ourselves as God's beloved, we embark on a transformative journey toward cultivating genuine self-love and holistic well-being.

Embracing the truth that we are God's beloved holds transformative power, for it is in the awareness of His love that we find the strength to navigate life's challenges and grow in spiritual maturity. Recognizing ourselves as God's beloved is pivotal for several reasons.

Firstly, awareness of God's love serves as an anchor for our identity. In a world where external influences and societal standards often attempt to define us, understanding that we are beloved by God provides a solid foundation. It shields us from the detrimental effects of comparison, insecurity, and the relentless pursuit of external validation.

Secondly, the acknowledgment of being God's beloved is a catalyst for spiritual growth. As the Scripture affirms, it is the goodness of God that draws us to repentance (Romans 2:4). When we grasp the depth and constancy of God's love, it fuels our desire to align our lives with His will. Awareness of His love becomes the driving force behind our pursuit of righteousness and transformation.

However, several factors can obscure our recognition of being God's beloved. Among them are feelings of guilt, shame, inadequacy, comparison, and busyness. These hindrances can cloud our spiritual vision, preventing us from fully experiencing and internalizing God's love.

To better recognize ourselves as God's beloved, we can adopt practical strategies. Firstly, engaging in regular self-reflection and prayer helps us confront feelings of guilt and shame, allowing God's love to bring healing and restoration. Additionally, cultivating gratitude and contentment counters the toxic effects of comparison and inadequacy, fostering a deep sense of being loved as we are.
Moreover, carving out intentional moments of stillness and solitude in our busy lives creates space for God's love to permeate our awareness. By identifying and addressing these barriers, we open ourselves to the life-transforming truth that we are God's beloved, allowing His love to shape our identity and influence every aspect of our lives.

Understanding the dynamics of self-love introduces a profound concept of limiting access and establishing boundaries. Those who truly love themselves recognize the value of setting limits on who gets unrestricted entry into the sacred realms of their lives. This involves a careful consideration of who deserves to touch us, speak into our lives, reside in our minds, lead us spiritually, and become intertwined with our souls on an emotional level.

Self-love is a protective force that acknowledges not everyone is entitled to live rent-free in our minds or wield influence over our decisions. It prompts us to scrutinize the individuals seeking access and ask whether they genuinely contribute to our well-being and personal growth. In essence, self-love becomes a barrier against those who may only bring toxicity, negativity, or dissonance into our lives.

Consider the analogy of ourselves as Rolls-Royces and others as Rolls-Royces selling themselves cheap. Those who understand their worth recognize that they are not relegated to the clearance rack, accessible to anyone willing to make minimal efforts. Instead, they position themselves behind checkpoints and clearances, demanding a level of investment that aligns with their inherent value.

Understanding your worth also involves recognizing the maintenance fees associated with allowing someone access to your heart. While someone might have the allure to catch your attention, the critical question is whether they possess what it takes to enhance and embrace your value. Not everyone is equipped to appreciate, uplift, and honor the unique qualities you bring to the table.

The lesson often learned through experience is that not everyone deserves access to the depths of your being. It's crucial to distinguish between offering an act of love, such as acknowledgment, and allowing someone unbridled access. Self-love teaches us to discern, to evaluate the intentions and contributions of those seeking entry, ensuring that the access granted aligns with the enhancement of our well-being rather than diminishing our value. In the end, understanding your worth becomes a compass guiding you to establish boundaries and limits that safeguard the sanctity of your heart and soul.

Self-care is often misunderstood as selfishness, but in reality, it is a vital practice that enables individuals to care for others more effectively. The Bible encourages us to cast our cares on God because He cares for us (1 Peter 5:7). However, many individuals find themselves overwhelmed by the weight of caring for others and neglecting their own well-being. It's crucial to understand that self-care is not only acceptable but also necessary.

The analogy of casting cares on God implies that there is a limit to what an individual should carry. Just as God cares for us, He desires us to care for ourselves within the boundaries of His grace. It is not an act of selfishness but a recognition of our limitations and a commitment to maintaining our physical, emotional, and spiritual health.

Empathy, a beautiful quality, can turn detrimental when it transforms into emptying oneself for others without replenishing. People often find themselves caring too much about the opinions of others, neglecting their own needs in the process. Recognizing that God cares about every aspect of our lives, including how we delegate our care, empowers us to prioritize self-care without guilt.
Self-care is an act of stewardship. God entrusted us with the care of our bodies, minds, and spirits. Neglecting self-care diminishes our ability to fulfill our responsibilities and serve others effectively. Just as an empty well cannot quench the thirst of others, an empty individual cannot provide the necessary care to those around them.

Understanding the boundaries of care and practicing self-care is not only biblical but also a wise approach to life. God does not call us to carry burdens beyond what He has graced us to handle. Learning to care for ourselves allows us to operate from a place of abundance, ensuring that we can pour into the lives of others without running dry. It is not an act of selfishness but an acknowledgment of God's design for holistic well-being.

The Power of "Yes" and "No" in Self-Care and Communication
In the teachings of Jesus, a profound lesson echoes through the ages: "But let your 'Yes' be 'Yes,' and your 'No,' 'No.' For whatever is more than these is from the evil one" (Matthew 5:37). This timeless wisdom emphasizes the importance of integrity and clarity in our communication, particularly when it comes to our commitments.

The Integrity of "Yes" and "No":
Our "yes" and "no" are more than mere words; they are solemn pledges and firm refusals, respectively. When we say "yes" to a commitment, it's a genuine and intentional agreement, signifying our dedication to follow through. On the other hand, when we say "no," it is a clear and unequivocal rejection, leaving no room for confusion or manipulation.

The Value of Your "Yes":
Your "yes" is a precious commodity, representing your time, energy, and commitment. It is the front door to the facility that houses your resources. Not everyone deserves access to your "yes," and being discerning about who gains entry is crucial. Your "yes" is a commitment that should align with your values, priorities, and, most importantly, God's guidance.

142

Guarding Your Resources:
Saying "yes" to the wrong person or commitment can divert resources intended for more important or God-ordained purposes. It's a strategic decision, a careful consideration of where your time and energy will be invested. Learning to protect your "yes" is not just about personal boundaries but also a spiritual discipline, ensuring that you steward your resources wisely.

The Art of Saying "No":
Saying "no" is not a negative act but a protective one. It's a necessary form of self-care and a demonstration of your commitment to stewarding the resources God has entrusted to you. Saying "no" randomly at times can be a revealing strategy. It helps discern those who genuinely care about you and respect your boundaries from those who might not have your best interests at heart.

Spiritual Discipline in Communication:
Embracing the teachings of Jesus regarding our "yes" and "no" is not only about effective communication but also a spiritual discipline. It reflects your dedication to clear and honest interactions, ensuring that your commitments align with your values and God's guidance.
In your journey of self-care and relational wisdom, let your "yes" and "no" be guided by integrity, purpose, and a commitment to steward your resources for God's glory.

Workbook-Personal Development Worksheet: Becoming the Person You Must Be 100

SELF-RELATABILITY

The 6 Pillars

Embarking on a journey to strengthen our relationship with ourselves involves navigating through the foundational pillars that uphold the fabric of our personal connection. These six pillars —authenticity, respect, empathy, humility, communication, and adaptability—serve as guiding principles, illuminating the path towards a more profound understanding and appreciation of who we are. As we delve into each of these pillars, we will unravel the transformative power they hold in cultivating a resilient and authentic relationship with ourselves, laying the groundwork for a more fulfilling and harmonious existence.

Authenticity Unveiled: Embracing the Undisputed Origin of Self

To be authentic is to embody an undisputed origin, to be genuine in the truest sense of the word. It signifies embracing the core of our being, unmasking the layers we've accumulated through experiences, societal expectations, and self-imposed ideals. Let's delve into the synonyms of authenticity — original, actual, real, true — to unravel the profound connection between being our genuine selves and fostering meaningful relationships:

1. Original:

Being authentic requires tapping into our original essence, the unaltered blueprint that God designed. Our originality is the unique fingerprint of our souls, untainted by external influences. Just as an original work of art holds intrinsic value, our authenticity is a masterpiece that carries inherent worth. In relationships, our original selves serve as the foundation upon which genuine connections are built.

2. Actual:

Authenticity calls for an unveiling of the actual self, unfiltered and unedited. It means presenting the reality of who we are, rather than a curated version. In relationships, embracing our actual selves fosters transparency and invites others to engage with the genuine person beneath the surface. It's an invitation for others to know and appreciate the unvarnished truth of our existence.

BE ORIGINAL

3. Real:
To be authentic is to be real — to live in truthfulness and sincerity. Authenticity dismantles the façades we may construct to conform to societal expectations. In relationships, realness establishes trust, creating an environment where individuals feel secure in being their true selves. It's a commitment to honesty that forms the bedrock of authentic connections.

4. True:
Authenticity aligns with truth, as being true to oneself involves an unwavering commitment to personal values, beliefs, and identity. In relationships, the truth of who we are resonates with others on a profound level. Genuine connections are forged when individuals recognize and celebrate each other's truths, fostering an environment of acceptance and understanding.

In the realm of relationships, authenticity becomes a magnet for God's best. When we are true to ourselves — our original, actual, real, and true selves — we align with the divine design instilled in us by our Creator. God's best for us is intricately connected to our willingness to be authentic. It involves recognizing that we are fearfully and wonderfully made, inviting God's transformative power into our lives and relationships.

As we unravel the layers and rediscover the undisputed origin of our selves, we pave the way for authentic connections that reflect the beauty of God's design. In the journey of authenticity, we attract not only the best versions of ourselves but also the best that God has in store for our relationships.

The Intrinsic Worth of Authenticity: A Parable of True Value
Consider the world of art, where masterpieces captivate hearts and minds, each stroke carrying the essence of the artist's soul. In this realm, authenticity holds immeasurable value. Let's delve into the analogy of an authentic piece of art versus a forgery to unveil the profound truth about the worth of being genuine in our relationships:

1. The Value of the Original:
In the art world, an original masterpiece possesses a value that transcends mere aesthetics. The brushstrokes, the artist's intent, the unique perspective — these elements contribute to the masterpiece's intrinsic worth. Similarly, in relationships, our original selves, untainted by imitation or pretense, carry a value that cannot be replicated. The depth of our experiences, the authenticity of our emotions, and the uniqueness of our character shape a masterpiece in the gallery of human connections.

2. Fake Imitations in Relationships:
Now, imagine a forgery attempting to mimic the beauty of an original artwork. In relationships, counterfeit personas may temporarily impress, but their lack of authenticity becomes glaring over time. People who present a façade, embellishing their lives or personalities, may seem like a hundred-dollar bill but lack the genuine value of an authentic one-dollar bill. The contrast is stark — the original, though seemingly less adorned, retains an enduring and indisputable value.

3. The Worth of Genuine Currency:
Consider the analogy of real currency. A genuine one-dollar bill will always hold more value than a counterfeit one hundred. Similarly, individuals who authentically represent themselves possess a depth of character that exceeds the superficial allure of those who project a false image. Authenticity is the true currency of relationships, and its worth surpasses any counterfeit attempts to inflate value.

4. The True Cost of Imitation:
In relationships, the cost of imitation is profound. Just as a fake $100 bill holds legal consequences, counterfeit interactions in relationships lead to the erosion of trust and authenticity. People may project an image of opulence or success, but when the truth is uncovered, the value diminishes. The enduring worth of genuine connections is built on authenticity, creating bonds that withstand the test of time.

In essence, the value of authenticity in relationships mirrors the art world's reverence for original masterpieces. Our genuine selves, with all our imperfections and uniqueness, are the true masterpieces in the gallery of human connection. In a world inundated with imitations, the authentic stands out, creating a lasting impact that far surpasses the fleeting allure of counterfeit connections. Just as art enthusiasts treasure the original, so do those who recognize the immeasurable worth of authenticity in relationships.

Unveiling the Masks
In the intricate dance of human interactions, people often don masks to navigate the complexities of relationships. These masks, metaphorical disguises donned to conceal authentic selves, are worn for various reasons – societal expectations, fear of judgment, or the desire to fit into predetermined molds. Understanding the common masks we wear provides a crucial insight into the dynamics of self-relationship. One prevalent mask is the façade of perfection. In a world that often values flawless exteriors, individuals may cloak their vulnerabilities behind a veneer of faultlessness. The fear of being perceived as imperfect can lead to the creation of a polished persona that deviates from their true selves. This façade, while offering a semblance of control, can hinder genuine self-connection.

Another common mask is the people-pleaser persona. Driven by a deep-seated need for external validation, individuals may adopt behaviors designed to appease others at the expense of their authenticity. This mask, though worn with good intentions, can obscure genuine emotions and desires, creating a barrier to cultivating a robust self-relationship.
The armor of invulnerability is yet another mask people may adopt. Fueled by past hurts or a fear of emotional exposure, individuals may craft a shield that deflects authenticity. This protective layer, although providing a sense of safety, can become a barrier to forming an intimate connection with oneself.

The impact of removing these masks on self-relationship is profound. It requires a courageous examination of one's fears, insecurities, and the societal pressures that prompt the adoption of these disguises. Unveiling the masks is a transformative process that involves acknowledging and embracing one's authentic self. It is an act of self-love, allowing the true self to step into the light, fostering a deeper, more genuine relationship with oneself. As the masks fall away, the raw beauty of authenticity emerges, paving the way for self-discovery and a more fulfilling connection with others.

Embracing the Canvas of Your True Self: A Personal Revelation
Allow me to share a personal journey that underscores the profound significance of embracing one's authentic self. During my middle and high school years, I found myself ensnared in the trap of societal expectations. Fueled by a desire to fit in and gain acceptance, I attempted to mold myself into a semblance of what I believed was culturally valuable.

In the quest for approval, I stifled my true Christian character, my ahead of my time intellegence, and my genuine love for learning. The narrative of popularity dictated that athleticism and conventional good looks were the coveted attributes, and I yearned to assimilate into that paradigm. The disparity between my authentic self and the perceived societal ideal left me feeling inadequate, overshadowed by the allure of conformity.

It wasn't until the pivotal age of 19, in the solitude of my dorm room, that God's gentle but compelling voice penetrated my heart. In that transformative moment, He affirmed that He had uniquely called and crafted me to be myself — a vessel through which He intended to impact the world. The revelation struck with an indescribable force, urging me to shed the mask of conformity and embrace the genuine contours of my being.

This newfound clarity propelled me into a journey of self-discovery and self-love. I began to release the shackles of societal expectations, acknowledging that trying to erase my true self to fit a predefined mold was a disservice to the purpose that God had instilled within me.
The journey of embracing my authentic self has not been without its challenges, but the freedom and fulfillment derived from living in authenticity far outweigh the fleeting allure of societal approval.

It became evident that people who fail to celebrate your authenticity are not your intended audience. God designed us to impress with our unique qualities and impact with our authentic selves, not to conform in an attempt to gain approval.

Today, I stand as a testament to the transformative power of embracing one's authentic self. The purpose that emerged from that pivotal moment of self-acceptance has allowed me to impact millions around the world. The journey towards authenticity is not about impressing those who fail to recognize your worth; it's about embracing the masterpiece that God has uniquely painted within you. As you embark on your journey, may you find the courage to unveil your true self, confident that your authenticity is the very essence through which you are destined to make a profound impact on the world.

Cultivating Authenticity for Better Self-Relatability

Embracing authenticity is a transformative journey that leads us back to our original selves, fostering a profound connection within. Here are practical steps to enhance self-relatability through the pillar of authenticity:

1. Self-Reflection: Begin by engaging in regular self-reflection. Take moments to ponder your thoughts, emotions, and actions. Ask yourself probing questions, exploring the motivations behind your choices. This introspective practice allows you to identify areas where authenticity may be compromised.

2. Embrace Vulnerability: Authenticity thrives in vulnerability. Allow yourself to be seen, flaws and all. Embracing vulnerability is not a sign of weakness but rather a testament to your courage. Share your true thoughts and emotions, even if they make you feel exposed, recognizing that authenticity is the birthplace of genuine connection.

3. Identify Core Values: Delve into your core values—those principles that define your beliefs and guide your decisions. Aligning your actions with these values strengthens authenticity. When you live in harmony with your deeply held beliefs, you reinforce a sense of self-integrity and coherence.

4. Shed Societal Expectations: Authenticity often involves shedding the layers of societal expectations that may have accumulated over time. Recognize that societal norms don't define your worth or identity. Allow your genuine self to emerge, irrespective of external pressures, and embrace the freedom that comes with being true to yourself.

5. Practice Mindfulness: Cultivate mindfulness to stay present in each moment. Authenticity flourishes when you're fully engaged in the now, allowing you to respond authentically to your thoughts and emotions. Mindfulness fosters self-awareness, a cornerstone of authentic living.

6. Learn from Setbacks: Understand that authenticity is a continuous process of growth. When setbacks occur, view them as opportunities for learning rather than failures. Reflect on these experiences, acknowledge the lessons they offer, and use them to refine your understanding of yourself.

7. Seek Genuine Connections: Surround yourself with individuals who encourage authenticity. Build relationships where you can express your true self without fear of judgment. Authentic connections provide a nurturing environment for personal growth and self-discovery.
By consciously integrating these practices into your life, you embark on a journey of self-discovery and self-affirmation. Authenticity becomes the bridge that reconnects you with your original self, laying the groundwork for a more profound and meaningful relationship with yourself.

The Ripple Effect: How Authenticity Transforms Relationships

The authenticity we cultivate within ourselves acts as a catalyst, permeating through various facets of our lives and relationships. Here's how being authentic with ourselves positively influences our connections with God, spouse, kids, friends, and those we serve in the marketplace:

1. Relationship with God: Authenticity is the cornerstone of a genuine relationship with God. When we approach our spirituality with openness and honesty, laying bare our true selves before the Divine, we create an authentic dialogue. God desires a relationship with our authentic selves, and as we embrace vulnerability in our connection with Him, our spiritual journey becomes a transformative and deeply personal experience.

2. Spousal Relationship: Authenticity is the glue that binds a marital relationship. When we are true to ourselves, we invite our spouses into an intimate connection, free from pretense. This openness fosters trust, emotional intimacy, and mutual understanding. Authenticity in marriage allows for growth as individuals and as a couple, deepening the bond between spouses.

3. Parent-Child Dynamics: Authenticity in parenting creates a safe space for children to navigate their own authenticity. When parents model genuine self-expression, children learn the value of embracing their true selves. Authenticity strengthens the parent-child bond, fostering communication and trust. It allows parents to guide and support their children in a way that aligns with the family's core values.

4. Friendships: Authenticity is the bedrock of meaningful friendships. True friends appreciate and connect with our genuine selves. When we are authentic in our friendships, we invite others to reciprocate, creating a supportive environment where individuals can grow together. Authentic friendships provide a refuge for shared experiences, empathy, and mutual encouragement.

5. Professional Relationships: In the marketplace, authenticity is a powerful asset. Authentic leaders and colleagues create an environment of trust and collaboration. When we bring our authentic selves to the workplace, we contribute to a positive and inclusive culture. Authenticity in professional relationships fosters innovation, effective communication, and a shared sense of purpose.

6. Service to Others: Authenticity enhances our ability to serve others with compassion and understanding. When we are genuine in our interactions, we create connections built on trust and empathy. Authentic service involves seeing others for who they truly are and meeting their needs with a sincere heart. By bringing our authentic selves into our service to others, we contribute to positive transformations in their lives.

In essence, the authenticity we cultivate within ourselves ripples through every relationship, enriching the fabric of our connections. It serves as a catalyst for deeper, more meaningful interactions, fostering a community where individuals feel seen, heard, and valued for their true selves.

Workbook-Authenticity Exploration Worksheet Page 102

Self-Respect

In the intricate dance of relationships, respect emerges as a central pillar, providing the foundational support for meaningful connections. At its core, respect is the recognition and acknowledgment of the inherent worth, dignity, and uniqueness of an individual. It goes beyond mere courtesy; it delves into a profound understanding of the divine artistry that shapes each person.

Self-respect, an essential component of this pillar, emanates from a deep reverence for the Creator's craftsmanship. The biblical adage that the fear of God is the beginning of wisdom holds a profound truth – a profound respect for God sets the stage for a healthy self-respect. When individuals comprehend the intricate design God has woven within them, they inherently develop a sense of self-worth and value.

Self-respect becomes a guiding force, influencing how individuals allow themselves to be treated by others. It serves as a compass, directing them away from relationships and interactions that compromise their dignity and self-worth. In essence, self-respect sets the standard for how individuals expect to be treated, fostering an environment where healthy boundaries and mutual regard flourish. The relationship between self-respect and respect for others is symbiotic. As individuals cultivate a deep appreciation for their own worth, they naturally extend that same respect to those around them. Respectful behavior becomes a natural outflow of recognizing the inherent value present in every individual, irrespective of differences or disagreements.

Respect, as a pillar of relatability, creates a harmonious atmosphere where individuals feel seen, heard, and valued. It forms the bedrock upon which healthy relationships are built, fostering an environment where diverse perspectives can coexist in unity. As you embark on the journey of relational growth, may you embrace the transformative power of respect – a force capable of enriching your connections and elevating the quality of your interactions with both yourself and others.

Insecurities: The Silent Eroder
Insecurities can stealthily infiltrate the fortress of self-respect, whispering doubts about one's worth and capabilities. Whether stemming from past experiences or societal expectations, insecurities cast shadows that distort the clarity of self-perception.
Neutralizing the Impact:
- Self-Reflection: Engage in introspection to identify the root causes of insecurities. Unearth these hidden fears and confront them head-on.
- Positive Affirmations: Counter negative thoughts with affirmations that reinforce your strengths and value. Consistent positive self-talk gradually weakens the grip of insecurities.
- Surround Yourself with Positivity: Cultivate relationships and environments that foster encouragement and positivity. A supportive community serves as a powerful antidote to the poison of insecurity.

By addressing insecurities through self-awareness and positive reinforcement, individuals can reclaim their self-respect and stand resilient in the face of doubt.

Comparisons: The Thief of Contentment
In a world where social comparison is almost inevitable, the act of measuring oneself against others becomes a subtle but potent underminer of self-respect. Constantly evaluating one's achievements, appearance, or life circumstances in relation to others can sow seeds of discontent and erode the foundation of self-worth.
Neutralizing the Impact:
- Cultivate Gratitude: Shift the focus from what others have to what you are grateful for in your own life. Gratitude counters the corrosive effects of comparison by fostering contentment.
- Set Personal Goals: Instead of benchmarking against others, set realistic and personalized goals. Celebrate your progress and achievements based on your unique journey.
- Mindful Awareness: Cultivate mindfulness to catch and redirect negative thought patterns associated with comparison. Being present in the moment allows you to appreciate your own worth.

By actively countering the habit of comparing oneself to others, individuals can safeguard their self-respect and find contentment in their unique journey, recognizing that each path is distinct and valuable.

Negative Self-Talk: The Silent Underminer
Negative self-talk, the internal dialogue that shapes one's perception of oneself, is a formidable force in either bolstering or undermining self-respect. When individuals engage in harsh self-criticism, harbor self-doubt, or perpetuate negative beliefs about their worth, it becomes a pervasive obstacle to maintaining a healthy level of self-respect.
Neutralizing the Impact:
- Practice Self-Compassion: Treat yourself with the same kindness and understanding that you would offer to a friend facing challenges. Develop a habit of self-compassion by acknowledging imperfections without harsh judgment.
- Affirmations: Counter negative self-talk with positive affirmations. Affirmations help rewire thought patterns and reinforce positive beliefs about oneself. Regularly affirming one's strengths and capabilities can fortify self-respect.
- Seek Support: Share your struggles with a trusted friend, family member, or mentor. Sometimes an external perspective can provide valuable insights and counteract the impact of negative self-talk.

By addressing negative self-talk head-on, individuals can create a more nurturing internal environment that upholds self-respect. This intentional shift in mindset contributes to a more positive self-image and reinforces the belief in one's inherent value.

The Fear of God: Foundation of Self-Respect and Wisdom
The scriptural injunction that "the fear of the Lord is the beginning of wisdom" (Proverbs 9:10) holds profound insights into the cultivation of self-respect and the acquisition of practical wisdom. The fear of God extends beyond mere trepidation; it encompasses a reverential awe and deep respect for the Creator and His divine design. This fear serves as the cornerstone upon which a robust framework of self-respect is erected.

Reverencing God's Design:
When individuals recognize and revere God as the master craftsman who intricately designed them, a transformative shift occurs. Understanding that each person is fearfully and wonderfully made (Psalm 139:14) fosters a sense of awe and appreciation for one's inherent value. This divine reverence becomes the bedrock upon which self-respect is anchored. It reframes the narrative, guiding individuals away from self-deprecation and toward an acknowledgment of their worthiness.

The Link Between Reverence and Wisdom:
The fear of God, transcending mere religiosity, sets the stage for the acquisition of wisdom. In a marriage, with children, or within the complexities of the workplace, wisdom becomes the practical application of divine principles. Reverencing God is the compass that directs individuals to navigate relationships, make ethical decisions, and embrace a lifestyle of honor and respect.

Wisdom as a Skill Cultivated Through Reverence:
Wisdom is not a static possession but a dynamic skill honed through a continual reverence for God's precepts. It involves applying divine truths in a manner that becomes second nature. A person who reverences God and walks in wisdom exhibits a distinct aura of self-respect and purpose. This emanation serves as an inspiration, influencing others to pursue a similar path of reverence and wisdom.

The Impact on Relationships:
Reverencing God has a cascading effect on relationships. A person who reveres the divine design within themselves establishes boundaries, refusing to allow others to handle them casually or disrespectfully. This extends to various spheres of life, such as marriage, parenting, and professional interactions. The fear of God becomes the guiding force that upholds self-respect and imparts the discernment to navigate relationships with wisdom.

In essence, the fear of God, far from inducing fearfulness, becomes the catalyst for profound self-respect and wisdom. It propels individuals to honor the divine imprint within themselves, fostering a lifestyle characterized by reverence, purpose, and impactful wisdom.

Negative Self-Talk: The Silent Underminer

Negative self-talk, the internal dialogue that shapes one's perception of oneself, is a formidable force in either bolstering or undermining self-respect. When individuals engage in harsh self-criticism, harbor self-doubt, or perpetuate negative beliefs about their worth, it becomes a pervasive obstacle to maintaining a healthy level of self-respect.

Neutralizing the Impact:

- Practice Self-Compassion: Treat yourself with the same kindness and understanding that you would offer to a friend facing challenges. Develop a habit of self-compassion by acknowledging imperfections without harsh judgment.
- Affirmations: Counter negative self-talk with positive affirmations. Affirmations help rewire thought patterns and reinforce positive beliefs about oneself. Regularly affirming one's strengths and capabilities can fortify self-respect.
- Seek Support: Share your struggles with a trusted friend, family member, or mentor. Sometimes an external perspective can provide valuable insights and counteract the impact of negative self-talk.

By addressing negative self-talk head-on, individuals can create a more nurturing internal environment that upholds self-respect. This intentional shift in mindset contributes to a more positive self-image and reinforces the belief in one's inherent value.

The Fear of God: Foundation of Self-Respect and Wisdom

The scriptural injunction that "the fear of the Lord is the beginning of wisdom" (Proverbs 9:10) holds profound insights into the cultivation of self-respect and the acquisition of practical wisdom. The fear of God extends beyond mere trepidation; it encompasses a reverential awe and deep respect for the Creator and His divine design. This fear serves as the cornerstone upon which a robust framework of self-respect is erected.

Reverencing God's Design:

When individuals recognize and revere God as the master craftsman who intricately designed them, a transformative shift occurs. Understanding that each person is fearfully and wonderfully made (Psalm 139:14) fosters a sense of awe and appreciation for one's inherent value. This divine reverence becomes the bedrock upon which self-respect is anchored. It reframes the narrative, guiding individuals away from self-deprecation and toward an acknowledgment of their worthiness.

The Link Between Reverence and Wisdom:

The fear of God, transcending mere religiosity, sets the stage for the acquisition of wisdom. In a marriage, with children, or within the complexities of the workplace, wisdom becomes the practical application of divine principles. Reverencing God is the compass that directs individuals to navigate relationships, make ethical decisions, and embrace a lifestyle of honor and respect.

Wisdom as a Skill Cultivated Through Reverence:

Wisdom is not a static possession but a dynamic skill honed through a continual reverence for God's precepts. It involves applying divine truths in a manner that becomes second nature. A person who reverences God and walks in wisdom exhibits a distinct aura of self-respect and purpose. This emanation serves as an inspiration, influencing others to pursue a similar path of reverence and wisdom.

The Impact on Relationships:

Reverencing God has a cascading effect on relationships. A person who reveres the divine design within themselves establishes boundaries, refusing to allow others to handle them casually or disrespectfully. This extends to various spheres of life, such as marriage, parenting, and professional interactions. The fear of God becomes the guiding force that upholds self-respect and imparts the discernment to navigate relationships with wisdom.

In essence, the fear of God, far from inducing fearfulness, becomes the catalyst for profound self-respect and wisdom. It propels individuals to honor the divine imprint within themselves, fostering a lifestyle characterized by reverence, purpose, and impactful wisdom.

Understanding how you should be treated and actively teaching others how to treat you are pivotal aspects of cultivating healthy relationships. First, self-awareness empowers you to recognize your intrinsic worth and establish clear boundaries. By acknowledging and respecting your own needs, you set the foundation for cultivating positive relationships. Furthermore, teaching others how to treat you involves effective communication, transparency, and consistent modeling of your expectations. This proactive approach ensures that the dynamics of your relationships align with your values and contribute to a harmonious and respectful environment. Ultimately, the interplay between learning how to be treated and teaching others is a crucial element in fostering relationships that are rooted in mutual understanding, respect, and fulfillment.

Teaching Yourself How to Be Treated:
- Time for Reflection: Take time to reflect on your values, needs, and boundaries. Understanding your worth is the first step in teaching yourself how you deserve to be treated.
- Educate on Boundaries: Clearly define your boundaries. Know what is acceptable and unacceptable in your interactions. When you enforce these boundaries, you send a powerful message about your expectations.
- Adapt a Positive Self-Talk: Cultivate a positive mindset. Remind yourself of your strengths and value. When you believe in your worth, it becomes easier to teach others how to treat you.
- Communicate Assertively: Practice assertive communication. Express your thoughts, feelings, and needs clearly and respectfully. Being open about your expectations allows others to understand how you want to be treated.
- Hold Firm to Principles: Stay committed to your core principles and values. Holding firm to these foundational beliefs provides a stable framework for teaching yourself how you want to be treated.

Teaching People How to Treat You:
- Transparency is Key: Be transparent about your expectations. Clearly communicate your needs and desires to others. When people know what you value, they are better equipped to align with those values.
- Exemplify Boundaries: Demonstrate your boundaries through consistent actions. When you consistently reinforce your limits, others learn to respect and adhere to them.
- Acknowledge Positive Behavior: Reinforce positive behavior with acknowledgment. When someone treats you well, express gratitude. This positive reinforcement encourages others to continue treating you with respect.
- Consistent Modeling: Model the behavior you desire. Treat others with the same level of respect and consideration that you expect. Leading by example is a powerful way to shape the dynamics of how you are treated.
- Hold Space for Growth: Recognize that people, including yourself, are capable of growth and change. Holding space for growth allows room for improvement in how you are treated, fostering a more positive and dynamic environment.

The Transformative Impact of Self-Respect on Relationships
Self-respect serves as the cornerstone of healthy and flourishing relationships across various spheres of life. Its influence extends far beyond personal well-being, significantly shaping the dynamics of interactions in marriage, parenting, the professional arena, family, and those under our influence.
- 1. Marriage:
  - In the context of marriage, self-respect establishes the foundation for mutual respect between partners. When individuals have a strong sense of self-worth, they are better equipped to communicate their needs, set boundaries, and engage in a relationship based on equality. This mutual self-respect fosters a partnership characterized by understanding, support, and shared growth.
- 2. Parenting:
  - Self-respect profoundly impacts parenting dynamics. Parents who prioritize self-respect model healthy behavior for their children. This modeling sets a standard for how individuals should be treated, teaching children the importance of self-worth and empowering them to establish their own boundaries in future relationships.
- 3. Professional Arena:
  - In the professional realm, self-respect contributes to a positive work environment. Individuals who respect themselves are more likely to foster respectful and collaborative relationships with colleagues, superiors, and subordinates. This, in turn, enhances teamwork, communication, and overall productivity within the workplace.

- 4. Family:
  - Within the family unit, self-respect is a powerful force that influences how family members interact. When each member values themselves, it creates an environment of mutual respect, open communication, and a shared commitment to the well-being of the family as a whole.
- 5. Influence on Others:
  - Those who exhibit self-respect naturally influence others around them. Whether in a mentorship role, leadership position, or any form of influence, individuals who uphold self-respect set a standard for how others should be treated. This influence ripples through various relationships, creating a positive and uplifting atmosphere.
- 6. Personal Growth:
  - Self-respect is intricately linked to personal growth. As individuals cultivate self-respect, they engage in continuous self-improvement and self-awareness. This personal growth positively impacts relationships, as it encourages adaptability, empathy, and a deeper understanding of oneself and others.

In essence, self-respect acts as a catalyst for building and nurturing strong, meaningful, and harmonious relationships across diverse aspects of life. Its transformative influence creates a ripple effect, fostering a culture of respect, understanding, and mutual support.

Navigating Disrespect: Setting Boundaries and Taking Action
Respecting oneself involves not only understanding one's worth but also knowing how to handle situations where that worth is undermined. Handling disrespect with grace and conviction requires a combination of setting clear boundaries and, when necessary, making tough decisions about who has a place in your life.
- 1. Set Clear Boundaries:
  - Establishing and communicating boundaries is paramount when faced with disrespect. Clearly articulate what behaviors are unacceptable and communicate these boundaries assertively. Whether in personal or professional relationships, let others know how you expect to be treated and what actions will not be tolerated.
- 2. Identify Disrespectful Behaviors:
  - Recognize the signs of disrespectful behavior. This may include belittling comments, dismissive attitudes, or actions that undermine your well-being. By identifying disrespectful behaviors early on, you empower yourself to address the issue proactively.
- 3. Communicate Assertively:
  - When faced with disrespect, it's crucial to communicate assertively rather than aggressively. Express your feelings and concerns calmly and directly. Use "I" statements to convey how the behavior affects you personally, fostering a constructive dialogue.
- 4. Evaluate Intent vs. Impact:
  - Consider the intent behind the disrespectful behavior versus its impact on you. Some actions may stem from ignorance rather than malice. Assessing the intent helps you decide whether the relationship can be salvaged through open communication and mutual understanding.
- 5. Give Feedback:
  - Offer feedback on the specific behaviors that crossed your boundaries. Be specific about what was inappropriate and why. This clarity helps the other person understand the impact of their actions and provides an opportunity for correction.
- 6. Establish Consequences:
  - Clearly communicate the consequences of continued disrespect. Let the individual know that persistent disregard for your boundaries will result in a change in the nature of the relationship. This may include limiting contact or, in extreme cases, ending the relationship altogether.
- 7. Cut Off Toxic Relationships:
  - Recognize when a relationship has become toxic and is consistently detrimental to your well-being. If efforts to address disrespect prove futile, it may be necessary to cut ties. This decision is about self-preservation, ensuring that you prioritize your mental and emotional health.
- 8. Seek Support:
  - Reach out to friends, family, or a support network for guidance and encouragement. Discussing your experiences with trusted individuals provides perspective and emotional support during challenging times.

153

- 9. Prioritize Self-Care:
  - After setting boundaries or making the tough decision to cut off a relationship, prioritize self-care. Focus on activities and relationships that uplift and rejuvenate you. Nurturing your well-being is essential after navigating disrespect.

Remember, respecting yourself means taking action when faced with disrespect. By setting clear boundaries, communicating assertively, and making decisions in alignment with your well-being, you empower yourself to cultivate healthy and respectful relationships.

Boosting Self-RESPECT: Practical Strategies
Respect is not only about how others treat you but also about how you treat yourself. Elevating your level of self-respect is a journey of self-discovery and self-care. Here are practical strategies to boost your self-respect, using points that spell "RESPECT":

- 1. Recognize Your Worth:
  - Acknowledge your inherent value and worth as a unique individual. Recognize your strengths, talents, and achievements. Affirm yourself daily with positive affirmations that reinforce your sense of self-worth.
- 2. Embrace Your Authenticity:
  - Embrace your true self and authenticity without apology. Celebrate your quirks, imperfections, and unique qualities that make you who you are. Refrain from comparing yourself to others and instead focus on being the best version of yourself.
- 3. Set Boundaries:
  - Establish clear boundaries to protect your physical, emotional, and mental well-being. Learn to say no to activities, relationships, or situations that compromise your values or drain your energy. Honor your boundaries and communicate them assertively to others.
- 4. Practice Self-Care:
  - Prioritize self-care activities that nurture your mind, body, and spirit. Engage in activities that bring you joy, relaxation, and fulfillment, whether it's meditation, exercise, hobbies, or spending time with loved ones. Make self-care a non-negotiable part of your routine.
- 5. Elevate Your Standards:
  - Set high standards for yourself in all areas of life, including relationships, career, and personal growth. Strive for excellence and pursue goals that align with your values and aspirations. Surround yourself with people who uplift and inspire you to be the best version of yourself.
- 6. Cultivate Positive Relationships:
  - Surround yourself with individuals who respect and value you for who you are. Foster relationships built on mutual respect, trust, and support. Distance yourself from toxic relationships or individuals who undermine your self-worth.
- 7. Take Ownership of Your Choices:
  - Take responsibility for your actions, decisions, and their consequences. Accept accountability for your mistakes and learn from them. By owning your choices, you empower yourself to make intentional decisions aligned with your values and goals.

Boosting your level of self-respect requires dedication, self-awareness, and commitment to personal growth. By practicing these strategies consistently, you can cultivate a deep sense of self-respect and appreciation for the unique individual that you are.

Workbook Pages
- **Boosting Self-RESPECT: Practical Strategies Worksheet 105**
- **Teaching Yourself How to Be Treated and Teaching People How to Treat You Worksheet 112**

SELF-EMPATHY UNVEILED

Definition of Empathy:
Empathy is the profound ability to understand and share the feelings of another. It transcends mere sympathy, as it involves actively entering into the emotional experience of another person. It requires a genuine openness to connect with the emotions, perspectives, and struggles of those around us. In essence, empathy is the bridge that links individuals, fostering a deeper connection through shared understanding.

Significance of Empathy in Relationships:
Empathy stands as a cornerstone in the architecture of meaningful relationships. It serves as a binding agent, cultivating compassion and understanding between individuals. In relationships, whether romantic, familial, or platonic, the ability to empathize creates a safe space for emotional expression. It bridges gaps in communication, allowing individuals to feel heard and validated. The significance of empathy lies in its capacity to build trust, fortify emotional bonds, and contribute to the overall health and resilience of relationships.

Exploring How Empathy Extends to Self-Relationship:
While empathy is often associated with understanding others, its extension to self-relationship is equally vital. Self-empathy involves turning inward with the same compassionate understanding one would offer to a friend. It entails acknowledging and validating one's own emotions, fears, and struggles without judgment. Understanding and embracing our own experiences contribute to a healthier self-relationship. Practicing self-empathy involves recognizing that our feelings are valid, even if they seem incongruent or challenging. By extending the same level of compassion to ourselves that we offer others, we create a foundation for self-love and acceptance. Ultimately, empathy, both outward and inward, becomes a transformative force that enhances the fabric of our connections with others and ourselves.

Navigating the Waters of Self-Empathy and Self-Sympathy:
Understanding the nuances between self-empathy and self-sympathy is crucial for fostering genuine growth and resilience.
Self-Empathy:
Self-empathy involves approaching our own experiences with an open heart and a willingness to understand.

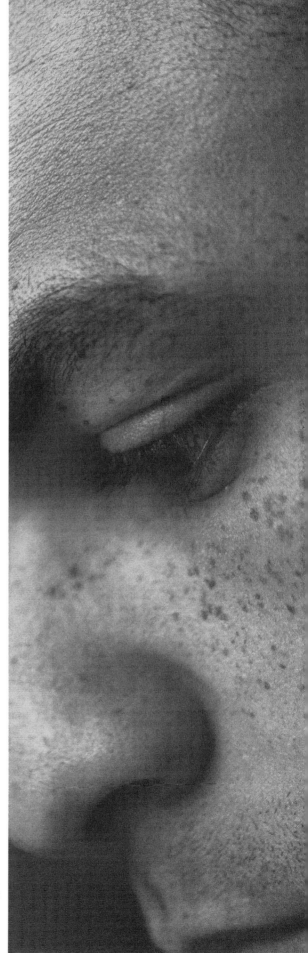

155

It's a compassionate acknowledgment of our feelings without falling into the trap of self-pity or victimization. When practicing self-empathy, we strive to recognize and validate our emotions without making excuses or perpetuating a mentality of helplessness. This approach empowers us to take responsibility for our feelings and actions, fostering a sense of agency in our lives.

Self-Sympathy (Victimization Mentality, Making Excuses, etc.):
On the other hand, self-sympathy often involves adopting a victimization mentality, where one sees themselves as constantly subject to external circumstances. This mindset may manifest in making excuses for our actions, blaming external factors for our challenges, and avoiding personal responsibility. While self-sympathy might offer temporary relief, it often hinders growth by perpetuating a cycle of disempowerment and a lack of accountability.

Breaking Free from the Chains of Self-Sympathy:
Differentiating between self-empathy and self-sympathy requires a conscious examination of our internal dialogue. It involves recognizing when we are making excuses, placing blame, or adopting a victim mentality. Breaking free from the chains of self-sympathy requires a shift in perspective – acknowledging challenges without surrendering to them. Instead of dwelling on the "why me?" narrative, self-empathy encourages a mindset that asks, "what can I learn from this?" It empowers us to take proactive steps toward positive change.

Cultivating a Culture of Accountability:
Embracing self-empathy means fostering a culture of accountability in our inner dialogue. It means holding ourselves responsible for our choices and actions while understanding the complexity of our emotions. By distinguishing self-empathy from self-sympathy, we create space for authentic self-reflection and personal growth. This process sets the stage for a healthier and more resilient self-relationship, laying the groundwork for a more empowered and fulfilled life.

Navigating the Depths: Recognizing and Understanding One's Own Emotions
In the ebb and flow of life, emotions act as the currents that shape our experiences. Many individuals, however, find themselves caught in the undertow of their emotions, allowing these powerful currents to dictate the motion of their moments. The key to breaking free from this tumultuous cycle lies in the intentional practice of recognizing and understanding one's own emotions.

1. The Unconscious Influence of Emotions:
Emotions, often subtle and nuanced, have a profound influence on our thoughts, decisions, and actions. When left unexamined, these emotions can become silent architects, constructing the landscape of our lives without our conscious consent. Recognizing this unconscious influence is the first step toward reclaiming agency over our emotional responses.

2. Unveiling Triggers and Root Emotions:
Emotions are not solitary entities but interconnected threads woven into the fabric of our experiences. By taking the time to unravel the layers, we can uncover the triggers that set off surface-level emotions and explore the deeper, root emotions beneath. This process is akin to untangling a knot, allowing us to understand the complex interplay of feelings within.

3. The Practice of Mindful Reflection:
Mindful reflection serves as a compass in the journey of recognizing and understanding emotions. It involves creating moments of stillness to tune into our emotional landscape. Through this intentional pause, we gain the clarity needed to discern the various emotions at play, their origins, and the narratives they may carry from the past.

4. Owning Emotions for Empowerment:
To truly practice self-empathy, we must own our emotions with a sense of empowerment. This ownership involves acknowledging that emotions, whether pleasant or challenging, are valid and carry valuable information. Owning our emotions shifts the dynamic from being passive recipients to active participants in our emotional experiences.

5. Crafting a Plan for Growth:
Understanding one's own emotions is not a passive endeavor; it is an active and transformative practice. Armed with insights into the triggers and root emotions, individuals can craft a personalized plan for growth. This plan may involve cultivating healthier coping mechanisms, seeking support, or engaging in practices that nurture emotional well-being.

6. Breaking Free from Emotional Bondage:
The practice of recognizing and understanding one's own emotions is a liberation from emotional bondage. It dismantles the chains that tether individuals to reactive patterns and provides the space needed to respond with intentionality. In this newfound freedom, individuals become architects of their emotional landscapes, constructing a life aligned with their values and aspirations.

In essence, the journey of recognizing and understanding one's own emotions is an expedition into self-discovery and empowerment. By embracing this practice, individuals cultivate a reservoir of self-empathy, ensuring that emotions become allies rather than silent architects of their lives.

Embracing Growth: The Impact of Self-Empathy on Personal Well-Being
Embarking on the transformative journey of self-empathy is not just an act of introspection; it is a catalyst for personal growth and enhanced well-being. The profound impact of self-empathy ripples through various dimensions of an individual's life, creating a positive and empowering trajectory.

Emotional Resilience and Coping Mechanisms:
One of the immediate fruits of self-empathy is the development of emotional resilience. By recognizing and understanding one's emotions, individuals equip themselves with a robust set of coping mechanisms. Instead of being swept away by the tide of challenges, they navigate the waters with a newfound sense of resilience, bouncing back from adversity with greater ease.

Improved Decision-Making and Clarity:
Self-empathy acts as a lantern illuminating the path of decision-making. When individuals are attuned to their emotions, they make decisions from a place of clarity and authenticity. The fog of uncertainty begins to lift, revealing a clearer understanding of personal values, aspirations, and the steps needed for personal and professional advancement.

Enhanced Interpersonal Relationships:
The impact of self-empathy extends beyond the individual to the realm of interpersonal relationships. As individuals develop a deeper understanding of their own emotions, they become more attuned to the feelings of others. This heightened empathy fosters healthier and more meaningful connections, as individuals can navigate relationships with a greater sense of compassion, patience, and understanding.

Stress Reduction and Mental Well-Being:
The practice of self-empathy serves as a potent stress-reduction tool. By acknowledging and understanding emotions, individuals prevent the accumulation of internal stressors that can manifest physically and mentally. This proactive approach to mental well-being creates a harmonious internal environment, reducing the likelihood of chronic stress-related ailments.

Empowerment and Self-Image:
Self-empathy is an empowering force that reshapes self-perception. As individuals recognize and validate their own emotions, a positive shift occurs in self-image. The internal dialogue transforms from self-criticism to self-compassion, fostering a more nurturing relationship with oneself. This, in turn, bolsters confidence and resilience in the face of life's challenges.

Cultivation of a Growth Mindset:
At the core of personal growth lies the cultivation of a growth mindset. Self-empathy is a powerful ally in this pursuit, encouraging individuals to view challenges as opportunities for learning and development. Embracing setbacks with self-compassion and a growth-oriented perspective fuels continuous improvement and resilience.

Barriers to Empathy in Self-Relationship

The journey toward self-empathy, though transformative, is not without its share of obstacles. Recognizing and understanding these barriers is essential in navigating the intricate path toward a more compassionate self-relationship.

1. Self-Criticism and Judgement:

A pervasive barrier to self-empathy is the tendency toward self-criticism and harsh judgment. Many individuals have internalized societal expectations and unrealistic standards, leading to a critical inner voice. Overcoming this barrier involves challenging these ingrained patterns and fostering a mindset of self-compassion, allowing room for growth and imperfection.

2. Fear of Vulnerability:

The fear of vulnerability can hinder the practice of self-empathy. Some individuals may perceive vulnerability as a weakness, fearing judgment from themselves or others. Embracing vulnerability requires reframing it as a strength, a courageous act that opens the door to self-understanding and authentic connection.

3. Cultural and Social Conditioning:

Cultural and social conditioning can shape individuals' perceptions of self-worth and acceptable emotional expressions. Messages from society about what is deemed "acceptable" or "normal" may create barriers to acknowledging and understanding one's own emotions. Breaking free from these conditioned responses involves challenging societal norms and embracing a more authentic, individualized approach to self-awareness.

4. Overemphasis on External Validation:

Relying excessively on external validation can impede the development of self-empathy. If individuals prioritize external opinions over their own internal compass, the journey toward understanding personal emotions becomes muddled. Shifting the focus inward, detached from external approval, is a crucial step in fostering self-empathy.

External Factors Affecting Self-Empathy:

1. Societal Expectations:

Societal expectations and norms can exert external pressures that hinder self-empathy. Cultural paradigms may discourage open dialogue about emotions or stigmatize certain feelings. Recognizing these external influences is vital for dismantling barriers and embracing a more authentic approach to self-understanding.

2. Time Constraints and Busy Lifestyles:

Modern lifestyles often prioritize productivity and efficiency, leaving little room for introspection. Time constraints can be a significant external barrier to practicing self-empathy. Cultivating the habit of making intentional time for self-reflection becomes crucial in overcoming this hurdle.

3. Digital Distractions:

Constant connectivity and digital distractions can divert attention from self-reflection. The barrage of external stimuli may drown out internal signals, hindering the development of self-awareness. Establishing boundaries with digital devices is essential in creating space for self-empathy practices.

4. Social Comparison and Influences:

The pervasive culture of social comparison, fueled by social media and societal standards, can distort perceptions of self-worth. External influences that foster comparison may obstruct the authentic exploration of one's emotions. A conscious effort to filter external influences and prioritize authentic self-connection is crucial.

Navigating Toward Empathy:
Recognizing these barriers, both internal and external, is the first step in navigating toward empathy in self-relationship. By dismantling these obstacles, you can pave the way for a more compassionate, authentic understanding of your own emotions, fostering a profound connection with yourself.

Developing Self-Empathy: Nurturing Compassion Over Criticism

Understanding the Importance of Nurturing Self-Compassion:
Self-compassion is the gentle, understanding response to one's own imperfections, failures, and challenges. It involves treating oneself with kindness, embracing one's humanity, and fostering a sense of warmth and understanding even in moments of difficulty. Unlike self-criticism, which often exacerbates negative emotions, self-compassion creates a supportive environment that encourages growth, resilience, and emotional well-being.

Contrasting Self-Compassion with Self-Criticism:

- Internal Dialogue: Self-compassion involves a dialogue infused with kindness and understanding. It acknowledges mistakes and setbacks as part of the human experience, offering encouragement to try again. In contrast, self-criticism tends to berate and amplify errors, creating a hostile internal environment that hinders growth.
- Impact on Well-Being: Nurturing self-compassion contributes to enhanced emotional well-being. It provides a foundation for coping with challenges, fostering resilience, and promoting a positive outlook. Conversely, self-criticism is often linked to increased stress, anxiety, and a negative impact on mental health.
- Relationship with Failure: Self-compassion allows individuals to approach failures with a sense of understanding and curiosity. It recognizes that everyone encounters obstacles and sees them as opportunities for growth. On the other hand, self-criticism can turn failures into overwhelming and demoralizing experiences, hindering the learning process.
- Encouraging Exploration: A self-compassionate mindset encourages exploration and experimentation without the fear of harsh judgment. This openness to new experiences fosters personal development and a willingness to step out of comfort zones. Conversely, self-criticism can paralyze individuals, leading to avoidance and a fear of failure.

Cultivating Self-Compassion in Daily Life:

- Mindful Awareness: Cultivate mindfulness to become aware of self-critical thoughts. Mindfulness allows individuals to observe their inner dialogue without attachment, creating space for self-compassion to emerge.
- Positive Self-Talk: Replace self-critical language with positive and affirming self-talk. Encourage oneself in the same way a supportive friend might offer words of comfort and motivation.
- Kindness to Imperfections: Embrace imperfections as part of the shared human experience. Recognize that nobody is flawless, and self-compassion lies in accepting oneself amid imperfections.
-

Developing self-empathy necessitates a shift from self-criticism to self-compassion. By fostering a kind and understanding relationship with yourself, you pave the way for a more resilient, emotionally healthy, and compassionately connected inner world. This shift becomes a powerful catalyst for navigating life's challenges with grace and embracing personal growth with open hearts and minds.

Cultivating Self-Empathy: A Journey through EMPATHY
Embarking on the path of cultivating self-empathy involves embracing a holistic approach represented by the acronym EMPATHY. Each letter encapsulates a key aspect of the transformative process:

- Empower Through Reflection:
  - Mindful Self-Reflection: Engage in regular moments of mindful self-reflection. Create a sacred space to explore your thoughts, emotions, and experiences without judgment.
  - Journaling Practice: Maintain a journal to document your inner journey. Write about your daily experiences, thoughts, and feelings. This practice enhances self-awareness and deepens the connection with your inner self.

- Mend with Self-Compassion:
  - Kindness Toward Yourself: Cultivate a habit of speaking to yourself with kindness. Replace self-critical thoughts with affirming and encouraging words. Treat yourself with the same compassion you would extend to a dear friend.
  - Acknowledging Imperfections: Embrace your imperfections as part of your unique journey. Instead of harsh judgment, recognize that mistakes and flaws contribute to your growth and development.
- Practice Active Listening (to Yourself):
  - Inner Dialogue Awareness: Be mindful of your inner dialogue. Notice how you speak to yourself and become aware of any negative patterns. Actively listen to your thoughts without immediate judgment.
- Acceptance of Emotions:
  - Permission to Feel: Grant yourself permission to experience the full spectrum of emotions. Avoid suppressing or invalidating your feelings. Understand that emotions are valid and offer valuable insights into your inner world. (Ephesians 4:26)
  - Name and Validate Emotions: Practice naming your emotions and acknowledging their presence. Validating your emotions allows you to honor your feelings and promotes self-understanding.
- Transformative Human Connection:
  - Community Engagement: Foster connections with supportive communities. Engage in conversations that promote empathy and understanding. Share your experiences and insights while being receptive to the perspectives of others.
  - Professional Support: Seek guidance from emotionally intelligent individuals or mentors who can provide a safe space for exploring your emotions and developing self-empathy.
- Harmony Through Godly Mindfulness (Philippians 4:8):
  - Mindful Prayer and Reflection: Integrate mindfulness into your prayer life. Meditate on virtues mentioned in Philippians 4:8—whatever is true, noble, right, pure, lovely, admirable, excellent, and praiseworthy.
  - Mindful Submission to God: Surrender your thoughts and emotions to God's sovereignty. Cultivate a mindful awareness of God's presence, recognizing His authority over your inner world.
- Yearning for Growth:
  - Goal Setting: Set realistic and achievable personal goals. Celebrate your accomplishments, no matter how small. Recognize that growth is a continuous process, and each step forward is a triumph.

Cultivating self-empathy is a gradual and intentional process. By embracing the holistic approach outlined by the EMPATHY framework, individuals can nurture a compassionate connection with themselves, leading to profound personal growth and well-being.

HUMILITY: A GUIDING LIGHT IN SELF-RELATIONSHIPS

Humility

Humility, in the context of self-relationships, is a virtue that transcends mere modesty or self-deprecation. It is a profound acknowledgment of our inherent dependency on God and a recognition of His sovereignty over our lives. True humility births a transformative mindset that shapes the way we perceive ourselves, fostering a healthier and more authentic relationship with our inner selves.

Definition of Humility:

At its core, humility is not about diminishing one's worth but about embracing a right perspective in relation to God and others. It involves a willingness to surrender our self-will to the divine, recognizing that God's wisdom far surpasses our limited understanding. In essence, humility is a posture of the heart that positions us to be receptive to God's guidance and transformative work in our lives.

How Humility Aids Self-Relationships:

- Self-Acceptance: Humility enables self-acceptance by fostering an authentic understanding of our strengths and weaknesses. It liberates us from the pressure of perfection, allowing us to embrace our uniqueness as God's handiwork.
- Embracing Growth: A humble mindset sees each experience, whether triumphant or challenging, as an opportunity for growth. Rather than viewing mistakes as failures, humility transforms them into stepping stones toward personal development.
- Inner Peace: By relinquishing the need for constant validation and recognition, humility brings inner peace. It shifts our focus from self-promotion to a contentment found in God's approval and purpose for our lives.
- Healthy Self-Reflection: Humility encourages healthy self-reflection, providing a balanced perspective on our actions and motivations. It allows us to confront areas of pride, self-centeredness, or insecurity, fostering a deeper understanding of ourselves.

161

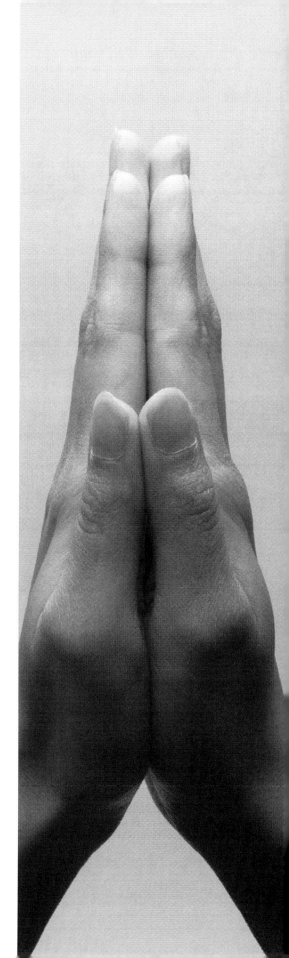

Characteristics of a Humble Mindset:
- Submission to God's Will: A humble mindset willingly submits to God's will, recognizing that His plans and purposes surpass our understanding. It is marked by a desire to align our goals with God's divine blueprint for our lives.
- Others-Centeredness: Humility shifts the focus from self to others. It cultivates a genuine concern for the well-being of those around us, fostering empathy, compassion, and a willingness to serve.
- Grace and Forgiveness: A humble mindset is characterized by the extension of grace, both to oneself and others. It acknowledges that everyone is a work in progress and that mistakes are opportunities for learning and growth.
- Continuous Learning: Humility thrives in an environment of continuous learning. It embraces the idea that wisdom is an ongoing pursuit, and each experience contributes to our development.

Navigating the Depths of Humility: Beyond Self-Deprecation
In the original design of humility, it is crucial to distinguish it from self-deprecation. While both concepts involve a form of self-reflection, humility takes a markedly different route. Self-deprecation tends to diminish one's value, often accompanied by a negative self-view that can undermine confidence and hinder personal growth. In contrast, humility fosters a healthy self-view grounded in an understanding of our identity in God.

Differentiating Humility from Self-Deprecation:
- Source of Evaluation: Humility draws its evaluation from God's truth and wisdom. It recognizes that our worth is derived from being created in God's image and redeemed by His love. On the other hand, self-deprecation often stems from comparing oneself to worldly standards or unrealistic expectations.
- Healthy Acknowledgment: Humility involves a healthy acknowledgment of strengths and weaknesses. It recognizes that each individual possesses unique qualities and areas for improvement. In contrast, self-deprecation tends to overly focus on perceived shortcomings without celebrating individual strengths.
- Confidence in God's Design: A humble mindset is confident in God's design. It acknowledges that God created each person with purpose and intention, fostering a sense of security and contentment. Self-deprecation, however, often leads to insecurity and a distorted self-image.

How Humility Fosters a Healthy Self-View:
- Embracing Imperfection: Humility creates a space where imperfections are not seen as failures but as opportunities for growth. It allows for a compassionate understanding of oneself, recognizing that God's grace covers areas of weakness.
- Gratitude for God's Work: A humble heart is grateful for God's transformative work. It acknowledges that personal growth is a continuous journey guided by the hand of the Creator. Gratitude becomes a cornerstone, shifting the focus from self-deprecation to appreciation for God's ongoing craftsmanship.
- Valuing Others: Humility fosters an appreciation for the diversity of gifts and talents in others. It enables a healthy recognition of one's strengths while appreciating and valuing the unique contributions of those around us.
- Authentic Confidence: True humility cultivates authentic confidence, not in one's abilities alone but in God's provision and guidance. It is a confidence rooted in understanding that God equips and empowers His children for the roles and purposes He has ordained.

Signs of Self-Deprecation: Unraveling the Patterns
Recognizing signs of self-deprecation is crucial for cultivating a healthier self-view. Let's delve into the subtleties that may indicate a self-deprecating mindset:
- Sole Focus on Shortcomings (S): Constantly dwelling on personal flaws and perceived inadequacies becomes a recurring pattern. Self-deprecators tend to magnify their shortcomings while overlooking their strengths.
- Ignoring Achievements (I): Achievements and successes are downplayed or dismissed. Individuals caught in self-deprecation often undermine their accomplishments, attributing them to luck or external factors rather than acknowledging their own efforts.
- Giving in to Negative Self-Talk (G): Internal dialogue is dominated by negative self-talk. A self-deprecating mindset feeds on a barrage of self-critical thoughts, creating a detrimental mental environment.
- Neglecting Self-Care (N): Prioritizing others' needs over personal well-being becomes a norm. Individuals may neglect self-care and compromise their physical, emotional, or mental health due to a lack of self-worth.

162

- Excessive Apologizing (S): Apologizing unnecessarily and taking on blame for situations, even when not at fault, characterizes a self-deprecating demeanor. This constant need to apologize stems from a sense of unworthiness.

Consequences of Self-Deprecation: Unraveling the Impact
- Stunted Personal Growth (S): Self-deprecation can hinder personal growth by fostering a mindset that discourages taking on new challenges. The fear of failure, rooted in self-doubt, becomes a significant barrier.
- Isolation from Relationships (I): Constant self-deprecation can lead to isolation from meaningful relationships. Others may find it challenging to connect with someone who consistently downplays their value and contributions.
- Nurturing Mental Health Struggles (G): The negative self-talk inherent in self-deprecation contributes to mental health struggles such as anxiety and depression. It perpetuates a cycle of negativity that affects overall well-being.
- Strained Interpersonal Connections (N): Neglecting personal needs and constantly apologizing can strain interpersonal connections. Others may feel burdened by the constant self-blame and lack of self-assurance.
- Sapped Emotional Energy (S): The energy invested in self-deprecating thoughts drains emotional reserves. This emotional exhaustion can hinder the ability to cope with stress and navigate life's challenges.

Recognizing these signs and understanding the consequences is the first step towards breaking free from the grip of self-deprecation. As we unravel these patterns, may it pave the way for a journey towards self-compassion, growth, and a more affirming self-view.

Navigating the Shadows: My Journey out of Self-Deprecation
In the early days of my ministry with UNPLUGGED, I found myself entangled in the intricate web of self-deprecation. Reflecting on those times, I vividly recall succumbing to the very signs that characterize this damaging mindset.

- *Sole Focus on Shortcomings:* I often found myself fixating on my perceived flaws and inadequacies. Every misstep, every imperfection, seemed magnified in my mind. The relentless pursuit of an unattainable perfection haunted my thoughts.
- *Ignoring Achievements:* Achievements, instead of being celebrated, were downplayed or dismissed. There was an innate fear of appearing prideful or boastful, leading me to undermine my accomplishments. I attributed success to external factors, almost as if luck, not effort, played the defining role.

In the realm of ministry, this translated into downplaying the impact of the work, the wisdom imparted, and even my own presence. There was a hesitancy to embrace the significance of the gifts bestowed upon me by God. I walked on tiptoes around my achievements, as if acknowledging them would shatter the fragile balance between humility and self-worth.

I remember moments of dimming my light, believing that humility required a muted existence. I hesitated to let my accomplishments shine, concerned about how it might be perceived by others. The fear of being seen as self-centered led to a habitual downplaying of the very gifts that were meant to illuminate the path for others.

It was a pivotal realization that shifted my perspective. I understood that my achievements, my wisdom, my very presence were not about me but about the divine purpose woven into the fabric of my being. Dimming my light didn't serve humility; it stifled the essence of the calling placed upon my life.

The journey out of self-deprecation became a lesson in embracing the fullness of God's gifts without fear of judgment. It was a realization that humility is not found in self-diminishment but in recognizing the Source of our strengths. Now, I encourage you not to succumb to the shadows of self-deprecation. Let your achievements shine, for they are reflections of God's grace and purpose. In doing so, you pave the way for others to find their own light and purpose without fear or reservation.

Humility Directed Inward: A Dance with Imperfections
At the heart of humility lies the ability to turn the gaze inward, acknowledging personal imperfections and embracing the inherent limitations of our humanity. This inward journey is an intimate exploration, a dance with the raw, unfiltered self.

Embracing Personal Imperfections: Humility, when directed inward, invites us to embrace our imperfections as integral parts of our unique design. Instead of viewing flaws as blemishes to be hidden, humility encourages us to see them as brushstrokes contributing to the masterpiece of our lives. In acknowledging our imperfections, we create space for authenticity, allowing our true selves to emerge without the suffocating weight of pretense.

This acceptance of imperfections is not a resignation to mediocrity but a celebration of the beauty that arises from embracing the imperfect. It's an admission that, in our vulnerabilities, we find connection with the shared human experience. Humility becomes a gentle guide, leading us away from the harsh judgment of self-criticism toward a compassionate understanding of our imperfect selves.

The Connection between Humility and Self-Acceptance: Humility and self-acceptance share an intricate dance, each movement influencing the other. As we humble ourselves, acknowledging our limitations and imperfections, we pave the way for genuine self-acceptance. It's a symbiotic relationship wherein humility creates the fertile ground for self-acceptance to take root, and in turn, self-acceptance nurtures the growth of humility.

To accept oneself requires a level of humility that transcends self-centeredness. It involves recognizing that our value is not solely determined by accomplishments or external validations. True self-acceptance is grounded in an understanding of our intrinsic worth, independent of societal standards or fleeting successes. Humility becomes the anchor, grounding us in the truth that our significance emanates from a source greater than ourselves.

This inward journey is transformative, leading to a profound sense of peace and contentment. It's a recognition that, in our imperfections and limitations, we find the fertile ground for growth and connection. As we navigate the delicate balance between humility and self-acceptance, we discover the freedom to be authentically ourselves, imperfections and all. The dance continues, a rhythmic interplay that guides us toward a deeper understanding of the beautifully imperfect individuals we are meant to be.

Navigating the Shadows: Unmasking False Humility
False humility, often disguised as a virtue, is a subtle adversary that can cast shadows on genuine humility. In its deceptive nature, false humility mimics the authentic trait, but beneath the surface, it conceals dangers that can erode both personal well-being and the foundations of relationships.
Defining False Humility: False humility manifests when individuals outwardly portray a modest demeanor while internally harboring a superiority complex. It's a performance, a carefully crafted façade aimed at garnering praise or maintaining an appearance of selflessness. Unlike genuine humility, which stems from an honest acknowledgment of one's imperfections, false humility is driven by a desire for admiration or recognition.

Dangers to Oneself: The peril of false humility lies in its impact on personal growth and authenticity. When individuals adopt a façade of humility, they create barriers to self-awareness. The reluctance to acknowledge genuine strengths and weaknesses hinders the development of a healthy self-concept. This self-deception can lead to stagnation, as the pursuit of growth becomes entangled in a web of false modesty.

Moreover, false humility can breed resentment and frustration. The internal dissonance between the projected modesty and the unacknowledged sense of superiority creates a breeding ground for inner conflict. This conflict can manifest as a distorted view of oneself, hindering the journey toward authenticity and genuine self-improvement.

Dangers to Relationships: In the realm of relationships, false humility can sow seeds of discord. When individuals feign humility for external approval, their interactions may be tainted with insincerity. Others may sense the inauthenticity, leading to strained connections. Trust, a cornerstone of healthy relationships, becomes compromised when humility is perceived as a performance rather than a sincere expression.

Furthermore, false humility can foster a power dynamic where individuals use their perceived modesty as a tool for manipulation. This subtle manipulation can erode the foundations of trust, hindering the potential for genuine connection and intimacy.

In essence, false humility poses a dual threat, undermining personal authenticity and casting a shadow over the authenticity of relationships. Recognizing and dispelling false humility requires a commitment to self-awareness and a genuine embrace of one's strengths and limitations. It is through this genuine humility that individuals can navigate the delicate balance between acknowledging their worth and appreciating the worth of others.

The Temptation of Pride and Ego in Self-Relationship
Defining Pride and Ego:
Pride signifies an excessive belief in one's abilities or achievements, often accompanied by an inflated sense of self-worth. It can manifest as a resistance to acknowledging faults or limitations, hindering genuine self-reflection.

Ego, closely related to pride, involves an individual's sense of self-importance and the desire for recognition. While a healthy ego is vital for self-esteem, an exaggerated ego can lead to arrogance, impeding authentic connections and self-awareness.

Counting the COST of Pride:
Investing in pride is akin to a risky venture with high costs and uncertain returns. Examining the repercussions of such an investment reveals a multi-faceted impact that extends beyond the individual.
- *Crisis in Relationships (C):* Pride often initiates a crisis in relationships. The refusal to admit fault or seek reconciliation can lead to fractured connections, as others struggle to breach the walls of a prideful heart.
- *Oblivion to Growth (O):* Pride creates an oblivion to personal growth. An unwillingness to learn from mistakes or acknowledge areas for improvement becomes a barrier to the continuous journey of self-discovery.
- *Siloed Isolation (S):* Pride constructs silos of isolation. The inability to authentically connect with others, fueled by an inflated self-perception, leads to a lonely journey devoid of genuine relationships.
- *Tainted Self-Perception (T):* Pride taints self-perception. The refusal to see oneself authentically can distort the alignment of actions with values and principles, creating a chasm between perceived and actual identity.

Unmasking the Roots of Pride:
Peeling back the layers of pride reveals intricate roots deeply embedded in the human psyche. Understanding these roots is instrumental in unraveling the motivations behind prideful behaviors.
- *Insecurity :* Pride often conceals insecurities. The need to project an image of invulnerability may stem from an underlying fear of rejection or inadequacy.
- *Denial of Vulnerability:* Pride is a defense against vulnerability. The fear of being perceived as weak or imperfect drives individuals to construct a facade of strength and infallibility.
- *Comparative Validation:* The habit of incessant comparison fuels pride. Seeking validation through perceived superiority becomes a coping mechanism to mask feelings of inadequacy.
- *Fear of Exposure:* Pride arises from a fear of exposure. The reluctance to be seen authentically may stem from a fear of judgment, leading to the construction of a protective shield.

Navigating the Waters Between Proud and Prideful: An Exploration of Identity
The nuances between being *proud* and being *prideful* form a delicate interplay in the realm of human emotions. Understanding this distinction is pivotal for cultivating humility and maintaining a grounded sense of self.

Proud: A Natural Emotion:
Feeling proud is a natural emotional response to significant elements in life. Whether it's accomplishments, heritage, faith, or personal growth, experiencing pride is an acknowledgment of the value attached to these aspects. It reflects a healthy recognition of one's efforts and the positive attributes that contribute to personal identity.

Being proud of one's heritage can be a celebration of cultural richness and diversity. Taking pride in accomplishments or personal growth reflects self-acknowledgment and the pursuit of excellence. Pride in faith signifies a deep connection to spiritual values and beliefs. In essence, feeling proud is a human response to the beauty and significance found in life's various dimensions.

The Pitfall of Prideful Identification:
The challenge arises when pride transforms into *prideful identification,* where personal worth becomes exclusively tied to achievements, heritage, faith, or self. This shift in focus from acknowledgment to identity creates an inflated sense of self-importance, leading to a distorted self-perception.

Identifying with accomplishments alone can breed arrogance, overshadowing the collaborative efforts that contribute to success. Tying one's identity solely to heritage may foster an exclusivist mindset, missing the opportunity to appreciate the richness of diverse cultures. Prideful identification with faith might lead to judgment and exclusion rather than embracing the universal principles of love and compassion.

The Humility in Divine Identity:
True humility begins when identity is anchored in something greater than personal achievements or attributes. Identifying with God serves as a transformative cornerstone, providing a stable foundation for humility. When individuals recognize themselves as children of God, the weight of His goodness and glory becomes the guiding force.

Acknowledging God's role in personal accomplishments humbles the heart, attributing success to divine grace. Viewing heritage through the lens of a shared human experience fosters unity rather than division. Identifying with God in faith aligns with the principles of love, mercy, and compassion, transcending exclusive attitudes.

The Filtering Lens of Divine Identity:
Divine identity acts as a filtering lens, allowing individuals to view accomplishments, heritage, faith, and self through the awareness of God's goodness. It keeps pride in check, preventing the distortion of self-perception. This perspective encourages a focus on purpose and service to others rather than self-centered pride.

In essence, the journey from being proud to avoiding prideful identification involves recognizing the divine thread woven into the fabric of personal identity. Humility flourishes when individuals find their worth in the context of something greater – the boundless love and grace of the Creator.

The Perils of Pride: A Scriptural Unraveling
The ancient wisdom of Proverbs warns us with stark clarity: "Pride goes before destruction, a haughty spirit before a fall" (Proverbs 16:18, ESV). This profound truth underscores the dangers of allowing pride to take root in our hearts, leading to a gradual descent into destruction.

A Warning in Proverbs:
The timeless wisdom encapsulated in Proverbs is a divine caution against the insidious nature of pride. The imagery of pride preceding destruction is vivid, offering a powerful metaphorical depiction of the perilous journey pride sets in motion.

God's Patience and Our Choices:
God, in His infinite mercy, often provides us with opportunities to recognize and rectify our prideful ways. The phrase "pride comes before a fall" suggests that God grants us time and grace to humble ourselves. Yet, the responsibility lies with us to discern these moments of divine patience and choose humility over pride.

The Entanglement of Pride:
The process of a fall rooted in pride begins innocuously. It starts with genuine pride in one's accomplishments—a healthy acknowledgment of hard work and success. However, when pride transforms into over-identification, becoming the sole definition of self, it begins to entangle like a web.

Over-Identification and the Fall:
Over-identification with accomplishments blinds individuals to their inherent vulnerabilities and need for God's grace. The fall begins when personal worth is solely tied to achievements, creating an inflated sense of self-sufficiency. The individual becomes ensnared in the web of their own pride, unable to see the impending peril.

Examples of the Unraveling:
Consider a successful entrepreneur who attributes their achievements solely to personal brilliance, disregarding the collective efforts and external factors that contributed to success. As this pride deepens, it blinds them to potential pitfalls and the need for continuous learning. The eventual fall may manifest as a business setback, exposing the limitations masked by pride.

Similarly, a person over-identifying with their physical appearance may experience a fall when faced with the inevitable changes that come with time. The pride in outward beauty, when unchecked, can lead to a profound sense of loss and identity crisis.

Humiliation as a Path to Humility:
God's design is gracious yet firm. If we persist in pride, relying on our self-sufficiency, life has a way of humbling us—sometimes in ways we could never anticipate. The business tycoon faces financial crises, and the beauty idol experiences aging. The humiliation in these moments serves as a pathway to humility.

Choosing Humility Over Humiliation:
The beauty of the divine warning is that it offers an invitation to choose humility willingly. By recognizing the signs of pride, acknowledging our dependence on God, and embracing humility, we sidestep the harsh lessons that humiliation might bring.

In essence, the cautionary wisdom in Proverbs beckons us to navigate life's journey with an awareness of our inherent need for God's grace. It invites us to choose the path of humility, avoiding the pitfalls that pride, if left unchecked, inevitably brings.

Overcoming Pride: A Path to Humility
P - Practice Self-Awareness
- Reflect on your thoughts, actions, and reactions to identify instances of pride.
- Cultivate mindfulness to catch prideful tendencies in the moment.
R - Replace Judgment with Understanding
- Shift from judging others to seeking understanding.
- Embrace empathy to comprehend different perspectives and experiences.
I - Invite Feedback and Reflection
- Encourage honest feedback from others about your behavior.
- Take time for self-reflection, considering how pride may be hindering personal growth.

D - Develop a Teachable Spirit
- Embrace a mindset of continuous learning and growth.
- Be open to receiving guidance and correction from others.

E - Eradicate Comparison
- Resist comparing yourself to others, recognizing individual strengths and weaknesses.
- Celebrate others' successes without feeling diminished in your own worth.

By actively addressing these points, individuals can navigate the challenging terrain of pride, paving the way for personal and relational growth through the development of humility.

Navigating Humility in the Hand of God: A Dive into 1 Peter 5:6-7 6 Humble yourselves, therefore, under the mighty hand of God so that at the proper time he may exalt you, 7 casting all your anxieties on him, because he cares for you.

The apostle Peter, through divine inspiration, provides profound insights into the dynamics of humility in the context of our relationship with God. The passage in 1 Peter 5:6-7, rendered in the English Standard Version, serves as a roadmap for understanding the responsibility, location, and timing inherent in embracing humility.

Responsibility in Humility:
The passage begins with a clear directive—humble yourselves. This choice is a responsibility we carry, signifying that humility is not merely a passive state but an intentional posture we adopt. The call to humility implies an awareness of our tendencies toward pride and a commitment to preventatively manage it.

Location Matters:
Peter's guidance on where we are to humble ourselves is equally crucial. "Under the mighty hand of God" emphasizes the location under God's sovereignty and will. This deliberate choice to place ourselves under God's hand signifies a surrender to His authority and a recognition of His mighty power. It's an acknowledgment that true humility is found not in self-elevation but in submitting to God's providence.

Choosing the Palm Over the Fingers:
However, the details matter in this divine geography. Humbling ourselves under God's hand is not a call to peer around the edges, attempting to dictate our own course. It's about positioning ourselves under the palm, a place of safety, nurture, and growth. Attempting to peek around God's fingers, seeking shortcuts or self-made paths to success, leads to a dangerous dance at the edges where the risk of falling off looms large.

Trust in God's Timing:
The passage further unfolds with the promise that, in due time, God will exalt us. This underscores the importance of trusting God's timing, a virtue often tested in seasons of waiting. Exalting ourselves prematurely may lead to instability and a fall, but under the careful timing of God, our elevation is secure and purposeful.

Casting Anxieties:
The following verse introduces a critical element often linked with pride—the anxiety of wanting things on our terms and timing. Casting all anxieties on God is an antidote to the impatience and restlessness that breed pride. Acknowledging that God cares for us is an anchor that steadies our hearts, allowing us to relinquish control and align our desires with His perfect plan.

Staying in His Palm:
In summary, humility is not just a precursor to exaltation; it's a posture that ensures we remain secure in God's hand. By humbling ourselves under His mighty hand, trusting His timing, and casting our anxieties on Him, we position ourselves for sustained growth and divine exaltation. The call is clear: stay in the palm, away from the precarious edges, and let God orchestrate the timing of your elevation.

Workbook-The HUMBLE Approach Worksheet + Journal 121

Strategies for Cultivating Humility: A HUMBLE Approach

Embracing humility is a transformative journey, and adopting intentional strategies can help us navigate this path and guard against the pitfalls of pride. Let's explore a HUMBLE approach, outlining key strategies to foster humility in our lives.

1. Humility in Reflection:
- Honest Self-Examination: Regularly reflect on your thoughts, actions, and motives. Honest self-examination fosters awareness of areas where pride may lurk.
- Understanding Imperfection: Embrace your imperfections as opportunities for growth. Acknowledge mistakes and learn from them rather than seeking to cover them up.

2. Understanding Others:
- Minds Open to Learning: Cultivate a mindset open to learning from others. Recognize that everyone, regardless of status or position, has something valuable to offer.
- Empathy in Interactions: Practice empathy in your relationships. Seeking to understand others' perspectives contributes to a humble disposition.

3. Mindful Gratitude:
- Acknowledging Blessings: Regularly express gratitude for the blessings in your life. Acknowledging the source of your blessings helps cultivate a humble heart.
- Celebrating Others: Celebrate the accomplishments of others genuinely. A humble spirit finds joy in the success of others without comparison or competition.

4. Bowing to a Higher Authority:
- Submission to God's Will: Surrender your plans and desires to God's will. Acknowledge a higher authority and trust in the divine timing of your life's journey.
- Seeking Divine Guidance: Consult God in decision-making. Rely on prayer and seek divine guidance to avoid relying solely on your understanding.

5. Lifting Others Up:
- Acts of Service: Engage in acts of service without seeking recognition. Humility is reflected in selfless acts that benefit others.
- Encouraging Language: Use words that uplift and encourage. Humble individuals inspire and motivate without diminishing others.

6. Elevating through Character:
- Consistent Integrity: Uphold a consistent standard of integrity. Humility is rooted in authenticity and a commitment to ethical conduct.
- Focusing on Character Growth: Prioritize character development over external validation. Humility seeks internal growth rather than external acclaim.

These strategies, encompassing the HUMBLE framework, provide a practical guide for fostering humility. By incorporating these principles into our daily lives, we can navigate the delicate balance between acknowledging our worth and recognizing the greatness of the divine, ensuring that humility remains a cornerstone of our character.

Embracing the Transformative Power of Humility in Self-Relationships

In the journey of self-discovery and relational harmony, humility emerges as a guiding force that profoundly impacts our connection with ourselves. As we reflect on the significance of humility in self-relationships, it becomes clear that this virtue serves as a transformative tool, shaping our perspective, fostering growth, and laying the foundation for authentic connections.

Summarizing the Importance of Humility:
- Balanced Perspective: Humility grants us a balanced perspective, allowing us to acknowledge our strengths without pride and embrace our weaknesses without shame. It provides a realistic self-view, free from the distortions of arrogance or self-deprecation.
- Continuous Growth: True humility fuels a commitment to continuous self-improvement. Instead of stagnation, a humble heart remains open to learning, adapting, and evolving on the journey toward personal growth.
- Submission to Divine Guidance: Humility in self-relationship involves submitting our plans and aspirations to the divine. By acknowledging our limited understanding, we trust in a higher design that surpasses our comprehension.

Encouragement for Embracing Humility:
- Self-Acceptance: Embracing humility is an act of self-acceptance. It invites us to appreciate the complexity of our being, recognizing both the strengths that make us unique and the imperfections that make us human.
- Empowering Transformation: Humility is not a sign of weakness but a source of empowerment. It empowers us to navigate the complexities of life with grace, acknowledging our need for God's guidance and the support of others.

COMMUNICATION WITH SELF

Understanding the Significance of Self-Communication: Navigating the Power Within

In the vast landscape of self-relationship, the resonance of words within our souls holds the key to unlocking profound transformations. Our inner world is a symphony of thoughts, interpretations, and reactions—an unceasing narrative that shapes our perceptions and influences our reality. To embark on the journey of effective self-communication is to navigate the continuous inner dialogue, recognizing its nuances, and unlocking the power inherent in the words we allow to vibrate within our souls.

Unceasing Narratives:

Our minds are engaged in a perpetual conversation with the world around us. Thoughts flow, interpretations unfold, and reactions emerge, forming the unceasing narrative of our inner world. Acknowledging this ongoing dialogue is the crucial first step toward gaining insight into the intricate patterns of our thoughts and the stories we tell ourselves. It is within this awareness that the seeds of transformation are planted.

The Power of Self-Talk:

Every word spoken within the inner chambers of our minds carries profound significance. Whether these words lean towards the positive or negative, our self-talk serves as the architect of our perceptions, beliefs, and, ultimately, our reality. Recognizing the nature of this internal dialogue bestows upon us a unique power—the power to consciously choose the words that shape our inner narrative. In this recognition lies the key to harnessing the potential of self-talk for positive transformation.

Impact on Emotions and Actions:

The words we choose in our inner dialogue are not mere whispers in the corridors of our minds; they are resonant echoes that profoundly impact our emotions and actions. Positive affirmations can elevate our spirits, fostering resilience and optimism, while negative self-talk may contribute to feelings of doubt, anxiety, or sadness. Understanding this impact becomes the compass that guides us through the vast seas of our internal world.

170

Setting Sail: Navigating the Inner Seas of Self-Communication:

- Mindful Observation: Cultivating mindfulness involves becoming keen observers of our thoughts without judgment. This practice allows us to discern recurring patterns, distinguishing between constructive and detrimental self-talk.
- Intentional Scripting: Deliberately choosing positive narratives sets the stage for empowerment. Words of encouragement, affirmation, and self-love contribute to a narrative that fosters well-being and resilience.

The ancient wisdom found in Proverbs 23:7, "As a man thinks in his heart, so is he," resonates as a guiding principle of profound significance. These words encapsulate the profound truth that the seeds of our thoughts, sown in the fertile soil of our hearts, bear the fruits that define our reality. As we delve into the intricacies of this timeless wisdom, we uncover the transformative power hidden within the realm of our inner dialogue.

The Creative Force of Thought:

The verse echoes the undeniable truth that our thoughts are not passive inhabitants of our minds; rather, they are architects actively shaping the reality we experience. The process begins in the heart—the epicenter of our desires, beliefs, and self-perception. What we think about ourselves, the world, and our place in it serves as the blueprint for the person we become.

Attracting What Resides Within:

"As a man thinks in his heart, so is he," unveils the profound principle that we don't attract what we merely desire; we attract who we are. Our inner dialogue and thought patterns mold our character, determining the essence of our being. In this cosmic dance, the energy we emit through our thoughts becomes a magnetic force, drawing towards us experiences, opportunities, and relationships that resonate with our inner narrative.

The Formula of Creation: "Speak Those Things That Be Not As Though They Were":

The wisdom extends beyond the realm of thought, introducing the dynamic concept of intentional speech. "Speak those things that be not as though they were" becomes a formula for creation—an invitation to verbalize our desires and aspirations with confidence. However, before we utter these words, our thoughts must conceive and nurture them.

Dreams as Seeds of Thought:

God, in His infinite wisdom, grants us dreams—glimpses of the end, the destination of our journey. These dreams serve as powerful catalysts, shaping our thoughts and influencing our inner dialogue. By showing us the end, God ignites the spark of belief within us, encouraging us to think and speak of a reality that is yet to manifest.

Harnessing the Inner Dialogue:

Our inner dialogue, the silent conversation within the chambers of our minds, emerges as the crucible where dreams take form and thoughts become reality. Practicing the transformative art of thinking positively, envisioning a bright future, and embracing self-affirming beliefs propels us towards personal growth and attracts the very reality we aspire to live.

In the sacred theater of our existence, the script is written in the language of thought, and the stage is set by the inner dialogue of the heart. May we, as conscious creators, harness the power within our thoughts and shape a reality that mirrors the beauty of our dreams.

The Art of Effective Self-Communication: Nurturing a Dialogue with Purpose

In the labyrinth of our thoughts, the art of effective self-communication becomes a guiding light, illuminating the path to self-awareness and personal transformation. Let us navigate the intricacies of this artistry, unveiling the key elements that empower us to sculpt a dialogue with purpose.

Clarity in Expressing Thoughts and Feelings to Oneself:

The first brushstroke on the canvas of effective self-communication is clarity—an artful expression of thoughts and feelings to oneself. Clarity acts as the language of the soul, enabling us to decipher the intricate emotions, desires, and convictions that reside within. By articulating our inner landscape with precision, we gain insight into the layers of our being, fostering a profound connection with the essence of who we are.

Developing a Positive and Constructive Inner Dialogue:
The inner dialogue, akin to a continuous narrative echoing within, holds the power to shape our worldview and influence our actions. To harness this power, we embark on the journey of developing a positive and constructive inner dialogue. This involves consciously steering our thoughts toward affirmations of self-worth, resilience, and gratitude. As architects of our mental landscape, we construct a sanctuary of positivity that nurtures growth, resilience, and a deep sense of well-being.

Identifying and Addressing Negative Self-Talk Patterns:
As guardians of our mental realms, we confront the shadows cast by negative self-talk patterns. Identifying these patterns is an essential step toward fostering a transformative dialogue with oneself. By recognizing the whispers of doubt, fear, or self-criticism, we can address them with the light of truth and self-compassion. This intentional confrontation dismantles the barriers that inhibit our journey to self-discovery, allowing us to redefine the narrative we tell ourselves.

In the symphony of effective self-communication, clarity, positivity, and the courage to confront negativity blend harmoniously. Together, these elements create a masterpiece—a dialogue with oneself that resonates with authenticity, purpose, and a profound understanding of the intricacies of the human spirit. As we refine this art, we embark on a transformative odyssey, unlocking the gates to self-awareness and unveiling the boundless potential within.

Cultivating Stillness: Nurturing the Art of Active Listening Within
In the hustle and bustle of life's tempests, finding moments of stillness becomes a vital anchor for the ship of our souls. Picture these moments as serene harbors where the tides of quiet reflection ebb and flow. Practicing stillness is not merely a pause in the symphony of life; it is a deliberate tuning into the whispers of our own needs and desires.

Quiet Times with God:
Amidst the cacophony of daily demands, frequenting quiet times with God acts as a sanctuary for the spirit. These moments of communion become a sacred dialogue where the ship's captain—our inner self—aligns its course with the divine compass. In the quiet recesses, we cultivate sensitivity in our spirit, honing the ability to discern the gentle nudges and tugs on the strings of our soul. The more attuned we become, the clearer the signals of our deepest needs and desires.

Creating Quiet Pockets Through the Day:
Imagine these quiet pockets as oases in the vast desert of our bustling routines. By intentionally creating moments of stillness throughout the day, we foster an environment where the ship's instruments—the mind, soul, and body—can be fine-tuned. Whether through short pauses, mindful breaths, or brief prayers, these quiet interludes allow us to intercept the signals that would otherwise be drowned in the noise of life's demands.

Cultivating Sensitivity in the Spirit:
Sensitivity in the spirit is like having a finely tuned instrument to detect the subtlest notes in life's melody. Engaging with the person of the Holy Spirit in these quiet times rejuvenates the spirit, making it proactive in safeguarding the sanctity of our internal dialogues. Spiritual disciplines become the sails that catch the wind of divine revelation, steering us away from treacherous waters where harmful thoughts and patterns lurk.

Intercepting Signals:
Every day, our souls and bodies emit signals—undiscovered treasures and potential dangers. Practicing active listening within helps us decode these signals. We become aware of the echoes of unresolved issues, the melodies of current emotions, and the symphony of bodily needs. In this attunement, we intercept the signals early, preventing them from becoming storms that threaten the serenity of our internal seas.

Attentiveness to Inner Dialogues:
Be cautious of the conversations within your sacred chambers. The inner dialogues shape the very fabric of our being. Engaging in conversations with negativity, past demons, or the echoes of our old selves is like navigating through dark corridors. By being attentive to every dialogue within, we take charge of the ship's helm, ensuring that our course aligns with the destination of purpose, joy, and spiritual abundance.

In the sanctuary of stillness, we find the strength to actively listen to the symphony within, harmonizing our ship's journey with the divine score of our authentic needs and desires.

Navigating the Depths Within: A Practical Guide to Being Intune with Yourself

Embarking on the journey of self-discovery requires an intentional tuning into the currents of your inner world. Let's embark on this exploration with the compass of practical steps, spelling out the path to becoming truly *Intune* with yourself.

1. Identify Your Triggers (I):
Recognize the signals that set off waves of emotions within you. By pinpointing specific triggers, you gain the ability to navigate these emotional waters more skillfully. Ask yourself: What situations, words, or actions consistently stir reactions in me? Identifying triggers is the first step toward gaining mastery over your emotional seas.

2. Nurture Spiritual Disciplines (N):
Cultivate practices that foster spiritual growth and connection. Whether it's prayer, meditation, or reading sacred texts, these disciplines act as the sails that harness the winds of divine guidance. As you engage in these practices, you become attuned to the subtle whispers of the Holy Spirit, providing a spiritual compass for your journey within.

3. Tune into Your Body (T):
Your body is an intricate instrument sending signals about your well-being. Pay attention to physical sensations, tensions, and discomfort. Practice mindful breathing to bring awareness to each breath, grounding yourself in the present moment. Your body, much like a finely tuned instrument, provides valuable insights into your inner symphony.

4. Unearth Core Values (U):
Explore and define your core values. What principles and beliefs form the bedrock of your identity? Unearthing these values helps you align your actions with your authentic self. Take time to reflect on what truly matters to you, steering your ship towards a destination that resonates with your deepest desires.

5. Name Your Emotions (N):
Acknowledge and name the emotions coursing through your being. Like the navigator plotting points on a map, labeling your emotions brings clarity to the inner landscape. Ask yourself: What am I feeling right now? By identifying and expressing your emotions, you become better equipped to navigate the complex seas of your inner world.

6. Embrace Self-Reflection (E):
Allocate intentional time for self-reflection. Create a personal harbor where you can contemplate your experiences, aspirations, and challenges. Journaling is a powerful tool for self-reflection, allowing you to document the ebb and flow of your thoughts and emotions. In this sanctuary of reflection, you gain insights that guide your ship's course.

Embark on this journey of becoming *Intune* with yourself, allowing the symphony within to harmonize with the divine melodies of your purpose and desires. As you navigate these practical steps, may your inner compass guide you toward a deeper connection with the authentic captain of your soul.

Guardians of the Inner Sanctum: The Imperative of Healthy Boundaries
Recognizing the profound impact of words, setting healthy boundaries becomes paramount, acting as vigilant gatekeepers for the sanctity of our minds and hearts. This is especially crucial when considering the voices that speak into our lives, shaping the trajectory of our journey.

1. Rising to the Level of Spoken Words:
It is an immutable truth that we often ascend or descend to the level of the words we allow to take root within us. Words possess the power to shape beliefs, attitudes, and ultimately, our actions. The spoken and unspoken narratives surrounding us contribute to the construction of our self-image and the possibilities we envision for ourselves.

2. Qualified Voices and Setting Boundaries:

Not every voice is qualified to wield influence over the contours of our destiny. Allowing unqualified voices to speak into our lives can inadvertently chart a course misaligned with our purpose. To mitigate this, establish boundaries that discern between voices that foster growth and those that sow seeds of doubt. Qualify those who earn the privilege of shaping your perspective and aspirations.

3. Speaking In vs. Speaking Over:

Understanding the distinction between "speaking in" and "speaking over" is pivotal. "Speaking in" involves internalizing constructive input, allowing it to contribute positively to personal growth. Conversely, "speaking over" entails ceding authority to external voices to define our limits and potential. It is imperative to be discerning, ensuring that those granted this authority are trustworthy guides on our journey.

4. Borrowing from Scripture: Affirmations as Shields:

In seasons where self-communication falters or external voices become discordant, the reservoir of divine truth within scripture becomes a wellspring of affirmation. Borrow strength from scriptural affirmations that echo God's perspective on your identity and purpose. These affirmations act as shields, repelling the arrows of negativity and doubt.

5. Boundaries with Self: Acknowledging Limits:

Even in the dialogue with oneself, boundaries play a crucial role. Acknowledge your own limits in self-communication. If your current state prevents you from speaking life and encouragement, borrow from scriptural affirmations until you regain the ability to do so authentically. Establishing boundaries with yourself ensures that your inner narrative aligns with divine truth.

Setting healthy boundaries safeguards the integrity of our inner sanctum. It empowers us to be intentional gatekeepers, allowing only words that affirm, inspire, and align with our divine purpose to shape our narrative. Let the boundaries you set be a testament to the reverence you hold for the sanctity of your mind and heart, ensuring that the words within contribute to the majestic story of your God-ordained journey.

Mastering the Inner Dialogue: Confronting and Transforming Self-Sabotaging Thoughts

The mind is a battleground where thoughts, both empowering and self-sabotaging, contend for dominance. Identifying and challenging self-sabotaging thoughts is a crucial step toward fostering a mindset that aligns with God's truth and purpose for our lives.

1. Unmasking Self-Sabotaging Thoughts:

Self-sabotaging thoughts often cloak themselves in familiar garments, disguising their destructive nature. Unmasking them requires a keen awareness of recurring negative patterns and the impact they have on your emotions and actions. Pay attention to thoughts that breed doubt, fear, or undermine your worth.

2. Interrogating the Origin:

To challenge self-sabotaging thoughts effectively, interrogate their origin. Ask yourself whether these thoughts align with divine truth or if they derive from past experiences, societal expectations, or distorted self-perceptions. Understanding the root allows you to address the underlying issues fueling negative thoughts.

3. The Power of Affirmation:

Affirmations are potent tools in dismantling self-sabotaging thoughts. Craft affirming and empowering messages rooted in God's promises and your true identity in Him. These affirmations counteract the negativity, fostering a mindset aligned with divine truth. Regularly declare these affirmations to fortify your mental landscape.

4. Replacement Strategy:

Replace destructive self-talk with intentional, empowering messages. When a self-sabotaging thought arises, consciously replace it with a positive, affirming statement. This replacement strategy reshapes your inner dialogue, reinforcing thoughts that uplift, encourage, and harmonize with God's perspective on your life.

5. Cultivating a Positive Mental Environment:
Challenge self-sabotaging thoughts by cultivating a positive mental environment. Surround yourself with influences that speak life and truth into your narrative. Engage in activities that nurture a positive mindset, such as reading uplifting literature, listening to inspiring messages, and spending time in prayer and meditation.

6. Accountability and Support:
Share your journey of challenging self-sabotaging thoughts with a trusted friend, mentor, or spiritual companion. Accountability and support create a dynamic where external perspectives contribute to the transformative process. Seek counsel from those who align with your pursuit of a positive and God-centered mindset.

7. Consistency and Patience:
Transformation takes time and consistent effort. Be patient with yourself as you navigate this process. Consistently challenge and replace self-sabotaging thoughts, recognizing that the renewal of the mind is a journey. Celebrate small victories, and embrace the transformative power of persistent, intentional thought management.

In mastering the inner dialogue, you empower yourself to confront and transform self-sabotaging thoughts. This journey is not about perfection but progress—an ongoing commitment to aligning your thoughts with God's truth. As you identify, challenge, and replace destructive self-talk, you pave the way for a mindset that reflects the beauty of God's design for your life.

Navigating the Inner Landscape: A Journey through Self-Communication
In the realm of self-communication, we've embarked on a profound journey, delving into the intricacies of the mind and the power embedded within our thoughts and words. Here, we've uncovered the significance of understanding the continuous inner dialogue—an ongoing narrative that shapes our perceptions, beliefs, and ultimately, our reality.

Key Reflections:
- The Power of Words: Every word spoken in the inner chambers of our minds holds significance. Whether positive or negative, our self-talk shapes our perceptions, beliefs, and reality. Acknowledging this power allows us to harness its potential for positive transformation.
- Affirmations as Anchors: Crafting affirmations rooted in God's promises and our true identity counteracts self-sabotaging thoughts. These affirmations serve as anchors, grounding our mindset in divine truth and empowering us to confront negativity.
- Cultivating a Positive Mental Environment: The choices we make in shaping our mental environment influence the quality of our thoughts. Surrounding ourselves with positive influences and engaging in uplifting activities contribute to a mindset aligned with God's perspective.
- Intuition and Self-Awareness: Active listening to one's own needs and desires involves tuning in to internal signals and emotions. Cultivating self-awareness through attentive listening allows us to catch warning signals early and prevent destructive patterns.
- Boundaries in Self-Communication: Setting healthy boundaries within self-communication involves clearly defining personal values and limits. Reinforcing these boundaries prevents the infiltration of destructive self-talk and preserves a space for God's truth to flourish.

Guidance Toward Adaptability:
As we conclude this exploration of self-communication, we transition to the final pillar of relatability—adaptability. The ability to adapt is essential in navigating the ever-changing landscapes of relationships, both with ourselves and others. Join us in unraveling the transformative power of adaptability, where resilience and openness pave the way for dynamic connections and a deeper understanding of God's design for our relational journey.

Workbook-Challenging Self-Sabotaging Thoughts Worksheet Page 124
Workbook-Setting Healthy Boundaries Worksheet Page 127

SELF-ADAPTABILITY

Cultivating Self-Adaptability: Navigating God's Pruning Process

Self-adaptability is the dynamic posture of the heart and mind that willingly engages with God's pruning process. It involves a conscious choice to submit and commit to the transformative work that God desires to accomplish in our lives. While relinquishing control to the invisible hand of God might challenge our innate desire for certainty and control, it is a crucial step on the path to relationship mastery and the fulfillment of God's purpose.

The Essence of Self-Adaptability:

Self-adaptability goes beyond a passive response to change; it is an active, intentional cultivation of a disposition that welcomes God's pruning and redirection. This mindset acknowledges the fluidity of God's plan and embraces the necessary adjustments and shifts that accompany His transformative work.

Submission and Commitment:

Embracing self-adaptability requires a dual commitment: submitting to God's leading and committing to the process, even when it involves discomfort or uncertainty. It demands a willingness to trust God's wisdom over our understanding and to surrender the areas of our lives that need refining.

Relinquishing Control for Relationship Mastery: While it is not easy to relinquish control, especially in a culture that values self-sufficiency, it is a crucial step toward relationship mastery with God. Just as the potter molds the clay, God desires to shape and refine us, but our willingness to yield is essential. Self-adaptability becomes a bridge between our desire for control and God's divine plan.

The Wilderness and the Promised Land Analogy:

Reflecting on the journey of the Israelites provides a poignant analogy for self-adaptability. Those who adapted to the challenges of the wilderness, trusting in God's guidance, entered the Promised Land. On the other hand, those who grumbled, resisted change, and longed for the familiarity of Egypt missed out on the destination God had prepared for them.

Warning Against Complacency:
This narrative serves as a cautionary tale in our lives. Like the Israelites, we may face wilderness seasons where self-adaptability is imperative. The warning is clear: those who resist growth and change risk missing out on the abundant life God has planned. Adaptability becomes a key to navigating the uncertainties of the wilderness, ushering us into the fulfillment of God's promises.

In the forthcoming sections, we will delve deeper into the facets of self-adaptability, exploring resilience, openness, and a growth mindset. By understanding and embracing these elements, we position ourselves to actively participate in God's transformative work, ultimately reaching the destination He has prepared for us. May this exploration inspire a willingness to submit, commit, and adapt, trusting in the hands of the Master Potter to mold us into vessels fit for His purpose.

Understanding the Divine Pruning Process: A Call to Self-Adaptability
God's pruning in our lives serves a profound purpose, intricately connected to the concept of self-adaptability. In our journey with Him, pruning is a vital process that ensures our continual growth and fruitful existence.

Significance of Bearing Fruit:
God desires us to bear fruit continuously, not merely for our individual benefit but as a source of nourishment for generations to come. A healthy tree and branches signify a life that is rooted in God, providing sustenance, shade, and a living testimony. Our lives become a beacon of hope, radiating God's transformative power and faithfulness.

Five Aspects God Prunes for Self-Adaptability:
- Pride (P): Pride hinders our receptivity to God's guidance and correction. To adapt, we must allow God to prune away the roots of pride, cultivating humility in our hearts.
- Rebellion (R): A spirit of rebellion resists God's authority and plans. Self-adaptability requires submitting to God's will, allowing Him to prune away the rebellious tendencies that hinder our growth.
- Unforgiveness (U): Unforgiveness creates barriers in our relationships, stunting our spiritual and emotional growth. Self-adaptability demands that we let go of grudges and allow God to prune away the roots of unforgiveness.
- Negative Thinking (N): Negative thought patterns can poison our minds and hinder our adaptability. God's pruning involves replacing negative thinking with a renewed, positive mindset that aligns with His truth.
- Entitlement (E): Entitlement can breed discontent and ingratitude. To adapt, we must allow God to prune away entitlement, cultivating a spirit of gratitude and contentment in all circumstances.

The Pruning Process and Self-Adaptability:
God prunes us not out of punishment but out of love. He desires to shape us into vessels that continually bear fruit, reflecting His glory. Self-adaptability is the key to embracing the pruning process with a willing heart. It involves acknowledging that, just as a vine needs pruning for optimal fruitfulness, our lives require divine adjustments to fulfill God's purposes.

The Metaphor of the Vine and Branches:
In John 15:2, Jesus describes this pruning process: "He cuts off every branch in me that bears no fruit, while every branch that does bear fruit he prunes so that it will be even more fruitful." This metaphor emphasizes God's desire for us to bear abundant fruit and the necessity of pruning for sustained growth.

As we explore self-adaptability, let us recognize the divine purpose in God's pruning. Embracing this process allows us to continually bear fruit, not only for our benefit but for the generations that will follow. May we approach God's pruning shears with humility and a readiness to adapt, trusting that His transformative work will yield a life that glorifies Him and blesses others.

Embracing Every Moment: The Power of Adaptability

The Endurance of Seasons: God often keeps us in specific seasons longer than we anticipate. These extended periods serve a purpose – they are times of seasoning. Just as a seasoned individual imparts flavor and richness to a situation, being seasoned in a particular season equips us to add depth, understanding, and preservation to key moments in the next season. The art of adaptation allows us to extract the essence of each season, ensuring that nothing is wasted.

The Dynamic Nature of Life:
Life is inherently dynamic, characterized by constant change and unpredictability. The ability to adapt becomes a survival skill, a passport that allows us to navigate the diverse landscapes of our existence. The static and rigid find themselves left behind, while the adaptable soar to new heights.

God's Search for the Adaptable:
God is in search of individuals who can navigate the unpredictable terrain of life. He seeks hearts that are willing to adapt, recognizing that adaptability is not a sign of weakness but a testament to resilience and trust in His providence. God is the ultimate orchestrator of change, and those who adapt willingly align themselves with His divine rhythm.

Shift in Perspective:
Embracing adaptability requires a fundamental shift in perspective. Instead of resisting change, we learn to welcome it as an opportunity for growth. Each twist and turn becomes a chance to discover new facets of God's plan and purpose for our lives. The unpredictable becomes a canvas for divine creativity.

Willingness to Adapt:
The willingness to adapt is an acknowledgment that our plans are subject to divine redirection. It is an admission that God's thoughts and ways are higher than ours (Isaiah 55:8-9), and His purpose transcends our limited understanding. The adaptable heart is open to the beauty hidden within unexpected moments, confident that even in change, God's hand remains steady.

A Divine Choreography:
Life's moments are like notes in a divine symphony, orchestrated by God. The adaptable soul dances to the rhythm of His melody, finding joy in each movement. When we resist adaptation, we risk missing the harmonious cadence of God's plans for our lives.

As we cultivate the art of adaptability, we position ourselves to embrace every moment as a unique opportunity for growth and divine intervention. God's call is clear – be willing to adapt, trusting that His purpose will unfold in the most unexpected yet beautiful ways. The dance of life becomes a divine choreography, and the adaptable heart finds its rhythm in God's eternal song.

The Power of Pivoting: Embracing Immediate Obedience
In the grand narrative of following God, the concept of pivoting emerges as a powerful principle. To pivot is to swiftly and decisively change direction in response to God's leading. It is an act of immediate obedience, a dance of faith where one adjusts their steps to align with the divine rhythm. This concept unfolds in the stories of the "immediately" and the "eventually" followers of Jesus.

The Immediately Followers:
When Jesus called His disciples, a distinct group responded with immediacy. Their response was not clouded by questions or concerns about the destination; instead, they immediately dropped their nets and followed Him (Matthew 4:19-20). This act of immediate obedience marked the beginning of their transformative journey with Christ. The immediately followers trusted in the wisdom of the One who called them, displaying a readiness to pivot at His command.

Pivoting with Swift Footwork:
The art of pivoting requires swift footwork – a willingness to move without hesitation. Just as a basketball player adjusts their stance in a split second to respond to the opposing team, believers must cultivate a spiritual agility that allows them to pivot at God's promptings. The immediately followers demonstrated this agility, embodying a trust that God's direction is always for their good (Romans 8:28).

The Eventually Followers:
On the other side of the spectrum are the eventually followers. These individuals, while intrigued by the call of Jesus, choose to contemplate and question before making a decision. They hesitate to drop their nets immediately, caught in the undertow of doubt and deliberation. The eventual followers may miss the pivotal moments that God orchestrates, as their response is delayed and lacks the immediacy that characterizes obedient discipleship.

Navigating the Unknown:
Pivoting often involves navigating the unknown. When God calls His people to pivot, the destination may not be fully revealed. It requires a trust that transcends understanding (Proverbs 3:5-6). The immediately followers, without a detailed itinerary, embraced the uncertainty, confident that the One leading them knew the way. The eventuallies, in their hesitation, grappled with the fear of the unknown, potentially missing out on the transformative journey God had prepared for them.

Shifting Perspectives:
The power of pivoting lies not only in the physical act of moving but also in the shift of perspective that accompanies it. When Jesus called the fishermen, He promised to make them fishers of men, altering their self-perception and purpose (Matthew 4:19). The pivot brought a new identity and mission. Those who pivot immediately are positioned for a shift in perspective, enabling them to see themselves and their purpose through God's lens.

Conclusion:
Pivoting is an essential aspect of the believer's journey. It calls for immediate obedience, swift footwork, and a willingness to navigate the unknown. The narratives of the immediately and eventually followers serve as mirrors, prompting reflection on our own readiness to pivot. In the dance of faith, may we be a people who pivot immediately, trusting that God's direction is always towards a destination of transformative purpose.

The Urgency of Immediate Obedience: Avoiding the Pitfalls of Delayed Response
Immediate obedience to God's directives is not merely a suggestion but a crucial element in the life of a believer. The biblical narratives are replete with examples illustrating the significance of swift and unwavering responses to God's commands. Understanding the importance of immediate obedience involves recognizing the dangers associated with delayed responses and cultivating the right attitudes to adapt seamlessly to God's leading.

Dangers of Delayed Obedience:
- Loss of Thrones: Saul's Tragic Tale: The narrative of Saul serves as a cautionary tale on the dangers of delayed obedience. In 1 Samuel 15, God gave Saul clear instructions through the prophet Samuel. However, Saul chose to delay his obedience, partially fulfilling the command. This seemingly surface-level disobedience had profound consequences – the loss of his throne. Immediate obedience is paramount, for delayed response might result in losing the very things God has entrusted to us, whether it be a position, relationship, or opportunity.
- Surface Worship vs. Obedient Heart: Saul's downfall highlights the inadequacy of a surface-level appearance of worship. His offering of sacrifices and preservation of spoils did not compensate for his disobedience (1 Samuel 15:22-23). True worship is not in external rituals but in an obedient heart. Delayed obedience may create a facade of religiosity, but it cannot overshadow the core requirement of surrendering to God's will.
- Impact on Family and Community: Achan's Story: In the book of Joshua, Achan's delayed obedience had a cascading effect on his entire family and the community (Joshua 7). His disobedience not only resulted in personal consequences but affected those connected to him. This narrative underscores the communal implications of delayed obedience, emphasizing that our actions have broader repercussions.

Cultivating Attitudes for Immediate Obedience:

- Sensitivity to God's Voice: Immediate obedience begins with sensitivity to God's voice. Developing a keen spiritual ear requires a consistent and intimate relationship with God through prayer, meditation, and a posture of listening.
- Submission and Humility: Swift obedience stems from a heart submitted to God's authority. A humble acknowledgment of our dependence on God positions us to obey without hesitation. Pride and self-reliance hinder immediate obedience.
- Adaptability to God's Timetable: Being adaptable to God's timetable is crucial. Immediate obedience may not always align with our preferred schedules or plans. Cultivating patience and trust in God's perfect timing enables seamless responses.

Immediate obedience is not an optional virtue; it is foundational to a thriving relationship with God. The stories of Saul and Achan underscore the dangers of delayed responses, emphasizing that unrepentant disobedience, even if it appears to linger, will eventually result in the loss of thrones and affect those connected to us. As we navigate the complexities of life, may our hearts be attuned to God's voice, submitted to His authority, and adaptable to His perfect timetable, ensuring that our obedience is immediate and unwavering.

Resilience: The Crucial Companion of Adaptability

Resilience, the capacity to bounce back from challenges and remain steadfast amid adversity, is an indispensable element of adaptability. In the intricate fabric of our lives, God intricately weaves trials and challenges to cultivate resilience, ensuring that we are well-equipped for the dynamic nature of relationships and family dynamics. The wisdom encapsulated in James 1:2-3 provides profound insights into the purpose of trials and their transformative role in fostering adaptability.

Trials: The Versatile Tools of God's Crafting:
James invites believers to "count it all joy" when encountering various trials, recognizing them as essential components of our growth journey. These trials serve as God's versatile tools, allowing us to experience the multifaceted nature of challenges. Consider life's trials as a trial period, a divine invitation to taste the next level of spiritual and relational growth. Just as a trial period with a service provider grants familiarity and ease of use, our trial periods in life equip us with the experiential knowledge needed for resilience. God, in His wisdom, allows us to undergo these trial periods so that, when the payment is due for our next season, we are not only familiar but resilient in our readiness for what lies ahead.

Adaptability through Versatility:
Versatility, the ability to handle diverse situations with ease, emerges from the diverse trials God allows in our lives. These trials act as a spiritual gym, where our adaptability muscles are exercised and strengthened. The "various trials" encompass a spectrum of experiences, ensuring that we are not one-dimensional but equipped to navigate the complexities of relationships and family dynamics.

Resilience as the Fruit of Adversity:
The testing of our faith in the crucible of trials produces patience – a key component of resilience. Resilience is not a passive endurance; it is an active, enduring strength that arises from the refining fires of challenges. Just as a metal becomes stronger through the process of tempering, our spirits become resilient through the trials that God permits. The goal is not merely endurance but to emerge "whole, complete, and lacking in nothing" – a testament to the transformative power of God's adaptive plan for our lives.

The Trial Period: Preparing for the Next Level:
Consider life's trials as a trial period, a divine invitation to taste the next level of spiritual and relational growth. Just as a trial period with a service provider grants familiarity and ease of use, our trial periods in life equip us with the experiential knowledge needed for resilience. God, in His wisdom, allows us to undergo these trial periods so that, when the payment is due for our next season, we are not only familiar but resilient in our readiness for what lies ahead.

Conclusion:
Resilience, cultivated through the various trials God allows, is the crucial companion of adaptability. As we navigate the challenges of life and relationships, may we embrace the diverse trials with joy, recognizing them as God's versatile tools crafting resilience within us. Our trial periods serve as preparatory stages for the next level, ensuring that we are not only familiar but robustly adaptable, ready to face the dynamic landscapes of relationships and family dynamics with enduring strength.

Embracing Openness: A Gateway to Adaptability
Openness involves being receptive to new perspectives, ideas, and experiences—an indispensable quality for fostering adaptability. This disposition not only opens the door to personal growth but also enriches the fabric of relationships and allows for a harmonious interplay of diverse perspectives.

Receptivity to New Perspectives:
Being adaptable requires a genuine willingness to listen and learn from others. Openness to new perspectives signifies a humble acknowledgment that wisdom and insight can be gleaned from various sources. Just as a tree that bends with the wind is less likely to break, a heart and mind open to diverse viewpoints are more resilient in the face of life's storms.

Welcoming Fresh Ideas:
Adaptability thrives in an environment where new ideas are not merely tolerated but welcomed. It's about recognizing that innovation and growth often emerge from the fertile ground of novel concepts. Just as a garden flourishes with a diverse array of plants, the landscape of our lives becomes vibrant when we cultivate a mindset that values and integrates fresh ideas.

Space for Personal Growth:
Openness creates a spacious arena for personal growth to unfold. Like a well-tended garden needs room for each plant to stretch its roots and reach toward the sun, individuals need space for their unique journeys of self-discovery and improvement. This involves being receptive not only to external influences but also to the inner promptings of growth and change.

Humility as a Companion to Openness:
At the heart of openness lies humility—the acknowledgment that our understanding is incomplete and there is always room to learn and grow. A humble spirit recognizes that personal growth is an ongoing journey, marked by the willingness to adapt and evolve. In relationships, humility fosters an atmosphere where each person's unique contributions are honored and valued.

The Intersection of Openness and Adaptability:
Openness and adaptability intersect seamlessly, creating a dynamic synergy. When we embrace openness, we invite the winds of change to shape us, much like a sail adjusts to the shifting breeze. This flexibility enables us to navigate the ever-changing seas of life with grace and resilience. Moreover, it allows us to adapt not just to external circumstances but to the evolving landscapes of our own understanding and beliefs.

Conclusion:
In the pursuit of adaptability, openness is both a gateway and a companion. By being receptive to new perspectives and ideas, and by allowing ample space for personal growth, we create a fertile ground for adaptability to flourish. Just as a garden that welcomes a variety of plants is more resilient to environmental changes, a life marked by openness becomes a canvas where adaptability paints its masterpieces, weaving together the threads of growth, humility, and harmonious relationships.

Learning and Unlearning: Navigating the Seas of Adaptability
The journey of adaptability is intertwined with the twin processes of learning and unlearning—a dynamic dance between acquiring new insights and shedding outdated beliefs and habits. In the ever-changing landscapes of life, the ability to learn and unlearn becomes a compass that guides us through uncharted waters, offering the promise of growth, resilience, and deeper understanding.

Importance of Letting Go:
Adaptability often begins with the courage to let go—letting go of outdated beliefs, habits, and perspectives that may no longer serve us. Just as a ship must cast off anchor to sail into new horizons, individuals must release the weight of obsolete ideas to navigate the evolving currents of life. This process involves acknowledging that what once provided stability might now hinder progress.

Willingness to Reevaluate Perspectives:
A crucial aspect of adaptability is the ongoing willingness to reevaluate and adjust perspectives. Like a sailor navigating changing tides, individuals must be open to recalibrating their understanding of situations, people, and even themselves. This flexibility in perspective allows for a more nuanced and accurate interpretation of the world, fostering adaptability in the face of diverse challenges.

Strategies for Intentional Learning and Unlearning:
Cultivating Curiosity:
- Embracing adaptability requires a curious mind—an eagerness to explore and discover. Cultivating curiosity sparks a desire for continuous learning, propelling individuals into new realms of knowledge and understanding.

Reflection and Self-Awareness:
- Intentional learning involves reflective practices that heighten self-awareness. Taking time to reflect on experiences, beliefs, and reactions provides valuable insights that guide the process of unlearning and adapting.

Seeking Diverse Perspectives:
- Actively seeking diverse perspectives is akin to navigating through varied landscapes. Exposure to different viewpoints challenges existing paradigms, fostering adaptability by broadening the scope of understanding.

Embracing a Growth Mindset:
- A growth mindset—believing that abilities and intelligence can be developed through dedication and hard work—encourages adaptability. It fosters resilience in the face of challenges and cultivates a willingness to learn from setbacks.

Learning and Unlearning: An Ongoing Voyage:
In the grand odyssey of life, learning and unlearning are continuous voyages. Each encounter, each challenge, and each new insight becomes a port of call where individuals can acquire new knowledge and shed old ways of thinking. The adaptability born from this dynamic process empowers individuals to navigate life's seas with confidence, responding to the ever-changing winds with a spirit of resilience and growth.

Learning and unlearning are the compass and sails of adaptability, guiding us through the unpredictable waters of life. By recognizing the importance of letting go, cultivating a willingness to reevaluate perspectives, and employing intentional strategies for continuous growth, individuals embark on a transformative journey where adaptability becomes not just a skill but a way of being—a dynamic dance with the rhythms of change and growth.

Patience as a Companion to Self-Adaptability: Nurturing Growth with Grace
In personal development, patience becomes a steady companion, blending resilience and strength into our journey.

Understanding the delicate relationship between patience and adaptability is essential for navigating the challenges of growth with grace and celebrating the milestones along the transformative odyssey.

Understanding the Relationship:
Patience and adaptability share an intimate bond, akin to the ebb and flow of the tides. Adaptability requires the capacity to endure the fluctuations of change, to gracefully accept that growth unfolds in its own time. Patience, in turn, is the gentle hand that guides us through the labyrinth of self-discovery, allowing the process to unfold organically rather than forcing predetermined timelines.

In the context of personal development, patience becomes the soil in which the seeds of adaptability can take root. It's the recognition that growth is a nuanced journey, with its ebbs and flows, and that forcing progress may hinder the very transformation we seek. Patience whispers that every step, no matter how small, contributes to the grand mosaic of self-evolution.

Navigating Challenges with Grace:
Patience becomes a beacon of light during the challenges inherent in personal growth. As we strive to adapt to new realities, confront obstacles, or dismantle outdated structures within ourselves, patience offers solace. It encourages a perspective that views setbacks not as roadblocks but as detours leading to unexpected revelations and lessons.

In the face of the unknown, patience allows for a measured response. It dissolves the urgency that often accompanies change, providing a space for contemplation, resilience, and the unwavering belief that the journey is as significant as the destination. Through patience, challenges become stepping stones rather than stumbling blocks, and the transformative process becomes a dance rather than a hurried march.

Celebrating Progress and Milestones:
Patience invites the art of celebration—a joyful acknowledgment of progress and milestones along the transformative journey. Each adaptation, no matter how incremental, is a cause for celebration. Rather than fixating on the distant horizon, patience prompts us to savor the beauty of the present, acknowledging the growth that has taken root within.

Celebration becomes a form of gratitude—a recognition of the resilience and adaptability that have brought us to this moment. It fuels motivation and propels us forward with renewed vigor. Patience and celebration, intertwined, create a harmonious rhythm in the dance of personal evolution, reinforcing the understanding that the journey itself is a destination worthy of celebration.

Conclusion:
In the symphony of personal growth, patience harmonizes with adaptability to create a melody of resilience and grace. Navigating challenges with patience transforms obstacles into opportunities, and celebrating progress becomes an affirmation of the journey's significance. Together, patience and adaptability guide individuals through the ever-changing landscapes of self-discovery, fostering a holistic and enduring transformation.

Workbook-Reflection Questions: Self Adaptability 129

183

7 SHIPS YOU MUST BOARD BEFORE YOU BOARD A RELATIONSHIPS

Embarking on the Seven Essential Ships Before Boarding a Relationship

Before setting sail into the seas of romantic relationships, it's crucial to board seven foundational ships: Sonship, Discipleship, Ownership, Stewardship, Friendship, Worship and Hardship. Each ship represents a vital aspect of personal development and spiritual alignment that will profoundly impact the success and fulfillment of your relationships.

1. **Sonship**: The Foundation of Identity: Sonship refers to your identity as a child of God. Understanding your worth and value in the eyes of your heavenly Father forms the bedrock of a healthy self-concept. By boarding the Sonship ship, you embark on a journey to discover who you are in Christ, gaining the security and assurance that comes from being unconditionally loved.

2. **Discipleship**: The Path to Growth: Discipleship involves a commitment to continual growth and learning, both individually and in the context of your faith. As a disciple, you embrace the teachings of Jesus, allowing His wisdom to shape your character and guide your decisions. Boarding the Discipleship ship ensures that you and your potential partner share a common foundation, fostering spiritual unity and mutual understanding.

3. **Ownership**: Taking Responsibility for Your Journey: Ownership is about taking responsibility for your life, choices, the impact you have on others, and even material aspects like ideas and residual income-producing assets. This ship emphasizes accountability, self-awareness, intentional living, and financial stewardship. By boarding the Ownership ship, you acknowledge your role in creating a healthy, thriving relationship. It's the vessel that empowers you to navigate challenges with maturity, contribute positively to the shared journey, and build a solid financial foundation.

4. **Stewardship**: Nurturing Resources for Abundance: Stewardship entails the wise and responsible management of resources entrusted to your care, including time, talents, finances, and relationships. By boarding the Stewardship ship, you commit to nurturing these resources with diligence and integrity, recognizing them as gifts from God. This journey empowers you to cultivate abundance in your life and relationships, fostering a sense of gratitude, purpose, and fulfillment.

184

5. **Friendship**: The Anchor of Relational Bonds: Friendship serves as the anchor that secures and strengthens all other relationships. By cultivating genuine friendships, you create a supportive network of companions who uplift, encourage, and journey alongside you through life's joys and challenges. Boarding the Friendship ship involves investing time, effort, and care into building meaningful connections based on mutual trust, respect, and shared experiences. This voyage enriches your relational landscape, providing a foundation of warmth, understanding, and companionship that enhances every aspect of your life.

6. **Worship**: Elevating the Spirit in Reverence: Worship is the act of expressing reverence, adoration, and gratitude towards God, acknowledging His sovereignty and goodness. Becoming a worshiper entails cultivating a deep and intimate connection with the divine, where your heart is attuned to His presence and your life reflects His glory. By boarding the Worship ship, you prioritize the pursuit of God's presence above all else, aligning your desires, thoughts, and actions with His will. This foundational journey of worship prepares your heart to receive and give love in its purest form, laying the groundwork for a relationship grounded in spiritual unity, devotion, and divine purpose.

7. **Hardship**: Navigating Challenges with Resilience and Faith: Hardship is an inevitable part of the human experience, encompassing trials, setbacks, and adversity that we encounter along life's journey. Boarding the Hardship ship involves facing these challenges with courage, resilience, and unwavering faith, recognizing them as opportunities for growth and transformation. By embracing hardship as a precursor to relationship readiness, you cultivate inner strength, perseverance, and a deep reliance on God's grace.

In the upcoming sections, we will delve into each ship, exploring the profound significance it holds for your personal and relational well-being. As you prepare to embark on this transformative voyage, remember that the strength of your relationships is deeply intertwined with the strength of your individual foundation. By consciously embracing Sonship, Discipleship, and Ownership, you lay the groundwork for a relationship that is anchored in purpose, growth, and shared responsibility.

BOARDING SON-SHIP

Sailing the First Ship: Embracing Sonship
Embarking on the ship of sonship is not just the first step but a foundational prerequisite for navigating the vast seas of relationships. This ship equips us with indispensable skills and perspectives that are crucial for successfully sailing other relational vessels. If we fail to comprehend what it means to be a child of God, we'll find ourselves ill-prepared to fulfill the diverse roles of a spouse, parent, friend, or any other relational capacity.

Foundational Understanding:
Understanding sonship is akin to grasping the helm of the ship that steers our identity. As children of God, we're not merely adopting a title; we're embracing a profound reality that reshapes how we perceive ourselves and, consequently, how we interact with the world. The foundational understanding of God as our Father transforms our worldview, dictating the course of every other relationship we embark upon.

Shifting Roles:
The revelation of sonship has a domino effect on our various roles. Knowing God as our Father shifts every other role we hold. Whether it be a spouse, parent, friend, or colleague, the lens through which we view these roles changes. Sonship fosters qualities like love, grace, and forgiveness, and these characteristics become the sails that carry us through the diverse waters of relational dynamics.

Satan's Resistance:
The enemy of our souls vehemently opposes the revelation of sonship. Satan understands that a person who fully comprehends their identity as a child of God becomes fortified against his attacks. The assurance of being God's beloved child is an anchor that holds firm in the face of doubt, insecurity, and the onslaught of the adversary. By undermining sonship, Satan seeks to create relational turbulence, leaving individuals adrift and vulnerable to the storms of life.

186

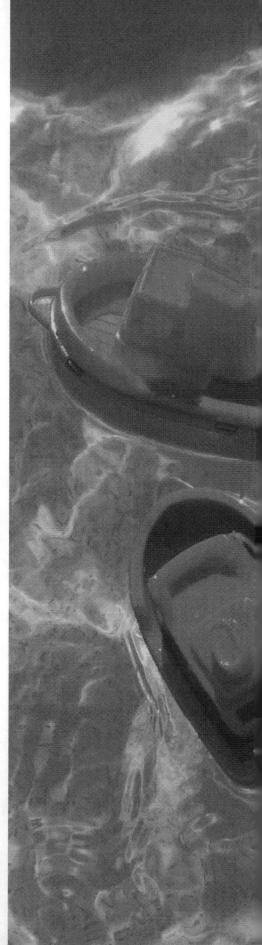

The Theology of Adoption: Embraced by God's Choosing

The theological concept of adoption is a profound and transformative truth woven throughout the fabric of Scripture. It signifies not merely a legal transaction but a divine embrace, a choice made by God to claim us as His own. Let's delve into the theological richness of adoption and the implications it carries for our understanding of God's love and our identity.

Biblical Foundation:
The Bible unfolds the narrative of adoption, revealing God's heart as the ultimate adoptive Father. Ephesians 1:5 (ESV) declares, "He predestined us for adoption to himself as sons through Jesus Christ, according to the purpose of his will." This verse encapsulates the divine intent behind adoption. It's not an afterthought but a predestined plan birthed in the heart of God.

Chosen and Desired:
Adoption communicates a powerful truth: we are chosen and desired by God. In the cultural and legal context of biblical times, adoption wasn't merely about providing a home for the orphaned; it was about intentionally selecting a child to become an heir. God's choice to adopt us into His family is an act of intentional love, signifying His desire to take on the responsibility that is us.

The Essence of God's Love:
The theological depth of adoption unveils the essence of God's love. It's not a generic or distant affection; it's an intimate, intentional, and sacrificial love. God's decision to adopt us is a demonstration of His commitment to us, regardless of our flaws or shortcomings. Romans 8:15 (ESV) beautifully captures this essence: "For you did not receive the spirit of slavery to fall back into fear, but you have received the Spirit of adoption as sons, by whom we cry, 'Abba! Father!'"

Humbling Grace:
Adoption should profoundly humble us. The realization that the Creator of the universe chose us, with all our imperfections, should leave us awestruck. It's an undeserved grace that shatters any notion of earning or merit. We are not adopted into God's family based on our performance but solely by His grace.

Identity and Inheritance:
Adoption shapes our identity and secures our inheritance. As adopted children of God, we inherit the promises and blessings of the Kingdom. Galatians 4:7 (ESV) declares, "So you are no longer a slave, but a son, and if a son, then an heir through God." Our identity is rooted in being cherished sons and daughters of the Almighty, destined for an eternal inheritance.
In conclusion, the theology of adoption weaves together the threads of God's love, choice, and grace. It transforms our understanding of relationship with God, grounding us in the assurance that we are not mere servants but cherished members of God's family, adopted with intentional love and divine purpose.

Overcoming Barriers to Embracing Adoption: Unveiling the Truth
While the concept of adoption carries profound theological significance, embracing this truth can be hindered by various barriers rooted in our understanding, experiences, and misconceptions. Let's explore some common obstacles that may impede our recognition and full embrace of the reality of adoption in God's family.

1. Orphan Spirit:
One prevalent hindrance is what's often termed an "orphan spirit." This mindset stems from feelings of rejection, abandonment, or unworthiness, which may have originated from past experiences or broken relationships. Recognizing God's choice to adopt us as sons and daughters becomes challenging when overshadowed by a lingering sense of orphanhood.

2. Performance-Based Identity:
A performance-based identity fosters the belief that we must earn love and acceptance. If we carry this mindset into our spiritual understanding, the unconditional love inherent in adoption becomes a challenging concept. Embracing the truth that God chose us, not based on our merits but His grace, requires a shift away from performance-oriented thinking.

3. Misconceptions about God's Character:
Misconceptions about God's character can erect barriers to embracing adoption fully. If we perceive God as distant, harsh, or punitive, accepting His invitation to be adopted into His family becomes a daunting prospect. The journey to embracing adoption often involves dismantling distorted views of God's nature and replacing them with the truth of His love.

4. Fear of Rejection:
The fear of rejection can be a potent inhibitor. Even with the assurance of God's unconditional love, our fear of rejection can prompt hesitation in fully embracing the reality of adoption. Confronting this fear involves understanding that God's love transcends human experiences of rejection and stands as an unshakable foundation.

5. Lack of Understanding:
Sometimes, the hindrance is rooted in a lack of understanding or awareness. Many believers may not fully grasp the depth and significance of adoption in God's plan. Increasing our knowledge and meditating on Scriptures that expound on this truth can dismantle the barriers of ignorance.

Overcoming and Embracing the Truth:
To overcome these hindrances, intentional steps are crucial. Engaging in deep, personal reflection, seeking God through prayer, and immersing oneself in Scriptures that unveil the beauty of adoption are essential. Additionally, fostering a supportive community that reinforces these truths can create an environment conducive to embracing the reality of being chosen and adopted by God.

In essence, recognizing and embracing the truth of adoption requires a transformative shift in our thinking and a surrendering of barriers that hinder us from fully experiencing the depth of God's love and the privileges of being His cherished sons and daughters.

Transformative Impact of Embracing Sonship on Relationships: Unveiling a New Paradigm
Embracing sonship isn't merely a theological concept; it's a profound truth that carries the power to reshape and elevate every facet of our relationships. The impact of recognizing ourselves as beloved sons and daughters of God resonates across various dimensions, fostering healthier connections and deeper intimacy.

1. Identity Clarification:
Embracing sonship provides a secure foundation for our identity. As we understand ourselves as valued and chosen by God, it dispels insecurities and fosters a sense of self-worth. This clarity cascades into our relationships, freeing us from seeking validation or identity in others.

2. Mutual Respect and Honor:
Recognizing our sonship in God's family instills a deep sense of honor and respect for ourselves and others. When we comprehend the profound value God places on each individual, it naturally translates into how we view and treat those around us. Relationships become a space where honor and respect flourish.

3. Authentic Connection:
Embracing sonship dismantles the need for pretense or performance in relationships. Authenticity becomes the hallmark of our interactions. Knowing that God accepts us as we are, we extend the same grace to others, fostering genuine and vulnerable connections that transcend superficiality.

4. Purpose-Driven Relationships:
Understanding our identity as sons and daughters aligns us with a higher purpose. Relationships cease to be solely transactional or driven by personal agendas; instead, they become conduits for fulfilling God's overarching mission. Shared purpose strengthens bonds and adds depth to our connections.

5. Empathy and Compassion:
Sonship cultivates empathy by reminding us of God's compassion toward us. When we grasp the depth of God's love and mercy, it becomes a wellspring for extending the same to those around us. Compassion becomes a natural outflow, fostering understanding and support in our relationships.

6. Gracious Forgiveness:
The knowledge of our sonship encourages a culture of forgiveness. Understanding the magnitude of God's forgiveness toward us empowers us to extend grace to others. Relationships marked by forgiveness create an environment where individuals can grow and thrive despite imperfections.

7. Empowering Leadership:
For those in leadership roles, embracing sonship transforms leadership styles. Leaders guided by the example of God's fatherhood exhibit servant leadership, empowering and uplifting those under their care. This paradigm shift promotes healthier dynamics in family, workplace, or community leadership.

In essence, embracing sonship serves as a catalyst for a paradigm shift in how we approach and navigate relationships. It touches the core of our being, reshaping attitudes, fostering a culture of love and grace, and infusing purpose into our connections with others. The transformative impact extends far beyond personal growth, influencing the collective dynamics of families, communities, and societies.

Workbook-Embracing Sonship Worksheet: Navigating the Journey to Deeper Relationships 132

BOARDING DISCIPLE-SHIP

Boarding the Ship of Discipleship: Nurturing Christlike Character

In the vast sea of relationships, the ship of Discipleship stands as a crucial vessel, ready to equip individuals with the skills and virtues needed to navigate the challenges and joys of connections with others. Discipleship, in the context of relationships, is the intentional pursuit of Christlikeness and disciplined living. This ship becomes the training ground where individuals learn to deny self, carry their cross, and follow the example set by Christ.

Understanding Discipleship:
Discipleship is more than acquiring knowledge; it's a transformative journey of embodying the teachings and character of Christ. As we follow Him, we engage in disciplines that shape our attitudes, actions, and interactions. The call to deny oneself signifies a surrender of personal desires to align with the higher purpose of Christ.

Scriptural Foundation:
The foundational scripture for Discipleship in relationships comes from Matthew 16:24 (ESV): "If anyone would come after me, let him deny himself and take up his cross and follow me." This profound statement encapsulates the essence of Discipleship—surrendering personal desires, embracing the challenges, and wholeheartedly following the ways of Christ.

Learning Christlikeness:
On the ship of Discipleship, individuals learn the disciplines that cultivate Christlike character. These may include humility, love, forgiveness, and self-control. Embracing these disciplines enables us to sail through relationships with grace, compassion, and a spirit of service.

Disciplines for Relationship Sailing:
- Humility: Acknowledging our imperfections and valuing others above ourselves.
- Love: Practicing unconditional love, mirroring Christ's love for us.
- Forgiveness: Extending forgiveness as a continual practice in relationships.
- Self-Control: Disciplining our responses, emotions, and actions for positive relational outcomes.

190

The Cross-Carrying Journey:
Taking up one's cross involves embracing the challenges and sacrifices that come with relationships. It's about enduring difficulties, offering forgiveness, and staying committed even when faced with trials. Discipleship teaches us that genuine relationships often require self-sacrifice and perseverance.

Following Christ's Example:
As we follow Christ's example in relationships, we prioritize sacrificial love, servant leadership, and a commitment to the well-being of others. This ship equips us with the tools to navigate storms, showing us that relationships thrive when built on the foundation of Christlike character.

Conclusion:
Discipleship, as a ship in the relational seas, offers transformative experiences that enable individuals to embody Christ's teachings and virtues. As we embark on this ship, we equip ourselves not only to sail relationships effectively but also to leave a lasting impact through our Christlike influence. In the following sections, we will delve into the specific disciplines that empower us to become disciplined followers of Christ in the context of relationships.

Navigating the Waters of Desires and Disciplines in Relationships
In the vast expanse of relational seas, the difference between desires and disciplines becomes a navigational compass determining the course and outcome of our connections with others. Desires serve as the initial winds that propel us into relationships, fueled by attraction, affection, and longing. However, it is the sturdy sails of disciplines that ensure we not only embark on the journey but successfully reach the shores of fruitful, lasting relationships.

Understanding Desires:
Desires are the currents that set relationships into motion. They are the sparks that ignite the flame, prompting us to seek companionship, intimacy, and connection. Desires fuel the initial excitement and enthusiasm, often inspiring us to take the first steps into the sea of relationships.

The Discipline of Endurance:
As the initial winds of desires propel us forward, we encounter the inevitable storms and challenges that characterize any relationship. This is where disciplines come into play. Endurance, a vital discipline, allows us to withstand the tempests and navigate the rough waters. Like a ship enduring through a storm, a disciplined mindset ensures that we weather challenges with resilience and commitment.

The Example of Christ's Discipline:
The epitome of discipline is found in the life of Jesus Christ. He faced temptations, endured hardships, and withstood immense pressure—all while remaining disciplined in His purpose. His journey demonstrates that desires may initiate the relationship, but it is discipline that ensures its enduring success.

Disciplines as Steadfast Anchors:
Disciplines in relationships serve as anchors, grounding us in values, principles, and actions that withstand the shifting tides. Faithfulness, consistency, honor, respect, and patience are disciplines that, when practiced consistently, contribute to the stability and longevity of relationships. They prevent us from drifting aimlessly and guide us toward the shared goals of the relationship.

The Hard Work of Disciplines:
While desires initiate the voyage, the hard work of relationships is sustained by disciplines. It's the commitment to doing what must be done every time it must be done—regardless of circumstances. This disciplined mindset acknowledges that relationships require intentional effort, sacrifice, and perseverance.

Conclusion: Desires may set the sails, but it is disciplines that navigate relationships through storms and propel them toward the shores of fulfillment. As we continue our journey through the relational seas, we recognize that desires are the starting point, but disciplines are the guiding stars that ensure we stay the course. In the upcoming sections, we will delve into specific disciplines that empower individuals to navigate relationships successfully and enjoy the promised fruits that lie ahead.

Embracing Christlike Disciplines for Effective Relationship Navigation

To sail relationships effectively, adopting Christlike disciplines is paramount. These disciplines serve as guiding principles, shaping our character, actions, and interactions with others. Here are some key Christlike disciplines to embrace daily:

1. Love (Agape Love):
- Definition: Unconditional, sacrificial love.
- Application: Choosing to love others regardless of their actions, showing kindness, forgiveness, and selflessness.

2. Patience:
- Definition: Enduring difficulties or waiting without frustration.
- Application: Remaining calm in challenging situations, allowing time for personal and relational growth.

3. Humility:
- Definition: A modest view of oneself, valuing others above oneself.
- Application: Putting the needs and interests of others before our own, acknowledging our imperfections.

4. Forgiveness:
- Definition: Choosing to pardon offenses and let go of resentment.
- Application: Extending forgiveness to others, just as Christ forgave us, fostering reconciliation and healing.

5. Self-Control:
- Definition: Exercising restraint over one's impulses and emotions.
- Application: Managing reactions, resisting temptations, and maintaining composure in various situations.

6. Generosity:
- Definition: Giving freely and abundantly to others.
- Application: Sharing resources, time, and compassion with a generous heart, expecting nothing in return.

7. Servanthood:
- Definition: A willingness to serve and meet the needs of others.
- Application: Seeking opportunities to serve and uplift others, embodying a humble and selfless attitude.

8. Compassion:
- Definition: Deep awareness of and sympathy for another's suffering.
- Application: Showing empathy and understanding, actively seeking to alleviate the pain or struggles of others.

9. Truthfulness:
- Definition: Consistent honesty and integrity in words and actions.
- Application: Communicating transparently, avoiding deceit, and upholding honesty in all interactions.

10. Grace:
- Definition: Unmerited favor and kindness.
- Application: Extending grace to others, recognizing that everyone falls short and deserves compassion and understanding.

11. Joy:
- Definition: A deep sense of happiness and contentment.
- Application: Cultivating joy in relationships, choosing gratitude and focusing on positive aspects, even amidst challenges.

12. Gentleness:
- Definition: Considerate and mild in behavior and temperament.
- Application: Responding with gentleness and humility, avoiding harshness or aggressiveness.

13. Faithfulness:
- Definition: Loyalty and commitment to promises and responsibilities.
- Application: Upholding commitments, staying true to one's word, and demonstrating loyalty in relationships.

Conclusion: Embracing Christlike disciplines daily not only shapes our character but also transforms the way we engage with others. These disciplines serve as a compass, guiding us through the complexities of relationships and enabling us to sail effectively toward shared goals. As we integrate these disciplines into our daily lives, we cultivate an environment of love, grace, and understanding, fostering flourishing relationships that honor God and bless those around us.

The Transformative Impact of Discipleship on Relationships

Embracing discipleship is akin to setting sail on a purposeful journey that transforms not only our individual lives but also the landscape of our relationships. Let's delve into the profound impact discipleship has on various facets of our connections with others.

1. Deeper Connections through Understanding:

Discipleship compels us to adopt a posture of humility and empathy, mirroring Christ's example. As we seek to understand the hearts and struggles of those around us, relationships deepen. The discipline of putting others first, as modeled by Jesus, fosters a genuine connection built on compassion and shared understanding.

2. Mutual Growth in Relationships:

Discipleship invites us to walk alongside others in their personal and spiritual journeys. In relationships, this translates into shared pursuits of growth and development. Couples, friends, and family members engaged in discipleship together experience a mutual sharpening effect, enhancing their collective well-being.

3. Enhanced Communication:

The discipline of discipleship emphasizes the importance of truthful and respectful communication. Applying these principles in relationships transforms the way we express ourselves. Clear, honest, and uplifting communication becomes a hallmark, minimizing misunderstandings and promoting harmony in interactions.

4. Authenticity Breeds Trust:

Christ's discipleship model underscores the value of authenticity. In relationships, this authenticity becomes a powerful force, breaking down barriers and fostering trust. As we embrace discipleship, we learn to be genuine about our struggles and victories, creating an environment where others feel safe to do the same.

5. Steadfast Support in Community:

Discipleship emphasizes the communal aspect of faith and growth. Translating this into relationships means becoming steadfast supporters. Through thick and thin, discipleship teaches us to bear one another's burdens, providing unwavering support in the diverse landscapes of life.

6. Character Transformation:

The transformative power of discipleship extends to character development. As we intentionally mold our character after Christ's example, relationships witness a profound change. Love, patience, kindness, and other virtues become the building blocks of our interactions, contributing to healthier, more positive connections.

In essence, discipleship is the wind that propels our relational sailboat. It aligns our compass with the values of Christ, guiding us through the ebbs and flows of human connections. Relationships touched by discipleship are characterized by understanding, growth, transparent communication, authenticity, consistent support, and a shared journey toward transformed character. As we navigate these relational waters, discipleship becomes the beacon guiding us toward the harbor of fulfilling and Christ-centered connections.

The Ever-Expanding Horizon of Discipleship: A Lifelong Journey

Discipleship is not a destination but an ongoing voyage, an endless pursuit of aligning our lives with the teachings and character of Christ. This perpetual journey of learning, growing, and becoming more like Him is the powerhouse that propels us toward greater depths in our relationships.

Consider this: even if granted a millennium of existence, we would only skim the surface of what it truly means to be a husband, father, friend, or any other relational role. It's a lifelong process that necessitates a continual walk with Christ, a commitment to sitting at His feet and imbibing the wisdom, love, and grace that only He can provide.

A poignant illustration of this truth is found in the biblical account of Mary and Martha. As Jesus visited their home, Martha busied herself with serving, while Mary chose to sit at the feet of Jesus, absorbing His teachings. When Martha expressed her concern to Jesus, expecting Him to reprimand Mary, Jesus gently corrected her. He highlighted that Mary had chosen the one thing necessary—being at His feet, learning from Him. This choice, Jesus emphasized, would endure and impact her life in ways that temporal service could not.

In our relationships, the concept remains the same. The commitment to discipleship—sitting at the feet of Jesus, imbibing His wisdom and grace—becomes the anchor that keeps our journey in sync with the divine. Here's why:

1. Continuous Growth:
Discipleship ensures that our relationships don't stagnate but, instead, constantly evolve. It's an acknowledgment that we can always learn more, love more deeply, and serve more compassionately. The journey never ends because Christ's lessons are inexhaustible.

2. Deeper Understanding:
As we sit at the feet of Jesus, our understanding of love, forgiveness, patience, and other virtues deepens. This richer understanding translates into a profound impact on our interactions with others. Discipleship enriches the quality of our relationships by shaping us into vessels of Christ-like love.

3. Guidance in Challenges:
Navigating the challenges within relationships requires a steady hand and a wise heart. Discipleship provides the compass and wisdom needed to weather storms and maintain a Christ-centered course, ensuring that we respond to trials with grace and wisdom.

4. Sustaining Grace:
The grace we receive at the feet of Jesus sustains us through the ebb and flow of relational dynamics. Whether in moments of joy or hardship, discipleship is the source of sustaining grace that empowers us to love, forgive, and persevere.

Embracing the truth that discipleship is a lifelong journey is akin to acknowledging that the horizon of relational possibilities with Christ is boundless. It's not a burden but a privilege— the privilege of continual transformation and the joy of becoming vessels through which Christ's love flows into our relationships. So, let us choose, like Mary, the one thing necessary: to be at His feet, learning, growing, and becoming vessels of His transformative love in all our relationships.

Workbook-Reflection Questions on Discipleship + Discipleship Spark Activity: A Journey Through the Gospels Page 136

-

BOARDING
OWNWER-SHIP

Navigating the Ship of Ownership: Cultivating Purpose and Generational Wealth

As we journey through the seas of relationships, the third ship we encounter is Ownership—a vessel that imparts crucial lessons on embracing our purpose, establishing our identity, and creating generational wealth. Ownership is not just about possessing material things; it's about understanding who we are, why we're here, and the legacy we desire to leave behind.

Understanding Purpose:

Ownership begins with a profound understanding of our purpose. Like a captain charting a course for uncharted waters, embracing our purpose guides our decisions, actions, and interactions in relationships. Purpose gives us direction, infuses our endeavors with meaning, and serves as a compass in navigating the complexities of life. Owning our purpose means recognizing the unique gifts, talents, and passions bestowed upon us, acknowledging that we are vessels designed for a specific journey.

Establishing Identity:

Just as a ship bears its name proudly across its bow, Ownership teaches us to establish and own our identity. In the context of relationships, understanding who we are is crucial for authentic connections. Owning our identity involves embracing our strengths and weaknesses, acknowledging past experiences, and continually growing into the person we aspire to be. Authenticity becomes the wind in our sails, propelling us forward with genuine connections and meaningful relationships.

Creating Generational Wealth:

Ownership extends beyond the immediate horizon of our lives—it sets sail towards creating generational wealth. Just as a fleet of ships passes down seafaring wisdom through the ages, so too does the legacy of ownership leave a lasting impact on future generations. This involves not only accumulating financial resources but also building a foundation of values, principles, and wisdom that can withstand the tests of time. Ownership empowers us to be stewards of the resources we've been entrusted with, ensuring that our legacy becomes a beacon for those who follow.

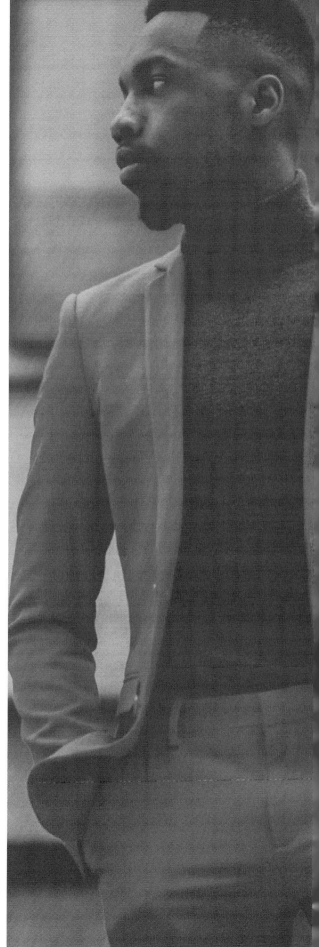

195

In the context of relationships, ownership encourages us to take responsibility for our roles and contributions. Whether in marriages, parenting, friendships, or community engagements, the principles of ownership guide us to be intentional and purpose-driven. As we navigate this ship, we learn to set our course based on a deeper understanding of who we are, live authentically, and leave a legacy that echoes through generations.

The next leg of our relational journey explores how embracing ownership can impact and enrich the dynamics of our connections, empowering us to sail confidently towards shared goals and objectives.

The Shackles of Non-Ownership: Breaking Free from Bondage
In the vast seas of relationships, there exists a stark contrast to the liberating voyage of ownership—the entanglement of non-ownership. Many individuals find themselves ensnared by forces beyond their control, becoming possessed rather than possessors. Non-ownership manifests in various forms, such as addictions, unhealthy dependencies, soul ties, and insecurities, casting shadows that cripple relationships and hinder personal growth.

The Chains of Addiction:
One of the prevalent ways non-ownership manifests is through addiction. Whether it's substances, habits, or destructive patterns of behavior, these vices become the puppeteer, dictating the course of one's life and relationships. Addictions erode personal agency, leaving individuals beholden to the next fix or momentary escape. In relationships, the chains of addiction drag down connections, infusing them with instability and unpredictability.

Unhealthy Dependencies:
Non-ownership often takes the form of unhealthy dependencies on others. When individuals derive their identity, worth, or purpose solely from external sources, they become enslaved to the expectations and opinions of others. Relationships, then, are marred by codependency and a constant need for validation. The inability to stand independently can lead to a stifling atmosphere, preventing the flourishing of genuine connections.

Soul Ties and Emotional Bonds:
Soul ties, formed through unhealthy emotional connections, can become like anchors weighing down relationships. When individuals are unable to sever detrimental ties from the past, these emotional entanglements hinder the ability to fully engage in present connections. The residue of past experiences and relationships can cast a shadow over current partnerships, preventing the free flow of authentic interaction.

Insecurities as Shackles:
Non-ownership thrives in the soil of insecurities. When individuals are bound by self-doubt, fear and a lack of self-acceptance, relationships bear the brunt of these insecurities. The constant need for reassurance, the fear of vulnerability, and the inability to express one's authentic self all contribute to a toxic atmosphere, stifling the growth of healthy connections.

Breaking free from the shackles of non-ownership is an essential step toward cultivating thriving relationships. The journey involves acknowledging these entanglements, understanding their roots, and actively pursuing a path of ownership. As we explore the seas of relationships, embracing ownership becomes the wind in our sails, propelling us toward genuine connections, purposeful living, and the legacy we were destined to leave. The forthcoming discussions will delve deeper into the transformative power of ownership and its profound impact on the dynamics of relationships.

Signs Someone is OWNED

Understanding the signs that someone is owned can be vital for recognizing internal struggles and barriers to healthy relationships. Here are indicators that may suggest a person is owned:

- Overpowered by External Validation (O):
  - Seeking Approval: Constantly seeking approval and validation from others, unable to define self-worth independently.
  - Conforming to Expectations: Preferring to conform to external expectations rather than expressing authentic beliefs.
- Withdrawn from Personal Purpose (W):
  - Lack of Passion: Displaying disinterest or apathy towards personal passions and goals.
  - Unclear Objectives: Struggling to articulate or pursue meaningful life objectives and lacking a sense of direction.
- Neglecting Relationships (N):
  - Communication Barriers: Difficulty in expressing emotions and thoughts openly, hindering effective communication.
  - Limited Emotional Investment: Showing little emotional investment in relationships, resulting in surface-level connections.
- Escaping Responsibility (E):
  - Procrastination: Chronic procrastination and avoidance of tasks that require responsibility.
  - Financial Irresponsibility: Poor management of finances, neglecting long-term financial goals.
- Destructive Relationships (D):
  - Toxic Connections: Maintaining relationships that are harmful, abusive, or detrimental to personal well-being.
  - Enabling Negative Influences: Allowing external influences to dictate decisions, often leading to destructive outcomes.

More points
- Avoidance of Accountability:
  - Blame-shifting: Frequently blaming external factors or other people for personal challenges.
  - Excusing Behavior: Creating justifications to avoid taking responsibility for actions and their consequences.

Conclusion:

Recognizing these signs in oneself or others provides an opportunity for self-reflection and growth. It's essential to acknowledge these patterns and take intentional steps toward breaking free from external influences, fostering personal ownership, and building healthier relationships. If you observe these signs in someone close to you, offering support and understanding can be a meaningful contribution to their journey of self-discovery and empowerment.

Navigating the Seas of Ownership: Empowered Relationships

In the divine blueprint of creation, God envisioned humanity as stewards, custodians, and owners of the resources, talents, and relationships bestowed upon them. This paradigm of ownership isn't rooted in selfish ambition but is a reflection of God's desire for His children to fully embrace their identity, purpose, and the transformative power that comes with being owners. As we embark on the ship called ownership, we encounter profound lessons that fortify relationships and infuse them with purpose and vitality.

Understanding Identity:

Ownership begins with a deep understanding of one's identity. When individuals recognize themselves as masterpieces meticulously crafted by the Creator, they gain a sense of self-worth and purpose. This clarity of identity becomes the bedrock upon which healthy relationships are built. Instead of seeking validation from others, individuals can contribute authentically to relationships, bringing their true selves to the forefront.

Cultivating Purpose:
On the ship of ownership, individuals unearth their unique purpose and calling. God has endowed each person with specific gifts, talents, and passions meant to contribute to the world and enhance relationships. Understanding and embracing this purpose propels individuals to navigate relationships with intentionality. Purpose becomes a guiding star, steering connections toward shared goals and meaningful collaboration.

Creating Resources:
Ownership empowers individuals to create and steward resources wisely. Whether it's time, talents, or material possessions, the ability to generate resources ensures a bountiful journey. In relationships, this translates to the capacity to give generously, invest in shared endeavors, and create an environment where both parties can flourish. Ownership cultivates a spirit of abundance rather than scarcity.

Building Generational Wealth:
Generational wealth isn't solely confined to financial assets; it extends to the rich connection of values, wisdom, and relational legacies passed down through generations. The ship of ownership teaches individuals to invest in relationships, leaving a legacy that transcends the temporal. Families, friendships, and communities become beneficiaries of the wealth generated through intentional ownership.

Fostering Accountability:
Ownership demands accountability. When individuals recognize their responsibility in relationships, they become accountable for their actions, words, and contributions. This accountability fosters trust, transparency, and a shared commitment to the well-being of the relationship. In owning both successes and shortcomings, individuals create a culture of honesty and growth.

Embracing Transformation:
Ownership is a transformative journey. As individuals embrace the ship of ownership, they undergo a process of refinement and growth. This personal transformation positively impacts relationships. Instead of being stagnant or complacent, individuals continuously seek opportunities for improvement, inspiring those around them to embark on their own transformative journeys.

In the vast expanse of relationships, the ship of ownership emerges as a beacon of empowerment and purpose. God invites His children to step onto this vessel, where the lesson learned and the treasures discovered profoundly impact the dynamics of relationships. As we set sail, we recognize that true ownership is a gift that empowers us to navigate the seas of relationships with wisdom, grace, and a profound sense of purpose.

Becoming an Owner: Practical Steps for Empowered Living

Embarking on the transformative journey of ownership is a deliberate and empowering choice. To become an owner is to step into the fullness of who you are, embracing your identity, purpose, and the responsibility to steward your relationships and resources wisely. Here are practical steps, represented by the points in the word "OWNER," to guide you on this empowering path:

O - Own Your Identity:
- Reflection: Take time to reflect on your unique qualities, strengths, and values.
- Affirmations: Affirm your worth and identity daily, grounding yourself in God's perspective.
- Authenticity: Embrace and express your true self without fear of external expectations.

W - Work with Purpose:
- Discover Purpose: Explore your passions, talents, and interests to identify your purpose.
- Set Goals: Establish clear and achievable goals aligned with your purpose.
- Intentionality: Infuse purpose into daily tasks, making intentional choices that align with your calling.

N - Nurture Relationships:
- Communication: Foster open and honest communication in your relationships.
- Invest Time: Dedicate quality time to building and nurturing connections.
- Generosity: Give generously of your time, resources, and love to strengthen relationships.

E - Excel in Stewardship & Embrace Accountability
- Time Management: Efficiently manage your time, prioritizing tasks and relationships.
- Resource Stewardship: Wisely steward your financial and material resources.
- Embrace Accountability:
    o Self-Accountability: Hold yourself accountable for your actions and decisions.
    o Transparent Communication: Encourage open dialogue within your relationships.
    o Learn and Grow: Embrace mistakes as opportunities for growth and improvement.

R - Reflect on Legacy:
- Legacy Planning: Consider the impact you want to leave on future generations.
- Values Clarification: Clearly define the values you want to pass down to your descendants.
- Intentional Living: Make decisions today that contribute to a positive and enduring legacy.

By embracing these practical steps, you actively cultivate the mindset and habits of an owner. Each intentional choice contributes to the overall empowerment of your life and relationships. Remember, becoming an owner is an ongoing process of growth, and as you consistently apply these principles, you'll find yourself navigating the seas of life with purpose, authenticity, and a profound sense of responsibility.

Workbook-Becoming an OWNER Worksheet Page 140

BOARDING STEWARD-SHIP

Embarking on Relationship Success: The Essence of Boarding Stewardship

Before one can navigate the intricate waters of a relationship, there lies a profound need for individual readiness and thoughtful preparation. This crucial prerequisite is encapsulated in the concept of "Boarding Stewardship" — the deliberate and mindful practice of stewarding oneself before extending that stewardship to another person in the journey of love.

Understanding Stewardship:

Stewardship, in its essence, is the responsible and intentional management of something entrusted to one's care. In the realm of relationships, it signifies the conscientious handling of one's own emotional, mental, and spiritual well-being before embracing the shared odyssey with a partner. Stewardship involves a commitment to nurture, protect, and contribute positively to the relational space that two individuals are about to co-create.

Practicing Individual Stewardship:

- **Self-Discovery and Self-Care:**
  - Before boarding a relationship, individuals must embark on a journey of self-discovery. Understanding one's values, passions, and personal aspirations forms the bedrock of individual stewardship. Moreover, practicing self-care ensures that one brings a healthy and whole self into the shared space of a relationship.
- **Emotional Intelligence and Healing:**
  - Emotional readiness is a vital aspect of boarding stewardship. Individuals must engage in the process of self-reflection, addressing past wounds, and cultivating emotional intelligence. Healing from previous relationship experiences ensures that emotional baggage does not hinder the potential for a thriving connection.
- **Establishing Personal Boundaries:**
  - Stewardship involves the establishment of clear and healthy boundaries. Individuals need to identify their needs, communicate them effectively, and respect the boundaries of others. This practice creates a foundation of respect and sets the stage for robust interpersonal dynamics.

- **Values Clarification:**
  - Understanding personal values and life goals is paramount. Individual stewardship demands clarity on what one holds dear and the direction in which they envision their life moving. Aligning personal values helps in assessing compatibility with a potential partner.

Benefits of Boarding Stewardship:

1. **Mutual Growth and Understanding:**
   - Practicing individual stewardship facilitates mutual growth and understanding within a relationship. Both individuals, having invested in personal development, can bring enriched perspectives to the partnership.
2. **Effective Communication:**
   - Communication skills are honed during individual stewardship. The ability to express oneself, actively listen, and navigate conflicts with emotional intelligence contributes to the creation of a communicatively healthy relationship.
3. **Healthy Relationship Foundation:**
   - The practice of stewardship lays the groundwork for a robust foundation. It ensures that both individuals enter the relationship with a sense of self-awareness, promoting an environment conducive to trust, respect, and shared aspirations.
4. **Resilience in Adversity:**
   - Individual stewardship equips individuals with the resilience needed to weather the storms of life. Facing challenges becomes a joint venture where both partners contribute from a place of strength and self-assurance.

In conclusion, boarding stewardship is a precursor to relationship success. It signifies the acknowledgment that fostering a healthy connection requires a commitment to individual growth and well-being. By practicing stewardship before boarding a relationship, individuals set sail with a compass of self-awareness, emotional resilience, and a clear understanding of their values. This intentional preparation becomes the wind that propels the relationship towards harmonious horizons, ensuring a voyage marked by mutual respect, understanding, and enduring love.

Workbook-Stewardship Readiness Worksheet: Preparing to Board a Relationship 142

Preparation for Relationship Boarding: Stewardship as a Prerequisite

Before embarking on the journey of a romantic relationship, individuals can benefit immensely from the practice of stewardship. Stewarding key aspects of one's life lays a solid foundation and cultivates the attributes needed for a healthy and thriving partnership. Let's explore five critical elements of stewardship—time, money, personal resources, emotional well-being, and personal growth—and understand how they serve as preparatory steps for boarding a meaningful relationship.

1. **Stewardship of Time:**
   - **Preparation Principle:** Investment in Self-Discovery
   - Time is a valuable currency in the preparation for a relationship. Stewarding time involves dedicating moments to self-reflection, personal growth, and understanding one's values and priorities. By investing time in self-discovery, individuals gain a clearer sense of who they are and what they seek in a partner, laying the groundwork for a more intentional relationship.

2. **Stewardship of Finances:**
   - **Preparation Principle:** Financial Responsibility
   - Effective stewardship of money is a crucial aspect of preparing for a relationship. It involves budgeting, saving, and understanding one's financial habits. Financial responsibility not only ensures individual financial well-being but also contributes to building a stable and harmonious foundation for future shared finances within a relationship.

3. **Stewardship of Personal Resources:**
   - **Preparation Principle:** Cultivation of Individual Strengths
   - Personal resources encompass talents, skills, and capabilities. Stewarding personal resources involves honing individual strengths, developing skills, and pursuing passions. This preparation enhances self-confidence and contributes to a more fulfilled and well-rounded individual ready to bring their unique qualities into a relationship.

4. **Stewardship of Emotional Well-Being:**
   - **Preparation Principle:** Cultivation of Emotional Resilience
   - Emotional well-being is a cornerstone of relationship readiness. Stewarding emotional health involves self-awareness, the ability to manage emotions, and cultivating resilience. Individuals who prioritize their emotional well-being are better equipped to navigate the complexities of relationships and contribute positively to their partner's emotional landscape.

5. **Stewardship of Personal Growth:**
   - **Preparation Principle:** Commitment to Continuous Improvement
   - Personal growth is an ongoing journey. Stewarding personal growth means actively seeking opportunities for self-improvement, learning, and evolving as an individual. This commitment to continuous improvement not only enhances one's own life but also enriches the potential contributions to a future relationship.

Benefits of Stewardship in Relationship Preparation:

1. **Clarity of Purpose:**
   - Stewarding time and resources provides individuals with clarity about their life goals and relationship expectations. This clarity is fundamental for building a purposeful and aligned partnership.

2. **Financial Stability:**
   - Effective financial stewardship ensures financial stability, reducing potential stressors in a relationship. It establishes a solid foundation for responsible financial decisions within the context of a partnership.

3. **Individual Strengths and Contributions:**
   - Stewarding personal resources allows individuals to recognize and leverage their unique strengths. This, in turn, enhances their ability to make meaningful contributions to the relationship.

4. **Emotional Resilience:**
   - Stewarding emotional well-being fosters emotional resilience. Individuals who prioritize emotional health are better equipped to navigate challenges and maintain a supportive emotional environment within a relationship.

5. **Commitment to Growth:**
   - Stewardship of personal growth reflects a commitment to continuous improvement. Individuals who embrace growth as a lifelong journey contribute to the dynamic evolution of a relationship, fostering a culture of mutual development.

BOARDING
FRIEND-SHIP

Before embarking on the journey of romantic or familial relationships, there is a foundational ship that one must board—a ship named Friendship. Friendship serves as the bedrock upon which all other relationships are built, offering stability, trust, and companionship in the tumultuous seas of life. In fact, Jesus Himself emphasized the significance of friendship when He declared to His disciples, "I no longer call you servants, because a servant does not know his master's business. Instead, I have called you friends" (John 15:15).

Friendship is not merely a casual acquaintance or a superficial connection; rather, it is a deep bond rooted in mutual respect, understanding, and shared experiences. It involves genuine care and concern for one another's well-being, as well as a willingness to offer support and encouragement in times of need. Like the sturdy hull of a ship, friendship provides a solid framework for navigating the complexities of human relationships.

The importance of friendship extends beyond the realm of interpersonal dynamics; it also shapes our character and influences the way we interact with others. Learning to be a good friend lays the groundwork for cultivating empathy, communication skills, and conflict resolution strategies—essential components of healthy relationships. By honing our ability to be genuine, loyal, and compassionate friends, we equip ourselves with the tools necessary to foster meaningful connections with romantic partners, family members, and colleagues alike.

Furthermore, friendship fosters a sense of belonging and acceptance, allowing individuals to express themselves authentically without fear of judgment or rejection. In the safe harbor of friendship, we find refuge from the storms of life and experience the joy of companionship—a joy that enriches our lives and enhances our overall well-being.

Ultimately, the ship of Friendship serves as a guiding light in the vast ocean of relationships, illuminating the path towards deeper connections, lasting love, and genuine intimacy. By recognizing the foundational role of friendship and nurturing this sacred bond in our lives, we pave the way for richer, more fulfilling relationships with those around us.

203

Selectivity in friendships is paramount due to the valuable resources exchanged within these relationships, such as time, understanding, and energy. Before extending friendship, it's crucial to first establish a solid foundation by nurturing relationships with God and oneself. To be a friend of God entails cultivating a deep connection through reverence, trust, and communion with the divine. Personally, I believe that beyond any title or position, the pinnacle of relational honor lies in being recognized as a friend of God.

Being your own best friend is equally vital, as it involves self-awareness, self-compassion, and self-respect. By nurturing a positive and supportive relationship with oneself, individuals gain clarity on their values, boundaries, and aspirations. This self-awareness serves as a compass for selecting friends who align with one's personal growth journey and aspirations.

The friendship with God and oneself serves as a guiding principle when considering potential friendships. It instills discernment, allowing individuals to differentiate between relationships that nurture growth and those that may hinder it. Additionally, these foundational friendships provide a source of strength and stability, enabling individuals to navigate the complexities of human relationships with wisdom and grace. Ultimately, by prioritizing friendship with God and oneself, individuals establish a strong framework for cultivating meaningful and mutually enriching friendships with others.

ecognizing signs that indicate you or someone else may not be fulfilling the role of a good
riend is crucial for fostering healthy relationships. Below are signs, organized into the acronym
SIGNS," that may suggest areas for improvement:

1. Selfishness: If you frequently prioritize your own needs and desires over those of your
   friends, it may indicate a lack of consideration and empathy.
2. Ignoring: Consistently failing to listen attentively, show interest, or respond to your friend's
   messages or calls can signal neglect and disregard for their feelings.
3. Gossiping: Engaging in gossip or spreading rumors about your friends behind their backs
   undermines trust and mutual respect, damaging the foundation of your friendship.
4. Negativity: Constantly expressing pessimism, criticism, or judgment towards your friends'
   ideas, actions, or life choices can create a toxic atmosphere and erode their self-esteem.
5. Self-Centeredness: If your interactions with friends consistently revolve around discussing
   your own problems, achievements, or interests without showing genuine interest in theirs, it
   may indicate a lack of reciprocity and empathy.

n the flip side, signs that your friend may not be fulfilling the role of a good friend include:

1. Selfishness: If your friend frequently prioritizes their own needs and desires over yours, it
   may indicate a lack of consideration and empathy for your feelings.
2. Ignoring: If your friend consistently fails to listen attentively, show interest, or respond to
   your messages or calls, it may signal neglect and disregard for your friendship.
3. Gossiping: If your friend engages in gossip or spreads rumors about you behind your back, it
   undermines trust and mutual respect, damaging the foundation of your friendship.
4. Negativity: If your friend constantly criticizes or judges your ideas, actions, or life choices, it
   can create a toxic atmosphere and erode your self-esteem.
5. Self-Centeredness: If your friend's interactions with you consistently revolve around
   discussing their own problems, achievements, or interests without showing genuine interest
   in yours, it may indicate a lack of reciprocity and empathy.

ecoming a better friend is a journey of growth and self-awareness, characterized by intentional
:tions and genuine care for others. Here are some points, organized into the acronym
RIEND," to guide you on this journey:
1. Foster Trust: Cultivate trust by being reliable, honest, and confidential. Keep your promises,
   maintain confidentiality, and demonstrate consistency in your words and actions. Trust forms
   the foundation of strong friendships.
2. Respect Boundaries: Respect your friend's boundaries by being mindful of their preferences,
   needs, and limitations. Avoid pressuring them into situations they're uncomfortable with and
   be understanding of their personal space and autonomy.
3. Initiate Communication: Take the initiative to reach out and stay connected. Regular
   communication, whether through calls, texts, or in-person meetings, shows that you value
   the relationship and are invested in maintaining it.
4. Empathize: Practice empathy by putting yourself in your friend's shoes and seeking to
   understand their feelings, perspectives, and experiences. Listen actively, validate their
   emotions, and offer support without judgment.
5. Nurture Growth: Support your friend's personal growth and development by encouraging
   their aspirations, celebrating their achievements, and providing constructive feedback when
   needed. Be their cheerleader and advocate for their success.
6. Demonstrate Kindness: Show kindness through small gestures of thoughtfulness,
   compassion, and generosity. Offer a listening ear, lend a helping hand, and express
   appreciation for your friend's presence in your life.
·member, being a better friend is not about perfection but about making a genuine effort to
ow care, support, and appreciation for the people in your life who matter to you.

BOARDING
WOR-SHIP

Worship stands as a foundational boat to board
before setting sail into the vast sea of
relationships. It's more than just a Sunday routine
or a melodic chorus sung from our lips; true
worship emanates from the depths of our being,
from our spirits. In John 4:23-24, Jesus articulates
this truth when he speaks of worshiping God in
spirit and truth. Worshiping in spirit means
engaging with God from the very core of who we
are—our personality, gifts, talents, and deepest
convictions. It's a profound expression of
authenticity, where our entire being is laid bare
before the Creator, uninhibited by pretense or
performance.

Moreover, worship in spirit encompasses a lifestyle
of reverence and devotion, extending far beyond
the confines of a church sanctuary. It's a continual
posture of adoration, gratitude, and surrender,
woven into the fabric of our everyday lives.
Whether we're at work, at home, or in the midst of
our daily routines, our worship flows seamlessly
from our spirits, infusing every moment with
purpose and meaning.

Yet, worship in truth is equally essential. It
requires a sincere and unfiltered approach to God,
free from the trappings of hypocrisy or
superficiality. It's about aligning our hearts and
minds with the reality of who God is—His
character, His promises, and His will for our lives.
True worship acknowledges God for who He truly
is, acknowledging His sovereignty, His grace, and
His unending love.

In a world teeming with distractions and false
idols, worship in spirit and truth serves as a
beacon of authenticity and devotion. It's a clarion
call to break free from the shackles of superficial
religiosity and to embrace a genuine, heartfelt
connection with the Divine. When we worship God
from the depths of our spirits, uninhibited by
external influences or distractions, we not only
honor Him but also cultivate a fertile soil for
healthy, thriving relationships.

For in worshiping God authentically, we learn to
love and relate to others with the same sincerity
and reverence. Our relationships become infused
with the same spirit of worship, marked by
authenticity, humility, and genuine care for one
another. Thus, before embarking on the voyage of
relationships, let us first board the boat of
worship, setting sail with hearts ablaze with the
fire of true adoration and devotion.

ow idol worship SINKS relationships and how true worship SAILS them:

NK Relationships:

..**Selfishness:** Worshiping other things can lead to a self-centered mindset, where our desires and needs take precedence over the well-being of others. Relationships suffer when one party prioritizes their own interests above mutual respect and consideration.

?.**Insecurity:** When we worship worldly ideals such as material possessions or social status, we inevitably foster feelings of inadequacy and comparison. This insecurity can breed jealousy and mistrust in relationships, undermining the foundation of trust and intimacy.

;.**Neglect:** Idolizing worldly pursuits can result in neglecting our relationships. Whether it's prioritizing work over spending time with loved ones or investing excessive energy into personal hobbies, neglect can lead to feelings of abandonment and resentment in relationships.

!.**Keeping Up Appearances:** Worshiping external standards of success or beauty often leads to a facade of perfectionism. In relationships, this facade can create a barrier to genuine connection, as individuals feel pressured to maintain a flawless image rather than embracing vulnerability and authenticity.

IL Relationships:

..**Sincerity:** Worshiping God holistically fosters sincerity in relationships, as we learn to approach others with honesty and transparency. Genuine worship cultivates a heart of humility and authenticity, laying the groundwork for meaningful connections built on trust and mutual respect.

?.**Alignment:** When we worship God as the ultimate authority in our lives, our values and priorities align with His divine will. This alignment spills over into our relationships, guiding us to prioritize love, forgiveness, and compassion in our interactions with others.

;.**Intimacy:** Worshiping God cultivates intimacy in relationships by nurturing a deep spiritual connection with Him. As we draw near to God in worship, His love fills our hearts and overflows into our relationships, fostering a profound sense of closeness and unity with those around us.

!.**Loyalty:** Worshiping God instills a sense of loyalty and commitment in relationships. As we acknowledge God's faithfulness and steadfast love, we are inspired to mirror these qualities in our interactions with others, remaining steadfast in our loyalty and support through the ups and downs of life.

embracing worship as a holistic lifestyle, we navigate the waters of relationships with grace d wisdom, steering clear of the pitfalls that threaten to sink them. Instead, we set sail on a urney marked by sincerity, alignment, intimacy, and loyalty, guided by the unshakeable undation of our worshipful devotion to God.

conclusion, worship is not merely an act of devotion reserved for religious rituals or sacred aces; it is a transformative lifestyle that permeates every aspect of our being and lationships. By worshiping God holistically, from the depths of our spirits and in alignment th His truth, we cultivate sincerity, alignment, intimacy, and loyalty in our interactions with hers. Worship guides us to prioritize love, compassion, and forgiveness, fostering deep nnections and mutual respect in all relationships. It empowers us to navigate the complexities human interaction with grace and wisdom, steering clear of the pitfalls of selfishness, security, neglect, and superficiality. Boarding the ship of worship before entering a lationship is essential, as it lays the foundation for a thriving journey characterized by thenticity, alignment with divine values, intimate connection, and unwavering loyalty. timately, worship is the compass that guides us through the seas of life, illuminating the path flourishing relationships and fulfilling our purpose in God's grand design.

orkbook Reflecting on Your Worship Practices Worksheet Page 144A

BOARDING HARD-SHIP

Boarding the Hardship Ship: Preparing for the Challenges of Relationships

Life's journey is often fraught with trials and tribulations, and navigating through hardship is an essential precursor to embarking on the voyage of relationships. Just as a sailor must weather storms at sea to become an experienced captain, individuals must endure trials and tough times before entering into marriage and parenthood. The apostle Paul's words in Romans 5:3-5 offer profound wisdom in this regard, reminding us that suffering produces endurance, endurance produces character, and character produces hope.

In the context of relationships, this passage takes on new significance. Suffering, whether it be personal struggles, relational conflicts, or external challenges, is an inevitable part of any partnership. By embracing these hardships and allowing them to shape us, we develop the endurance necessary to weather the storms that may come our way. Just as muscles grow stronger through resistance training, our capacity to love and persevere in relationships is fortified through adversity.

Moreover, enduring hardships cultivates character, molding us into individuals of integrity, empathy, and resilience. In the crucible of suffering, we are stripped of superficiality and pretense, revealing the core of who we are and what we value. This character development is essential for healthy relationships, as it fosters trust, authenticity, and mutual respect.

As character takes root in our lives, it breeds hope —the confident expectation of God's faithfulness and provision. This hope becomes the anchor that sustains us through the storms of life, anchoring our relationships in the unshakeable foundation of God's love. When we face challenges in marriage, parenting, or any other relational context, it is this hope that empowers us to persevere, to forgive, and to extend grace to one another.

Ultimately, the journey of boarding the Hardship Ship before entering into relationships is not one of despair but of anticipation. It is a recognition that through the trials and tribulations of life, we are being prepared and refined for the beautiful and rewarding adventure of love, companionship, and family. Just as a skilled sailor navigates rough waters with confidence, so too can we navigate the complexities of relationships with courage and faith, knowing that God's love sustains us through every trial and hardship.

Navigating Trials in Relationships: Finding Joy in Every Stage
James 1:2-4 ESV serves as a beacon of guidance for individuals embarking on the journey of relationships, reminding us to find joy even amidst trials of various kinds. This call to count it all joy underscores the importance of maintaining a perspective of gratitude and trust in God's sovereignty, regardless of the challenges we encounter. Joy is not merely an emotion but a posture of the heart—a steadfast assurance that God is at work in all circumstances.

In every stage of our relationships, whether in courtship, marriage, parenting, or friendship, we are called to count it all joy. This requires cultivating a mindset of joyfulness that transcends our circumstances. Rather than waiting for trials to pass before finding joy, we must learn to rejoice even in the midst of adversity. This shift in perspective empowers us to face challenges with resilience and optimism, knowing that God is using every trial to shape and mold us for His purposes.

God tests our faith not to cause us harm but to strengthen and refine it. A faith that has not been tested remains shallow and susceptible to doubt. By allowing trials to test our faith, God deepens our trust in Him and strengthens our spiritual resilience. In relationships, this tested faith becomes the bedrock of our commitment and trust in one another, enabling us to weather storms together and emerge stronger on the other side.

Steadfastness, the product of tested faith, is essential for navigating the complexities of relationships. Just as a ship's anchor provides stability amidst turbulent waters, so too does steadfastness anchor our relationships in the unchanging truth of God's love and faithfulness. Patience plays a crucial role in this process, allowing steadfastness to have its full effect. As we patiently endure trials, we grow in maturity and completeness, lacking nothing that is essential for building healthy, thriving relationships.

In conclusion, James 1:2-4 offers a profound perspective on the role of trials in shaping our character and relationships. By counting it all joy and allowing steadfastness and patience to have their full effect, we are equipped to navigate the complexities of relationships with grace and resilience. As we embrace trials as opportunities for growth and refinement, we become better prepared to serve and love others in the variousness of marriage, parenting, and all other relational spheres.

Workbook: Finding Joy in Trials - James 1:2-4 Page 144E

209

THE RELATIONSHIP MENTALITY.

The Relationship Mentality is a foundational mindset that governs how individuals approach and navigate their interactions with others. It encompasses a set of attitudes, beliefs, and perspectives that shape one's behavior, communication, and expectations within relationships. At its core, the Relationship Mentality involves recognizing the interconnectedness of all relationships—whether with God, oneself, a spouse, children, friends, or colleagues—and understanding the importance of fostering healthy, meaningful connections.

Mental readiness, within the context of the Relationship Mentality, refers to a state of preparedness and maturity in one's approach to relationships. It involves being emotionally resilient, spiritually grounded, and psychologically equipped to handle the challenges, uncertainties, and complexities inherent in interpersonal dynamics. A mentally ready individual understands that relationships require effort, commitment, and continuous growth, and they are willing to invest the necessary time and energy to nurture and sustain these connections.

The importance of having a Relationship Mentality and being mentally ready for relationships cannot be overstated, especially given the unpredictability and volatility often associated with human interactions. Many individuals enter relationships without fully understanding the responsibilities, sacrifices, and compromises that accompany them. Instead, they may be driven by a desire for companionship, validation, or fulfillment without considering the deeper implications and demands of building and maintaining healthy relationships.

Unfortunately, this lack of mental readiness can lead to disillusionment, conflict, and ultimately, the breakdown of relationships. Without a solid foundation rooted in the Relationship Mentality, individuals may struggle to communicate effectively, resolve conflicts constructively, or maintain a sense of mutual respect and understanding. Moreover, they may find themselves ill-equipped to navigate the inevitable challenges, setbacks, and disappointments that arise in relationships.

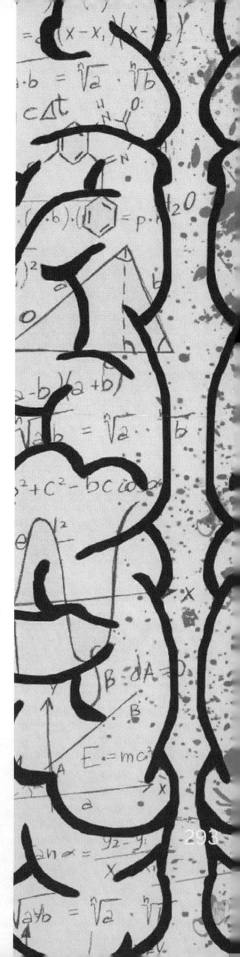

It is essential to recognize that developing a Relationship Mentality and cultivating mental readiness is a journey that requires self-awareness, introspection, and personal growth. It involves examining one's beliefs, attitudes, and behaviors, as well as addressing any unresolved issues or emotional baggage that may hinder relational success. By embracing a mindset centered on authenticity, empathy, humility, and resilience, individuals can enhance their capacity to form and sustain meaningful connections, thereby enriching their lives and the lives of those around them.

The Mindset: Attitudes, Beliefs, and Perspectives

The mindset is the lens through which individuals perceive, interpret, and respond to the world around them. It encompasses a set of attitudes, beliefs, and perspectives that shape behavior, communication, and expectations within relationships. Our minds are akin to sophisticated computers with various settings—divine settings (original), depraved settings (flesh and carnal settings), and demonic settings (dark influence). It is our choice which settings we allow our minds to be set to, and these choices profoundly impact our interactions and relationships.

Divine Settings (Original)

1. Love: Choosing to approach relationships with a mindset of love involves selflessly seeking the well-being and flourishing of others, even at personal cost.
2. Joy: Cultivating joy in relationships involves finding delight and contentment in the blessings and connections shared with others, despite challenges or circumstances.
3. Peace: Pursuing peace entails seeking harmony, reconciliation, and tranquility in relationships, promoting unity and understanding.
4. Patience: Exercising patience involves enduring difficulties and challenges in relationships with grace and forbearance, trusting in God's timing and provision.
5. Kindness: Practicing kindness means extending compassion, generosity, and goodwill toward others, fostering warmth and goodwill in relationships.
6. Goodness: Embracing goodness involves acting with integrity, honesty, and moral excellence in relationships, promoting trustworthiness and righteousness.
7. Faithfulness: Demonstrating faithfulness entails remaining steadfast, loyal, and committed to others, even in the face of adversity or temptation.
8. Gentleness: Cultivating gentleness involves showing tenderness, humility, and sensitivity in interactions with others, fostering empathy and understanding.
9. Self-Control: Exercising self-control means mastering one's impulses, desires, and emotions, promoting balance, discipline, and maturity in relationships.
10. By setting our minds to the fruit of the spirit settings, we can cultivate healthy, nurturing, and fulfilling relationships that reflect the love, grace, and character of God.

Depraved Settings (Flesh and Carnal Settings)

1. **Selfishness:** Selfishness manifests as a focus on one's own desires, needs, and interests at the expense of others. It leads to conflict, resentment, and relational dysfunction.
2. **Pride:** Pride manifests as arrogance, superiority, and an unwillingness to admit fault or seek help. It hinders genuine connection, humility, and cooperation in relationships.
3. **Manipulation:** Manipulation involves using deceit, coercion, or control tactics to influence others for personal gain. It erodes trust, authenticity, and mutual respect in relationships.
4. **Dishonesty:** Dishonesty entails lying, deceit, or deception to conceal truth or manipulate others. It undermines trust, integrity, and the foundation of healthy relationships.
5. **Inflexibility:** Inflexibility manifests as rigidity, stubbornness, or resistance to change or differing viewpoints. It impedes compromise, growth, and effective communication in relationships.
6. **Communication Barriers:** Communication barriers include poor listening skills, defensiveness, and passive-aggressive behavior. They hinder understanding, empathy, and resolution in relationships.

Demonic Settings (Dark Influence)

- Deception: Deception involves the distortion or concealment of truth, often fueled by malicious intent or manipulation. It sows seeds of discord, distrust, and division in relationships.
- Malice: Malice manifests as ill will, spite, or a desire to harm others emotionally or physically. It breeds resentment, hostility, and toxic relational dynamics.
- Control: Control entails exerting power or dominance over others, often through coercion, manipulation, or intimidation. It stifles autonomy, freedom, and authentic expression in relationships.
- Isolation: Isolation involves cutting off or alienating individuals from supportive networks or healthy relationships. It fosters dependency, loneliness, and vulnerability to manipulation or abuse.
- Negativity: Negativity manifests as a pervasive focus on pessimism, criticism, or cynicism, draining energy and joy from relationships. It undermines morale, optimism, and resilience.
- Exploitation: Exploitation involves taking advantage of others for personal gain, often at their expense or detriment. It erodes trust, reciprocity, and the sanctity of relationships.

In summary, the mindset we choose to adopt profoundly influences the quality and dynamics of our relationships. By consciously aligning our attitudes, beliefs, and perspectives with divine settings—embracing authenticity, respect, empathy, humility, effective communication, and adaptability—we can cultivate healthy, fulfilling connections that honor God and enrich our lives. Conversely, yielding to depraved or demonic settings leads to dysfunction, discord, and relational breakdown. Therefore, it is imperative to guard our minds and intentionally set them on the path of righteousness and wisdom, ensuring that our relationships thrive in love, truth, and grace.

Mental readiness is crucial for navigating the complexities of life and relationships effectively. Our minds must be prepared to RESPOND, ENDURE, ACTIVATE, DISCERN, and be YIELDED to ensure we approach challenges and opportunities with wisdom and resilience.

1. **Respond**: Our minds must be mature enough to respond thoughtfully rather than react impulsively. Reacting often leads to hasty decisions or emotional outbursts that can harm relationships. By cultivating self-awareness and emotional regulation through practices like mindfulness and self-reflection, we can train our minds to pause and respond with intentionality and grace.
2. **Endure**: Mental readiness involves developing the endurance to persevere through difficulties without losing hope. Instead of seeking quick fixes or immediate gratification, we must adopt a marathon mindset, trusting in God's faithfulness to sustain us through the long haul. Building spiritual resilience through prayer, meditation, and reliance on God's promises strengthens our ability to endure trials and challenges.
3. **Activate**: Our minds should be proactive in seeking solutions and opportunities amidst adversity. Problem-solving skills and creativity are essential for activating positive outcomes. Whether it's brainstorming solutions, seeking advice from mentors, or nurturing a mindset of innovation, activating our mental faculties empowers us to overcome obstacles and pursue growth and success.
4. **Discern**: Mental readiness requires the ability to discern truth from deception, right from wrong. Cultivating discernment involves deepening our understanding of God's word and aligning our perspectives with His truth. Regular study of scripture, seeking wise counsel, and prayerful reflection enable us to make wise choices and navigate moral complexities with clarity and conviction.
5. **Yielded**: Finally, our minds must be yielded to the guidance and transformation of the Holy Spirit. Surrendering our thoughts, desires, and plans to God's leading allows Him to shape our character and direct our steps according to His purposes. Yielding to the Holy Spirit's work within us enables spiritual growth, wisdom, and alignment with God's will.

By intentionally developing mental readiness in these areas, we equip ourselves to face life's challenges with resilience, wisdom, and faith, ultimately fostering personal growth and relational flourishing.

Workbook: Cultivating Mental Readiness Worksheet Page 144G

BUILDING GOD-CENTERED MARITAL FOUNDATIONS

Transitioning from Self to Union: Building God-Centered Marital Foundations

As we bid adieu to the exploration of the intricate relationship with self, we now embark on a new chapter that delves into the sacred union of two souls—a journey into the heart of marital relationships. From the introspective shores of self-discovery, we now set sail toward the boundless horizon of companionship and union, with marriage as our compass. This transition signifies not just a shift in focus but a deepening of connections—a call to build and strengthen the very foundations that support enduring marriages.

The threads of self-awareness and adaptability, woven meticulously in the fabric of our individual lives, will now intertwine with those of our life partners. It is a transition that beckons us to cast a unified gaze toward the divine blueprint, recognizing the importance of a solid foundation for a union that is destined to endure. The objective is clear: to cultivate a marriage firmly rooted in the soil of God's love—a marriage that stands resilient against the tests of time and the changing tides of life.

As we navigate through the stages of dating, courtship, and marital commitment, let us set sail with hearts open to the divine currents that guide us. The sections that follow will explore the nuances of building a foundation that withstands the storms, cherishing the moments of calm, and embracing the promise lands of love and unity that lie ahead.

May this exploration be not just a guide but a transformative journey, where God's presence is not just acknowledged but actively sought to illuminate the path of marital fulfillment.

Preparing for Marriage: God's Role in Arranging Marriages

Before we delve into the intricacies of marriage, let's take a moment to address those who are currently navigating the realms of courtship and dating—those who stand at the threshold of a life-altering decision. In this crucial section, the focus is on the importance of ensuring you are walking hand in hand with the right life partner, a journey marked by divine guidance and the orchestration of God's hand in the matchmaking process.

The concept of seeking God's guidance in choosing a life partner is not just a quaint notion but a profound truth woven into the fabric of lasting marriages. As you consider taking the next step with your significant other, it is paramount to recognize that marriage is more than a social contract; it is a sacred covenant designed by the Creator Himself. Therefore, the foundation upon which this covenant rests must be laid with careful consideration and divine discernment.

Allowing God to play a central role in the matchmaking process is not a relinquishment of personal choice but a surrender to the One who knows the depths of our hearts and the intricacies of our individual journeys. God's role in arranging marriages is not limited to a mere stamp of approval; it is an invitation to embark on a shared expedition guided by His wisdom, love, and purpose.

In this section, my earnest desire is to impress upon you the gravity of the commitment you are considering. Marriage is not a casual endeavor but a sacred pilgrimage, and your choice of a life partner is a decision that resonates throughout your earthly journey. As we explore this concept together, let it serve as a mirror reflecting the depth of your connection with your significant other and, more importantly, the alignment of your union with God's divine plan.

May this exploration be a source of confirmation for those walking in God's intended path and a revelation for those who may need to reassess their journey. Let God's guiding hand illuminate the path ahead, unveiling the beauty of a marriage founded on His eternal wisdom and boundless love.

Choosing in God's Will: A Foundation for Lasting Marriages
The decision to marry is one of the most significant choices individuals make in their lives, and seeking alignment with the will of God is paramount. Choosing a life partner is a pivotal decision that influences the course of one's journey and, consequently, the fulfillment of God's purpose for their lives. Understanding the importance of being in God's will when considering marriage is essential for building a foundation that withstands the tests of time.

1. Divine Alignment:
Being in God's will means aligning your choices with His divine purpose for your life. When choosing a life partner within God's will, you position yourself to walk the path He has laid out for you, enhancing the likelihood of a purpose-driven and fulfilling marriage.

2. Missing God's Best:
Choosing a partner outside of God's will might mean settling for what is good instead of receiving His best. God's perfect will ensures that you are with someone perfectly suited for your unique purpose and calling, whereas stepping outside His will could lead to missed opportunities and unfulfilled potential.

3. Impact on Kingdom Building:
Marriage is not just about personal happiness but also about contributing to God's kingdom. Being in God's will in your choice of a life partner ensures that your union is not only fulfilling for you individually but also contributes to God's greater purpose on Earth.

4. Navigating Challenges:
Marriage comes with its challenges, and being in God's will provides a strong foundation to face those challenges together. Couples who have sought God's guidance in their union are better equipped to navigate difficulties, relying on His wisdom and grace.

5. Free Will and God's Permissive Will:
Understanding the concepts of God's perfect will and His permissive will is crucial when it comes to making life-altering decisions, such as choosing a life partner.

God's Perfect Will:
God's perfect will represents His divine plan, which is tailor-made for each individual. It encompasses the ideal path that God has laid out for someone's life, including their choice of a life partner. It reflects God's best for His children, aligning with His purposes, values, and overarching plan for their lives. When individuals seek God's perfect will, they position themselves to experience the highest level of fulfillment, blessings, and divine alignment.

God's Permissive Will:

God's permissive will, on the other hand, acknowledges the freedom of human choice. God allows individuals to exercise their free will, even if their choices may deviate from His ideal plan. While God's permissive will may encompass situations or decisions that are not His absolute best, it is within the boundaries of His overarching sovereignty. God permits certain choices, understanding the complexity of human decisions and their consequences.

In the context of choosing a life partner, seeking God's perfect will involves actively aligning one's desires and decisions with God's revealed plan. It means trusting in His wisdom and understanding that His perfect will is designed to lead to the highest level of joy, purpose, and compatibility in marriage.

Conversely, God's permissive will allows individuals to make choices outside of His ideal plan. This doesn't imply that God endorses or desires those choices, but rather, He permits individuals to exercise their free will. Choosing a partner within God's permissive will may still lead to a fulfilling life, but it might lack the fullness of blessings and alignment that comes with God's perfect will. It's important to note that understanding God's perfect will and permissive will requires seeking His guidance through prayer, discernment, and aligning one's heart with the principles outlined in His Word. Ultimately, seeking God's perfect will in the choice of a life partner is an act of faith, trusting that His plan is far superior to our own understanding.

Loneliness vs. God's Presence:

Choosing to be alone in God's will is far better than being with someone outside of it. Loneliness in the will of God is accompanied by His comforting presence, while being in a relationship outside His will may lead to the absence of His guidance and peace.

Understanding that God's will is not restrictive but liberating is key. It provides a framework within which individuals can experience true freedom and joy, knowing that their choices are guided by a loving and all-knowing Creator. In the journey of choosing a life partner, seeking God's will ensures that the foundation of the relationship is anchored in divine purpose and promises.

The Divine Art of Matchmaking: Why God Alone Qualifies

Understanding the qualifications that render God uniquely fit for this role unveils the depth of His knowledge, love, and intimate understanding of each individual. First and foremost, God knows you in a way that surpasses self-awareness. He understands the intricacies of your character, the hidden corners of your heart, and the unique blend of qualities that make you who you are. This intimate knowledge surpasses any human understanding, ensuring that the match God orchestrates is finely tuned to the essence of your being.

Moreover, God comprehends your purpose. He knows the path He has designed for you and the kind of partner who will not only walk beside you but also contribute to the fulfillment of your purpose. In divine matchmaking, God aligns two individuals whose journeys complement and enhance one another, creating a union that resonates with purpose and shared vision.

God's knowledge extends to the realm of preferences, including those of a physical nature. While physical attraction is not the sole foundation of a lasting relationship, God understands its importance. He knows what captivates your heart, what kindles desire within you, and even the intricacies of your sexual preferences. The divine Matchmaker is attentive to every facet of your being, ensuring that the union He arranges encompasses both spiritual compatibility and physical resonance.

Trusting God's matchmaking expertise involves recognizing that He has not just someone good for you but someone who is the best for you. The waiting period is not a delay but an opportunity for God to prepare both individuals for the journey ahead. It is an acknowledgment that God's timing is perfect, and His best is worth waiting for.

In essence, God's qualifications as the Matchmaker stem from His omniscience, wisdom, and unbounded love. His involvement in arranging marriages transcends human understanding, weaving together stories of love, purpose, and fulfillment that extend beyond the earthly realm. As you embark on the journey of seeking a life partner, rest in the assurance that the divine Matchmaker is orchestrating a love story that reflects His perfect plan for your life.

God's Confirmation in Marriage: A Steady Anchor in Turbulent Waters

Marriage, a sacred covenant, is a journey marked by various seasons, each presenting its unique challenges and joys. In the midst of these undulating waves, the importance of God's confirmation becomes paramount. It serves as a guiding light, illuminating the path of commitment and anchoring couples in the assurance of His divine orchestration.

1. Confidence Amidst Uncertainty:
- God's confirmation provides unwavering confidence during moments of uncertainty. In the heat of disagreements or in the face of life's storms, the assurance that your spouse is indeed the one chosen by God becomes a steadfast anchor, keeping the marriage resilient.

2. Sustaining Commitment Through Challenges:
- Marriage is not immune to challenges, and there will be times when doubts may surface. God's confirmation acts as a potent reminder, reinforcing the commitment made before Him. It becomes a touchstone during trials, urging couples to hold fast to each other with the knowledge that they are walking the path God has laid out.

3. Preventing Premature Departure:
- In the absence of God's confirmation, the turbulence of marital discord may tempt individuals to prematurely depart from the union. However, with the divine assurance that this is the person God intended for you, the commitment is fortified, and couples are encouraged to weather the storms together, trusting in God's overarching plan.

4. Consistent Confirmations:
- God's confirmation is not a one-time event; it is a continuous reassurance that unfolds throughout the journey of marriage. It manifests in various ways – through random confirmations, serendipitous moments, or the unveiling of new dimensions in the relationship. These consistent affirmations reinforce the truth that what is from God has an inherent quality of confirmation.

5. Strengthening the Bond:
- The confirmation of God's hand in your marriage serves to deepen the bond between spouses. It fosters an environment where love, trust, and understanding can thrive, creating a relationship that withstands the test of time and external pressures.

-

As a testament to the divine foundation of marriage, God's confirmation is not just a one-time proclamation but an ongoing dialogue between the couple and their Creator. It is a lifeline that keeps the marital vessel secure in God's purpose, even when the seas are tempestuous. Having personally navigated through arguments, disagreements, and challenging moments in my own marriage, I distinctly recall the times when God's confirmation illuminated our path. It was during these moments, often right after heated disagreements, that His reassurance blinked like a guiding light, reinforcing the divine orchestration of our union.

Divine Qualifications: Why We Are Not Fit to Choose

In the complex dance of relationships, the idea that we, as individuals, are not qualified to pick our life partner might initially raise eyebrows. Society often emphasizes personal autonomy and the pursuit of individual desires. However, when it comes to the intricacies of marriage and the lifelong journey with a partner, there are several compelling reasons why we fall short in the realm of matchmaking.

Firstly, our limited knowledge of ourselves poses a significant obstacle. While we may have a grasp of our surface-level preferences and immediate desires, the depths of our character, long-term goals, and the intricacies of our purpose often elude our understanding. God, on the other hand, possesses an omniscient awareness of our being, allowing Him to discern not just what we want but what we truly need.

Secondly, our perspectives are inherently finite. We view the world through the lens of our experiences, shaped by cultural influences, personal biases, and evolving emotions.

Secondly, our perspectives are inherently finite. We view the world through the lens of our experiences, shaped by cultural influences, personal biases, and evolving emotions. This limited perspective hinders our ability to foresee the challenges and triumphs that lie ahead in a lifelong commitment. God, as the divine orchestrator, sees the entirety of our lives and can weave together the stories of two individuals in a way that surpasses our human foresight.

Moreover, our desires can be swayed by temporary emotions and external pressures. What we find appealing in a potential partner today may be influenced by fleeting trends or societal expectations. Our understanding of compatibility can be clouded by the transient nature of human emotions. God's perspective, rooted in eternal wisdom, ensures that the matches He makes are grounded in enduring principles rather than fleeting sentiments.

The discernment required for choosing a life partner goes beyond our individual capacity. It involves an understanding of not just our present selves but our future selves — the person we are becoming. God, as the divine Matchmaker, comprehends the intricate journey each person is on and aligns individuals whose paths intersect with divine precision.

As you reflect on your relationship, ask yourself: Did you pick this person, or did God pick them for you? The realization that divine wisdom surpasses our finite understanding invites a profound sense of trust in the One who is intricately involved in the details of our lives, including the sacred union of marriage. Trusting God's qualifications as the ultimate Matchmaker opens the door to a love story written with divine precision and purpose.

Navigating Red Flags: Seeing Clearly Before Marriage
In the excitement and anticipation of a romantic relationship, it's not uncommon for individuals to overlook red flags that may signal potential challenges ahead. The early stages of love can create a euphoric atmosphere that blurs judgment, leading many to dismiss warning signs that might otherwise be apparent. Understanding why people often miss these red flags is crucial for fostering a healthy and discerning approach to relationships.

1. Rose-Colored Glasses:
During the initial phases of a relationship, individuals tend to wear metaphorical rose-colored glasses, emphasizing the positive qualities of their partner while downplaying or completely disregarding any negative aspects. This optimistic bias can cloud judgment and make it challenging to see red flags clearly.

2. Desire for Connection:
The human desire for connection and companionship can sometimes override our ability to critically assess a potential partner. Loneliness or a strong yearning for love might lead someone to minimize or ignore warning signs in the hope of filling an emotional void.

3. Fear of Confrontation:
Confronting red flags often involves difficult conversations and potential conflict. Fear of rocking the boat or jeopardizing the relation-ship may lead individuals to downplay or dismiss clear warning signs, choosing temporary peace over addressing underlying issues.

4. Idealization of Love:
Societal expectations and romantic ideals often paint an unrealistic picture of love and relationships. This idealization can create a perception that true love conquers all, including significant red flags. The belief that love should be perfect can hinder a realistic assessment of a relationship.

5. Personal Blind Spots:
Individuals might have personal blind spots, areas where their own insecurities, unmet needs, or past experiences influence their judgment. These blind spots can prevent them from recognizing red flags that, if acknowledged, would demand a closer examination of their own emotional well-being.

Addressing red flags before marriage is crucial, as these warning signs often become more pronounced over time. What may seem like a minor concern early on could develop into a significant challenge later in the relationship. Being attentive to your instincts, seeking guidance from trusted friends or mentors, and prioritizing open communication with your partner are essential steps in navigating red flags and ensuring a more informed and resilient foundation for your marital journey. Ignoring red flags now may mean confronting them later, and the price of overlooking them can be steep in the context of a committed, long-term relationship.

Signs to Examine in Your Prospect:
- Selfishness: If your prospect consistently prioritizes their own needs and desires above those of the relationship, demonstrating a lack of willingness to compromise and collaborate, it may indicate unreadiness for the selflessness required in marriage.
- Indecisiveness: If your partner struggles with making important decisions or exhibits a pattern of wavering commitments, it might suggest an uncertainty about long-term commitments, a crucial aspect of a stable marriage.
- Unresolved Baggage: Unaddressed emotional baggage or past traumas can significantly impact a person's ability to engage in a healthy, committed relationship. Signs of unresolved issues should be carefully considered before entering into marriage.
- Lack of Shared Goals: Fundamental misalignment in life goals, such as career aspirations, family planning, or spiritual beliefs, may indicate that your prospect is not on the same page regarding foundational aspects crucial for a successful marriage.
- Communication Challenges: If there are persistent difficulties in expressing feelings, resolving conflicts, or maintaining open and honest communication, it could signal a potential struggle in navigating the complexities of married life.

Signs to Examine in Yourself:
- Independence Overload: If you find it challenging to envision a life intertwined with another person or struggle with the idea of relying on someone else, you may need to assess your readiness for the interdependence required in marriage.
- Fear of Commitment: A deep-seated fear or avoidance of long-term commitments might indicate an internal resistance to the responsibilities and permanence that come with marriage.
- Unresolved Personal Issues: Personal insecurities, unresolved traumas, or a lack of self-awareness can hinder your ability to contribute positively to a marital partnership. Addressing these issues before marriage is crucial.
- Inability to Compromise: If you consistently resist compromising or adapting to another person's needs, it may signal a challenge in navigating the give-and-take nature of a marital relationship.
- Unrealistic Expectations: Expecting perfection or viewing marriage as a solution to personal problems can set the stage for disappointment. Realistic expectations grounded in mutual growth and support are essential for a healthy marriage.

Examining these signs in both your prospect and yourself provides an opportunity for introspection and ensures a more informed decision about whether marriage is the right step at this moment in your lives. Marriage is a sacred covenant that requires emotional maturity, mutual understanding, and a shared commitment to growth.

Navigating the Decision Crossroads: Pursuing God's Perfect Will
Embarking on the journey of deciding whether to continue pursuing a relationship or to release it into God's hands is an emotionally charged expedition. Letting go of someone you envisioned a future with, especially if soul ties have woven a connection, is no easy feat. However, it is crucial to remember that lasting happiness is found only on the path God has paved.

As you stand at this crossroads, examine the evidence before you. What signals, red or green, are present? Red flags serve as serious warnings, pointing to aspects in either you or your potential partner that could jeopardize the union. These demand careful consideration. Yellow flags, on the other hand, caution you to slow down, suggesting that although the relationship aligns with God's will, the timing may not be right for marriage. Reflecting on my own journey, I recall instances where yellow flags prompted my wife and me to decelerate, ensuring that our readiness for marriage matched God's timetable.

Green flags signify readiness in specific areas for the commitment of marriage. Individuals may exhibit a spectrum of these flags, signifying strengths and readiness in some areas but potential challenges in others. While someone may possess numerous green flags, a couple of red flags in character may outweigh the positive qualities. It's crucial to assess the overall balance.

The white flag, the flag of surrender, symbolizes acknowledgment that the journey may be over. It's a recognition that the relationship, despite your hopes and efforts, may not align with God's perfect will. Surrendering to His plan often involves courageously facing the reality that it might be time to end or temporarily pause the relationship.

Therefore, take heed of the flags – red, yellow, green – and be attuned to the white flag, surrendering to God's perfect timing and plan. The decision may be challenging, but trusting in God's wisdom will lead to a path of enduring joy and fulfillment.

In navigating the intricate path of serious dating, it becomes paramount to scrutinize the very fabric of your relationship. These questions serve as guiding beacons, illuminating the landscape of your connection. As you delve into these inquiries, you unearth not just the present dynamics but also glimpses of the future you might share. Each question is a compass, pointing to potential red flags demanding careful consideration, yellow flags prompting a pause for reflection, and green flags signaling readiness for a deeper commitment. As you confront these questions with openness and honesty, you unveil the true nature of your compatibility, values, and aspirations. The journey of serious dating is a period of exploration, and these questions offer a compass to navigate the uncharted waters, helping you discern whether your relationship is poised to set sail or if it's time to anchor in different harbors.

1. What values and beliefs are non-negotiable for both of us in a marriage?
   - Red Flag: Misaligned core values or beliefs may lead to significant conflicts down the road.
   - Yellow Flag: Differences in values are present but open for discussion, suggesting the need for further exploration.
   - Green Flag: Shared and compatible values, creating a solid foundation for a thriving marriage.
2. How do we handle conflicts and disagreements?
   - Red Flag: Frequent intense conflicts, disrespect, or inability to resolve issues could pose a threat to the relationship.
   - Yellow Flag: Some conflicts arise, but they are addressed with a willingness to communicate and find resolution.
   - Green Flag: Healthy conflict resolution, demonstrating effective communication and mutual respect.
3. What role does faith play in our individual lives and our potential marriage?
   - Red Flag: Stark differences in religious beliefs or commitment to faith may lead to challenges in building a spiritual foundation.
   - Yellow Flag: Differences in faith exist, requiring ongoing conversations to find common ground.
   - Green Flag: Shared or compatible faith, allowing for the development of a strong spiritual connection.
4. How do we navigate major life decisions and changes?
   - *Red Flag:* Inability to make decisions together or support each other during significant changes may signify challenges in partnership.
   - *Yellow Flag:* Some difficulties in decision-making or adapting to change, requiring further exploration and compromise.
   - *Green Flag:* Demonstrated ability to make joint decisions and adapt to life changes collaboratively.
5. Do we share a vision for our future, including family, career, and lifestyle goals?
   - *Red Flag:* Divergent long-term goals may lead to future conflicts and dissatisfaction.
   - *Yellow Flag:* Some misalignments in future aspirations, necessitating open communication and compromise.
   - *Green Flag:* Shared vision and goals for the future, providing a sense of direction and unity.
6. How do we handle financial matters individually, and what approach will we take in marriage?
   - *Red Flag:* Significant financial disagreements or irresponsible financial behaviors can strain a marriage.
   - *Yellow Flag:* Some differences in financial habits that require open communication and planning for the future.
   - *Green Flag:* Shared financial values and responsible money management for a secure marital foundation.

7. How do we maintain our individual identities while building a life together?
- Red Flag: A lack of individual autonomy or pressure to conform entirely may lead to feelings of suffocation.
- Yellow Flag: Struggling to strike a balance between individuality and unity, requiring ongoing discussion.
- Green Flag: Healthy respect for individual identity within the context of a committed relationship.

8. How do we handle external influences, such as family, friends, and societal expectations?
- Red Flag: Overwhelming influence or interference from external sources may impact the relationship negatively.
- Yellow Flag: Difficulty navigating external influences, requiring clear boundaries and communication.
- Green Flag: Healthy boundaries and the ability to prioritize the relationship amidst external pressures.

9. What are our expectations regarding roles and responsibilities within a marriage?
- Red Flag: Misaligned expectations regarding roles and responsibilities may lead to unmet needs and frustrations.
- Yellow Flag: Differences in expectations that require open dialogue and compromise for a harmonious partnership.
- Green Flag: Shared expectations and a clear understanding of respective roles, fostering a balanced and collaborative union.

10. How do we approach personal growth and self-improvement within the context of our relationship?
- Red Flag: Resistance to personal growth or conflicting trajectories of individual development may hinder the relationship.
- Yellow Flag: Some differences in personal growth approaches, requiring mutual support and understanding.
- Green Flag: A shared commitment to personal growth, supporting each other's journeys toward becoming the best versions of themselves.

11. What are our expectations and approaches to parenting, including discipline, values, and involvement?
- Red Flag: Stark differences in parenting styles or expectations may lead to conflicts and challenges in co-parenting.
- Yellow Flag: Varied expectations in parenting that require thorough discussion and alignment for a unified approach.
- Green Flag: Shared values and compatible parenting styles, providing a solid foundation for a harmonious family life.

Workbook-Serious Dating Evaluation Worksheet Page 145

Strategies for Graceful Offboarding: Navigating the Path to God's Best
Breaking off a relationship, especially when the evidence suggests it's not aligned with God's perfect will, can be a daunting task. However, implementing practical strategies can make this process more manageable and pave the way for the brighter future God has in store.

Build Trust in God's Timing:
- Begin by fostering trust in God's unwavering wisdom and perfect timing. Remember that His plans for your life far exceed any relationship you may be tempted to cling to out of fear or uncertainty.

Examine the Evidence:
- Delve into the reasons why this person might not be the one. Write down specific instances or patterns that indicate misalignment with God's perfect will. Facing the evidence head-on provides clarity and reinforces your decision.

Consider the Consequences:
- Reflect on the potential consequences of continuing a relationship that lacks divine alignment. Envision the future implications on your emotional, spiritual, and mental well-being. This foresight can serve as motivation to step away for a season or permanently.

Reflect on Your Initial State:
- Assess your mindset and emotional state when you initially boarded this relationship. Were there insecurities or fears that contributed to your decision? Understanding your initial vulnerabilities helps you make more informed choices moving forward.

Create a Support System:
- Surround yourself with a support system of trusted friends, family, or mentors who can offer guidance and encouragement during this challenging time. Having a community that understands your journey is invaluable.

Seek Professional Counsel:
- Consider seeking professional counseling or pastoral guidance. A neutral third party can provide insights and tools to navigate the complexities of disentangling from a relationship.

Establish Boundaries:
- Establish clear boundaries for communication and interaction as you navigate the offboarding process. This will help both parties maintain emotional distance and facilitate a smoother transition.

Focus on Personal Growth:
- Shift your focus toward personal growth and self-discovery. Use this time to deepen your relationship with God, understand yourself better, and cultivate the qualities that align with His purpose for your life.

Remember that offboarding is not a sign of failure but an act of courage and obedience to God's higher plan. By taking intentional steps and relying on His grace, you can gracefully navigate this transition and set the stage for the abundant blessings He has in store.

Navigating Uncharted Waters: The Art of Compassionate Relationship Offboarding
While a face-to-face conversation is often the most compassionate and respectful way to address the complexities of a relationship, there are situations where it might be challenging due to emotional intensity or potential hostility. In such cases, a well-crafted letter allows for thoughtful expression without immediate reactions. It provides the recipient with the opportunity to process the information at their own pace. However, it's important to emphasize the willingness to engage in further discussion if the person desires it. The key is to approach this delicate situation with empathy, kindness, and a genuine concern for both parties' emotional well-being.

Honest and Heartfelt Conversation About Our Relationship
I hope this message finds you well, and I want to express my gratitude for the time we've spent together. Our journey has been filled with valuable moments, and I appreciate the connection we've shared.

After much prayer, reflection, and consideration, I believe it's important for us to have an open and honest conversation about our relationship. I deeply value the time we've spent getting to know each other, and it's not without careful consideration that I share my thoughts.

As we've navigated this journey, I've been seeking God's guidance and clarity on our relationship. I believe it's crucial for us to align ourselves with His will and purpose for our lives. In doing so, I've come to a realization that our paths may not be perfectly aligned with His plan for our futures.

This is a difficult message for me to convey, and I hope you understand that my intention is rooted in respect and sincerity. I believe that God has unique plans for each of us, and it's important for us to be in harmony with His design for our lives.

I would like us to take some time for personal reflection and prayer, seeking God's wisdom and discernment in this matter. It's my hope that we both prioritize our individual walks with God during this time of transition.

I am open to discussing this further, and I believe that our faith and trust in God will guide us through this process. If you feel it would be beneficial, we can arrange a time to talk in person or over the phone.

Thank you for your understanding, and I wish you nothing but the very best on your journey. May God's grace and guidance be with you always.

Healing After Relationship Offboarding: Navigating Singleness with Purpose

H - Harnessing Self-Reflection:
Take time to introspect and understand the lessons learned from the relationship. Reflect on personal growth and identify areas for improvement.

E - Embracing Independence:
Cultivate a sense of self-sufficiency and embrace the opportunity to rediscover personal interests and hobbies. Enjoy the freedom that comes with being single.

A - Acceptance and Forgiveness:
Acknowledge and accept the emotions that accompany the end of a relationship. Practice forgiveness, both for yourself and your former partner, to release any lingering resentments.

L - Learning from the Past:
Extract valuable insights from the relationship's conclusion. Consider what worked well and what didn't, using this knowledge to shape future choices.

Remember, healing is a gradual process, and each individual's journey is unique. Embrace this time of self-discovery and allow it to pave the way for a future filled with healthier and more fulfilling connections.

Embracing a New Season: Unlearning and Relearning Singleness

As you embark on the journey of rediscovering yourself in the realm of singleness, it's essential to acknowledge the significance of unlearning and relearning. This process involves shedding misconceptions, societal pressures, and past relationship paradigms to embrace God's design for this unique season.

Unlearning involves letting go of preconceived notions about singleness that may have been influenced by cultural expectations or personal experiences. It's about dismantling any negative beliefs that hinder the full enjoyment and purpose of this season. Whether you've just come out of a relationship or have been navigating singleness for a while, unlearning provides the necessary space to declutter your mind and heart.

Relearning is the intentional pursuit of God's perspective on singleness. It's about understanding the purpose and beauty inherent in this season of life, recognizing it as an opportunity for growth, self-discovery, and spiritual development. By immersing yourself in God's truth and wisdom, you can reshape your mindset and expectations, aligning them with His perfect plan.

Unveiling the Purpose of Unlearning and Relearning:

Letting Go of Cultural Pressures (L):
- Unlearn societal pressures that may have ingrained false timelines and expectations about when and how relationships should unfold. Relearn God's timing and His perfect plan for your life.

Breaking Free from Relationship Stereotypes (B):
- Unlearn stereotypes that may have shaped your perception of what a relationship should look like. Relearn the biblical foundation of relationships and marriage, understanding God's design for companionship.

Rediscovering Personal Identity (R):
- Unlearn any tendencies to find identity solely in a relationship. Relearn your identity in Christ, understanding that your worth and purpose extend beyond your relationship status.

Navigating the Freedom of Singleness (N):
- Unlearn the fear or apprehension associated with singleness. Relearn how to navigate the freedom this season provides for personal exploration, pursuing passions, and deepening your relationship with God.

Embracing Contentment (E):
- Unlearn the idea that contentment is solely linked to relationship status. Relearn how to find contentment and joy in your relationship with God and the journey He has set before you.

Letting Go of Cultural Pressures (L): Redefining Timelines and Expectations

In the process of unlearning and relearning singleness, a pivotal aspect involves letting go of cultural pressures that dictate timelines and expectations regarding relationships. Society often imposes rigid expectations, urging individuals to conform to predetermined timelines for dating, marriage, and family-building. This can lead to unnecessary stress, comparison, and a sense of inadequacy if these expectations aren't met.

Unlearning these cultural pressures requires a deliberate effort to disentangle your beliefs from societal norms. This might involve challenging the notion that a specific age is the "right" time to settle down or questioning the idea that being single equates to a lack of fulfillment. Letting go of these pressures allows you to embrace the uniqueness of your journey and understand that God's timing transcends societal expectations.

Relearning involves seeking God's perspective on time and relationships. God operates outside the constraints of worldly timelines, and His plans are purposeful and perfect. The Bible reminds us in Ecclesiastes 3:1 that "there is a time for everything, and a season for every activity under the heavens." This truth invites you to relinquish the pressure to conform to cultural timelines and instead trust in God's sovereign timing

Key Steps in Letting Go and Relearning:
Reflection and Awareness:
- Take time to reflect on any societal pressures or expectations that have influenced your views on singleness and relationships. Be aware of the cultural narratives that may have shaped your mindset.

Aligning with God's Word:
- Seek guidance from the Scriptures to understand God's timeless principles for relationships. Recognize that His timing may differ from societal norms, and His plans are designed for your ultimate good.

Personalizing Your Journey:
- Embrace the idea that your path is uniquely yours. Unlearn the comparison trap and allow God to unfold His plan for your life at His perfect pace.

Focusing on Growth:
- Relearn the concept of growth and personal development. Use this season to invest in self-discovery, spiritual maturity, and pursuing the passions God has placed within you.

Cultivating Patience:
- Understand that letting go of cultural pressures is an ongoing process. Relearning patience is essential, trusting that God's timing is impeccable and that His plan for your life surpasses societal expectations.

By letting go of cultural pressures and relearning God's timeless truths, you free yourself from unnecessary burdens and open your heart to the beauty of God's unique plan for your singleness. This transformative journey sets the stage for a deeper, more purposeful understanding of the season you're in.

Breaking Free from Relationship Stereotypes (B): Unlearn and Relearn for God's Design
In the pursuit of unlearning and relearning singleness, an integral aspect is breaking free from relationship stereotypes. Societal stereotypes often shape our perception of what a relationship should look like, setting unrealistic expectations and fostering unhealthy comparisons. To embark on the journey of unlearning, it is crucial to identify and dismantle these stereotypes that may have influenced your view of relationships.

Unlearning involves recognizing the impact of relationship stereotypes and challenging their validity. Common stereotypes may include unrealistic portrayals in media, societal pressure to conform to specific roles, or the notion that relationships are the primary source of personal fulfillment. Breaking free from these stereotypes allows you to approach relationships with a fresh perspective, unburdened by unrealistic expectations.

Relearning centers on understanding God's design for companionship and relationships as outlined in the Bible. This entails immersing yourself in the biblical principles that govern healthy, God-centered relationships. Scriptures such as Genesis 2:18, which states, "It is not good for the man to be alone. I will make a helper suitable for him," provide the foundational understanding that God created companionship to be a source of support, love, and mutual growth.

Key Steps in Breaking Free and Relearning:

Identifying Stereotypes:
- Reflect on the stereotypes that may have shaped your views on relationships. Recognize how these stereotypes might have influenced your expectations and beliefs.

Questioning Cultural Narratives:
- Unlearn societal narratives that may promote unhealthy relationship ideals. Challenge the notion that relationships should conform to worldly standards rather than aligning with God's timeless truths.

Exploring Biblical Foundations:
- Relearn the biblical foundations of relationships by studying Scriptures that provide insight into God's design for companionship. Seek wisdom from passages that highlight the qualities of a healthy and God-honoring relationship.

Understanding Mutual Growth:
- Embrace the concept that relationships, when aligned with God's design, become a platform for mutual growth and support. Unlearn the idea that relationships are solely for personal fulfillment and recognize their broader purpose.

Cultivating Realistic Expectations:
- Relearn the importance of cultivating realistic expectations in relationships. Understand that God's design emphasizes love, commitment, and shared spiritual values rather than conforming to societal stereotypes.

Breaking free from relationship stereotypes and relearning God's design for companionship empowers you to approach relationships with authenticity and a biblical foundation. This transformative process enables you to embrace the beauty of God's plan for relationships and fosters a healthier and more purposeful perspective on companionship.

Rediscovering Personal Identity (R): Unlearn and Relearn for Christ-Centered Identity
In the journey of unlearning and relearning during singleness, a crucial aspect is rediscovering personal identity. Often, individuals may unknowingly find their identity solely within the context of a relationship, defining themselves by their partner or their relationship status. Unlearning this tendency is vital for fostering a healthy, Christ-centered identity.

Unlearning involves recognizing and letting go of the ingrained belief that your identity is solely derived from being in a relationship. This process requires self-reflection to identify any tendencies to seek validation, purpose, or worth exclusively through the lens of your relationship status. Unlearn the idea that a relationship defines your value. Relearning centers on understanding and embracing your identity in Christ. As a child of God, your worth and purpose extend beyond any relationship status. Relearning your identity in Christ involves immersing yourself in the biblical truth that you are fearfully and wonderfully made (Psalm 39:14) and that your true identity is found in being a beloved creation of God.

Key Steps in Rediscovering Personal Identity:
Acknowledging Dependency Tendencies:
- Unlearn any tendencies to depend on a relationship for a sense of identity. Acknowledge moments when you may have sought validation or worth through being in a relationship.

Embracing Individuality:
- Unlearn the notion that your identity is solely tied to being part of a couple. Reclaim your individuality and recognize the unique qualities and gifts that make you who you are apart from any romantic relationship.

Affirming Identity in Christ:
- Relearn your identity in Christ by affirming the biblical truth about your creation and purpose. Embrace passages that highlight God's love for you, irrespective of your relationship status.

Cultivating Personal Growth:
- Unlearn the belief that personal growth is primarily linked to being in a relationship. Relearn that personal growth is a continuous journey independent of your relationship status. Seek opportunities for self-improvement and development.

Connecting with God's Promises:
- Relearn the promises God has for you as an individual. Explore Scriptures that affirm God's plan for your life and the unique purpose He has designed for you.

By unlearning the tendency to find identity solely in a relationship and relearning your identity in Christ, you cultivate a strong foundation for singleness. This transformative process empower you to embrace your individuality, recognize your inherent worth, and navigate singleness with secure and Christ-centered identity.

Navigating the Freedom of Singleness (N): Unlearn and Relearn for Embracing Freedom
In the unlearning and relearning journey during singleness, navigating the freedom this season offers is a crucial aspect. Often, societal expectations or personal fears can create apprehension about being single. Unlearning these fears and embracing the true freedom of singleness is essential for personal growth and fulfillment.

Unlearning involves recognizing and letting go of any fear or apprehension associated with singleness. This may include societal pressures, personal insecurities, or the misconception that being single equates to incompleteness. Unlearn the notion that singleness is a limitation rather than an opportunity for exploration and growth.

Relearning centers on understanding and embracing the freedom that singleness provides. This involves viewing singleness not as a lack but as a unique season for personal exploration, pursuing passions, and deepening your relationship with God. Relearn that singleness is a valuable and purposeful phase of life.

Key Steps in Navigating the Freedom of Singleness:
Unlearning Societal Expectations:
- Identify and unlearn any societal expectations or pressures that have contributed to apprehension about being single. Challenge the notion that your worth is determined by you relationship status.
Embracing Personal Exploration:
- Relearn the freedom for personal exploration that singleness offers. Explore your interests, hobbies, and goals without the constraints of a relationship. See singleness as an opportuni for self-discovery and growth.
Pursuing Passions and Goals:
- Unlearn the idea that being in a relationship is a prerequisite for pursuing passions or achieving goals. Relearn that singleness provides the space and time to wholeheartedly pursue your aspirations and dreams.
Deepening Relationship with God:
- Relearn the importance of using this season to deepen your relationship with God. Recogniz that singleness allows for undivided focus on your spiritual journey, fostering a deeper connection with God.
Cultivating Independence:
- Unlearn any dependencies that hinder the cultivation of independence. Relearn the strength and fulfillment found in embracing independence during the season of singleness.

By unlearning the fear or apprehension associated with singleness and relearning how to navigate the freedom this season provides, you empower yourself to make the most of this unique phase. Singleness becomes a time of purposeful exploration, personal growth, and a deepening connection with God.

Embracing Contentment (E): Unlearn and Relearn for Lasting Joy
In the journey of unlearning and relearning during singleness, embracing contentment is a vita aspect. Often, there is a societal misconception that contentment is solely linked to one's relationship status. Unlearning this notion and relearning how to find contentment and joy in your relationship with God and the journey He has set before you is essential for lasting fulfillment.

Unlearning involves shedding the idea that your relationship status determines your level of contentment. Recognize and let go of the societal pressure that suggests being in a relationshi is the sole source of happiness. Contentment should not be contingent upon your relationship status.
Relearning centers on discovering and embracing the true sources of contentment and joy. This involves finding fulfillment in your relationship with God, understanding that He is the ultimat source of lasting joy. Relearn that contentment is a state of the heart, not a reflection of exter circumstances.

Key Steps in Embracing Contentment:

Unlinking Contentment from Relationship Status:
- Unlearn the societal idea that contentment is only achievable when in a relationship. Challenge the belief that a partner is the primary source of joy and fulfillment.

Finding Joy in God's Presence:
- Relearn how to find joy and contentment in your relationship with God. Understand that true and lasting joy comes from a deep connection with Him, transcending any temporary circumstances.

Appreciating the Journey:
- Unlearn the rush to reach the destination of a relationship and embrace the journey of singleness. Relearn to appreciate and find contentment in the present, understanding that each phase has its unique blessings.

Cultivating Gratitude:
- Relearn the art of cultivating gratitude for the blessings in your life. Shift your focus from what you lack to the abundance of goodness surrounding you, fostering a content and joyful spirit.

Investing in Personal Growth:
- Unlearn the idea that a relationship is the primary avenue for personal growth. Relearn that singleness provides ample opportunities for self-improvement, skill development, and personal enrichment.

By unlearning the notion that contentment is solely linked to relationship status and relearning to find lasting joy in your relationship with God and the journey He has set before you, you embark on a path of true fulfillment. Embracing contentment becomes a choice rooted in spiritual connection and a deeper understanding of God's purpose for your life.

In conclusion, the journey of unlearning and relearning during singleness is a transformative process that allows you to redefine and rediscover the true essence of this unique season. Singleness, often viewed as a waiting period, is, in fact, a gift in itself—an invaluable opportunity to master your gifts, understand your identity in Christ, and cultivate contentment rooted in a deep relationship with God. Unlearning societal misconceptions about singleness frees you from unnecessary pressures and expectations, enabling a relearning process where you recognize the divine purpose and potential within this phase. It is a time to invest in personal growth, pursue passions, and develop the qualities that will not only enhance your life but make you a remarkable gift to the one God has ordained for you. Through unlearning and relearning, singleness becomes a season of preparation, a gift that empowers you to embrace your uniqueness, discover your purpose, and ultimately become a blessing to the person destined to share the journey of life with you.

Dating vs. Courting

In the realm of relationships, unlearning conventional dating practices and embracing the concept of courtship can be a transformative journey. Unlike the often casual and aimless nature of dating, courtship represents a purposeful and intentional approach to romantic relationships. Courtship, in essence, is a "ship" set on a deliberate course towards a destination, viewing the relationship as a vessel navigating the waters of shared values, commitment, and mutual growth.

Unlearning the world's view of dating involves stepping away from the culture of casual connections and short-lived romances, where the emphasis is often on immediate gratification and fleeting experiences. Instead, courtship places a higher value on shared values, emotional compatibility, and a commitment to pursuing a God-centered relationship.

One significant difference lies in the intention behind courtship. While dating may involve casual encounters and uncertain commitments, courtship is marked by a focused pursuit of marriage. It involves a clear understanding of shared goals, values, and spiritual alignment between partners. Courtship encourages a deeper connection, fostering emotional intimacy without compromising the sanctity of marriage.

Furthermore, courtship emphasizes the involvement of families and mentors, recognizing the importance of community input in the decision-making process. It brings accountability and wisdom into the relationship, providing a solid foundation for a lasting marriage.

By unlearning the societal norms associated with dating and embracing the intentional principles of courtship, individuals can create a relational framework that aligns with God's design for romantic unions. This shift in perspective not only transforms the nature of relationships but also contributes to building lasting marriages centered on shared faith, values, and a commitment to mutual growth.

in the context of courtship, dating takes on a more intentional and purposeful role. Dating, in its original sense of meeting up on a particular date, becomes a tool within the broader framework of courtship. Under the umbrella of courtship, meaningful and purpose-driven dates can serve as opportunities for individuals to get to know each other, build connection, and assess compatibility with a potential life partner.

Contrary to the cultural norms of dating, where the emphasis often leans towards casual encounters and immediate gratification, courtship redefines the dating process. It discourages the superficial and worldly aspects of modern dating culture, where individuals may engage in multiple relationships without a clear commitment to a shared future.

In the pursuit of courtship, the focus shifts from actively seeking a partner through various dating channels, including online platforms, to immersing oneself in God's purpose. The idea is that as individuals grow and mature in their God-given purpose, they naturally become aligned with someone who shares similar values and goals. God doesn't require us to play matchmaker, instead, He desires us to trust in His timing and guidance as we navigate the journey of purpose.

Engaging in purpose-driven activities and pursuing personal growth become the primary focus, allowing God to orchestrate divine connections. Rather than relying on our efforts to be seen or available on dating sites or through other conventional dating methods, courtship encourages us to be so immersed in our purpose that God, in His perfect timing, brings the right person into our lives.

Dating, when approached within the framework of courtship, becomes a tool for intentional connection and exploration, fostering relationships that align with God's design for lasting unions. It emphasizes the importance of allowing God to be the ultimate matchmaker, trusting in His wisdom to lead us to a partner who complements our purpose and journey.

Navigating the period between the end of one relationship and the beginning of another is a crucial time for personal development and growth. Singleness is not merely a transitional phase but an opportunity for a profound transformation—a time to wait, serve, and prepare for the weight of marriage. The biblical wisdom encapsulated in the verse "those who wait on the Lord shall renew their strength" takes on a nuanced significance in the context of singleness.

Waiting on the Lord isn't a passive act but an active engagement with God's purpose. It involves serving, seeking, and surrendering to His guidance during this season of singleness. Picture it like being a waiter or waitress at a restaurant. While waiting for the main course, the waiter is actively engaged in preparing, serving, and ensuring everything is in order. Similarly, in the season of singleness, individuals are called to actively participate in the divine process of becoming the person God intended them to be.

This season of singleness is akin to a training ground, where individuals are equipped with the skills, resilience, and wholeness required to navigate the weightiness of marriage. God uses this time to mold and shape singles, ensuring they carry the right weight to endure the challenges and responsibilities of a marital relationship. Like diligent waiters and waitresses in a bustling restaurant, singles are honing their spiritual, emotional, and relational muscles, preparing to carry the weight of a God-ordained marriage.

During this interim, healing becomes a priority—a process of shedding the weight of pain, bitterness, and unresolved issues. It is a time to gain emotional intelligence, cultivate healthy habits, and develop the self-awareness needed for the journey ahead. Singleness, in essence, becomes a powerful time of waiting, serving, and transforming—a divine preparation for the weightiness of a God-centered marriage. The wait is not passive but an active pursuit of God's purpose, ensuring that when the right person comes, both individuals are ready to embark on the weighty but fulfilling journey of marriage.

Entering into marriage is akin to embracing a substantial weight, and understanding the gravity of this commitment is essential for singles contemplating the journey ahead. The weight of marriage is not to be underestimated, as it demands a significant level of emotional, spiritual, and relational maturity. Here are six reasons why singles must actively engage in losing or gaining weight during their season of singleness:

- W - Wisdom: Marriage requires a profound level of wisdom to navigate the complexities, challenges, and decision-making processes that arise. The weight of marital responsibilities necessitates a wisdom gained through life experiences, self-awareness, and a deep understanding of God's principles.
- E - Emotional Resilience: Emotional resilience is a critical aspect of the weight individuals carry in marriage. Singles must develop the capacity to bounce back from disappointments, conflicts, and the inevitable ups and downs of life. Emotional maturity gained in singleness contributes to the strength needed to weather the storms of marital life.
- I - Intimacy: True intimacy is more than physical; it involves emotional, spiritual, and intellectual connection. Singles must gain the weight of understanding themselves intimately and learn to cultivate deep connections with God and others. This foundation becomes crucial for fostering intimacy within marriage.
- G - Godly Character: The weight of marriage requires individuals to possess a godly character, marked by virtues such as love, patience, kindness, and forgiveness. Developing these character traits during singleness is essential, as they form the bedrock of a healthy and thriving marital relationship.
- H - Holistic Health: Physical, emotional, and spiritual health contribute to the overall well-being required to bear the weight of marriage. Singles must actively pursue holistic health during their season of singleness, laying the foundation for a robust and enduring marital union.
- T - Teamwork: Marriage is a partnership that thrives on teamwork. Singles must gain the weight of collaboration, learning to communicate effectively, resolve conflicts amicably, and navigate shared responsibilities. Developing teamwork skills in singleness ensures a smoother transition into the collaborative nature of marriage.

Understanding these six facets—wisdom, emotional resilience, intimacy, godly character, holistic health, and teamwork—illuminates the weightiness of marriage. Singles are encouraged to actively engage in losing detrimental weights such as unhealthy habits, unresolved issues, and emotional baggage while gaining the weight of positive attributes that contribute to a thriving marriage. By purposefully navigating their season of singleness, individuals position themselves to embrace the weight of marriage with readiness and resilience.

In conclusion, evaluating your relationship before embarking on the voyage of marriage is a crucial step in ensuring a strong and enduring union. Assessing the flags, whether red, yellow, or green, provides invaluable insights into the health and readiness of your relationship. Taking the time to navigate the harbor of singleness allows you the opportunity to shed the weight of unaddressed issues and gain the strength needed for the challenges of marriage. Staying anchored in singleness is not a setback but a strategic preparation for the right ship that will come to harbor. It's a season to grow, heal, and align with God's perfect plan. May this section empower you to make the best decision for your future, guided by wisdom, prayer, and a deep connection with the One who orchestrates the perfect timing of each relationship.

Workbook-Marriage Readiness Worksheet Page 150

RELATIONSHIP WITH SPOUSE

Spousal Connection

The beauty of marriage lies not only in its joys but also in the journey of overcoming hurdles and growing together. It is essential to recognize that any marriage, regardless of its current state, possesses the potential for profound transformation. The key lies in the shared commitment of both partners to embark on a journey of renewal.

Belief becomes a cornerstone in this transformative process. The belief that, with faith, prayer, and dedication, a marriage can be reshaped and aligned with the divine purpose it was intended for. This foundational belief sets the stage for the remarkable power of Christ to enter and rebuild the marital foundation. As we delve into the exploration of Christ-centered marriages, let us carry this belief with us—a belief that serves as a beacon of hope, guiding couples toward the path of profound marital transformation.

Exploring the foundational design of marriage in the context of God's original plan is a crucial step in understanding its significance as the cornerstone of human relationships. As we delve into the biblical definition of marriage, it's essential to recognize that God intended this sacred union to be between a man and a woman who, together, possess the fundamental traits and qualities needed to embark on the journey of building a family. Moreover, it involves a shared commitment to allowing God to continually cultivate and refine those qualities as they progress through the various stages of marriage.

The scriptural foundation for the sanctity of marriage is evident in Hebrews 13:4, which declares, "Let marriage be held in honor among all." This divine injunction emphasizes the significance of marriage being honored, esteemed, and revered. Satan, however, seeks to undermine this honor by distorting the beauty and sanctity of marriage in the minds of individuals. His tactics involve perverting the perception of marriage or convincing people to dismiss it altogether.
Marriage, as God designed it, is a beautiful and purposeful institution that serves as a refining crucible for both the husband and wife. It creates a safe and nurturing environment for the next generation to be nurtured and prepared to impact the world positively. When marriages are held in honor, society experiences stability, flourishing communities, and a cycle of positive influence through generations.

Conversely, when marriages are not held in honor, society bears the weight of various consequences. Dysfunctional families, broken homes, and the erosion of foundational values contribute to societal unrest and moral decline. It becomes evident that honoring the divine blueprint for marriage is not just a matter of personal fulfillment but has far-reaching implications for the flourishing of individuals, families, and communities. As we explore the role of Christ as the foundation of marriages, let us first appreciate the profound significance of God's original design for this sacred union. Within the rich fabric of biblical symbolism, Christ is often depicted as the cornerstone—a pivotal component crucial for building a strong and unwavering foundation. This metaphor holds profound significance when applied to marriages,

emphasizing that nothing is truly worth building if Jesus is not the cornerstone of the union. A cornerstone, in architectural terms, serves as the principal foundation stone, connecting and aligning the entire structure. It bears the weight of the entire edifice and ensures its stability and endurance over time. Similarly, Christ serves as the cornerstone of our marriages, providing the essential alignment, support, and strength needed to withstand the tests of time.

Exploring this biblical metaphor illuminates the unique qualities that make Christ the ideal cornerstone for marriages. Firstly, a cornerstone is carefully selected and precisely placed, symbolizing the intentional choice of Christ at the very foundation of a marital union. It is not a haphazard decision but a deliberate and purposeful commitment to build upon the solid rock of Christ's teachings and principles.

Furthermore, a cornerstone is unyielding and unshakable, providing a firm and unwavering foundation for the entire structure. Similarly, when Christ is the cornerstone of a marriage, it establishes an unshakable foundation. The challenges and storms of life may come, but a marriage anchored in Christ remains steadfast, rooted in the timeless truths and promises of God.

The value of a cornerstone lies not only in its initial placement but in its ability to endure. Similarly, Christ as the cornerstone ensures that the foundation of a marriage is not just strong in the beginning but remains robust throughout the journey. His teachings, love, and grace become the bedrock upon which the marriage is built, sustaining it through the various seasons and challenges that may arise.

In essence, establishing Christ as the cornerstone of a marriage is a deliberate choice to build upon the unshakable foundation of His love, wisdom, and guidance. As couples embrace this biblical metaphor, they fortify their union with the enduring strength that comes from aligning their lives with the cornerstone that is Christ.

The timeless parable of building on sand versus building on rock, as told by Jesus in the Gospel of Matthew, serves as a profound metaphor for the choices we make in constructing the foundations of our lives, including marriages. The parable illustrates the stark contrast between those who choose the easy and expedient path, symbolized by building on sand, and those who invest time, effort, and intentionality into constructing a solid foundation on rock.

Building on sand represents the desire for quick results, immediate gratification, and shortcuts in the construction process. The sandy foundation may seem convenient at first, offering a seemingly swift solution, much like the allure of quick fixes or impulsive decisions in a marriage. However, this foundation lacks the depth and stability required to withstand the storms that life inevitably brings.

On the other hand, those who choose to build on rock are characterized by a commitment to lasting, enduring foundations. The process of finding and establishing the rock may take more time and effort, reflecting a deliberate choice to prioritize long-term stability over immediate convenience. This approach signifies a willingness to invest in the marriage journey, patiently crafting a foundation that can weather the challenges and uncertainties of life.

The question then becomes, "Are you building your marriage to pass or to last?" The distinction lies in the intentions and choices made during the construction phase. Marriages built to pass may focus on temporary pleasures, surface-level fixes, and the avoidance of deeper, more challenging aspects. These marriages may lack the resilience needed when faced with trials.

Conversely, marriages built to last embrace the patient and intentional process of finding the rock, symbolizing a commitment to enduring strength and stability. The investment of time, prayer, communication, and shared values contributes to a foundation that can withstand the test of time.

As we delve into the signs of whether a marriage is built on sand or rock, it's essential to reflect on the choices made in the construction phase and assess the foundation upon which the marriage stands. Building on the rock requires patience, wisdom, and a focus on lasting, Christ-centered principles, ensuring that the marriage remains unshakable in the face of life's storms.

Signs a Marriage is Built on Sand:
S - Superficial Communication:
Communication in a marriage built on sand tends to be shallow and lacks depth. Superficial conversations dominate, avoiding meaningful discussions about emotions, goals, and challenges. The foundation remains vulnerable to erosion due to the absence of open and honest communication.

A - Avoidance of Conflict Resolution:
In marriages built on sand, conflicts are often ignored or suppressed rather than addressed constructively. Avoidance becomes the norm, preventing the couple from strengthening their foundation through healthy conflict resolution. Over time, unresolved issues accumulate, weakening the structure.

233

N - Neglect of Emotional Connection:
A marriage built on sand may prioritize external appearances over emotional connection. The couple might neglect the emotional needs of each other, leading to a lack of intimacy and understanding. The foundation becomes brittle when emotional bonds are disregarded.

D - Dependency on External Factors:
When a marriage relies heavily on external factors such as material wealth, societal expectations, or fleeting pleasures, it stands on shaky ground. The foundation built on sand is susceptible to external pressures, lacking the internal strength needed to weather storms.

Signs a Marriage is Built on the Rock:
R - Rooted in Shared Values:
A marriage built on the rock is grounded in shared values and principles. The couple aligns their lives with Christ-centered values, creating a solid foundation that withstands the shifting sands of societal trends and external pressures.

O - Open and Honest Communication:
Communication in a rock-solid marriage is characterized by openness and honesty. The couple engages in meaningful conversations, addressing both joys and challenges. The foundation is strengthened through transparent communication, fostering a deeper connection.

C - Commitment to Conflict Resolution:
In marriages built on the rock, conflicts are seen as opportunities for growth. The couple commits to resolving issues constructively, learning from challenges, and fortifying their foundation through shared problem-solving.

K - Koinonia: Spiritual Intimacy:
Koinonia, or spiritual intimacy, becomes a cornerstone of rock-solid marriages. The couple nurtures their relationship with God, fostering spiritual unity. This shared spiritual foundation provides strength and resilience amid life's uncertainties.

Assessing the signs within a marriage can reveal whether it is built on sand or the rock. Recognizing and addressing areas of vulnerability can guide couples toward strengthening their foundation and building a marriage that endures.

Embracing Renewal: Rebuilding on a Firm Foundation
In the journey of marriage, there comes a moment when the realization dawns that the foundation may not be as solid as initially thought. It's a pivotal point, a crossroads where a decision must be made – to demolish the existing structure and rebuild anew or to continue navigating a shaky foundation. While the idea of starting over might seem daunting, it carries within it the potential for incredible transformation and renewal.

Consider this phase as a renovation project. Many couples, faced with the need for a stronger foundation, have opted for a controlled demolition – tearing down the old to make way for something new, resilient, and more beautiful. It's not a moment for self-condemnation but an opportunity for rebirth. God, in His grace, has already paid for the renovation; all that's required is a willingness to rebuild.

This rebuilding process is not about beating oneself up for past mistakes but rather acknowledging that growth often involves tearing down what no longer serves the purpose. It's an invitation to construct something greater, more aligned with God's design for marriage. Just as a home can be reconstructed into a larger and more secure structure, marriages too can experience renewal, provided the commitment to rebuild on a firm foundation is unwavering.

Choosing to rebuild is an act of faith, acknowledging that God's grace extends even to the rebuilding process. It is better to engage in a controlled demolition, guided by internal decisions to address weaknesses, than to risk the potential collapse resulting from both internal and external pressures. Through God's guidance and a shared commitment to rebuild, couples can witness their marriage transforming into a resilient and enduring structure, firmly grounded on the Rock.

Demolishing the Foundations of Sand: Steps Towards Renewal
For couples who find themselves standing on shaky ground, the realization that your marriage may have been built on sand can be both disheartening and liberating. The good news is that acknowledging this truth is the first step towards renewal. Just as a house can be rebuilt, marriages too can undergo a transformative process, starting with the demolition of foundations that lack stability.

- Reflection and Acknowledgment: Begin by reflecting on the current state of the marriage. Acknowledge the weaknesses and vulnerabilities that have become apparent. This introspection is not meant to assign blame but to gain clarity on the areas that need attention.
- Open and Honest Communication: Establish a safe space for open and honest communication. Share your feelings, concerns, and aspirations for the marriage. This is a crucial stage for understanding each other's perspectives and laying the groundwork for the rebuilding process.
- Seek Professional Guidance: Consider seeking the assistance of a marriage counselor or therapist. A neutral third party can provide insights and strategies to navigate challenges. Professional guidance can contribute significantly to the healing and rebuilding journey.
- Identify Specific Weaknesses: Pinpoint the specific areas where the foundation may be weak. Whether it's issues of trust, communication breakdown, or unaddressed conflicts, identifying these weaknesses is essential for targeted and effective reconstruction.
- Mutual Commitment to Change: Renewal requires a mutual commitment to change. Both partners must be willing to invest time, effort, and energy into rebuilding the marriage. Establish shared goals and a vision for the renewed relationship.
- Forgiveness and Letting Go: Let go of past grievances and forgive each other. Carrying the baggage of past mistakes hinders the rebuilding process. Embrace forgiveness as a powerful tool for healing and moving forward.
- Rebuilding Through Small Acts: Start the rebuilding process through small, intentional acts of love and kindness. Focus on rebuilding trust, improving communication, and fostering a renewed sense of connection.
- Cultivate a Christ-Centered Focus: Shift the focus of the marriage towards Christ. Invite Him into the process of renewal, seeking His guidance and grace. A Christ-centered foundation provides the stability needed for lasting transformation.

Remember, the process of demolishing and rebuilding is a journey. It requires patience, resilience, and a shared commitment to creating a marriage firmly grounded on the unshakable Rock. With dedication and faith, couples can embark on this transformative path towards renewal.

Cultivating Resilient Faith: The Third Rope in Marital Storms
In marriage, storms are not a matter of "if" but "when." They may manifest as financial strains, communication breakdowns, or unexpected life events, challenging the very core of the marital bond. Often, couples find themselves reaching for their faith as a lifeline only when the storm is already raging. However, the key to navigating these marital storms with grace lies in cultivating and activating a robust faith in God during the calm before the tempest.

1. Activating Faith in the Calm:
Many couples inadvertently wait until the storms are upon them to activate their faith. However, a faith cultivated in times of calm becomes a powerful anchor when the waves of challenges crash against the marital ship. The proactive approach involves intentionally strengthening the spiritual bond during seasons of tranquility, allowing faith to become a well-practiced resource.

2. Resilience: The Foundation of Marriage:
Resilience is the bedrock of any enduring marriage. It is the ability to bend without breaking, to weather the storms without losing sight of the shared journey. This resilience is not solely a product of human strength; it draws from a deeper well—the reservoir of faith. Couples resilient in their faith find themselves not merely surviving storms but emerging from them stronger and more united.

3. The Third Rope: Tethering to the Holy Spirit:

Imagine marriage as a ship navigating the unpredictable seas of life. The first two ropes represent the husband and wife, working together to steer and stabilize the vessel. However, a third rope is crucial—the Holy Spirit. Without this divine connection, the marital ship lacks the guidance, strength, and sustenance needed to weather storms. Allowing the Holy Spirit to be an active participant in the marriage transforms it from a two-person endeavor to a divinely orchestrated journey.

4. Proactive vs. Reactive Faith:

Proactive faith involves intentionally seeking God, praying together, and building a spiritual foundation before the storms arrive. Reactive faith, on the other hand, is a desperate reach for God in the midst of chaos. While both approaches can lead to restoration, the former allows couples to face challenges with a faith that has been nurtured and practiced.

5. Anchoring in the Unseen:

The storms of marriage often test what cannot be seen with the naked eye—trust, commitment, and the unseen hand of God. Cultivating faith in the unseen aspects of the marriage journey enables couples to navigate challenges with an assurance that, even when they can't see the way, God is intricately involved.

In summary, building a resilient marriage requires more than human effort; it demands a connection to the divine. The third rope, tethered to the Holy Spirit, ensures that the marital ship remains steady during the storms. Couples who activate and cultivate their faith in times of calm find themselves equipped to face any tempest, secure in the knowledge that, with God as their guide, their marriage can withstand and flourish in the face of adversity.

Navigating Marital Storms: Lessons from the Sea of Galilee
In the chronicles of the Sea of Galilee, we find poignant narratives of Jesus' disciples grappling with tempests while out on the water. These incidents offer profound insights into the dynamics of faith and the assurance of God's presence in the midst of life's storms.

1. The Sleeping Savior:

One stormy night, the disciples found themselves battling turbulent waves, fearing for their lives. In the stern of the boat, amidst the chaos, lay Jesus, sound asleep. This seemingly paradoxical scene underscores a profound truth—having Jesus on board is the assurance of safety. When life's storms threaten to overwhelm us, the key is not the absence of challenges but the presence of the Master. His restful demeanor in the midst of the storm challenges us to trust in His sovereignty even when circumstances appear dire.

Often, our marriages encounter storms that evoke fear, doubt, and anxiety. Yet, the lesson here is that with Jesus at the helm, we can rest assured that His presence transforms our fears into tranquil assurance. His calm can permeate our hearts, teaching us to sleep in the boat of our relationships, trusting in the One who governs the winds and waves.

2. The Delayed Savior

In a poignant sequel to the Sea of Galilee narratives, we encounter a remarkable episode where Jesus deliberately sent his disciples ahead without His physical presence. This intentional act served as a test of their faith, challenging them to navigate the waters in His absence. As they set sail, unbeknownst to them, a storm brewed on the horizon, and the waters became tumultuous.

The divine silence during their struggle is a testament to a profound truth—sometimes, God's voice is heard most clearly in the midst of our challenges. In marriage, there are moments when God seems silent, especially when facing trials. The disciples' experience resonates with the uncertainties that can engulf our relationships, leaving us to grapple with doubts and fears in the absence of apparent divine intervention.

Yet, as the disciples battled the tempest, something extraordinary occurred. Jesus, who initially sent them on this journey, met them walking on the very waters they feared. His presence, though not immediately visible, transcended the storm. This transformative moment highlights a profound reality: Christ may seem absent or silent, but He is always aware of our struggles and, at the appointed time, reveals Himself, walking over what terrifies us.

In the context of marriage, this narrative beckons us to recognize that even when God seems silent, His omniscient eyes are fixed on our journey. The storms may assail, but Jesus will meet us, walking over the challenges that threaten to engulf us. His silent testing of our faith is not an abandonment but a preparation for a revelation of His power and authority over the very things we dread.

The disciples, initially gripped by fear, were astounded at Jesus' presence. Likewise, in our marriages, when God breaks His silence, revealing Himself in the midst of our struggles, we are left awe-struck by His ability to transcend the storm. This narrative serves as an encouragement for couples navigating the seas of marital challenges. Even in moments of divine silence, trust that Jesus is walking over your fears, ready to bring peace and reassurance to your relationship.

In conclusion, this episode accentuates the profound truth that God's silence does not equate to abandonment. Instead, it serves as a canvas upon which His miraculous interventions are painted. As we navigate the marital seas, let us find solace in the reality that the One who commands the winds and waves will meet us, walking over the very challenges that threaten to capsize our relationship.

In conclusion, these two instances on the Sea of Galilee illuminate the essence of faith in the marital journey. Jesus' presence and promises are our anchors in turbulent times. As we navigate the seas of marriage, let us find solace in the truth that with Jesus on board and His promises as our compass, we can calmly face any storm, knowing that the One who calms the seas resides within us.

Cultivating Unshakeable Faith in Your Marriage
Building a resilient and unshakeable faith in your marriage is a proactive and ongoing process. Rather than waiting until storms arrive, couples can intentionally strengthen their faith before, during, and after challenges. Here's a guide using the acronym FAITH to help you cultivate a robust foundation for your marital journey:
1. Foundation in Christ:
Establishing your marital foundation on the cornerstone of Christ is paramount. Prioritize shared spiritual practices, such as prayer, Bible study, and attending church together. A solid foundation in Christ ensures that your faith is deeply rooted, providing stability when storms arise.

2. Anticipate Challenges:
Anticipating challenges does not mean expecting the worst, but rather acknowledging that difficulties are a natural part of life. Couples can prepare for storms by maintaining open communication, addressing issues promptly, and seeking wise counsel when needed. Proactively discussing potential challenges builds resilience.

3. Intentional Spiritual Growth:
Regularly invest in your spiritual growth as individuals and as a couple. This involves personal prayer and study, as well as joint efforts to deepen your understanding of God's Word. Intentional spiritual growth provides a reservoir of strength to draw from during challenging times.

4. Trust in God's Promises:
Immerse yourselves in the promises found in Scripture. Trusting in God's faithfulness and His promises for your marriage serves as an anchor during storms. Reflecting on biblical assurances fosters confidence in God's ability to guide you through any trial.

5. Hold Onto Hope:
Hope is a powerful antidote to despair. Maintain a hopeful outlook by focusing on the positive aspects of your relationship, cherishing shared memories, and envisioning a future together. Holding onto hope enables you to face challenges with optimism and determination.

In summary, cultivating unshakeable faith in your marriage is an intentional journey that involves building a foundation in Christ, anticipating challenges, investing in intentional spiritual growth, trusting in God's promises, and holding onto hope. By consistently nurturing your faith, you empower your marriage to withstand the storms and emerge stronger, reaffirming the unyielding bond you share.

Nurturing Spiritual Intimacy for a Stronger Connection

Spiritual intimacy in marriage is the deep, shared connection between spouses that transcends the physical and emotional realms, reaching into the spiritual dimensions of their lives. It involves a shared commitment to grow spiritually individually and as a couple. Strengthening spiritual intimacy is not just about praying together or attending church; it's about fostering a joint pursuit of God's heart and a desire for spiritual growth that permeates every aspect of married life.

1. Shared Spiritual Desires:
A key aspect of spiritual intimacy is a shared desire for things of God. When both partners have a genuine hunger for spiritual matters, it creates a strong foundation for growth. Shared spiritual desires include a commitment to prayer, studying Scripture together, and engaging in activities that deepen your collective understanding of God.

2. Individual Spiritual Growth:
While shared spiritual pursuits are crucial, individual spiritual growth is equally important. Each spouse should have a personal relationship with God, engaging in personal prayer, studying the Bible independently, and cultivating a deep, individual connection with God. This ensures that your spiritual foundation is not solely reliant on your partner but is robust and self-sustaining.

3. Strengthening the Marriage Collectively:
Couples who prioritize spiritual intimacy find that it strengthens every other aspect of their marriage. A shared faith becomes the anchor during challenging times, providing comfort, wisdom, and perspective. Collectively growing spiritually enables couples to navigate life's complexities with a united front, fortified by their shared commitment to God.

4. Prayerful Independence:
Developing the ability to pray independently is crucial for spiritual intimacy. Each partner should feel comfortable communicating with God individually, fostering a personal connection. This independence ensures that even when physically apart, the spiritual bond remains strong, contributing to a resilient and enduring connection.

5. Growing Together, Growing Deeper:
Spiritual growth is a journey that deepens over time. Couples who invest in spiritual intimacy understand that it's not a destination but a continuous process. As you grow together, your connection deepens, creating a resilient bond that withstands the tests of time and trials.

In conclusion, nurturing spiritual intimacy in marriage involves cultivating shared spiritual desires, prioritizing individual spiritual growth, strengthening the marriage collectively, developing prayerful independence, and understanding that spiritual growth is a journey. A marriage rooted in spiritual intimacy becomes a haven of strength, resilience, and enduring love.

Cultivating Spiritual Intimacy: Practical Strategies for Couples

Cultivating spiritual intimacy in your marriage involves intentional efforts and shared commitment. Here are practical strategies to strengthen the spiritual connection between you and your spouse:
- 1. Prioritize Shared Spiritual Activities:
    - Make time for shared spiritual activities such as praying together, attending church services, or participating in Bible studies as a couple. These shared experiences contribute to a deeper understanding of each other's spiritual journey.
- 2. Establish a Joint Prayer Routine:
    - Create a regular routine for joint prayer. Whether it's daily, weekly, or as fits your schedule, coming together in prayer fosters a sense of unity and shared purpose in your spiritual walk.
- 3. Read and Discuss Scripture Together:
    - Choose a book of the Bible or a devotional to read together. Discussing the passages and insights can open up meaningful conversations about your faith and how it applies to your marriage.

- 4. Attend Spiritual Retreats or Workshops:
  - Invest in attending spiritual retreats or marriage workshops that focus on enhancing your spiritual connection. These events provide dedicated time for reflection, learning, and growth as a couple.
- 5. Encourage Individual Spiritual Practices:
  - Support and encourage each other's individual spiritual practices. Whether it's personal prayer time, journaling, or reading spiritual literature, recognizing and fostering these practices strengthens your collective spiritual foundation.
- 6. Incorporate Faith into Daily Life:
  - Integrate your faith into your daily life. This can include praying together before meals, discussing spiritual insights, or finding ways to apply your faith to challenges you face as a couple.
- 7. Serve Together:
  - Engage in acts of service together. Volunteering or serving others as a couple not only strengthens your bond but also provides opportunities to live out your faith in practical ways.
- 8. Seek Guidance and Mentorship:
  - Consider seeking guidance from a spiritual mentor or joining a couples' small group. Having mentors or a community to share experiences and insights can enrich your spiritual journey as a couple.
- 9. Celebrate Spiritual Milestones:
  - Acknowledge and celebrate spiritual milestones in your marriage. Whether it's commemorating the anniversary of a significant spiritual moment or celebrating answered prayers, these milestones reinforce your shared spiritual journey.
- 10. Foster a Culture of Grace:
  - Create a culture of grace within your marriage. Understand that spiritual growth is a lifelong process, and both of you will experience highs and lows. Approach each other with love, patience, and understanding as you navigate your spiritual paths together.

By implementing these practical strategies, couples can actively cultivate spiritual intimacy, fostering a connection that becomes the cornerstone of a thriving and enduring marriage.

Overcoming Marital Obstacles: Navigating Spiritual Warfare in Marriage
Marriage, while a beautiful union, often encounters challenges that require intentional navigation. It's essential to recognize that some obstacles are part of the human experience, while others may have a spiritual origin. In this section, we will delve into identifying common challenges in marriage and understanding the spiritual warfare that can impact the marital bond

1. Recognizing Common Challenges:
Marital challenges come in various forms, including communication breakdowns, financial stress, intimacy issues, and external pressures. Understanding that these challenges are part of the shared human experience helps couples approach them with empathy and a united front.

2. The Reality of Spiritual Warfare:
Spiritual warfare involves unseen battles that can affect the spiritual, emotional, and physical aspects of marriage. Satan seeks to undermine the foundation of marriage by sowing discord, fostering resentment, and creating distractions. By recognizing the spiritual dimension, couples can address challenges with a strategic and prayerful mindset.

3. Wrestling Against Spiritual Forces:
The apostle Paul reminds us that our struggle is not against flesh and blood but against spiritual forces (Ephesians 6:12). Couples engaged in spiritual warfare should be aware of the tactics used to sow division and strife in marriages. Identifying these tactics allows couples to unite against the true enemy.

4. Prayer as a Weapon:
Prayer is a powerful weapon in spiritual warfare. Couples are encouraged to pray together, seeking God's guidance, protection, and wisdom for their marriage. Regular prayer not only fortifies the marital bond but also invites God's presence into the challenges faced.

5. Seeking Professional and Pastoral Support:
While spiritual warfare is a reality, it's important to acknowledge the role of human emotions and experiences. Seeking professional counseling or pastoral guidance provides couples with tools to navigate challenges effectively. These support systems can help address deep-seated issues and offer practical solutions.

6. Fostering Unity and Communication:
Satan's strategy often involves creating division within marriages. Couples can counteract this by fostering unity and open communication. Establishing a safe space for honest dialogue allows spouses to share their feelings, concerns, and aspirations, fostering a deeper connection.

7. Building a Spiritual Defense:
Couples can build a spiritual defense by investing in their individual spiritual growth. Reading and meditating on Scripture, engaging in regular prayer, and participating in spiritual activities together create a foundation that withstands the attacks of the enemy.

8. Relying on God's Word:
God's Word serves as a source of strength and guidance. Couples facing challenges can find solace and wisdom by grounding their responses and decisions in biblical principles. The Bible offers timeless truths that illuminate the path to marital harmony.

Navigating spiritual warfare in marriage requires couples to be vigilant, prayerful, and intentional in fostering a Christ-centered bond. By identifying common challenges and understanding the spiritual dimension, couples can overcome obstacles and emerge stronger in their marital journey.
Discerning and Transforming Marriage Challenges into Opportunities

In the journey of marriage, challenges are inevitable, but the way couples approach and navigate them can make all the difference. Recognizing these obstacles before they become insurmountable is a key aspect of effective spiritual warfare. Here, we will explore common challenges faced by marriages and how building on a Christ-centered foundation can turn these hurdles into opportunities for growth and strength.

1. Communication Breakdown:
Challenge: Misunderstandings, unmet expectations, and poor communication can lead to strife.
Opportunity: Christ-centered communication involves active listening, empathy, and grace. Facing communication challenges becomes an opportunity to deepen understanding and strengthen connection.

2. Financial Stress:
Challenge: Financial pressures can strain marriages and create tension.
Opportunity: Trusting God's provision and managing resources in alignment with biblical principles turns financial challenges into opportunities for financial stewardship and unity.

3. Intimacy Issues:
Challenge: Physical and emotional intimacy struggles can cause marital discord.
Opportunity: A Christ-centered approach to intimacy involves selflessness and vulnerability, transforming challenges into opportunities for deeper emotional and physical connection.

4. External Pressures:
Challenge: External influences, such as societal expectations or family dynamics, can impact marital harmony.
Opportunity: Building a Christ-centered marriage provides a solid foundation that can withstand external pressures, fostering unity and resilience.

5. Trust Issues:
Challenge: Betrayal or mistrust can erode the foundation of a marriage.
Opportunity: Christ's example of forgiveness and restoration offers an opportunity for couples to rebuild trust through grace, humility, and commitment.

6. Divergent Priorities:
Challenge: When spouses have different priorities, conflicts may arise.
Opportunity: Aligning priorities with Christ's teachings allows couples to find common ground, transforming divergent paths into an opportunity for shared purpose.

7. Parenting Challenges:
Challenge: Disagreements or challenges in parenting can strain a marriage.
Opportunity: Embracing a Christ-centered approach to parenting provides couples with shared values, turning parenting challenges into opportunities for collaboration and unity.

8. Time Management Struggles:
Challenge: Busy schedules and competing demands can lead to neglect.
Opportunity: Prioritizing Christ in the marriage schedule transforms time management challenges into opportunities for intentional connection and spiritual growth.

9. Spiritual Stagnation:
Challenge: A lack of spiritual growth can impact the overall health of a marriage.
Opportunity: Prioritizing joint spiritual practices, such as prayer and studying Scripture, turns spiritual stagnation into an opportunity for shared growth and deepening faith.

10. Resentment and Unforgiveness:
Challenge: Holding onto resentment can poison the marital relationship.
Opportunity: Embracing Christ's teachings on forgiveness allows couples to turn resentment into an opportunity for healing and restoration.

Discerning these challenges early on and addressing them through a Christ-centered lens empowers couples to transform obstacles into opportunities for growth, connection, and enduring love. By relying on the principles of Christ, marriages can navigate challenges with resilience, fostering a bond that withstands the tests of time.

Fortifying Marriages: Equipping for Spiritual Warfare
In the sacred union of marriage, spiritual warfare is a reality that couples must face. The apostle Paul's metaphor of the whole armor of God, detailed in Ephesians 6:10-18, provides profound wisdom for couples seeking to fortify their marriage against the schemes of the enemy. As the Scriptures remind us, "For we do not wrestle against flesh and blood, but against the rulers, against the authorities, against the cosmic powers over this present darkness, against the spiritual forces of evil in the heavenly places" (Ephesians 6:12, ESV).

Marriages are prime targets for the adversary, who seeks to sow discord, confusion, and division. Therefore, couples must be vigilant, keeping their heads on a swivel and staying alert to the spiritual battles that may impact their relationship. The foundation of Christ is the bedrock of marital resilience, but it is equally essential to be armed and ready for the battles that may come.

The Bible teaches us that one can put a thousand to flight, but two can put ten thousand to flight (Deuteronomy 32:30). This exponential impact can only be realized when couples stand united against the common enemy, and this unity is compromised when marital conflicts become a battlefield. As we delve into the armor of God, let us explore each piece as a vital component in safeguarding the sacred bond of marriage.

In the unseen realms, a battle rages, and as couples committed to a Christ-centered marriage, it is crucial to comprehend the nature of this conflict. The scripture, "For we do not wrestle against flesh and blood, but against the rulers, against the authorities, against the cosmic powers over this present darkness, against the spiritual forces of evil in the heavenly places," unveils the spiritual warfare that seeks to infiltrate marriages. Recognizing that your struggle is not against your spouse but against a formidable adversary with a well-organized system is the first step.

Satan's subtle tactics, woven into various aspects of society, aim to divide and conquer. From media messages to societal pressures, the enemy strategically exploits weaknesses, hurts, and insecurities. By understanding the scouting report the enemy holds on each individual and relationship, couples can unveil the schemes designed to hinder unity and cleaving. To stand strong, couples must identify the true source of their conflicts and unite against the common enemy seeking to sow discord in their marriage.

Activity: "The Demon's Scouting Report" 166

The Belt of Truth: Holding Couples Together

The first piece of the whole armor of God is the belt of truth. In a marriage, truth serves as the binding force that holds couples together in authenticity and transparency. Just as a soldier's belt secures the armor and weapons, the belt of truth in marriage provides stability and strength.

In the context of marriage, truth involves openness, honesty, and a commitment to genuine communication. It means laying bare one's heart, sharing dreams and fears, and being truthful about one's own shortcomings. The belt of truth also involves aligning marital values with God's eternal truths, ensuring that the foundation of the relationship is built on unshakable principles.

When couples wear the belt of truth, they fortify their union against the lies and deceptions the enemy may attempt to introduce. As truth becomes the undergirding force in a marriage, couples stand firm, resilient in the face of challenges. This foundational piece of armor enables couples to navigate the complexities of life, secure in the knowledge that they are bound together by the truth that sets them free (John 8:32, ESV).

As we embark on this exploration of the armor of God, may couples embrace the belt of truth, anchoring their relationship in openness, honesty, and alignment with God's eternal truths. The journey of fortifying marriages against spiritual warfare begins with the commitment to stand united in truth, ensuring that the bonds of love remain unbreakable in the face of any challenge.

Navigating True vs. Truth in Marriage: Tightening the Belt of Unity

In marriage, couples often encounter situations that initially seem true. The reality of challenges, conflicts, and uncertainties is undeniable and can, at times, cast a shadow on the marital bond. However, the key to fortifying marriages lies not merely in acknowledging what is true but, more importantly, in anchoring the relationship in God's eternal truth.

True situations are the tangible circumstances and experiences that couples encounter—financial struggles, communication breakdowns, or external pressures, to name a few. While these situations may be genuine and impactful, they should not be the sole focus. In the spiritual realm of marriage, the concept of truth transcends the immediacy of circumstances and beckons couples to look beyond the surface.

God's truth, as revealed in His Word, serves as an unchanging anchor for couples navigating the complexities of life. While true situations may threaten to loosen the belt of unity, embracing the higher truth of God's promises tightens the bond between husband and wife. The biblical principle of leaving and cleaving (Genesis 2:24) underscores the importance of prioritizing the higher truth over the immediate situation.

Focusing on the truth while going through a true situation is a pivotal practice for couples. It involves aligning personal perspectives and responses with God's eternal truths, creating a unified front against the schemes of the enemy. The belt of unity is tightened when couples turn to God's Word for guidance, seeking His truth to illuminate the path through challenges.

In the marriage journey, situations may arise that threaten to pull couples apart. The loosening of the belt of unity occurs when attention is solely directed toward the true circumstances without anchoring them in God's enduring truth. As couples navigate the complexities of life, the call to become one flesh extends beyond physical unity to a profound connection to a higher truth.

Embracing God's truth in the midst of true situations allows couples to endure, persevere, and strengthen their marital foundation. The belt of unity remains firm, securely holding them together as they face the storms of life. In the chapters of marital resilience, the commitment to tighten the belt of unity by focusing on God's truth ensures that, even in the face of true challenges, couples stand united and fortified against the schemes of the enemy.

Workbook-The Belt of Truth: Holding Couples Together - Worksheet 168

Satan's Assault on Marital Unity: Unveiling His Strategy

In the spiritual battleground of marriage, Satan cunningly orchestrates his assault on the unity and resilience of couples. His primary tactic involves redirecting their focus from God's eternal truth to the temporal and often turbulent realities of true situations. The enemy recognizes that when couples fixate on the immediate challenges, conflicts, and uncertainties they face, the belt of unity becomes vulnerable to loosening. Satan thrives in the chaos of relational discord, desiring to create rifts and separations by urging couples to prioritize the true circumstances over God's unchanging truth.

By steering couples away from the higher truth revealed in Scripture, Satan seeks to breed doubt, mistrust, and division within marriages. He understands that a unified couple grounded in God's truth poses a formidable threat to his schemes. When the belt of unity remains tightened through a shared commitment to God's promises, couples are equipped to withstand the enemy's attempts to sow discord and strife. Recognizing Satan's tactics and choosing to anchor in God's truth fortify marriages against the assaults on their unity. In the face of spiritual warfare, couples can stand firm, confident that God's truth prevails over the transient challenges that seek to undermine their marital foundation.

Truth Scriptures

Embarking on a journey to fortify the spiritual foundation of your marriage, we delve into timeless truths from the Bible. These verses, each holding profound wisdom, serve as the threads of a belt that secures and strengthens the fabric of your marital bond. From the divine design of leaving and cleaving to the enduring qualities of love outlined in 1 Corinthians 13, these eternal truths provide a roadmap for couples navigating the complexities of married life. As we explore the significance of these Scriptures, remember that God's truth is the unerring guide, tightening the belt that holds your marriage together, even in the face of challenges and storms. Look up these scriptures and take sometime to process through these truths.

- Ephesians 5:31: This verse emphasizes the concept of leaving and cleaving, highlighting the importance of unity and commitment. By holding fast to each other, couples reinforce the truth that they are a united front, and their commitment is grounded in God's design for marriage.
- 1 Corinthians 13:4-7: Known as the "Love Chapter," these verses describe the characteristics of love. By embodying these qualities, couples strengthen their bond and maintain a truthful perspective, focusing on the enduring and selfless nature of love.
- Philippians 2:3-4: Encouraging humility and consideration for each other's needs, this passage fosters an environment of selflessness. By prioritizing each other's interests, couples maintain a truthful understanding of mutual respect and care.
- Colossians 3:14: The centrality of love in this verse underscores its binding nature. Love becomes the unifying force that holds everything together. Couples, by choosing love, tighten the belt of truth, reinforcing the harmonious fabric of their relationship.
- 1 Peter 4:8: Stressing the covering nature of love, this verse suggests that love overlooks faults. Embracing this truth allows couples to extend grace and forgiveness, creating an atmosphere of acceptance and understanding.
- Proverbs 3:5-6: Trusting in the Lord and acknowledging Him in all aspects of life, including marriage, provides a foundation built on God's wisdom. Couples, by relying on this eternal truth, tighten the belt of truth by placing their trust in God's guidance.
- Matthew 19:6: Jesus affirms the divine joining of husband and wife. Understanding that God is the architect of their union helps couples recognize the sacredness of their bond, reinforcing the truth of their connection.
- 1 Corinthians 7:3-5: This passage speaks about mutual responsibility in marital intimacy. By respecting each other's needs and rights, couples acknowledge the truth that their bodies belong to each other, fostering a sense of unity and equality.
- Proverbs 18:22: Recognizing the gift of a spouse as a blessing from the Lord reinforces the truth of God's providence in bringing them together. Gratitude for this gift tightens the belt of truth by acknowledging God's role in their union.
- Mark 10:9: Jesus reinforces the permanence of marriage. By internalizing this truth, couples approach challenges with the understanding that their commitment is steadfast, creating a solid foundation for their relationship.

Incorporating these biblical truths into their daily lives, couples can fortify the belt of truth in their marriage, creating a resilient and God-centered foundation.

The Breastplate of Righteousness: Guarding Hearts in Love"
As we transition from the foundational Belt of Truth, we arrive at the Breastplate of Righteousness —an essential piece of armor designed to protect the heart. In the spiritual sense, righteousness is not merely a set of moral actions but a state of being declared righteous through faith in Christ. Understanding this is crucial for couples navigating the intricate landscape of love.

In relationships, hearts are vulnerable to a myriad of emotional arrows—arrows of insecurity, unworthiness, guilt, shame, condemnation, fear, perfectionism, and the relentless need to people-please. These silent heart concerns can corrode the very foundation of a marriage, eroding the confidence and joy that love should bring. This is where the Breastplate of Righteousness, modeled after the imputed righteousness of Jesus, plays a pivotal role.

When we recognize and embrace the truth that our righteousness comes from Christ, our hearts find a secure refuge. The righteousness imputed by Jesus covers us, shielding us from the condemnation of sin and the unrealistic expectations that may be imposed on ourselves or our partners. As individuals, this understanding liberates us from the burdens of perfectionism and the need to earn love. The Breastplate ensures that we don't have to strive for an unattainable perfection, and we don't have to exhaust ourselves in the pursuit of pleasing everyone around us.

In the marriage context, the Breastplate of Righteousness safeguards the collective heart of the relationship. It fosters an environment where forgiveness can flourish, where partners can extend grace to one another, understanding that true righteousness comes from Christ alone. A marriage anchored in the righteousness of Jesus becomes a sanctuary for hearts, a place where imperfections are embraced, and love is freely given and received.

Let us, therefore, be intentional about wearing this Breastplate of Righteousness in our relationships. By aligning our hearts with the truth of Christ's imputed righteousness, we create a love fortified against the enemy's attempts to sow discord and discontent. May the righteousness of Jesus be the unyielding guard around our hearts and the heart of our marriages.

Unmasking Satan's Schemes: Undermining Hearts in Marriage"
In the cosmic battlefield of marriage, Satan employs subtle yet destructive tactics to undermine the very hearts that form the core of our relationships. His sinister plot involves exploiting vulnerabilities such as insecurities, condemnation, and perfectionism, seeking to create fault lines within the sacred bond. Understanding these schemes is paramount for couples as they navigate the complexities of love.

One of Satan's primary strategies is to fuel insecurities. He whispers lies that sow seeds of doubt about self-worth and adequacy, fostering an atmosphere of inadequacy within individuals and, consequently, the marriage. These insecurities, if left unguarded, become breeding grounds for resentment, jealousy, and comparison, corroding the foundations of love.
Condemnation is another weapon in Satan's arsenal. He capitalizes on past mistakes, regrets, and guilt, aiming to erode the sense of righteousness imputed by Christ. By keeping hearts burdened with shame and unforgiveness, he creates division between spouses, hindering the free flow of grace and understanding.

Furthermore, Satan exploits the desire for perfection, luring individuals into a relentless pursuit of flawlessness. This insidious quest, often fueled by societal standards and unrealistic expectations, burdens hearts with an unattainable ideal. In marriage, the relentless pursuit of perfection can lead to discontent, frustration, and a perpetual feeling of inadequacy.

On the flip side, Satan cunningly twists the concept of grace, attempting to turn it into a license for sin. By convincing individuals that grace abounds, he seeks to undermine the commitment to righteousness and holy living. However, the Apostle Paul vehemently challenges this perspective, proclaiming, "Shall we continue in sin, that grace may abound? God forbid" (Romans 6:1-2, ESV). Paul's words remind us that while grace is abundant, it is not a justification for perpetual sin.

As couples navigate the tumultuous waters of marriage, it is crucial to unmask these schemes and fortify their hearts with the Breastplate of Righteousness. Recognizing the tactics Satan employs to undermine hearts allows couples to stand firm in the truth of Christ's imputed righteousness. By guarding their hearts against insecurities, condemnation, and the pursuit of perfection, couples can foster an environment where grace, forgiveness, and love flourish. May the imputed righteousness of Jesus be the impenetrable shield that protects the hearts of couples from Satan's subtle yet destructive schemes.

Understanding and embracing the biblical concept of righteousness is paramount for couples seeking to safeguard their hearts in the intricate dance of marriage. Righteousness, when imputed through faith in Jesus Christ, serves as a protective shield against the onslaught of insecurities, condemnation, and the relentless pursuit of perfection. The following scriptures offer profound insights into the transformative power of righteousness, reminding couples that their worth is anchored in Christ's righteousness, not in their own efforts. As they delve into these passages, couples are invited to reflect on the immeasurable grace that covers their shortcomings, the freedom found in Christ's righteousness, and the assurance that, through Him, they stand blameless before God.

Romans 3:22 (ESV):
- "The righteousness of God through faith in Jesus Christ for all who believe. For there is no distinction."
- Explanation: This foundational verse underscores that righteousness is a gift from God, attainable through faith in Jesus Christ. It nullifies any distinction among believers, emphasizing that all who believe share in this divine righteousness.

2 Corinthians 5:21 (ESV):
- "For our sake he made him to be sin who knew no sin, so that in him we might become the righteousness of God."
- Explanation: This powerful verse encapsulates the divine exchange that occurred on the cross. Christ, sinless, took on our sin, and in return, believers are granted the righteousness of God. It exemplifies the grace that covers and transforms.

Philippians 3:9 (ESV):
- "And be found in him, not having a righteousness of my own that comes from the law, but that which comes through faith in Christ, the righteousness from God that depends on faith."
- Explanation: Paul emphasizes the futility of self-righteousness derived from adherence to the law. True righteousness is found in Christ through faith, reinforcing the importance of reliance on Him.

Isaiah 61:10 (ESV):
- "I will greatly rejoice in the Lord; my soul shall exult in my God, for he has clothed me with the garments of salvation; he has covered me with the robe of righteousness, as a bridegroom decks himself like a priest with a beautiful headdress, and as a bride adorns herself with her jewels."
- Explanation: This poetic imagery depicts God clothing believers with the garments of salvation and adorning them with the robe of righteousness. It symbolizes a profound spiritual transformation that occurs through God's grace.

Jeremiah 23:6 (ESV):
- "In his days Judah will be saved, and Israel will dwell securely. And this is the name by which he will be called: 'The Lord is our righteousness.'"
- Explanation: The assurance that the Lord is our righteousness brings security and salvation. Knowing that our righteousness is anchored in God fosters a sense of peace and confidence in marital relationships.

Matthew 6:33 (ESV):
- "But seek first the kingdom of God and his righteousness, and all these things will be added to you."
- Explanation: Prioritizing the pursuit of God's kingdom and righteousness is a foundational principle. Trusting that God's righteousness encompasses all aspects of life, including marriage, reinforces reliance on Him.

As you meditate on these scriptures, may you find solace, strength, and a deepened understanding of the imputed righteousness that fortifies your hearts in the face of marital challenges.

Activity: "Guarding Your Hearts with the Breastplate of Righteousness" 171

Peaceful Places

Transitioning from the Breastplate of Righteousness to the Shoes of Peace signifies a crucial shift in the armor of God that every couple should grasp. Just as the breastplate guards the heart, the shoes play a pivotal role in determining the couple's stance and movement in the spiritual realm. The Shoes of Peace represent a commitment to maintaining a peaceful perspective and creating an atmosphere of harmony, not just within the marriage but also in the surrounding relational landscape.

In marriage, the importance of being peaceful individuals cannot be overstated. Peace is not merely the absence of conflict but a proactive pursuit of serenity, understanding, and cooperation. Choosing peace means adopting a perspective that prioritizes unity and seeks resolution over contention. It is an intentional commitment to fostering an environment where love and understanding can thrive.

By wearing the Shoes of Peace, couples embrace the mindset that their goal is to seek peace in all circumstances. This perspective influences their interactions, decisions, and reactions, creating an atmosphere where tensions are diffused, and love can flourish. The absence of peace can be a breeding ground for misunderstandings, resentment, and division within a marriage. Conversely, a commitment to peace paves the way for effective communication, mutual support, and shared growth.

Maintaining a peaceful atmosphere is not only important within the confines of the marital relationship but also extends to the broader relational landscape. As couples navigate various social, familial, and professional spheres, the Shoes of Peace enable them to bring a spirit of tranquility wherever they go. Their commitment to peace becomes a testimony of God's transformative power, radiating a positive influence on those around them.

In essence, the Shoes of Peace empower couples to be ambassadors of harmony, carrying the transformative message of God's love and grace wherever their journey takes them. As they step forward in the journey of marriage, may their every stride be marked by the pursuit of peace, creating a lasting impact on their relationship and the world around them.

Satan relentlessly schemes against marriages, particularly in the realm of peace. His devious strategy involves stripping away the Shoes of Peace, leaving couples vulnerable to slipping into conflict and chaos. Picture this: instead of having shoes with a firm grip, Satan desires to put bowling shoes on couples, making them skid across the battlefield of marriage with no traction, no stability, and no groundedness.

The Shoes of Peace are designed to provide a secure grip, enabling couples to stand firm and unshaken in the face of challenges. Satan, however, seeks to create an environment where couples are easily pushed from a peaceful stance to engaging in problematic behaviors. By robbing them of the grip that the Shoes of Peace offer, he aims to instigate chaos, sow discord, and breed conflict within the sacred bond of marriage.

A lack of peace in marriage not only invites unnecessary strife but also makes couples more susceptible to being pushed and pulled in various directions by external pressures. Satan delights in the vulnerability of couples who, without the firm grip of peace, find themselves slipping into contentious conversations, resentful attitudes, and hurtful actions. In the absence of peace, every step becomes precarious, increasing the likelihood of stumbling into destructive behaviors that can harm the foundation of the relationship.

The adversary desires couples to be volatile and ready to cause problems, and what better way to achieve this than by removing the firm footing provided by the Shoes of Peace? Bowling shoes on the battlefield symbolize a lack of stability, making couples prone to sliding into arguments, bitterness, and emotional turmoil. Satan's ultimate goal is to see marriages unravel and disintegrate, leaving a trail of broken relationships and wounded hearts.

As couples navigate the complexities of life, the Shoes of Peace become indispensable for maintaining a steady and unyielding stance. Guarded by the grip of peace, couples can confidently traverse the challenges of marriage, fully aware that their steps are secure and their foundation is unshakable. May couples resist the schemes of the enemy, keep their Shoes of Peace firmly on, and stand united against the forces that seek to undermine the sanctity of their marital journey.

In the journey of marriage, maintaining peace is crucial for building a resilient and lasting relationship. Peace serves as the stabilizing force that keeps couples grounded, fostering unity, understanding, and harmony. The Bible provides an invaluable guide on cultivating and preserving peace in various aspects of life, including marriage. These scriptures offer timeless wisdom and encouragement, acting as a compass to help couples safeguard their feet from slipping into conflict and discord.

- Philippians 4:6-7 (ESV): "Do not be anxious about anything, but in everything by prayer and supplication with thanksgiving let your requests be made known to God. And the peace of God, which surpasses all understanding, will guard your hearts and your minds in Christ Jesus."
- Explanation: This scripture highlights the connection between prayer, thanksgiving, and the peace of God. It encourages couples to bring their concerns and requests to God, trusting that His peace will guard their hearts and minds, fostering tranquility within the marriage.
- Colossians 3:15 (ESV): "And let the peace of Christ rule in your hearts, to which indeed you were called in one body. And be thankful."
- Explanation: Here, the emphasis is on allowing the peace of Christ to govern hearts. Allowing this divine peace to rule creates an environment where gratitude flourishes, promoting a spirit of unity and understanding in marriage.
- James 3:17-18 (ESV): "But the wisdom from above is first pure, then peaceable, gentle, open to reason, full of mercy and good fruits, impartial and sincere. And a harvest of righteousness is sown in peace by those who make peace."
- Explanation: The wisdom from God promotes peace and is accompanied by qualities that nurture healthy relationships. Couples are encouraged to sow seeds of righteousness in their marriage by cultivating a peaceful and understanding atmosphere.
- Isaiah 26:3 (ESV): "You keep him in perfect peace whose mind is stayed on you because he trusts in you."
- Explanation: Trusting in God brings perfect peace. Couples are reminded that anchoring their minds on God, especially during challenging times, leads to a state of peace that surpasses understanding.
- Romans 12:18 (ESV): "If possible, so far as it depends on you, live peaceably with all."
- Explanation: This scripture encourages couples to take personal responsibility for living peaceably. While external factors may contribute to conflict, the emphasis is on individuals doing their part to maintain peace within the marriage.
- Psalm 34:14 (ESV): "Turn away from evil and do good; seek peace and pursue it."
- Explanation: Actively pursuing peace is a commitment. This scripture encourages couples to actively seek and pursue peace in their interactions, emphasizing the importance of intentional efforts toward harmony.
- John 14:27 (ESV): "Peace I leave with you; my peace I give to you. Not as the world gives do I give to you. Let not your hearts be troubled, neither let them be afraid."
- Explanation: Jesus promises a unique peace that goes beyond worldly understanding. Couples are encouraged to lean on this divine peace, finding reassurance in Christ's gift, and to reject fear and troubled hearts.

These scriptures collectively reinforce the idea that cultivating peace in marriage is both a spiritual and intentional endeavor. By aligning their hearts with God's principles of peace, couples can strengthen their relationship and fortify their feet against slipping into the pitfalls of discord and strife.

Workbook-Assessing Your Marriage Shoes for a Firm Grip" 173

From the Shoes of Peace to the Shield of Faith: A Firm Foundation for Marital Defense

As we lace up our shoes of peace, preparing to navigate the diverse terrains of marriage, we find ourselves stepping onto the ground of unshakable faith. The shield of faith stands as the extension of our armor, encompassing us and safeguarding our hearts from the fiery darts of the adversary. Faith is not merely a passive piece of armor; it is an active force that intercepts, deflects, and nullifies the attacks aimed at our individual lives and marriages.

Understanding Faith:
At its core, faith is a profound trust and confidence in God's promises and character. It is the substance of things hoped for and the evidence of things not seen (Hebrews 11:1). Faith goes beyond mere belief; it is an unwavering conviction that God is true to His Word, and His promises are sure. This robust trust forms the foundation of the shield that guards our hearts and marriages.

The Role of Faith in Marital Defense:
Our marriages are not immune to the assaults of doubt, confusion, and insecurity. The shield of faith, however, acts as a powerful deterrent against these attacks. Picture faith as an invisible force field extending around you and your spouse. As the enemy hurls his darts—whispers of doubt, seeds of discord, or waves of insecurity—your shield of faith intercepts and extinguishes them before they can penetrate your hearts.

Deflecting Doubt and Insecurity:
Doubt and insecurity often target the core of marital relationships, seeking to undermine the foundation of trust and unity. However, an activated shield of faith deflects these assaults. When doubt attempts to cast shadows on your marriage, faith reminds you of God's promises for your relationship. In moments of insecurity, faith reaffirms your identity in Christ, reinforcing the truth that you are fearfully and wonderfully made.

Proactive Faith in Marriage:
The shield of faith is not reactive; it is a proactive defense mechanism. It prompts couples to cultivate a robust and active faith by consistently seeking God together, praying over their marriage, and aligning their actions with God's Word. A marriage fortified by faith becomes a united front against the schemes of the enemy.

Living With an Extended Shield:
Encouragingly, the shield of faith is not constrained by personal shortcomings or past mistakes. It extends beyond individual limitations, creating a collective protection for the marriage. As couples strengthen their faith together, the shield becomes broader, covering a wider expanse of potential attacks.

In conclusion, as we transition from the shoes of peace, firmly grounded in a peaceful and unified stance, we extend our shield of faith, an invisible yet powerful defense against the enemy's attempts to destabilize and destroy. In the arena of marriage, where doubts and insecurities may arise, faith stands as an impenetrable barrier, ensuring that the fiery darts fall harmlessly to the ground, leaving the marriage unscathed and fortified.

Satan's Cunning Strategies Against the Shield of Faith: Unveiling the Enemy's Tactics
In the realm of spiritual warfare, Satan, the adversary, employs cunning strategies to compromise and weaken the shield of faith. Recognizing that faith is the bedrock of our defense against his schemes, he craftily seeks to dismantle this essential piece of our spiritual armor. Let us unveil some of the adversary's tactics designed to hinder, weaken, and ultimately render ineffective the shield of faith.

1. Doubt as a Poisonous Dart:
Satan understands that doubt is a potent toxin to faith. He strategically injects doubt into the minds of believers, causing them to question God's promises, provision, and even His character. By fostering uncertainty, he hopes to paralyze the believer, making the lifting of the shield of faith a cumbersome task.

2. Undermining Identity in Christ:

Another insidious tactic involves undermining the believer's identity in Christ. Satan seeks to plant seeds of insecurity and unworthiness, convincing individuals that they are not truly loved, forgiven, or valued by God. When believers lose sight of their identity in Christ, their confidence in God's promises—critical to the shield of faith—is eroded.

3. Encouraging Self-Reliance:

The enemy is keen on redirecting faith toward human strength, achievements, or self-reliance. By fostering trust in personal abilities, resources, or the reliability of others, Satan aims to divert faith away from its rightful place in God. This misguided faith, misplaced in human capabilities, proves inadequate when faced with spiritual attacks.

4. Deceptive Appeals to Alternative "Shields":

Satan tempts believers to rely on alternative "shields" that seem sturdy but crumble under the weight of spiritual onslaughts. These may include relying solely on financial security, relationships, or success as shields against life's challenges. While these elements may offer temporary reassurance, they lack the enduring strength of the shield of faith anchored in God.

5. Disconnection from the Source:

Ultimately, Satan desires to sever the connection between believers and the source of their faith—God Himself. By encouraging spiritual apathy, neglect of prayer, and distancing from God's Word, he weakens the lifeline that activates and sustains the shield of faith. When the shield is disconnected from its source, its protective power diminishes.

6. Weariness and Spiritual Fatigue:

Satan understands that prolonged spiritual battles can lead to weariness and fatigue. In this state, believers may be tempted to lower or abandon their shields altogether. By wearing down their spiritual stamina, Satan hopes to exploit moments of vulnerability.

As couples navigate the challenges of life and marriage, they must be vigilant against these cunning strategies. Recognizing the enemy's tactics allows believers to fortify their faith, lift the shield with unwavering confidence, and thwart Satan's attempts to compromise their spiritual defenses. Strengthened by a united shield of faith, couples can stand firm against the schemes of the adversary, securing the protection God designed for their marriage.

The Importance of Faith Scriptures
In the battleground of marriage, the shield of faith is our paramount defense against the enemy's attempts to sow doubt, confusion, and insecurity. Just as a skilled warrior trains with their shield to ward off attacks, couples must fortify their faith through the timeless truths found in God's Word. These faith scriptures serve as both a source of encouragement and a powerful tool to reinforce the shield, ensuring that it remains sturdy and steadfast. As couples delve into these verses, they not only cultivate a shared faith but also anchor themselves in the unchanging promises of God, creating an impenetrable defense against the schemes of the enemy.

1. Hebrews 11:1 (ESV) - Understanding the Essence of Faith:

"Now faith is the assurance of things hoped for, the conviction of things not seen."
This foundational verse defines the essence of faith, highlighting the unwavering confidence in God's promises. As couples face challenges, this scripture reminds them that their faith is rooted in the certainty of God's unseen but trustworthy character.

2. Romans 10:17 (ESV) - Building Faith Through God's Word:

"So faith comes from hearing, and hearing through the word of Christ."
This scripture emphasizes the role of God's Word in nurturing faith. Couples are encouraged to consistently immerse themselves in the Scriptures, knowing that faith is strengthened as they hear and internalize the truths found in God's Word.

3. Mark 11:24 (ESV) - Praying in Faith:
"Therefore I tell you, whatever you ask in prayer, believe that you have received it, and it will be yours."
This verse underscores the connection between faith and prayer. As couples pray together, they learn to approach God with unwavering confidence, trusting that He hears their petitions and is faithful to respond according to His perfect will.

4. 2 Corinthians 5:7 (ESV) - Walking by Faith, Not by Sight:
"For we walk by faith, not by sight."
This scripture encourages couples to navigate their marital journey with a reliance on faith rather than relying solely on what is visible. It reinforces the idea that faith provides a supernatural perspective that transcends the limitations of human understanding.

5. Ephesians 6:16 (ESV) - The Shield of Faith:
"In all circumstances take up the shield of faith, with which you can extinguish all the flaming darts of the evil one."
This verse, directly addressing the shield of faith, reminds couples of the shield's purpose and effectiveness. It serves as a powerful reminder that faith is the key to extinguishing the fiery darts of the enemy.

6. Hebrews 11:6 (ESV) - Pleasing God Through Faith:
"And without faith, it is impossible to please him, for whoever would draw near to God must believe that he exists and that he rewards those who seek him."
This scripture highlights the integral role of faith in pleasing God. Couples are encouraged to approach their relationship with God and each other with a deep-seated belief in His existence and His faithfulness to reward those who seek Him.

7. James 1:6 (ESV) - Seeking Wisdom in Faith:
"But let him ask in faith, with no doubting, for the one who doubts is like a wave of the sea that is driven and tossed by the wind."
This verse challenges couples to approach God with unwavering faith, emphasizing that doubt can lead to instability. It encourages them to seek God's wisdom in faith, knowing that He provides generously to those who believe.

8. Philippians 4:6-7 (ESV) - Experiencing Peace Through Faith:
"Do not be anxious about anything, but in everything by prayer and supplication with thanksgiving let your requests be made known to God. And the peace of God, which surpasses all understanding, will guard your hearts and your minds in Christ Jesus."

This scripture links faith with peace, illustrating how a trusting heart, expressed through prayer, leads to God's transcendent peace guarding hearts and minds. Couples are encouraged to anchor their anxieties in faith.

Incorporating these faith scriptures into their daily lives, couples establish a firm foundation for their shield of faith. Each verse becomes a reinforcing layer, making the shield more resilient against the enemy's attempts to weaken their trust in God and each other.

Workbook-Faith Assessment and Strengthening Activity for Couples: 175

Targeting the Mind: Satan's Quest for Headshots
In the spiritual battleground of marriage, the mind stands as a primary arena where fierce battles unfold. Satan, aware of the mind's susceptibility, strategically launches attacks to sow seeds of doubt, fear, and unworthiness. The Helmet of Salvation becomes a crucial piece of armor, shielding and preserving the mental well-being of individuals within a marriage.

The Battlefield of the Mind:
Satan's tactics often involve infiltrating thoughts, stirring up insecurities, and challenging the very foundations of one's identity. Many couples find themselves grappling with silent struggles within their minds, potentially leading to disconnection and discord. Recognizing the importance of a protective helmet is essential to maintaining mental stability amidst spiritual warfare.

The Power of the Gospel:
The Gospel serves as the transformative force that fortifies the Helmet of Salvation. Justification, the understanding that God pursued and declared individuals as His sons and daughters, provides a shield against feelings of unworthiness. Sanctification, the ongoing process of God's work in shaping individuals, offers assurance that growth and improvement are continual. Glorification, the promise of eternal life in heaven, secures the mind against the fear of losing salvation.

Stability Amidst Spiritual Warfare:
Salvation, anchored in the Gospel, stabilizes the mind for battle. Knowing that one is justified, sanctified, and glorified provides a mental anchor against the enemy's attempts to create doubt and turmoil. The Helmet of Salvation grants clarity, assuring individuals within the marriage that they are eternally secure, loved, and being continually transformed.

Combatting Distractions:
Distractions in the form of doubts, fears, and feelings of inadequacy can lead to marital discord. The Helmet of Salvation not only guards against these distractions but also empowers individuals to focus on the truth of their identity in Christ. It ensures that the mind remains steadfast, undeterred by the enemy's attempts to create chaos within.

The Unified Mindset:
A marriage is profoundly impacted when both partners wear the Helmet of Salvation. Shared understanding and belief in the Gospel provide a unified mindset, fostering mental resilience and stability. Couples equipped with the Helmet of Salvation can face challenges with a confidence grounded in the eternal security found in Christ.

In the ongoing spiritual warfare of marriage, the Helmet of Salvation stands as a powerful defense, ensuring that the minds of individuals within the union are guarded against the enemy's assaults. By embracing the transformative power of the Gospel, couples can navigate the battlefield of the mind with unwavering assurance and mental stability.

Targeting the Mind: Satan's Quest for Headshots
In the relentless spiritual warfare that unfolds within the context of marriage, Satan strategically aims for what could be considered "headshots" – assaults on the minds of individuals. Recognizing the significance of protecting the mind with the Helmet of Salvation becomes paramount in thwarting the enemy's relentless attempts to destabilize couples.

The Vulnerable Mind:
Satan understands that an unprotected mind is susceptible to a barrage of attacks. The mind, left unguarded, becomes a battlefield where doubt, fear, and insecurity can run rampant. By targeting the thoughts and perceptions of individuals within a marriage, the enemy aims to create division, discord, and a sense of unworthiness.

The Power of Doubt:
Doubt, one of Satan's primary weapons, seeks to erode the foundations of faith, trust, and unity within a marriage. By instilling uncertainty about salvation, personal worth, and the steadfastness of God's promises, the enemy endeavors to create a breeding ground for relational turmoil. Without the Helmet of Salvation, doubt can penetrate and wreak havoc on the mental stability of individuals.

Assaulting Identity:
The enemy often launches assaults on the core identity of individuals within a marriage. Attacks on self-worth, value, and righteousness aim to undermine the very essence of who God created them to be. In the absence of the protective Helmet of Salvation, these assaults can lead to internal conflicts and a distorted self-perception.

The Helmet's Defensive Role:
The Helmet of Salvation serves as the ultimate defense against headshots targeted by the enemy. By embracing the truths of justification, sanctification, and glorification found in the Gospel, individuals within a marriage can fortify their minds against doubt and insecurity. The helmet becomes a shield, deflecting the arrows of the enemy and preserving mental well-being.

Unity in Defending the Mind:
Couples, united in wearing the Helmet of Salvation, stand resilient against the enemy's attempts to create division and confusion. A shared commitment to the truths of the Gospel fosters a unified defense, ensuring that both partners are equipped to withstand the assaults on their minds. The Helmet becomes a symbol of unity, protecting the collective mental strength of the marriage.

The Battle for Renewed Minds:
Scripture urges believers to renew their minds continually (Romans 12:2). The Helmet of Salvation facilitates this renewal by safeguarding against the toxic influences of the enemy. As couples prioritize the protection of their minds, they engage in a proactive stance against the adversary's attempts to disrupt their marital harmony.

In the ongoing spiritual warfare, the enemy seeks headshots, aiming to disrupt the minds of individuals within marriages. The Helmet of Salvation emerges as the essential defense, guarding against doubt, fear, and attacks on identity. Couples, understanding the gravity of this spiritual battle, can stand firm in unity, preserving the sanctity of their minds and fortifying their marriage against the assaults of the enemy.

Guarding Minds with the Helmet of Salvation: Scripture Guide
Protecting the minds of individuals within a marriage is vital for maintaining a strong, unified relationship. The Helmet of Salvation serves as a powerful defense against the enemy's attempts to destabilize mental well-being. Here is a selection of scriptures that couples can delve into, understanding the importance of salvation and the Gospel in safeguarding their minds:

. Romans 8:1-2 (ESV):
- *Explanation:* This passage declares the freedom from condemnation for those in Christ Jesus. Embracing salvation means no longer being held captive by guilt or fear, offering a foundation for a secure and guilt-free mind.
. Ephesians 6:17 (ESV):
- *Explanation:* The Helmet of Salvation is explicitly mentioned in the armor of God. This scripture emphasizes the defensive role of salvation in protecting the mind against the schemes of the enemy.
. 2 Corinthians 10:5 (ESV):
- *Explanation:* The apostle Paul encourages believers to take every thought captive to obey Christ. Understanding salvation empowers individuals to combat negative thoughts, ensuring a renewed and Christ-centered mindset.
Philippians 4:7 (ESV):
- *Explanation:* The peace of God, which surpasses all understanding, guards hearts and minds in Christ Jesus. Salvation brings a transformative peace that shields against anxiety and insecurity.
Romans 12:2 (ESV):
Explanation: The call to be transformed by the renewal of the mind is anchored in the Gospel. Salvation initiates a process of mind renewal, aligning thoughts with God's truth.
Colossians 3:1-2 (ESV):
Explanation: Setting minds on things above is a reflection of being raised with Christ. Salvation redirects focus, preventing the mind from being ensnared by earthly concerns.

7. 1 Peter 1:3 (ESV):
  • Explanation: This passage celebrates the living hope we have through the resurrection of Jesus Christ. Salvation offers a living hope that guards against despair and hopelessness.
8. Titus 3:5 (ESV):
  • Explanation: The washing of regeneration and renewal of the Holy Spirit is tied to salvation. Recognizing the transformative work of salvation helps individuals maintain a spiritually renewed mind.
9. Romans 10:17 (ESV):
  • Explanation: Faith comes from hearing, and hearing through the word of Christ. Regular exposure to the Gospel strengthens faith, providing an unwavering defense against doubts.
10. John 14:6 (ESV):
- Explanation: Jesus declares Himself as the way, the truth, and the life. Understanding salvation through Christ solidifies truth in the mind, countering the enemy's attempts to distort reality.

Exploring these scriptures collectively allows couples to fortify their minds with the Helmet of Salvation. As they internalize the truths of the Gospel, their thoughts become anchored in Christ, creating a unified defense against the enemy's assaults on their mental well-being.

Empowering Marriages with the Sword of the Spirit: The Word of God
In the arsenal of spiritual weaponry, the Sword of the Spirit, identified as the Word of God, stands out as the only offensive weapon provided to believers. The importance of knowing and wielding this weapon cannot be overstated, as it holds the power to shape reality and repel the schemes of the enemy. The Word of God is not merely a static text; it is a living force that sustains the entire cosmos. The sun and the moon, in all their celestial glory, continue their dance in the sky because of the enduring power of God's Word. Likewise, when couples and individuals engage with and stand on the Word, they tap into a force that transcends human understanding. It becomes a shield against the assaults of the enemy and a beacon guiding them through the challenges of life.

Understanding the Word of God is akin to being proficient with a powerful weapon. Every soldier, whether in times of war or peace, constantly hones their skills with their weapon, knowing that readiness is key to facing unexpected attacks. Similarly, believers need to invest time daily in delving into the Scriptures, becoming familiar with the promises, principles, and precepts contained within. The Word is not to be left untouched, gathering dust; it is a dynamic tool that requires continuous practice and engagement.

Unfortunately, there is a tendency to become complacent or bored with the Word, neglecting the very weapon that could provide victory in life's battles. The enemy recognizes the potential impact of believers who are skilled in using the Sword of the Spirit. Hence, daily immersion in the Word is not just a spiritual discipline; it is a strategic move to fortify marriages against unforeseen attacks.

Couples must cultivate a lifestyle of daily engagement with the Scriptures, allowing the Word of God to permeate their thoughts, conversations, and decisions. The more proficient they become in handling the Sword of the Spirit, the more adeptly they can counter the enemy's tactics and fortify their marriage against any assault. As the Word becomes an integral part of their lives, couples wield a powerful weapon that shapes their reality and ensures victory in the face of adversity.

Faith Assessment and Strengthening Activity for Couples: 175

Battling Satanic Strategies: Safeguarding the Efficacy of God's Word
In the spiritual warfare that unfolds in the realm unseen, Satan employs cunning strategies to weaken believers' proficiency with the Sword of the Spirit – the Word of God. Recognizing the transformative potential of God's Word, the enemy seeks to diminish its impact in the lives of individuals and couples, hindering its role as a surgical instrument for renewal and a supernatural weapon for dismantling strongholds.

Satan understands that when the Word of God is wielded with precision, it acts as a surgical instrument in the hands of the Divine Surgeon. God's Word has the power to penetrate the deepest recesses of the human heart, laying bare the wounds and maladies that hinder spiritual growth and marital harmony. The enemy aims to distort this perception, encouraging indifference or distraction when engaging with the Scriptures. By doing so, he obstructs the transformative work the Word can perform, leaving individuals and marriages vulnerable to the wounds of the past and present.

Moreover, Satan recognizes that the Word of God is not just a personal instrument but a supernatural weapon with the potential to alter the course of entire communities and nations. Couples who stand united, armed with the Word, become formidable forces capable of tearing down the strongholds of darkness in their families, neighborhoods, cities, regions, and even globally. Consequently, the adversary strives to undermine the collective impact of God's Word by fostering division, distractions, and distortions within marital relationships.

In a world inundated with noise and distractions, Satan seeks to drown out the transformative power of the Word, rendering it ineffective in renewing minds and healing wounds. By subtly steering couples away from the consistent and intentional study of God's Word, he hopes to keep them from fully realizing its potential in their lives and relationships. However, couples who remain vigilant, recognizing the enemy's tactics, can fortify their commitment to daily engagement with the Scriptures. In doing so, they not only safeguard their own hearts and marriages but also become conduits for the supernatural power of God's Word to impact the broader spheres of influence around them.

In the spiritual battlefield of marriage, where unseen forces seek to disrupt, divide, and deceive, the Word of God serves as our mighty weapon. These scriptural darts, infused with the power and authority of God's truth, are declarations of faith aimed at the enemy. Each statement is a proclamation of victory, rebuke, and defiance against the schemes of darkness. As couples stand united, these darts become a powerful tool, piercing through the spiritual realm with the force of divine authority. In using these scriptural darts, couples engage in spiritual warfare, confident that the promises of God's Word will prevail over every tactic of the adversary. With unwavering faith and armed with the truth, couples can declare their authority in Christ and witness the transformational impact of God's Word on their marriage.

Scriptural Darts for Warfare Against the Enemy

- *Dart of Rebuke (James 4:7):* "Satan, in the authority of Jesus' name, we rebuke you. Submit to God, and flee from our marriage. Your schemes have no power here."
- *Dart of Defeat (Colossians 2:15):* "By the triumph of the cross, we declare your defeat, Satan. Every weapon formed against us is nullified. We stand victorious in Christ."
- *Dart of Exorcism (Luke 10:19):* "In Jesus' name, we exercise authority over all demonic influences. No evil shall harm our marriage, for we tread upon serpents and scorpions."
- *Dart of Disruption (Isaiah 54:17):* "Every tongue that rises against our marriage in judgment, we condemn. This is our heritage as servants of the Lord, and our righteousness is from Him."
- *Dart of Division (Matthew 12:25):* "Satan, your kingdom divided against itself cannot stand. We declare unity and harmony in our marriage, rendering your divisive tactics powerless."
- *Dart of Deception (2 Corinthians 2:11):* "We are not ignorant of your schemes, Satan. Your attempts to deceive our minds are thwarted by the light of God's truth. We stand firm in discernment."
- *Dart of Chains Broken (Isaiah 58:6):* "Every yoke of bondage you seek to impose is shattered. We declare freedom and release from every chain you try to bind around our marriage."
- *Dart of Fearlessness (2 Timothy 1:7):* "For God has not given us a spirit of fear, but of power, love, and a sound mind. Satan, your tactics of fear are replaced with the courage bestowed by God."
- *Dart of Confusion (1 Corinthians 14:33):* "Satan, the author of confusion, we reject your attempts to sow discord. The God of peace reigns in our hearts and home."
- *Dart of Victory (Romans 8:37):* "We are more than conquerors through Christ who loves us. Satan, your attempts are futile, for our victory is secured by the blood of the Lamb."

These scriptural darts, aimed at the enemy with unwavering faith, declare the authority and victory of Christ over every scheme and strategy of the adversary.

Workbook-Activity: Scriptural Surgery and Weaponization 178

Putting On the Whole Armor of God: A Strategic Imperative
The biblical exhortation to "put on the whole armor of God" is not a casual suggestion but a strategic imperative for every believer, especially within the sacred union of marriage. The metaphor of armor conveys the comprehensive protection required in the spiritual battlefield of life and relationships. Each piece of the armor is not an optional accessory but a vital component, harmoniously working together to fortify the individual and the marriage.

When Ephesians 6:11 emphasizes putting on the "whole armor of God," it underscores the indispensability of completeness. Just as a soldier wouldn't venture into battle with crucial gaps in their protective gear, believers must ensure that every aspect of God's armor is actively worn. A helmet without a breastplate or a shield left behind renders the warrior vulnerable. In the same vein, a marriage without the entirety of God's protective covering risks exposure to the schemes of the enemy.

Putting on the whole armor of God is a deliberate and ongoing practice. It requires cultivating a warrior's mindset within the marital relationship, recognizing that, even in moments of tranquility, the battle is ongoing. Regular practice, intentional implementation of each piece of the armor, and maintaining a vigilant posture ensure that couples are equipped for the challenges and victories that accompany the journey of marriage. The whole armor of God is not just a defensive measure; it positions couples to stand firm, resilient and fortified against the schemes of the enemy.

The Warrior's Mentality: Navigating Seasons of War and Peace in Marriage
In the narrative of Gideon's selection of soldiers, a profound lesson emerges about the mentality of war and its relevance to the ebb and flow of seasons within marriage. God's specific instructions to Gideon reveal not only the criteria for selection but also the crucial importance of the warriors' mindset. This mindset is a guiding principle that couples can apply to navigate the varying seasons of their relationship.

Imagine the scene at the water's edge: soldiers who bowed down, immersing their faces in the water, versus those who brought the water to their mouths, remaining vigilant. The latter group, with heads on a swivel, alert to their surroundings, were chosen for the battle ahead. In this, we glean a powerful metaphor for the marriage journey – the need for a mentality of war.

In marriage, as in life, there are distinct seasons, including times of refreshing peace and moments that demand a warrior's resolve. It's tempting to lower our guard during periods of tranquility, to bow down and immerse ourselves in the comfort of peace. Yet, the call remains to keep our heads on a swivel, to remain vigilant even in moments of refreshment.

This warrior's mentality acknowledges that seasons of peace are not the signal to retire from readiness but a brief reprieve before the next engagement. It recognizes that, in marriage, there will be good times and challenges, but neither should catch us off guard. Instead, the mentality of war prepares couples for both the serenity of peace and the demands of battle.

Enjoying the harmonious moments is essential, but the call is to be simultaneously watchful, keeping heads on a swivel. This mindset prevents complacency and ensures that couples are prepared for the unexpected shifts and challenges that may arise. In embracing the mentality of war, couples fortify their relationship, ready to stand firm in unity against the schemes that may threaten the sacred bond of marriage.

THE BIBLICAL NATURE OF HUSBAND AND WIFE IN STRONG MARRIAGES

In the divine orchestration of marriage, God has intricately woven together the unique characteristics of a man and a woman, crafting complementary roles that harmonize and balance each other. From the very essence of their being, individuals carry traits and qualities designed by God, evolving and maturing through the various stages of life to fulfill specific functions within the sacred covenant of marriage. Understanding these roles becomes paramount as it allows couples to grasp the intricate dance of partnership that God has set in motion.

The importance of comprehending the biblical roles of a husband and wife lies not only in recognizing their individual identities but also in realizing the divine intention behind these roles.

Each role contributes distinct strengths and perspectives to the union, forming a harmonious whole. As couples delve into the depth of these roles, they uncover the blueprint for a flourishing marriage, understanding the unique ways each partner complements and completes the other.

Equally significant is the emphasis on intentionality for a strong marital foundation. Once individuals comprehend the distinct roles designed by God, they are empowered to be intentional in their actions and attitudes.

Intentionality becomes the compass guiding couples through the various seasons of marriage, steering them away from distractions and ensuring that their union remains purposeful and functional.

In essence, understanding the biblical nature of husband and wife serves as a cornerstone for building a strong marriage. It is not merely a static acknowledgment of roles but an active participation in God's divine design, where intentionality becomes the driving force for a thriving, God-honoring marital relationship.

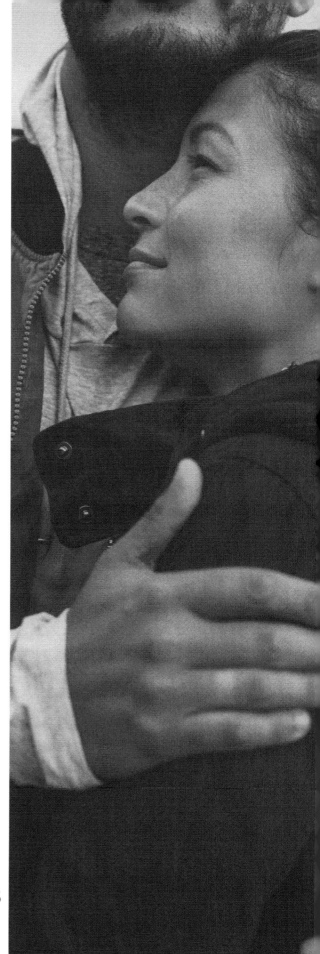

Starting with the Biblical Roles of a Husband
The Husband as the Spiritual Leader:
In the divine order of marriage, God has entrusted men with the role of spiritual leadership. This leadership is not meant to be exerted from the realm of the soul or the body but is to emanate from the deepest core of a man's being—the spirit, guided by the Holy Spirit. Unfortunately, many men miss the mark when it comes to spiritual leadership. Some might be led by their physical desires or the yearning of their souls for completeness, neglecting the higher call to lead from the spirit. True spiritual leadership aligns all other aspects of life under the guidance of the Holy Spirit, bringing harmony to a husband's role.

Exploring the Biblical Model of Spiritual Leadership:
Delving into the biblical model of spiritual leadership unveils a portrait of servant leadership, much like Christ Himself, who came not to be served but to serve. A husband's spiritual leadership is marked by humility, selflessness, and a deep commitment to the well-being and growth of his spouse. Leading by example in faith becomes paramount—demonstrating unwavering trust in God, humility in seeking His guidance, and an unyielding commitment to the principles of love, grace, and forgiveness.

Qualities of Spiritual Leadership:
- Humility: A spiritually leading husband walks in humility, recognizing that true strength lies in surrendering to God's will and serving others.
- Prayerfulness: An essential quality of spiritual leadership is a consistent and fervent prayer life, seeking God's wisdom, guidance, and covering for the marriage.
- Faithfulness: A husband's commitment to faithfulness, not only in marital fidelity but also in unwavering trust in God's plan, is a hallmark of spiritual leadership.
- Servanthood: In mirroring Christ's example, a spiritually leading husband embodies a servant's heart, putting the needs and growth of his spouse above his own.
- Encouragement: Fostering an atmosphere of encouragement and support, a spiritually leading husband uplifts and empowers his wife in her faith journey.

Understanding and embodying these qualities forms the foundation for a husband's spiritual leadership, contributing to the strength and vibrancy of the marital relationship.

Leading by Example: A Man's Impact Beyond His Home
A man's role as a spiritual leader extends far beyond the walls of his home; it becomes a beacon that illuminates the path for others in his sphere of influence. Leading by example is not merely a duty; it's a profound responsibility that shapes the character and trajectory of those around him.

Impact on His Wife:
When a man leads by example in his faith, his wife witnesses firsthand the transformative power of a Christ-centered life. His commitment to prayer, humility, and sacrificial love creates a safe and nurturing environment within the marriage, fostering a partnership built on trust, mutual respect, and spiritual growth.

Impact on His Children:
For his sons, a father's example becomes a blueprint for authentic manhood—rooted in integrity, humility, and strength underpinned by gentleness. His daughters, observing the way he cherishes and respects their mother, learn invaluable lessons about love, self-worth, and the qualities to seek in a future spouse. The impact extends to grandchildren, creating a generational legacy of faith.

Impact on Fatherless Kids:
In a broader sense, a man's example carries weight for those who may lack a father figure. By embodying Christ-like qualities, he becomes a source of guidance and inspiration for fatherless kids, offering them a glimpse into the transformative power of a relationship with God.

Impact in Business and Community:
Beyond the family unit, a man's example resonates in his professional and community engagements. A leader who operates with integrity, humility, and a commitment to service influences the culture of his workplace and community. Co-workers, employees, and acquaintances observe the consistency between his beliefs and actions, creating an environment where ethics and compassion thrive.

Shaping the World:
Ultimately, a man leading by example contributes to shaping the world around him. His commitment to embodying Christ-like virtues ripples through various spheres, challenging societal norms and fostering a culture of compassion, respect, and love. By consistently reflecting the heart of Christ, he becomes a catalyst for positive change, influencing both the present and the future.

Christ-Like Heart:
A man's heart, aspiring to be Christ-like, is characterized by love, compassion, and a commitment to service. In imitating the humility and sacrificial love of Christ, he becomes a living testament to the transformative power of a life surrendered to God. This Christ-like heart not only impacts his immediate relationships but radiates outward, leaving an indelible mark on the world.

Emulating Christ: Examples for Cultivating Christ-Likeness
Jesus Christ, as the ultimate model of humility, love, and self-sacrifice, provides timeless examples for men to emulate in their pursuit of Christ-likeness. By embodying these qualities, husbands and fathers can positively impact their families and the world around them, bringing glory to God.

Servant Leadership:
Example: Washing the disciples' feet (John 13:1-17).
- *Impact:* Cultivating a heart of service and humility within the family and community.

Compassion for Others:
Example: Healing the sick, feeding the hungry (Matthew 14:14, 15:32-39).
- *Impact:* Fostering a compassionate and caring atmosphere, extending love to those in need.

Forgiveness and Grace:
Example: Forgiving sins and offering grace (Luke 7:48, John 8:1-11).
- *Impact:* Establishing an environment of forgiveness and grace within the family, promoting reconciliation.

Unwavering Faith and Trust in God:
Example: Praying in Gethsemane (Matthew 26:36-46).
- *Impact:* Encouraging a steadfast faith and trust in God, even in challenging times.

Teaching Through Parables:
Example: Parables to convey spiritual truths (Matthew 13:3-9, Luke 15:3-7).
- *Impact:* Using wisdom and effective communication to impart important lessons to family and others.

Prioritizing Relationship with God:
Example: Withdrawing to pray (Mark 1:35, Luke 5:16).
- *Impact:* Emphasizing the importance of personal communion with God and spiritual discipline.

Resisting Temptation:
Example: Overcoming Satan's temptations in the wilderness (Matthew 4:1-11).
- *Impact:* Instilling the importance of resisting temptation and relying on God's strength.

Inclusive Love and Acceptance:
Example: Welcoming sinners and outcasts (Matthew 9:10-13, Luke 19:1-10).
- *Impact:* Cultivating a family environment of inclusive love and acceptance.

Enduring Persecution with Dignity:
Example: Enduring the cross for the sake of humanity (Philippians 2:8).
- *Impact:* Encouraging resilience and dignity in the face of challenges, trusting in God's purpose.

Praying for Others:
Example: Interceding for others, even those who crucified Him (Luke 23:34, John 17:20-21).
- *Impact:* Instilling a habit of fervent prayer for the well-being of family, friends, and the world.

By consciously seeking to emulate these examples from the life of Jesus, husbands and fathers can contribute to a Christ-like atmosphere that profoundly impacts their families and extends God's glory to the world.

Workbook-Servant Leadership Assessment and Development Worksheet for Husbands
180

The Husband as the Provider and Protector: Holistic Provision

God's design for husbands encompasses the roles of provider and protector, reflecting the profound responsibility to care for and safeguard their families. This role, however, extends beyond mere financial support. To be a holistic provider and protector, a husband must embrace the multifaceted aspects of provision, addressing spiritual, mental, emotional, and physical needs alongside financial responsibilities.

1. Spiritual Provision:
A husband's duty involves cultivating a spiritually enriching environment within the family. This includes leading in prayer, fostering spiritual discussions, and encouraging a relationship with God. By prioritizing spiritual growth, he becomes a provider of eternal values and guidance.

2. Mental and Emotional Provision:
A holistic provider attends to the mental and emotional well-being of his family. This involves being an empathetic listener, offering emotional support, and creating a nurturing atmosphere. Providing mental and emotional stability contributes to a healthy family dynamic.

3. Physical Provision:
Basic necessities like shelter, food, and clothing are fundamental to physical provision. A husband is called to ensure the physical needs of his family are met, creating a secure and comfortable environment. This role includes maintaining the overall well-being and health of the family.

4. Financial Provision:
While financial provision is a crucial aspect, it is only one component of the husband's role. Providing financially ensures the family's material needs are met, allowing them to thrive in other areas. However, being solely focused on finances at the expense of spiritual, mental, and emotional provisions is an incomplete form of protection.

5. Holistic Protection:
True protection extends beyond physical safety. A holistic protector shields his family from spiritual attacks, emotional distress, and mental challenges. By addressing every facet of provision, a husband becomes a comprehensive protector, fostering an environment where his family can flourish and overcome adversities.

6. Being a One-Dimensional Provider:
A husband who limits his provision to a single dimension, such as financial support alone, may neglect the vital needs in other areas. This can result in an imbalance, hindering the family's overall well-being. A complete provider ensures a well-rounded and thriving family life.

In essence, the husband's role as a provider and protector is to emulate God's character by supplying for the diverse needs of his family. A holistic approach ensures a balanced and flourishing family life, creating an environment where each member can reach their full potential under the loving care and protection of their husband and father.

Workbook-Holistic Provision Assessment and Development Worksheet for Husbands 186

261

Embracing Responsibility: The Power of Response
Responsibility is a profound concept for men, encapsulating the idea of having the ability to respond. To effectively handle the diverse responsibilities that come with leading a family, a man needs more than just reactive capabilities. God calls men to be proactive and equipped with divine abilities, responding to situations with wisdom, love, and strength.

1. Spiritual Discernment:
A Man's Response: Cultivating a strong relationship with God provides the spiritual discernment needed to lead a family. When faced with spiritual decisions or challenges, a man must respond by seeking divine guidance through prayer and aligning his actions with God's Word.

2. Emotional Intelligence:
A Man's Response: Emotional intelligence is crucial in understanding and responding to the feelings of his spouse and children. A man should be attentive to emotions, responding with empathy, patience, and effective communication to foster emotional well-being within the family.

3. Financial Stewardship:
A Man's Response: Responsible financial management involves budgeting, saving, and making sound financial decisions for the family's well-being. A man responds by ensuring financial stability, avoiding unnecessary debt, and providing for both immediate needs and future goals.

4. Conflict Resolution:
A Man's Response: Conflicts are inevitable in any relationship. A responsible man responds to conflicts with humility, actively listening, and seeking resolutions that prioritize the unity and harmony of the family. He models effective conflict resolution for his spouse and children.

5. Time Management:
A Man's Response: Balancing work, family, and personal time requires effective time management. A responsible man responds by prioritizing quality time with his family, setting boundaries, and being present during significant moments in their lives.

6. Nurturing Relationships:
A Man's Response: Building and nurturing healthy relationships with his spouse and children is a key responsibility. A man responds by investing time, expressing love and affirmation, and fostering an environment where every family member feels valued and cherished.

7. Providing Physical Security:
A Man's Response: Physical protection involves creating a safe and secure environment for the family. A responsible man responds by ensuring the home is a refuge, addressing safety concerns, and actively taking measures to protect the well-being of his loved ones.

8. Continuous Learning:
A Man's Response: A responsible man acknowledges that growth is an ongoing process. He responds by actively seeking opportunities for personal and professional development, staying informed about evolving family dynamics, and adapting to the changing needs of his loved ones.

In essence, responsibility is not just about reacting to situations; it's about having the ability to respond with intentionality, wisdom, and divine guidance. A man, equipped with these abilities, becomes a pillar of strength and support for his family, navigating the complexities of life with grace and purpose.

Workbook-Embracing Responsibility: The Power of Response - Husband's Worksheet 189

Navigating the Silent Struggles: A Husband's Journey to Healing
Acknowledging the Unseen Burdens
In the intricate nature of masculinity, being a man, husband, and father comes with its unique set of challenges. Society often places expectations and pressures on men, projecting an image of unwavering strength and self-sufficiency. However, behind the façade of stoicism, there lies a battlefield of unseen burdens. The enemy strategically targets the core identity of a man, aiming to erode the very foundation of God's image in him. Having walked this path myself, I understand the weight that accompanies these roles. Yet, the journey to healing begins with a humble acknowledgment of our need for divine assistance. God is not only the sustainer but the healer, ready to transform our struggles into a testimony of His grace.

The Veil of Silent Struggles
Silent struggles often shroud the hearts of men, concealing the vulnerabilities that society deems as weaknesses. The pressure to conform to societal expectations can lead men to wear a veil of strength, suppressing the internal battles they face. This perceived necessity for unyielding toughness can create isolation, hindering men from seeking the support they desperately need. The truth is, vulnerability is not synonymous with weakness; it is the gateway to authentic strength. In this section, we unveil the hidden battles men face, shedding light on the importance of tearing down the veil and embracing the healing power of transparency. The journey to wholeness starts with acknowledging that behind every silent struggle, there is a man yearning for restoration.

Emotional Battles
"It's hard for a man to become emotionally intelligent if emotions are irrelevant to him."
The journey through emotional battles for men can be likened to navigating a landscape where emotions are often dismissed as irrelevant. This societal perspective hinders the development of emotional intelligence, creating a struggle for men to understand and articulate their own emotions. In reality, men grapple with a spectrum of conflicting emotions, including vulnerability, fear, and the pressure to conform to societal expectations of stoicism.

Internal Pressures
One of the silent challenges men face revolves around internal pressures, particularly the expectation to perpetually embody strength. Society imposes a rigid framework on men, dictating that they should always be resilient, unwavering, and impervious to emotional turmoil. The idea that men should never cry reinforces an unrealistic standard, causing internal conflict as men navigate the delicate balance between societal expectations and their authentic emotional experiences.

Emotional Suppression
Men, like anyone else, require emotional outlets to maintain mental and spiritual well-being. Emotional suppression, driven by societal norms, can lead to an accumulation of unresolved emotions. This silent struggle underscores the importance of having healthy outlets.
Personally, I find solace in activities like long drives, lifting heavy weights, and contemplative walks. These serve as avenues to vent, reflect, and connect with God, allowing a release of emotions that might otherwise become toxic. Dispelling the myth that men shouldn't cry is essential, as tears serve as a natural and necessary release, cleansing the soul from accumulated burdens. Recognizing and embracing these emotional facets contributes to a more authentic and resilient emotional life for men.
\David's Emotional Resilience at Ziklag: A Biblical Model for Men
The biblical account of David at Ziklag provides a powerful illustration of emotional resilience, showcasing how men can navigate deep emotional turmoil while remaining anchored in their faith. In this narrative, David and his men return to Ziklag to find their families taken captive, sending them into a profound state of grief and distress.

Authentic Expression of Emotion:
David's initial response is characterized by raw and genuine emotion. The text reveals that "David and the people who were with him raised their voices and wept until they had no more strength to weep" (1 Samuel 30:4, ESV). This vivid portrayal dispels the notion that men should suppress their emotions, emphasizing the importance of authentic expression, even in the face of overwhelming grief.

Seeking God in the Midst of Emotion:
Crucially, amid his intense emotional state, David turns to God. He doesn't let his emotions dictate his actions but rather seeks divine guidance. "And David inquired of the Lord, 'Shall I pursue after this band? Shall I overtake them?'" (1 Samuel 30:8a, ESV). David's example illustrates that men can bring their emotions to God, seeking His counsel and finding strength in divine guidance.

Recovering All Through Purposeful Action:
God's response to David's inquiry provides clear instructions on pursuing and recovering what was lost. "Pursue, for you shall surely overtake and shall surely rescue" (1 Samuel 30:8b, ESV). Despite the emotional turmoil, David receives a divine directive, and he takes purposeful action. This narrative highlights that men can operate in their God-given purpose even in the midst of emotional distress, trusting in God's guidance for recovery.

Embracing Emotional Healing and Restoration:
Ultimately, David and his men recover all that was taken, showcasing the possibility of restoration after deep emotional pain. This biblical account serves as a model for men, demonstrating that they can navigate the spectrum of emotions, seek God's guidance, and still operate in purpose, ultimately experiencing recovery and restoration.In today's context, men can draw inspiration from David's example at Ziklag, understanding that emotions, when filtered through a reliance on God, can lead to a resilient and purposeful life, even in the face of adversity.

Navigating Men's Emotional Landscape: Balancing Passion and Regulation
Men, like everyone else, are intricate beings with a broad spectrum of emotions. While embracing and expressing emotions is healthy, it's crucial for men to regulate their emotional responses to avoid potential detriments to family life. Unchecked emotions, such as anger, lust, or an overwhelming desire for success, can have profound effects on relationships. Understanding the roots of these emotional challenges is the first step toward emotional regulation.

Root Wounds Contributing to Emotional Turmoil:
Many emotional struggles in men find their roots in unhealed wounds. Past traumas, unmet needs, or unresolved issues can become the breeding ground for emotional challenges. For example, anger may be a response to feeling powerless or unheard, while an insatiable desire for success may stem from a deep-seated need for validation. Identifying these root wounds is a crucial aspect of emotional intelligence.

Practical Strategies for Emotional Regulation:
- Self-Awareness: Encouraging men to develop self-awareness is fundamental. This involves recognizing triggers and understanding the emotional responses they elicit. Journaling, reflection, and seeking therapy are effective tools for fostering self-awareness.
- Mindfulness and Meditation: Incorporating mindfulness practices can help men stay present and regulate their emotional responses. Techniques such as deep breathing, meditation, or mindfulness exercises can contribute to emotional balance.
- Healthy Outlets: Providing healthy outlets for emotions is essential. Engaging in physical activities like exercise, sports, or creative pursuits can channel intense emotions in a positive direction.
- Effective Communication: Men need to cultivate effective communication skills to express their emotions constructively. This involves not only identifying and communicating feelings but also actively listening to their partner's emotions.
- Seeking Support: Men should feel empowered to seek support when needed. Whether through friendships, mentorship, or professional counseling, having a support system helps in processing and regulating emotions.

Balancing Passion and Regulation: Passion is a beautiful aspect of masculinity, but it must be balanced with emotional regulation. Rather than suppressing emotions, the goal is to understand, regulate, and channel them in a way that aligns with biblical principles. Men are called to be passionate leaders, but this passion should be tempered with emotional intelligence, ensuring that it contributes positively to family life. In embracing emotional regulation, men not only safeguard their families from potential detriments but also foster an environment of emotional health and resilience within the home. By addressing root wounds and implementing practical strategies, men can navigate their emotional landscapes in a way that aligns with God's design fo husbands and fathers.

- **Emotional Regulation Worksheet for Husbands + Journal 192**
- **REGULATE Emotions Worksheet for Men 197**

265

Navigating the Mental Landscape: Renewing the Mind for Intentional Husbandhood

Men often face a multitude of mental health challenges as they strive to fulfill their roles as husbands and fathers. The weight of responsibility, societal expectations, and the constant need to provide holistic support can lead to significant mental struggles. Addressing these challenges requires a deliberate effort to renew the mind, cultivating a mentality that allows men to be intentional and involved in their marriages while trusting God with what they can't control.

Stress and Anxiety:
The relentless pressure to meet societal expectations and fulfill various roles often contributes to high levels of stress and anxiety among men. The weight of providing financial stability, emotional support, and leadership can become overwhelming. This mental strain not only affects the individual but also seeps into marital dynamics, potentially causing tension and emotional distance.

Societal Expectations:
Men are often bombarded with societal expectations that dictate they must embody strength, resilience, and unwavering confidence. These expectations can create a mental battleground where men feel the need to present an image of invulnerability, even when facing internal struggles. The fear of falling short of these expectations can lead to stress, anxiety, and a sense of inadequacy.

Understanding the Mental Struggles:
Having been through the mental and emotional challenges that come with the responsibilities of husbandhood and fatherhood, I empathize with the difficulties men face. Balancing career, family, and personal well-being is a formidable task, and it's essential to acknowledge the mental struggles that accompany these roles.

Renewing the Mind:
Renewing the mind involves actively challenging negative thought patterns and replacing them with God's truth. Recognizing that it's okay not to have everything under control and seeking God's guidance allows men to cultivate a mentality that prioritizes trust over constant worry. Romans 12:2 encourages believers to be transformed by the renewal of their minds, emphasizing the importance of aligning thoughts with God's perspective.

Trusting God and Being Present:
A key aspect of navigating mental health challenges is trusting God with what is beyond human control. Recognizing that God is the ultimate provider and sustainer allows men to release the burden of perfection. Trusting God doesn't mean shirking responsibility but rather acknowledging His sovereignty and seeking His guidance in every aspect of life. This trust empowers men to be present in their marriages, knowing that God is at work in areas beyond their capacity.

In summary, addressing the mental struggles of husbands involves intentional efforts to renew the mind, replacing societal expectations with God's truth, and cultivating a mentality grounded in trust. By embracing God's perspective, men can navigate the challenges of husbandhood with a renewed sense of purpose, mental resilience, and the ability to be actively involved in their marriages.

Regulating Emotions: A Blueprint for Men

Navigating the intricate landscape of emotions can be a challenging yet essential aspect of being intentional husbands. The ability to regulate emotions empowers men to lead with wisdom, empathy, and authenticity. Here's a blueprint to help men regulate their emotions, fostering emotional intelligence and resilience:
  - Reflect:
Take moments for self-reflection to understand the root causes of emotions. Identifying the source helps in addressing underlying issues rather than merely reacting to surface-level triggers.

  - Express:
Create healthy outlets for emotional expression. Whether through open communication with a trusted friend, spouse, or journaling, finding ways to express emotions prevents internal build-up and fosters a more balanced emotional state.

G - Guard:
Guard the mind against negative influences. Be mindful of the content consumed, as it can significantly impact emotions. Choose uplifting and positive sources that contribute to emotional well-being.

U - Understand:
Strive to understand the complexity of emotions. Recognize that emotions are a natural part of the human experience, and seeking to understand their purpose helps in managing them effectively.

L - Learn:
Continuously educate oneself on emotional intelligence. Attend workshops, read books, or engage in activities that promote emotional literacy. Learning about emotions equips men with the tools to navigate them with greater finesse.

A - Acknowledge:
Acknowledge the validity of emotions without judgment. Emotions are neither good nor bad; they are signals indicating internal states. Acknowledging them fosters self-compassion and a healthier emotional landscape.

T - Take Breaks:
Recognize when a pause is needed. Taking breaks allows time for emotions to settle and for a more measured response. It prevents impulsive reactions that may be regretted later.

E - Exercise:
Physical activity plays a significant role in emotional regulation. Regular exercise releases endorphins, contributing to a more positive mood and providing a constructive outlet for stress.

Regulating emotions is not about suppressing them but rather about developing a healthy relationship with one's internal world. By implementing these strategies, men can proactively engage with their emotions, fostering emotional resilience and creating a more stable foundation for intentional husbandhood.

Navigating the Blueprint of Husbands' Love: Ephesians 5:25-31

The Apostle Paul, under divine inspiration, provides a profound blueprint for husbands in Ephesians 5:25-31, unraveling principles that illuminate the sacrificial and sanctifying love husbands are called to exemplify.

1. Love Your Wives - The Power of "Your":
The significance of the term "your" in "love your wives" emphasizes the individuality and uniqueness of the marital bond. Husbands are summoned to love their wives personally, acknowledging and valuing them as distinct individuals, each deserving of a tailored, sacrificial love.

2. Christ's Model - Sacrificial and Sanctifying Love:
Drawing a parallel with Christ and the church, husbands are urged to mirror Christ's sacrificial love. Christ's selfless act of giving himself up for the church illustrates the depth to which husbands are to sacrificially invest in their wives' well-being. This sacrificial love is not passive but actively seeks the sanctification of the wife, cleansing her through the transformative power of God's Word.

3. Washing with the Word - Wisdom and Leadership:
The imagery of washing with the word underscores the husband's role in leading with wisdom and spiritual guidance. As Christ uses His wisdom to sanctify the church, husbands are called to lead with divine wisdom, ensuring their wives are nurtured, matured, and spiritually cleansed through the transformative influence of God's Word.

4. Love Your Wives as Your Own Bodies:
The command to love wives as one's own body establishes a connection so profound that the well-being of the wife becomes inseparable from the husband's own. This directive encourages husbands to nurture and cherish their wives, fostering an environment where both partners flourish individually and collectively.

5. Leaving and Cleaving - Creating Unity:
The scripture echoes the timeless principle of leaving one's parents to cleave to one's spouse, emphasizing the establishment of a new, unified entity. Husbands are encouraged to prioritize their marital union, creating a sacred bond that surpasses all other earthly ties.

In embracing these principles, husbands can embody the sacrificial, sanctifying love outlined in Ephesians 5, fostering a marital relationship that reflects the divine union of Christ and the church.

1. Reflect on Your Personalized Love: How can you intentionally express love to your wife in a way that acknowledges her individuality and uniqueness, demonstrating a love that is tailored specifically to her needs and desires?
2. Sacrificial Love in Action: In what practical ways can you actively give of yourself for the well-being of your wife, mirroring Christ's sacrificial love? Consider both tangible acts of service and emotional support that embody selflessness.
3. Leading with Wisdom: How can you enhance your role as a spiritual leader in your marriage, using divine wisdom to guide and nourish your wife? Reflect on how your leadership can contribute to her spiritual growth and well-being, washing her with the transformative power of God's Word.

The biblical exhortation in 1 Peter 3:7 offers profound insights into how husbands are called to relate to their wives. The passage begins by urging husbands to "live with your wives in an understanding way." This goes beyond mere cohabitation; it emphasizes a depth of connection and comprehension. Husbands are encouraged to actively seek to understand their wives – their emotions, thoughts, dreams, and struggles. It involves empathetic listening, genuine interest, and a commitment to knowing and appreciating the uniqueness of each woman.

Furthermore, husbands are instructed to "show honor to the woman as the weaker vessel." The term "weaker vessel" does not imply inferiority but acknowledges potential physical vulnerabilities. This brings attention to the responsibility husbands bear in providing protection and honor. Opening doors, ensuring their safety, and displaying acts of chivalry are expressions of this honor. It's a recognition of the husband's role as a protector, creating an environment where the wife feels cherished and valued.

The phrase "since they are heirs with you of the grace of life" emphasizes equality in spiritual inheritance. Both husband and wife share the same standing before God as heirs of His grace. This truth dispels any notion of superiority or inferiority based on gender. Husbands are called to recognize and honor the shared spiritual identity they have with their wives.

The warning in the concluding part of the verse is striking – "so that your prayers may not be hindered." This underscores the significance God places on the way husbands treat their wives. It suggests a direct connection between the quality of the marital relationship and the effectiveness of a husband's prayers. It emphasizes that a lack of understanding, honor, and equality in the marital relationship can hinder spiritual vitality and communion with God. In essence, the way a husband treats his wife is inseparable from his relationship with God. If a husband chooses not to adhere to these principles, it indicates that God will not incline His ear to the prayers concerning the husband's business, ministry, or other endeavors for success. This underscores the profound impact of marital dynamics on a husband's spiritual life and the importance of aligning with God's principles in all aspects of life.

- How am I currently living with my wife in an understanding way, considering her unique needs, emotions, and perspectives? How can I improve in ensuring that her thoughts and feelings are fully understood and valued?
- In what practical ways am I actively showing honor to my wife as the "weaker vessel," recognizing and valuing her strengths and vulnerabilities? What specific actions or gestures can I incorporate to enhance the atmosphere of honor in our relationship?
- Do I view my wife as a co-heir with me in the grace of life, and am I fostering an environment that reflects equality, respect, and shared responsibilities in our relationship? How can I better collaborate with my wife and ensure that we both thrive as equal partners in our marriage?
- Reflect and Write: Take some time to write out your prayers and aspirations for your business, ministry, or personal success. What specific requests are you consistently bringing before God?
- Follow-up Question: Examine Your Habits: Now, consider your current habits and actions as a husband. In what ways do your behaviors, attitudes, or treatment of your wife align or misalign with the principles of honoring and understanding her as outlined in 1 Peter 3:7? How might any inconsistencies be hindering the effectiveness of your prayers?

10 Gentleman Things to Show Honor to Your Wife:
1. Open Doors: Consistently open doors for your wife as a gesture of respect and honor.
2. Pull Out Chairs: Extend the courtesy of pulling out her chair when you're dining together.
3. Offer Your Arm: When walking together, offer your arm for her to hold onto, showcasing protection and care.
4. Surprise Acts of Kindness: Regularly surprise her with small acts of kindness, such as leaving a sweet note or bringing her favorite treat.
5. Express Gratitude: Regularly express your appreciation for her efforts and contributions to the relationship and family.
6. Take Initiative: Be proactive in taking on responsibilities and tasks without waiting to be asked, demonstrating your commitment and support.
7. Listen Attentively: Show genuine interest and actively listen when your wife is expressing herself, creating a space for her thoughts and feelings to be heard.
8. Plan Thoughtful Dates: Plan dates or activities that align with her interests, showing that you value and prioritize her preferences.
9. Compliment Sincerely: Offer sincere and specific compliments regularly, highlighting qualities you admire in her.
10. Create Shared Rituals: Establish shared rituals or traditions that strengthen your bond, such as regular date nights or weekend getaways.

10 Ways to Live in a More Understanding Way with Your Wife:

1. Practice Empathy: Strive to understand your wife's perspective and emotions, putting yourself in her shoes.
2. Effective Communication: Foster open and honest communication, creating an environment where both of you feel comfortable expressing thoughts and feelings.
3. Active Listening: Practice active listening by giving your full attention and responding thoughtfully to what your wife is sharing.
4. Learn Her Love Language: Understand and cater to her love language, ensuring your expressions of love align with her preferences.
5. Acknowledge Differences: Embrace and appreciate the differences between you and your wife, recognizing that diversity can strengthen your relationship.
6. Celebrate Achievements: Acknowledge and celebrate your wife's achievements, both big and small, fostering a sense of support and encouragement.
7. Be Patient: Cultivate patience, especially in moments of disagreement or misunderstanding, allowing space for resolution and growth.
8. Prioritize Quality Time: Make an intentional effort to spend quality time together, nurturing the emotional connection between you.
9. Learn and Grow Together: Pursue personal and relational growth together, attending workshops or reading books on marriage to enhance understanding.
10. Apologize and Forgive: Be quick to apologize when necessary and practice forgiveness, creating a foundation of grace and humility in your relationship.

Understanding the Headship in Marriage:
In 1 Corinthians 11:3, the Apostle Paul offers a profound insight into the divine order within marriage. The verse asserts, "But I want you to understand that the head of every man is Christ, the head of a wife is her husband, and the head of Christ is God." This establishes a clear hierarchy designed by God, providing valuable principles for the role of Christ as the head of the husband and the husband as the head of the wife.

Christ as the Head:
For a husband, acknowledging Christ as the head is not merely a theological concept but a daily surrender to the lordship of Jesus. This means seeking divine guidance, wisdom, and alignment with Christ's character in every decision and action. As the head, Christ leads with sacrificial love, selflessness, and a commitment to the well-being and spiritual growth of the husband.

Husband as the Head:
Understanding the husband's role as the head involves spelling out the key elements:
- H: Humility over Hierarchy: Being the head doesn't imply dominance; instead, it calls for humility. The husband is to emulate Christ's servant-leadership, prioritizing the needs and growth of his wife.
- E: Edifying and Encouraging: The headship involves building up and encouraging the wife in her journey. The husband, in partnership with Christ, plays a pivotal role in his wife's spiritual, emotional, and personal development.
- A: Accountability to God: As the head, the husband is accountable to God for the stewardship of his role. This underscores the responsibility of seeking God's guidance and aligning decisions with biblical principles.
- D: Decision-Making with Discernment: Headship doesn't mean making unilateral decisions bu' involves seeking discernment from Christ. The husband's decisions should reflect the love, wisdom, and grace modeled by Christ.

Embracing the divine order outlined in 1 Corinthians 11:3 fosters a harmonious and flourishing marital relationship, where Christ is acknowledged as the ultimate authority, guiding husbands t lead with love, humility, and divine wisdom.

Being Intentional and Attentive as a Husband:
Being a husband goes beyond mere existence; it calls for intentionality and a keen attentiveness to the details that shape a flourishing marriage. Understanding what it means to be intentional and attentive involves spelling out the key elements:

D - Deliberate Acts of Love:
Being intentional means consistently engaging in deliberate acts of love. This could range from expressing affection through words and deeds to surprising gestures that communicate thoughtfulness and care. A husband actively seeks opportunities to demonstrate love in ways tha resonate with his wife's heart.

E - Empathetic Listening:
Part of being attentive involves empathetic listening. A husband actively listens to his wife, seeking to understand her thoughts, feelings, and concerns. This requires genuine interest and a commitment to creating a safe space for open communication.

T - Thoughtful Gestures:
Attention to detail manifests through thoughtful gestures. This could be remembering significan dates, anticipating needs, or surprising with gestures that align with the wife's preferences. Thoughtfulness communicates a deep understanding of the spouse's individuality.

A - Anticipation of Needs:
An intentional husband anticipates the needs of his wife. This involves proactively addressing challenges, providing support, and creating an environment where the wife feels understood an cared for. Anticipating needs fosters a sense of security and partnership.

- Investment in Quality Time:

Quality time is a vital detail that contributes to a thriving marriage. Being intentional means prioritizing meaningful moments together, whether through shared activities, conversations, or experiences. This investment strengthens the emotional bond between husband and wife.

. - Leverage on Love Languages:

Understanding and leveraging each other's love languages is key. Being intentional involves discovering and consistently incorporating the wife's love language into expressions of affection. This tailored approach ensures that love is communicated in a way that resonates most deeply.

5 - Spiritual Alignment:

Being attentive includes a spiritual dimension. A husband actively cultivates spiritual alignment with his wife, encouraging shared values, prayer, and a collective pursuit of spiritual growth. This intentional focus strengthens the foundational aspects of the marriage.

Embracing intentionality and attentiveness in marriage involves a daily commitment to actively participate in the details that contribute to a thriving and deeply connected relationship. This intentional approach positions the husband to be a source of love, understanding, and support.

Workbook-Getting to Know Your Wife: Memory Challenge 199

272

Embracing Gentleness: A Biblical Imperative for Husbands in Marriage
Colossians 3:19, from the English Standard Version, provides a profound insight into the role of husbands within the marital relationship. The verse succinctly instructs husbands to love their wives and emphasizes the importance of avoiding harshness in their interactions.

Harshness in a marriage can have detrimental effects on the emotional well-being of wives. It creates an environment of tension, fear, and insecurity, hindering the growth of trust and intimacy. Harsh words or actions can erode the foundation of a healthy marriage, leaving wives feeling unloved, unappreciated, and emotionally wounded.

To be gentle with one's wife involves cultivating an atmosphere of understanding, compassion, and patience. It requires active listening, empathy, and a willingness to acknowledge and validate her feelings. Gentle husbands strive to communicate with kindness and respect, avoiding the use of hurtful language or demeaning gestures. They prioritize emotional support, recognizing that a gentle approach fosters an environment where love can thrive and marriages can flourish.

Practicing gentleness also involves being attuned to the unique needs and sensitivities of one's wife. It means taking the time to understand her perspective, appreciating her individuality, and responding to her with tenderness. A gentle husband seeks to build up rather than tear down, recognizing that love is not only expressed through words but also through actions that reflect kindness and consideration.

In essence, Colossians 3:19 calls husbands to a higher standard of love—one that actively avoids harshness and embraces the transformative power of gentleness. It encourages husbands to create a marital atmosphere where love is evident not only in moments of joy but also in the way conflicts are handled and daily interactions are conducted. By adhering to this biblical principle, husbands can contribute to the flourishing of their marriages, fostering an environment where both spouses can thrive and grow in love.

Unveiling Harshness: Examples to Avoid
In examining the guidance of Colossians 3:19, it's crucial for husbands to be mindful of their words and actions to prevent any manifestation of harshness. Let's explore examples that align with the points spelling out H-A-R-S-H:

1. **Hasty Criticism (H):** Expressing immediate disapproval without thoughtful consideration can be perceived as harsh. This might involve criticizing your wife's ideas, decisions, or actions without understanding her perspective. **Strategy:** Practice patience and seek to understand before expressing disapproval. Engage in open communication, asking questions to gain insight into your wife's perspective.
2. **Aggressive Responses (A):** Reacting with aggression, whether verbally or physically, can instill fear and insecurity in the marital relationship. This includes raising one's voice, slamming doors, or engaging in confrontations. **Strategy:** Develop healthy ways to channel frustration or anger. Consider taking a brief break to cool off before discussing challenging topics. Explore non-confrontational communication techniques.
3. **Reckless Disregard (R):** Ignoring or dismissing your wife's feelings, needs, or opinions demonstrates a lack of regard. This can make her feel unimportant or undervalued, contributing to emotional distance. **Strategy:** Cultivate active listening skills. Make a conscious effort to show genuine interest in your wife's feelings and opinions. Regularly check in on her emotional well-being.
4. **Sarcastic Remarks (S):** Employing sarcasm in communication may seem harmless, but it can carry undertones of mockery or contempt. Sarcastic remarks can be hurtful, eroding the foundation of trust and respect. **Strategy:** Foster open and honest communication. If humor is part of your relationship, ensure it is always kind-hearted and mutually enjoyable. If in doubt, opt for sincerity over sarcasm.
5. **Hurtful Comparisons (H):** Drawing unfavorable comparisons between your wife and others, whether subtly or explicitly, can be deeply hurtful. It undermines her sense of worth and creates a toxic atmosphere. **Strategy:** Celebrate and appreciate your wife's uniqueness. Focus on her strengths and positive qualities. Practice gratitude for the qualities that make her distinct and valuable.

Being aware of these examples helps husbands steer clear of harsh behaviors and fosters an environment where love and gentleness can thrive in accordance with biblical principles.

Understanding the root causes of harshness is essential for those who struggle with this behavior. Identifying these underlying issues can pave the way for personal growth and transformation. Let's delve into five root causes, using points that spell "**H-A-R-S-H**":

1. Hurts from the Past (H): Harshness can often be a defense mechanism stemming from unresolved hurts or traumas in one's past. Individuals may project their pain onto others, using harsh words or actions as a way to guard themselves from further emotional injury. Addressing past wounds through therapy or self-reflection can be a crucial step in breaking this cycle.
2. Anger Management Issues (A): Uncontrolled anger is a significant contributor to harsh behavior. If a person struggles to manage and express anger appropriately, it can manifest as harsh criticism, aggressive responses, or hurtful comparisons. Learning healthy ways to cope with and express anger, such as through communication or stress-relief techniques, is pivotal for overcoming this root cause.
3. Resentment and Unforgiveness (R): Harshness can be fueled by deep-seated resentment or unforgiveness. Holding onto grudges or past grievances can poison relationships and lead to the expression of harsh words. Engaging in forgiveness practices, both towards others and oneself, can alleviate the emotional burden and contribute to a more compassionate demeanor.
4. Stress and Overwhelm (S): Individuals facing high levels of stress or overwhelming situations may inadvertently channel their frustrations into harsh interactions. The pressures of life, work, or personal challenges can take a toll on emotional regulation. Implementing stress management techniques, setting realistic expectations, and seeking support can mitigate the impact of stress-related harshness.
5. Insecurity and Low Self-Esteem (H): Harshness can be a manifestation of one's own insecurities and low self-esteem. A person may project their feelings of inadequacy onto others, using criticism or hurtful remarks as a way to assert control or mask their own vulnerabilities. Building self-awareness, practicing self-compassion, and seeking affirmation in healthy ways are crucial steps in addressing this root cause.

By recognizing and addressing these root causes, individuals can embark on a journey of self-discovery and healing, fostering a more positive and compassionate approach in their interactions with others.

Processing Harshness: A Journey to Self-Discovery and Healing

Harshness in our interactions often finds its roots in deeper emotional struggles. Understanding and addressing these underlying issues is a transformative journey toward personal growth and healing. This worksheet is designed to guide you through the process of recognizing and working through the root causes of harshness in your life.

1. Reflect on Past Hurts:

- Take some time for self-reflection. Consider moments from your past that may have left lasting emotional wounds.
- Write down specific experiences or traumas that might contribute to your current struggles with harshness.
- Reflect on how these past hurts may have shaped your emotional responses in your present relationships.

Processing and Healing:

- Consider seeking therapy or counseling to address unresolved issues from your past.
- Engage in journaling as a way to express and understand your emotions related to past hurts.

2. Explore Anger Management:

- Evaluate how you currently handle anger. Are there patterns of uncontrolled anger that lead to harsh behavior?
- Identify specific triggers that tend to provoke anger and harsh responses.
- Explore alternative, healthier ways to express and manage anger.

Processing and Healing:

- Learn and practice anger management techniques, such as deep breathing or mindfulness exercises.
- Consider joining anger management support groups or seeking guidance from a mental health professional.

3. Confront Resentment and Unforgiveness:

- Examine areas of your life where resentment or unforgiveness might be lingering.
- List any grudges or grievances you are holding onto, whether towards others or yourself.
- Explore the idea of forgiveness and its potential impact on your emotional well-being.

Processing and Healing:
- Practice forgiveness exercises, starting with small steps and gradually addressing deeper issues.
- Consider discussing your feelings with a trusted friend, mentor, or spiritual advisor.

4. Address Stress and Overwhelm:
- Evaluate the stressors in your life, both external and internal.
- Identify areas where you feel overwhelmed and how this might contribute to harsh responses.
- Explore practical stress management techniques that resonate with you.

Processing and Healing:
- Establish a self-care routine that includes activities to help alleviate stress.
- Seek support from loved ones or professionals to navigate challenging situations.

5. Confront Insecurity and Low Self-Esteem:
- Reflect on moments when you feel the need to assert control through harsh behavior.
- Explore underlying insecurities or feelings of inadequacy that may contribute to these behaviors.
- Identify positive affirmations and aspects of self-worth to focus on.

Processing and Healing:
- Engage in self-awareness exercises to understand and challenge negative self-perceptions.
- Seek positive affirmations from supportive sources and work on building self-esteem.

Remember, this journey is personal, and progress takes time. Be patient with yourself and celebrate small victories along the way. Seeking professional help can provide valuable support in navigating and healing from these root causes of harshness.

Navigating Disagreements with Love: A Blueprint for Husbands

Engaging in disagreements, corrections, or challenges within a marriage is inevitable, but the manner in which these interactions occur is crucial for maintaining a healthy and loving relationship. Let's explore a blueprint for husbands to correct, challenge, or disagree with their wives in a manner that spells "L-O-V-E":

L - Listen Actively: Before expressing your disagreement, take the time to actively listen to your wife's perspective. Demonstrate genuine interest and empathy, ensuring that she feels heard and understood. Listening lays the foundation for a respectful and constructive conversation.

O - Offer Empathy: Empathy is a powerful tool in navigating disagreements. Put yourself in your wife's shoes, striving to understand her emotions and point of view. Expressing empathy communicates that you value her feelings and are open to a collaborative resolution.

V - Validate Feelings: Acknowledge and validate your wife's feelings, even if you may not fully agree with her perspective. Validating her emotions creates an atmosphere of mutual respect and ensures that she feels acknowledged, fostering a sense of security in the relationship.

E - Express Calmly and Clearly: When expressing your disagreement, do so calmly and clearly. Avoid harsh language, raised voices, or demeaning remarks. Clearly articulate your viewpoint while maintaining a tone of love and respect. Effective communication is key to finding common ground.

Reflection Questions:

1. **Listen Actively (L):** How can you improve your active listening skills during disagreements? Are there specific habits or distractions you need to address to become a better listener?
2. **Offer Empathy (O):** In what ways can you show more empathy during disagreements? How can you ensure that your wife feels understood and supported emotionally?
3. **Validate Feelings (V):** Reflect on past disagreements. Have you effectively acknowledged and validated your wife's feelings, even when you disagreed with her perspective?
4. **Express Calmly and Clearly (E):** How can you ensure that your expressions during disagreements remain calm and clear? Are there specific communication techniques you can adopt to avoid escalation?

By implementing these principles of love during disagreements, husbands can foster an environment where differences are addressed with respect and understanding, contributing to the overall health and strength of the marital relationship.

Navigating Lust in Husbandhood: A Call to Holiness in Relationships

Lust, as defined in a biblical context, refers to an intense, inappropriate desire for someone, often of a sexual nature. The implications of lust on husbandhood are profound, impacting not only the individual but also the dynamics within a marriage and family. The scriptural foundation for understanding the severity of lust is found in the teachings of Jesus in Matthew 5:28 (ESV): "But I say to you that everyone who looks at a woman with lustful intent has already committed adultery with her in his heart."

Breaking down this scripture, Jesus goes beyond the external actions, emphasizing the significance of one's internal thoughts and desires. The message is clear: lust is not a trivial matter; it strikes at the very core of marital fidelity. It challenges husbands to cultivate purity not only in their outward actions but also in the sanctuary of their hearts.

The prevalence of lust among men can be attributed to various factors, including past experiences and exposure to explicit content. Society, through media and cultural norms, often bombards individuals with sexual imagery, setting unrealistic standards and distorting healthy expectations within marriages. Many husbands, having been exposed to explicit content or engaged in premarital sexual activities, may carry unrealistic sexual expectations into their marriages.

The impact of lust on wives and families is significant. When a husband harbors lustful desires, it can create an emotional and relational distance. Wives may feel objectified, undervalued, or unable to meet unrealistic expectations set by external influences. The sacred bond of intimacy within marriage is affected, as the purity and exclusivity intended for the marital relationship become compromised.

Moreover, the pervasive influence of pornography has played a role in shaping sexual expectations. The performances in pornographic content often involve unrealistic scenarios and behaviors that are not reflective of genuine, intimate connections between spouses. This, in turn, can lead to dissatisfaction within marriages and even addiction to explicit content.

Recognizing the impact of lust on husbandhood requires a commitment to holiness and a reevaluation of the sources that shape one's sexual expectations. Husbands are called to actively guard their hearts, seeking purity in thought and action. Communication within marriages is essential, as open dialogue about sexual expectations, struggles, and desires can foster understanding and intimacy.

Addressing issues related to lust may involve seeking professional counseling or guidance, especially if it has developed into an addiction. Husbands are encouraged to embark on a journey of self-reflection, repentance, and intentional efforts to cultivate purity within their hearts and marriages. By upholding biblical principles and fostering genuine, loving connections, husbands can contribute to the sanctity and strength of their marriages and families.

Overcoming Lust: A Path to Purity in Husbandhood

Navigating the challenges of lust requires intentional efforts and a commitment to pursue purity and holiness in husbandhood. Let's explore practical ways to overcome lust, using points that spell "L-U-S-T":

L - Leverage Accountability: Establishing accountability mechanisms is crucial in the journey to overcome lust. Husbands can confide in a trusted friend, mentor, or join a support group where they can openly discuss struggles, share victories, and receive guidance without judgment.

U - Understand Triggers: Identifying and understanding triggers for lustful thoughts is a key step in overcoming them. Husbands should reflect on situations, environments, or specific content that tends to stimulate inappropriate desires. Awareness of triggers enables proactive avoidance and helps in cultivating self-control.

S - S - See the Sin for Its True Nature: Recognizing the true nature of lust and understanding its potential consequences is a crucial aspect of overcoming this challenge. Husbands should cultivate a clear understanding of the destructive impact of lust on their relationships, emotional well-being, and spiritual health. Seeing the sin for what it truly is involves acknowledging that it goes beyond a momentary desire, recognizing its potential to sabotage trust, intimacy, and the sanctity of the marital bond. This awareness serves as a powerful motivator to resist the allure of lustful thoughts and behaviors, fostering a commitment to pursue purity for the sake of a thriving and God-honoring marriage.

T - Transform Thought Patterns: Overcoming lust involves reshaping thought patterns. Husbands can actively redirect their minds when inappropriate thoughts arise by focusing on positive aspects, engaging in prayer, or meditating on scripture. Transforming thought patterns requires consistent effort and a commitment to renewing the mind.

By embracing these strategies, husbands can embark on a transformative journey towards purity and holiness. Overcoming lust is not an isolated endeavor but a collaborative effort that involves seeking support, understanding personal triggers, accessing professional guidance, and actively engaging in the process of renewing one's mind. Pursuing purity not only strengthens the marital bond but also aligns with biblical principles, fostering a relationship characterized by love, respect, and intimacy.

Overcoming Lust: A Path to Purity in Husbandhood - Worksheet 201

278

THE BIBLICAL ROLES OF A WIFE: A HELPER AND SUPPORT

Understanding the biblical roles of a wife begins with a foundational perspective on the divine purpose of marriage. In the Bible, a wife is described as a companion, partner, and helpmate to her husband. Genesis 2:18 (ESV) expresses this beautifully: "Then the Lord God said, 'It is not good that the man should be alone; I will make him a helper fit for him.'"

Biblical Definition:
A wife, in the biblical context, is a God-ordained partner designed to complement her husband. The term "helper" does not imply subservience but emphasizes a supportive and cooperative role within the marital union.

Helper and Support:
The idea of a wife as a helper denotes a woman who stands by her husband's side, providing invaluable support and assistance. This biblical role encompasses various aspects, including emotional, spiritual, and practical support.

Emotional Support:
A husband often faces challenges and stresses in life, and a wife's role as a helper involves offering emotional support. This can include being a listening ear, providing comfort, and offering encouragement during difficult times. The wife's ability to create a safe and nurturing emotional environment contributes significantly to the overall well-being of the marriage.

Spiritual Support:
In the realm of spirituality, a wife plays a crucial role as a spiritual companion. This involves praying together, sharing spiritual insights, and fostering a joint commitment to faith. The wife, as a helper, assists in cultivating a spiritually enriched atmosphere within the marriage.

Practical Assistance:
Practically, a wife is often instrumental in managing the affairs of the household. This includes responsibilities such as maintaining the home, managing finances, and raising children. By actively participating in these practical aspects, a wife fulfills the role of a helper by lightening her husband's load and contributing to the harmony of the family.

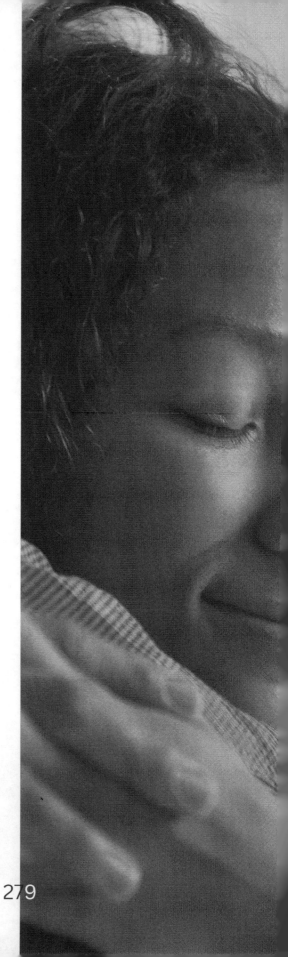

Partnership in Decision-Making:
The biblical concept of a helpmate also signifies a partnership in decision-making. A wife's input, wisdom, and perspective are valued in the collaborative process of navigating life's choices. This shared decision-making enhances the strength and unity of the marital bond.

In essence, the biblical roles of a wife as a helper and support underscore the dynamic partnership that marriage is intended to be. As a wife embraces her role with love, wisdom, and commitment, she becomes an indispensable asset to her husband, fostering a relationship that reflects the divine design for marriage.

The Precious Role of a Wife: More Valuable than Jewels

Proverbs 31:10 beautifully declares, "An excellent wife who can find? She is far more precious than jewels." This verse highlights the immeasurable worth and honor that comes with the role of being a wife. It serves as a reminder to every wife that her role is not just significant but incredibly valuable.

Understanding one's worth is fundamental to a thriving marriage. A wife's sense of self-worth directly impacts the vitality of her relationship. When a woman recognizes her preciousness, it creates a foundation for a healthy and fulfilling marriage. Unfortunately, relationships can face unnecessary challenges when a woman struggles with a lack of self-worth.

The key for a woman to walk in the preciousness of being a wife is to know that she is more valuable than any jewel or position she may desire. Sometimes, in the pursuit of external achievements or recognition, wives may inadvertently cheapen themselves. The profound truth is that the ultimate goal for every wife should be to embody the essence of an excellent wife—a woman who prioritizes the sacred and honorable role of being a wife.

Embracing the preciousness of a wife involves recognizing one's intrinsic value and worthiness. It means understanding that the role of a wife is not defined by external accomplishments but by the love, dedication, and support she brings to her marriage. A precious wife is one who, aware of her own worth, contributes to the flourishing of her relationship with love, grace, and wisdom.

In conclusion, Proverbs 31:10 encourages every wife to embrace the preciousness of her role. More valuable than any jewel, the honor of being a wife is foundational to a thriving marriage. By acknowledging her intrinsic worth and prioritizing the essence of an excellent wife, a woman can navigate the complexities of marriage with confidence, grace, and the recognition that she is indeed a precious gem in the eyes of her partner and, ultimately, in the eyes of God.

Recognizing Your Intrinsic Worth: A Journey to Embracing Your Precious Role

Understanding your worth as a wife is an essential aspect of cultivating a thriving marriage. The biblical perspective in Proverbs 31:10 highlights that you are more precious than jewels, emphasizing the immeasurable value that comes with the role of being a wife. This worksheet aims to guide you on a journey to recognize and embrace your intrinsic worth as you navigate the precious role of a wife.

1. **Reflect on Proverbs 31:10:**
   - Take some time to meditate on the verse. How does it make you feel to be described as more precious than jewels?
   - Consider writing down your initial thoughts and emotions that arise as you reflect on the biblical perspective of your worth.
2. **Identify External Influences:**
   - Explore any external influences or societal expectations that may contribute to feelings of inadequacy or diminished self-worth.
   - List specific pressures or comparisons that you may be subjecting yourself to in your pursuit of external achievements.
3. **Define Your Intrinsic Value:**
   - Separate your sense of worth from external accomplishments. Define the qualities and attributes within yourself that contribute to your intrinsic value.
   - Write down aspects of your character, love, dedication, and support that you bring to your marriage, recognizing these as integral to your worth.

- **Embrace the Essence of an Excellent Wife:**
  - Reflect on what it means to embody the essence of an excellent wife. How can you prioritize the sacred and honorable aspects of your role?
  - Consider practical ways you can contribute to the flourishing of your relationship with love, grace, and wisdom.
- **Affirmation and Declarations:**
  - Create a list of positive affirmations and declarations about your worth as a wife. Use phrases that resonate with your newfound understanding of being more precious than jewels.
  - Read these affirmations daily to reinforce a positive self-image and cultivate a sense of worthiness.
- **Seek Support and Encouragement:**
  - Reach out to friends, family, or a support group to share your journey of recognizing your intrinsic worth.
  - Seek encouragement from those who value and appreciate your role as a wife.

Remember, your worth is not determined by external standards but by the love, dedication, and support you bring to your marriage. Embracing the preciousness of your role involves recognizing and celebrating your intrinsic value. As you navigate this journey, may you find confidence, grace, and fulfillment in being a precious gem in the eyes of your partner and, most importantly, in the eyes of God.

Workbook-Recognizing Your Intrinsic Worth: A Journey to Embracing Your Precious Role 202

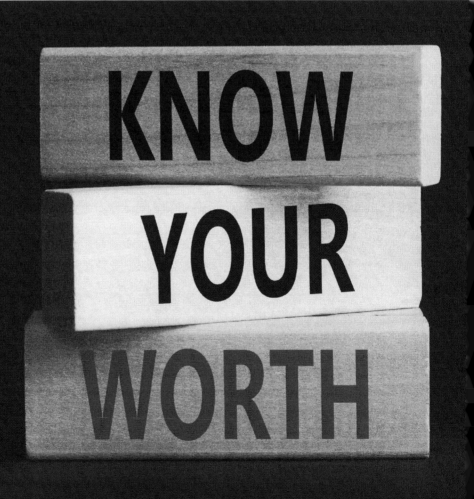

The Favor of a Wife: A Good Thing Found

Proverbs 18:22 beautifully expresses the significance of finding a wife, declaring, "He who finds a wife finds a good thing and obtains favor from the Lord." This verse underscores the profound favor that a wife brings into her husband's life, and by extension, the blessing she becomes in the eyes of the Lord.

- F - Foundational Support:
  - One of the markers of the favor a wife provides is the foundational support she offers. A wife becomes a source of strength, encouragement, and unwavering support for her husband. Like a pillar in the home, she contributes to the stability and resilience of the marital foundation.
- A - Affectionate Companion:
  - A wife's favor is often seen in the role of an affectionate companion. She brings warmth, love, and companionship into her husband's life, creating a haven of emotional connection and intimacy. Her presence becomes a constant source of joy and comfort.
- V - Valuable Partner:
  - As a valuable partner, a wife collaborates with her husband in the journey of life. Whether facing challenges or celebrating victories, her partnership adds depth and richness to their shared experiences. Together, they navigate the complexities of life, growing individually and as a couple.
- O - Overflow of Blessings:
  - The favor of a wife extends beyond the marital relationship, ushering in an overflow of blessings. The positive impact she has on her husband's life ripples into various aspects bringing favor not only into their home but also into the broader scope of their interactions with others.
- R - Relational Harmony:
  - The favor of a wife contributes to relational harmony within the marriage. Through effective communication, empathy, and a willingness to understand her husband, she fosters an environment of unity. Her efforts in promoting peace and understanding create a harmonious atmosphere that positively impacts the overall well-being of the relationship.

Reflecting on Proverbs 18:22, wives are encouraged to ponder the unique favor they bring into their husband's lives. It prompts a contemplation of the ways they provide foundational support, affectionate companionship, valuable partnership, and the overflow of blessings. Recognizing and embracing these aspects can deepen the appreciation for the special role wives play in the lives of their husbands and the favor they bring into their homes.

Workbook-Proverbs 18:22 Reflection Worksheet: Unveiling Your Impact as a Wife 20!
The Favor You Provide Him 206

282

7 Things a Man Wants to Find in His Wife:
1. **Love and Affection:**
    - A man desires to experience genuine love and affection from his wife, creating a deep emotional connection.
2. **Respect and Admiration:**
    - Mutual respect is crucial. A man wants a wife who not only respects him but also admires his qualities and achievements.
3. **Companionship:**
    - A fulfilling marriage includes a strong sense of companionship. A man seeks a wife with whom he can share his life's journey, joys, and challenges.
4. **Trustworthiness:**
    - Trust is the foundation of a strong marriage. A man looks for a wife he can trust completely, both in good times and challenging moments.
5. **Support and Encouragement:**
    - A supportive wife who encourages him in his pursuits and stands by him during difficulties is invaluable to a man.
6. **Shared Values and Goals:**
    - Common values and shared life goals contribute to a sense of unity. A man wants a wife with whom he can build a life aligned with their shared vision.
7. **Physical Intimacy and Connection:**
    - Physical intimacy is an essential aspect of marriage. A man desires a wife with whom he can share a deep and fulfilling physical connection.

Ways God Favors Men Through a Wife:
1. **A Helper and Companion (Genesis 2:18):**
    - God designed a wife to be a helper suitable for her husband. She becomes a companion, offering support and partnership in life.
2. **Completing and Enhancing (Genesis 2:24):**
    - The biblical concept of becoming one flesh highlights how a wife completes and enhances a man's life, creating a harmonious unity.
3. **A Source of Blessing (Proverbs 18:22):**
    - Finding a wife is seen as obtaining favor from the Lord. God's blessing is inherent in the gift of a loving and supportive wife.
4. **A Partner in Prayer (1 Peter 3:7):**
    - A wife is described as a fellow heir of the grace of life. Together, a husband and wife can be partners in prayer, seeking God's guidance and blessings.
5. **A Crown to Her Husband (Proverbs 12:4):**
    - A wife is likened to a crown, symbolizing honor and favor. Her presence brings dignity and favor to her husband's life.
6. **Wisdom and Counsel (Proverbs 31:26):**
    - A virtuous wife is described as one who speaks with wisdom and faithful instruction. God's favor is evident when a wife provides wise counsel to her husband.
7. **A Fountain of Joy (Proverbs 5:18):**
    - God's favor is seen in the joy a man finds in his wife. The relationship is designed to be a source of joy, companionship, and mutual fulfillment.

The Wife as the Nurturer: Cultivating a Biblical Home Environment
In exploring the biblical roles of a wife, a fundamental aspect is her identity as a nurturer. The term "nurturer" carries profound significance, reflecting the unique abilities and responsibilities bestowed upon wives within the context of marriage and family life.

Differentiating Roles: Nurturing a Husband vs. a Son
It's crucial to distinguish between nurturing a husband and a son, as these roles require nuanced approaches. While a mother nurtures her son in his formative years, a wife's nurturing role toward her husband involves emotional support, encouragement, and fostering an environment conducive to growth and unity. Understanding this distinction helps wives navigate their dual roles within the family.

God-Designed Nurturing Trait: A Source of Strength for Husbands
The nurturing trait instilled in wives by God serves as a source of strength for husbands. In the complexities of life, a husband may face challenges that demand emotional and psychological support. A wife, functioning as a nurturing partner, offers solace, understanding, and encouragement, creating a safe space where her husband can find respite from life's demands.

Prioritizing the Home: A Biblical Foundation
A wife's nurturing role is firmly rooted in biblical principles that prioritize the home. The Bible emphasizes the significance of a woman's role in creating a nurturing home environment. This underscores the idea that a wife's primary focus should be her home, not external pursuits such as career ambitions or social media endeavors. By placing the home at the forefront, a wife aligns with biblical teachings that highlight the importance of a harmonious and nurturing family life.

Emphasizing Biblical Foundation: Nurturing as a Reflection of God's Love
The biblical foundation of nurturing as a wife extends beyond earthly responsibilities. It reflects God's design for love and care within the family structure. A nurturing wife embodies qualities that align with God's intention for families to be a source of support, love, and growth. By embracing this role, a wife contributes to the overall well-being of her husband and the family unit, establishing a strong foundation for spiritual and emotional flourishing.

In essence, the nurturing role of a wife encompasses the intentional cultivation of an environment where love, understanding, and support thrive. This biblical perspective reinforces the vital contribution wives make to the well-being and stability of their families, emphasizing the divine purpose behind their nurturing role.

- Reflecting on Your Role as a Helper:
  - In what specific ways do you currently support and assist your husband as his helper, considering both practical and emotional aspects of support?
- Exploring Your Nurturing Role:
  - How do you express your nurturing qualities within the family, creating an environment that fosters emotional well-being and growth for both your husband and children?
- Prioritizing the Home:
  - In what practical ways do you prioritize and invest in your home, aligning with the biblical foundation that emphasizes the importance of a nurturing and harmonious family environment?

Building and Tearing: The Practical Dynamics of a Woman's Influence
In the intricate dance of daily life, a woman's practical actions and decisions play a pivotal role in either building or tearing down the home she has been entrusted to steward. Let's explore the practical dynamics of how a woman builds her home and the potential pitfalls that might contribute to tearing it down.

Building:
B - Blueprint of Love:
A woman builds her home by creating a blueprint infused with love. This involves intentional planning, considering the needs and desires of each family member. Her thoughtful approach sets the foundation for a loving and harmonious home.

U - Unifying Efforts:
Building a home requires a unified effort. A wise woman engages her family in shared responsibilities, fostering a sense of teamwork and collaboration. Through mutual contribution, the home becomes a collective project where everyone plays a vital role.

I - Investment in Relationships:
The core strength of a home lies in its relationships. A woman builds her home by investing time and energy in nurturing meaningful connections with each family

L - Lifelong Learning:
A commitment to lifelong learning is a cornerstone of a thriving home. A woman builds her home by cultivating a culture of curiosity, growth, and adaptability. This commitment ensures that the home evolves positively over time.

D - Domestic Excellence:
Practical skills in managing the domestic sphere contribute significantly to building a comfortable and well-functioning home. From efficient organization to creating a welcoming atmosphere, a woman's commitment to domestic excellence enhances the overall quality of her home.

Tearing:
T - Toxic Communication:
One of the subtle ways a woman might contribute to tearing down her home is through toxic communication. Negative words, criticism, or harsh tones can erode the emotional foundation of a home, creating an environment of tension and discord.

E - Emotional Neglect:
Emotional neglect is a powerful force that can undermine the fabric of a home. When a woman unintentionally neglects the emotional needs of her family members, it creates a void that can lead to dissatisfaction and disconnection.

A - Absence of Boundaries:
The absence of healthy boundaries can contribute to tearing down a home. A woman must establish and maintain boundaries that protect the emotional and physical well-being of her family, ensuring a balanced and respectful environment.

R - Resentment and Unforgiveness:
Harboring resentment and unforgiveness can act like corrosive agents within a home. A woman must actively work towards resolving conflicts, promoting forgiveness, and cultivating an atmosphere of grace to prevent the destructive impact of resentment.

S - Straying from Priorities:
When priorities become skewed, and external demands take precedence over the needs of the family, a home is at risk of being torn down. A woman must be vigilant in aligning her actions with the core priorities that contribute to the well-being of her home.

Understanding the practical dynamics of building and tearing down empowers a woman to navigate her role with wisdom, intentionality, and a commitment to nurturing a flourishing home.

Building and Tearing Worksheet: Assessing Your Impact on Your Home

Building:

1. Blueprint of Love:
- Reflect on your approach to planning and organizing your home. Are you intentional in considering the needs and desires of each family member? How can you enhance your blueprint to foster a more loving and harmonious home?

2. Unifying Efforts:
- Evaluate how you engage your family in shared responsibilities. Do you foster a sense of teamwork and collaboration? Identify areas where you can further encourage mutual contribution to make the home a collective project.

3. Investment in Relationships:
- Consider the time and energy you invest in nurturing meaningful connections with each family member. Are there specific relationships that need more attention? How can you strengthen the bonds that hold your home together?

4. Lifelong Learning:
- Assess your commitment to lifelong learning within your home. How do you cultivate a culture of curiosity, growth, and adaptability? Identify areas where you can promote continuous positive evolution within your home.

5. Domestic Excellence:
- Reflect on your practical skills in managing the domestic sphere. How do you contribute to creating a comfortable and well-functioning home? Identify areas where you can enhance your commitment to domestic excellence.

Tearing:

6. Toxic Communication:
- Examine your communication patterns. Are negative words, criticism, or harsh tones present in your interactions? Identify strategies to foster positive communication and eliminate toxic elements.

7. Emotional Neglect:
- Reflect on how you attend to the emotional needs of your family members. Are there areas where unintentional emotional neglect occurs? Identify ways to bridge emotional gaps and strengthen connections.

8. Absence of Boundaries:
- Evaluate the boundaries you have established to protect the emotional and physical well-being of your family. Are there areas where healthy boundaries are lacking? Identify and implement boundaries that contribute to a balanced and respectful environment.

9. Resentment and Unforgiveness:
- Reflect on your approach to conflict resolution and forgiveness. Are there lingering feelings of resentment or unforgiveness? Identify steps you can take to actively work towards resolution and cultivate an atmosphere of grace.

10. Straying from Priorities:
- Assess how well your actions align with the core priorities that contribute to the well-being of your home. Are external demands taking precedence over family needs? Identify ways to realign your priorities to nurture a flourishing home.

Use this worksheet to reflect on your impact on your home and identify actionable steps to strengthen its foundation through wisdom, intentionality, and a commitment to nurturing a thriving environment.

Navigating Harmony: A Wife's Warning from Proverbs
In the intricate nature of marital dynamics, Proverbs offers timeless wisdom that resonates with a clear warning for wives about the potential consequences of certain behaviors. Let's delve into Proverbs 21:19, which states, "It is better to live in a desert land than with a quarrelsome and fretful woman," and also consider the parallel verse about a contentious woman driving others to the rooftop.

Proverbs 21:19 - The Desert Land Dilemma:
This scripture vividly illustrates the impact of a quarrelsome and fretful woman on the atmosphere of a home. The comparison to a desert land implies a desolate and inhospitable environment. A quarrelsome woman is one who is prone to arguments, disputes, and constant bickering. This verse suggests that a man might find the solitude of a desert preferable to the turmoil and strife associated with a quarrelsome wife. The desert, while harsh, is at least free from the relational strife that can accompany constant conflict in the home.

Proverbs 21:9 - The Rooftop Retreat:
The parallel verse emphasizes the undesirable nature of contention within a household. A contentious woman is one who is likely to provoke disagreements and conflicts. The imagery of seeking refuge on the rooftop rather than enduring strife inside the house underscores the profound discomfort that can arise when a woman becomes contentious. This metaphorical retreat speaks to the instinctual desire to distance oneself from an environment marked by conflict.

Emotional Regulation and Household Harmony:
For wives, these verses serve as a poignant reminder of the impact their emotional disposition can have on the household. Emotional regulation is a key element in fostering a harmonious home environment. Quarrelsomeness and fretfulness, if left unchecked, can create an emotional desert where peace withers, and the relational landscape becomes barren.

Navigating Shemotions: Understanding and Regulating Emotional Currents in Marriage
In the intricate dance of marriage, emotions often become the silent orchestrators of the relationship's ebb and flow. The term "shemotions" encapsulates the unique emotional currents that many women navigate within their marriages. These emotions, deeply rooted in personal experiences, societal expectations, and the complexities of relationships, can become powerful forces that shape the dynamics of a marriage.
Understanding Shemotions:
1. Shattered Expectations:
- Women often carry expectations, both self-imposed and influenced by societal norms. When these expectations are shattered—whether in the form of unmet needs or unrealized dreams—it gives rise to emotions such as disappointment, frustration, and a sense of inadequacy.
2. Hormonal Flux:
- The intricate interplay of hormones, particularly during life stages like pregnancy, postpartum, and menopause, can contribute to emotional fluctuations. Understanding the physiological aspect of these emotions is essential in navigating the associated challenges.
3. Relationship Traumas:
- Past traumas, whether from previous relationships or childhood, can cast a long shadow on the emotional landscape of a woman. Unresolved traumas may manifest as trust issues, fear of vulnerability, or difficulty in expressing emotions openly.
4. Societal Pressures:
- Societal expectations often place a unique burden on women, influencing their perceptions of success, beauty, and the roles they play. The pressure to meet these expectations can lead to emotions such as anxiety, self-doubt, and a constant quest for validation.
Damaging Effects of Unregulated Shemotions:
1. Communication Breakdown:
- Unregulated shemotions can contribute to communication breakdowns within a marriage. Misunderstandings, unexpressed needs, and emotional distance may result from the inability to navigate and communicate complex emotions.

2. Erosion of Intimacy:
- Intimacy flourishes in an environment of emotional openness and vulnerability. When shemotions are left unregulated, the erosion of intimacy becomes a potential consequence, hindering the deep connection that marriage thrives on.

3. Impact on Mental Health:
- Prolonged emotional turbulence can take a toll on mental health. Conditions such as anxiety and depression may surface, impacting not only the individual but the overall marital ecosystem.

4. Strain on Marital Bonds:
- The cumulative effect of unregulated shemotions can strain the foundational bonds of marriage. Trust may be compromised, and the overall stability of the relationship may be at risk.

The Importance of Emotional Regulation:

1. Navigating Storms with Grace:
- Emotional regulation empowers women to navigate the storms of shemotions with grace. By developing the ability to understand, express, and manage emotions, women can foster an environment of emotional safety within the marriage.

2. Cultivating Effective Communication:
- Emotional regulation enhances communication skills, allowing women to express their needs, desires, and concerns in a constructive manner. Effective communication is the bridge that connects emotional worlds within a marriage.

3. Preserving Intimacy:
- Emotional regulation is a key ingredient in preserving intimacy. It allows for vulnerability, trust, and mutual understanding to flourish, creating a space where the marital bond deepens over time.

4. Fostering Mental Well-being:
- Prioritizing emotional regulation contributes to overall mental well-being. By addressing shemotions in a healthy way, women can proactively manage stress, anxiety, and other emotional challenges, promoting mental resilience.

In essence, navigating shemotions is an integral aspect of the marital journey for many women. Understanding the origins of these emotions, recognizing their potential impact, and embracing the importance of emotional regulation are pivotal steps in fostering a marriage characterized by empathy, connection, and enduring love.

Practical Habits for Emotional Well-Being:
To avoid the pitfalls described in Proverbs, wives are encouraged to cultivate habits that contribute to emotional well-being:
- Self-awareness: Regularly assess emotional states and identify triggers for negativity.
- Open communication: Establish a culture of open dialogue to address concerns and prevent emotional bottlenecks.
- Seeking support: Build a network of support, including friends, family, or counselors, to share concerns and seek guidance.
- Healthy outlets: Engage in activities that provide emotional release and promote a positive mindset.
- Conflict resolution: Develop healthy conflict resolution skills, emphasizing understanding and compromise.

Creating a Haven, Not a Desert:
A wise wife recognizes her role in shaping the emotional climate of her home. By embracing emotional regulation and fostering an environment of peace, understanding, and support, she contributes to the flourishing of her household. The choice to create a haven instead of a desert lies within the daily decisions and habits that wives cultivate for the well-being of their families.

Reflect on your recent interactions with your spouse. Have you noticed any patterns of quarrelsomeness or fretfulness? How might these patterns be impacting the overall atmosphere of your home?

Evaluate your emotional regulation habits. Are there specific triggers or situations that tend to lead to contention or fretfulness? How can you proactively implement healthier emotional practices to create a more harmonious household?

emotion Regulation Worksheet: Navigating Emotional Currents in Marriage 208

Embracing the Vital Role of Respect for Men

The concluding part of Ephesians 5:33 emphasizes the crucial role of a wife in fostering a respectful and supportive atmosphere within the marriage. The directive for the wife to see that she respects her husband is not a mere suggestion but a powerful insight into the dynamics of a thriving relationship. This perspective challenges wives to intentionally and perceptively consider how they view and treat their husbands.

To begin with, the phrase "let the wife see" prompts introspection. It urges wives to assess their perceptions of their husbands. Do they truly see their husbands for who they are, appreciating their virtues and recognizing their potential? Often, past experiences, whether in childhood or previous relationships, can cloud one's vision. Therefore, it becomes essential to discard lenses tainted by disrespect or negative influences and instead adopt a perspective aligned with respect for God's creation.

Respecting one's husband involves acknowledging the inherent goodness and worth within him. It requires seeing beyond any flaws or shortcomings and recognizing the positive qualities that contribute to the relationship. This approach goes beyond mere acknowledgment; it involves actively affirming and appreciating the unique strengths and qualities that make the husband who he is.

Moreover, the call to respect carries a transformative power. Many men thrive on respect, and when they receive it within the confines of their marriage, it can be a catalyst for positive change and growth. Wives play a pivotal role in cultivating an environment where respect is not only given but also reciprocated. It involves creating a space where both partners feel valued, understood, and supported.

For some women, the challenge lies in overcoming learned behaviors or cultural attitudes that may inadvertently manifest as disrespect. The nurturing of respect involves a continuous process of self-awareness and intentional efforts to replace disrespectful habits with affirming and constructive communication.

In essence, the directive to let the wife see that she respects her husband is an invitation to cultivate a marriage where both partners feel seen, appreciated, and empowered. It is a recognition of the transformative impact that respect can have on the dynamics of a relationship, fostering an atmosphere where love and mutual understanding can flourish.

Ways Unintentional Disrespect May Creep In

Respect is a crucial element in a thriving marriage, and often, unintentional actions or habits can inadvertently convey disrespect. It's essential for wives to be aware of potential pitfalls that might undermine the respect they desire to show their husbands. Consider the following points to ensure unintentional disrespect doesn't sneak into your relationship:

1. Withholding Appreciation
Sometimes, failing to express gratitude for your husband's efforts can unintentionally communicate a lack of appreciation. Take time to acknowledge and thank him for the things he does, whether big or small, to foster an atmosphere of respect.

2. Ignoring Boundaries
Disrespect can emerge when personal boundaries are overlooked. Be mindful of your husband's need for space, time alone, or specific preferences. Respecting his boundaries is a crucial aspect of fostering a healthy and respectful relationship.

3. Nonchalant Communication
Your communication style can unknowingly convey disrespect if it becomes nonchalant or dismissive. Ensure you are actively engaged in conversations, offering your full attention and validating his thoughts and feelings.

4. Neglecting Input
Disregarding your husband's opinions or ideas, even unintentionally, can diminish the sense of respect in your relationship. Make a conscious effort to value his input and consider his perspective in decision-making.

5. Grumbling or Complaining

Constant grumbling or complaining about various aspects of life, including your marriage, can wear down the atmosphere of respect. Instead, focus on constructive communication and find solutions together.

6. Unsupportive Actions

Actions that lack support or encouragement can communicate disrespect. Ensure you actively support your husband's goals, dreams, and endeavors, demonstrating your belief in his capabilities.

7. Tone of Voice

The tone used in communication can significantly impact how a message is received. Pay attention to your tone, ensuring it conveys respect and love rather than unintentional negativity or frustration.

8. Ignoring Emotional Needs

Every husband has emotional needs, and failing to address them can be unintentionally disrespectful. Be attuned to your husband's emotions and strive to meet his needs with empathy and understanding.

9. Non-Verbal Cues

Non-verbal cues such as eye-rolling, sighs, or dismissive gestures can communicate disrespect without a word spoken. Be mindful of your body language and strive for gestures that convey love and respect.

10. Grasping for Control

Attempting to control every aspect of your husband's life, even with good intentions, can be perceived as disrespect. Allow space for his autonomy and decisions, fostering an environment of mutual respect.

By being aware of these potential pitfalls, wives can actively work to eliminate unintentional disrespect from their marriages and create a foundation of love and mutual respect.

Signals of Emotional Distance: Unveiling Signs of Disrespect

In the intricate dance of marriage, subtle shifts in behavior can often signal deeper issues. Recognizing the signs of emotional distance is crucial for a wife to address potential challenges in her marriage. Let's explore these indicators through the lens of RESPECT:

Silence: A sudden increase in silence or a lack of open communication can signify emotional withdrawal. If your husband has become reticent and less willing to engage in conversation, it may indicate that he feels disrespected or unheard.

Impaired Intimacy: Emotional distance can manifest in a decline in physical intimacy. If your husband appears less interested in physical connection, it might be a reflection of emotional distance resulting from perceived disrespect.

Growing Frustration: Increased frustration or irritability may be a red flag. If your husband seems perpetually on edge or easily agitated, it could be a response to feeling disrespected or undervalued.

Neglect of Shared Activities: A diminishing interest in shared activities and hobbies may indicate a sense of detachment. If your husband withdraws from the activities you once enjoyed together, it could be a sign of emotional distance.

Expression of Displeasure: Your husband may communicate his displeasure indirectly, expressing dissatisfaction with sarcasm, critical remarks, or passive-aggressive behavior. Such expressions may be indicative of unaddressed feelings of disrespect.

Sudden Independence: A desire for increased personal space or a newfound independence might signify emotional distancing. If your husband seeks more time alone or engages less in joint decision-making, it could be a response to perceived disrespect.

By attentively observing these signs, a wife can gain insights into potential issues and take proactive steps to foster an atmosphere of respect and understanding within the marriage. Addressing these subtle cues with open communication and a commitment to mutual respect can help bridge emotional gaps and strengthen the marital bond.

Respecting Men: Understanding the Core Desires"
Respect is a foundational element in the framework of a healthy and thriving marriage. For men, feeling respected is not merely a preference; it is a deep-seated need that profoundly influences their well-being and the dynamics of the relationship. Let's explore the core desires of men using the acronym RESPECT:

- Recognition: Men desire recognition for their efforts, achievements, and contributions. Feeling acknowledged and appreciated for the value they bring to the marriage fosters a sense of significance. Wives can express recognition through verbal affirmations, acknowledging their husband's strengths, and appreciating his unique qualities.
- Encouragement: Encouragement is a powerful expression of respect. Men appreciate wives who believe in their capabilities and provide uplifting words during challenges. An encouraging environment empowers husbands to overcome obstacles, knowing that their spouse stands by them.
- Support: Supporting a man in his pursuits, dreams, and endeavors communicates a profound level of respect. Whether it's a career aspiration, a personal goal, or a shared vision for the future, wives can actively participate in and champion their husband's journey. A supportive partner bolsters a man's confidence and self-esteem.
- Patience: Patience is a virtue that husbands deeply value. Recognizing that everyone has flaws and imperfections, men appreciate wives who exhibit patience and understanding during moments of weakness. Patience allows space for personal growth and fosters an environment where both partners can thrive.
- Expressiveness: Men often appreciate clear and direct communication. Being able to express thoughts, feelings, and expectations openly contributes to a sense of respect. Wives can demonstrate respect by fostering open communication channels, allowing their husbands to share their perspectives without judgment.
- Consistency: Consistency in words and actions is vital for establishing a sense of security and respect in marriage. Men thrive in environments where expectations are clear, and actions align with verbal affirmations. Consistency builds trust and reinforces the foundation of mutual respect.
- Trust: Trust is a cornerstone of respect in a marriage. Men deeply value a wife's trust in their decision-making, character, and commitment. Cultivating a relationship based on trust involves transparency, reliability, and a shared commitment to building a strong foundation.

Understanding and embodying these elements of respect can transform the dynamics of a marriage, creating a space where both partners feel valued, affirmed, and deeply connected. It requires intentional efforts to consistently express respect in various facets of the relationship, ultimately contributing to the overall health and longevity of the marriage.

Workbook Building a Foundation of Respect: A Practical Activity for Wives" Page 211

Submission: A Divine Dance in Marriage

Ephesians 5:22-33 provides profound insights into the dynamics of submission within marriage, illuminating the divine design for the union between husband and wife.

Submission Defined:

When Paul instructs wives to "submit to your own husbands, as to the Lord," he introduces a concept often misunderstood in contemporary culture. Submission within marriage is not about inferiority or oppression; rather, it's a voluntary and respectful yielding. It involves a wife recognizing her husband's God-given role as the leader of the family and willingly aligning herself under his leadership.

Submission as Unto the Lord:

The phrase "as to the Lord" is pivotal in understanding the nature of submission. It implies that a wife's submission is ultimately an act of reverence and obedience to God. By submitting to her husband in a way that mirrors her submission to the Lord, a wife acknowledges the divine order established by God in marriage.

Worldly Attacks on Biblical Submission:

In the current cultural landscape, the concept of submission has come under significant scrutiny. The world often misinterprets biblical submission as an antiquated and oppressive idea. This misunderstanding contributes to a distorted view of marriage, hindering couples from experiencing the fullness of God's design.

The Problem of Distorted Perspectives:

When the biblical concept of submission is attacked or misunderstood, it can lead to distortions in marital relationships. Some may view submission as a power struggle, causing tension and discord. Others may reject the idea altogether, missing out on the beautiful dance of mutual submission and sacrificial love that God intends for marriages.

Restoring God's Design:

To counteract the worldly attacks on submission, couples must turn to the biblical model and seek God's guidance for their marriage. Submission is not about dominance or control but rather a harmonious partnership where both spouses contribute to the flourishing of the marriage. Embracing biblical submission requires humility, trust, and a commitment to honoring God in the marital relationship.

The Beauty of Mutual Submission:

The concept of submission in Ephesians 5 is part of a reciprocal exchange between spouses. While wives are called to submit, husbands are called to sacrificial love. This mutual submission fosters a dance of unity, where both partners contribute to the well-being of the marriage.

In conclusion, Ephesians 5:22-33 invites couples to embrace the divine dance of submission within marriage. By understanding and applying biblical principles, couples can counter the world's attacks, restoring the beauty and purpose of submission in a Christ-centered union.

Navigating Submission: What to Submit to and What to Avoid

Submission is a biblical principle that requires careful navigation within the context of marriage. Ephesians 5:22-33 instructs wives to submit to their husbands, but it's essential to discern what aspects deserve submission and what should be avoided.

Submit to Spiritual Leadership:

A wife should willingly submit to her husband's spiritual leadership. This involves recognizing and respecting his role as the spiritual head of the household. Submitting in this area means actively participating in spiritual practices together, seeking God's guidance, and supporting each other's faith journey.

Avoid Submitting to Unbiblical Commands:

While submission is encouraged, a woman should never submit to commands or requests that go against biblical principles. If a husband asks his wife to compromise her faith, values, or engage in unethical behavior, she is called to stand firm in her commitment to God's Word.

Submit to Love and Cherishing:
Wives are called to submit to their husbands' sacrificial love and cherishing. This means allowing the husband to express love in his unique way and recognizing his efforts to care for and cherish his wife. Submission in this context fosters an atmosphere of love and mutual respect.

Avoid Submitting to Abuse or Mistreatment:
Submission does not equate to enduring abuse or mistreatment. A woman should never submit to behavior that causes harm, whether physical, emotional, or verbal. God's design for marriage does not endorse any form of abuse, and seeking help in such situations is both wise and biblically supported.

Submit to Shared Decision-Making:
In healthy marriages, submission involves collaborative decision-making. A wife can submit to the joint process of discussing and deciding important matters. This fosters a sense of unity and partnership, allowing both spouses to contribute to the well-being of the family.
Avoid Submitting to Unilateral Decision-Making:
Submission does not mean surrendering individual agency. Wives should avoid submitting to unilateral decision-making where their opinions, desires, or insights are disregarded. God's design for marriage encourages mutual respect and consideration.

Submit to Mutual Growth:
A wife can submit to the journey of mutual growth and development. This includes supporting each other's personal and relational growth, encouraging individual pursuits, and working together to become the best versions of themselves.

Avoid Submitting to Stagnation:
Submission should not lead to stagnation or complacency. A woman should avoid submitting to a mindset or lifestyle that hinders personal and relational growth. God's desire for marriage is a continuous journey of becoming more Christ-like.

In conclusion, understanding what to submit to and what to avoid is crucial for a healthy and God-honoring marriage. Wives are called to submit to God's design while discerning when to stand firm against anything that deviates from biblical principles.

TIPS for Navigating Unacceptable Behavior in a Husband
Navigating a situation where a husband exhibits behavior that a wife shouldn't submit to can be challenging. Here are some practical tips to consider, using the acronym TIPS:
1. TALK Openly:
Initiate open and honest communication with your husband. Share your concerns and feelings about the behavior you find unacceptable. Create a safe space for dialogue, allowing both of you to express your thoughts.

2. IDENTIFY Boundaries:
Clearly define your boundaries and communicate them with kindness and firmness. Let your husband know the specific behaviors that are causing distress and explain why they are unacceptable to you. Establishing boundaries is crucial for maintaining a healthy relationship.

3.PRAY Together:
Prayer can be a powerful tool for transformation. Encourage your husband to join you in prayer, seeking God's guidance and wisdom. A shared spiritual journey can foster connection and open the door for positive change.

4. SUPPORT Positive Change:
Acknowledge and support any positive changes your husband makes. Reinforce behaviors that align with your values and express appreciation for efforts to improve. Positive reinforcement can be a motivating factor for personal growth. SEEK Professional Help: If the behavior persists or escalates, consider seeking professional assistance. Marriage counselors or therapists can provide guidance, facilitating conversations and offering strategies for addressing problematic behavior.

Remember, the goal is not to control or manipulate but to foster a healthy and respectful relationship. If, despite your efforts, the behavior persists and poses a threat to your well-being, seeking professional help becomes even more critical. Always prioritize your safety and emotional health in any situation.

Learning from the Proverbs 31 Woman: A Woman of Virtue
The Proverbs 31 Woman serves as an exemplary model for women, offering timeless wisdom that transcends generations. Here are key lessons that women can glean from her virtuous character:
Vision and Purpose (Proverbs 31:10-12):
- The Proverbs 31 Woman has a clear vision for her life and family. Women can learn the importance of setting goals, cultivating a sense of purpose, and aligning their actions with a greater vision.

Hard Work and Diligence (Proverbs 31:13-19):
- She is known for her industrious nature. Women can draw inspiration from her commitment to hard work, resourcefulness, and diligence in managing her responsibilities.

Compassion and Generosity (Proverbs 31:20):
- The Proverbs 31 Woman extends her hand to the needy. Women can cultivate a heart of compassion, embracing opportunities to share kindness and generosity with those around them.

Integrity and Honor (Proverbs 31:25):
- She is clothed with strength and dignity. Women can prioritize integrity in their character, maintaining a sense of honor, self-respect, and moral uprightness in all aspects of life.

Wisdom and Communication (Proverbs 31:26):
- The Proverbs 31 Woman speaks with wisdom. Women can learn the value of cultivating wisdom in their speech, ensuring that their words uplift, encourage, and convey wisdom in various situations.

Family and Marriage (Proverbs 31:27-28):
- She looks well to the ways of her household. Women can prioritize the well-being of their families, creating a nurturing environment and investing in the growth and success of their marriages and children.

Fear of the Lord (Proverbs 31:30):
- The fear of the Lord is the foundation of her life. Women can learn the importance of cultivating a deep reverence for God, aligning their lives with His principles, and seeking His guidance in all endeavors.

By reflecting on these lessons from the Proverbs 31 Woman, women can find inspiration to live purposefully, contribute positively to their families and communities, and embody the virtues that lead to a life of fulfillment and impact.

Workbook-Activity: Assessing and Building Proverbs 31 Qualities Page 214

Shifting Into the 6 Pillars of Relatability in Marriage

Welcome to a transformative journey, an exploration that transcends the ordinary and delves deep into the heart of your marital connection. At the core of every thriving marriage lies the essence of relatability—an artful dance of connection, understanding, and shared goals. In the forthcoming chapters, we will unravel the intricacies of the 6 Pillars of Relatability, each representing a vital dimension aimed at fortifying the bonds that tie you and your spouse together.

Relatability is not a passive experience; it's a deliberate choice to honor individuality, nurture understanding, and propel both partners towards shared aspirations. Within each pillar, we confront challenges head-on, offer profound insights, and present practical strategies that serve as tools to strengthen your marital bond. This journey is not just about recognizing your existing strengths; it's about identifying opportunities for intentional growth and enhancement.

As you embark on this exploration, envision the 6 Pillars as guiding lights, illuminating the path to more profound and meaningful connection with your spouse. These pillars are not rigid structures but fluid dimensions, responding to the unique contours of your relationship. Let's delve into the first of these dimensions, the foundational pillar of *Authenticity*, unraveling the challenges, insights and strategies that will empower you to authentically relate in your marriage.

Authenticity in Marriage: Did They Marry the Real You?

The foundation of a thriving marriage is authenticity—the freedom to be genuinely oneself and to accept one's partner in their truest form. It prompts a crucial question: Did they marry the real you? Often, the journey of courtship involves presenting the best version of ourselves, but as the relationship deepens, the importance of authenticity becomes increasingly evident.

1. Unveiling the Real You:
Authenticity begins with the courage to unveil the real you. It's about allowing your partner to see beyond the curated image presented during courtship. This involves sharing vulnerabilities, dreams, and quirks that make you uniquely you. Proverbs 12:22 highlights the value of honesty, emphasizing that those who deal truthfully are pleasing to the Lord. In marriage, honesty lays the groundwork for authenticity.

2. Embracing Imperfections:
Authenticity embraces imperfections—the messy, unfiltered aspects of life. Marriage is a journey of growth and acceptance, and acknowledging imperfections fosters an environment where both partners can evolve together. Romans 15:7 encourages believers to accept one another just as Christ accepted them, setting a powerful example for marital authenticity through acceptance.

3. Building Trust Through Transparency:
Trust is a cornerstone of any healthy marriage, and transparency is its building block. Sharing transparently about one's thoughts, feelings, and experiences builds trust over time. Authenticity allows couples to navigate challenges together, fostering a deepened connection. Proverbs 3:3-4 speaks of trusting in the Lord and doing good, a principle applicable in marriage where trusting in each other contributes to goodness in the relationship.

4. Navigating Challenges Authentically:
Authenticity shines brightest in moments of challenge. Being authentic during disagreements or tough times involves expressing genuine feelings and concerns. Ephesians 4:25 underscores the importance of putting away falsehood and speaking truthfully to one another. Navigating challenge authentically strengthens the marital bond and builds resilience.

5. Growing Together Authentically:
Authenticity is not static; it's a dynamic process of growth. As individuals evolve, so does the marriage. Couples who grow together authentically find joy in each other's journeys. Ecclesiastes 4:9-10 emphasizes the value of companionship and mutual support, reflecting the beauty of growing together on the authentic path of marriage.

In essence, authenticity in marriage is about creating a space where both partners can be true to themselves and feel unconditionally accepted. It's a journey of continuous discovery, where the real you is not only embraced but celebrated, laying the groundwork for a resilient and fulfilling marital relationship.

Encouraging Authenticity in Marriage: Trusting God's Transformative Power

Embracing authenticity within the sacred covenant of marriage is not only a liberating journey for individual souls but a transformative process that enriches the union itself. Here are five compelling reasons why spouses must choose to be their true selves and trust in God's guiding hand throughout the authentic journey:

1. Genuine Connection:

Authenticity fosters a profound connection between spouses. When individuals bring their true selves to the relationship, it creates a space for genuine understanding and acceptance. Trusting God in this process means acknowledging that He designed marriage to be a place of authentic connection, where hearts intertwine without the need for pretense.

2. Strengthening Intimacy:

True intimacy flourishes in an atmosphere of authenticity. By being transparent about dreams, fears, and aspirations, spouses cultivate a deeper emotional intimacy.

3. Navigating Challenges Together:

Authenticity equips couples to face challenges as a united front. By embracing each other's genuine selves, spouses build resilience and unity in confronting life's trials. Trusting God through challenges involves relying on His wisdom to guide the authentic responses needed to navigate the complexities of marriage.

4. Sustainable Growth:

Individual and marital growth are intricately linked to authenticity. When spouses allow themselves to evolve authentically, it paves the way for sustainable personal and relational growth. Trusting God in this journey means relying on His transformative power to guide the growth process and make all things beautiful in His time (Ecclesiastes 3:11).

5. Creating a Legacy of Love:

An authentic marriage becomes a beacon of love for future generations. Children, friends, and family witness the beauty of genuine connection and are inspired by the legacy of love rooted in authenticity. Trusting God in this legacy-building process means surrendering to His divine plan, believing that He orchestrates beauty from the genuine hearts surrendered to Him.

Trusting God throughout the journey of authenticity involves leaning into His promises, especially the assurance that He makes crooked paths straight (Isaiah 45:2). By surrendering to His guidance, spouses can navigate the sometimes unpredictable terrain of authenticity with confidence, knowing that God's transformative power is at work, bringing beauty and strength to their marriage.

Consequences of Avoiding Authenticity in Marriage

When couples avoid being authentic, choosing instead to hide behind masks or withhold their true selves, several consequences may emerge, impacting the overall health and longevity of the relationship.

Erosion of Trust:

Authenticity is the cornerstone of trust. When spouses are not genuine with each other, it erodes the foundation of trust within the relationship. Trust is fragile, and once broken, it can be challenging to rebuild.

Communication Breakdown:

Authenticity fuels open and honest communication. Without it, couples may experience a breakdown in communication. Important conversations become elusive, and partners may resort to surface-level interactions, missing out on the depth that authentic communication provides.

Emotional Disconnection:

The essence of emotional intimacy lies in being vulnerable and authentic with one another. Avoiding authenticity leads to emotional disconnection, as partners may struggle to truly understand and empathize with each other's experiences and feelings.

Resentment and Unresolved Issues:
Suppressing true thoughts and feelings can lead to the accumulation of resentment. Unresolved issues fester beneath the surface, creating a breeding ground for animosity and tension that can erupt unexpectedly, causing damage to the relationship.

Identity Loss:
Marriage is a union of two unique individuals. Without authenticity, individuals may feel pressured to conform or suppress aspects of their identity to fit societal or spousal expectations. This can lead to a sense of identity loss, affecting self-esteem and overall fulfillment.

Stagnation in Personal Growth:
Authenticity encourages personal growth within the context of the marriage. When spouses avoid being true to themselves, personal development may stagnate. The relationship, instead of being a catalyst for growth, becomes a hindrance.

Impact on Intimacy:
True intimacy involves sharing one's authentic self, both emotionally and physically. When authenticity is lacking, intimacy can be compromised. Partners may feel a sense of distance, hindering the development of a deeper, more profound connection.

Long-Term Relationship Strain:
While a lack of authenticity may not immediately lead to the dissolution of a marriage, it can create enduring strain. Over time, the accumulated consequences may strain the relationship, making it more challenging to navigate challenges and find shared meaning.

Navigating Towards Authenticity:
Couples can reverse these consequences by Intentionally cultivating authenticity in their marriage. Through open communication, vulnerability, and a commitment to understanding one another, spouses can create a relationship that thrives on genuine connection, mutual support, and enduring love. Remember, the journey toward authenticity is ongoing, and each step taken strengthens the bond between partners.

Practical Steps Towards Marital Authenticity: Cultivating Openness and Honesty
Fostering authenticity in marriage involves intentional steps that cultivate an environment of openness and honesty. Here are practical strategies for couples seeking to embark on the journey of authenticity:
1. Honest Communication:
Encourage open and honest communication. Create a safe space where both spouses feel free to express their thoughts, feelings, and concerns without fear of judgment. Establish regular times for meaningful conversations, allowing each partner to share their authentic selves.

2. Vulnerability:
Embrace vulnerability as a strength. Share personal experiences, dreams, and fears. Vulnerability fosters a deeper connection as it allows spouses to witness and understand each other's authentic responses to life. Acknowledge that vulnerability is not a sign of weakness but a pathway to intimacy.

3. Active Listening:
Practice active listening. When your spouse shares, give them your full attention. Seek to understand not just the words spoken but the emotions and intentions behind them. Active listening builds trust and demonstrates a genuine desire to connect on a deeper level.

4. Mutual Respect:
Cultivate mutual respect. Recognize and honor each other's individuality. Respecting differences paves the way for authenticity, allowing spouses to be true to themselves without the fear of rejection. Remember that God designed each person uniquely, and that uniqueness should be celebrated.

. Shared Goals and Dreams:
dentify and pursue shared goals and dreams. Discussing aspirations and working towards
ommon objectives strengthens the bond between spouses. Sharing dreams allows for mutual
upport, creating a foundation for authenticity as both partners contribute to the realization of
ach other's desires.

. Transparency in Decision-Making:
e transparent in decision-making processes. Whether big or small, involve your spouse in
mportant decisions. Transparency builds trust and ensures that both partners are actively
articipating in shaping their lives together. Transparency also reduces the chances of
isunderstandings and fosters a sense of unity.

. Quality Time Together:
rioritize quality time together. Engage in activities that allow for genuine connection. Quality
me fosters an atmosphere where authenticity naturally thrives. Whether it's a shared hobby,
ate nights, or simple moments of togetherness, invest time in deepening your connection.

. Embrace Growth Together:
cknowledge that personal and marital growth is a continuous process. Embrace the changes
nat come with growth and commit to evolving together. Authenticity is not stagnant; it
volves with the growth of individuals and the marriage. Embracing growth ensures that
uthenticity remains a dynamic and enriching aspect of the relationship.

nplementing these practical steps requires commitment and patience. However, as spouses
vest in creating an environment of openness and honesty, they lay the foundation for a
arriage characterized by authenticity, deep connection, and enduring love.

arital Authenticity Worksheet: Navigating Challenges and Fostering Open Conversations 218

Mutual Respect

Foundational Importance of Respecting One Another:

Respect is the soil from which the roots of a strong marriage draw sustenance. In a relationship, respect goes beyond mere courtesy; it encompasses recognizing the inherent worth, dignity, and autonomy of one's partner. This foundational importance is underscored in Ephesians 5:33, which instructs husbands to love their wives and wives to respect their husbands. This biblical wisdom emphasizes the reciprocal nature of respect, highlighting its role in nurturing a harmonious marital bond.

When spouses respect each other, they acknowledge and honor the unique qualities, perspectives, and boundaries each brings to the union. It sets the stage for an egalitarian partnership where decisions are made collaboratively, and the autonomy of each person is valued. The foundation of respect provides a stable platform upon which a thriving marriage can be built.

Contribution to a Healthy and Thriving Marriage:

A marriage characterized by mutual respect becomes a fertile ground for growth, both individually and as a couple. Respect creates an atmosphere where differences are celebrated rather than criticized. In embracing the uniqueness of one's partner, couples foster an environment of acceptance, promoting emotional safety and vulnerability.

Communication, a vital artery of any marriage, flourishes in an atmosphere of mutual respect. Spouses feel heard, understood, and validated, leading to effective conflict resolution and a deeper connection. Proverbs 15:1 speaks to the impact of gentle words, emphasizing their power to turn away wrath. Mutual respect paves the way for gentleness in communication, reducing the likelihood of hurtful exchanges.

Moreover, mutual respect is a key player in cultivating intimacy. When spouses feel respected, they are more likely to be open, trusting, and emotionally available. This intimacy extends beyond the physical realm, encompassing the shared emotional, intellectual, and spiritual aspects of the marital bond.

In conclusion, the significance of mutual respect in marriage cannot be overstated. It forms the bedrock upon which a healthy and thriving relationship is constructed. As couples embrace the call to respect and honor one another, they embark on a journey of profound connection, where love deepens, and the marriage becomes a testament to the enduring power of mutual respect.

Navigating Challenges to Mutual Respect in Marriage: Strengthening the Foundation

While mutual respect is a vital element in a healthy marriage, it is not immune to challenges that can strain this foundation. Recognizing and navigating these challenges is crucial for preserving the fabric of respect within the marital relationship.

Communication Breakdowns:

One common challenge to mutual respect is communication breakdowns. When spouses struggle to effectively convey their thoughts and feelings or fail to actively listen, misunderstandings can arise. These breakdowns may lead to unintentional disrespect, as one partner may feel unheard or invalidated. Overcoming this challenge involves investing time and effort in developing strong communication skills, including active listening and expressing oneself with clarity and empathy.

Differing Expectations:

Differing expectations can create tension and hinder mutual respect. Each partner may bring unique expectations about roles, responsibilities, or expressions of love and respect. Misaligned expectations can lead to unmet needs and feelings of disappointment, potentially eroding mutual respect. Addressing this challenge requires open and honest communication about expectations, allowing both spouses to understand and accommodate each other's perspectives.

Cultural and Gender Differences:

Cultural and gender differences can also pose challenges to mutual respect. Each partner may come from a distinct cultural background with varying beliefs and customs. Additionally, societal expectations related to gender roles may influence perceptions of respect. Overcoming these challenges involves fostering cultural competence, embracing diversity, and engaging in ongoing dialogue to understand and appreciate each other's unique backgrounds.

Balancing Individual Autonomy and Partnership:

Another challenge arises in balancing individual autonomy with the partnership. While mutual respect thrives on acknowledging each other's independence, finding the right balance can be tricky. Overemphasis on individual autonomy may lead to a lack of consideration for the needs of the partnership, while too much focus on the partnership may stifle individual growth. Navigating this challenge involves ongoing negotiation and compromise, ensuring that both spouses feel respected in their individual pursuits while nurturing the collective bond.

Addressing Past Hurts:

Past hurts and unresolved conflicts can cast a shadow over mutual respect. If either partner carries emotional baggage from previous relationships or experiences, it may impact their ability to trust and respect their spouse fully. Confronting and addressing past hurts through open communication, forgiveness, and seeking professional help if necessary can contribute to healing and rebuilding mutual respect.

In essence, acknowledging and addressing these challenges head-on is essential for maintaining and strengthening mutual respect in a marriage. By actively working through these obstacles, couples can fortify the foundation of their relationship and create a space where respect continues to thrive and deepen.

Cultivating Mutual Respect in Marriage: Practical Strategies for Strengthening Your Bond

Building and maintaining mutual respect in a marriage requires intentional effort and commitment. Consider implementing these practical strategies to foster a relationship grounded in respect and understanding.

Open and Honest Communication:

Encourage an environment of open and honest communication. Create regular opportunities to discuss feelings, expectations, and concerns. Ensure that both partners feel heard and valued, fostering a sense of mutual respect. Practice active listening, seeking to understand before being understood.

Establish Shared Values and Goals:

Identify and establish shared values and goals within your marriage. This provides a common foundation that aligns both partners, fostering a sense of unity and shared purpose. When working towards shared objectives, mutual respect is strengthened as you recognize each other's contributions to achieving common aspirations.

Set and Respect Boundaries:

Establish clear boundaries and respect each other's personal space and autonomy. Boundaries help define individual needs and expectations. Respecting these boundaries demonstrates an understanding of each other's autonomy, contributing to an atmosphere of mutual respect.

Prioritize Empathy:

Cultivate empathy by putting yourself in your partner's shoes. Understand their perspectives, experiences, and emotions. This empathetic approach fosters a deeper connection and appreciation for each other, reinforcing mutual respect.

Practice Gratitude:

Express gratitude for your partner's contributions, both big and small. Acknowledging and appreciating each other's efforts enhances feelings of value and respect. Regularly verbalize your gratitude and celebrate each other's strengths.

6. Seek Compromise and Collaboration:
When conflicts arise, approach problem-solving with a spirit of compromise and collaboration. Focus on finding solutions that honor both partners' needs and preferences. This collaborative approach reinforces a sense of equality and mutual respect within the decision-making process.

7. Maintain Individual Identities:
While fostering unity, recognize and celebrate each other's individual identities. Allow space for personal growth and pursuits. This acknowledgment of individuality contributes to a healthy balance between partnership and autonomy, enhancing mutual respect.

8. Continuous Learning and Adaptation:
Marriage is a journey of continuous learning and adaptation. Stay curious about your partner's evolving interests, perspectives, and goals. Embrace growth together and be willing to adapt to changes, reinforcing a commitment to understanding and respecting each other at every stage of life.

9. Regularly Check-In:
Schedule regular check-ins to discuss the state of your marriage. This intentional practice provides an opportunity to address concerns, celebrate successes, and ensure that both partners feel heard and supported. Consistent communication strengthens the foundation of mutual respect.

10. Seek Professional Guidance:
If challenges persist, consider seeking professional guidance. Marriage counseling or therapy can offer valuable insights, tools, and strategies to navigate difficulties, fostering an environment of mutual respect and understanding.

By implementing these practical strategies, couples can actively nurture a relationship built on mutual respect, creating a foundation for a fulfilling and enduring marriage.

Workbook-Cultivating Mutual Respect: Worksheet for Couples Page 220

The Essence of Empathy in Marriage: Fostering Connection and Compassion

Defined as the ability to understand and share the feelings of another, empathy forms the bedrock of emotional connection between spouses. In the dance of daily life, empathy allows partners to step into each other's shoes, fostering a deep and meaningful understanding.

Empathy goes beyond mere sympathy; it involves actively engaging with and validating the emotions of one's spouse. It is the compass that guides couples through the terrain of shared experiences, allowing them to navigate joys and sorrows with a sense of unity. By acknowledging and resonating with each other's feelings, spouses create an emotional bridge that strengthens the foundation of their relationship.

One of the defining features of empathy is its power to cultivate compassion within a marriage. When spouses make a conscious effort to comprehend and share in each other's emotional experiences, a compassionate atmosphere is nurtured. Compassion begets patience, kindness, and a willingness to support each other through life's challenges. This, in turn, leads to a more resilient and harmonious relationship.

Empathy is the key that unlocks the door to effective communication in marriage. When both partners feel heard and understood, conflicts are approached with a spirit of collaboration rather than confrontation. Empathetic listening allows spouses to express vulnerability without fear of judgment, creating a safe space for open and honest communication.

In the journey of marriage, moments of joy are magnified, and burdens are lightened when empathy is present. Celebrating victories becomes a shared experience, and navigating difficulties becomes a joint effort. The essence of empathy lies not only in understanding the spoken words but also in deciphering the unspoken emotions that reside in the heart of one's spouse.

In conclusion, empathy is the heartbeat of a compassionate and connected marriage. It transforms ordinary moments into extraordinary memories, for in the warmth of empathy, couples find solace, understanding, and the enduring strength to weather the seasons of life together.

Navigating the Challenges of Showing Empathy in Marriage

While empathy is a cornerstone of a healthy and thriving marriage, navigating its terrain comes with its own set of challenges. Understanding and addressing these challenges is crucial for couples committed to fostering a deeper connection and sustaining a compassionate relationship.
Communication Barriers:

- One common challenge in showing empathy is overcoming communication barriers. Misunderstandings, assumptions, or ineffective communication styles can hinder the accurate interpretation of a spouse's emotions. It's essential for couples to work on their communication skills, ensuring that their expressions of empathy are clear and genuinely understood.

Emotional Exhaustion:

- The demands of daily life, career pressures, and individual stressors can lead to emotional exhaustion. In such instances, spouses may find it challenging to summon the emotional energy required for empathetic engagement. Recognizing the signs of emotional fatigue and implementing self-care practices are vital in overcoming this challenge.

Differing Perspectives:
- Individuals bring unique perspectives, experiences, and emotional triggers into a marriage. Understanding and respecting these differences require intentional effort. Couples may encounter challenges when trying to empathize with emotions or situations that are unfamiliar or triggering. Patience, open-mindedness, and a willingness to learn from each other can help bridge these gaps.

Unresolved Resentments:
- Lingering resentments from past conflicts can create a barrier to empathetic responses. Unresolved issues may lead to a defensive mindset, making it difficult for spouses to genuinely empathize with each other's emotions. Addressing and resolving underlying conflicts is essential for creating an environment where empathy can flourish.

Cultural and Gender Differences:
- Cultural and gender differences can influence how individuals express and perceive empathy. Couples navigating these differences may face challenges in understanding each other's emotional cues or expectations. Open and respectful dialogue about cultural or gender-related perspectives can aid in overcoming these challenges.

External Stressors:
- External stressors, such as financial pressures, family dynamics, or health concerns, can impact a spouse's ability to express empathy consistently. Recognizing the influence of external stressors and finding ways to support each other during challenging times is crucial in maintaining an empathetic connection.

Lack of Emotional Literacy:
- Some individuals may struggle with identifying and articulating their emotions accurately. This lack of emotional literacy can pose challenges in expressing and receiving empathy. Couples can work together to enhance their emotional intelligence and create a safe space for emotional expression.

In the face of these challenges, a commitment to ongoing communication, mutual understanding, and continuous personal and relational growth is essential. Couples who actively address and overcome these challenges pave the way for a marriage grounded in genuine empathy and lasting connection.

Cultivating Emotional Literacy for Empathetic Connections

Emotional literacy is a foundational element in building empathy within a marriage. It involves the ability to recognize, understand, and effectively manage one's own emotions, as well as the capacity to interpret and respond to the emotions of others. In the context of marriage, developing emotional literacy is key to fostering deep connections and providing the necessary emotional support.

1. Self-Reflection and Recognition: Start by engaging in self-reflection to understand your own emotions. Take time to identify and label your feelings, exploring the underlying causes and triggers. This self-awareness lays the groundwork for recognizing and validating your partner's emotions.

2. Active Listening Skills: Strengthen your emotional literacy by honing active listening skills. Pay close attention to both verbal and non-verbal cues during conversations with your spouse. This includes observing body language, facial expressions, and tone of voice. Actively listening fosters a deeper understanding of your partner's emotional state.

3. Empathy Mapping: Create an "empathy map" by considering your spouse's perspective. This involves understanding their feelings, thoughts, and needs in various situations. Empathy mapping encourages you to step into your partner's shoes, promoting a more nuanced understanding of their emotional world.

4. Journaling Emotions: Keep a personal journal to track and express your emotions. Regularly jotting down your feelings allows you to process and make sense of your emotional experiences. This practice not only enhances your emotional literacy but also helps you stockpile empathy by ensuring you are attuned to your own emotional needs. Engaging in regular self-reflection and journaling provides a dedicated space for individuals to explore and understand their own emotions. By documenting thoughts and feelings, spouses can enhance their self-awareness, leading to improved emotional literacy. This practice encourages open communication about personal emotions within the marriage.

5. Seek Feedback and Communication:Encourage open communication with your spouse about emotional needs. Seek feedback on how well you are understanding and responding to their emotions. Creating a safe space for mutual expression fosters emotional literacy and strengthens the empathetic connection between partners.

Empathy Building Exercises:
Actively incorporating empathy-building exercises into the marital routine can strengthen emotional understanding. Couples can participate in activities that involve taking on each other's perspectives or sharing vulnerable experiences. These intentional exercises create opportunities to practice empathy and deepen emotional connections.

Regular Emotional Check-Ins:
Establishing a routine of emotional check-ins creates a safe space for spouses to openly share their feelings. Setting aside dedicated time to discuss emotions, concerns, and joys allows each partner to feel heard and understood. This practice fosters a culture of empathy and reinforces emotional connection.

Stockpiling Empathy:
Stockpiling empathy involves actively replenishing your emotional reserves so that you can consistently support your spouse. This can be achieved through self-care practices, maintaining healthy boundaries, and seeking emotional support from friends or professionals when needed. Just as you invest in your physical well-being, tending to your emotional health ensures you have the capacity to empathize with your partner.

Cultivating emotional literacy is an ongoing process that significantly contributes to building empathy in marriage. By understanding your own emotions, actively listening, and seeking to comprehend your spouse's perspective, you create a foundation for empathetic connections. Stockpiling empathy ensures that you approach marital interactions with emotional intelligence and a reservoir of understanding.

Workbook-Activity: Enhancing Emotional Intelligence and Empathy in Marriage Page 222

305

Embracing Humility in Marriage: A Transformative Pathway

Introducing humility into the intricate dance of marriage can be a transformative and enriching experience. In the context of marital relationships, humility takes center stage as a key player in fostering understanding, grace, and resilience.

Defining Humility:
At its core, humility involves a genuine acknowledgment of one's own limitations and a willingness to consider and appreciate the perspectives, needs, and experiences of others. In marriage, humility becomes a cornerstone for building a strong foundation, allowing both partners to navigate the complexities of life with openness and grace.

Transformative Impact:
The transformative impact of humility is profound. When humility is woven into the fabric of a marriage, it paves the way for a more compassionate and forgiving atmosphere. Instead of harboring haughty perspectives, partners are better equipped to approach each other's mistakes and shortcomings with understanding, patience, and a commitment to growth.

Conflict Resolution and Harmony:
Humility plays a pivotal role in conflict resolution within a marriage. Rather than engaging in power struggles or placing blame, humble individuals are more inclined to seek solutions collaboratively. Humility fosters active listening, a crucial element in understanding each other's needs and perspectives, thereby contributing to a more harmonious relationship.

Filtering Through Grace and Understanding:
In the journey of marriage, both spouses are bound to make mistakes. The lens through which these mistakes are filtered can make a significant difference. Humility encourages spouses to view each other's imperfections through the lens of grace and understanding. This shift in perspective allows room for growth, fostering an environment where learning and forgiveness thrive.

306

The Pitfalls of Pride and Perfection:
Conversely, pride and a pursuit of perfection can become silent destroyers of marriages. The unwillingness to admit fault or acknowledge one's limitations can create barriers, hindering the free flow of communication and understanding. Embracing humility serves as an antidote to these pitfalls, nurturing a relationship culture built on vulnerability, authenticity, and mutual support. In conclusion, humility is not a sign of weakness but a source of strength in marriage. It opens doors to deeper connection, compassion, and growth. As spouses embark on the journey of humility, they lay the groundwork for a resilient and thriving relationship that withstands the tests of time.

Overcoming Ego and Pride: Navigating the Path to Humility
Marriage, a union of two individuals with unique perspectives and backgrounds, often encounters the formidable foes of ego and pride. These adversaries can pose significant challenges to the cultivation of humility within the marital dynamic. Addressing and overcoming these barriers is crucial for fostering a healthy and thriving relationship.

Common Challenges Related to Ego and Pride:
Ego and pride, if left unchecked, can manifest in various ways within a marriage. These challenges may include resistance to admitting fault, a reluctance to seek compromise, and a general unwillingness to consider the needs and perspectives of one's spouse. These barriers can create a divisive atmosphere, hindering the growth and unity of the marital bond.

Strategies for Overcoming Personal Barriers:
Overcoming personal barriers to practicing humility requires intentional effort and self-reflection. One strategy involves cultivating self-awareness—acknowledging and understanding one's own triggers, insecurities, and defense mechanisms. By recognizing these aspects, individuals can take proactive steps to address and mitigate the impact of ego and pride on their interactions with their spouse.

Humility vs. Humiliation:
A crucial distinction to make in the pursuit of humility is recognizing the difference between genuine humility and humiliation. Humility involves a willingness to acknowledge one's imperfections without demeaning oneself. It's an act of strength that fosters growth and connection. On the other hand, humiliation results from subjugating oneself under demeaning circumstances. It's vital for individuals not to compromise their self-worth in the pursuit of humility, ensuring that they stand up for themselves and maintain a healthy sense of dignity.

Standing Up for Yourself:
While humility is a commendable virtue, it doesn't mean succumbing to unjust treatment or accepting humiliation. It's essential for individuals to stand up for themselves when faced with disrespectful or demeaning behavior. Setting healthy boundaries and communicating assertively can be crucial in maintaining one's self-respect within the marital relationship.

Seeking Professional Help:
In instances where ego and pride create persistent challenges in a marriage, seeking professional help can be a constructive step. Marriage counselors and therapists provide a neutral and supportive space for couples to navigate these complex dynamics, offering guidance and tools to overcome barriers and cultivate humility.

In conclusion, overcoming ego and pride is a journey of self-discovery and intentional growth. By addressing these challenges head-on, individuals can pave the way for a more humble, compassionate, and resilient marriage.

Applying Humility in Conflicts: Navigating Turbulent Waters with Grace
Conflict is an inevitable aspect of any marriage, and how couples navigate disagreements can significantly impact the health of their relationship. Applying humility in conflicts is a transformative approach that promotes understanding, empathy, and unity, even in the midst of turbulent waters.

Practical Ways to Apply Humility:
During conflicts, applying humility involves a conscious effort to prioritize understanding over being understood. One practical way is active listening—taking the time to genuinely hear and comprehend your spouse's perspective before expressing your own. This act of humility creates a space for open communication and fosters an environment where both partners feel valued.

Another strategy is to avoid blame and focus on shared responsibility. Humility encourages couples to view conflicts as joint challenges rather than assigning fault. By acknowledging each other's contributions to the disagreement, couples can collaboratively work towards resolutions that strengthen their connection.

Preventing Escalation Through Humility:
The role of humility in preventing the escalation of conflicts is profound. When both partners approach disagreements with a humble mindset, there is a reduced likelihood of defensive reactions and counter-attacks. Humility allows individuals to pause, reflect, and choose response that contribute to resolution rather than escalation.

A key aspect of preventing escalation is the willingness to apologize and seek forgiveness. Humility empowers individuals to acknowledge their mistakes and express remorse when necessary. Apologizing doesn't diminish one's value; rather, it enhances it by demonstrating a commitment to growth and relational harmony.

Transformative Power of Humility:
Humility possesses a transformative power that can reshape the dynamics of a marriage. It softens hearts, fosters emotional connection, and builds resilience. When couples approach conflicts with humility, they create a foundation for trust and mutual respect, allowing their relationship to weather challenges and emerge stronger.

Examples of humility in action include spouses admitting when they are wrong, expressing vulnerability, and actively working towards compromise. These acts not only diffuse immediate conflicts but also contribute to the overall strength and longevity of the marital bond.
In conclusion, applying humility in conflicts is a deliberate choice that couples can make to nurture a healthier and more resilient marriage. By embracing humility, couples create an environment where conflicts become opportunities for growth, understanding, and lasting harmony.

Nurturing Harmony Through Humility: The Path to Purposeful Unity
Marriage, much like a symphony, thrives when there is harmony between partners. Humility serve as the conductor, orchestrating a harmonious marital environment where mutual understanding and appreciation flourish. This connection between humility and harmony plays a pivotal role in ensuring that a marriage stays on track in pursuing its goals.

The Link Between Humility and Harmony:
Harmony in marriage is not a result of perfect circumstances but rather the intentional efforts of both partners to cultivate a balanced and cooperative relationship. Humility becomes the bridge that spans differences and unites individuals in their pursuit of shared goals. By embracing humility, couples create an atmosphere where each partner's strengths complement the other's weaknesses, leading to a harmonious synergy.

Fostering Mutual Understanding:
Humility fosters mutual understanding by dismantling the barriers of pride and defensiveness. In a humble environment, partners feel safe expressing their thoughts, feelings, and aspirations without fear of judgment. This open communication paves the way for a deepened understanding of each other's perspectives, needs, and desires.

One practical way humility fosters understanding is through empathy—the ability to step into each other's shoes and see the world from their viewpoint. This empathetic understanding creat a resonance that contributes to the overall harmony of the relationship.

Cultivating Appreciation Through Humility:

Appreciation is a key component of marital harmony, and humility plays a central role in cultivating it. When partners approach each other with humility, they recognize and value the unique contributions each brings to the marriage. This recognition fosters a culture of appreciation where both partners feel acknowledged and affirmed.

Moreover, humility enables couples to navigate challenges without harboring resentment. Instead of holding onto grudges, humble individuals choose forgiveness and grace, ensuring that past conflicts don't disrupt the harmonious flow of their marriage. Resentment, on the other hand, often stems from pride and can act as a disruptive force, hindering the pursuit of shared goals.

Pride and Resentment: Hindrances to Purposeful Unity:

Pride and resentment, if left unchecked, act as formidable obstacles to purposeful unity in marriage. Pride blinds individuals to their own faults and obstructs the path to compromise. Resentment, born from unresolved conflicts, erodes the foundation of harmony, creating discord that disrupts the pursuit of common goals.

By contrast, humility clears the way for purposeful unity. It allows couples to set aside personal agendas and work collaboratively towards their shared vision. In a humble and harmonious marriage, partners find strength in unity, ensuring that their collective purpose remains the guiding force in their journey together.

In essence, nurturing harmony through humility is a conscious and ongoing process that couples can embark upon to fortify the foundation of their marriage. By embracing humility, couples create a space where purposeful unity thrives, propelling them forward on a shared path toward their goals and aspirations.

Workbook-Humbling Hearts: A Self-Reflection Worksheet for Couples 224

Navigating Marital Waters: The Essence of Effective Communication

Effective communication stands as a cornerstone in the foundation of a thriving marriage, fostering understanding, connection, and unity. In contrast, defective communication can create rifts, misunderstandings, and unnecessary conflict. Let's delve into the distinctions between effective and defective communication, underlining the pivotal role of effective communication in nurturing a strong and resilient marital relationship.

Defining Effective Communication:
Effective communication in marriage involves the clear, open, and respectful exchange of thoughts, feelings, and information between spouses. It goes beyond the mere exchange of words; it encompasses active listening, empathy, and a genuine effort to understand one another. This form of communication fosters a safe and supportive environment for both partners to express themselves.

Significance of Effective Communication:
Effective communication is the lifeblood of a healthy marriage. It establishes a bridge of understanding between spouses, ensuring that both parties feel heard, valued, and acknowledged. It promotes emotional intimacy, laying the groundwork for a deep and meaningful connection. When couples communicate effectively, they navigate challenges, celebrate victories, and grow together, fostering a resilient and enduring bond.

Understanding Defective Communication:
On the flip side, defective communication involves patterns that hinder understanding and create discord. This may include ineffective listening, defensive responses, or the use of hurtful language. Defective communication can lead to misunderstandings, resentment, and a breakdown in emotional connection, eroding the very fabric of the marital relationship.

The Role of Communication in Building Resilience:
Effective communication acts as a vital tool for building resilience in a marriage. It allows couples to address challenges, express needs, and work through conflicts in a constructive manner. When spouses communicate effectively, they create a buffer against the inevitable storms of life, weathering difficulties together and emerging stronger as a united front.

Navigating Challenges in Communication: Building Bridges, Not Barriers
Effective communication is the lifeblood of a healthy marriage, serving as a vital bridge that connects hearts and minds. However, this journey is not always smooth, and couples often face challenges that can strain their ability to communicate effectively. Identifying and understanding these hurdles is crucial for building bridges, not barriers, in marital communication.

Ineffective Listening:
One common challenge in communication is ineffective listening. It's not merely hearing words but truly understanding the message conveyed. Often, spouses may be physically present but mentally distant, missing the nuances and emotions behind the words. Active and empathetic listening is key to overcoming this challenge, as it fosters a deeper connection and ensures that both partners feel heard and valued.

Hurtful Language:
The use of hurtful language is a potent weapon that can inflict lasting wounds on a marriage. Words have the power to build up or tear down, and when used irresponsibly, they can create chasms of pain. Couples must be mindful of their language, choosing words that uplift and heal rather than wound. Ephesians 4:29 encourages speaking only words that edify and impart grace, emphasizing the transformative impact positive communication can have on a marriage.

Satan's Interference:
It's essential to recognize that effective communication is not only a human endeavor but a spiritual one as well. Satan, the adversary, seeks to disrupt and divide marriages by sowing discord and misunderstanding. Being aware of this spiritual battle allows couples to approach communication with prayer, seeking God's guidance and protection against the schemes of the enemy.

Addressing these challenges requires intentionality, patience, and a commitment to fostering an environment where open and honest communication can thrive. As couples navigate these obstacles together, they not only strengthen their ability to communicate effectively but also fortify the foundation of their marriage, ensuring that the bridges of understanding remain resilient against the storms of miscommunication.

Navigating Communication with Wisdom: Insights from James 1:19
In the wisdom of James 1:19, a treasure trove of guidance is offered for navigating the intricate landscape of communication in marriage. The opening words, "Know this, my beloved brothers," serve as a clarion call to pay earnest attention to the ensuing counsel. Understanding that we are beloved by God, recipients of His unfailing love, forms the foundation for dismantling barriers to communication. When secure in our beloved identity, we can approach conversations with confidence, free from the shackles of resentment, insecurities, and defensiveness.

The scriptural formula unfolds with a threefold directive:
Be Quick to Hear:
The urgency to be swift in listening is a potent antidote to communication breakdowns. When spouses prioritize active and attentive listening, they open the gateway to understanding, empathy, and connection. The quicker we are to truly hear and comprehend each other's perspectives, the more profound the outcomes of our communication become.

Slow to Speak:
The injunction to be deliberate and unhurried in speech is a cornerstone of effective communication. Slow, thoughtful speech allows for measured responses, reducing the likelihood of misunderstandings and preventing the escalation of conflicts. This deliberate pace provides room for the Holy Spirit to guide words, fostering an environment of mutual respect and understanding.

Slow to Anger:
The wisdom of being slow to anger is a powerful prescription for marital harmony. It invites couples to refrain from seeking triggers or reasons for frustration, choosing instead a path of patience and forbearance. By cultivating an atmosphere where anger is not easily kindled, spouses can engage in discussions with a calm spirit, enhancing the prospects for fruitful dialogue.

In essence, James 1:19 provides a blueprint for communication suffused with wisdom, love, and patience. Beloved by God, spouses can embrace the invitation to be quick to hear, slow to speak, and slow to anger. As they weave these principles into the fabric of their communication, marriages are enriched, strengthened, and graced with the enduring bonds of understanding and connection.

The Power of a Soft Answer: Insights from Proverbs 15:1
Proverbs 15:1 encapsulates profound wisdom on the dynamics of communication, offering a timeless principle for nurturing harmonious relationships. The scripture asserts, "A soft answer turns away wrath, but a harsh word stirs up anger." This succinct verse invites reflection on the tone and tenor we infuse into our interactions, especially within the sacred space of marriage.

Operating at a Higher Frequency:
The call to provide a soft answer is a beckoning toward a higher frequency of communication. In a world often resonating with harshness, cultivating a gentle and soft demeanor becomes a transformative practice. Frequent communion with God throughout the day acts as a tuning fork, attuning our spirits to the divine frequency. This spiritual alignment empowers us to respond to life's challenges and relational dynamics with grace and gentleness.

Guarding Against Daily Frustrations:
In the hustle and bustle of daily life, it's easy to accumulate frustrations and grievances. Proactively tapping into God's presence ensures that we don't carry the weight of these challenges into our marriages. A softened heart, nurtured through continuous connection with God, positions us to respond gently, turning away the potential of wrath that may seek to manifest.

Choosing Soft Words Over Harsh Words:
The choice between soft and harsh words is pivotal in shaping the atmosphere of our relationships. Soft words, birthed from a cultivated relationship with God, carry the fragrance of love, understanding, and compassion. They have the power to de-escalate tension, fostering an environment where wrath finds no fertile ground to take root.

Capitulating Wrath for Life:
Wrath, when left unchecked, can capsize relationships, leaving a trail of destruction. A soft answer becomes a life raft, skillfully navigating the turbulent waters of disagreement and conflict. Choosing gentleness over harshness not only preserves the sanctity of our relationships but also contributes to the abundant life God desires for us.

In conclusion, Proverbs 15:1 extends an invitation to operate at a higher frequency, to guard against daily frustrations, and to choose soft words over harsh ones. Embracing this wisdom enables us to turn away wrath, ushering in a life-giving atmosphere in our marriages and families.

Constructive Communication: Lessons from Ephesians 4:29
In Ephesians 4:29, the Apostle Paul imparts profound wisdom regarding the power of our words and the impact they can have on the dynamics of our relationships, especially within the sacred covenant of marriage. The scripture admonishes, "Let no corrupting talk come out of your mouth, but only such as is good for building up, as fits the occasion, that it may give grace to those who hear."

The Essence of Giving Grace:
At the heart of this scripture lies the essence of giving grace through our words. Grace is an unmerited favor and kindness extended toward others. In the context of marriage, giving grace involves offering understanding, patience, and support to our spouses, even in the midst of challenges. It means acknowledging their journey, celebrating their victories, and embracing them with love, regardless of imperfections.

Guarding Against Corrupting Talk:
Corrupting talk extends beyond explicit negativity; it encompasses any dialogue that undermine the well-being of the hearer or contradicts God's redemptive work in their lives. As spouses, our responsibility is to be vigilant gatekeepers of our speech, ensuring that our words align with God's purpose for our loved ones. This involves refraining from sowing seeds of doubt, discouragement, or negativity that may hinder the growth of God's plans.

Speaking to Build Up:
The scripture advocates for communication that builds up rather than tears down. It encourages mindful selection of words that contribute to the edification and growth of our spouses. Constructive communication involves being intentional about the impact our words have on the hearer, fostering an atmosphere of encouragement, affirmation, and empowerment.

Fitting the Occasion:
Being attuned to the occasion means cultivating awareness in our communication. It requires a present and engaged approach, considering the context, emotions, and needs of the moment. Effective communication is not a one-size-fits-all endeavor but rather a tailored expression that meets the unique requirements of the situation.

Granting Grace to the Hearers:
The ultimate reward of adhering to the principles outlined in Ephesians 4:29 is the bestowal of grace upon the hearers. Our words, when seasoned with grace, become instruments of God's love and understanding. They pave the way for deeper connections, stronger bonds, and a marital environment where both spouses feel valued, appreciated, and accepted.

In conclusion, Ephesians 4:29 implores us to communicate with intentionality, refraining from corrupting talk and embracing a language that builds up, fitting the occasion. By doing so, we partake in the beautiful act of giving grace to our spouses, fostering a relationship grounded in love, understanding, and mutual respect.

Seasoned Speech: Insights from Colossians 4:6
Colossians 4:6 offers a profound insight into the art of communication, urging believers to let their speech always be gracious and seasoned with salt. This biblical guidance transcends mere language; it encapsulates the skillful practice of preserving and enhancing relationships through intentional, grace-infused communication.

Skillful Art:
Communication, portrayed as a skillful art in this scripture, involves more than the mere exchange of words. The call to let our speech be seasoned with salt invites us to approach communication as an intentional craft. Like a seasoned chef carefully choosing the right blend of spices, our words should enhance and preserve the relationships we engage in.

Preserving and Persevering:
Just as salt serves as a preservative, our words have the power to either preserve or perish. Speaking gracious and uplifting words can act as a preservative for the hearts and minds of our spouses. It guards against the corrosive effects of negativity and criticism, allowing them to persevere through life's challenges.

Adding Flavor to Dialogue:
The analogy of seasoning with salt suggests that our speech adds flavor to the otherwise mundane and routine aspects of our interactions. Gracious words enhance the quality of dialogue, making our communication more palatable and enjoyable. Just as salt enhances the taste of food, our words can enrich the essence of our relationships.

Answering Each Person:
The scripture emphasizes the need for our speech to be contextually relevant—seasoned in a way that aligns with the unique needs of each person. This tailored approach to communication involves understanding the individual nuances, concerns, and aspirations of our spouses. It reflects an empathetic stance that recognizes and responds to the specific needs of the hearer.

Empathetic Communication:
Practicing empathetic communication becomes the gateway to developing the skill of seasoned speech. When we empathize with our spouses, we gain insight into their emotional landscape, enabling us to respond with the grace and understanding that this scripture encourages. Empathy becomes the conduit through which our words can truly season the conversations we have.

In conclusion, Colossians 4:6 invites us to view communication as a skillful art, where our words act as both preservatives and enhancers. By seasoning our speech with grace and empathy, we add flavor to our interactions, preserving and elevating the relationships we cherish.

Here are examples of gracious and seasoned-with-salt responses in a marriage:

- Conflict Resolution:
  - Instead of saying: "You always do this, you never consider my feelings!"
  - Say: "I've noticed we've been struggling with this. Can we talk about how we both feel and find a solution together?"
- Encouragement:
  - Instead of saying: "You're so lazy; you never help around the house!"
  - Say: "I appreciate your efforts. Can we discuss how we can share responsibilities more effectively?"
- Expressing Needs:
  - Instead of saying: "You never spend time with me; you're always busy!"
  - Say: "I miss spending quality time together. Can we find a balance that works for both of us?"
- Apologizing:
  - Instead of saying: "Well, if you hadn't done that, I wouldn't have reacted that way!"
  - Say: "I'm sorry for my reaction. I could have handled that better. Can we talk about what happened?"
- Discussing Finances:
  - Instead of saying: "You're so irresponsible with money!"
  - Say: "Let's work together to create a budget that aligns with our financial goals. What do you think?"
- Supporting Each Other:
  - Instead of saying: "You never understand what I'm going through!"
  - Say: "I'm going through a tough time, and I need your support. Can we talk about how you can support me?"
- Expressing Feelings:
  - Instead of saying: "You're so inconsiderate; you never think about my feelings!"
  - Say: "I felt hurt when that happened. Can we discuss how we can better understand each other's feelings?"
- Gratitude:
  - Instead of saying nothing about a thoughtful gesture.
  - Say: "I noticed the effort you put into [specific action]. It meant a lot to me. Thank you!"

These responses incorporate grace, understanding, and empathy, contributing to an atmosphere of mutual respect and fostering positive communication in the marriage.

Emphasizing the Significance of Adaptability in a Thriving Marriage

Adaptability stands as a cornerstone in the foundation of a thriving marriage, offering couples the capacity to weather storms and embrace the sunshine together. It is a dynamic quality that allows partners to navigate the ebb and flow of life, reinforcing the resilience of their union. Recognizing its significance opens the door to a marriage that not only endures challenges but flourishes in the face of them.

Introducing the Idea of Growth and Change in the Marital Journey
The marital journey is an odyssey marked by growth and change. As couples embark on this expedition together, they encounter various landscapes that shape and mold them. Understanding that change is not only inevitable but an integral part of the journey fosters a mindset that positions couples to evolve and adapt, ensuring their connection remains vibrant and enduring.
Understanding Adaptability in Marriage

Defining Adaptability in the Context of a Marital Relationship
Adaptability in marriage is the art of navigating the twists and turns of life in tandem. It involves a conscious and flexible approach to the challenges and opportunities that arise, recognizing that each partner brings their uniqueness to the relationship. A marriage grounded in adaptability acknowledges that circumstances may shift, but the commitment to growth and unity remains steadfast.

Discussing the Role of Flexibility and Openness to Change
Flexibility and openness to change are the building blocks of adaptability in marriage. Being flexible means recognizing that plans may alter, expectations may shift, and both partners may undergo transformations. It involves a willingness to embrace the unexpected, fostering an environment where change is not feared but seen as an opportunity for growth. Openness to change cultivates an atmosphere where communication flows freely, allowing partners to navigate the ever-evolving landscape of their shared life. Together, flexibility and openness create a resilient framework that can withstand the tests of time, ensuring a marriage that remains vibrant and responsive to the journey it undertakes.

Navigating the 70/30 Reality: Embracing Adaptability in Marriage
In the intricate dance of marriage, there exists a reality often described as the 70/30 principle. This principle acknowledges that there will be seasons when one partner may need to carry a heavier load, adapting to the shifting dynamics of life. Understanding and embracing this truth is essential for building a resilient and lasting marriage.

I vividly recall a season in our marriage when my wife was expecting our daughter, Hannah. We found ourselves spending weeks in the hospital, navigating the uncertainties of pregnancy. During that time, the weight of responsibility fell heavily on my shoulders. I had to adapt swiftly, lifting the heaviest load of our marriage at that particular moment. It was a season that required flexibility, understanding, and a willingness to carry more than my fair share.

As life unfolded, my wife transitioned into the beautiful role of motherhood. Yet again, adaptability became paramount. I needed to adjust to the changes, recognizing that her role, needs, and priorities had transformed. This wasn't an isolated incident; it was an ongoing process of being flexible and understanding as we both evolved individually and within the context of our partnership. Marriage, in its essence, is a selfless sport, a league that demands teamwork and a deep understanding of the ever-shifting dynamics between partners. Being adaptable is not a luxury but a necessity. There will be times when the playbook you once relied on becomes obsolete, and you must learn new strategies together.

Moreover, life-altering moments may arrive, shifting the landscape permanently. What worked in the early stages of our marriage may no longer be effective as we continue to grow and change. Adapting to these changes is not just a choice; it's a requirement for a marriage that thrives. In conclusion, the 70/30 reality teaches us that adaptability is the cornerstone of a successful marriage. It's about being willing to carry the heavier load when necessary, adjusting to the changing seasons of life, and continuously learning and growing together. Embracing this reality ensures that the bond between spouses remains strong and resilient, capable of weathering any storm that comes their way.

Navigating Changes Together: A Journey of Growth
Marriage is a dynamic journey marked by various changes and transitions, a narrative that unfolds in chapters of growth, challenges, and shared experiences. Understanding the nature of these changes and learning how to navigate them together is crucial for the strength and longevity of a marital bond.

One significant change that couples often encounter is the arrival of children. The transition to parenthood brings a wave of joy, responsibility, and adjustments. From sleepless nights to the transformation of roles and priorities, becoming parents requires adaptability and teamwork. Navigating this change involves open communication, sharing responsibilities, and embracing the new identity that parenthood brings.

Career changes represent another common juncture in the marital journey. Whether it's a job switch, relocation, or a shift in professional priorities, these changes impact both partners. Navigating career transitions requires mutual support, understanding each other's aspirations, and fostering an environment where both individuals can thrive in their respective pursuits. The ebb and flow of financial circumstances can also introduce significant changes. From periods of abundance to seasons of financial strain, couples need to work together to manage resources wisely, communicate openly about financial goals, and support each other through financial challenges. This shared responsibility helps build resilience and unity in the face of economic fluctuations.

Health challenges, both physical and mental, are changes that can profoundly impact a marriage. Facing illnesses, injuries, or mental health struggles together requires empathy, patience, and a commitment to walk alongside each other through the healing process. Navigating health changes involves seeking professional help, fostering emotional support, and maintaining open lines of communication.

The empty nest phase, when children leave home, is yet another transformative period. Couples must rediscover and invest in their relationship, adapting to the newfound freedom and pursuing shared interests. This transition provides an opportunity for couples to deepen their connection and rekindle the romance that may have taken a backseat during the busy parenting years.

In essence, navigating changes together is about recognizing that the only constant in life and marriage is change itself. Couples who approach these transitions with a united front, open communication, and a commitment to mutual support are better equipped to weather the storms and emerge stronger. Embracing change as a shared adventure fosters a resilient partnership capable of thriving through every season of life.

Navigating Vulnerability in Times of Change: Embracing Adaptability and Trust in God
The vulnerability of relationships during periods of change and transition underscores the importance of adaptability and unwavering trust in God. Recognizing that adaptability serves as a shield against the unpredictability that change brings, couples can find strength in the third and unchanging cord of their relationship—God. Amidst the uncertainty, trusting God, the immutable rock, becomes a stabilizing force that guides couples through the challenges of transformation.

1. Vulnerability and Adaptability: Change introduces an element of vulnerability into relationships. It disrupts routines, alters dynamics, and exposes couples to uncertainties. In such times, adaptability becomes a cornerstone for navigating the unpredictable nature of change. Couples who cultivate a spirit of adaptability are better equipped to face the challenges, adjusting their expectations and responses as needed.

2. The Unchanging Nature of God: Amidst the flux of change, the unchanging nature of God provides a solid foundation. God is immutable, and His reliability becomes a source of comfort and strength. Couples can lean on His consistency, finding assurance in His promises and steadfast love. Trusting in God's unchanging character empowers couples to weather the storms of transition with a sense of stability.

3. Embracing God's Guidance: Change often leads to unfamiliar territories, and couples may feel disoriented. Trusting God involves acknowledging His omniscience and seeking His guidance. Couples can turn to God in prayer, individually and together, seeking wisdom and discernment as they navigate the unknown. Surrendering to God's guidance fosters a deeper sense of security and purpose.

4. Knowing God Knows the Way: In moments of change, uncertainty can breed anxiety. Trusting God involves recognizing that He knows the way even when couples might feel lost. God's omniscience extends beyond human understanding, providing assurance that He is leading them through the transitions. Couples can find comfort in surrendering their anxieties to God, allowing His peace to prevail.

5. The Third Cord in Marriage: The Bible speaks of a threefold cord that is not easily broken (Ecclesiastes 4:12). In marriage, this third cord is God Himself. During times of change, couples are reminded that their relationship is not sustained by their efforts alone but is securely anchored in the unchanging nature of God. Turning to God as the third cord reinforces their connection and resilience.

In conclusion, vulnerability during change is inevitable, but couples can fortify their relationship by embracing adaptability and trusting in God's unchanging nature. As couples navigate the uncertainties together, placing their trust in the third cord of their relationship ensures that they emerge from times of change with strengthened bonds and a deeper reliance on the God who remains constant amidst life's transitions.

Navigating the Rapids: Overcoming Challenges in Adaptability

Adaptability is a crucial aspect of a thriving marriage, yet it is not without its challenges. Couples often find themselves navigating tumultuous waters when faced with change, and understanding and overcoming these challenges is paramount to fostering a positive marital environment. In this section, we delve into common challenges against adaptability and provide strategies for overcoming resistance and maintaining a positive attitude.

1. Fear of the Unknown: The fear of the unknown can be a significant roadblock to adaptability. Couples may feel apprehensive about changes, especially when they are uncertain about the outcomes. To overcome this, fostering open communication and addressing concerns collaboratively is essential. Sharing hopes and concerns allows spouses to navigate uncertainties together, transforming fear into shared courage.

2. Comfort Zone Resistance: Humans naturally seek comfort and familiarity. Stepping out of the comfort zone can be challenging, especially when it involves adapting to new circumstances. Couples can combat this resistance by gradually introducing change, celebrating small victories, and reinforcing the idea that growth often occurs just beyond the comfort zone.

3. Communication Breakdown: A breakdown in communication can hinder adaptability. Misunderstandings, unspoken expectations, and lack of clarity can contribute to resistance. Establishing a foundation of transparent communication, active listening, and empathy helps mitigate these challenges. Regular check-ins provide opportunities to address concerns and align expectations.

4. Differing Perspectives: Couples may encounter challenges when their perspectives on change differ. While one spouse may embrace it, the other may resist. Bridging this gap requires intentional dialogue, seeking understanding, and finding common ground. Recognizing and valuing each other's perspectives fosters a sense of unity amid change.

5. Lack of Flexibility: Rigidity poses a significant challenge to adaptability. A lack of flexibility can hinder a couple's ability to adjust to new circumstances. Encouraging flexibility through practices such as compromise, understanding, and a willingness to adjust plans helps cultivate adaptability as a shared trait.

6. Past Traumas and Resentments: Past traumas or unresolved resentments can amplify resistance to change. Couples should acknowledge and address past wounds through open conversations, seeking professional guidance if needed. Healing past hurts creates a foundation for embracing change without the burden of unresolved issues.

In conclusion, adapting to change in marriage requires a concerted effort to address and overcome challenges. By acknowledging fears, fostering open communication, and embracing a mindset that views challenges as opportunities for growth, couples can cultivate adaptability, strengthening the resilience of their marriage in the face of life's inevitable changes.

Practical Strategies for Increasing Adaptability in Marriage

Adaptability is a key factor in building a resilient and thriving marriage. Here are practical strategies to enhance adaptability within the marital relationship:

- Open Communication:
  - Foster a culture of open and honest communication.
  - Encourage the expression of thoughts, feelings, and concerns without judgment.
  - Actively listen to your spouse, seeking to understand their perspective.
- Flexibility in Expectations:
  - Embrace the reality that expectations may need to evolve over time.
  - Be open to adjusting personal and shared goals as circumstances change.
  - Cultivate flexibility in roles and responsibilities within the marriage.
- Shared Decision-Making:
  - Involve both partners in decision-making processes.
  - Collaboratively discuss major life changes, considering each other's needs and desires.
  - Recognize that decisions may need to be revisited and revised as circumstances shift.
- Cultivating Emotional Intelligence:
  - Develop self-awareness to understand personal emotional responses.
  - Practice empathy to better comprehend your spouse's emotions.
  - Build a vocabulary for expressing emotions effectively.
- Mindfulness Practices:
  - Incorporate mindfulness techniques to stay present in the moment.
  - Practice mindfulness individually and as a couple to reduce stress and enhance adaptability.
  - Explore activities such as meditation or deep-breathing exercises together.
- Setting Growth Goals:
  - Establish both individual and shared growth goals.
  - Regularly revisit and revise growth goals as personal and collective circumstances change.
  - View challenges as opportunities for learning and personal development.
- Creating Rituals of Connection:
  - Develop rituals that foster connection and strengthen the marital bond.
  - Establish routines for checking in with each other during times of change.
  - Celebrate small wins and shared achievements regularly.
- Prioritizing Self-Care:
  - Recognize the importance of self-care for both partners.
  - Encourage each other to engage in activities that promote well-being.
  - Understand that self-care contributes to individual resilience and adaptability.
- Seeking Professional Support:
  - Consider seeking the guidance of a marriage counselor or therapist during significant life changes.
  - Utilize professional support to navigate challenges and enhance adaptability.
- Cultivating a Growth Mindset:
  - Embrace a growth mindset that sees challenges as opportunities for learning and growth.
  - View changes in circumstances as part of the dynamic nature of life.
  - Foster a shared perspective that encourages adaptability as a pathway to marital resilience.

By incorporating these practical strategies, couples can enhance their ability to adapt, navigate change, and fortify the foundation of a resilient and thriving marriage.

Workbook-Adaptability in Marriage Worksheet 232

NAVIGATING TOWARDS SHARED HORIZONS IN YOUR RELATIONSHIP

Shared Mission and Desired Outcome

Just as a ship needs a destination, marriages thrive when couples have a shared mission – a collective purpose that unites them in the pursuit of common goals. This shared mission becomes the wind in their sails, propelling them forward through the challenges and triumphs of their journey. It transforms the ordinary into the extraordinary, grounding the couple's odyssey in a shared sense of purpose.

Moreover, a thriving relationship necessitates a shared desired outcome. This is the vivid panorama that couples paint together, illustrating the future they wish to create. It involves envisioning the type of partnership they aspire to be, the family they hope to nurture, and the impact they aim to make on the world. This shared vision becomes a magnetic force, drawing them toward a future that aligns with their deepest values and aspirations.

Legacy Planning: Crafting a Lasting Impact

Legacy planning adds a profound layer to this odyssey, emphasizing the enduring impact a couple can have on future generations. It involves intentional choices that contribute to the legacy they leave behind – a legacy of love, wisdom, and shared values. A relationship without consideration for legacy is like a ship without a course, susceptible to drifting away from its intended path.

In the absence of a vision, relationships may perish. They risk being consumed by the routine and challenges of daily life, losing sight of the bigger picture. It is in this context that intentional navigation becomes paramount. Couples must actively engage in shaping their shared vision, revisiting their mission, and continually recalibrating their course toward the divine destination they aspire to reach.

Importance of Intentional Navigation

Intentional navigation signifies a deliberate and conscious effort to steer the relationship in the desired direction.

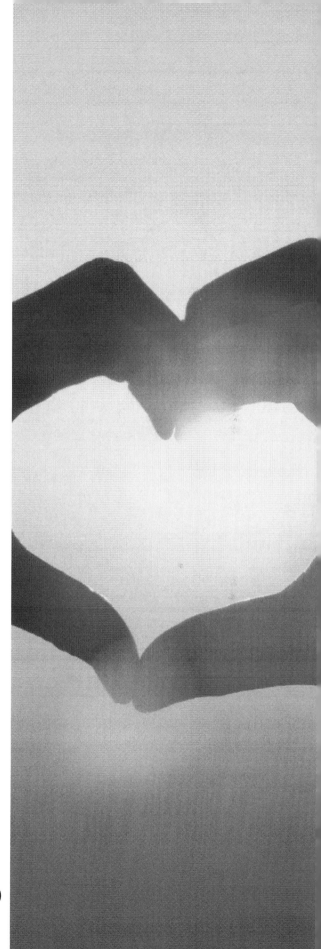

It involves regular communication, joint decision-making, and a commitment to growing together. Without intentional navigation, a relationship may succumb to the currents of life's challenges, drifting away from the shared vision that initially set it in motion.

In the following sections, we will explore practical strategies for couples to embark on this intentional journey, including legacy planning, treating their relationship with a strategic mindset, and developing mission and vision statements. As we delve into these aspects, let us keep in mind that a relationship without a vision perishes, but one with a shared divine destination flourishes with purpose and enduring love.

Navigating the Divine Destinies of Marriage: Unveiling the Journey
In the intricate dynamics of marital relationships, the concept of a "divine destination" emerges as a profound and spiritually charged notion. It signifies desired places, both figurative and literal, where God intends married couples to be fruitful, multiply, subdue, and have dominion for His glory. These divine destinations are not singular but myriad, reflecting the intricate design of God's plan for couples to traverse unique landscapes and explore specific waters in their journey together.

To comprehend the essence of a divine destination, it is imperative to recognize that these are not mere wishful destinations conjured by human desires. Instead, they are intricately woven into the fabric of God's overarching plan for couples. The scriptural foundation for this concept is rooted in the command given to humanity in Genesis, emphasizing the importance of marital unity in fulfilling God's purposes.

Moses, a towering figure in biblical history, serves as both an exemplar and a cautionary tale in understanding the dynamics of divine destinations. His journey, from receiving instructions at the burning bush to leading the Israelites through the wilderness, showcases the transformative power of obedience to God's will. Moses encountered numerous trials, confronted Pharaoh, witnessed miraculous plagues, and even parted the Red Sea. Yet, despite his remarkable achievements, a moment of disobedience cost him entry into the promised land.

Moses' story serves as a stark reminder that obedience to God's instructions is paramount in reaching the divine destinations set before couples. His disqualification from entering the promised land echoes a powerful truth – that windows of opportunity in God's plan can close due to disobedience. This narrative underscores the gravity of marital obedience, urging couples to take seriously the journey God has set before them and to navigate it with a collective heart that desires alignment with His divine will.

The warning in Moses' tale is not meant to instill fear but to emphasize the sacred nature of marriage and legacy. Couples are called to stay in the flow of God's purpose, ensuring that their collective obedience propels them toward the divine destinations God has ordained for them. The journey requires a commitment to remaining in His will, aligning their hearts with His, and actively participating in the unfolding narrative of their shared purpose.

In reflection, defining a divine destination involves contemplating the long-term goals and aspirations that align with God's plan for couples. It requires a heart that seeks His will, a commitment to obedience, and a recognition of the sacred nature of the journey. As couples embark on this odyssey, they are encouraged to stay attuned to the divine orchestrations of their union, ever mindful of the destinations that God, in His infinite wisdom, has set before them.

enerational Blessings: Transforming Legacies

the intricate mosaic of marriage, the concept of legacy planning extends beyond material ossessions; it encompasses the spiritual, mental, emotional, physical, and financial heritage passed down through the ages. While not everyone may come from a lineage of ealth, the wisdom embedded in a marriage can pave the way for a wealthy family to emerge. he scriptural wisdom that guides this notion asserts that a wise person, and by extension a ise marriage, leaves an inheritance for their children's children.

he sacred responsibility of legacy planning involves thinking beyond the immediate and onsidering the profound impact on future generations. It's an intentional and forward-inking approach that transcends the constraints of the present. Even if a couple has yet to elcome children into their lives, the vision extends to "children's children," reflecting the esire for a holistic inheritance that touches every facet of their descendants' lives.

ne biblical wisdom encapsulated in leaving an inheritance for "children's children" nderscores the divine intent for generational blessings to flow through families. It challenges e notion of generational curses and neglect, urging couples to become conduits of God's ansformative power. The goal is not merely financial prosperity but a comprehensive and nduring legacy that encompasses spiritual richness, mental fortitude, emotional well-being, nysical health, and financial stewardship.

od's design for marriage includes being proactive in breaking generational cycles of hardship, eglect, and spiritual poverty. It envisions a legacy where each succeeding generation stands n the shoulders of the one before, propelled forward by the collective wisdom, blessings, and re that flow through the family lineage. This intentional approach serves as a pipeline for lvancing God's kingdom on Earth.

the journey of legacy planning, couples are invited to see themselves as architects of a ture where their descendants inherit more than material wealth. They become custodians of narrative that champions spiritual abundance, mental resilience, emotional well-being, ysical health, and financial stewardship. It's a vision that aligns with God's desire for milies to be conduits of His transformative grace, ensuring that the ripple effects of nerational blessings continue to touch lives for years to come.

e challenge is not merely to accumulate wealth for personal comfort but to steward sources in a way that leaves an indelible mark on the history of family. The vision of a ealthy family emerging from humble beginnings is rooted in the understanding that true alth goes beyond the tangible; it encompasses the intangible richness that shapes the aracter and destiny of generations. As couples embark on the journey of legacy planning, ey embrace the sacred role of being vessels through which God's blessings flow, creating a nerational impact that echoes through the corridors of time.

orkbook-Legacy Builders Worksheet: Building a Lasting Heritage for Generations 234

321

Unlocking Family Prosperity: Building a Legacy through Entrepreneurship

In the intricate dance of life, many couples find themselves entrapped in the conventional narrative of working a job, earning a paycheck, and navigating the perpetual uncertainties of employment. However, there exists an untapped reservoir of potential within the sacred union of marriage – the creation of a family business. The concept of a family business extends beyond financial gains; it encapsulates the synergy of unique gifts, talents, and expertise that couples can seamlessly blend to build a legacy that transcends generations.

One of the most overlooked threats to a couple's financial stability is the unawareness of how their individual giftings can be woven together to form a robust family business. In the modern era, where job security is precarious, couples often find themselves one job loss away from financial vulnerability. While traditional employment has its merits, it lacks the resilience and legacy-building potential inherent in a family business.

The societal narrative ingrained in us from an early age emphasizes the pursuit of education, excelling within established systems, and funneling our skills into corporate frameworks. Yet, the hidden truth lies in the untapped potential within each couple – the capacity to birth and nurture a family business. Imagine a scenario where you and your spouse channel your creativit skills, and passions into a revenue-generating venture that you collectively own and operate.

In ancient times, almost every family engaged in a form of family business, serving as a safety net for provision and a means of bartering in times of hardship. Today, the idea of a family business serves as a beacon of financial empowerment and resilience. It's more than a source o income; it's a vehicle for passing down values, skills, and a thriving enterprise to future generations.

The Bible echoes this principle in its portrayal of inheritance. It states, "The inheritance of fathers is houses and wealth" (Proverbs 19:14). This inheritance, symbolized by lands and houses, signifies a legacy where children don't start from scratch. Instead, they inherit the fruit of their parents' labor – a family business that becomes a source of provision, stability, and generational wealth.

Creating a family business isn't just about breaking free from the cycle of job dependence; it's about constructing a robust legacy that ensures children and grandchildren won't need to start over. It's about sowing the seeds of entrepreneurship, resilience, and financial wisdom into the fabric of the family. The family business becomes a conduit for dreams, a reservoir of hidden wealth, and a testament to the potential unlocked when couples align their unique giftings in pursuit of a shared vision.

In essence, the family business isn't merely a revenue-generating idea; it's a paradigm shift, a journey toward financial independence, and a legacy-building endeavor that echoes through th corridors of time. As couples ponder their hidden wealth-building potential, they open the doo to a transformative journey – one where the entrepreneurial spirit within the family becomes a beacon of prosperity for generations to come.

Unlocking Purposeful 5-9: A Blueprint for Personal and Generational Wealth

In the rhythmic cadence of life, the conventional 9-5 job often dominates our daily existence, consuming the lion's share of our time and energy. However, within the margins of our after-work hours lies an untapped reservoir of potential – the transformative 5-9, where purpose meets passion, and the seeds of generational wealth are sown.

Understanding the Pivot: The pivotal moment arises when individuals recognize the need to pivot from a traditional 9-5 mindset to the entrepreneurial spirit of the 5-9. This shift is a conscious decision to leverage after-work hours for personal and financial growth. It's about acknowledging that true prosperity often lies outside the confines of a paycheck.

Learning the Marketplace: Purposeful 5-9 hours begin with dedicated learning. Individuals should immerse themselves in understanding the marketplace they aspire to serve. Whether through courses, books, or mentorship, acquiring knowledge during these hours sets the stage for informed decision-making and market acumen.

Becoming the Person for the Business: The 5-9 is the opportune time to invest in personal development. Becoming the person capable of running a successful business involves cultivating skills, refining leadership qualities, and nurturing the resilience needed for entrepreneurship. This transformative journey unfolds during these purposeful hours.

Creating Income-Generating Products: As the foundation is laid, attention shifts to crafting income-generating products. Whether it's a service, a digital product, or a tangible offering, the 5-9 becomes the workshop for turning ideas into reality. This is the phase where passion converges with strategy to birth a product that resonates with the intended audience.

Positioning for Impact: The purpose-driven entrepreneur seeks not only financial gain but also positive impact. The 5-9 hours provide the canvas for positioning oneself as a force for good in the marketplace. Engaging with the community, fostering relationships, and aligning the business with impactful initiatives become the focal points.

Primetime Family Hours: One of the invaluable aspects of purposeful 5-9 is that it often aligns with primetime family hours. These hours become sacred ground for collaborative planning and creation. Couples, in particular, can maximize this time to build their family business, nurture shared visions, and lay the groundwork for generational wealth.

Guarding Against Distractions: Distractions lurk in the form of entertainment, gossip, and the vortex of social media. Guarding against these distractions is paramount during the purposeful 5-9. The mantra becomes clear: while distracted, something is subtracted. Opting for intentional and focused use of these hours is a key to sustained success.

Maximizing Weekends: While the 5-9 may vary based on individual schedules, weekends emerge as a potent force for planning generational wealth. These days, free from the constraints of traditional work hours, offer extended periods for strategic thinking, collaborative efforts, and executing plans for the family business.

In conclusion, the purposeful 5-9 is not merely a time frame; it's a mindset shift. It's a commitment to investing in personal growth, cultivating entrepreneurial skills, and strategically planning for generational wealth. As the 9-5 may pay the bills, it's the 5-9 that has the potential to secure a legacy and redefine the trajectory of a family's financial future.

Workbook-Unlocking Purposeful 5-9: A Blueprint for Personal and Generational Wealth
Worksheet 240

Developing Mission and Vision Statements for Your Relationship

Proverbs 29:18 wisely declares, "Where there is no vision, the people perish," emphasizing the transformative power of having a clear vision. This truth resonates profoundly in the context of marriages and families – without a shared vision, the fabric of unity can unravel. Your decision t either envision prosperity or risk perishing is pivotal in shaping the destiny of your relationship.

Crafting a mission statement serves as the foundational compass that guides your relationship. Much like a ship needs a navigational chart to traverse the vast seas, a mission statement encapsulates shared values and purpose, providing direction even in stormy waters. It becomes the anchor that grounds your relationship in a common purpose, fostering resilience and unity during life's challenges. Drawing inspiration from Ephesians 5:2, a mission statement is an embodiment of sacrificial love, outlining the commitment to mutually uplifting one another on the journey of life.

Concurrently, creating a vision statement amplifies the power of forward-thinking. Proverbs 29:18's assertion finds resonance here – a well-crafted vision statement outlines the desired future for your relationship. It serves as a beacon on the horizon, drawing you and your partner toward a shared destination. This shared vision becomes the motivating force that propels your relationship forward, transcending daily routines and momentary challenges. It's a collective dream, a shared narrative, and a portrayal of the prosperous future you desire.

When developing mission and vision statements, consider the unique essence of your relationship. Reflect on the values that bind you, the purpose that unites you, and the aspiration that fuel your collective journey. A thoughtful mission statement becomes the moral compass, while a vision statement paints a vivid picture of the future you aim to build together. Remember the decision to craft these statements is a declaration of commitment to prosperity – a deliberate step toward a thriving, purposeful, and enduring relationship.

Defining Mission and Vision Statements for Your Relationship

Mission and vision statements are powerful tools that encapsulate the essence, purpose, and aspirations of a relationship. They provide a guiding framework, shaping the trajectory of your shared journey. Let's delve into what these statements are, what they do, and explore examples, including a personal vision and mission statement for a family:

Mission Statement: A mission statement serves as a compass, outlining the fundamental purpose and values of your relationship. It answers the question, "Why do we exist?" This statement encapsulates the core principles that guide daily actions, decisions, and interactions. A well-crafted mission statement aligns both partners toward a shared objective, fostering unity and purpose. It's a declaration of your commitment to the foundational principles that define your relationship.

Vision Statement: A vision statement is a forward-looking declaration that outlines the desired future of your relationship. It serves as a source of inspiration, providing a vivid picture of the aspirations and achievements you aim to realize together. While a mission statement focuses on the present, a vision statement paints a compelling picture of the future you wish to build. It ignites motivation, aligning both partners toward a shared, aspirational destination.

My Vision and Mission Statement for my Family:

Vision Statement: To journey for over 50 years in a marriage that honors God, marriage, and family. To serve as a beacon of hope and an example of love throughout the decades. To be steadfast stewards of our legacy and to be recognized as a family that mentors the next generation of families for God's glory.

Mission Statement: Each day, the Eze family purposefully engages in the transformative practice of love and stewardship. By embracing these principles, we ensure that our marriage becomes a living testament, continuously growing a legacy that is not only seen but deeply felt—a legacy that honors God and reflects the beauty of love, the wisdom of stewardship, and the prosperity that emanates from the heart of our commitment.

Workbook-Family Vision and Mission Statement Worksheet 243

Cohesive Merger: Unifying Family Core Values

In the intricate dance of family life, the cohesion of family core values forms the foundation upon which a resilient and purposeful home is built. Family core values represent the collective principles that the entire family holds dear. The intertwining of these values is a dynamic and essential process that contributes to the strength and unity of the family unit.

The Unyielding Importance of Core Values: Family core values serve as the compass that directs the choices and behaviors of each family member. These values are not mere words on paper; they are the embodiment of what the family collectively cherishes and upholds. In the face of challenges, they become the anchor that prevents the family from drifting apart. Therefore, the creation of core values is not a task to be taken lightly; rather, it is a profound undertaking that requires thoughtful consideration and introspection.

Creating a Sturdy Foundation: It is paramount to craft core values that are firm and unmovable, akin to the bedrock upon which a sturdy structure is built. These values should not be swayed by passing trends or external pressures. Instead, they should reflect the timeless principles that the family deems non-negotiable. The creation of such unyielding values ensures that the family is rooted in a stable foundation, capable of weathering the storms of life.

The Significance of Alignment: When family core values align seamlessly, a powerful synergy is unleashed. This alignment brings forth a sense of unity and shared purpose, fostering an environment where each family member feels seen, understood, and supported. It is not about stifling individuality but the connection of values that harmoniously coexist, enhancing the collective strength of the family.

Guardians of Identity: Core values are the guardians of a family's identity. They define what the family stands for, creating a unique signature that distinguishes it from others. As individual members contribute their personal values to the collective pool, a rich and vibrant synergy is created, reflecting the diversity and strength of the family's character.

Immovability in the Face of Change: In a world that is constantly evolving, core values become the immovable constants that provide stability. As circumstances shift and external influences ebb and flow, the family can rely on these steadfast values to navigate challenges with resilience and unity. They act as a guiding light, illuminating the path forward even in the darkest of times.

In essence, the cohesive merger of family core values is not a one-time task but a continuous process of refinement and alignment. It requires open communication, mutual respect, and a commitment to upholding the principles that matter most. As families embark on this journey of value creation, they sow the seeds of a resilient and purposeful legacy that will endure for generations to come.

Here are eleven core values every family can consider, along with sample core value statements that they can use or modify according to their own beliefs and preferences:

- **Reverence for God and His Principles:**
  - Core Value Statement: "At the foundation of our family is a deep reverence for God and His principles. We seek to align our lives with His guidance, cultivating a home where His love, wisdom, and grace prevail."
- **Love and Compassion:**
  - Core Value Statement: "In our family, we value love and compassion, treating each other with kindness and empathy, fostering a home filled with warmth and understanding."
- **Integrity and Honesty:**
  - Core Value Statement: "We uphold the highest standards of integrity and honesty. Our family is built on trust, transparency, and doing what is right even when no one is watching."
- **Faith and Spiritual Growth:**
  - Core Value Statement: "Our family is grounded in faith. We commit to growing spiritually together, relying on God's guidance and nurturing a strong foundation in our beliefs."
- **Respect and Appreciation:**
  - Core Value Statement: "Respect is at the core of our family. We appreciate each member for their uniqueness, honoring diverse perspectives and treating one another with dignity."
- **Communication and Openness:**
  - Core Value Statement: "Open and honest communication is a cornerstone of our family. We create a safe space for sharing thoughts and feelings, fostering understanding and unity."
- **Unity and Teamwork:**
  - Core Value Statement: "We are a united team. Our family values collaboration, working together to overcome challenges, celebrate victories, and support each other's dreams."

- **Generosity and Sharing:**
  - Core Value Statement: "Generosity defines our family. We joyfully share our time, resources, and love with others, recognizing the blessings we've received and extending them to those in need."
- **Gratitude and Positivity:**
  - Core Value Statement: "Gratitude is our attitude. We choose to focus on the positive aspects of life, expressing thankfulness for each other and the blessings that surround us."
- **Resilience and Perseverance:**
  - Core Value Statement: "Our family is resilient. We face challenges with strength and perseverance, learning and growing through difficulties, and emerging stronger together."
- **Quality Time and Bonding:**
  - Core Value Statement: "We prioritize quality time together. Our family values shared experiences, creating lasting memories through meaningful interactions and bonding moments."

Feel free to customize these core value statements to align with the specific values, beliefs, and aspirations of your family. Adapt them to reflect what matters most to you and your loved ones.

The Void Without Core Values: Navigating the Perils of Poor Values

In the absence of intentional core values, a family may find itself adrift in a sea of uncertainty, facing numerous challenges that can erode the very fabric of their unity. The importance of having core values as a family cannot be overstated, as they serve as the guiding principles that shape decisions, interactions, and the overall trajectory of the family's journey. Let's delve into the perils of poor values and the transformative power that intentional core values bring to family life.

1. Lack of Direction:
- Peril: Families without core values often lack a clear sense of direction. This absence of guiding principles can lead to confusion, indecision, and a collective sense of being lost. Without a moral compass, family members may make choices based on individual whims rather than shared values.

2. Fragmented Unity:
- Peril: Poor or undefined values can result in fragmented unity. When each family member operates according to their own set of principles, conflicts arise, and a sense of cohesion diminishes. The lack of a unifying foundation can strain relationships and create a sense of isolation within the family unit.

3. Vulnerability to External Influences:
- Peril: Families without established core values are more susceptible to external influences. The absence of a solid value system can leave the family vulnerable to societal pressures, cultural trends, and peer influences, potentially leading to decisions that do not align with the family's best interests.

4. Ethical Dilemmas:
- Peril: The absence of clear core values may result in ethical dilemmas. When faced with challenging situations, family members may struggle to make decisions that align with a shared moral framework, leading to internal conflicts and potential moral compromises.

5. Erosion of Trust:
- Peril: Trust is a foundational element of strong families. Poor values or a lack thereof can contribute to an erosion of trust among family members. When there's uncertainty about the principles that guide each person, it becomes challenging to build and maintain trust in the family.

6. Inconsistent Parenting:
- Peril: In families without established values, parenting approaches may lack consistency. This inconsistency can create confusion for children, who benefit greatly from a stable and predictable environment. Core values provide a framework for consistent parenting and a shared approach to nurturing and guiding children.

7. Strained Communication:
- Peril: Effective communication is essential for healthy family dynamics. Without core values, communication can become strained as family members may struggle to express their needs, expectations, and concerns in a way that resonates with others. Establishing values fosters a common language and understanding.

8. Missed Opportunities for Growth:
- Peril: Families without core values may miss valuable opportunities for growth. The intentional pursuit of shared values provides a platform for learning, resilience, and collective progress. Without this foundation, families may struggle to navigate challenges and capitalize on opportunities for personal and relational growth.

he Transformative Power of Core Values: In contrast, families with intentional core values xperience a transformative journey. Core values serve as a guiding light, illuminating the path orward and fostering a strong, resilient family unit. By embracing and practicing shared values, amilies create a foundation of trust, unity, and purpose that withstands the tests of time. The ourney of defining and living by core values is a proactive step toward building a legacy of trength, connection, and enduring love within the family.

Workbook-Family Core Values Worksheet 246

ere is a list of biblical core values along with references and suggested core value statements r families:

- **Love**
  - Reference: 1 Corinthians 13:4-7
  - Core Value Statement: "In our family, we choose to love one another genuinely, practicing patience, kindness, and humility. We believe love is the foundation that binds us together."
- **Faith**
  - Reference: Hebrews 11:1
  - Core Value Statement: "Our family places its trust in God, living with unwavering faith in His promises and relying on His guidance in all aspects of our lives."
- **Hope**
  - Reference: Romans 15:13
  - Core Value Statement: "We hold onto hope in our family, seeking joy and peace through our trust in God's plan, knowing that He is the source of our ultimate hope."
- **Humility**
  - Reference: Philippians 2:3-4
  - Core Value Statement: "In our family, we embrace humility, valuing others above ourselves and putting their interests before our own. We choose a posture of selflessness."
- **Forgiveness**
  - Reference: Colossians 3:13
  - Core Value Statement: "Forgiveness is a cornerstone in our family. We bear with one another, offering grace and forgiveness as we've been forgiven by our Heavenly Father."
- **Compassion**
  - Reference: Ephesians 4:32
  - Core Value Statement: "Our family is characterized by compassion. We are kind-hearted, forgiving, and seek to reflect the mercy of Christ in our interactions with each other and the world."
- **Integrity**
  - Reference: Proverbs 10:9
  - Core Value Statement: "Integrity is our guide. In our family, we choose paths of honesty and uprightness, knowing that a life of integrity brings security and trust."
- **Generosity**
  - Reference: 2 Corinthians 9:7
  - Core Value Statement: "We are a generous family, understanding that giving is an expression of love. We give with joy and cheerfulness, reflecting God's generous heart."
- **Justice**
  - Reference: Micah 6:8
  - Core Value Statement: "Our family seeks justice. We act justly, love mercy, and walk humbly with our God, advocating for fairness and righteousness in our interactions with others."
- **Gratitude**
  - Reference: 1 Thessalonians 5:18
  - Core Value Statement: "Gratitude is our attitude. In all circumstances, we give thanks, acknowledging that a heart of gratitude transforms challenges into opportunities for growth."

el free to use or modify these core value statements to align them with the specific values d convictions of your family.

Cultivating a Thriving Partnership: Embracing Teamwork and Mutual Support

Unlike a solitary endeavor, marriage is a shared journey where the success and growth of one are inherently linked to the success and growth of the other. Cultivating a mindset of teamwork within the union of marriage is not merely a choice; it is the cornerstone of building a foundation that withstands the tests of time.

Team Mentality vs. Me Mentality: The fundamental difference between a team mentality and a "me" mentality lies in perspective. A "me" mentality places individual needs, desires, and victories at the forefront, often neglecting the collaborative potential of a united front. On the other hand, a team mentality views marriage as a partnership where both individuals contribute their strengths, support each other's weaknesses, and celebrate shared victories. It's a shift from "what's best for me" to "what's best for us."

The Power of Teamwork: Teams, whether in sports or any other realm, achieve success through collaboration, coordination, and a shared vision. Similarly, a marriage that operates with a teamwork mentality taps into the combined strengths of both partners, creating a synergy that propels them forward. From navigating challenges to pursuing shared goals, the power of teamwork lies in the understanding that the success of the team is the success of each individual within it.

Every Home as a Winning Sports Organization: Consider a successful sports organization – a winning team is not just a collection of talented individuals; it's a group that operates cohesively, each member playing a vital role in achieving a common goal. Similarly, every home has the potential to function as a winning organization when teamwork becomes the heartbeat of the marriage. Roles are defined, communication is streamlined, and there is a collective commitment to the success and well-being of the family unit.

Prioritizing Emotional and Spiritual Growth: Teamwork extends beyond the tangible aspects of managing a household or pursuing shared goals; it deeply influences the emotional and spiritual growth of individuals within the marriage. Prioritizing emotional growth involves fostering an environment where open communication, vulnerability, and mutual understanding thrive. Spiritual growth, on the other hand, connects the couple on a deeper level, anchoring their relationship in shared values and a higher purpose.

In essence, cultivating a thriving partnership through teamwork and mutual support transforms marriage from a mere coexistence to a dynamic collaboration. It involves intentional choices, selflessness, and a commitment to the success of the team. As couples embrace the power of teamwork, they unlock the full potential of their union, creating a foundation that not only survives but flourishes through the seasons of life.

Team-Winning Elements: Translating Success from Sports to Family

In the playbook of a successful sports organization, certain winning elements consistently emerge, and these principles can seamlessly translate to the context of a winning family organization. Drawing parallels between the two realms not only reveals the common threads that underpin success but also provides a roadmap for families to build a resilient and thriving unit.

Good Owner (God): In the sports world, a successful team often has a visionary and supportive owner who sets the tone for the organization's culture. In the family dynamic, God assumes the role of the ultimate Owner – providing the overarching vision, values, and purpose. Aligning the family's vision with God's divine plan establishes a foundation for success, imbuing the family organization with a sense of direction and purpose.

Winning Culture (Kingdom Culture): A winning sports organization is characterized by a culture excellence, teamwork, and a commitment to shared values. Similarly, a winning family organization thrives on a Kingdom Culture, where love, respect, and spiritual growth form the bedrock. Infusing Kingdom principles into the family culture fosters an environment where each member is valued, contributing to the overall success of the family unit.

olid Coach and General Manager (The Holy Spirit): Behind every successful sports team is a olid coaching staff and general manager who guide, strategize, and empower the players. In he family context, the Holy Spirit assumes this role – providing guidance, wisdom, and mpowerment. Seeking the Holy Spirit's counsel ensures that the family is led by divine visdom, navigating challenges with resilience and unity.

roven Playbook (The Bible): While sports teams follow a playbook to navigate the game uccessfully, families have a proven playbook – the Bible. The scriptures provide timeless rinciples, offering guidance on love, forgiveness, resilience, and the foundations of a uccessful family life. Families that anchor their strategies in the wisdom of the Bible find nduring solutions to the challenges they face.

layers Bought into the Coach's System (Husband and Wife): A winning sports team thrives 'hen players fully buy into the coach's system, working together for a common goal. Similarly, ie husband and wife in a family organization form the core players who, when aligned in urpose and commitment, create a formidable team. Their partnership, rooted in love and nared values, becomes a driving force for the success of the family.

hampionship or Bust Focus: Successful sports teams maintain a championship or bust ientality, constantly striving for excellence. In a winning family organization, the focus is on ursuing spiritual and emotional growth, a resilient marriage, and a harmonious home nvironment. The commitment to a championship-level family life becomes the driving force ehind every decision and action.

ounce Back from Losses with Lessons Learned: In sports, losses are inevitable, but resilient ʾams bounce back, having learned valuable lessons. Similarly, challenges and setbacks are art of family life. A winning family organization acknowledges these setbacks, learns from ʾem, and approaches each new day with renewed determination and wisdom.

; families draw inspiration from the winning elements of successful sports organizations and ʾe proven playbook of the Bible, they discover that the principles of excellence, teamwork, ʾd a shared vision are universal. By aligning their family playbook with these timeless inciples, families can build a winning organization that thrives, not just for the present, but r generations to come.

orkbook-Family Championship Organization Assessment Worksheet 249

329

Engaging in a Family Championship Activity, encompassing elements like team name and mascot creation, designing family jerseys, setting championship goals, planning game nights, and hosting annual awards ceremonies, serves as more than just a lighthearted family pastime. These activities hold profound significance in strengthening the familial bond, fostering teamwork, and contributing to the overall well-being of the family unit.

1. Building Identity and Unity: Creating a team name and mascot allows each family member to contribute to the family's identity. This collaborative process fosters a sense of belonging and unity as every member has a stake in defining who the family is and what it represents. It's a shared endeavor that encourages individual expression within the context of a collective identity.

2. Expressing Individuality and Creativity: Designing family jerseys provides a creative outlet for each family member. It allows them to express their unique personalities and interests while contributing to a collective theme. This not only showcases the individuality within the family but also encourages a celebration of differences.

3. Goal Setting and Achievement: The concept of championship trophy goals introduces the idea of setting and working towards common objectives as a family. This exercise instills a sense of purpose and direction, encouraging family members to support each other in reaching these goals. Celebrating achievements with a tangible representation like a trophy reinforces the value of teamwork and perseverance.

4. Promoting Teamwork and Communication: A planned team-building game night serves as an opportunity for family members to engage in activities that promote teamwork, communication, and laughter. These games encourage collaboration, strategic thinking, and effective communication, fostering a positive and supportive family dynamic.

5. Recognizing and Celebrating Contributions: An annual family awards ceremony is a time for reflection and celebration. Recognizing each family member's unique contributions, achievements, and growth over the year reinforces a positive family culture. It cultivates an atmosphere where every individual feels valued and acknowledged for their role in the family's journey.

6. Creating Lasting Memories: These activities contribute to the creation of lasting memories for the entire family. Whether it's the excitement of choosing a team name, the laughter shared during game nights, or the pride in receiving a family award, these moments become cherished memories that bind family members together and contribute to the family's shared history.
In essence, the Family Championship Activity is not just about fun and games; it's a deliberate investment in the emotional, social, and psychological well-being of the family. It sets the stage for a supportive and thriving family environment where each member feels seen, valued, and an integral part of the team.

As we conclude this exploration into cultivating a thriving relationship with your spouse and family, my earnest prayer is that these insights and activities have served as a source of inspiration and motivation for you. I hope they have sparked a transformative shift in your mindset regarding the roles of husband and wife, leading you to aspire to create a winning culture within your marriage.

May these principles have provided a compass, offering direction for your marital journey and emphasizing the importance of flowing in the guidance of the Holy Spirit. While acknowledging that no marriage is perfect, my hope is that yours is perfectly positioned for growth, understanding, and love.

As we prepare to transition to the next chapter, focusing on the crucial aspect of raising and nurturing the next generation, consider the impact of creating a family culture where your children not only survive but thrive under your guidance. Your role as parents is pivotal in shaping an environment where your children can flourish, discover their potential, and grow into individuals who contribute positively to the world.

I am grateful for the opportunity to share in this journey with you, and I trust that the forthcoming discussions on family culture and child-rearing will further enrich your understanding and provide practical insights. May your family continue to be a testament to the transformative power of intentional and God-guided relationships. Until the next chapter, may your union be blessed with growth, joy, and an enduring commitment to each other.

RELATIONSHIP WITH CHILDREN

A Father's Perspective

I embark on this chapter with a heart filled with both excitement and humility. As of the writing of this book, I am a newly minted father to a beautiful daughter named Hannah, who, at the time of writing this section, is 18 months old. The principles and perspectives shared in this section are not just theoretical musings; they are born out of the practical journey my wife and I have embarked upon in raising our beloved daughter.

This chapter is a product of our intentional choices, prayers, and discussions about the values and environment we wish to cultivate for our daughter. However, it doesn't stop there. It extends to the hundreds of children, some connected more closely than others, whom I've had the privilege to guide, mentor, and be a father figure for, over a span of more than a decade.

Having counseled over 200 kids ranging from kindergarten to high school and maintaining close relationships with many who are now navigating the challenges of college and adult life, I've played a significant role in shaping perspectives on parenting. This section is not only informed by scriptural exegesis but also by the experiential reality of being a father and a father figure to numerous young minds.

As you delve into these principles, know that they are deeply rooted in a thorough understanding of scripture, a decade-long experience in counseling children, and the everyday challenges and joys of raising my own daughter. It is my sincere hope that these insights, reflections, and practical advice will serve as a source of inspiration and guidance in your parenting journey.

May these words resonate with you and bring clarity, encouragement, and wisdom as you navigate the beautiful yet complex terrain of parenting. Let us embark on this chapter with a shared commitment to raising our children in an environment where they can flourish and grow into the unique individuals they were created to be.

NURTURING A GROWTH ENVIRONMENT FOR CHILDREN

Setting the Stage: The Profound Impact of Parenting
Parenting, from a biblical perspective, is not merely a biological or societal role but a sacred and divine calling. It transcends the physical act of bringing a child into the world; it is a stewardship of a precious life entrusted by God. Understanding the gravity of this role is paramount, as it sets the stage for the profound impact that parenting can have on a child's growth and development.

Defining Parenting Biblically: From a biblical standpoint, parents are more than caretakers or providers. They are spiritual guides, mentors, and stewards appointed by God to nurture a child in the ways of righteousness and wisdom. The Bible teaches that children are a heritage from the Lord (Psalm 127:3), emphasizing the responsibility of parents to raise them in the fear and admonition of the Lord (Ephesians 6:4). This definition elevates parenting to a sacred calling with eternal implications.

The Goal of Parenting: The overarching goal of raising a child should extend beyond mere survival or conformity. It is not about impressing or imposing predetermined expectations upon them but about making a lasting impact. Parenting is a deliberate effort to equip children holistically, preparing them to leave the parental home and create homes of their own. It's about instilling a hope within them that extends beyond the confines of their immediate surroundings, influencing the world through their unique gifts and personalities.

The Challenge of Unqualified Parents: Unfortunately, in the contemporary landscape, the profound calling of parenting is sometimes undertaken by individuals who may not be adequately equipped or mature enough for the task. This is a pressing concern, as the impact of unqualified parenting can reverberate through generations. Children raised by individuals who are still grappling with their own issues may face challenges in their holistic development.
In acknowledging the profound impact of parenting, it is crucial to recognize the need for intentionality, humility, and a continuous commitment to growth as parents. The journey of parenting is not a solitary endeavor; rather, it is a collaborative effort with God as the ultimate guide. As we navigate the intricacies of this divine calling, let us strive to impact our children in ways that transcend the immediate and echo into eternity.

God's Perspective: Valuable Creations in His Image

Understanding God's perspective on children is foundational to effective and purposeful parenting. The Scriptures provide profound insights into how God views and values children. Let's explore three key scriptures that illuminate God's divine perspective:

1. Psalm 127:3 (ESV) - "Behold, children are a heritage from the Lord, the fruit of the womb a reward." In this verse, children are described as a heritage or inheritance from the Lord. The imagery suggests that God entrusts parents with the stewardship of His precious gifts. Children are not merely the result of biological processes; they are intentional blessings bestowed by God. Recognizing this truth shifts the focus from viewing children as possessions to understanding them as entrusted treasures.

2. Matthew 18:10 (ESV) - "See that you do not despise one of these little ones. For I tell you that in heaven their angels always see the face of my Father who is in heaven." Jesus, in this verse, emphasizes the significance of children by cautioning against despising them. The mention of angels assigned to children underscores their special status in God's eyes. Children have a direct connection to the heavenly realm, symbolizing their intrinsic value. This scripture reinforces the idea that God's view of children extends beyond their physical presence, encompassing their spiritual significance.

3. Mark 10:14-16 (ESV) - "Let the children come to me; do not hinder them, for to such belongs the kingdom of God." In this passage, Jesus rebukes those who try to keep children away, affirming that the kingdom of God belongs to them. He uses children as examples of the humility and trust required to enter God's kingdom. This scripture highlights the purity and sincerity inherent in children, qualities that God values. It challenges adults to approach God with childlike faith and underscores the Kingdom's openness to those with a child's heart.

God's perspective on children is clear throughout the Bible — they are treasured creations made in His image. The scriptures above showcase the divine intentionality behind each child's existence and emphasize the responsibilities and privileges associated with parenting. As parents, recognizing and embracing God's view of children provides a solid foundation for nurturing, guiding, and cherishing the precious lives entrusted to our care.

Adopting God's Views on Children: A Transformative Approach to Parenting

Understanding and adopting God's views on children is not merely a theological concept but a transformative approach to parenting that shapes the very fabric of family dynamics. Here are key reasons why it is crucial to align our perspectives with God's divine view of children:

1. Acknowledging Their Inherent Value: Embracing God's perspective on children acknowledges their inherent value as intentional creations of the Almighty. This recognition shifts the paradigm from viewing children as mere biological outcomes to understanding them as valuable beings entrusted to our care. Every child is a unique expression of God's creativity, designed with purpose and significance.

2. Shaping Parental Priorities: God's view on children influences how parents prioritize their roles. When parents recognize that children are a heritage and reward from the Lord, it reframes the priorities within the family. Parenting becomes a sacred stewardship, emphasizing the need for intentional guidance, nurturing, and the provision of a godly environment for each child to thrive.

3. Fostering Compassion and Respect: Understanding that children have angels in heaven and are under divine care fosters a sense of compassion and respect. It encourages parents to treat their children with dignity, recognizing the spiritual dimension of their existence. This perspective discourages actions or attitudes that despise or undermine the well-being of children.

4. Cultivating a Kingdom-Centric Environment: Jesus' affirmation that the kingdom of God belongs to children challenges parents to create a kingdom-centric environment at home. This involves fostering an atmosphere of humility, trust, and childlike faith. Aligning with God's view prompts parents to prioritize spiritual development and nurture the qualities that make the kingdom accessible to the young hearts in their care.

5. Guiding Through God's Principles: God's views on children, as revealed in scripture, provide a roadmap for parenting guided by divine principles. Parents who adopt these principles find themselves relying on the wisdom of the Creator to navigate the complexities of raising children. This alignment with God's perspective becomes a source of strength, guidance, and assurance in the parenting journey.

6. Promoting a Legacy of Faith: Adopting God's views on children sets the foundation for instilling a legacy of faith. It involves imparting spiritual truths, modeling godly character, and creating an environment where children can grow in their relationship with God. This legacy extends beyond immediate family dynamics, influencing generations to come.

In essence, adopting God's views on children is not just a theoretical alignment but a transformative journey that impacts parenting philosophies, daily interactions, and the overall atmosphere within the family. It invites parents to partner with God in the sacred task of raising children, recognizing the profound responsibility and privilege embedded in this divine partnership.

God's Original Design for Parenting: Embracing Biblical Principles

Delving into the pages of the Bible reveals profound insights into God's original design for parenting. From the creation narrative to various teachings and examples throughout scripture, the Bible offers timeless wisdom on the role of parents and the principles that guide the upbringing of children.

1. Stewardship of Souls: The Bible paints a vivid picture of parenting as a sacred stewardship of souls. Parents are entrusted with the responsibility of nurturing and guiding the spiritual, emotional, and physical well-being of their children. Proverbs 22:6 (ESV) encourages parents to "Train up a child in the way he should go; even when he is old, he will not depart from it." This principle underscores the lifelong impact of parental guidance.

2. Modeling Godly Character: Parents are called to model godly character, providing a tangible representation of faith, love, and integrity. Ephesians 6:4 (ESV) instructs, "Fathers, do not provoke your children to anger, but bring them up in the discipline and instruction of the Lord." This emphasizes the importance of nurturing an environment where children witness the practical application of biblical principles.

3. Teaching God's Word: Deuteronomy 6:6-7 (ESV) beautifully captures the essence of incorporating God's Word into everyday life: "And these words that I command you today shall be on your heart. You shall teach them diligently to your children, and shall talk of them when you sit in your house, and when you walk by the way, and when you lie down, and when you rise." The emphasis here is on an immersive, continual impartation of God's truth.

4. Disciplining with Love: The Bible advocates for discipline within the framework of love and guidance. Proverbs 13:24 (ESV) wisely states, "Whoever spares the rod hates his son, but he who loves him is diligent to discipline him." Discipline is portrayed not as harsh punishment but as a form of loving correction aimed at the child's growth and well-being.

5. The Blessings of Children: Psalm 127:3-5 (ESV) affirms the blessings inherent in children: "Behold, children are a heritage from the Lord, the fruit of the womb a reward. Like arrows in the hand of a warrior are the children of one's youth. Blessed is the man who fills his quiver with them!" This perspective shifts the narrative from viewing children as burdens to recognizing them as precious gifts and sources of joy.

6. Parenting as a Rewarding Position: Embracing God's original design for parenting transforms the perception of parenthood from a daunting task to a rewarding position. It invites parents to partner with God in the profound journey of shaping lives, influencing generations, and contributing to the divine narrative of family.

In conclusion, God's original design for parenting is rooted in love, stewardship, and the holistic development of children. It provides a roadmap for parents to navigate the complexities of raising children, imparting timeless principles that stand the test of time. Embracing this divine design positions parents to experience the profound rewards and blessings embedded in the sacred calling of parenthood.

Stewardship of Souls: Nurturing Lifelong Impact

Parenting, according to the Bible, is intricately woven into the concept of stewardship of souls. This profound responsibility involves being entrusted with the spiritual, emotional, and physical well-being of children. Imagine this stewardship as holding the delicate yet resilient fabric of a child's soul, a fabric that is shaped by the hands of those entrusted with its care.

Entrusted with a Soul: Being entrusted with a soul implies more than meeting the immediate needs of a child. It requires cultivating an acute ability to respond to the nuanced, intricate needs of a child rather than merely reacting to them. When parents prioritize their well-being, ensuring that their own emotional and spiritual needs are met, they are better equipped to attend to the unique requirements of their children. A nurtured parent can be a nurturing steward of a child's soul.

Training and Being Under Training: Proverbs 22:6 (ESV) offers a timeless principle: "Train up a child in the way he should go; even when he is old, he will not depart from it." Training involves intentional, purposeful guidance, imparting values and principles that shape the trajectory of a child's life. Yet, there's a reciprocal aspect to this principle — parents need to be under training themselves. A commitment to continuous learning and growth ensures that parents are equipped with the wisdom and insight needed to effectively train their children.

The Way They Should Go: The phrase "the way he should go" is laden with significance. It's not a rigid directive imposed on a child; instead, it's an invitation into a journey imbued with purpose and meaning. Parents are called to instill principles that elucidate not just the 'what' but the 'why' — why they should embark on this particular path. The current trajectory of a parent's life should align with the route they desire their child to take. It's about living out these principles authentically, creating a compelling narrative that beckons the child to follow.

Early Impartation and Lifelong Impact: Parents are tasked with instilling principles early in a child's life. The goal is to allow the child to witness the tangible, seen promises of these principles. When children can see the positive outcomes of values lived out authentically, it serves as a powerful motivator for them to embrace the same principles. The promise encapsulated in the verse unfolds over a lifetime — when they are old, they will not depart from these foundational truths. As parents impart wisdom, they set in motion a cycle of generational blessing where children become carriers of enduring principles, passing them on to future generations.

In essence, stewardship of souls in parenting involves a delicate dance of responding to needs, continuous training, guiding along a purposeful path, and early impartation of timeless principles. This stewardship is not just a duty; it's an invitation to be part of a narrative that spans generations — a narrative where children, equipped with enduring values, impact the world with the legacy of their upbringing.

Workbook-Stewardship of Souls Worksheet 251

Modeling Godly Character: Crafting a Positive Environment for Instruction

Parenting goes beyond laying down rules; it's a call to embody godly character, creating an atmosphere where instructions are received positively. Ephesians 6:4 (ESV) provides essential guidance: "Fathers, do not provoke your children to anger, but bring them up in the discipline and instruction of the Lord."

In understanding the emotional impact of our actions, it's crucial to evaluate the responses they provoke in our children. The link between our emotional state and their openness to instruction requires intentional consideration. We must strive to model emotions that encourage a receptive atmosphere, fostering an environment where they feel valued.

Reflecting on our temperament and parenting style is an essential step in transforming our approach. Considering how our upbringing influences our methods allows us to intentionally align our temperament with godly character. This transformation not only impacts our interactions but also sets the tone for the positive reception of instructions.

A key principle lies in building up our children before introducing disciplines. Creating an environment where they feel loved and valued ensures they are brought into disciplines willingly, understanding the purpose and benefits rather than being forced into compliance. As parents, our role is to guide, creating an atmosphere where disciplines flow naturally.

Imagine our children flowing into disciplines willingly, understanding the importance of aligning with godly principles. Fostering an atmosphere devoid of fear or resentment is vital. By emphasizing the positive aspects of learning and growth, we pave the way for our children to willingly follow godly principles, making disciplines a constructive experience.

The source of our instructions holds great significance. Evaluating whether our disciplines and instructions align with biblical principles or are influenced by personal opinions or cultural norms is crucial. Emphasizing the importance of aligning our parenting with the teachings of the Lord ensures that our children are guided by divine wisdom.

Lastly, our delivery style when communicating instructions plays a vital role. The patience, love, and compassion exemplified by the Lord should be mirrored in our approach. Striving to convey instructions in a manner that draws our children closer to God's truth ensures that our parenting reflects divine principles.

In essence, modeling godly character in parenting involves intentional self-reflection and transformation. Our temperament, emotional expressions, and delivery style profoundly impact our children's receptiveness to instruction. Aligning these aspects with biblical principles creates an environment where godly character is not just preached but lived out, shaping our children's understanding of faith, love, and integrity.

Negative Outcomes of Provoking Anger in Children: A Cautionary Perspective

Parenting, with its inherent challenges, demands a thoughtful and intentional approach. Provoking anger in children, whether through unchecked temperaments, a lack of emotional regulation, ineffective delivery, or a reluctance to apologize, can have profound negative outcomes. Here, we delve into the potential repercussions of such actions, urging parents to consider the long-term effects on their children's well-being.

1. **Strained Parent-Child Relationship:** Provoking anger creates an environment of tension and strain in the parent-child relationship. The child may perceive the parent as an adversary, hindering the development of a secure and trusting bond. This strain can persist into adolescence and adulthood, affecting the overall quality of the parent-child connection.
2. **Emotional Distress and Resentment:** Children who frequently experience anger-provoking situations may internalize feelings of emotional distress. Resentment towards the parent may build over time, impacting the child's mental and emotional well-being. Such emotional distress can manifest in various aspects of their life, potentially affecting relationships, self-esteem, and overall happiness.
3. **Inhibited Communication and Expression:** A child subjected to anger-provoking situations may develop a fear of expressing themselves openly. Inhibited communication can hinder the child's ability to share thoughts, feelings, and concerns. This inhibition may extend to relationships outside the family, impacting their social and emotional development.
4. **Behavioral Issues and Acting Out:** Children often externalize their emotional turmoil through behavior. Anger-provoking situations can contribute to behavioral issues, including defiance, aggression, or withdrawal. These behavioral manifestations are often a cry for help, signaling underlying emotional distress that needs attention and understanding.
5. **Impact on Mental Health:** Long-term exposure to anger-provoking environments can have a detrimental impact on a child's mental health. The stress and emotional turmoil may contribute to anxiety, depression, or other mental health challenges. Addressing the root cause of these issues often requires a concerted effort to change the dynamics within the family.
6. **Cycle of Negative Parenting Patterns:** Children learn from the behaviors modeled by their parents. If a parent consistently provokes anger without resolution, the child may internalize this pattern as acceptable. This learned behavior can perpetuate negative parenting patterns across generations, creating a cycle that is challenging to break.
7. **Diminished Self-Esteem and Self-Worth:** Children who experience frequent anger-provoking situations may internalize a sense of inadequacy. The repeated exposure to negativity can diminish their self-esteem and self-worth. This, in turn, may impact their confidence, resilience, and overall outlook on life.

In conclusion, the negative outcomes of provoking anger in children underscore the profound responsibility parents have in shaping their children's emotional well-being. By recognizing the potential consequences of such actions, parents can make intentional efforts to foster an environment of love, understanding, and emotional safety, laying the foundation for a healthy and positive parent-child relationship.

Nurturing Emotional Resilience in Children: A Call for Compassion and Understanding

In the complex landscape of parenting, it's paramount for parents to recognize that children, in their formative years, lack the emotional regulation skills that adults have developed over time. Children do not possess the cognitive tools to navigate and regulate their emotions with the proficiency of adults. Therefore, it is essential to approach parenting with an extra layer of compassion and understanding.

Children's brains are still in the process of maturation, and their minds are not equipped to manage emotional complexities in the same way adults do. Provoking anger or creating emotionally charged environments without offering guidance and support can set the stage for detrimental consequences. Children are vulnerable, and the impact of emotional distress on their mental well-being should not be underestimated.

When children face consistent emotional turmoil without the necessary support mechanisms, it can potentially pave the way for struggles with depression and even thoughts of self-harm. The emotional world of a child is intricate and delicate, requiring a parent's gentle guidance and nurturing. Parents play a crucial role in teaching children how to navigate their emotions, fostering resilience, and laying the groundwork for a healthy emotional life.

In light of this, parents are urged to exercise patience, empathy, and a deep understanding of their children's emotional limitations. By recognizing and respecting the developmental stage of their child's mind, parents can create an environment that promotes emotional growth, resilience, and a strong foundation for mental well-being. It is through this compassionate approach that parents contribute significantly to the emotional health and future success of their children.

Workbook-Parenting Reflection Worksheet 253

340

Checklist: Assessing and Addressing Negative Outcomes of Anger Provocation in Children

Parenting is a complex journey that requires constant self-reflection and adjustment. If you're concerned about the potential negative outcomes of anger-provoking situations with your child, use this checklist to assess and implement strategies for positive change:

1. Strained Parent-Child Relationship:
    o Assessment: Notice any tension or strain in your relationship with your child.
    o Strategy: Prioritize one-on-one time with your child, engage in activities they enjoy, and foster open communication. Seek professional help if needed.
2. Emotional Distress and Resentment:
    o Assessment: Observe signs of emotional distress or resentment in your child.
    o Strategy: Create a safe space for your child to express emotions. Apologize when necessary and engage in open dialogue to address and heal emotional wounds.
3. Inhibited Communication and Expression:
    o Assessment: Evaluate your child's willingness to express themselves openly.
    o Strategy: Encourage open communication, actively listen, and validate their feelings. Be approachable and willing to discuss any concerns or issues.
4. Behavioral Issues and Acting Out:
    o Assessment: Monitor your child's behavior for signs of distress or acting out.
    o Strategy: Implement consistent and fair discipline, emphasizing positive reinforcement. Seek professional guidance to understand and address underlying emotional challenges.
5. Impact on Mental Health:
    o Assessment: Be attentive to signs of anxiety, depression, or mental health struggles.
    o Strategy: Prioritize your child's mental well-being. Consider therapy or counseling to address deeper emotional issues and work towards creating a supportive environment.
6. Cycle of Negative Parenting Patterns:
    o Assessment: Reflect on your parenting patterns and their potential impact on your child.
    o Strategy: Break the cycle by seeking guidance from parenting resources, attending parenting classes, and fostering a commitment to positive change.
7. Diminished Self-Esteem and Self-Worth:
    o Assessment: Gauge your child's self-esteem and confidence levels.
    o Strategy: Encourage and affirm your child regularly. Provide opportunities for them to excel and showcase their unique talents. Be intentional about building their self-worth.

Remember, as a parent, it's never too late to make positive changes. Consistent efforts to create a loving, understanding, and emotionally safe environment can have a profound impact your child's well-being and the overall dynamics of your parent-child relationship.

The power of a sincere apology, coupled with adjusted behavior, holds transformative potential in a child's life. Apologizing to a child demonstrates humility and acknowledges their emotions, fostering a sense of respect and understanding. However, the true impact lies the commitment to changed behavior that follows the apology. It's not merely about saying sorry; it's about actively showing remorse through actions. Children are perceptive and intuitive, and they internalize the authenticity of an apology by observing the adjustments in parent's behavior. When a parent takes responsibility for their actions, articulates a genuine apology, and then consistently modifies their behavior to align with their words, a profound shift occurs in the child's perception. They learn that mistakes are part of the human experience, but accountability, sincere apologies, and intentional changes are the keys to growth and emotional resilience. This process instills in children a sense of security, trust, and the belief that they are valued and respected. A well-executed apology, coupled with sustained behavioral adjustments, becomes a powerful tool for teaching children about empathy, forgiveness, and the capacity for positive change in relationships. It creates a foundation for healthy emotional development, fostering a culture of openness and understanding within the parent-child dynamic.

Workbook-Apology and Behavior Adjustment Worksheet 256

Foundations of Faith: Diligently Teaching God's Truth to the Next Generation
In the profound wisdom of Deuteronomy 6:6-7 (ESV), the Scriptures unveil a timeless directive for parents, guiding them on the path of imparting God's truth to their children. The commandment emphasizes the centrality of God's words, urging parents to internalize these truths within their hearts. The journey begins with a personal commitment to live out the commandments and statutes of the Lord, serving as a living testimony to the transformative power of God's Word.

The foundational principle lies in instilling the fear of the Lord, a reverential awe and respect for His divine authority. This fear is not born out of dread but out of an understanding of His wisdom, love, and sovereignty. Teaching children to keep the commandments becomes a holistic endeavor, encompassing not just the adherence to rules but the cultivation of a heart posture that aligns with God's principles.

Verses 4-5 further enrich the teaching, encapsulating the fundamental truth of the oneness of God and the wholehearted love and devotion owed to Him. As parents, the responsibility is not merely to instruct but to reveal the nature and character of God through their lives. Children are to see in their parents a reflection of God's oneness, love, and undivided devotion.

The manner in which this teaching is to be carried out is marked by diligence and continuity. It extends beyond formal instruction to a seamless integration into daily life. Whether sitting in the house, walking along the way, lying down, or rising, the conversation and demonstration of God's truth should be woven into the fabric of every moment. Repetition becomes a key ally in the learning process, reinforcing God's principles in the hearts and minds of children.

This immersive approach does not advocate for a forced religion but rather a flowing relationship with God. Parents are called to walk in the Spirit, demonstrating a life led by God's wisdom and anointing. When discussions about God are infused with the power of the Holy Spirit, children witness not just words but a tangible manifestation of God's presence. The fruit of this diligent teaching becomes evident in the character, decisions, and choices of both parents and children.

In essence, Deuteronomy beckons parents to embark on a journey of holistic and continuous spiritual education, where the fear of the Lord, love for His commandments, and the revelation His character shape the very essence of family life. The promise echoes through the ages – a life well-lived in obedience to God's principles, ensuring not only longevity but a flourishing legacy that echoes the goodness of the Lord.

Reflection Questions
1. How can you ensure that the teachings and commandments of the Lord are consistently on your heart and mind?
2. In what practical ways can you diligently incorporate God's truth into everyday life, especially when interacting with your children?
3. Reflect on your own journey of fearing the Lord and keeping His commandments. How can you model and share this reverence for God with your children?

avigating the landscape of discipline when it comes to parenting has, unfortunately, led to vo extremes. On one side, there's the risk of abusive practices, where discipline morphs to harmful actions that leave lasting scars on a child's physical and emotional well-being. n the other side, the pendulum can swing towards sparing the rod to an extent that it sters an environment of rebellion, as the absence of structure and correction fails to still essential values and boundaries. Striking a balance is crucial, and it begins with the cognition that effective discipline is not a one-size-fits-all approach.

isciplining with love implies a comprehensive understanding of the term "discipline" self. It involves cultivating a disciplined mindset within parents before addressing the havior of their children. Physical discipline, while permissible, should always be veloped in love, ensuring that correction is constructive rather than punitive. The notion "sparing the rod" is not a call to abstain from correction but an encouragement to correct ligently, with a focus on the child's overall well-being.

key aspect of disciplining with love is self-discipline on the part of parents. This involves notional regulation, avoiding unrealistic expectations, and practicing empathy. Before any rm of correction is administered, it's vital for parents to reflect on their own emotional ate, ensuring that the response is rooted in love rather than frustration. Unrealistic pectations can lead to unfair punishments, and attempting to live vicariously through a ild's achievements can cloud the judgment of what is genuinely beneficial for them.

timately, the goal of disciplining with love is to create an atmosphere where correction is act of love, not an expression of anger or control. It is about guiding a child toward derstanding the consequences of their actions, fostering growth, and building character. approaching discipline with diligence, self-awareness, and an unwavering commitment the well-being of the child, parents can embody the biblical principle of disciplining th love, leaving a lasting impact on their child's development.

ltivating Positive Behavior: The Parental Influence

rental behavior plays a pivotal role in shaping the conduct and demeanor of children. ten, negative behaviors in children can be traced back to patterns or actions within the me environment. Recognizing and addressing these contributing factors is essential for ltivating positive behavior in children. Here are five common parental behaviors that can rease negative behavior in children:

.Neglect or Lack of Attention:
  o Children crave attention and connection with their parents. When parents are consistently absent or preoccupied, children may resort to negative behaviors as a way to seek attention, even if it's negative attention. Quality time and genuine engagement are vital for fostering positive behavior.

.Inconsistency in Discipline:
  o Inconsistency in enforcing rules and consequences can lead to confusion and frustration for children. When rules are not consistently applied, children may exhibit negative behaviors as they test boundaries. Establishing clear and consistent expectations provides a stable foundation for positive behavior.

.Disrespectful Communication:
  o The way parents communicate with each other and with their children sets a powerful example. Disrespectful or aggressive communication styles can be mirrored by children, contributing to negative behavior. Creating a culture of respectful and open communication fosters a healthier emotional environment.

Modeling Negative Coping Mechanisms:
  o Children observe and mimic the coping mechanisms of their parents. If parents resort to negative ways of handling stress, conflict, or emotions, children may adopt similar methods. Modeling healthy coping strategies and emotional regulation is crucial for encouraging positive behavior.

Unrealistic Expectations:
  o Setting expectations that are too high or unrealistic for a child's developmental stage can lead to frustration and negative behavior. Children need age-appropriate challenges and gradual growth. Unrealistic expectations may result in feelings of inadequacy and manifest as challenging behaviors.

343

Addressing these behaviors requires self-awareness and a commitment to creating a positive an nurturing home environment. By fostering open communication, providing consistent discipline, and modeling healthy behaviors, parents can significantly influence and shape positive conduct in their children.

1. Self-Reflection on Attention and Connection:
   o How often do I intentionally set aside quality time to engage with my child without distractions?
   o In what ways can I enhance my presence and attentiveness during interactions with my child?
2. Evaluation of Consistency in Discipline:
   o Am I consistent in enforcing rules and consequences within the household?
   o How can I establish clearer expectations and maintain consistency in disciplining my child?
3. Assessment of Communication Styles:
   o What communication patterns do I model for my child, especially during moments of stress or conflict?
   o How can I improve and model respectful communication within the family?
4. Exploration of Coping Mechanisms:
   o Have I noticed any negative coping mechanisms in my child that may mirror my own behaviors?
   o What positive coping strategies can I demonstrate and encourage to promote emotional well-being?
5. Reflection on Realistic Expectations:
   o Are my expectations aligned with my child's developmental stage, and are they realistic?
   o How can I adjust my expectations to provide age-appropriate challenges for my child's growth?

These reflection questions are designed to encourage self-awareness and contemplation on specific aspects of parenting that influence a child's behavior. Taking the time to reflect on these questions can guide parents in fostering a more positive and supportive home environment.

Workbook-Before You Discipline Worksheet 257

The Joy Of Children

Children, as described in Psalm 127:3-5 (ESV), are indeed a heritage and reward from the Lord, contributing immeasurable blessings to the lives of their parents. A parent's perspective on their child plays a pivotal role in shaping the dynamics of the parent-child relationship and influencing the child's development. Here are five ways children are a blessing to parents who, in turn, bless their children:

1. **Joy and Fulfillment:**
   - Children bring immeasurable joy and fulfillment to their parents. Their laughter, curiosity, and unique personalities infuse life with moments of happiness and wonder. A parent's ability to appreciate and savor these joyful experiences enhances the overall well-being of the family.

2. **Purpose and Meaning:**
   - Parenting instills a profound sense of purpose and meaning in the lives of parents. Nurturing and guiding a child through various stages of growth contribute to a deeper understanding of one's role in shaping the future. The journey of parenthood brings a sense of significance and legacy.

3. **Unconditional Love and Connection:**
   - Children have a remarkable capacity to evoke unconditional love in their parents. The bond forged between parent and child creates a connection that withstands challenges and endures throughout a lifetime. This depth of love fosters emotional resilience and support within the family.

4. **Learning and Growth:**
   - Parents often experience personal growth and self-discovery through the challenges and joys of parenting. The responsibility of guiding a child's development encourages continuous learning, adaptability, and the acquisition of new skills. This dynamic process of learning and growing together strengthens the parent-child relationship.

5. **Legacy and Impact:**
   - Children represent a legacy and the opportunity to make a positive impact on future generations. Parents who invest time, wisdom, and love into their children contribute to a legacy that extends beyond their own lives. The values, principles, and lessons imparted to children become a lasting testament to the impact of intentional parenting.

6. **Reciprocal Care in Old Age:**
   - The kindness and care extended to children during their formative years often result in reciprocal gestures of love and support as parents age. A foundation of respect and compassion built through positive interactions pays dividends in later years. Children who have experienced genuine care and affection are more likely to reciprocate by providing emotional and physical support to their aging parents. This reciprocal care becomes a source of comfort and companionship, fostering a harmonious relationship between parents and adult children in the later stages of life.

Embracing the blessings of children involves adopting a perspective that values the unique contributions each child brings to the family. As parents recognize and celebrate these blessings, they create an environment where their children, in turn, feel valued, loved, and equipped to navigate life's journey. The reciprocal nature of blessings between parents and children establishes a foundation for a flourishing and harmonious family life.

Threads of Influence: Navigating the Impact of Childhood Experiences on Parenting
As parents, we are not detached entities; rather, we are products of the very formative years that shaped our worldview, values, and coping mechanisms. The impact of our upbringing resonates in the way we parent, often revealing itself in both subtle nuances and overt patterns.

Understanding Parental Influence: Our childhood experiences, be they nurturing or challenging, hold a powerful sway over the dynamics of our own families. The echoes of how we were raised manifest in our parenting styles, shaping the atmosphere we cultivate for our children. It's a reflection of the lessons learned, the wounds endured, and the coping mechanisms developed during our early years.

The Unseen Threads: Sometimes, the influence of our past is subtle, like an unseen current guiding the course of a river. Our attitudes, communication styles, and responses to challenges are often deeply ingrained patterns inherited from our own upbringing. These unseen threads intertwine with our interactions with our children, subtly molding their perceptions, emotional responses, and understanding of the world.

Healing for the Sake of Generations: Many parents carry wounds from their formative years, wounds that have yet to heal. Unresolved issues from childhood can inadvertently perpetuate cycles of toxicity, passing down patterns that echo through generations. Without intentional healing, parents risk subjecting their children to the shadows of their own unaddressed traumas.

Intentional Healing as a Parental Duty: Recognizing the potential impact of our childhood experiences is the first step towards intentional healing. It requires a courageous exploration of our own narratives, acknowledging both the strengths and vulnerabilities shaped by our upbringing. As parents, we carry the responsibility of breaking the chains of negative patterns, ensuring that our children inherit a legacy of resilience, understanding, and love.

Breaking the Chains: Healing is not only a personal journey but a profound gift to the next generation. It involves breaking the chains of negative cycles, consciously choosing a different path for our children. By addressing our own wounds, we create a space for our children to thrive, unburdened by the weight of unresolved traumas.

In essence, reflecting on personal experiences is not a nostalgic exercise; it's a deliberate act of breaking free from the shackles of the past. As parents, we have the power to rewrite the narrative, to heal and create an environment where our children's childhoods are marked by love, resilience, and the freedom to forge their own paths. The journey of healing is not only a gift to ourselves but a legacy of strength and wholeness for the generations that follow.

Unraveling the Past: Breaking Free from the Chains of Childhood Wounds in Parenting"
The journey towards effective and compassionate parenting necessitates the courageous act of identifying patterns and wounds from past experiences. Satan, ever cunning in his schemes, strategically targets the formative years, seeking to sow seeds of discord and pain that can manifest in destructive patterns in adulthood.

The impact of personal history on parenting styles is profound, and Satan's malevolent strategy becomes evident as parents unwittingly perpetuate the wounds they themselves endured during the crucial years from 0 to 12. Recognizing the vulnerability of children during this formative period, Satan aims to inflict as many wounds as possible, knowing that the developing minds and hearts of children lack the capacity to process hurt or disqualify negative words effectively. The absence of a fully developed prefrontal cortex during these years leaves children unable to reason, making them particularly susceptible to the enduring effects of childhood wounds.

The insidious nature of Satan's strategy lies in burying these hurts deep within individuals, creating a ticking time bomb that often detonates in adulthood. By the time individuals reach 18 and beyond, the wounds inflicted in their early years resurface, compounding the pain and affecting their relationships, especially as parents.

The cycle continues as these wounded individuals, now parents themselves, unintentionally pass on the pain to their children, perpetuating a legacy of generational wounds.

However, the redemptive power of healing offers a glimmer of hope. The journey of identifying and acknowledging these patterns and wounds provides an opportunity to break free from the chains of generational pain. By embarking on the path of healing, parents can interrupt the destructive cycle, fostering an environment where children can experience the fullness of a loving and nurturing childhood. The time to stop the perpetuation of wounds is now, offering a chance for restoration, redemption, and the creation of a new legacy marked by healing and wholeness.

Workbook-Healing Generational Wounds Worksheet 259

Healing from Childhood Wounds: The "HEAL" Approach
Healing from childhood wounds is a transformative journey that involves intentional and thoughtful steps. The "HEAL" approach provides a framework for parents seeking to address and overcome the impact of past wounds on their parenting.

- **H - Honest Reflection:**
  - Begin by honestly reflecting on your childhood experiences.
  - Acknowledge and identify moments that may have left emotional wounds.
  - Be open to exploring the connection between past experiences and your current emotional state.
- **E - Embracing Self-Compassion:**
  - Cultivate self-compassion as you navigate your healing journey.
  - Understand that everyone carries some form of emotional baggage, and it's okay to acknowledge your wounds.
  - Treat yourself with the kindness and understanding you would offer to a friend in a similar situation.
- **A - Active Awareness:**
  - Develop an active awareness of your triggers and emotional responses.
  - Pay attention to situations that evoke strong emotions, and explore their roots in your past.
  - By being consciously aware, you can start to break the automatic patterns influenced by childhood wounds.
- **L - Learning and Unlearning:**
  - Engage in continuous learning about the impact of childhood experiences on adult behavior.
  - Embrace opportunities for unlearning harmful patterns and replacing them with healthier alternatives.
  - Seek resources, therapy, or support groups that provide tools for personal growth and healing.

By adopting the "HEAL" approach, parents can embark on a transformative journey toward healing from childhood wounds. This intentional process not only benefits the individual but also contributes to creating a healthier and more nurturing environment for their children. Remember, healing is a gradual process, and each step taken brings you closer to breaking generational cycles and fostering positive change.

Creating an Activation Environment for Children: Nurturing Seeds of Potential

As parents, we bear the profound responsibility of cultivating an activation environment that fosters the growth and development of the seeds of potential planted within our children. An activation environment is not merely a physical space but a holistic atmosphere that nurtures every aspect of a child's being—emotionally, spiritually, and mentally. Understanding the significance of this environment is paramount in steering our children toward their God-given destinies.

Defining an Activation Environment: An activation environment is characterized by positivity, encouragement, and intentional nurturing. It is a space where children feel safe, loved, and supported in exploring their unique gifts and talents. This environment is free from excessive negativity, criticism, and unrealistic expectations. Instead, it thrives on affirmations, constructive guidance, and an atmosphere that propels children to reach their full potential.

The Role of Positivity and Nurturing: Positivity and nurturing serve as foundational pillars in the activation environment we create for our children. Positive reinforcement encourages a child's self-esteem and confidence, allowing them to believe in their abilities. Nurturing involves providing the necessary care, attention, and guidance that empower children to navigate challenges and celebrate successes.

In this environment, children are not only allowed but encouraged to dream, explore, and express themselves authentically. The home becomes a sanctuary where seeds of creativity, resilience, and faith are sown, watered, and allowed to flourish. The power of positivity and nurturing is transformative, shaping the way children perceive themselves, others, and the world around them.

Our Responsibility as Gardeners: Imagine our role as parents akin to that of gardeners. We are entrusted with the sacred task of tending to the soil, removing the weeds, and ensuring the conditions are optimal for growth. The seeds within our children are divinely placed, each with its unique purpose and potential. Our responsibility is to create an environment where these seeds can germinate, take root, and blossom into the extraordinary individuals they are destined to become.

In conclusion, the activation environment we establish within our homes profoundly influences the trajectory of our children's lives. It is a space where they learn not only about the world but also about themselves, their worth, and the boundless possibilities ahead. Let us embrace the calling to be intentional gardeners, sowing seeds of love, faith, and encouragement, and watch with joy as our children bloom into the magnificent creations God designed them to be.

The Impact of a Deactivating Environment on Children: Navigating the Shadows

In stark contrast to an activation environment that nurtures and encourages, a deactivating environment casts shadows over a child's growth, potentially hindering their emotional, spiritual, and mental well-being. Understanding the profound effects of such an environment is crucial for parents, as it prompts reflection on the atmosphere they are creating within the home.

Emotional Strain and Self-Esteem: A deactivating environment often inflicts emotional strain on children, leaving them vulnerable to feelings of inadequacy, self-doubt, and diminished self-esteem. Constant exposure to criticism, negativity, or a lack of affirmation can sow seeds of insecurity that may persist into adulthood. The emotional toll becomes evident in how children perceive themselves and their abilities.

Impaired Social and Emotional Development: Children raised in a deactivating environment may encounter challenges in their social and emotional development. The absence of positive reinforcement and nurturing guidance can hinder their ability to form healthy relationships, express themselves openly, and navigate complex emotions. This impairment may manifest in difficulties relating to peers, coping with stress, or adapting to various social situations.

Stifled Creativity and Exploration: Creativity thrives in an activation environment where children are encouraged to explore, experiment, and express themselves freely. Conversely, a deactivating environment stifles creativity by imposing limits, instilling fear of failure, or discouraging imaginative pursuits. The absence of a supportive atmosphere may restrain a child's natural curiosity and hinder the development of creative thinking.

isk of Learned Helplessness: Children exposed to persistent deactivation may develop learned elplessness, a mindset where they believe their actions have little impact on their circumstances. his learned helplessness can impede their motivation, resilience, and belief in their ability to ffect positive change. As a result, they may navigate life with a sense of powerlessness and a eluctance to pursue goals.

ong-Term Impact on Mental Health: The effects of a deactivating environment can extend into dulthood, contributing to mental health challenges such as anxiety, depression, and low self-orth. The emotional scars from childhood may shape one's perception of the world and self, fluencing the way they approach relationships, challenges, and personal fulfillment.

conclusion, the impact of a deactivating environment on children underscores the profound fluence parents wield in shaping their children's lives. Recognizing the signs of deactivation ompts a crucial self-reflection for parents, urging them to assess the atmosphere they are ltivating within the home. By fostering an environment of love, encouragement, and positive firmation, parents can empower their children to overcome shadows and thrive in the light of their ue potential.

ne Power of Positive Reinforcement: Cultivating a Growth Mindset in Children
ositive reinforcement stands as a cornerstone in shaping the growth mindset of children, laying the undation for their journey toward realizing their full potential. This approach involves knowledging and rewarding positive behavior, fostering an environment where children feel lued, encouraged, and motivated to embrace challenges. The impact of positive reinforcement tends beyond immediate behavioral changes; it nurtures a mindset that views effort, learning, and silience as key components of success.

ncouragement as a Catalyst for Growth: Encouragement plays a pivotal role in the power of sitive reinforcement. By expressing belief in a child's capabilities and emphasizing the portance of effort, parents provide the essential fuel for their growth journey. Encouragement comes a catalyst that propels children to take on challenges, explore new territories, and develop e confidence to confront obstacles.

aise that Fosters Intrinsic Motivation: While praise is a fundamental aspect of positive inforcement, its effectiveness lies in its ability to foster intrinsic motivation. Meaningful and ecific praise that focuses on a child's effort, determination, and specific achievements cultivates a nse of internal satisfaction and a desire for continual improvement. Intrinsic motivation becomes e driving force behind a child's pursuit of excellence.

firmation: Nurturing a Positive Self-Image: Affirmation contributes significantly to shaping a sitive self-image in children. When parents consistently affirm their children's strengths, iqueness, and worth, it creates a secure emotional foundation. A positive self-image enables ildren to approach challenges with resilience, viewing setbacks as opportunities for growth rather an obstacles to success.

ltivating a Growth Mindset: The essence of positive reinforcement lies in cultivating a growth ndset—a belief that abilities can be developed through dedication and hard work. This mindset powers children to embrace challenges, learn from failures, and persist in the face of setbacks. It sitions them to see their intelligence and talents as dynamic qualities that can be enhanced with ort.

e Ripple Effect on Behavior and Attitude: Positive reinforcement initiates a ripple effect, luencing both behavior and attitude. Children who experience consistent positive reinforcement more likely to exhibit pro-social behavior, engage in collaborative efforts, and approach rning with enthusiasm. The ripple effect extends beyond behavior, shaping a positive and imistic attitude toward themselves, others, and the world around them.

conclusion, the power of positive reinforcement in fostering a growth mindset cannot be rstated. Parents play a pivotal role in creating an environment where encouragement, praise, and rmation converge to activate the inherent potential within their children. By intentionally ploying positive reinforcement strategies, parents contribute to the development of resilient, fident, and motivated individuals ready to navigate life's challenges with a mindset geared ard growth and success.

Examples of Encouragements, Praise, and Affirmations for Creating an Activation Environment
Encouragements:
1. "I believe in your ability to figure this out. Take your time, and I'm here to help if you need it."
2. "Your effort and determination are truly impressive. Keep going; you're making great progress."
3. "Mistakes are a natural part of learning. Learn from them, and you'll become even stronger."
4. "Your curiosity and eagerness to learn new things inspire me. Keep exploring and discovering."
5. "Your unique perspective brings so much creativity to our family. Embrace what makes you special."

Praise:
1. "I noticed how you handled that situation with kindness. Your empathy toward others is remarkable."
2. "Your commitment to finishing your tasks, even when they're challenging, shows real perseverance."
3. "The way you approached that problem with creativity and resourcefulness is truly commendable."
4. "I'm impressed by the responsibility you've shown in taking care of your responsibilities. Well done!"
5. *"Your dedication to practicing and improving your skills is paying off. I can see the progress you're making."

Affirmations:
1. "You are valued just as you are. Your worth is not determined by achievements or mistakes."
2. "Your uniqueness is a gift to the world. Embrace all the qualities that make you who you are."
3. "I appreciate your kindness and the positive energy you bring to our family. You are a joy to be around."
4. "Your perspective matters, and your voice is important. I'm grateful for the insights you share."
5. "You are capable of handling whatever challenges come your way. I have confidence in your abilities."

These examples demonstrate the power of positive language in creating an activation environment for children. By incorporating such encouragements, praise, and affirmations into daily interactions, parents can nurture a mindset of growth, resilience, and self-worth in their children.

Creating Your Personalized Encouragements, Praises, and Affirmations Worksheet
Encouragements:
1. Think about a challenging situation your child is currently facing. Write an encouragement that expresses your belief in their ability to navigate and overcome it.
2. Encouragement: _____
3. Reflect on a recent effort or project your child undertook. Craft an encouragement acknowledging their hard work and dedication.
4. Encouragement: _____
5. Consider a mistake or setback your child experienced. Write an encouragement that emphasizes the importance of learning and growth from such experiences.
6. Encouragement: _____
7. Focus on a unique quality or talent your child possesses. Create an encouragement that celebrates and encourages them to embrace their individuality.
8. Encouragement: _____
9. Think about a goal or aspiration your child has. Develop an encouragement that motivates them to pursue it with determination and enthusiasm.
10. Encouragement: _____

Praises:
1. Identify a specific act of kindness or empathy your child displayed. Write a praise recognizing their compassionate behavior.
2. Praise: _____
3. Highlight a responsibility or task your child successfully completed. Craft a praise acknowledging their sense of responsibility and accomplishment.
4. Praise: _____
5. Recall a problem-solving moment where your child demonstrated creativity. Write a praise commending their inventive thinking.
6. Praise: _____
7. Acknowledge consistent effort and progress your child has made in a particular skill or area. Develop a praise focusing on their dedication.

- Praise: _____
- Identify a positive change in behavior or attitude. Write a praise recognizing the positive transformation you've observed.
- Praise: _____

Affirmations:

- Create an affirmation that emphasizes your child's intrinsic value, separate from achievements.
- Affirmation: _____
- Craft an affirmation celebrating your child's unique qualities and encouraging them to embrace their individuality.
- Affirmation: _____
- Develop an affirmation expressing gratitude for the positive energy your child brings to the family.
- Affirmation: _____
- Write an affirmation that reinforces the importance of your child's voice and perspective.
- Affirmation: _____
- Craft an affirmation instilling confidence in your child's ability to handle challenges and uncertainties.
- Affirmation: _____

Use this worksheet to tailor personalized encouragements, praises, and affirmations that resonate with your child's unique qualities and experiences.

_____
_____
_____
_____
_____
_____
_____
_____
_____
_____
_____
_____
_____
_____
_____
_____
_____
_____
_____
_____
_____
_____
_____
_____
_____
_____
_____
_____
_____
_____

Strategies for Encouraging Curiosity in Children

Cultivating a sense of curiosity in children is an invaluable investment in their overall development. Curiosity serves as a catalyst for learning, creativity, and critical thinking, laying the foundation for a lifetime of exploration and growth. As parents and educators, guiding this curiosity can be both fulfilling and instrumental in shaping a child's journey of discovery.

1. Fostering an Inquisitive Environment: Create an atmosphere that encourages questions and exploration. Offer a variety of age-appropriate books, puzzles, and educational toys that pique their interest. A rich learning environment stimulates curiosity and provides endless opportunities for discovery.

2. Model Curiosity: Children often mirror the behavior of their caregivers. Demonstrate curiosity in your daily life by asking questions, exploring new topics, and expressing genuine interest in the world around you. Modeling a curious mindset sets a powerful example for your child to emulate.

3. Encourage Open Communication: Establish open lines of communication where your child feels comfortable expressing their thoughts and questions. Foster an environment where curiosity is met with encouragement rather than criticism. This promotes a positive association with curiosity and learning.

4. Explore Diverse Subjects: Expose your child to a broad range of subjects and activities. Introduce them to science, art, music, nature, and more. Diversifying their experiences not only broadens their knowledge base but also sparks curiosity in various areas, helping them discover their interests.

5. Support Hands-On Learning: Facilitate hands-on learning experiences that engage multiple senses. Activities such as experiments, art projects, and nature walks provide tangible encounters that enhance curiosity. These experiences make learning enjoyable and memorable.

6. Connect Curiosity to Values: Guide your child in channeling their curiosity toward positive and constructive endeavors. Discuss how curiosity can lead to personal growth, understanding others, and making a positive impact on the world. Aligning curiosity with values empowers children to navigate their inquisitiveness responsibly.

7. Embrace Questions and Provide Answers: Welcome your child's questions and provide thoughtful, age-appropriate answers. If you don't know the answer, explore the question together. This collaborative approach not only satisfies their curiosity but also demonstrates that learning is an ongoing, shared journey.

8. Use Technology Wisely: Leverage age-appropriate educational apps, websites, and interactive platforms that align with your child's interests. Technology can be a valuable tool for expanding their horizons and delving deeper into subjects that capture their curiosity.

9. Celebrate Curiosity: Acknowledge and celebrate your child's curiosity-driven accomplishments, no matter how small. Reinforce the idea that curiosity is a commendable quality, fostering a positive attitude toward exploration and learning.

10. Guard Against Unhealthy Curiosity: While encouraging curiosity, it's essential to guide children away from inappropriate or harmful inquiries. Establish boundaries and explain the importance of respecting others' privacy and maintaining moral values.

In summary, cultivating curiosity in children is a dynamic and intentional process that involves creating an environment conducive to exploration, modeling curiosity, and providing diverse learning opportunities. By nurturing their inquisitiveness, parents and educators contribute to a child's holistic development, setting the stage for a lifelong love of learning.

Fostering Creativity in Children: Unleashing the Power of Imagination

Creativity is an innate gift bestowed upon each child, a reflection of the divine Creator who designed them with limitless potential for innovation. As parents and educators, recognizing the profound significance of fostering creativity in a child's life is key to unlocking the doors of boundless imagination and potential.

God, the Ultimate Creator: At the core of fostering creativity in children lies an acknowledgment of God as the ultimate Creator. In the opening chapters of the Bible, God reveals Himself as the masterful architect of the universe, the One who spoke creation into existence. Recognizing that children are made in the image of this creative God prompts us to create environments that nurture and celebrate their innate creativity.

Strategies for Encouraging Creativity:
1. **Provide Open-Ended Activities:** Offer activities that have no predetermined "right" or "wrong" answers, allowing children to explore, experiment, and express their unique ideas without fear of judgment.
2. **Encourage Divergent Thinking:** Foster an atmosphere where children are encouraged to generate a variety of ideas and solutions to a given problem. Divergent thinking expands their capacity for creativity.
3. **Cultivate a Love for Learning:** Sparking curiosity and a love for learning nurtures creativity. Expose children to a wide range of subjects and encourage them to explore areas that captivate their interest.
4. **Value and Display Their Creations:** Showcasing a child's creations, whether it's a drawing, a story, or a craft, communicates the value of their creative efforts. This affirmation bolsters their confidence and motivates continued exploration.
5. **Embrace Mistakes as Learning Opportunities:** Create an environment where making mistakes is viewed as a natural part of the learning process. Encourage children to learn from errors and find creative solutions.

Unleashing the Power of Imagination: Imagination is a gateway to creativity, allowing children to envision possibilities beyond the constraints of reality. By fostering creativity, we empower children to harness the power of their imagination. This skill not only enhances their problem-solving abilities but also equips them for a future where innovation is a valuable asset.

In essence, fostering creativity in children is an invitation to participate in the divine act of creation. It involves providing them with the tools, opportunities, and encouragement needed to explore the vast landscape of their imagination. As parents and educators, let us embrace our roles as stewards of creativity, cultivating an environment where each child's unique gifts and ideas can flourish, contributing to a world enriched by their innovative contributions.

Promoting Self-Expression: Nurturing the Unique Identity of Your Child
The journey of parenting is a dynamic process that involves recognizing and embracing the individuality of each child. One crucial aspect of this journey is promoting self-expression, allowing your child to explore and express their unique identity. Understanding the importance of self-expression is pivotal for a child's emotional and psychological well-being.

Every child is wonderfully made, with distinct personality traits, quirks, and innate ways of being themselves. As parents, it is our responsibility to create an environment that not only acknowledges but also celebrates these individual differences. Often, societal expectations or parental desires can unintentionally stifle a child's ability to express themselves authentically. It's essential to resist the temptation to mold them into predefined expectations and instead value the inherent uniqueness they bring to the world.

Practical approaches to fostering an environment that supports and values self-expression include actively listening to your child. Pay attention to their thoughts, feelings, and ideas, and encourage them to communicate openly. Create a safe space where they feel comfortable expressing themselves without fear of judgment. This involves fostering an atmosphere of acceptance, where differences are celebrated rather than criticized.

Another vital aspect is providing diverse opportunities for self-expression. Engage your child in various activities such as art, music, writing, or sports, allowing them to discover and develop their talents and interests. Be open to exploring different outlets and mediums that resonate with their unique personality.

Encourage creativity by letting them make choices and express their preferences. Whether it's choosing their clothes, room decor, or extracurricular activities, empowering your child to make decisions contributes to a sense of autonomy and self-expression. This autonomy helps build their confidence and fosters a positive self-image.

Moreover, guide them in understanding and managing their emotions. Teach them healthy ways to express their feelings and thoughts, whether through words, art, or other constructive outlets. Creating an emotional vocabulary and validating their experiences empowers children to navigate their internal world with confidence.

In conclusion, promoting self-expression in your child is a journey that requires intentional effort and an unwavering commitment to embracing their uniqueness. As you guide them in discovering and expressing their authentic selves, you contribute to their emotional well-being and lay the foundation for a healthy self-image that will positively impact their future relationships and endeavors.

Conclusion: Cultivating an Activation-Focused Environment for Lifelong Growth
In this exploration of creating an activation-focused environment for our children, we have delved into key principles that contribute to their holistic development. As parents, recognizing the uniqueness of each child and actively fostering an atmosphere that encourages self-expression, curiosity, and creativity lays the foundation for a journey of lifelong growth.
Summarizing the key points, we've underscored the significance of:
1. **Promoting Self-Expression:** Acknowledging and celebrating the individuality of each child, providing a safe space for them to express themselves authentically.
2. **Fostering Creativity:** Recognizing creativity as a vital aspect of a child's life and implementing strategies to nurture and encourage creative thinking.
3. **Encouraging Curiosity:** Cultivating a sense of curiosity in children while emphasizing the importance of controlled curiosity that aligns with positive activation.

These principles are not mere guidelines but transformative pathways that contribute to the long-term well-being of our children. An activation-focused environment serves as the fertile ground where the seeds of God-given potential can sprout, grow, and mature into the unique individuals they were created to be.

The benefits of such an environment extend beyond childhood, shaping the trajectory of their lives. Children raised in an atmosphere that values their distinctiveness, encourages exploration, and supports their natural curiosity are more likely to develop a growth mindset. This mindset equips them to face challenges with resilience, adaptability, and an eagerness to learn throughout their lives.

Emphasizing the long-term benefits, we envision children who grow into adults unafraid of embracing their uniqueness, who approach life with a sense of wonder and curiosity, and who contribute positively to the world around them. As parents, the investment made in creating an activation-focused environment becomes a legacy—a legacy of empowered, confident, and compassionate individuals who impact the world in meaningful ways.

May the principles shared in this exploration guide you on a transformative parenting journey, and may the activation-focused environment you cultivate be a source of joy, growth, and lifelong fulfillment for your children.

Avoiding the "Disappointment" Narrative: Nurturing Positive Self-Esteem in Children

In our journey as parents, it's crucial to recognize the profound impact our words have on our children's self-esteem. One term that merits thoughtful consideration is the use of the word "disappointment" in our interactions with them. While parents may employ it with the intention of guiding their children toward certain decisions, it's essential to understand the potential negative consequences associated with this narrative.

The term "disappointment" carries a weight that can significantly influence a child's self-perception. When parents express disappointment in their children's choices, behaviors, or outcomes, it can inadvertently create an environment of control. Children may internalize this disappointment as a form of parental disapproval, shaping their beliefs about their own worth and capabilities.

Parents often use the term as a subtle means of steering their children in a preferred direction. However, the impact goes beyond the immediate situation, influencing a child's sense of self-worth and confidence. The disappointment narrative can instill fear and anxiety, making children hesitant to take risks or make decisions autonomously.

It's important to recognize that children are highly perceptive, and the language we use becomes ingrained in their self-talk. When disappointment becomes a recurring theme, children may start associating their worth with the ability to meet parental expectations. This can lead to a pattern of seeking external validation and approval, hindering the development of a healthy, internalized self-esteem.

As parents, fostering an environment that encourages open communication, understanding, and positive reinforcement is crucial. Instead of framing discussions in terms of disappointment, consider emphasizing constructive feedback, guidance, and affirmation. This approach helps children view challenges as opportunities for growth rather than potential sources of disappointment.

Ultimately, the goal is to create a narrative that cultivates resilience, self-confidence, and a positive self-image in children. By choosing language that uplifts rather than discourages, we contribute to the development of emotionally secure individuals who are better equipped to navigate life's challenges with confidence and self-assurance.

The Weight of Unrealistic Expectations: Navigating the Pitfalls of Parental Pressure
Unrealistic expectations can cast a heavy shadow on the parent-child dynamic, significantly contributing to the disappointment narrative. It's crucial for parents to engage in self-reflection and understand the potential harm that arises from imposing undue pressure on their children. The roots of these expectations often lie in the internal motivations of parents, which can range from a desire to live vicariously through their children to seeking external validation or succumbing to societal pressures.

One common source of unrealistic expectations is the parental aspiration to see their children fulfill unfulfilled dreams or aspirations. While it's natural for parents to wish the best for their children, the line blurs when these aspirations become unattainable or are driven by the parent's unmet desires. Children are unique individuals with their own talents, interests, and pathways, and imposing unrealistic expectations can stifle their authenticity and hinder the development of a healthy self-image.

The desire to showcase achievement can also fuel unrealistic expectations. Parents, driven by societal benchmarks or comparisons with other families, may inadvertently burden their children with expectations that exceed their capabilities or interests. The pressure to conform to predefined notions of success can create an environment where children feel compelled to meet external standards rather than pursuing their passions.

Moreover, the intensity of parental love and concern can sometimes manifest as an overwhelming desire for the child's success. This well-intentioned but misguided approach can inadvertently communicate to children that their worth is contingent on meeting specific benchmarks. Such expectations may lead to anxiety, fear of failure, and a diminished sense of self-worth.

To navigate this challenge, parents must engage in honest self-examination, acknowledging their motivations and addressing any unrealistic expectations they may harbor. Embracing a mindset that prioritizes the individuality of each child allows for a more supportive and nurturing environment. Rather than projecting unattainable goals onto their children, parents can encourage them to explore their interests, discover their strengths, and define success in their own terms.

In conclusion, understanding the weight of unrealistic expectations and their impact on the disappointment narrative is a vital step toward fostering a healthy parent-child relationship. By creating an environment that values authenticity, individual growth, and open communication, parents can empower their children to navigate life with resilience and confidence.

Workbook-Parental Expectations and Feelings Reflection Worksheet 263

Encouraging Positive Reinforcement and Constructive Feedback: Nurturing Growth in Children
In the journey of parenting, fostering a positive and supportive environment is crucial for the well-being and development of children. Two key elements that play a pivotal role in shaping this environment are positive reinforcement and constructive feedback.

Positive reinforcement involves acknowledging and praising desirable behaviors in children. It serves as a powerful tool to counteract disappointment and build a foundation of confidence and self-esteem. Recognizing and celebrating small achievements, efforts, or positive attitudes can create a ripple effect, motivating children to continue making positive choices. This practice fosters a sense of accomplishment, reinforcing the belief that their actions are valued and appreciated.

Constructive feedback, on the other hand, is an essential aspect of guiding children toward growth and resilience. It differs from criticism in that it focuses on specific behaviors rather than the child's character. Constructive feedback provides insights into areas of improvement while highlighting strengths, creating a balanced perspective. By offering guidance and suggestions for improvement, parents can empower their children to learn from mistakes, develop resilience, and cultivate a growth mindset.

How to Offer Feedback and Support: Building a Foundation of Growth and Resilience
In the journey of parenting, offering feedback and support in a constructive manner is pivotal for the emotional well-being and development of children. Here are practical strategies for parents to navigate this crucial aspect of nurturing their children:

1. **Choose the Right Time and Place:** Timing is essential when providing feedback or support. Choose a moment when both you and your child are calm and receptive. Find a quiet and comfortable space where you can have an open conversation without distractions.
2. **Use Positive Language:** Frame your feedback in a positive and affirming manner. Instead of focusing solely on what needs improvement, highlight the strengths and efforts of your child. Positive language fosters a sense of encouragement and reinforces a growth mindset.
3. **Be Specific and Clear:** Clearly articulate the behavior or action you are addressing. Specific feedback helps children understand the context and allows them to identify areas for improvement. Avoid vague statements and provide concrete examples.
4. **Active Listening:** Before offering feedback, take the time to actively listen to your child's perspective. Understanding their thoughts and feelings creates a supportive environment. Acknowledge their emotions and let them know you value their input.
5. **Balance Positive and Constructive Feedback:** While addressing areas for improvement, balance it with positive feedback. Recognize and celebrate achievements, efforts, or positive attitudes. This balanced approach reinforces a sense of accomplishment and motivates continued positive behavior.
6. **Offer Emotional Support:** Beyond feedback, be a source of emotional support for your child. Create an environment where they feel comfortable sharing their thoughts and concerns. Provide reassurance and empathy, letting them know you are there for them no matter what.
7. **Encourage Independence:** Support your child in developing independence and problem-solving skills. Instead of providing all the answers, guide them in finding solutions. This empowers them to take ownership of their actions and decisions.
8. **Celebrate Progress:** Acknowledge and celebrate the progress your child makes. Whether it's a small improvement or a significant achievement, recognizing their efforts reinforces a sense of accomplishment and encourages a positive outlook.
9. **Maintain Open Communication:** Foster open and honest communication with your child. Encourage them to express their thoughts, feelings, and concerns. Be approachable and willing to discuss various topics, creating a foundation for trust.
10. **Express Unconditional Love:** Regardless of the feedback or challenges, consistently express your unconditional love and support. Knowing they are loved irrespective of their successes or failures contributes to a secure and nurturing environment.

incorporating these strategies, parents can navigate the delicate balance of offering feedback and support in a constructive manner. This approach lays the groundwork for a positive parent-child relationship, fostering growth, resilience, and emotional well-being in children.

Navigating the Pressures on Children: Understanding the Modern Challenges

In the rapidly evolving landscape of today's world, children are subjected to a myriad of pressures, both societal and academic, that previous generations might not have encountered. It imperative for parents to recognize and comprehend these challenges, fostering an open and supportive environment. Here, we delve into the complexities of navigating the pressures on children and the potential impact on their well-being:

1. Societal Pressures: The advent of technology has interconnected the world, exposing children to a vast array of societal pressures. Social media, peer comparisons, and the constant barrage o information can contribute to feelings of inadequacy and the pursuit of unrealistic standards. Parents must actively engage with their children to understand the dynamics of social interactions online and offline. Encourage open communication, emphasizing that value is not determined by external validations.

2. Academic Pressures: The educational landscape has become increasingly competitive, placing substantial academic burdens on children. High expectations, rigorous schedules, and the fear o failure can lead to stress and anxiety. Parents should foster a balanced approach to academics, recognizing that each child has unique strengths and challenges. Create an environment where learning is valued over grades, and where mistakes are seen as opportunities for growth rather than failures.

3. Formation of a Parent-Child Partnership: To effectively navigate these pressures, it is essentia to establish a partnership with your child. This involves active listening, empathy, and creating safe space for them to express their concerns. Understand that the pressures they face may diffe significantly from what you experienced in your own childhood. Encourage a two-way dialogue, where both parent and child contribute to finding solutions and coping mechanisms.

4. Impact on Well-being: The cumulative effect of societal and academic pressures can take a to on a child's well-being. Increased stress levels, anxiety, and a sense of isolation are potential consequences. As parents, being attuned to changes in behavior, mood, or academic performanc is crucial. Addressing these challenges requires a combination of emotional support, guidance, and the cultivation of resilience.

5. Building Resilience: Equip your child with the tools to navigate and overcome pressures by instilling resilience. Teach them problem-solving skills, coping mechanisms, and the importance of self-care. Emphasize that setbacks are a natural part of life and an opportunity for growth. B fostering resilience, parents empower their children to face challenges with confidence and adaptability.

In conclusion, understanding the pressures on children in the modern era is a crucial step in effective parenting. By acknowledging these challenges, parents can proactively work towards creating an environment that promotes resilience, emotional well-being, and a healthy balance between societal and academic expectations. The key lies in forming a strong parent-child partnership that fosters communication, empathy, and mutual understanding.

Developing Coping Mechanisms: Nurturing Resilience in Children

Teaching children effective coping mechanisms is not only a means of navigating current challenges but also an investment in lifelong skills. Here, we explore strategies to help children build resilience and cope with the pressures they encounter:

Acknowledge Feelings and Provide Validation: Start by creating an environment where children feel safe expressing their emotions. Acknowledge their feelings without judgment, and let them know that it's okay to experience a range of emotions. Validation lays the foundation for healthy coping, allowing children to process and navigate stress.

Teach Mindfulness and Relaxation Techniques: Introduce mindfulness and relaxation exercises as tools for managing stress. Simple practices like deep breathing, meditation, or journaling can help children center themselves amidst pressure. These techniques empower them to regain control over their emotions and thoughts.

Encourage Problem-Solving Skills: Teach children the art of problem-solving. Equip them with the ability to break down challenges into manageable parts and brainstorm potential solutions. Fostering a proactive mindset enables children to approach difficulties with resilience, viewing them as opportunities for growth.

Foster a Growth Mindset: Instill in children the concept of a growth mindset, emphasizing that challenges are a natural part of learning and development. Encourage a positive attitude towards setbacks, framing them as stepping stones to success rather than insurmountable obstacles. This mindset shift promotes resilience in the face of adversity.

Affirm Their Worth and Identity: Constantly reaffirm your child's inherent worth and identity, independent of external achievements. Remind them that their value is not determined by grades, societal expectations, or performance in various activities. Understanding their worth in the eyes of God provides a foundational source of affirmation and security.

Share Stories of Overcoming Adversity: Narratives have the power to inspire and motivate. Share stories of individuals who have overcome challenges and adversities, emphasizing that everyone faces difficulties. Highlight the lessons learned, the growth achieved, and the resilience developed through those experiences.

Emphasize the Concept of Pressure Making Diamonds: Introduce the idea that pressure, when managed appropriately, can lead to resilience and strength. The analogy of pressure creating diamonds underscores the transformative potential of challenges. Help children view pressure as an opportunity for growth and character development.

In conclusion, developing coping mechanisms in children is an essential aspect of parenting. By imparting these life skills, parents empower their children to navigate the pressures of life with resilience, adaptability, and a positive mindset. Remember that the goal is not to shield children from challenges but to equip them with the tools to face challenges head-on, knowing they are loved, valued, and capable of overcoming adversity.

Living by Example: The Power of Caught vs. Taught

In the intricate journey of parenting, the adage "caught, not taught" encapsulates a profound truth — the influence of parental behavior speaks louder than words. Children are incredibly perceptive, absorbing the nuances of their surroundings, and as parents, living by example becomes a potent tool for instilling values. Here, we delve into the significance of "caught vs. taught" and the transformative impact it has on shaping a child's character:

1. Model the Values You Wish to Instill: Children are keen observers, mirroring the behaviors an attitudes they witness in their parents. If you aspire to instill honesty, integrity, kindness, or an other virtue, embodying these values in your daily life is paramount. Consistency between words and actions reinforces the authenticity of your teachings.

2. Create a Home Environment Aligned with Principles: The home serves as the primary crucible where a child's character is forged. Establish an environment that reflects the principles you want your children to embrace. A home imbued with love, respect, and positive communication fosters a nurturing space where children can thrive emotionally, socially, and spiritually.

3. Foster Healthy Communication: Model effective and respectful communication within the family. The way conflicts are resolved, and conversations are conducted leaves an indelible imprint on a child's understanding of interpersonal dynamics. By navigating disagreements with empathy and open communication, parents teach valuable lessons in conflict resolution and emotional intelligence.

4. Prioritize Self-Care and Well-Being: Demonstrate the importance of self-care and well-being by prioritizing your physical, mental, and emotional health. When children witness their parents valuing and investing in their own well-being, they internalize the significance of self-care as a essential aspect of a balanced and fulfilling life.

5. Embrace a Growth Mindset: Cultivate a growth mindset by approaching challenges with resilience and a positive attitude. Share your own experiences of learning from mistakes, adapting to change, and embracing challenges as opportunities for growth. This mindset shift encourages children to view setbacks not as failures but as stepping stones toward improvemen

6. Express Empathy and Compassion: Infuse your interactions with empathy and compassion. Show kindness not only to family members but also to those outside the immediate circle. Acts generosity, understanding, and compassion resonate deeply with children, shaping their worldview and fostering a sense of social responsibility.

7. Acknowledge Imperfections and Apologize: No one is perfect, and admitting mistakes is a powerful lesson in humility and accountability. When parents acknowledge their imperfections and genuinely apologize when necessary, it creates a safe space for children to do the same. Th vulnerability fosters trust, strengthens the parent-child bond, and instills the value of accountability.

In essence, living by example is a dynamic and ongoing process. It requires self-reflection, intentionality, and a commitment to embodying the principles you aim to instill in your childre As you navigate the landscape of parenthood, remember that the values you live are the values your children are likely to internalize. By embracing this truth, you wield the transformative power of "caught vs. taught" in shaping the character and worldview of the next generation.

Worksheet-Living by Example: Worksheet 265

Age-Specific Considerations: Nurturing Growth at Every Stage
Understanding the Unique Needs of Each Age Group

A. Infancy to Age 6: Foundational Years
- **Establishing Security:**
  - Focus on creating a secure and loving environment.
  - Build trust through consistent care and responsive parenting.
  - Encourage exploration in a safe space to promote early development.
- **Cultivating Connection:**
  - Prioritize bonding and attachment through nurturing interactions.
  - Respond promptly to the child's needs, fostering a sense of safety.
  - Introduce age-appropriate stimulation for cognitive development.
- **Introduction to Values:**
  - Begin subtly introducing foundational values through stories and interactions.
  - Model kindness, empathy, and respect to lay the groundwork for character development.
  - Establish routines that provide a sense of predictability and security.

B. Ages 7-12: Nurturing Independence and Character Development
- **Encouraging Independence:**
  - Allow for age-appropriate decision-making to foster independence.
  - Provide opportunities for responsibility and self-sufficiency.
  - Encourage the development of hobbies and interests.
- **Character Building:**
  - Emphasize the importance of honesty, integrity, and empathy.
  - Teach problem-solving skills and effective communication.
  - Foster a growth mindset by celebrating effort and resilience.
- **Balancing Structure and Freedom:**
  - Maintain a balance between structure and flexibility.
  - Set clear expectations while allowing room for creativity.
  - Provide guidance on time management and responsibilities.

C. Ages 13-18: Addressing Adolescence
- **Fostering Responsibility:**
  - Encourage accountability and responsibility for actions.
  - Discuss the consequences of decisions and choices.
  - Support the development of organizational and planning skills.
- **Navigating Identity and Self-Discovery:**
  - Acknowledge and validate their evolving sense of identity.
  - Facilitate open communication about self-discovery.
  - Encourage healthy relationships and self-expression.
- **Preparing for Adulthood:**
  - Offer guidance on future goals and career exploration.
  - Discuss financial literacy and basic life skills.
  - Support their transition into adulthood with mentorship and practical advice.

D. 18 and Beyond: Preparing for Adulthood
- **Guiding Independence:**
  - Provide guidance on major life decisions without imposing.
  - Encourage autonomy and self-sufficiency.
  - Offer support as they navigate challenges and successes.
- **Cultivating Lifelong Learning:**
  - Emphasize the importance of continuous learning and personal growth.
  - Support higher education or vocational pursuits.
  - Encourage a proactive approach to lifelong learning and adaptability.
- **Building a Supportive Relationship:**
  - Transition into a role of mentorship and friendship.
  - Maintain open communication and be a source of encouragement.
  - Recognize their achievements and celebrate their independence.

Understanding the specific needs and challenges at each stage allows parents to tailor their approach, fostering a supportive and growth-oriented environment throughout their child's journey to adulthood.

The Intersection of Parenting and Friendship: Navigating Evolving Dynamics
Balancing Authority and Companionship
In the intricate dance of parenting, finding the sweet spot between being an authority figure and a friend is a delicate yet crucial balance. Recognizing that the dynamics between parents and children evolve over time, it's essential to cultivate a relationship that respects the roles of both authority and companionship.

Balancing Roles:
- **Establishing Authority:**
  - Emphasize the importance of respect and obedience.
  - Set clear boundaries and expectations.
  - Communicate with authority while maintaining empathy.
- **Being a Companion:**
  - Foster open communication and active listening.
  - Share experiences and interests to create a bond.
  - Demonstrate understanding and empathy in moments of vulnerability.

Cultivating an Evolving Relationship:
- **Childhood to Adolescence:**
  - During childhood, prioritize establishing authority to provide a sense of security.
  - As adolescence approaches, gradually introduce elements of companionship, respecting their growing autonomy.
  - Communicate openly about the changing dynamics and expectations.
- **Adolescence to Adulthood:**
  - Transition into a more supportive and companionable role during the adolescent years.
  - Encourage independence while offering guidance.
  - As they enter adulthood, shift towards a peer-like relationship while maintaining a foundation of respect.
- **Open Communication:**
  - Regularly check in on their comfort level with the evolving relationship.
  - Be receptive to feedback and adjust your approach accordingly.
  - Discuss expectations openly to avoid misunderstandings.

Navigating Challenges:
- **Maintaining Respect:**
  - Ensure that the friend-like dynamics do not compromise the respect owed to a parent.
  - Clearly communicate non-negotiable boundaries while fostering a sense of shared decision-making.
- **Addressing Conflicts:**
  - Approach conflicts with a blend of understanding and authority.
  - Encourage open dialogue to resolve issues collaboratively.
  - Model healthy conflict resolution for a constructive relationship.

Embracing Mutuality:
- **Shared Interests:**
  - Find common interests to strengthen the bond.
  - Engage in activities that foster a sense of camaraderie.
  - Celebrate shared achievements and milestones.
- **Supporting Independence:**
  - Acknowledge and support their journey towards independence.
  - Offer guidance when needed, respecting their autonomy.
  - Celebrate their successes and be a source of encouragement.

Balancing the roles of authority figure and friend requires adaptability, effective communication and a keen awareness of the evolving needs of your child. By navigating these dynamics with intentionality, parents can foster a relationship that stands the test of time, supporting their children as they navigate the various stages of life.

Navigating Extremes: The Dangers of Authoritarianism and Over-Friendliness in Parenting

Parenting is a delicate dance, and finding the right balance between authority and friendship is paramount. However, veering towards extremes—being overly authoritative or overly friendly—can pose significant dangers to the parent-child relationship and the child's overall development.

The Pitfalls of Authoritarian Parenting:

- **Strained Relationship:** Authoritarian parenting, characterized by strict rules and a lack of flexibility, often leads to strained relationships. The child may feel stifled, fostering resentment and hindering open communication.
- **Rebellion and Secrecy:** Excessive control may lead to rebellion or secretive behavior in children. Fear of punishment might discourage honesty, and children may resort to hiding aspects of their lives to avoid repercussions.
- **Impact on Self-Esteem:** Constant enforcement of rules without room for understanding can erode a child's self-esteem. Authoritarian parenting may instill obedience, but it often comes at the cost of stifling creativity and individuality.

The Pitfalls of Over-Friendliness:

Lack of Boundaries: Overly friendly parents may struggle to set and enforce boundaries. Children need structure and guidance, and the absence of clear boundaries can lead to confusion and a sense of insecurity.

Role Confusion: When parents prioritize friendship over authority, children may struggle to distinguish between parental and peer relationships. This role confusion can impact the child's ability to respect authority figures outside the home.

Missing Guidance: Overly friendly parents might shy away from providing necessary guidance or correction, fearing it will jeopardize the friendship. However, children need parental guidance to navigate challenges and make informed decisions.

Striking the Right Balance:

Clear Communication: Establish open communication about expectations and rules. A balance can be struck by explaining the reasons behind rules and fostering a sense of understanding rather than just enforcing compliance.

Flexibility with Boundaries: While maintaining necessary boundaries, allow flexibility where appropriate. This demonstrates a level of trust and understanding, contributing to a healthier parent-child relationship.

Consistent Support: Aim to be a supportive figure while maintaining an authoritative stance when needed. Children need to feel secure in the knowledge that their parents are both supportive and capable of guiding them.

Embracing the Middle Ground:

Adaptability: Parenting is not a one-size-fits-all journey. Being adaptable and responsive to your child's changing needs allows for a dynamic relationship that evolves with time.

Modeling Healthy Relationships: Strive to model a balanced and healthy relationship, showing that authority and friendship can coexist harmoniously. This sets a positive example for children to emulate in their own relationships.

Navigating the dangers of extremes in parenting requires a nuanced approach, understanding that the healthiest parent-child relationships thrive in the middle ground—where authority is wielded with empathy, and friendship is built on a foundation of respect. Balancing these elements creates an environment where children feel secure, understood, and supported in their journey to adulthood.

Authentic Parenting: Fostering Relatability and Connection

Authenticity is the cornerstone of building deep and meaningful connections, and this holds true in the parent-child relationship. When parents embrace authenticity, it creates an atmosphere of trust, relatability, and mutual understanding.

1. Open Communication: Authentic parenting encourages open and honest communication. When parents are authentic about their thoughts, feelings, and experiences, it sets the stage for children to feel comfortable sharing their own thoughts and concerns. This openness fosters a sense of trust, strengthening the bond between parent and child.

2. Vulnerability and Empathy: Being authentic involves embracing vulnerability. Parents who share their struggles, challenges, and even mistakes demonstrate to their children that it's okay not to be perfect. This vulnerability cultivates empathy, as children see their parents as real people navigating life's complexities. It creates an environment where children feel understood and supported.

3. Relating to Real Experiences: Authenticity allows parents to relate to their children through real experiences. Sharing personal stories, successes, and setbacks provides children with relatable examples that resonate with their own lives. This relatability helps children navigate their own challenges, knowing they are not alone in their journey.

4. Building a Genuine Connection: Authenticity builds a genuine connection between parent and child. When children witness their parents being true to themselves, it strengthens the emotional connection. This connection becomes a source of comfort and support, especially during times of difficulty or uncertainty.

5. Modeling Authenticity: Children learn by example, and when parents model authenticity, it encourages children to be authentic in their own lives. This modeling sets the foundation for healthy relationships, as children internalize the value of being true to oneself and embracing authenticity in their interactions with others.

6. Respecting Individuality: Authentic parenting respects the individuality of each family member. It recognizes that everyone is unique with their own perspectives, strengths, and weaknesses. This acknowledgment fosters an environment where each family member feels valued for who they are, promoting a sense of belonging and acceptance.

7. Embracing Imperfections: Authenticity involves embracing imperfections. Parents who acknowledge their own imperfections demonstrate resilience and the importance of learning and growing. This mindset encourages children to approach challenges with a positive attitude, understanding that mistakes are opportunities for growth.

8. Nurturing Self-Expression: Authentic parenting encourages self-expression. When parents express their true selves, it validates the importance of individuality and creativity. This validation, in turn, empowers children to explore and express their own identities, fostering a supportive environment for personal growth.

In essence, authenticity in parenting is a powerful force that transforms the parent-child relationship. It creates an atmosphere where children feel seen, heard, and accepted for who they are. By embracing authenticity, parents lay the foundation for a lifelong connection based on trust, understanding, and mutual respect.

Cultivating Authentic Parenting: Self-Reflection Worksheet 267

Fostering Relatability through Respectful Parenting

In the intricate dance of parenthood, one of the key elements that significantly contributes to relatability with children is the practice of respectful parenting. When parents approach their children with respect, recognizing their unique identities and honoring their personhood, it lays the groundwork for a relationship built on mutual understanding and connection.

The Power of Respect in Relatability:

1. **Valuing Individual Perspectives:** Respecting children involves acknowledging and valuing their individual perspectives. Each child is a unique individual with thoughts, feelings, and opinions that deserve consideration. By actively recognizing and respecting their viewpoints, parents open the door to meaningful conversations and shared understanding.

2. **Creating an Atmosphere of Trust:** Respect is foundational to building trust within the parent-child relationship. When children feel respected, they are more likely to trust their parents with their thoughts, concerns, and struggles. This trust forms the basis of open communication and a deeper connection, contributing to a sense of relatability.

3. **Encouraging Open Dialogue:** Respectful parenting encourages open dialogue where children feel safe expressing themselves. When children know their voices are heard without judgment, it creates an environment where they are more likely to share their thoughts and feelings. This open communication fosters relatability and strengthens the parent-child bond.

4. **Modeling Healthy Relationships:** Parents serve as powerful role models for their children. When they demonstrate respect in their interactions, both within the family and in external relationships, children learn valuable lessons about healthy relationships. This modeling contributes to the development of interpersonal skills and enhances relatability.

5. **Affirming Autonomy and Independence:** Respecting children involves recognizing and affirming their autonomy and budding independence. While guidance and boundaries are crucial, allowing space for children to make age-appropriate decisions cultivates a sense of independence. This respectful approach contributes to children feeling seen and understood, enhancing relatability.

Becoming More Respectful as a Parent:

Active Listening: Actively listening to your child without interruption or judgment is a powerful way to show respect. Make a conscious effort to understand their perspective before responding. This practice communicates that their thoughts and feelings are valued.

Mindful Communication: Choosing words carefully, maintaining a calm tone, and practicing patience contribute to respectful communication. Mindful communication involves being aware of the impact of your words and expressions, fostering an atmosphere of respect.

Empathy and Understanding: Cultivate empathy by putting yourself in your child's shoes. Understanding their emotions and experiences, especially during challenging moments, allows you to respond with empathy. This empathetic approach enhances respect and relatability.

Setting Realistic Expectations: Respecting your child's capabilities and developmental stage involves setting realistic expectations. Avoiding unrealistic demands allows your child to thrive in an environment where they feel understood and respected for who they are.

Apologizing When Necessary: Acknowledging mistakes and offering genuine apologies when warranted is a crucial aspect of respectful parenting. This vulnerability demonstrates that everyone, including parents, can learn and grow. It teaches children the importance of taking responsibility for one's actions.

Celebrating Individuality: Embrace and celebrate your child's individuality. Recognize their strengths, interests, and unique qualities. By affirming their identity, you communicate that they are valued and respected, fostering a deeper connection.

Establishing Consistent Boundaries: Respecting your child involves setting and maintaining consistent boundaries. Clearly communicate expectations and consequences in a manner that is fair and respectful. Consistent boundaries provide a sense of security and contribute to relatability.

Learning and Growing Together: Approach parenting as a journey of continual learning and growth, both for you and your child. Embrace the opportunity to learn from each other, creating an atmosphere of mutual respect and shared experiences.

In essence, respectful parenting forms the bedrock of a relationship characterized by relatability, trust, and understanding. By consistently practicing respect, parents not only foster a healthy and positive environment but also lay the foundation for a lasting and meaningful connection with their children.

Workbook-Respectful Parenting Reflection Worksheet 269

Cultivating Empathy and Humility in Parenting

Parenting with empathy and humility is fundamental to building a strong, trusting relationship with your child. These qualities contribute to relatability and foster a supportive environment for emotional growth. Here's a discussion on the importance of empathy and humility, along with practical ways to enhance these aspects in your parenting:

Understanding Empathy:
Empathy involves recognizing, understanding, and sharing the feelings of another. In the parent-child relationship, empathy creates a bridge that connects the emotional experiences of both parties. When parents demonstrate empathy, children feel seen, heard, and validated in their emotions.

- **Active Listening:**
  - **Practice Presence:** Be fully present when your child is expressing their feelings. Put aside distractions and actively engage in the conversation.
  - **Reflective Responses:** Respond to your child's emotions with reflective statements. For example, "It sounds like you're feeling..."
- **Validate Emotions:**
  - **Normalize Feelings:** Let your child know that it's okay to feel a range of emotions. Avoid dismissing or belittling their feelings.
  - **Use Affirming Language:** Offer statements like, "I understand it can be tough," or "It's okay to feel this way."
- **Shared Experiences:**
  - **Share Your Feelings:** Open up about your own emotions and experiences. This vulnerability creates a sense of connection.
  - **Connect Through Stories:** Share stories or experiences from your past that relate to your child's current emotions.

Embracing Humility:
Humility involves a willingness to acknowledge one's limitations, learn from mistakes, and treat others with respect. In the parent-child relationship, humility allows for mutual understanding and growth.

- **Apologizing When Necessary:**
  - **Model Apology:** Demonstrate the importance of taking responsibility for mistakes. Apologize when you've made an error or misjudgment.
  - **Share Your Process:** Explain how you're learning and growing as a parent, reinforcing the idea that everyone is on a journey of improvement.
- **Learning Together:**
  - **Admitting Lack of Knowledge:** It's okay not to have all the answers. Acknowledge when you're unsure and express a willingness to learn together.
  - **Explore New Things:** Embrace new experiences and learning opportunities with your child. This shared exploration strengthens the parent-child bond.
- **Seeking Input:**
  - **Ask for Their Perspective:** Invite your child to share their thoughts and opinions. Show that you value their insights and consider their perspectives.
  - **Collaborative Decision-Making:** Involve your child in age-appropriate decision-making processes. This fosters a sense of agency and shared responsibility.

Promoting Relatability:
- **Shared Vulnerability:**
  - **Express Your Vulnerabilities:** Share moments of vulnerability with your child. This openness encourages them to share their feelings without fear of judgment.
  - **Normalize Imperfections:** Emphasize that everyone makes mistakes, and it's a natural part of learning and growing.

- **Empathetic Actions:**
  - Show Compassion: Demonstrate acts of kindness and compassion toward others. Your child learns empathy by observing your actions.
  - Encourage Acts of Kindness: Guide your child in performing acts of kindness, nurturing their ability to understand and care for others.
- **Regular Check-Ins:**
  - Emotionally Check-In: Regularly ask your child how they're feeling. This fosters open communication and demonstrates your ongoing interest in their well-being.
  - Share Your Feelings Too: Model emotional expression by sharing your feelings during these check-ins.

Effective Communication and Adaptability in Parenting

Effective communication and adaptability are crucial components for building strong and relatable parent-child relationships. As a parent, your ability to communicate openly, listen actively, and adapt to your child's evolving needs contributes significantly to a healthy and connected family dynamic.

Importance of Effective Communication:

1. **Open Dialogue:** Effective communication involves creating an environment where your child feels comfortable expressing themselves. Encourage open dialogue by actively listening without judgment, allowing your child to share their thoughts, feelings, and concerns.
2. **Clarity in Expression:** Be clear and concise in your communication. Avoid ambiguous or confusing language, and ensure that your child understands your expectations, values, and the reasons behind your decisions.
3. **Encouraging Questions:** Foster a culture where questions are welcome. Encourage your child to ask questions, and provide thoughtful and age-appropriate answers. This promotes a sens of curiosity and intellectual engagement.
4. **Active Listening:** Actively listen to your child's perspective. This means not only hearing the words but understanding the emotions and intentions behind them. Reflecting on what your child communicates demonstrates empathy and validates their experiences.
5. **Consistent and Open Feedback:** Establish a feedback loop in which both you and your child can express your thoughts and feelings. Consistent, open feedback helps in addressing concerns, resolving conflicts, and reinforcing positive behaviors.

Becoming More Effective in Communication:

1. **Reflective Listening:** Practice reflective listening by paraphrasing your child's statements. This ensures that you understand their message accurately and allows your child to feel heard and valued.
2. **Non-Verbal Cues:** Pay attention to non-verbal cues such as body language and facial expressions. These cues often convey emotions that may not be expressed verbally, providir additional insights into your child's feelings.
3. **Empathetic Responses:** Respond to your child's emotions with empathy. Acknowledge their feelings, even if you don't agree with their perspective. This creates a connection and encourages emotional openness.
4. **Age-Appropriate Communication:** Tailor your communication style to your child's age and developmental stage. Use age-appropriate language, and adjust the complexity of your explanations to ensure understanding.
5. **Quality Time:** Dedicate quality time to communicate with your child. Engage in activities together, and use these moments as opportunities to share thoughts, dreams, and experiences.

Importance of Adaptability:

1. **Understanding Growth Phases:** Children go through various growth phases, and their needs, interests, and communication styles change. Being adaptable involves recognizing and adjusting to these phases to maintain a strong connection.
2. **Flexibility in Parenting Styles:** Understand that each child is unique, and what works for on may not work for another. Be flexible in your parenting style, adapting your approach to su the individual needs and personalities of your children.
3. **Adapting to Changes:** Life is dynamic, and unexpected changes are inevitable. Adaptability involves navigating changes such as relocation, family dynamics, or external circumstances while maintaining stability and support for your child.
4. **Learning and Growing Together:** Embrace a mindset of continuous learning and growth, bot for yourself and your child. Adaptability includes being open to new ideas, perspectives, an experiences, fostering an environment of mutual learning.
5. **Navigating Challenges:** Challenges are a part of life, and adaptability enables you to naviga them effectively. Teach your child problem-solving skills and resilience, emphasizing that challenges are opportunities for growth.

Becoming More Adaptable as a Parent:

- **Open Communication about Changes:** Discuss changes openly with your child, explaining the reasons behind them and addressing any concerns. This transparency builds trust and helps your child feel secure in times of change.
- **Prioritizing Flexibility:** Prioritize flexibility in your daily routines. While structure is essential, allowing room for spontaneity and adjustment communicates that adaptability is a valued trait.
- **Learning from Mistakes:** Model adaptability by acknowledging and learning from your mistakes. Demonstrate that setbacks are opportunities for growth and that adapting to new circumstances is a positive skill.
- **Seeking Input from Your Child:** Involve your child in decision-making processes when appropriate. Seeking their input empowers them, fosters a sense of responsibility, and communicates that their opinions are valued.
- **Embracing Change Together:** Approach changes as a team. Emphasize that the family unit can adapt and overcome challenges together, reinforcing a sense of unity and shared responsibility.

By prioritizing effective communication and adaptability, you create a foundation for a relatable and supportive parent-child relationship. Consistently practicing these skills demonstrates to your child that their thoughts and feelings are valued, fostering a deep and lasting connection.

Conclusion: Nurturing Lasting Connections in Parenting

As we conclude this exploration into the multifaceted world of parenting, it is evident that the journey is a dynamic and evolving process. Parenting is not a one-size-fits-all endeavor; instead, it's a unique and personal expedition filled with joys, challenges, and continuous learning. The intricacies of raising children involve a delicate balance of guidance, support, an adaptability.

Throughout this chapter, we delved into various aspects of parenting, from establishing a foundation of love and security to navigating the complexities of communication and adaptability. Understanding the profound impact of our actions, words, and attitudes on our children's development has been a recurring theme.

Key Takeaways:
1. **Foundation of Love:**
   o Building a foundation of love and security lays the groundwork for a child's emotional well-being and self-esteem.
2. **Communication and Connection:**
   o Effective communication and active listening are the cornerstones of building strong, relatable relationships with our children.
3. **Adaptability and Flexibility:**
   o Being adaptable and flexible in our parenting styles enables us to navigate the ever-changing landscape of our children's growth and development.
4. **Positive Reinforcement:**
   o Positive reinforcement fosters a growth mindset, encouraging children to explore, learn and develop resilience.
5. **Respect and Empathy:**
   o Treating children with respect and empathy reinforces their worth as individuals and nurtures a sense of security.
6. **Authenticity and Humility:**
   o Modeling authenticity and humility cultivates a relatable and trustworthy parent-child relationship.
7. **Navigating Challenges:**
   o Recognizing the pressures and challenges children face allows parents to provide guidance, instill coping mechanisms, and foster resilience.
8. **Age-Specific Considerations:**
   o Addressing the unique needs of children at different developmental stages is essential for effective parenting.
9. **Friendship and Authority:**
   o Balancing the roles of authority figures and companions contributes to a harmonious parent-child relationship.
10. **Reflective Parenting:**
   o Regular self-reflection enables parents to identify and address patterns, fostering personal growth and a healthier family environment.

In the grand opportunity of parenting, the threads of love, communication, adaptability, and positive reinforcement weave together to form a resilient and enduring bond between parents and children. While challenges may arise, viewing them as opportunities for growth and learning transforms the parenting journey into a shared adventure.

As parents, let us embrace the privilege and responsibility of shaping the next generation. Ma our homes be filled with love, laughter, understanding, and the unwavering commitment to guide our children towards a future of possibilities. Parenthood is not merely a role; it is a journey of connection, growth, and the profound joy of witnessing our children flourish into t unique individuals they are destined to become.

RELATIONSHIP WITH OTHERS

Extended Family

Navigating the intricate landscape of family roles beyond the immediate household, especially for singles or those managing diverse family connections, presents a unique set of joys and challenges. Jesus himself offered profound insights into the concept of family when confronted by his biological relatives expressing concern about his ministry. In response, he expanded the definition of family, emphasizing the significance of spiritual kinship and those who align with one's purpose and values.

In Matthew 12:46-50 (ESV), we find Jesus challenging traditional notions of family: "While Jesus was still talking to the crowd, his mother and brothers stood outside, wanting to speak to him. Someone told him, 'Your mother and brothers are standing outside, wanting to speak to you.' H replied to him, 'Who is my mother, and who are my brothers?' Pointing to his disciples, he said, 'Here are my mother and my brothers. For whoever does the will of my Father in heaven is my brother and sister and mother.'"

Understanding that family extends beyond biological ties is fundamental. While biological relatives hold significance, true family encompasses those who provide support, encouragemen and guidance in our journey through life. Yet, it's imperative to maintain a healthy balance between honoring familial connections and preserving individual autonomy. Each family member, regardless of their role, contributes to the complex dynamics of family dynamics, offering unique perspectives and contributions.

Acknowledging and navigating family dynamics involves grappling with roles, expectations, an boundaries. From the dutiful son or daughter to the doting uncle or aunt, family roles carry weight and responsibility. However, honoring these roles shouldn't come at the expense of individual well-being or self-respect. Setting clear boundaries and communicating openly with family members is essential to maintaining healthy relationships and preserving personal integrity.

Balancing individual needs with family unity requires a delicate dance of compromise and understanding. While family cohesion is invaluable, it shouldn't overshadow the importance of individual autonomy and self-care. Healthy relationships thrive on mutual respect, empathy, an reciprocity, where each member feels valued and supported while maintaining their unique identity.

Navigating the complex terrain of extended family relationships requires introspection, patience, and resilience. It's an ongoing journey of self-discovery and growth, where individual learn to honor their familial connections while staying true to themselves. By fostering open communication, setting healthy boundaries, and cultivating empathy and understanding, individuals can navigate their family roles with grace and integrity.

Ultimately, the ability to balance family obligations with personal autonomy contributes to a sense of fulfillment and well-being. Embracing the richness of extended family connections while prioritizing individual needs fosters harmonious relationships and lays the foundation fo a fulfilling life journey.

For singles, navigating outside family pressures about marriage and feeling constantly used can be challenging. Here's a guide to help singles create boundaries and sustain confidence in the face of these pressures:

1. Clarify Your Values and Goals: Take time to reflect on your values, aspirations, and priorities regarding marriage and relationships. Define what you want and what you're willing to tolerate in your personal life. Knowing yourself and your goals will help you establish boundaries that align with your values.

2. Communicate Your Boundaries Clearly: Be upfront and assertive about your boundaries with family members and others who pressure you about marriage. Clearly communicate your decisions and preferences regarding your relationship status and timeline for marriage. Set boundaries around discussing your personal life and politely but firmly redirect conversations when they veer into uncomfortable territory.

3. Practice Self-Validation: Develop a strong sense of self-worth and confidence independent of external validation, including societal or family expectations about marriage. Remind yourself that your worth is not determined by your relationship status and that it's okay to prioritize personal growth, career, or other interests before pursuing marriage.

4. Establish Personal Boundaries: Set boundaries around your time, energy, and resources to avoid feeling overwhelmed or used by others' expectations. Learn to say no to requests or demands that conflict with your priorities or values. Focus on self-care and activities that bring you fulfillment and joy, independent of relationship status.

5. Seek Support from Like-Minded Individuals: Surround yourself with friends, mentors, or support groups who respect your decisions and offer encouragement and understanding. Connect with other singles who share similar values and experiences, providing mutual support and validation in navigating societal pressures about marriage.

6. Redirect External Pressure: When faced with intrusive questions or comments from family members or others, respond assertively but diplomatically. Politely deflect inquiries about your relationship status and emphasize your focus on personal growth, career, or other interests. Reframe the conversation to topics that you're comfortable discussing or redirect attention away from your personal life.

7. Stay True to Yourself: Trust your instincts and intuition when it comes to making decisions about your personal life and relationships. Avoid succumbing to external pressure or rushing into marriage due to societal expectations. Stay true to your values, goals, and timeline, and trust that the right relationship will come in due time, on your own terms.

Creating and sustaining boundaries as a single person in the face of outside family pressures about marriage requires self-awareness, assertiveness, and self-validation. By clarifying your values, communicating your boundaries clearly, and prioritizing self-care and personal growth, you can navigate external pressures with confidence and maintain autonomy over your life choices.

Workbook Navigating Outside Family Pressures Worksheet For Singles Page 273

Married Couples

Establishing boundaries with extended family members is essential for maintaining a healthy and harmonious marriage. Here's how married couples can create boundaries effectively while respecting both their marriage and their relationships with outside family:

1. **Understand the Concept of "Cleave and Leave":** Embrace the biblical principle of leaving one's parents and cleaving to one's spouse. Recognize that while family relationships are important, the marital relationship takes precedence. Understand that establishing boundaries is not a rejection of family but a necessary step in building a strong marital foundation.

2. **Communicate Openly and Honestly:** Have open and honest discussions with your spouse about your expectations regarding boundaries with extended family. Clearly define what behaviors or interactions are acceptable and unacceptable, and agree on a unified approach to addressing boundary issues.

3. **Set Clear and Firm Boundaries:** Identify specific boundaries that you and your spouse need to establish with outside family members. This may include limits on visits, involvement in decision-making, financial support, or interference in marital disputes. Communicate these boundaries respectfully but firmly, emphasizing the importance of protecting your marriage and maintaining autonomy.

4. **Enforce Boundaries Consistently:** Once boundaries are set, enforce them consistently and without exceptions. Be prepared to assertively but respectfully reinforce your boundaries when they are violated. Consistency is key to ensuring that outside family members understand and respect your limits.

5. **Address Boundary Violations Promptly:** If outside family members overstep boundaries, address the issue promptly and directly. Approach the situation calmly and assertively, expressing your concerns and reiterating the importance of respecting your marriage and autonomy. Avoid escalating conflicts or becoming defensive, but stand firm in defending your boundaries.

6. **Seek Support and Guidance if Needed:** If boundary issues persist or become contentious, seek support and guidance from a trusted third party, such as a therapist, counselor, or religious leader. A neutral mediator can provide perspective and help facilitate constructive conversations with outside family members.

7. **Maintain Flexibility and Compromise:** While it's important to establish firm boundaries, be willing to evaluate and adjust them as needed based on changing circumstances or family dynamics. Practice flexibility and compromise with your spouse to find solutions that balance your needs with the expectations of outside family members.

Creating boundaries with outside family members requires open communication, mutual respect, and a united front from both spouses. By establishing clear boundaries and addressing boundary violations promptly and assertively, married couples can protect their marriage and foster a supportive environment for growth and intimacy.

Workbook Navigating Outside Family Pressures Worksheet For Singles 275

Healing from past family wounds is a vital step towards achieving emotional well-being and building healthy relationships. Many individuals carry deep-seated wounds from their family of origin, which can significantly impact their current relationships and hinder their ability to form a family of their own. To embark on a journey of healing, it's essential to employ strategies that address these wounds effectively. Here are four ways individuals can heal from the wounds of the family, using the points that spell HEAL:

H: Honor Your Feelings and Experiences Acknowledging and honoring your feelings and experiences is the first step towards healing from past family wounds. It's important to recognize and validate the pain, anger, sadness, or confusion that may arise from past experiences. By allowing yourself to feel and express these emotions in a safe and supportive environment, you can begin to release the emotional burden carried from past wounds. This process of emotional acknowledgment and validation lays the foundation for deeper healing and transformation.

E: Earn from the Pain and Not Just Burn from the Pain Rather than allowing past pain to consume and overwhelm you, strive to find meaning and purpose in your experiences. Embrace the opportunity to learn and grow from your past wounds, using them as catalysts for personal growth and transformation. By reframing your perspective and viewing challenges as opportunities for learning and development, you can turn pain into wisdom and resilience. Embracing this mindset empowers you to transcend the limitations imposed by past wounds and cultivate a sense of empowerment and self-awareness.

A: Address Unresolved Issues Healing from past family wounds requires addressing unresolved issues and traumas that continue to impact your life. Take proactive steps to explore and understand the root causes of your pain and distress, whether through therapy, counseling, or self-reflection. By confronting and processing unresolved issues, you can release pent-up emotions, break free from harmful patterns, and gain clarity and insight into your experiences. This process of exploration and resolution paves the way for deep healing and emotional liberation.

L: Liberate Yourself Through Forgiveness Forgiveness is a powerful tool for healing from past family wounds and releasing the emotional burdens carried from past hurts. While forgiveness does not excuse or condone the actions of others, it frees you from the grip of resentment, anger, and bitterness. By choosing to forgive those who have wronged you, you reclaim your power and autonomy, refusing to allow past wounds to define or control you. Forgiveness is a process of letting go and moving forward with compassion and grace, allowing you to cultivate inner peace, healing, and wholeness.

In summary, healing from past family wounds requires a holistic approach that honors your feelings, finds meaning in your experiences, addresses unresolved issues, and embraces forgiveness. By embracing these principles of healing, individuals can embark on a journey of self-discovery, empowerment, and transformation, breaking free from the shackles of the past and stepping into a future filled with healing, hope, and possibility.

375

Identifying true family members within our extended network can be both comforting and essential for our emotional well-being and sense of belonging. Here are some signs or traits to look for when determining if a family member is truly family:

F: Fosters Unconditional Love - A true family member demonstrates unconditional love and acceptance, regardless of differences or disagreements. They offer support, empathy, and encouragement without expecting anything in return.

A: Available in Times of Need - Genuine family members are there for you when you need them most. They offer their time, resources, and emotional support during challenging moments without hesitation or judgment.

M: Mutual Respect - Respect is a fundamental aspect of any healthy relationship, and true family members treat each other with genuine respect and dignity. They value your opinions, boundaries, and autonomy, fostering mutual respect in all interactions.

I: Invests in Relationships - Family members who are truly invested in the relationship prioritize spending quality time together, creating meaningful memories, and nurturing the bond through regular communication and shared experiences.

L: Listens with Empathy - Effective communication is essential in any relationship, and true family members listen with empathy and understanding. They validate your feelings, offer support, and communicate openly and honestly without judgment.

Y: Your Cheerleader - A true family member celebrates your successes, no matter how big or small, and genuinely cheers you on in your endeavors. They offer encouragement, praise, and unwavering support as you pursue your dreams and goals.

These signs or traits can help you identify those family members who truly embody the essence of family and contribute positively to your life. By nurturing relationships with individuals who exhibit these qualities, you can cultivate a strong support system and experience the joys of genuine familial bonds.

376

Stewarding Influence

In the dynamic landscape of modern relationships, the concept of stewarding influence holds profound significance, especially in spheres where our interactions extend beyond the confines of immediate family or close friends. Whether we're engaging with individuals online, navigating the intricate dynamics of the marketplace, mentoring aspiring talents, or serving within our communities, the way we wield our influence can shape destinies and catalyze transformative growth.

At the heart of stewarding influence lies a commitment to selflessness—an unwavering dedication to prioritizing the well-being and development of those we have the privilege to serve. Rather than seeking personal gain or recognition, true stewardship entails leveraging our giftings, resources, and experiences to empower others to realize their fullest potential. It's about selflessly pouring into the lives of others, nurturing their aspirations, and guiding them along the path toward their goals.

The power of influence cannot be underestimated. Each interaction, whether fleeting or enduring, carries the potential to leave an indelible mark on the lives of those we encounter. As stewards of influence, we bear the responsibility to wield this power judiciously, mindful of the impact our words, actions, and choices may have on others' journeys. By approaching our relationships with humility, empathy, and a genuine desire to uplift and inspire, we create environments conducive to growth, learning, and transformation.

In the realm of mentorship, stewarding influence takes on added significance. Mentors occupy a position of trust and authority, guiding and shaping the trajectories of those under their tutelage. It's essential for mentors to recognize the weight of their influence and to wield it with integrity, wisdom, and compassion. By fostering nurturing, empowering relationships with their mentees, mentors can impart invaluable wisdom, provide constructive guidance, and instill the confidence and resilience needed to navigate life's challenges.

Similarly, in the digital age, where online platforms serve as hubs for connection and engagement, stewarding influence requires a nuanced approach. As content creators, thought leaders, or influencers, our words and actions carry immense weight in shaping the perspectives, attitudes, and behaviors of our audience. It's incumbent upon us to use our platforms responsibly, disseminating messages that uplift, educate, and inspire rather than propagate divisiveness or negativity.

Ultimately, stewarding influence is not merely about exerting control or authority but about embodying servant leadership—a model characterized by humility, empathy, and a genuine commitment to the growth and well-being of others. By embracing this ethos and leveraging our influence for the greater good, we can cultivate communities marked by mutual respect, empowerment, and collective progress.

Poor Stewardship

In the intricate web of relationships, the stewardship of influence plays a pivotal role in shaping the dynamics and outcomes of our interactions. However, when influence is wielded carelessly or irresponsibly, it can have detrimental effects on the fabric of relationships. Poor stewardship of influence often manifests in various forms, ranging from manipulation and coercion to neglect and exploitation, all of which erode trust, breed resentment, and undermine the foundations of healthy relationships.

One of the most common pitfalls of poor influence stewardship is the tendency to prioritize self-interest over the well-being of others. When individuals use their influence solely for personal gain or to further their own agendas without regard for the needs or feelings of those they impact, it creates an imbalance of power and fosters an environment of exploitation. This self-serving approach to influence can lead to feelings of betrayal, disillusionment, and ultimately, the breakdown of trust within relationships.

Another detrimental aspect of poor influence stewardship is the misuse of authority or position to manipulate or control others. Whether in familial, professional, or social contexts, individuals in positions of power may abuse their influence to coerce compliance, suppress dissent, or exert undue pressure on others to conform to their desires. This misuse of authority not only violates the autonomy and dignity of individuals but also breeds resentment and animosity, ultimately corroding the bonds of trust and mutual respect essential for healthy relationships.

Furthermore, poor stewardship of influence often involves neglecting the impact of one's words and actions on others, leading to inadvertent harm or damage to relationships. Whether through careless remarks, thoughtless decisions, or lack of consideration for the feelings of others, individuals may unwittingly undermine the trust and goodwill they have cultivated with their loved ones, colleagues, or peers. Such disregard for the consequences of one's influence can result in feelings of hurt, betrayal, and alienation, straining relationships and eroding the foundation of mutual respect and understanding.

Additionally, the failure to recognize and take responsibility for the consequences of one's influence can perpetuate cycles of dysfunction and toxicity within relationships. When individuals refuse to acknowledge the harm they have caused or dismiss the concerns of those affected by their actions, it perpetuates a culture of denial and defensiveness that impedes meaningful resolution and reconciliation. This lack of accountability further exacerbates tensions and conflicts, making it difficult to repair and restore damaged relationships.

In essence, poor stewardship of influence undermines the very essence of healthy relationships, which are built on foundations of trust, respect, and mutual empowerment. By recognizing the profound impact of our words and actions on others and committing to wield our influence with integrity, empathy, and humility, we can cultivate environments characterized by authenticity, understanding, and genuine connection.

Stewarding our influence effectively is crucial for fostering positive and meaningful relationships. To ensure our impact is constructive and empowering, we can adopt strategies that align with the principles of stewardship. Here are key points to consider, each corresponding to a letter in the word "STEWARD":

- S - Stay Authentic: Authenticity forms the bedrock of impactful influence. By staying true to ourselves and our values, we build trust and credibility with others. Authenticity allows us to connect with people on a deeper level and inspire them through genuine expression.
- T - Transparency in Communication: Transparency fosters openness and trust in relationships By communicating openly and honestly, we create a safe space for dialogue and collaboration. Transparency also helps prevent misunderstandings and conflicts, leading to more harmonious interactions.
- E - Empower Others: Effective influence involves empowering others to reach their full potential. Instead of seeking to control or dominate, we should strive to uplift and support those around us. Empowering others cultivates a culture of mutual respect and collaboration, where everyone feels valued and encouraged to succeed.
- W - Walk in Empathy: Empathy is the cornerstone of compassionate influence. By putting ourselves in others' shoes and seeking to understand their perspectives, feelings, and needs, we can forge deeper connections and foster empathy-driven relationships. Walking in empathy promotes harmony and understanding in our interactions.
- A - Act with Integrity: Integrity is non-negotiable when it comes to stewarding influence. Acting with integrity means aligning our words, actions, and values consistently. Integrity builds credibility and trust, ensuring that our influence is perceived as authentic and reliable
- R - Respect Boundaries: Respecting boundaries is essential for healthy influence dynamics. We must recognize and honor the boundaries of others, whether they are physical, emotional or psychological. Respecting boundaries demonstrates empathy, sensitivity, and respect for individual autonomy.
- D - Demonstrate Humility: Humility is a hallmark of effective influence. By acknowledging our limitations, embracing feedback, and admitting mistakes, we demonstrate humility and authenticity. Humility fosters humility and openness, inviting collaboration and mutual growth.

By adopting these stewardship principles, we can leverage our influence to create positive impact, build meaningful relationships, and foster a culture of empowerment and growth.

Friendships play a crucial role in our lives, shaping our experiences, perspectives, and overall well-being. Proverbs 27:17 aptly captures the essence of friendships, stating, "As iron sharpens iron, so one person sharpens another." This powerful metaphor illustrates the transformative nature of friendships, highlighting how friends have the ability to uplift, challenge, and inspire us to become the best versions of ourselves.

Just as iron sharpens iron, healthy friendships sharpen and refine us, encouraging personal growth, accountability, and mutual support. Friends who embody the qualities of authenticity, respect, empathy, humility, effective communication, and adaptability are invaluable assets in our lives. They provide us with a safe space to be ourselves, offering unconditional love, understanding, and acceptance.

In the journey of life, we encounter various trials, challenges, and opportunities for growth. During these times, friends serve as trusted companions, walking alongside us, offering guidance, encouragement, and wisdom. They provide a listening ear, offering invaluable insights and perspectives that help us navigate life's complexities with clarity and resilience.

Moreover, friendships thrive on reciprocity and mutual respect. Just as we benefit from the positive influence of our friends, we also have a responsibility to be good friends in return. Cultivating the qualities of authenticity, respect, empathy, humility, effective communication, and adaptability within ourselves allows us to contribute positively to our friendships, fostering a nurturing and supportive environment for mutual growth and development.

However, it's essential to recognize that not all friendships are healthy or beneficial. Just as iron can rust and dull over time, toxic or one-sided friendships can hinder our personal growth and well-being. It's crucial to discern which friendships align with our values, goals, and overall well-being, and to invest our time and energy in relationships that uplift and empower us.

In summary, friendships are a cornerstone of our lives, providing us with companionship, support, and personal growth opportunities. As we journey through life, let us cherish and nurture the friendships that sharpen and refine us, cultivating relationships built on authenticity, respect, empathy, humility, effective communication, and adaptability. By surrounding ourselves with friends who embody these qualities, we can navigate life's challenges with courage, grace, and resilience, knowing that we are never alone on this journey.

Building on the profound impact of friendships, it's essential to recognize the significance of selective companionship. Just as Jesus had various groups of people in his life with different levels of intimacy and influence, we too must discern who we allow into our inner circle. Jesus had the crowd who followed Him for miracles, the Pharisees who opposed Him, the seventy who aided His ministry, the twelve disciples who were His close companions, and within them, the three with whom He shared extraordinary experiences. Similarly, we encounter individuals with varying levels of connection and influence in our lives, and it's crucial to be discerning about who we allow close.

Jesus exemplified the importance of selective companionship by not revealing His full self to everyone. He reserved intimate moments and deeper revelations for a select few, demonstrating the wisdom of discerning friendships. In our own lives, we should prioritize quality over quantity when it comes to friendships, seeking relationships characterized by authenticity, respect, empathy, and mutual support. Instead of striving to have numerous acquaintances, focus on cultivating a few genuine friendships that nurture your well-being and personal growth.

Before befriending others, it's vital to cultivate a deep friendship with God, as He is the ultimate source of fulfillment, contentment, and companionship. When God is our closest friend, we find solace, wisdom, and unconditional love that sustain us in all circumstances. By prioritizing our relationship with God above all else, we establish a foundation of strength and security that enables us to navigate friendships with discernment and wisdom.

Moreover, it's essential to be your own best friend, nurturing a positive and compassionate relationship with yourself. Being your own best friend means treating yourself with kindness, understanding, and respect, just as you would a dear friend. Embrace self-care practices that nourish your mind, body, and spirit, and cultivate a mindset of self-compassion and self-acceptance. When you are your own best friend and prioritize your relationship with God, you approach friendships from a place of wholeness and authenticity, enhancing your ability to form healthy and fulfilling connections with others.

In conclusion, while friendships are vital for personal growth and support, it's essential to be selective about the company we keep. Just as iron sharpens iron, healthy friendships sharpen and refine us, but toxic or one-sided relationships can hinder our progress. By surrounding ourselves with friends who embody authenticity, respect, empathy, and humility, and by prioritizing our relationship with God and being our own best friend, we cultivate a network of relationships that uplift and empower us on our journey through life.

Rebounding from Failure: A Path to Growth in Relationships

Failure is an inevitable aspect of the human experience, and it manifests in various dimensions of our lives, including our relationships with God, self, spouse, and children. However, the key lies not in avoiding failure but in how we rebound from it. Embracing failure as an opportunity for learning and growth can transform setbacks into stepping stones toward stronger, more resilient relationships.

1. Relationship with God:
- **Embrace Grace:** Understand that everyone falls short, and God's grace is sufficient. Failure does not diminish His love or willingness to guide you.
- **Learn and Repent:** Identify areas of spiritual growth and seek forgiveness when needed. Use failures as a catalyst for deepening your understanding of God's mercy.

2. Relationship with Self:
- **Self-Compassion:** Cultivate self-compassion by acknowledging that everyone makes mistakes. Treat yourself with the same kindness you'd offer a friend in a similar situation.
- **Reflection and Adjustment:** Reflect on the factors that led to the failure and consider adjustments. Use failures as insights into areas where personal growth is possible.

3. Relationship with Spouse:
- **Open Communication:** Discuss failures openly with your spouse, fostering a culture of transparency and understanding. Share lessons learned and jointly plan for improvement.
- **Rebuilding Trust:** If trust is affected, take intentional steps to rebuild it. Consistency in positive changes and open communication are vital in this process.

4. Relationship with Children:
- **Model Resilience:** Demonstrate resilience by acknowledging your mistakes and showing that failures can be transformative. Teach children that learning from mistakes is a valuable life skill.
- **Apologize and Make Amends:** Apologize sincerely when needed, and actively work towards making amends. This teaches children the importance of accountability and forgiveness.

5. Relationship with Others:
- **Extend Grace to Others:** Understand that others also experience failures. Extend grace to them as you would want grace extended to you.
- **Learn from Interactions:** Analyze interpersonal failures, seeking to understand the root causes. Use these insights to refine your communication and relational skills.

Key Principles for Rebounding:
- **Ownership:** Take responsibility for your actions and decisions. Avoid blame-shifting and instead focus on areas where personal growth is possible.
- **Humility:** Embrace humility in acknowledging mistakes. A humble attitude fosters a culture of learning and collaboration.
- **Adaptability:** Be adaptable in your approach, recognizing that failure often provides an opportunity for course correction and improvement.
- **Continuous Learning:** Cultivate a mindset of continuous learning. Treat failures as lessons that contribute to your ongoing personal and relational development.

In essence, rebounding from failure is not only possible but essential for personal and relational growth. By embracing failure as a teacher rather than an adversary, you pave the way for deeper connections, increased resilience, and a more fulfilling journey in your relationships with God, self, spouse, and children.

Workbook: Rebounding From Failure Worksheet 271

ebound from Failure:

1. **Reflect**: Take time to reflect on what went wrong in the relationship and the role you played in its failure. Acknowledge mistakes and areas for improvement.
2. **Evaluate**: Assess the lessons learned from the failed relationship and identify patterns or behaviors to avoid in future relationships.
3. **Boundaries**: Establish clear boundaries in future relationships to protect yourself from repeating past mistakes and ensure mutual respect and healthy dynamics.
4. **Openness**: Be open to new experiences and relationships, while being mindful of red flags and potential warning signs.
5. **Understand**: Seek to understand your emotions and reactions to the failure, and consider seeking professional help or support if needed.
6. **Nurture**: Focus on self-care and personal growth to rebuild your confidence, self-esteem, and emotional resilience. + **Navigate**: Take proactive steps to navigate any unresolved issues or lingering emotions from past relationships through therapy, counseling, or self-help resources.
7. **Determination**: Approach new relationships with determination and commitment to apply the lessons learned from past failures and create healthier dynamics.

Prevent Severe Failure:

1. **Prioritize** Communication: Foster open, honest communication with your partner to address concerns, express needs, and resolve conflicts promptly.
2. **Respect**: Cultivate mutual respect and appreciation in your relationship, valuing each other's opinions, boundaries, and autonomy.
3. **Emotional** Intelligence: Develop emotional intelligence skills to manage and express emotions in healthy ways, reducing the risk of emotional outbursts or conflicts.
4. **Vigilance**: Stay vigilant for signs of relationship distress or dissatisfaction, and address issues proactively before they escalate into severe problems.
5. **Engagement**: Stay actively engaged in your relationship, investing time, energy, and effort into nurturing the connection and keeping the bond strong. + Education: Invest in relationship education and resources to learn effective communication, conflict resolution, and relationship-building skills.
6. **Negotiation**: Practice negotiation and compromise in decision-making, respecting each other's needs and finding mutually satisfactory solutions.
7. **Transparency**: Be transparent and honest with your partner about your thoughts, feelings, and intentions, fostering trust and intimacy in the relationship. + **Teamwork**: Approach your relationship as a team, collaborating and supporting each other through challenges, changes, and growth opportunities.

LAST THOUGHTS

As we come to the conclusion of this journey through the intricate complexities of relationships, I hope you have found clarity, insight, and inspiration to navigate the relational landscape of your life with greater wisdom and intentionality. Throughout these pages, we have explored the profound interconnectedness of our relationships with God, self, spouse, children, and others, recognizing that each thread contributes to the fabric of our existence in unique and meaningful ways.

I pray that this book has served as a catalyst for deeper understanding and engagement with your relationships, illuminating the interdependence that binds them together. May you recognize the inherent value and significance of each connection, understanding that they are not isolated entities but integral components of a larger relational ecosystem.

By embracing the interconnectedness of your relationships, may you cultivate greater relatability and resilience, navigating life's challenges and joys with grace and fortitude. May you find strength in the bonds you share with others, drawing sustenance from the wellspring of love, support, and connection that flows through each relationship.

As you reflect on the insights gleaned from these pages, I pray that you feel empowered to chart a course toward divine destinations, guided by the compass of faith and anchored in the harbor of love. May your relationships be a source of joy, fulfillment, and purpose, serving as beacons of light in a world often shrouded in darkness.

If you find yourself in need of further assistance on your relational journey, whether it be overcoming relationship neglect, navigating relationship strain, or fostering deeper connection, know that help is available. Scan the QR codes below or go to **mycoachjosh.com** to explore opportunities for group coaching (**Relationship Mastery** or **Fulfillment Elite**) or to join a community of like-minded individuals committed to relational growth and transformation (**Lifework Communities**).

Remember, you are not alone on this journey. You have the capacity to relate and excel in every relationship and area of your life. May you walk forward with confidence, knowing that you are equipped with the tools, insights, and support needed to thrive in the beautiful tapestry of relationships that shape your life. - **Coach**

End-of-Book Relationship Assessment

Congratulations on completing "The Purpose of Relationships"! Now, let's take some time to reflect on your journey and measure your growth in various aspects of relationships. Please rate each statement below on a scale from 1 to 10, with 1 being "Strongly Disagree" and 10 being "Strongly Agree."

1. Relating with God:
   o I feel closer to God now compared to when I started this book. ____
   o My prayer life has deepened, and I feel more connected spiritually. ____
   o I am more consistent in practicing spiritual disciplines such as meditation, prayer, or worship. ____
2. Relating with Self:
   o I have a better understanding of myself, my values, and my needs. ____
   o I practice self-care regularly and prioritize my well-being. ____
   o I have developed healthier habits and coping mechanisms for managing stress and emotions. ____
3. Relating with Spouse (if applicable):
   o My communication with my spouse has improved. ____
   o I am more attentive and supportive of my spouse's needs and feelings. ____
   o Our relationship has grown stronger, and we feel more connected emotionally and spiritually. ____
4. Relating with Children (if applicable):
   o I spend quality time with my children and actively engage in their lives. ____
   o I have become more patient and understanding as a parent. ____
   o My children feel loved, supported, and respected in our relationship. ____
5. Relating with Other Relationships:
   o I have developed healthier boundaries in my relationships with friends, family, or colleagues. ____
   o I am better at resolving conflicts and maintaining positive relationships. ____
   o I actively invest time and effort into nurturing meaningful connections with others. ____
6. Overall Growth:
   o I feel more fulfilled and content in my relationships now. ____
   o I have noticed positive changes in my interactions and dynamics with others. ____
   o I am committed to continued growth and improvement in my relationships. ____

After rating each statement, take a moment to review your scores and reflect on areas where you've made significant progress as well as areas that may still need attention. Remember that growth is a journey, and every step forward is worth celebrating!

THE PURPOSE OF RELATIONSHIPS

lifework

COACH JOSH

10:00

mycoachjosh.com

WORKBOOK

BY JOSHUA EZE

RELATE

Relationship Mastery &
Fulfillment Elite Coaching Programs

The Purpose Of Relationships
Workbook

RELATE
The Card Game

Scan the QR codes to discover more about the additional resources that support "The Purpose of Relationships" book.

374

Made in United States
Orlando, FL
16 November 2024

53948852R00217